A History of the Great War

John Buchan

Copyright © BiblioLife, LLC

This book represents a historical reproduction of a work originally published before 1923 that is part of a unique project which provides opportunities for readers, educators and researchers by bringing hard-to-find original publications back into print at reasonable prices. Because this and other works are culturally important, we have made them available as part of our commitment to protecting, preserving and promoting the world's literature. These books are in the "public domain" and were digitized and made available in cooperation with libraries, archives, and open source initiatives around the world dedicated to this important mission.

We believe that when we undertake the difficult task of re-creating these works as attractive, readable and affordable books, we further the goal of sharing these works with a global audience, and preserving a vanishing wealth of human knowledge.

Many historical books were originally published in small fonts, which can make them very difficult to read. Accordingly, in order to improve the reading experience of these books, we have created "enlarged print" versions of our books. Because of font size variation in the original books, some of these may not technically qualify as "large print" books, as that term is generally defined; however, we believe these versions provide an overall improved reading experience for many.

A HISTORY OF
THE GREAT WAR

BY
JOHN BUCHAN

VOLUME II

BOSTON AND NEW YORK
HOUGHTON MIFFLIN COMPANY
1923

CONTENTS.

BOOK II. (*Continued*).

THE BELEAGUERED FORTRESS.

XXVI. THE OPENING OF THE DARDANELLES CAMPAIGN
(September 1, 1914–April 27, 1915) . . . 1
  The First Hint of an Eastern Diversion—Discussions in the War Council—Lord Kitchener, Lord Fisher, and Mr. Churchill—Subsidiary *versus* Divergent Operations—Topography and History of the Dardanelles—Justification for the Naval Attack—Fortifications of the Straits—The Naval Attack and its Results—The Origin of the Military Expedition—Sir Ian Hamilton—The Tactical Problem—The Battle of the Landing.

XXVII. THE SECOND BATTLE OF YPRES (April 17–May 24, 1915) 42
  Germany's Spring Policy in the West—The Taking of Hill 60—The Gas Attack—The Second Battle of Ypres—Its Results—The Ruined City—The Political Situation in Britain during April and May—The Formation of a Coalition Government.

XXVIII. THE ALLIED WESTERN OFFENSIVE IN THE SUMMER
OF 1915 (April 5–June 17) 70
  Germany's Summer Strategy—The French in Alsace and Lorraine—The French Advance in Artois—The British Attack at Festubert—The Summer's Stagnation—The War in the Air.

XXIX. THE RUSSIAN RETREAT FROM THE DONAJETZ
(April 28–June 21, 1915) 89
  Russia's Position in April—Hindenburg's Plan—Mackensen attacks—Retreat of the Russian Armies—The Loss of Przemysl and Lemberg—The Russian Position at Midsummer.

XXX. THE BEGINNING OF ITALY'S CAMPAIGN (April 26–
August 21, 1915) 111
  Sonnino's Diplomacy—The Treaty of London—Italy declares War on Austria—Italy's Strategic Position—The First Engagements on the Frontiers—The Beginning of the Isonzo Campaign—Italy declares War on Turkey.

CONTENTS.

XXXI. THE FIRST YEAR OF WAR: A RETROSPECT (June 28, 1914–June 28, 1915) 139
The Military Result—Germany's Calculations—Her Strength and Weakness—The Position of the Allies—The British Problem of Men and Munitions—British Finance—The Allies' Lack of Central Direction—The Neutral States—The Naval Position—The Leaders.

XXXII. THE ASIAN AND AFRICAN CAMPAIGNS (October 1914–July 9, 1915). 173
Transcaucasia—The Mesopotamian Campaign—The Capture of Nasiriyeh and Kut—The Cameroons—The War in German South-West Africa—The Surrender of the Enemy.

XXXIII. THE ABANDONMENT OF WARSAW (June 22–August 5, 1915) 189
Germany exploits her Success—The Crushing of the Warsaw Salient—The Advance of Mackensen and Linsingen—The Advance of Gallwitz—Comparison with Napoleon's Invasion—Prince Leopold enters Warsaw.

XXXIV. GALLIPOLI: THE BATTLES FOR KRITHIA (April 29–July 31, 1915) 206
The Attack of 6th May—The Australasian Corps at Sari Bair—The Battle of 4th June—The Withdrawal of the larger Warships—Kitchener's Difficulties—The Action of 21st June—The Action of 12th July—Arrival of British Reinforcements.

XXXV. THE STRAINING OF AMERICA'S PATIENCE . . 221
America's Temper—Reasons for her Hostility to Germany—The Difficulties of immediate Intervention—President Wilson—German Activities in America—Dr. Dumba.

XXXVI. GALLIPOLI: THE NEW LANDING (August 6–27, 1915) 237
The New Plan—Suvla Bay and its Neighbourhood—The New British Divisions—The Preliminary Attack at Cape Helles—The Anzac Advance on Koja Chemen—The Landing at Suvla—Its Failure.

XXXVII. THE GREAT RUSSIAN RETREAT (August 5–September 30, 1915) 256
The essential Russian Weakness—Germany's Next Step—The Russian Armies' Retreat to the Bug—The Fall of Kovno and Novo Georgievsk—The Fall of Brest Litovsk—The Fall of Grodno—The Retreat from the Vilna Salient—The first Russian Counter-strokes—Political Changes.

XXXVIII. CHAMPAGNE AND LOOS (September 23–October 2, 1915) 287
The Allied Line in the West—The Policy of the New Advance—The Great Bombardment—The Attack in Champagne—The French Attack in Artois—The British Subsidiary Attacks—The Battle of Loos—The Achievement of the 15th Division—Summary and Criticism.

CONTENTS.

XXXIX. THE BALKAN LABYRINTH 325
　　　The various Balkan States—Geography and History of the Peninsula—The Treaty of Berlin—The Balkan League—The First and Second Balkan Wars—Bulgaria's Discontent—King Ferdinand—Greece and Venizelos—Failure of Allied Diplomacy.

XL. BULGARIA ENTERS THE WAR (September 19–October 15, 1915) 343
　　　Bulgaria's Alliance with Germany—Mackensen's Army—The Intrigues at Sofia—The Position of Greece—The Allies send Troops to Salonika.

XLI. THE OVERRUNNING OF SERBIA (September 19, 1915–January 25, 1916) 358
　　　Serbia's Military Position—Mackensen's Problem—The Advance of Gallwitz and Kovess—Bulgaria's Flank Attack—Fall of Uskub—Fall of Nish—The Serbian Retreat to the Adriatic—The Allies in Salonika—The Austrian Conquest of Montenegro.

XLII. GALLIPOLI: THE EVACUATION (August 21, 1915–January 9, 1916) 380
　　　Sir Ian Hamilton recalled—Sir Charles Monro's Report—Kitchener's Visit to Gallipoli—The Evacuation of Suvla and Anzac—The Evacuation of Helles—A Miraculous Exploit.

XLIII. MESOPOTAMIA: THE BAGDAD EXPEDITION (October 21–December 3, 1915) 394
　　　The Turkish Massacres in Armenia—Trouble in Persia—The Question of an Advance to Bagdad—The Chief Responsibility for it—Townshend reaches Laj—The Battle of Ctesiphon—The Retreat to Kut.

XLIV. THE SECOND WINTER IN THE EAST AND WEST . 407
　　　The Fighting at Riga and Dvinsk—The Russian Attack on Czernovitz—The Aftermath of the Loos and Champagne Battles—The Winter Hardships—Sir John French surrenders his Command—His Qualities and Defects.

XLV. THE POLITICAL SITUATION IN FRANCE AND BRITAIN (October 1, 1915–January 26, 1916) . 428
　　　Popular Anxiety—The New Ministry in France—Criticism of the French Staff—The Situation in Britain—The Censorship—Edith Cavell—The New General Staff—British Finance—The Recruiting Problem—The Derby Report—The Military Service Bill—Parallel with American Civil War.

XLVI. SOME SIDE-LIGHTS ON THE GERMAN TEMPER . . 451
　　　The Growth of the *Politiques*—German Military Opinion—Views of German Financiers—The Popular Mind—Bethmann-Hollweg.

XLVII. AMERICA AT THE CROSS-ROADS 465
　　　The Purpose of the Allies—American Ideals—Mr. Wilson's increasing Difficulties—Mr. Elihu Root's Speech—The Problem for America narrowed and clarified

CONTENTS.

XLVIII. THE POSITION AT SEA (January 24, 1915–February 29, 1916) 477
> Tirpitz's Plan—The Allied and German Losses at Sea—The German Submarine Campaign — The *Baralong* Incident—The British Blockade—German Commerce Raiders—The Work of the British Fleet.

XLIX. THE WAR IN THE ÆGEAN AND IN AFRICA (October 1915–May 1916) 493
> Stalemate at Salonika—Bulgaria's Temper—The Position in Constantinople—The Defences of Egypt—The Defeat of the Senussi—The Conquest of the Cameroons—Germany's Principles of Colonization.

L. THE RUSSIAN FRONT IN THE SPRING OF 1916 (January 11–April 18) 512
> The Battles of Lake Narotch—Yudenitch takes Erzerum—Capture of Trebizond.

LI. THE FALL OF KUT (December 3, 1915–April 29, 1916) 527
> The Siege of Kut—The Relieving Force—The Battle of 6th and 7th January—The Battles of 13th and 21st January—The Attempt of 7th to 8th March—The Attempt of 5th April—The Last Efforts—Fall of Kut—The Responsibility of the Government of India.

LII. THE BATTLE OF VERDUN: FIRST STAGE (February 21–April 10, 1916) 539
> The Reasons for Falkenhayn's Plan—Nature of Verdun Area—The French Position—The Attack of 21st February—The Crisis at Douaumont—Pétain's Scheme of Defence—The German Attack west of the Meuse—The Struggle for Vaux—The Flank Attack at Avocourt—The Position on 10th April—Pétain—The Achievement of the French Soldier.

ILLUSTRATIONS

VOLUME II

RIGHT HONOURABLE DAVID LLOYD GEORGE	*Frontispiece*
GASSED	42
From a painting by John S. Sargent, R.A.	
THE SALT LAKE, SUVLA BAY	238
From a painting by Norman Wilkinson	
MARSHAL HENRI-PHILLIPPE PÉTAIN	554
From a photograph by Melcy, Paris	
VERDUN ON THE MEUSE, BEFORE BOMBARDMENT	566
From a painting by A. Renaud	

LIST OF MAPS.

1. The Gallipoli Peninsula 32
2. The Second Battle of Ypres 56
3. The Spring Campaign in Artois, 1915 78
4. The Italian Battle-ground 122
5. The Mesopotamian Campaign 178
6. The Campaign in South-west Africa 186
7. The German Advance from the Donajetz to the Eve of the Fall of Warsaw 196
8. The Gallipoli Peninsula: Anzac and Suvla Areas 252
9. The German Advance from Warsaw to Vilna . . 280
10. Champagne 298
11. The Fighting in Artois, September 1915 . . . 302
12. The Battle of Loos 318
13. Race Distribution in the Balkans 330
14. The Serbian Campaign 374
15. Riga and Dvinsk 410
16. The Western Frontier of Egypt 502
17. The Cameroons 508
18. The Erzerum Campaign 524
19. Mesopotamia: the Kut Area 534
20. The Verdun Area 572

A HISTORY OF THE GREAT WAR

CHAPTER XXVI.

THE OPENING OF THE DARDANELLES CAMPAIGN.

September 1, 1914–April 27, 1915.

The First Hint of an Eastern Diversion—Discussions in the War Council—Lord Kitchener, Lord Fisher, and Mr. Churchill—Subsidiary *versus* Divergent Operations—Topography and History of the Dardanelles—Justification for the Naval Attack—Fortifications of the Straits—The Naval Attack and its Results—The Origin of the Military Expedition—Sir Ian Hamilton—The Tactical Problem—The Battle of the Landing.

TOWARDS the close of 1914 the mind of the British Cabinet was much exercised by the deadlock in the West. To some of its members it seemed, in spite of Sir John French's hopefulness, that the German defence was impenetrable except by an attrition so slow that success would entail the bankruptcy of the conqueror. They believed victory to be certain, but wished it to come soon, and would fain have ended the war before the great drafts on Britain's man-power fell due. In this impatience there was a sound strategical instinct. There were no flanks to be turned in France and Flanders, but vulnerable flanks might be found elsewhere. The main gate of the enemy's beleaguered fortress was strongly held, but there were various back doors which might be found unguarded. Above all, they desired to make use of all the assets of Britain, and in the campaign in the West, since Sir John French's scheme of an advance by the coast road had been discarded, there was no direct part which the British navy could play. But in other regions a joint enterprise might be possible, where the sea-power of Britain could be used to decisive purpose.

Accordingly, we find during the winter a great scheme-making among Ministers and their technical advisers. Lord Fisher favoured a combined military and naval attack on the Schleswig-Holstein coast, for which he produced a colossal programme of new construction. His aim was to get behind the German right wing on land, and with the assistance of Russia to clear the Baltic. The enterprise seems to have been blessed at various times by Mr. Lloyd George and Mr. Churchill, but it faded from the air as it became clear that an immediate attack by Sir John French on a large scale was out of the question. The entry of Turkey into the war convinced the Government that, if a blow was to be struck in a new area, that area must be the Near East. Mr. Lloyd George's fancy dwelt on Salonika. He was anxious, with the co-operation of Greece and Russia, to strike at the flank of the Teutonic League, and for the purpose to transfer a large British army to Serbia. The scheme was strongly opposed by military opinion, which pointed to the poor communications in Serbia for an advance and the extreme danger of depleting the British front in the West; and, though Lord Kitchener was prepared at one time to agree to a modification of it, the project died when Greece refused her assistance. A third alternative remained, which, compared with the other two, was sane and reasonable—to clear the Dardanelles and strike at Constantinople.

The Dardanelles campaign is one of the most pitiful, tragic, and glorious episodes in British history. It can be judged to-day as fairly as it is ever likely to be judged, for sufficient details have been given to the world. But in telling its story certain obscure preliminaries have to be determined before the responsibility for its inception can be fixed. Four matters must be recounted ere a verdict can be passed: the discussions in the Cabinet before the naval action was decreed; the claims of the enterprise as a whole to be considered as a divergent or, in the alternative, as a subsidiary operation; the wisdom of the attack by ships alone; and the grounds upon which we entered upon, and the plan which governed, the larger military operations.*

* The subject was investigated by the Dardanelles Commission, which issued two reports (Cd. 8490 and Cmd. 371). The findings of the Commission need not be regarded as final, but the reports include most of the material evidence. For the much-disputed tale of the Cabinet discussions, see also Sir G. Arthur's *Life of Kitchener* (1920), and Lord Fisher's *Memories* (1919). Among the mass of general literature Sir C E. Callwell's *The Dardanelles* (1919), and H. W. Nevinson's *The Dardanelles Campaign* (1918), seem to be especially valuable. Sir Ian Hamilton has written the story from his own point of view in his *Gallipoli Diary* (1920), and Mr. John Masefield's *Gallipoli* (1916) is the saga of a great feat of arms.

I.

The Cabinet of twenty-two members which in August was responsible for the conduct of the war speedily revealed itself as too large, cumbrous, and miscellaneous a body for the secret and efficient transaction of business. Accordingly, towards the end of November, a special committee was created from it under the name of the War Council, which could act without further reference. Various Ministers, such as Sir Edward Grey, Lord Crewe, and Mr. Lloyd George, attended occasionally, but the regular members were the Prime Minister, the First Lord of the Admiralty, and the Secretary for War, who were assisted by their naval and military advisers. Of the three the strongest personality was Lord Kitchener. The outbreak of war had dispersed the old General Staff overseas, and Kitchener was virtually his own General Staff, and to a large extent Commander-in-Chief as well as War Secretary. His great experience, his unique public prestige, and the consciousness that he represented in his person the whole military authority of Britain made it hard for his colleagues to differ from his views. This difficulty was increased by the fact that he was unfamiliar with councils, had no facility in debate or in self-expression, and was apt to issue his conclusions as verdicts without argument or apologies. After him the First Lord was the most forceful figure, for Mr. Asquith's leisurely dialectic was ill suited to the rough business of war. Mr. Churchill was more than a distinguished Minister of the Crown; he was an enthusiast in his department, and had as sound a knowledge of military science as most staff officers. His active mind was for ever exploring new roads to victory, and from him and from the First Sea Lord at his elbow was bound to come the initiative in ideas.

As early as 1st September he had suggested to Kitchener the plan of seizing the Dardanelles by means of a Greek army, and so admitting a British fleet to the Sea of Marmora. On 25th November he proposed to the War Council to strike at the Gallipoli peninsula as a feint, but Kitchener decided that the movement was premature. But the matter remained in the minds of the War Council, and during December we find Kitchener discussing with Sir John Maxwell, then commanding in Egypt, the possibility of landing forces at Alexandretta in the Gulf of Iskanderun, to strike at the communications of any Turkish invasion of Egypt. On January 2, 1915, a new complexion was given to things by an appeal for help from Russia, then struggling on the

Bzura and in the Caucasus. Kitchener resolved that Russia's request must be met, and next day pledged himself to a demonstration against the Turks, telling Mr. Churchill that he considered the Dardanelles the only likely plan. On the 2nd, too, Lord Fisher had also informed the First Lord that he thought that the attack on Turkey held the field, " but only if it is immediate." Mr. Churchill telegraphed to Vice-Admiral Carden on the 3rd asking if he considered that it was possible to force the Dardanelles by the use of ships alone, and received the answer that they might be forced " by extended operations with a large number of ships." As far back as 1906 the General Staff had reported on this very point and had come to an adverse decision, and Admiral Sir Henry Jackson, whom Mr. Churchill had asked for a memorandum, was no less discouraging. On the 11th Vice-Admiral Carden telegraphed his plan in detail, and the Admiralty Staff which examined it were more than dubious about its merits. At a meeting of the War Council on the 13th Mr. Churchill explained the Carden scheme, and Kitchener declared that it was worth trying. The Council accordingly instructed the Admiralty to prepare for a naval expedition in February " to bombard and take the Gallipoli peninsula, with Constantinople as its objective."

It is clear that the chief patron of the scheme was Mr. Churchill. His principal naval advisers were either hostile or half-hearted, and assented only on the understanding that in case of failure the attack could instantly be broken off. In the Council itself Lord Fisher and Sir Arthur Wilson kept silence, conceiving it to be their duty to answer questions when asked, but not to volunteer advice. But the former, though wavering sometimes between two opinions, was on the whole against the enterprise. He knew a good deal about the subject, having served under Hornby during the Russo-Turkish War when that admiral lay off Constantinople, and having, as First Sea Lord in 1904, fully investigated the whole problem of forcing the Dardanelles. The more he looked at Mr. Churchill's policy the less he liked it, and on the 25th he wrote to the Prime Minister stating his objections. After a private meeting between Mr. Asquith, Mr. Churchill, and Lord Fisher on the 28th, a War Council was held, in which the First Lord carried his colleagues with him. For a moment it seemed as if Lord Fisher would resign, but he was persuaded to remain, apparently because he thought that the naval attack, even if it failed, need not involve serious losses. But on the feasibility of the operation he was still unconvinced, and he had with him the best naval opinion. Unfortunately, the naval authorities, out of a scrupulous regard for etiquette, left on the minds of the War Council the impression that they were not hostile to the scheme so much upon its technical merits as because they would have preferred a different objective in a totally different region. That appears to have been the view of Mr. Asquith and Lord Kitchener; it cannot have been Mr. Churchill's, who had precise knowledge of the technical naval objections but believed that new developments in gunnery had nullified them, and was prepared to force his opinion against the experts. That day, the 28th of January, the decision to attack the Dardanelles by the fleet alone was finally ratified.

At this point it will be well to pause and consider two points which are vital if we are to form a judgment on the enterprise—the relation of such a plan to the general strategy of the war, and the kind of problem which an unsupported naval attack involved.

In the first place, it is necessary to be clear on the meaning of the terms "subsidiary" and "divergent" operations. The first is properly a term of praise; the second of blame. Every great campaign must produce one or more subsidiary operations. A blow may be necessary at the enemy's line of supply, or a halting neutral may require to have his mind made up for him, or some piece of enemy property, strategically valuable, deserves to be gathered in. Such operations are, strictly speaking, part of the main campaign, and success in them directly subserves the main object of the war. A "divergent" operation, on the contrary, has no relation to the main effort, except that it is directed against the same enemy. Success in it is compatible with utter failure in the chief campaign, and does not necessarily bring the issue one step nearer. It usually involves some wasting of the force available for the main theatre, and it means a certain dissipation of the energy and brain-power of the high commands. The history of Britain is strewn with the wrecks of divergent operations, and a few instances may make their meaning clear. In the years 1793-4, when it was our business to scotch the Revolutionary Government of France by striking at its head, we set out on adventures in every quarter of the globe. We took six West Indian islands—strategically as important as the North Pole; we landed in Haiti; we sent a force under the Duke of York to the Netherlands; we held Toulon as long as we could; we seized Corsica; we sent an expedition to La Vendée. The consequence was that we succeeded nowhere, and the Revolutionary Government at the end of that time was stronger than ever. Next year, 1795, while things were going badly for us on other battle-grounds, we chose to send an expedition to Cape Town, to attack Demerara, and to make a disastrous landing on an island in Quiberon Bay. And so we continued to indulge our passion for outlandish geography, while France grew in strength and the star of Napoleon rose above the horizon. Take the year 1807. We sent a force under Sir Home Popham to the Cape, which proceeded to South America, took Buenos Aires, and presently lost it. We projected an expedition to Valparaiso, and another against Mexico. These ventures, as a matter of fact, were utter failures; but had they been successful they would have in no way helped the main purpose of the war. For in Europe Napoleon was moving from strength to strength. Eighteen hundred and seven was the year of Friedland and of the Treaty of Tilsit.

Let us attempt to set down the principles which govern legitimate subsidiary operations, and separate them from the illegitimate divergent type. There is first the question of locality. Obviously it is not necessary that the minor campaign should be fought in the same area as the major. Wellington wore down the strength of the French in the Peninsula, though the main theatre of war, the place where the big stake lay, was central Europe. In the American Civil War the eyes of the world were fixed on the lines of the Potomac, but the real centre of gravity was Vicksburg and the operations on the Mississippi. Nor, again, is it necessary that even the major campaign should be fought in or adjoining the enemy's home country. In the Seven Years' War France was conquered at Plassey and at Quebec, because it was for an overseas empire, for the domination of India and America, that the combatants fought. The locality of a subsidiary operation matters nothing, provided—and this is the first principle—the operation directly subserves the main object of the war. In other words, the operation, if successful, must be profitable. In the second place, there must be a reasonable chance of success. A subsidiary operation, thoroughly justified by general strategy, may be a blunder if it is undertaken with forces too weak to surmount the difficulties. If the force is not strong enough to effect the object, then, however desirable the object, the force would have been better left at home. Thirdly, any force used for the subsidiary operation must not seriously weaken the operations in the main theatre, unless the former operation is so vital that in itself it becomes the centre of gravity of the campaign. Waterloo was a battle which is rightly regarded as one of the decisive fights of the world, but the Allies at Waterloo won by a very narrow margin. At the time Wellington's seasoned veterans of the Peninsula were for the most part involved in the woods and swamps of the Canadian frontier. That was inevitable; but had they been sent there as part of a strategic purpose with the European situation what it was on Napoleon's return from Elba, it would have exactly illustrated the danger we are discussing. In the present war it was clear from the start that Germany must be conquered in Europe, and that the main campaign must be that on the lines from the North Sea to the Alps, and from the Baltic to the Bukovina. Germany had set the battle plan, and her antagonists could not choose but accept the challenge. Any weakening of these lines so as to compromise their strength for the sake of a subsidiary operation was clearly inadvisable by all the principles of war.

Whether the Dardanelles expedition violated the second and the third of these canons will be discussed in due course. But the application of the first—the value of the objective sought, and its relation to the central purpose of the Allies—can be made clear by a few general considerations. What were the ends to be attained by the forcing of the Dardanelles?

The Sea of Marmora and the winding straits that link it with the Ægean and the Euxine form a water frontier of some two hundred miles between Asia and Europe. This meeting-place of the East and the West has been the source of some of the most momentous events in human history. The story begins in the twilight of legend. As the traveller approaches the Dardanelles from the south he sees on his right, in front of the Bithynian Olympus, the hill called Kag Dagh, which is that Mount Ida whence the gods watched the siege of Troy. In the plain between it and the sea flow Simois and Scamander, once choked with famous dead. There by the hill of Hissarlik stood "windy Ilium." The current of the Dardanelles made the Straits difficult for laden merchantmen, and it was the fashion to unload the ships at their mouth, tow them empty through the Straits, and carry the goods on pack horses across the plain of Troy. But Priam, King of Troy, exacted an unconscionable tribute from the harassed Greek traders, and the Trojan war was fought to abolish the impost. So, if we are to accept the speculations of modern scholars, it was not a woman's face that launched the thousand ships, but an early craving for tariff reform. Across the Dardanelles Leander swam to meet his mistress Hero, the priestess of Aphrodite. There at the Narrows, Xerxes, seeking to conquer Europe, transported his armies by a bridge of boats on their way to Thermopylæ and Platæa; and a century and a half later Alexander the Great led his troops by the same passage to the conquest of Asia. On its shores St. Paul heard the cry from Macedonia, "Come over and help us." At first Constantine would have built his capital there, but he preferred the Bosphorus, where stood the old Greek colony of Byzantium, for centuries the emporium of the Euxine commerce. The new city which rose around the Golden Horn became the ruling centre of the Roman Empire. The transference of authority was a stroke of genius, for while the West went down in ruins before the incursions of the barbarian, Byzantium preserved for a thousand years the forms of Roman imperialism and the culture of the ancient world. The Dardanelles was designed by nature as a protection to the capital on the Bosphorus against any naval incursion from the south. But the Greek emperors of Byzantium, though they maintained formidable armies, seem to have neglected all questions of naval defence. In particular they made no serious attempts to fortify the approach from the Ægean. In the thirteenth century the Crusaders, forgetting the object of their expedition, and lured by the plunder of a rich capital, found little difficulty in bringing the Venetian fleet to the Dardanelles, and placing a Flemish count on the throne of Byzantium. Had they cared to maintain their conquest, they might have erected a formidable barrier against the Turk. But this Latin Empire was short-lived, and the Greek monarchs who followed the Counts of Flanders had neither the energy nor the means to meet the danger that soon threatened them from Asia. In the space of a hundred years the Ottoman Turks, nomads from Central Asia, had made themselves masters of the Near East. They held the Asiatic shore of the Sea of Marmora, and Constantinople, weak and wealthy, was the inevitable object of their ambition. In 1358 they crossed the Narrows of the Dardanelles, occupied Gallipoli, and made the rocky peninsula a base for their career of European conquest. Presently they had overrun the Balkan lands, and their capital was Adrianople. The territory of the Eastern Empire was now confined to a few hundred square miles around the walls of the great city. The end came on May 29, 1453, when Mahommed II., the stern, black-bearded conqueror whose portrait hangs to-day in the Sultan's Treasure House, breached the walls of Constantinople and ended the reign of the Palæologi.

The Turks were a martial people, with an eye for military needs.

From the outset the Sultans of Constantinople realized that the defence of their capital and the existence of their empire depended upon their security against naval attack. Until the rise of the Russian power in comparatively modern times there was no danger from the Black Sea. But it was all important to bar the western entrance of the Sea of Marmora, and the Turks had no sooner occupied Gallipoli than they began to fortify the Dardanelles. The " Castles of Europe and Asia " were erected at the entrance, which to-day have been replaced by the forts of Sedd-el-Bahr and Kum Kale. Higher up at the Narrows Sestos and Abydos were fortified—the " inner castles " of old descriptions. Besides these shore defences a fleet of galleys and sailing craft was always kept at Gallipoli on a war footing. In the year 400 the conspirator Gainas had led his Goths in rafts across the channel, and midway had been scattered by the Roman galleys. From that day till 1654 no attempt was made, save by the Turks, against the passage. In the latter year the Norwegian Adelen, acting as an Admiral of Venice, fought and defeated a Turkish fleet at the mouth of the Dardanelles, and seized Tenedos; but the shore forts barred all further progress. The Turks seemed to have found the expedient which would make their capital secure. Nevertheless in 1807 the Straits were passed. A British admiral, Sir J. T. Duckworth, was sent by Collingwood from Cadiz with a powerful squadron to detach the Sultan from the French alliance. He had orders to demand the surrender of the Turkish fleet, and in case of refusal to bombard Constantinople. Duckworth's feat was remarkable, not because he encountered any effective resistance, but because of the risks he ran and the light which his experience casts upon all similar enterprises. It was no easy matter to convey a squadron of line-of-battle ships and frigates under sail through the narrow winding waters and against the heavy currents of the Dardanelles. The " castles " at the entrance opened fire, as did the Narrows forts, but with little effect. A show of resistance by a Turkish squadron at Gallipoli ended in its prompt destruction by a detachment under Sir Sidney Smith. Duckworth anchored before Constantinople, and it seemed as if his mission were successful. But the French agent there, Sebastiani, induced the Sultan to prolong negotiations till heavy batteries had been erected on the sea front. Duckworth might have silenced these, but by this time he had begun to see the difficulties of his position. Warships that had run past the forts of the Dardanelles without subduing them and without leaving garrisons to secure the passage were in grave jeopardy.

When their supplies of food, water, and ammunition were exhausted they could receive no more except by the grace of their enemies It was this consideration that compelled Duckworth to retire before his mission was accomplished. He ran through the Dardanelles into the Ægean with the tide and the wind in his favour. The Turkish batteries opened fire—chiefly clumsy mediæval cannon throwing stone balls, and mounted on slides formed of parallel balks of timber. They could not be trained to right or left, but could fire only when a ship came opposite their muzzles. Yet even this primitive artillery was formidable: several of our ships were hit and badly damaged, and there was some loss of life. Duckworth's experience was such as to increase the reputation of the Dardanelles defences.

For a decade after 1820 all Europe was arrayed against Turkey, and between her and Russia there was constant bickering. Presently the position changed, the Western Powers grew apprehensive of Russia's Mediterranean designs, and were more inclined to support Turkey against her. It is unnecessary to enter into the details of the troubled diplomacy of these years, but we may note that in 1841, by a treaty signed by Russia, Britain, Prussia, Austria, and France, Turkey's right to keep the Dardanelles closed was made part of the public law of Europe.* No ship of war could pass the Straits without the express permission of the Sultan, and all merchantmen were to be examined at the entrance and show their papers. When the Crimean War broke out, the alliance of the Sultan was the necessary prelude to the passing of the Straits by the British and French fleets. The first step taken was the fortification of the Isthmus of Bulair, on the advice of Sir John Burgoyne, and its occupation by the Allied troops. The isthmus, a neck of land less than three miles wide between the Gulf of Saros and the Sea of Marmora, connects the Gallipoli peninsula with the mainland of Thrace. French and English engineers surveyed the ground and constructed a line of entrenchments from sea to sea. At that time there was much ill-informed criticism of these steps, and some impatience that lines should be fortified so far from the theatre of war. But the policy was wholly right. All operations on the Black Sea shores or on the Danube must depend upon a secure line of communications through the Dardanelles, and the Dardanelles could not be secure unless the Gallipoli peninsula were held.

* In 1871, when Russia denounced the clauses of the Treaty of Paris which forbade her to maintain a fleet in the Black Sea, a further convention was signed in London, confirming the treaty of 1841 and extending its provisions to the Bosphorus.

Since Duckworth's day the Straits had only once been passed, and again by a British admiral. When in 1877, during the Russo-Turkish War, the Russian advance from the Danube seemed to imperil Constantinople, our Mediterranean Fleet was sent to Besika Bay, and the Admiralty discussed with its commander, Sir Geoffrey Phipps Hornby, how it should be used to prevent a hostile occupation of the Turkish capital. In those days it was a first principle of our foreign policy that Russia should not have Constantinople. The British Cabinet hesitated, at times inclining to a direct support of the Turks, at others contemplating the possibility of having to meet the united forces of a victorious Russia and a subservient Turkey. It was anticipated that if our fleet attempted the Dardanelles, Turkey might oppose it, or the Russians be in possession of the northern shore. Hornby reported that, although the defences of the Straits had been greatly improved, he did not think the batteries would prevent him reaching the Sea of Marmora. But in a dispatch dated August 10, 1877, he pointed out that even after the Dardanelles were passed the situation of our fleet would be critical. He felt so strongly on the subject that he urged the Government to send a British force to occupy the Bulair lines, which the Turks were then putting into a state of defence. This, however, would have committed the Government to a definite policy, and nothing was done. In January 1878, when the Russians arrived before Constantinople, Hornby was directed to enter the Straits, and had actually brought up his fleet to the entrance when he was stopped by a telegram from the Admiralty. On 12th February he was ordered to pass the Straits without waiting for the Sultan's permit, and "if fired upon and his ships struck, to return the fire, but not to wait to silence the forts." As it happened, he passed through without fighting, and anchored in the Sea of Marmora. There he spent some anxious days. He did not trust the Turkish commandant at Bulair, and expected at any moment to hear that the Russians had seized the lines there and cut off his squadron from supplies by getting command of the Dardanelles defences. A rupture with Russia, however, was avoided, and Hornby's naval demonstration undoubtedly strengthened the hands of the British Government in the negotiations which ended with the Treaty of Berlin.

The history of the Dardanelles has been thus fully sketched because, without some knowledge of it, it is not easy to understand the importance of the Straits to Turkey. Against a naval Power like Britain or France they were the last defence of the capital, and that capital, more than any other great city of the world, was the palladium of the Power which had its seat there. It was almost all that was left to the race of Osman of their once splendid European possessions. It had been the base for those proud expeditions against Vienna and the Hungarian plains when Turkey was still a conquering Power. It had been the prize for which her neighbours had lusted, and which she had still retained against all rivals. It was, in a real sense, the sign visible of Turkey's existence as a sovereign state. If Constantinople fell Turkey would fall, and the doom of the capital was sealed so soon as the Allied battleships, with their communications secure behind them, entered the Sea of Marmora.

The strategic importance of the forcing of the Dardanelles in a war with Turkey was therefore clear beyond all doubt. But in how far would the fall of Constantinople influence the decision of the main European conflict? In the first place, it would to some extent simplify Russia's problem, and release troops for Poland and Galicia. There was the possibility that a mere threat to the capital might lead to a revolution which would overthrow the shaky edifice of Enver's rule. The bulk of the Turkish people did not share the passion for Germany felt by the Committee of Union and Progress, and advices from Constantinople during those days seemed to point to the imminence of a rising which would make a clean sweep of the Young Turk party, and restore the Sultan to his old place at the side of France and Britain. Again, the opening of the passage between the Black Sea and the Ægean would give Russia the means for exporting her accumulated wheat supplies. The lack of these was increasing the cost of bread in Western Europe, and the restriction of Russian exports had made the rate of exchange set violently against her, so that she was paying in some cases thirty times the normal price for her foreign purchases. She also stood in sore need of a channel for the entrance of war munitions. Archangel had been closed since January, the trans-Siberian line was a costly and circuitous route for all but her imports from Japan, while entries by Norway and Sweden were at the best precarious. But the main strategic value of the Dardanelles plan lay in its effect upon hesitating neutrals. Italy at the moment was still in the valley of indecision, and the downfall of Turkey and its influence upon the Balkan States would impel her to action. Turkey's defeat would have an effect upon the Balkan position like the addition of a new chemical to a compound—it would leave none of the constituents unaltered. Greece, Rumania, and Bulgaria had all of them national interests and purposes which compelled them to keep a watchful eye on each other, and which made it difficult for any one of them to move without its neighbour. Bulgaria, who had borne the heavy end of the Turkish campaign, had lost the prize of victory. Three compacts had been violated to her hurt, and she was deeply distrustful of all the Great Powers, and especially of Russia. German financiers had befriended her in 1913, when France and Britain had stood aside, and her Stambolovists had always looked to Austria as their ally. A secret treaty with Austria had indeed been concluded a month after the outbreak of the war. With Greece and Serbia—especially with the latter— she had a bitter quarrel over the delimitation of territory after the Balkan wars, and she had little cause to forget Rumania's intervention. At the same time her geographical position made it highly perilous for her to join the Teutonic League, unless its victory were assured. Her attitude was therefore a circumspect neutrality; but the first Allied guns that spoke in the Sea of Marmora would compel her to a decision. With Bulgaria decided, Greece and Rumania would follow suit. Rumania was faced with a complex situation from which she was slowly disentangling herself under the pressure of events. If her southern frontiers were safe it seemed likely that she would make her choice, and her geographical situation and her well-equipped army of nearly half a million would make her an invaluable ally. Greece in such circumstances could not stand apart. With Turkey out of action and the Balkans united on the Allies' side, the most critical part of the main campaign—the long front of Russia—would be greatly eased. When the Italian guns sounded on the Isonzo and the Rumanian force took the Austrian right wing in flank, the balance against Russian arms might be redressed.

In a speech made later in the year Mr. Churchill defined the prize at which he aimed: " Beyond those four miles of ridge and scrub on which our soldiers, our French comrades, our gallant Australian and New Zealand fellow-subjects are now battling, lie the downfall of a hostile empire, the destruction of an enemy's fleet and army, the fall of a world-famous capital, and probably the accession of powerful allies. The struggle will be heavy, the risks numerous, the losses cruel ; but victory, when it comes, will make amends for all. There never was a great subsidiary operation of war in which a more complete harmony of strategic, political, and economic advantages has combined, or which stood in truer relation to the main decision which is in the central theatre. Through the Narrows of the Dardanelles and across the ridges of the Gallipoli peninsula lie some of the shortest paths to a triumphant peace." The language may have been over-coloured, but substantially the claim was just. A Dardanelles expedition directly subserved the main object of the war. An attack by ships alone, an attack that in case of failure could be promptly suspended, would not, it may fairly be argued, have weakened the Allies' strength in the main theatre, though Kitchener may well have reflected that in the East it was not wise for Britain to put her hand to the plough and then turn back. It remains to consider whether the enterprise fulfilled the third of the conditions of a wise subsidiary operation : whether the plan gave a reasonable chance of success.

A naval attack on the Dardanelles without the co-operation of a military force would be a battle of ships against forts, and it had long been widely held by experts that in such a contest the advantage would lie with the forts. What were the grounds and the historical warrant of this opinion ? There is a letter of Nelson's, written on July 29, 1794, at the time when we were driving the French from Corsica and preparing to reduce the forts of Calvi. It had been suggested that the attack should be made from the sea, but Nelson demurred. He wrote to Lord Hood : " I took the liberty of observing that the business of laying wood before walls was much altered of late, and even if they had no hot shot, which I believed they had, that the quantity of powder and shot which would be fired away on such an attack could be much better directed from a battery on shore." Armour-clads replaced wooden walls, and high-explosive shells superseded red-hot shot, but it still remained true that shore batteries were a more effective weapon of assault against fortifications than even the heaviest guns mounted in the most powerful ships. For a little there was some disposition to believe that improvements in naval artillery and the increase of armoured protection might turn the scale in favour of the ships. But modern progress in armaments was as advantageous to the fort as to the ship, and one of the highest living authorities [*] had argued that, if anything, the advantage of the fort had increased since Nelson's day. He had even suggested what at first seemed a startling paradox, that the old wooden battleship, with its tiers of smooth-bore guns, could

[*] Lord Sydenham in his standard work on *Fortification*.

at close range pour into a land battery a more formidable fire, with a better chance of scoring effective hits, than the modern battleship with its few heavy guns at long range, even though these were weapons of the highest precision, fitted with telescopic sights, and directed by the aid of range-finders and observers.

In former times, though the shore battery generally beat the ship, there were exceptional cases when the victory lay with the latter. Such were Exmouth's attack on Algiers in 1816, and the exploit at Acre in 1840 But neither was a true test. The Algerian and Egyptian gunners not only shot badly, but allowed the hostile fleet to come up and anchor at close quarters without opening fire. It was the memory of these successes which led the Allied admirals in the Crimean War to believe that in the same way they could silence the forts on the sea front at Sebastopol. The attempt, made on October 17, 1854, ended disastrously, with six ships out of action and more than 500 men killed and wounded. A year later, on the anniversary of the Sebastopol bombardment, the forts of Kinburn were silenced by a naval attack. Napoleon the Third's three floating batteries, the *Dévastation*, *Lave*, and *Tonnant*, were engaged in the operations —the first of ironclads, and the pioneers of all modern armoured fleets. This event produced a new theory, and for some time it was supposed that the coming of the armoured ship had changed the conditions of the problem. But all subsequent experience belied this view. In the American Civil War the repeated naval assaults on Charleston ended in failure. It is true that in the attack on New Orleans Admiral Farragut succeeded in passing the forts that defended the narrow waterway of the Mississippi, but he did not attempt to silence them. He steamed past them, and then had the city at his mercy on its unprotected flank. His feat—not an attack on forts, but an evasion of them—would have been impossible had the river channel been protected by a modern mine-field. The most significant incident, perhaps, was our bombardment of Alexandria in 1882. At first sight it would seem to prove that a fleet could in a few hours and with trifling losses master forts on land. But the careful study of the bombardment which was made by an American Commission with the assistance of British naval officers, put the matter in a very different light. Our squadron was the most powerful which up to that date had ever operated against forts. One of the ships, the old *Inflexible*, was the Dreadnought of her day. We expended a great quantity of ammunition—about 1,740 heavy projectiles, 7-inch and upwards, including 88 rounds from the guns of the *Inflexible*, together with 1,400 smaller shells, and about 33,500 bullets from machine guns and rifles. The conditions were perfect—close range, calm weather, no mines, and highly incompetent opponents. Yet it was proved that not more than three of the Egyptian guns were directly put out of action by our fire. The whole defence system was bad. Most of the pieces were mounted *en barbette* over a low parapet that gave hardly any cover to the gunners. The guns at one fort were placed in front of a barrack wall, which stopped and exploded scores of shells that otherwise would have flown harmlessly overhead. What would have happened under better conditions was shown by the fact that a small battery of disappearing guns, constructed some years before by an American officer, Colonel Chaillé-Long, was never silenced, and was firing the day after the bombardment. Had not the forts surrendered, twenty-eight guns could have opened fire next day, when our fleet was almost bankrupt of ammunition. The natural deduction from the Alexandria bombardment was that a naval attack on modern forts, well armed and adequately manned, would be a highly critical operation, would most probably end in failure, and could only succeed at the cost of serious loss.

This conclusion was so generally accepted that during the Spanish-American War the United States Navy Department repeatedly warned the admirals that battleships and heavy cruisers must not be risked in close-range action with forts. All that the navy ventured upon was a long-range bombardment of the Spanish coast fortifications, attacks that were little more than demonstrations, for no serious attempt was made to silence the land batteries. A few guns mounted on Socapa Point at Santiago, and very badly served, were sufficient to prevent Admiral Sampson from risking a close attack. It was the same in the Russo-Japanese War. Admiral Togo never risked his battleships and cruisers in a close attack on the sea batteries of Port Arthur. There were occasional long-range bombardments with no result, and the reduction of the fortress was due to the attack by land. Similarly Tsing-tau in the present war fell not to Admiral Kato's squadron, but to General Kamio's army.

It might be said, however, that though ships were not likely to silence forts, forts could not prevent ships running past them. The argument was not relevant to the case of the Dardanelles, where in the long run not only a passage, but the occupation of the passage, was necessary, as Hornby found in 1878. But in any case it was unsound, for the development of submarine mines and torpedo warfare had made it all but impossible to evade the fort. A mine-field in a channel, protected by a few well-mounted guns, with searchlights and quick-firers to prevent mine-sweeping by night, was for a fleet a practically impassable barrier. The minefield could not be disposed of until the fort had been destroyed.

Such being the accepted doctrine among naval and military students of the question, it may well be asked why the scheme of forcing the Dardanelles by a naval attack alone was ever accepted by the British Government. It was known that very high naval authority was opposed to it; it was equally true that certain naval authorities approved of it, and that Mr. Churchill was its impassioned advocate. On what grounds? There was an idea abroad that new conditions had been introduced into the problem, and there was the usual tendency to exaggerate the effect of a new weapon. The Dreadnought, the long-range gun, the submarine, had each been hailed as about to revolutionize warfare. It was presumed that the huge high-explosive shells of the modern warship would make land batteries untenable, not by silencing their guns one by one, but by acting like flying mines, the explosion of which would shatter the defences and produce a panic among the gunners. Once the forts were thus temporarily overcome, landing parties would complete the task, the mine-fields would be cleared, and the passage be won. It was also anticipated that with the long range of the newest naval guns the forts could be bombarded from a distance at which their own armament would be ineffective. The notion was that the outer forts at the entrance to the Straits could be silenced by the converging fire of a number of ships from the open sea, while the attack on the inner forts would be carried on by individual fire from ships in the Gulf of Saros, which, with airplanes to direct them, would send their shells over the hills of the Gallipoli peninsula. These two factors —aerial reconnaissance and the increased range of naval guns —were believed to have changed the whole conditions of the enterprise.

It would be unfair to say that there was no colour for this forecast. But it erred in strangely neglecting and underestimating other factors in the situation, and in unduly simplifying the problem. It was not a mere question of a duel between the guns of the fleet and those of the permanent fortifications. Had it been, there would have been much to be said for the optimistic view

But the defences of the Dardanelles had been organized on a system which took the fullest advantage of natural features, and was based on past experience and a scientific knowledge of modern warfare. It was no improvised Turkish expedient, but the work of the German General Staff. It contemplated an attack, not only by a fleet, but by a large military force acting in conjunction. When, therefore, the Allies, to the surprise of their enemies, decided upon a mere naval attack, the problem of the defence was immensely simplified.

To appreciate the difficulties of the attack we must consider briefly the topography of the Straits. Their northern shore is formed by the peninsula of Gallipoli, a tongue of land some fifty miles long, which varies in width from twelve to two or three miles. The country is a mass of rocky ridges rising to a height of over 700 feet from the sea. The hills are so steep and sharply cut that to reach their tops is in many places a matter of sheer climbing. There was little cultivation; there were few villages, and no properly engineered roads. Most of the land was covered with a dense scrub from three to six feet high, with stunted forests in the hollows. Communications were so bad that the usual way from village to village was not by land, but by boat along the inner or outer coast. At the head of the Dardanelles, on the European side, lay the town and harbour of Gallipoli, the headquarters of the naval defence of the Straits. The southern shore is also hilly. Near the entrance on the Asiatic side there is the flat and marshy plain of Troy, which is bounded on the east by hills running to 3,000 feet. On both sides the high ground overhangs the sea passage, and on the north side for about twelve miles the hills form a line of cliffs, with narrow half-moons of beach at the base, and here and there a stream making a gully in the rampart. As everywhere in the Mediterranean, there is practically no tide, but a strong current, rising to four knots, sets continuously down the Straits from the Sea of Marmora. North-easterly winds are prevalent, and before the days of steam these often closed the passage for weeks at a time to ingoing traffic.

There were two groups of forts. The first was at the entrance—on the north side, Cape Helles and Sedd-el-Bahr, with one or two adjacent batteries; on the opposite shore, Kum Kale and Orkanieh. None of these forts were heavily armed, for it was recognized that in any case they would be at a disadvantage against a long-range attack from a fleet in the open sea. The entrance forts were merely the outposts of the real defence. The second group was at the

Narrows. Fourteen miles from the mouth the Straits close in to a width of about three-quarters of a mile. Up to this point their general course has been from south-west to north-east, but now the channel makes a short turn directly northward before resuming its original direction. There is thus within a distance of a few miles a sharp double bend, and guns placed in position at the water's edge could cross their fire against ships ascending the Straits, which would also be brought under end-on fire from guns at the top of the Narrows. At the entrance to the Narrows were the forts of Chanak, or Sultanieh Kalessi, on the Asiatic side, and Kilid Bahr, on the European. The slopes above the latter were studded with batteries, some commanding the approach to the Narrows, others commanding the seaway towards Gallipoli. Along both sides, but especially between Chanak and Nagara, the low ground was lined with batteries. It was possible to attack the forts at the entrance to the Narrows at fairly long range from the wider channel below the bend, but there was no room to bring any large number of ships into action at the same time. Once the entrance was passed all fighting must be at close range.

But the strength of the defence did not depend only on the batteries. An attacking fleet had other weapons to face besides the guns. There was first the obstruction of the channel by submarine mines. To get rid of these by sweeping was nearly impossible, for the light vessels, which alone could be employed, had to face not only the fire of the forts but that of mobile guns on the higher ground. Again, the descending current could be used to send down drift-mines upon the attacking ships. The artillery defence was further supplemented by howitzer batteries on the heights, difficult to locate, easy to move if located, and therefore almost impossible to silence. It was clear that a fleet endeavouring to force a channel thus defended was at the gravest disadvantage. There was only one way to complete success—the co-operation of a land army. By that means there was a chance of gaining possession of the heights behind the forts, attacking them in reverse, assisting the fleet to silence them, and then destroying the mine-field. Only a landing force, too, could deal with the mobile batteries.

It is a simple matter to be wise after the event, and it is easy to judge a military problem pedantically, without allowing for the chances of war. Every operation is to some extent a gamble, even after all the unknown quantities seem to have been determined. History showed a clear verdict on the handicap of a contest between ships and forts, without the assistance of a land army. History, too, showed that to pass the Dardanelles was a perilous achievement, unless the invader held the Gallipoli peninsula, and so could secure his supplies and his retreat. But it is permissible sometimes to defy history and create new precedents —laudable if the attempt succeeds, excusable if it fails. The attack by ships alone cannot be fairly classed as a divergent operation. Even if the weight of historical evidence was against success, there were new features in the problem not yet assessed, and on account of that unknown x and of the extreme value of the prize to be won even a prudent statesman might have felt justified in taking the odd chance. Again, the question of keeping open the communications behind was not so vital as in Hornby's day, for a fleet which passed the Dardanelles could pass the undefended Bosphorus, join up with the Russians in the Black Sea, and find a new base at Odessa or Sebastopol. We must judge the mind of the originators by the knowledge which they possessed in January, not by the damning revelations of March. The chief responsibility for the naval attempt must rest with Mr. Churchill, and it seems fair to conclude that that attempt, since it seemed possible to make it with a strictly limited liability, was a legitimate venture of war.

II.

On November 3, 1914, an Anglo-French squadron had appeared at the Dardanelles and for ten minutes bombarded the forts at the entrance. The order had been given by the British Admiralty, and the purpose seems to have been to draw the fire of the forts and ascertain if they possessed long-range guns. Such premature action was a blunder, for it put the enemy on the alert, and during the three months that followed no further step was taken, though by the end of January 1915 the island of Tenedos had been seized, while Greece tolerated the use of Lemnos, where the great inlet of Mudros supplied a valuable base for naval operations. By the middle of February a considerable naval force, French and British, had been concentrated at the entrance to the Straits. With two exceptions, the larger British ships were of the pre-Dreadnought class; but there were also present the *Inflexible*, which had been in the Battle of the Falkland Islands, and the new super-Dreadnought, the *Queen Elizabeth*. The latter belonged to the most recent and most powerful class of battleship in the world. She was one of a group of five which, when war began, were still in the builders' hands, and in the ordinary course she would not have been commissioned till the late summer of 1915. Her main armament was made up of eight 15-inch guns, so mounted as to give a fire of four guns ahead or astern, and of the whole eight on either side.

The operations against the outer forts began on Friday, 19th February. The ships engaged were the *Inflexible, Agamemnon, Cornwallis, Vengeance,* and *Triumph*—British; and the *Bouvet, Suffren,* and *Gaulois*—French; covered by a flotilla of destroyers.[*] The naval force was under the command of Vice-Admiral Sackville Carden, and the French squadron was under Rear-Admiral Guépratte. Behind the battle-line lay the new mother-ship for seaplanes, the *Ark Royal,* named after Howard's flagship in the war with the Spanish Armada. From her aircraft were sent up to watch the fire of the battleships and signal the result. The action began at 8 a.m. It was clear that the forts at Cape Helles, on the point of the peninsula, and at Kum Kale, on the opposite shore, were frequently hit, and at times seemed to be smothered in bursting shells. It was harder to make out what was happening to the low earthworks of the batteries about Sedd-el-Bahr. All morning the bombardment continued; it was like target practice, for not a single shot was fired in reply. Admiral Carden came to the conclusion that the forts had been seriously damaged, and at a quarter to three in the afternoon gave the order to close in. What followed showed that aerial observation of long-range fire was no easy matter. As the ships steamed nearer, the hitherto silent and apparently destroyed forts began to shoot. They made bad practice, for no one of the six ships that had shortened range was hit. By sundown the European batteries were quiet again, but Kum Kale was still firing, when, on account of the failing light, Admiral Carden withdrew the fleet.

For some days there was bad weather, but by the morning of Thursday, 25th February, it had sufficiently improved for operations to be resumed. At 10 a.m. on that day the *Queen Elizabeth, Agamemnon,* and *Irresistible,*[†] and the French battleship *Gaulois,* renewed the long-range bombardment of the outer forts. It was clear that these had not been seriously damaged by the action of

---

[*] *Inflexible*—17,250 tons, eight 12-inch guns, sixteen 4-inch guns; *Agamemnon*—16,750 tons, four 12-inch guns, ten 9 2-inch guns; *Cornwallis*—14,000 tons, four 12-inch guns, twelve 6-inch guns; *Vengeance*—12,950 tons, four 12-inch guns, twelve 6-inch guns; *Triumph*—11,980 tons, four 10-inch guns, fourteen 7.5-inch guns; *Bouvet*—12,200 tons, two 12-inch guns, two 10 8-inch guns, eight 5.5-inch guns, eight 4-inch guns; *Suffren*—12,730 tons, four 12-inch guns, ten 6.4-inch guns; *Gaulois*—11,260 tons, four 12-inch guns, ten 5.5-inch guns.

[†] 15,000 tons, four 12-inch and twelve 6-inch guns.

the 19th, and what injury had been done had been repaired in the interval. Once again the four forts, Sedd-el-Bahr, Cape Helles, Kum Kale, and Orkanieh, were attacked. Of these the first mounted six 10.2-inch guns, the second two 9.2-inch, the third four 10.2-inch and two 5 9-inch, and the fourth two 9 2-inch. Against the sixteen heavy guns of the forts the four ships brought into action twenty pieces heavier than anything mounted on the land, including the 15-inch guns of the *Queen Elizabeth*, the most powerful weapon ever used in naval war. The forts were thus greatly outmatched, and the long range of the *Queen Elizabeth's* guns enabled her to come into the fight at a distance where nothing from the land could possibly touch her. In an hour and a half the *Queen Elizabeth* and the *Agamemnon* had silenced the Cape Helles guns, but not before these had hit the latter ship, a shell fired at a range of six miles bursting on board her, with a loss of three men killed and five wounded. This was the only casualty suffered during the first stage of the bombardment. At 11.30 a m. the *Vengeance* and *Cornwallis* came into action, and, running into close range, silenced the lighter armament of the Cape Helles battery. The attack on the Asiatic forts was at the same time reinforced by two of the French ships, the *Suffren* and the *Charlemagne*, which poured in a heavy fire at a range of only 2,000 yards. Early in the afternoon the *Triumph* and the *Albion* [*] attacked Sedd-el-Bahr at close range. It said much for the courage and discipline of the Turkish artillerymen that, though they faced overwhelming odds, their last gun was not silenced till after 5 p.m.

Little daylight remained, but, covered by the battleships and destroyers, a number of North Sea trawlers at once set to work to sweep for mines in the entrance. The work was resumed next morning at sunrise, and the mine-field was cleared for a distance of four miles up the Straits. Then the *Albion, Vengeance,* and *Majestic* [†] steamed in between the headlands, and opened a long-range fire on Fort Dardanos, a work on the Asiatic side some distance below the Narrows. It was not heavily armed, its best guns being four 5 9 Krupps. As the battleships opened fire, a reply came not only from Dardanos but from several unlocated batteries at various points along the shore. The Turkish fire, however, did little harm, and we were able to attack the rear of the entrance forts and drive off several bodies of Turkish troops.

[*] 12,950 tons, four 12-inch guns, twelve 6-inch
[†] The oldest battleship type in the Navy; 14,900 tons, four 12-inch guns, twelve 6-inch.

One party near Kum Kale was driven across the bridge near the mouth of the river Mendere (the ancient Simois), and the bridge itself destroyed by shell fire. We believed that by this time the Turks had everywhere been forced to abandon the defences at the entrance, and landing parties of Royal Marines were sent ashore with explosives to complete the destruction of the guns in the forts. This they successfully accomplished, but near Kum Kale they encountered a detachment of the enemy, and, after a hot skirmish, had to fall back to their boats with a few casualties. On such slender basis the Turkish bulletins built up a report of landing parties everywhere repulsed with heavy loss. At this date it is clear that the Turks had nothing in the way of defences on the Gallipoli peninsula, apart from the shore forts.

The result of the day's operations was that we had cleared the entrance to the Straits. This was the easiest part of the problem, and only the beginning of the formidable task assigned to the Allied fleets. The real defence of the Dardanelles—the forts at the Narrows—had not been touched. Nevertheless, with that misleading optimism which has done so much to paralyze national effort, the press of France and Britain wrote as if the fall of the outer forts had decided the fate of Constantinople. In that city at the moment there was undoubtedly something of a panic among civilians, but the German and Turkish Staffs were in the best of spirits. They were greatly comforted by the time it had taken the powerful Allied fleet to destroy the outer forts, and they believed that the inner forts were impregnable. There long-range attacks would be impossible; no large number of ships could be brought simultaneously into action, and drifting mines and torpedoes could be used to supplement the artillery defence. Enver, not usually partial to the truth, was for once in a way correct when he told a correspondent: " The real defence of the Straits is yet to come. That lies where the difficult waterway deprives ships of their power to manœuvre freely, and obliges them to move in a narrow defile commanded by artillery and mines."

For a few days there were strong northerly winds, but in spite of the rough weather the mine-sweepers continued their work below the Narrows. On Thursday, 4th March, the battleships were again in action. Some attacked the forts inside the Straits, Dardanos and Soghandere, and a French cruiser in the Gulf of Saros demolished a look-out station at Cape Gaba Tepe. Among the ships engaged were the *Ocean* and the *Lord Nelson*.* A land-

* A sister ship of the *Agamemnon*—16,500 tons, four 12-inch guns, ten 9.2-inch.

ing party of Royal Marines near Kum Kale were driven back to their boats by a superior Turkish force with the relatively large loss of 22 killed, 22 wounded, and 3 missing. On 5th March there was a demonstration against Smyrna, a British and French detachment, under Vice-Admiral Peirse, bombarding the outer forts. The attack was not pushed, and was only intended to induce Enver to keep a considerable force in that neighbourhood.

On 6th March the weather was again fine, with a smooth sea, and a preliminary attempt was made on the Narrows forts. On the preceding day some of the ships had entered the Straits and drawn the fire of the forts at Kilid Bahr. There was an explosion in one of them, and after that it ceased firing. On the morning of the 6th the *Vengeance, Albion, Majestic, Prince George,** and *Suffren* steamed into the Straits and attacked the forts on both sides just below the Narrows. The fire was chiefly directed against Dardanos on the Asiatic, and Soghandere on the European shore —works which may be regarded as the outposts of the main Narrows defence. The attacking ships were struck repeatedly by shells, but no serious damage was done, and there was no loss of life. This attack from inside the Straits was, however, a secondary operation. The main attack, from which great results were expected, was made by the *Queen Elizabeth, Agamemnon,* and *Ocean* from the Gulf of Saros, on the outer side of the Gallipoli peninsula. Lying off the point of Gaba Tepe, they sent their shells over the intervening hills, with airplanes directing their fire. Their target was two of the forts at Chanak, on the Asiatic side of the Narrows, about twelve miles off. These forts had a very heavy armament, including 14-inch guns, and it was hoped to destroy them by indirect fire, to which they had no means of replying. The Turks replied from various points on the heights of the peninsula with well-concealed howitzers and field guns, and three shells struck the *Queen Elizabeth.* Next day, 7th March, the attack was renewed. The *Agamemnon* and *Lord Nelson,* firing at a range of from 12,000 to 14,000 yards, supported by four French battleships, the *Bouvet, Charlemagne, Gaulois,* and *Suffren,* attacked from inside the Straits and engaged the forts on both sides of the Narrows. Chanak, which the *Queen Elizabeth* had been trying to demolish the day before, brought its heavy guns into action. The *Gaulois, Agamemnon,* and *Lord Nelson* were hit several times, but we believed that we had put the forts below Chanak and Kilid Bahr out of action. Subsequent experi-

* A sister ship of the *Majestic.*

ence showed that it was a difficult matter permanently to silence forts. Under the heavy fire of the ships it was hard to keep the guns constantly in action, not so much on account of any serious damage, but because the batteries were flooded with stifling vapours from the shells, and it was necessary to withdraw the men until the air cleared. Further, the defenders had been ordered to economize ammunition, and to reserve their fire for the closer attack which they believed would follow. The fact, therefore, that a fort ceased firing was no proof that it had been really silenced. Again and again during these operations we heard of forts being silenced, which next day or a few days after could bring most of their guns into action.

The following week saw nothing but minor operations. On the 10th an attempt was made to shell the Bulair defences at long range, and the British warships shelled some new batteries of light guns which the Turks had established near Morto Bay, on the European side of the entrance to the Straits. The Turkish Government sent out a report that the Allied fleets had been unsuccessfully bombarding the defences at Sedd-el-Bahr and Kum Kale. The Allied press treated this as an impudent fiction, and pointed out that the forts there had been destroyed many days before. But the Turkish communiqué told the truth. We had destroyed the forts, but we had not occupied the ground on both sides of the entrance. The Turks had accordingly entrenched themselves strongly near the ruins and mounted guns, and these we attacked on 10th and 11th March. At that time, misled by the optimism of the newspapers, the ordinary man in France and Britain counted with certainty on the speedy news that our fleet was steaming through the Sea of Marmora on the way to Constantinople. When tidings came that the light cruiser *Amethyst* had on 15th March made a dash into the Narrows, he believed that the Turkish defence had collapsed. The *Amethyst's* enterprise was part of a mine-sweeping expedition, and also a daring reconnaissance in which the little ship drew the fire of the upper forts. She got but a short way, and lost heavily in the attempt. But her exploit, magnified through Greek channels, made the world believe that the Narrows defences had been seriously damaged, and that the time was ripe for a determined effort to force a passage. The combined fleet had now grown to a formidable strength, and included a Russian cruiser, the *Askold*, which appeared on 3rd March. Vice-Admiral Carden had been compelled by ill-health to relinquish the command, and Vice-Admiral John Michael de Robeck succeeded him.

The great effort was made on Thursday, 18th March. It was a bright, clear day, with a light wind and a calm sea. At a quarter to eleven in the forenoon, the *Agamemnon, Lord Nelson, Queen Elizabeth, Inflexible, Triumph,* and *Prince George* steamed up the Straits towards the Narrows. The first four ships engaged the forts of Chanak and the battery on the point opposite, while the *Triumph* and *Prince George* kept the batteries lower down occupied by firing at Soghandere, Dardanos, and Kephez Point. After the bombardment had lasted for an hour and a half, during which the ships were fired upon not only by the forts but by howitzers and field guns on the heights, the French squadron, *Bouvet, Charlemagne, Gaulois,* and *Suffren,* came into action, steaming in to attack the forts at short range. Under the combined fire of the ten ships the forts once more ceased firing. A third squadron then entered the Straits to push the attack further. This was made up of six British battleships, the *Albion, Irresistible, Majestic, Ocean, Swiftsure,** and *Vengeance.* As they steered towards Chanak the four French ships were withdrawn in order to make room for them in the narrow waters. But in the process of this change all the forts suddenly began to fire again, which showed that none of them had been seriously damaged. According to Turkish accounts, only one big gun had been dismounted.

Then came the first disaster of the day. The French squadron was moving down to the open water inside the Straits, being still under fire from the inner forts. Three large shells struck the *Bouvet* almost simultaneously, and immediately after there was a loud explosion, and she was hidden in a cloud of smoke. The first impression was that she had been seriously damaged by shell fire, but her real wound was got from one of the mines which the Turks were now sending down with the current. They had waited to begin this new attack till the narrow waterway was full of ships. As the smoke cleared, the *Bouvet* was seen to be heeling over. She sank in three minutes, in thirty-six fathoms of water, carrying with her most of her crew.

The attack on the forts continued as long as the light lasted. The mine-sweepers had been brought up the Straits in order to clear the passage in front, and to look out for drift-mines. An hour and a half after the *Bouvet* sank, the *Irresistible* turned out of the fighting line with a heavy list. She also had been struck by a mine, but she floated for more than an hour, and the destroyers took off nearly all her crew—a dangerous task, for they were the

* A sister ship of the *Triumph*—11,980 tons, four 10-inch, fourteen 7.5-inch guns.

target all the time of Turkish fire. She sank at ten minutes to six, and a quarter of an hour later another drift-mine struck the *Ocean*. The latter sank almost as quickly as the *Bouvet*, but the destroyers were on the alert, and saved most of her crew. Several of the other ships had suffered damage and loss of life from the Turkish guns. The *Gaulois* had been repeatedly hit; her upper works were seriously injured, and a huge rent had been torn in her bows. The *Inflexible* had been struck by a heavy shell, which killed and wounded the majority of the men and officers in her fire-control station, and set her on fire forward.

As the sun set most of the forts were still in action, and during the short twilight the Allied fleet slipped out of the Dardanelles. The great attack on the Narrows had failed—failed, with the loss of three battleships and the better part of a thousand men.

At first it was the intention of Admiral de Robeck to continue the attack, and the British Admiralty assented. But on 19th March Sir Ian Hamilton, who had seen part of the action, telegraphed to Kitchener that he had been reluctantly forced to the conclusion that the Dardanelles could not be forced by battleships alone, and by the 22nd De Robeck had come round to the same opinion. Lord Fisher felt himself bound to accept the view of the admiral on the spot, and though Mr. Churchill, supported by some of the younger naval officers, pressed for a renewal of the attack, he was compelled to bow to the opinion of his professional advisers. On the information at the disposal of the British Government it is hard to see what other course was open to them except to withdraw the fleet. Even if the enemy was running short of ammunition, the forts were sufficiently intact to protect the mine-field, and the mine-field barred the road for the great ships. Of the Allied fleet of sixteen battleships three had been sunk and four disabled long before they had come to the hardest part of their task. It is idle to discuss whether, had the action been persisted in even at the cost of more ships, the Turkish defence would have crumbled. Such discussions belong to the realm of pure hypothesis, and statesmen without a gift of prophecy must be content to decide on the gross and patent facts before them. Undoubtedly the Turks were gravely alarmed, and certain sections of the defence were ready to despair. But it is not less indubitable that, had the fleets attacked again, there would have been a stubborn resistance and such losses as would have left too weak a naval force for the joint operation now under contemplation. It was a gamble which no responsible Government could have justified to its people.*

III.

When the attack by ships alone was decided upon, small landing parties of marines had been contemplated; and early in February, before the bombardment began, the Government's notion of using troops rapidly extended. Even if the fleet succeeded to their full expectations soldiers would be needed to clear the shores of the Straits and guard the communications. The decision not to embark on an immediate offensive in the West and the failure of the Turkish assault on the Suez Canal had left Kitchener with certain forces at his disposal, and he was prepared to send the 29th Division to Salonika if Greece would join in the enterprise. When this scheme came to nought he was willing to use that division to assist the fleet at the Dardanelles. On 9th February he informed the War Council that if the Navy called for land forces they should be forthcoming; and on 16th February the Council decided to send the 29th Division at once to Lemnos, and to arrange, if necessary, for the dispatch of a force from Egypt. This decision marked the inception of the plan of military attack, into which the Government had drifted by slow and insensible stages.

A few days later Kitchener, alarmed by the position on the Russian front and by a grave appeal from Joffre, countermanded the sailing of the 29th Division, arguing that the Royal Naval Division and the Australians and New Zealanders from Egypt would be a sufficient force for the supplementary operations contemplated. This decision held, in spite of Mr. Churchill's protests, up to 10th March, by which time General Birdwood had reported on the problem—a loss of three weeks of valuable time. The 29th Division was ordered to embark on the 16th, and Sir Ian Hamilton, who had been appointed to command the land forces, left England on the 13th, arriving on the 17th at Tenedos. His instructions from Kitchener were of the vaguest kind, and showed the Government still hesitating between the naval and the conjoint schemes. He was to avoid a landing if possible; but if the fleet failed and a landing became imperative, none should be made

* For Enver's reported view see Dardanelles Commission (Cd. 8490), p 40. *Cf.* also Morgenthau's *Secrets of the Bosphorus*, chaps. xvii.-xviii.

until the full force available had assembled. Any landing on the Asiatic side was strongly deprecated. It may fairly be said that no commander-in-chief ever set out under a hazier charter.

But one sentence in these instructions was of the first importance: "Having entered on the project of forcing the Straits, there can be no idea of abandoning the scheme." Kitchener, whatever may be said of some of his colleagues, saw that the enterprise in its new form could not be run on any system of limited liability. It must be pushed to a triumphant conclusion, or it had better never have been dreamed of. Now the first point in such a venture is the number of available troops. No General Staff had worked out a plan for the conquest of the Gallipoli peninsula, our intelligence about Turkish preparations and strengths was vague, and the whole problem was in a mist of uncertainty. But sufficient was known to make it clear that the task was one of great difficulty and liable to indefinite extension. After the receipt of Birdwood's report Kitchener had no doubt that the Straits could only be forced by a large army. As early as 13th January he had calculated that at least 150,000 men would be required, and since then there had been no reason to lower the estimate. Everything would depend upon the first blow, and for that what force could he provide? At the outside not more than 70,000 men—the 29th Division, the Australian and New Zealand Corps of two divisions, the Royal Naval Division, and two French brigades. What reserves lay immediately behind them? At the most a couple of Territorial divisions, a second French division, and an Indian brigade. He had not provided a strength to ensure success for that first blow, which, having some of the advantages of surprise, was the most hopeful. Should the campaign be protracted, what reinforcements could he supply without weakening the fronts in Europe? He was aware that Joffre had a large scheme for a summer and autumn offensive, in which Britain was pledged to co-operate with all her strength. For that the new British divisions were assigned. The eternal dilemma of divergent operations was before him—an enterprise where victory might prove impossible except by courting defeat in a more vital area.

Kitchener, as his biographer has clearly shown,[*] at no time subscribed to the heresy that the Western front could be disregarded and the main effort of Britain switched on to a new theatre. He realized that the form of the campaign had been decreed in August by the German "outmarch"; he realized, what

[*] Sir George Arthur's *Life*, III., p. 111.

sundry of his colleagues forgot, that we were allies of France, and could not without her consent leave her to stand alone on what she regarded as the crucial battle-ground. Had the Allies indeed been gifted with supernatural insight they might have followed a different policy: forgone the Western offensive of 1915, for which they were not ready; held that line to the stalemate which Germany's preoccupation in Russia would not have permitted her to break; and concentrated on hacking their way through to Constantinople. They would have succeeded, and the final battle on the Western front would have come sooner. But this prescience is for the immortals and not for fallible men, and such a scheme would have been condemned as insane—and rightly condemned on the facts before them—by every competent soldier in the spring of 1915. The criticism of the British Government is not that it lacked the gift of second sight, but that it suffered itself to drift into a great venture without duly counting the cost. The ultimate responsibility must rest with Kitchener, who, overwhelmed with detail and unassisted by any competent staff, inexplicably lost his prudence and his firm hold upon military fundamentals. He consented to make the attempt with the loose fringes of Britain's military strength; but to any cool observer these forces were patently insufficient even for the first blow, and the demand for further troops must be refused, or, if granted, would lead to infinite difficulties in the Western theatre. The attack upon the Dardanelles by a land army had from the start every vice of a divergent operation.*

IV.

The officer appointed to the command of the Gallipoli expedition, Sir Ian Hamilton, had behind him forty-two years of service in British wars. He was a soldier of a type rare in modern armies —a man of wide culture, a poet, an accomplished writer, a brilliant talker, a liberal politician; but he had also proved himself a man of the most conspicuous gallantry, a skilled regimental

---

* As late as the beginning of March there was some hope of the co-operation of Greece. On 1st March the Prime Minister, M Venizelos, offered three Greek divisions. The King provisionally assented, but the offer was withdrawn, partly because of the opposition of M Streit and the Greek Staff under German influence, and partly because of the jealousy shown by Russia of Greece playing any part in connection with Constantinople. Russia also promised assistance in the shape of an army corps which was assembled at Odessa, and which, when the Dardanelles was forced, was to be transported across the Black Sea to the northern mouth of the Bosphorus.

leader, an able staff officer, and an efficient military administrator. In a high command in the field his reputation was still to make, and there were critics who, with the customary British distrust of imagination, argued ill of his prospects, detecting in him a certain caprice of temperament and volatility of mind which left his indubitable talents unco-ordinated. He was the man to undertake a forlorn hope, but was he the man, they asked, to give the forlorn hope a chance of success? That the venture was desperate and Sir Ian Hamilton's position one of immense difficulty no one can deny. The purpose of the Allies had already been betrayed by the abortive naval attack; he was warned that the whole business was on sufferance, that his troops were only lent to him temporarily, and that his task was a *coup de main*, since a prolonged campaign might well be out of the question. At the same time he had been solemnly adjured by Kitchener that there could be no retirement. He was given nothing in the shape of detailed instructions by the Government, and no information worth mentioning about the nature of the problem before him. He was left free to make his own schemes, but he had no freedom either in the appointment of his subordinate generals or in the requisition of troops. His objective was fixed for him, and the nature and size of his weapon determined by Kitchener; only the use of the weapon was left to his discretion.

Sir Ian Hamilton in his six months' command made no grave mistake; on the contrary, he faced a task of superlative hardness with courage, patience, and a remarkable elasticity of mind, and the ultimate failure can by no means be laid at his door. But in the medley of unjust criticism of which he was made the target one charge deserves examination. Long before the attack was launched he recognized the tenuity of his hopes. Most of his generals protested beforehand that the enterprise was impossible. He knew that once British troops landed on the peninsula there could be no turning back, and he was aware that any reinforcements would have to be wrung out of an unwilling Government. Was it not his duty to refuse to make the attempt when he had fully explored its slender chances—to resign rather than to be a party to the waste of gallant men? There were precedents for such a course. In 1796 Napoleon tendered his resignation when the Directory wished him to undertake a futile scheme, and, conversely, in 1800 he cancelled his orders to Moreau when he was unable to get that general to assent to their merits. But to demand such conduct of Sir Ian Hamilton was to be blind to the facts of the situation.

He had been ordered by Kitchener to make the attempt, and told that if Constantinople were taken the war would be won. These were his commands, which, as a soldier, he was bound to obey unless they were clearly proven to be insane. But, while the hazard seemed immense in those early days of April, it could not have been regarded as altogether beyond human powers to surmount; the very imperfection of the British intelligence left many unknown factors as a ground for hope. Had he resigned he would have been liable to the charge that he had refused through timidity a mission of the first importance, difficult but not patently impossible, and had failed in the true spirit of military discipline. Such a *gran rifiuto* would have been rejected by most soldiers; it was unthinkable in the case of a man of Sir Ian Hamilton's bold and sanguine spirit.

In appreciating the situation there seemed to him four places worthy of consideration for the landing of his army. There was the Asiatic coast, against which he had been expressly warned in Kitchener's instructions; in any case an advance in that quarter would have required greater strength than he possessed, and would have been in perpetual danger of flank and rear attacks from the Turkish forces in Asia Minor.* A second was at the neck of the peninsula at Bulair; but the place was strongly fortified, and too far from the Narrows, the real objective. The same argument applied against a landing at Enos at the mouth of the Maritza. He was therefore driven back to a landing on the peninsula itself, and it cannot be denied that he was right. There alone he could get the full co-operation of the fleet and protect his communications, and there alone would success give immediately the full strategical rewards.

The military elements of the peninsula were simple. To master it involved an assault from the Ægean, and the possible landing-places were few in number, small in extent, and clearly defined by the nature of the ground. Gaps must be found in the screen of yellow cliffs which fringed the sea. If we take the peninsula west of a line drawn north and south across the upper end of the Narrows, there were only two areas where troops could be disembarked. One of these was the various beaches round about Sedd-el-Bahr and Cape Helles; the other was on the Gulf of Saros, near Gaba Tepe, where the sandstone hills left a narrow space at the water's edge. Neither was good, and both were believed

* Liman von Sanders thought that the Asiatic landing would have been the wiser course. For the arguments in its favour see Callwell's *The Dardanelles*, chap. iv.

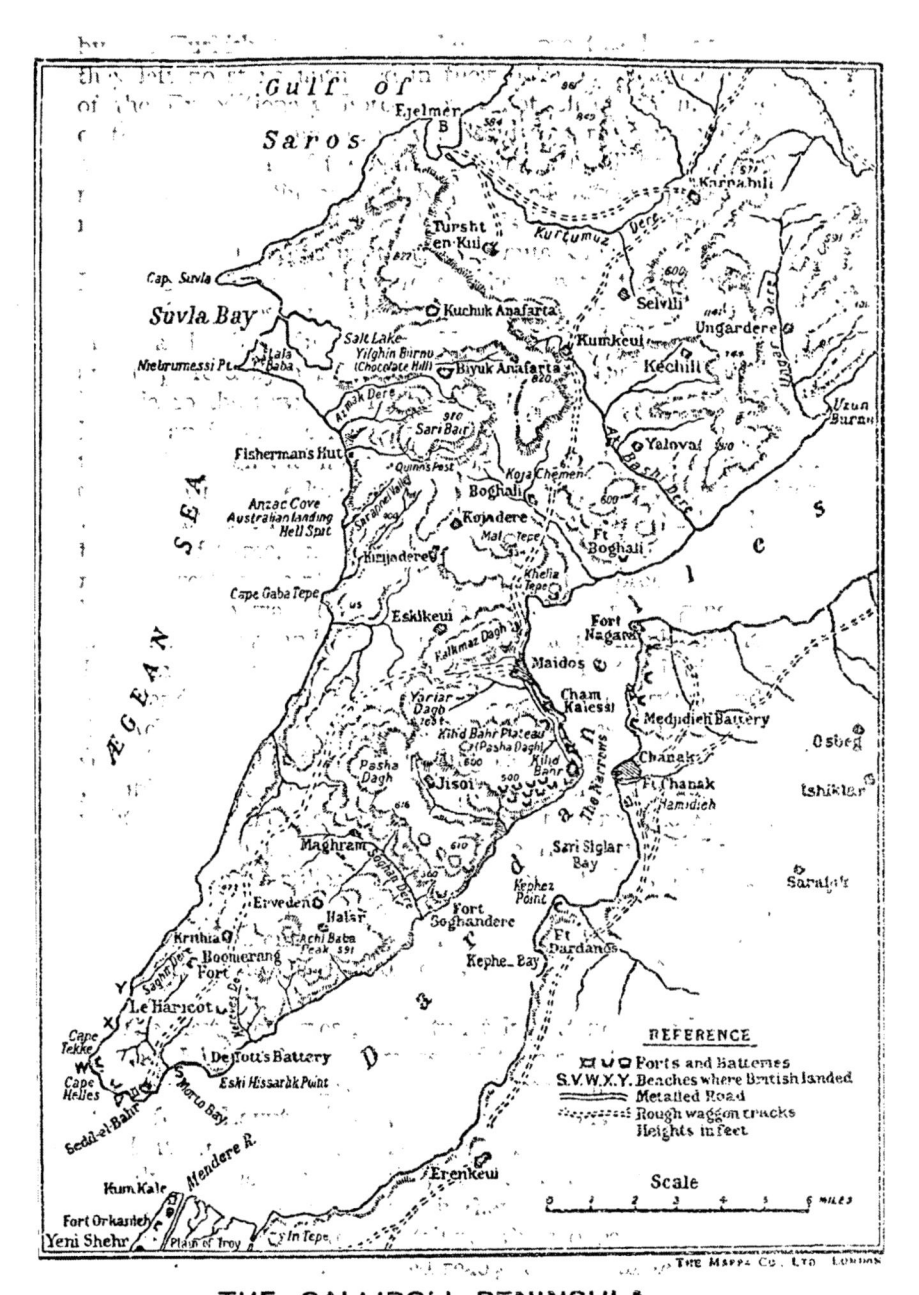

THE GALLIPOLI PENINSULA.

by the Turkish Staff to be wholly impracticable; nevertheless they left no stone unturned in their defence. The mere landing of the Expeditionary Force would not effect much. The hills of the Gallipoli peninsula may be said to form a natural fortress defending the rear of the Narrows forts. It will be seen from the map that behind the point of Kilid Bahr is a rocky plateau, which is more than 600 feet high, and extends inland for some five miles. Its highest ridge runs up to the summits known to the Turks as Pasha Dagh. These hills are a salient with the point towards the Gulf of Saros, and the sides curving back to the Dardanelles above and below Kilid Bahr. North the high ground continues, and is pierced by a pass, through which a rough track ran from Krithia to the town of Maidos, on the channel opposite Nagara. But to an invader coming from the west and aiming at Maidos the Pasha Dagh was not the only obstacle. West of it and south of Krithia rises the bold peak of Achi Baba, nearly 600 feet high, which sends out rocky spurs on both sides to the Dardanelles and the Gulf of Saros, and forms a barrier from sea to sea across the narrow western point of the peninsula. The problem before Sir Ian Hamilton was, therefore, plain enough in its general lines. He must effect a landing at the apex of the peninsula and at Gaba Tepe, in the Gulf of Saros. It would then be the business of the force landed at the first point to fight its way to Krithia, and carry the Achi Baba ridge, while the second force would advance from Gaba Tepe against the pass leading to Maidos. It might then be possible for the left wing of the first to come in touch with the right wing of the second, and together to force the Pasha Dagh plateau. If that movement succeeded the battle was won. He could bring up artillery to the plateau, which would make the European forts untenable. Moreover, he would dominate at short range the enemy's positions on the Asiatic side, and a combined attack by land and sea would give the Narrows to his hand.

The first steps were, unfortunately, attended with some confusion. Mudros Bay in Lemnos had been selected as the advanced base, and early in March the first Australian troops had landed there from Egypt. But when the divisions from England arrived it appeared that the ships had been faultily loaded—nobody's blame, for when they sailed there was no knowledge of the precise operations for which they would be required—and it was found necessary to redistribute the troops on the transports if they were to be disembarked ready for immediate action. This could not be done at Mudros, so there was nothing for it but to take the Expeditionary Force to Alexandria—a delay of some weeks, which enabled the Turks to complete their defences on the peninsula. The German Liman von Sanders had been appointed to the chief command, with Essad Pasha as his principal subordinate. Presently he had 40,000 troops there, with 30,000 men in immediate reserve, and had entrenched and fortified all the obvious landing-places. By the middle of April the hundred odd transports of the British army were back in Mudros. The force consisted of the 29th Division under General Hunter-Weston—eleven battalions of regulars and one of Scots Territorials; the Anzac Corps under Sir William Birdwood, made up of the Australian Division under General Bridges, and the composite New Zealand and Australian Division under General Sir A. J. Godley, with two brigades of mounted troops without their horses; the Royal Naval Division under General Paris, and a French Division under General d'Amade. None of the divisions were, as units, experienced in war, though the 29th consisted mainly of veterans from India and foreign stations; the Naval Division was a recent creation, as yet unprovided with artillery; the Australasian contingent had enjoyed but a short training as divisions; the French force had been hastily improvised, and contained a considerable number of native African troops. But the very heterogeneity and rawness of the army gave it a certain advantage in an enterprise outside the orthodox procedure of battle.

The day originally fixed for the attempt was 23rd April. But on the 20th a storm rose which for forty-eight hours lashed the Ægean. On the 23rd it abated, and that afternoon the first of the black transports began to move out of Mudros harbour. Next day the rest of the force followed, all in wild spirits for this venture into the unknown, so that they recalled to one spectator the Athenians departing for the Sicilian expedition, when the galleys out of sheer light-heartedness raced each other to Ægina.

That morning of Sunday, the 25th, was one of those which delight the traveller in April in the Ægean. A light mist fills the air before dawn, but it disappears with the sun, and all day there are clear skies, still seas, and the fresh, invigorating warmth of spring. The map will show the nature of the place chosen for the attempt. Gaba Tepe, on the north side of the peninsula, we have already noted. Round about Cape Helles there are five little beaches, originally nameless, but now for all time to be known by the letters accorded them by the British army. Beginning from the left, there is Beach Y, and, a little south of it, Beach X. Rounding Cape Tekke, we reach Beach W, where a narrow valley opens between the headlands of Tekke and Helles. Here there is a broad, semicircular stretch of sand. South of Helles is Beach V, a place of the same configuration as Beach W, but unpleasantly commanded by the castle and village of Sedd-el-Bahr at its southern end. Lastly, inside the Straits, on the east side of Morto Bay, is Beach S, close to the point of Eski Hissarlik. The landing at Gaba Tepe was entrusted to the Australian and New Zealand troops; that at the Helles beaches to the 29th Division, with some units of the Naval Division. It was arranged that simultaneously the French should land on the Asiatic shore at Kum Kale, to prevent the Turkish batteries from being brought into action against our men at Beaches V and S. Part of the Naval Division was detached for a feint farther north in the Gulf of Saros.

Let us assume that an airplane enabled us to move up and down the shores of the peninsula and observe the progress of the different landings. About one in the morning the ships arrive at a point five miles from the Gallipoli shores. At 1.20 the boats are lowered, and the troops line up on the decks. Then they embark in the flotillas, and the steam pinnaces begin to tow them shorewards in the hazy half-light before dawn.

The Australians destined for Gaba Tepe are carried in destroyers which take them in close to the shore. The operations are timed to allow the troops to reach the beaches at daybreak. Slowly and very quietly the boats and destroyers steal towards the land. A little before five an enemy's searchlight flares out. The boats are now in shallow water under the Gaba Tepe cliffs, and the men are leaping ashore. Then comes a blaze of rifle fire from the Turkish trenches on the beach, and the first comers charge them with the bayonet. The whole cliff seems to leap into light, for everywhere trenches and caverns have been dug in the slopes. The fire falls most heavily on the men still in the boats, who have the difficult task of waiting as the slow minutes bring them shoreward. The first Australians do not linger. They carry the lines on the beach with cold steel, and find themselves looking up at a steep cliff a hundred feet high. In open order they dive into the scrub, and scramble up the loose yellow rocks. By a fortunate accident the landing is farther north than was at first intended, just under the cliffs of Sari Bair. At Gaba Tepe the long slope would have given the enemy a great advantage in defence; but here there is only the forty-foot beach and then the cliffs. He who knows the Ægean in April will remember the revelation of those fringed sea walls and bare brown slopes. From a distance they look as arid as the Syrian desert, but when the traveller draws near he finds a paradise of curious and beautiful flowers—anemone, grape hyacinth, rock rose, asphodel, and amaryllis. Up this rock garden the Australians race, among the purple cistus and the matted creepers and the thickets of myrtle. They have left their packs at the foot, and scale the bluffs like chamois. It is an achievement to rank with Wolfe's escalade of the Heights of Abraham. Presently they are at the top, and come under the main Turkish fire. But the ground gives good cover, and they set about entrenching the crest of the cliffs to cover the boats' landing. This is the position at Sari Bair at 7 a m.

As we journey down the coast we come next to Beach Y. There at 7 a.m. all is going well. The 1st King's Own Scottish Borderers and the Plymouth battalion of the Naval Division, landing at a place which the enemy thought wholly impracticable, have without difficulty reached the top of the cliffs. . . . At Beach X things are even better. The *Swiftsure* has plastered the high ground with shells, and the landing ship, the *Implacable*, has anchored close to the shore in six fathoms of water. With scarcely a casualty the 2nd Royal Fusiliers have gained the cliff line. . . . There has been a harder fight at Beach W, between Tekke and Helles, where the sands are broader. The shore has been trenched throughout, and wired and mined almost to the water's edge, and in the scrub of the hinterland the Turkish snipers are hidden. The result is that, though our ships have bombarded the beach for three-quarters of an hour, they cannot clear out the enemy, and do not seem to have made much impression on the wire entanglements. The first troops have landed to the right under the cliffs of Cape Helles, and have reached the top, while a party on the left has scaled Cape Tekke. But the men of the 1st Lancashire Fusiliers who landed on the shore itself have had a fiery trial. They suffered heavily while still on the water, and on landing came up against unbroken lines of wire, while snipers in the valley in front and concealed machine guns and quick-firers rained death on them. Here we have had heavy losses, and at 7 a m. the landing has not yet succeeded.

But the case is more desperate still at Beach V, under Sedd-el-Bahr. Here, as at Beach W, there are a stretch of sand, a scrubby valley, and flanking cliffs. It is the strongest of the Turkish positions, and troops landing in boats are exposed to every type of converging fire. A curious expedient has been tried. A collier, the *River Clyde*, with 2,000 men of the 2nd Hampshires, 1st Dublin Fusiliers, and 1st Munster Fusiliers on board, as well as eight boat-loads towed by steam pinnaces, approached close to the shore. The boat-loads—the rest of the Dublin Fusiliers—suffered horribly, for when they dashed through the shallows to the beach they were pinned to the ground by fire. Three lines of wire entanglements had to be forced, and a network of trenches. A bank of sand, five or six feet high, runs at the back, and under its cover the survivors have taken shelter. In the steel side of the liner doors have been cut, which open and disgorge men, like some new Horse of Troy. But a tornado of shot and shell rained on her, and few of the gallant men who leaped from the lighters to the reef, and from the reef to the sea, reached the land. Those who did have joined their fellows lying flat under the sand bank on that beach of death. . . . At Beach S, in Morto Bay, all has gone well. Seven hundred men of the 2nd South Wales Borderers have been landed from trawlers, and have established themselves on the cliff tops at the place called De Totts Battery.

Let us go back to Sari Bair and look at the position at noonday. We are prospering there, for more than 10,000 men are now ashore, and the work of disembarking guns and stores goes on steadily, though the fire from inland is still deadly. We see a proof of it in a boat full of dead men which rocks idly in the surf. The great warships from the sea send their heavy shells against the Turkish lines, seaplanes are "spotting" for them, and wireless stations are being erected on the beach. Firing from the ships is not easy, for the morning sun shines right in the eyes of the gunners. The Royal Engineers are making roads up the cliff, and supplies are climbing steadily to our firing line. On the turf on the cliff top our men are entrenched, and are working their way forward. Unfortunately the zeal of the Australians has outrun their discretion, and some of them have pushed on too far, looking for enemies to bayonet. They have crossed three ridges, and have got to a ridge above Eskikeui within sight of the Narrows. In that pockety country such an advance is certain death, and the rash attack has been checked with heavy losses. The wounded are being brought in, and it is no light task getting them down the cliffs on stretchers, and across the beach and the bullet-splashed sea to the warships. Remember that we are holding a position which is terribly conspicuous to the enemy, and all our ammunition and water and food have to be dragged up these breakneck cliffs. Still the first round has been won, Indian troops are being landed in support, and we are firmly placed at Sari Bair.

As we move down the coast we find that all goes well at Beach X, and that the troops there are working their way forward, but that at Beach Y the Scottish Borderers are being heavily counter-attacked and are making little progress. The *Implacable* has knocked out of action a Turkish battery at Krithia which gave much annoyance to our men at Beach X. . . . At Beach W we have improved our position. We have cleared the beach and driven the Turks out of the scrub at the valley foot, and the work of disembarking men and stores is proceeding. Our right wing—the 4th Worcesters—is working round by the cliffs above Cape Helles to try and enfilade the enemy who are holding Beach V, where our men are still in deadly jeopardy. . . . The scene at Beach V is strange and terrible. From the deep water the *Cornwallis* and *Albion* are trying to bombard the enemy at Sedd-el-Bahr, and the 15-inch shells from the *Queen Elizabeth* are screaming overhead. The Trojan Horse is still lying bow on against the reefs, with her men unable to move, and the Turkish howitzers playing on her. If a man shows his head he is picked off by sharpshooters. The troops we have landed lie flat on the beach under cover of the sand ridge, unable to advance or retreat, and under a steady tornado of fire. . . . At Beach S things are satisfactory. Meantime the French landing at Kum Kale has achieved its purpose. Originally timed for 6 a m., it did not take place till 9 30. They had a skirmish with the Turks, partly on the height at Kum Kale, and partly on the Trojan plain. Then they advanced along the swell of ground near the coast as far as Yeni Shehr. Next evening they re-embarked, and joined our right wing at Beach S. They took 500 prisoners, and could have taken more had there been room for them in the boats. The Turk, who showed himself a dauntless fighter when fighting was the order of the day, surrendered with great complaisance and good-humour when the game was up. He had no crusading zeal in the business.

As darkness fell on that loud Sabbath, the minds of the Allied Staff may well have been anxious. We had gained a footing, but no more, and at the critical point it was but a precarious lodgment. The complexity and strength of the enemy's defence far surpassed our expectation. He had tunnelled the cliffs, and created a wonderful and intricate trench system, which took full advantage of the natural strength of the ground. The fire from our leviathans on the deep was no more effective against his entrenched positions than it had been against the forts of the Narrows.

Let us resume our tour of the beaches about 10 o'clock on the morning of the 26th. At Sari Bair the Australians are facing a counter-attack. It lasts for two hours, and is met by a great bombardment from our ships. The end comes when, about noon, the Australians and New Zealanders advance with the bayonet, and drive back the enemy. But all that day there is no rest for our troops, who are perfecting their trenches under a deluge of shrapnel. Their flanks are indifferently secured, and they have but the one landing-place behind them, from which their front line is scarcely a thousand yards distant. They are still clinging precariously to the coast scarp . . . At Beach Y things have gone badly. Our men there had advanced during the Sunday afternoon, and had been outflanked and driven back to the cliff edge. The Scottish Borderers lost their commanding officer and more than half their men. It was decided to re-embark and move the troops to Beach X, and as we pass the retreat is going on successfully under cover of the ships' fire. . . . At Beach X there has been a hard struggle. Last night we were strongly attacked there, and driven to the very edge of the cliffs, where we hung on in rough shelter trenches. This morning we are advancing again, and making some way. . . . At Beach W, too, there has been a counter-attack. Yesterday afternoon our right wing there, which tried to relieve the position on Beach V by an enfilading attack on the enemy, got among wire, and was driven back. During the night the Turks came on in force, and we were compelled to fling our beach parties into the firing line, bluejackets and sappers armed with whatever weapons they could find. This morning the situation is easier, we have landed more troops, and are preparing to move forward.

At Beach V the landing is still in its first stage. Men are still sheltering on the deadly beach behind the sand bank. We have gained some positions among the ruins which were once Sedd-el-Bahr, but not enough to allow us to proceed. Even as we look a final effort is beginning, in which the Dublin Fusiliers and the Munster Fusiliers distinguish themselves, though it is hard to select for special praise among the splendid battalions of the 29th Division. It continues all morning, most gallantly directed till he fell by Lieutenant-Colonel Doughty Wylie of the Headquarters Staff, and about 2 p.m. it is successful. The main Turkish trenches are carried, the debris of the castle and village are cleared, and the enemy retreat. The landing can now go forward, and the men who for thirty-two hours have been huddled behind the sand bank, enduring torments of thirst and a nerve-racking fire, can move their cramped limbs and join their comrades.

By the morning of Tuesday, the 27th, all the beaches—except Beach Y, which had been relinquished—were in working order, and the advance could proceed. The flanks were secure, and the front line was now more than a mile in advance of Beaches W and V. That day the Turkish gunners attempted to put a barrage of fire between the ships and the shore, but in spite of it the work of landing supplies went on swiftly. The scene on the beaches was like a gigantic shipwreck. It looked, so observers noted, as if an army with its stores had been washed ashore after a great gale or had saved themselves on rafts. That night our position at the apex of the peninsula ran from Eski Hissarlık on the Straits north-west to a point on the Gulf of Saros, 3,200 yards north-east of Cape Tekke. There was too little room for so large a force, and an advance was ordered for the 28th.

The main objective was Krithia village, and we found the road stoutly opposed. Our front was the 87th Brigade on the left, the 88th Brigade in the centre, and a French brigade on the right, with the 86th Brigade in reserve. In such a country a line has a tendency to "bunch" and become too thin in places. The result was that our progress was irregular, and under the strong Turkish counter-attacks we were too weak to hold all we won. The 87th Brigade advanced two miles, the maximum we were able to make good, though parties of the 88th Brigade got within a few hundred yards of Krithia village, and the French to within a mile. Still, by that evening we had securely won the butt of the peninsula, and our front ran from three miles north-west of Cape Tekke to a mile north of Eski Hissarlik.

So ended the opening stage of the Gallipoli campaign—the Battle of the Landing. It was a fight without a precedent. There had been landings—such as Abercromby's at Aboukir and Wolfe's at the cove west of Louisburg—fiercely contested landings, in our history, but none on a scale like this. Sixty thousand men, backed by the most powerful navy in the world, attacked a shore which Nature seemed to have made impregnable, and which was held by not inferior numbers of the enemy, in positions prepared for months, and supported by the latest modern artillery. The mere problem of transport was sufficient to deter the boldest. Every rule of war was set at nought. On paper the thing was impossible, as the Turkish army orders announced. By the text-books no man should have left the beaches alive. We were fighting against a gallant enemy who was at his best in defence and in this unorthodox type of battle. All accounts prove that the Turks fought with superlative boldness and courage, as well as with a reasonable chivalry. That our audacity succeeded was due to the unsurpassable fighting quality of our men—the regulars and Territorials of the 29th Division, the Naval Division, and not least to the dash and doggedness of the Australasian corps. Looking back with fuller knowledge, it is possible to question the wisdom of some of the details of the plan. It may be that a stronger force should have been landed on Beach Y; it is reasonable to urge that things might have gone differently had the bulk of the army been put ashore between Gaba Tepe and Suvla, which was strategically the most vulnerable part of the peninsula. But whatever be our judgment on its policy or its consequences, the Battle of the Landing must be acclaimed as a marvellous, an unparalleled feat of arms.

CHAPTER XXVII.

THE SECOND BATTLE OF YPRES.

April 17–May 24, 1915.

Germany's Spring Policy in the West—The Taking of Hill 60—The Gas Attack—The Second Battle of Ypres—Its Results—The Ruined City—The Political Situation in Britain during April and May—The Formation of a Coalition Government.

IN April the spirits of the Western Allies were not seriously dashed. Russia, after many vicissitudes, was believed to be making way in the Carpathians in the direction of the Hungarian plains. France was preparing for a great effort against the most vital portion of the German front, and in Britain it was thought that Sir John French would presently repeat on an extended scale the tactics of Neuve Chapelle, and do more than dint the opposing line. Such a season of confidence is often a precursor of misfortunes and black depression, and within a month's time a series of desperate actions on both East and West had convinced the world that Germany did not intend yet awhile to forgo her favourite part of the offensive. So far as the British front was concerned, the assault came where we were least ready. Our heavy guns had been largely taken from the northern section to assist the artillery preparation farther south. The French regulars had gone from the Ypres Canal to join the great concentration in Artois, and the Salient, that old cockpit of war, was held in very moderate strength. Suddenly, and almost without warning, it became the theatre of an attack which put our fortitude to a fiery trial.

The German major strategy was centred on the East, and for the moment she could send no weight of reserves to France and Flanders. Her purpose there was defensive, varied by such local counter-attacks as might be necessary for a prudent defence. Though thin in numbers, she was well provided with heavy guns

and shells, and in her new poison gas she had a weapon which she was eager to try should a favourable chance present itself. The device was not her own invention, having been suggested by a British chemist to Japan during the Russo-Japanese War. She was a little nervous about its use, and ever since Neuve Chapelle, after her fashion in such circumstances, had been circulating false reports of the use of gas by the Allies to prepare the world for her retaliation in kind. On the moral question it is needless to dogmatize. The use of gas was a breach of the rules of the Hague Convention which Germany had accepted, but she had made no secret of her attitude toward international compacts when they stood in the way of her interests. Gas and liquid fire were innovations—atrocious innovations they seemed to her enemies—but it is doubtful whether the suffering they caused was greater than the suffering from shell fire. A man who died in torture under chlorine might have suffered like agony from shrapnel. All the arguments against them might have been used with equal force by the mediaeval knight against gunpowder, by the old foot-soldier against high explosives, by the savage warrior against machine guns. The true point is that the innovation was not so much barbarous—all war is barbarous—as impolitic. Unless the weapon is so powerful as to break down all opposition, the innovator may find that he rouses a storm of resentment which nullifies the value of his device. Germany's opponents were not without their chemists, and could create a counter-weapon; and that Germany had been a pioneer in ugly methods was bound to exacerbate their feelings towards her and lower her moral prestige among neutrals—an unfortunate result for a Power which was daily beginning to realize more clearly that an unequivocal victory was beyond her hopes.

The First Battle of Ypres, which began on 20th October and ended with the repulse of the Prussian Guard on November 11, 1914, was fought on a battle-front stretching from Bixschoote in the north to Armentières in the south, over a broad salient whose first apex was Becelaere, and second Gheluvelt. The Second Battle of Ypres was confined to the northern segment of the Salient, between the Ypres Canal and the Menin road. Undoubtedly the Germans had no elaborate offensive purpose at the start. The battle began with a local counter-attack in return for our efforts at Hill 60, and when this attack prospered, owing to the surprise of the gas, it was pushed beyond its original aim. A proof is that there was no great massing of troops, as in the autumn battle; local reserves were brought up, but the German line was not thinned elsewhere. But in two respects the battles were akin. The second lasted almost exactly as long as the first —from Thursday, 22nd April, to Thursday, 13th May, when it slackened owing to the British thrust from Festubert. Like the first, too, it was fought against heavy odds. A crushing artillery preponderance and the use of poison gas were more deadly assets than any weight of numbers. For days our fate hung in the balance, dispositions grew chaotic in the fog of war, and it became a soldiers' battle, like Malplaquet and Albuera, where rules and text-books were forgotten, and we held by the sheer fighting quality of our men.

The map will show the peculiar difficulties of the Ypres Salient. Its nominal base was the line St. Eloi–Ypres–Bixschoote, but its real base was the town of Ypres itself. Ypres was as the hub of a wheel from which all the communications eastwards radiated like spokes. One important road crossed the canal at Steenstraate, and a few pontoon bridges had been built nearer Ypres; but all the main routes ran through the town—to Pilkem, to Langemarck, to Poelcappelle, to Zonnebeke, to Gheluvelt and Menin, besides the railway to Roulers. Virtually all the supplies and reserves for the troops holding the Salient must go through the neck of the bottle at Ypres. Now, early in November the Germans won gun positions at the southern re-entrant which enabled them to shell the town, and a bombardment was continued intermittently throughout the winter. A serious cannonade would gravely interfere with our communications, and we held the Salient with this menace perpetually before us. We could assume, therefore, that a heavy shelling of Ypres would be a preliminary to any German attack.

From the middle of November to the end of January the Salient was held by the French. On the 1st of February part of the French were withdrawn, and General Bulfin's 28th Division was brought north to replace them. By the 20th of April the Allied front was as follows: From the canal through Bixschoote to just east of Langemarck, and covering the latter place, was a French division of Colonial infantry. On the right of the French, to a point north-east of Zonnebeke, lay the Canadian Division, under General Alderson, General Turner's 3rd Brigade on the left, and General Currie's 2nd Brigade on the right. From north-east of Zonnebeke to the south-east corner of the Polygon Wood was the 28th Division, the 85th, 84th, and 83rd Brigades in order from left to right. At the corner of the Polygon Wood was Princess Patricia's Regiment from the 27th Division; and this division, under General Snow, continued the front east of Veldhoek along the ridge almost to Hill 60, where General Morland's 5th Division took over the line. The trenches we had received from the French were not good, especially in the section held by the Canadians and the 85th Brigade. They were very wet, and the dead were buried in the bottoms and the sides, so that to improve them was a gruesome and unwholesome task. Had it been possible, it would have been wiser to construct a wholly new line. Farther south the situation was better, and the 83rd Brigade and the 27th Division were more comfortably placed. Against this section was arrayed the left wing of the Duke of Würtemberg's IV. Army, whose headquarters were at Thielt.

To understand the significance of the events which began on 22nd April it is necessary to go back to what happened on the 17th, for, though the operations at Hill 60 were not strictly a part of the Ypres battle, they were a link in the chain of causes. Hill 60 was only a hill to the eye of faith, being no more than an earth heap from the cutting of the Ypres–Lille railway. Its advantage was that it gave a position from which the whole German front in the neighbourhood of Hollebeke Château could be commanded. It lay just east of the hamlet of Zwartelen, where the Household Brigade made their decisive charge on the night of 6th November. About seven in the evening of 17th April we exploded mines on the hill, won the top, entrenched ourselves in the shell craters, and brought up machine guns. Next day, Sunday, at 6 30, the Germans made a counter-attack in mass formation, which resulted in a desperate struggle at close quarters. Our machine guns mowed down the enemy, but he reached our trenches, and there was some fierce hand-to-hand fighting. Repeatedly during the day the attacks were renewed, but all were driven back, and by the evening we had expelled the enemy from the slopes of the hill with the bayonet. For the next three days there was no respite. The position was vital to the enemy if he would keep his Hollebeke ground, and a Saxon division was hurled against it, with the support of artillery and asphyxiating bombs. The hill formed a salient, and we were exposed to fire from three sides. On the 19th and 20th the cannonade continued, and on the evening of the latter day, about 6.30, there was another infantry attack which lasted for an hour and a half, while all the night parties with hand grenades worked their way up to our trenches. On Wednesday morning, the 21st, the enemy had established himself at one point on the slopes, at the north-east edge; but in the afternoon he was dislodged. Against an area 250 yards long by 200 deep tons of metal were flung, and for four and a half days the defenders lived through a veritable hell. But on Thursday, the 22nd, the hill was still ours, and there came a sudden lull in the attack—another such dangerous lull as that which in the previous October had preceded the launching of the thunderbolt.

Meanwhile, on Tuesday, the 20th, the bombardment of Ypres had begun. Suddenly into the streets of the little city, filled with their normal denizens and our own reserves, there fell the great 42-cm. shells. Fifteen children were killed at play, and a number of civilians perished in the debris. It was the warning for which we were prepared, and the High Command grew anxious. The destruction of Ypres served no military object in itself. It could only be a means to the blocking of the routes through which we supplied our lines in the Salient. It could not be aimed at Hill 60, where our communications had a free road to the west. It must herald an attack on the section between the canal and the Menin road.

The evening of Thursday, the 22nd, was calm and pleasant, with a light, steady wind blowing from the north-east. About 6.30 our artillery observers reported that a strange green vapour was moving over the French trenches. Then, as the April night closed in, and the great shells still rained upon Ypres, there were strange scenes between the canal and the Pilkem road. Back through the dusk came a stream of French soldiers, blinded and coughing and wild with terror. Some black devilry had come upon them, and they had broken before a more than human fear. Behind them they had left hundreds of their comrades stricken and dead, with froth on their lips and horrible blue faces. The rout surged over the canal, and the road to Vlamertinghe was choked with broken infantry and galloping gun teams lacking their guns. No discredit attached to those who broke, for the pressure was more than flesh and blood could bear. Some of the Zouaves and Turcos fled due south towards the Langemarck road, and in the early darkness came upon the Canadian reserve battalions. With amazement the Canadians saw the wild dark faces, the heaving chests, and the lips speechless with agony. Then they too sniffed something in the breeze, something which caught at their throats and affected them with a deadly nausea. The instant result was a four-mile breach in the Allied line. What was left of the French were back on the canal from Boesinghe to Steenstraate, where they were being pushed across by the German attack, and between them and the left of the Canadian 3rd Brigade were four miles of undefended country. Through this gap the Germans were pouring, preceded by the fumes of the gas, and supported by a heavy artillery fire.

The Canadians had suffered from the gas, but to a less extent than the French. With his flank in the air there was no course before General Turner except to refuse his left. Under the pressure of an attack by four divisions the 3rd Brigade bent inwards from a point just south of Poelcappelle till its left rested on the wood east of St. Julien, between the Langemarck and Poelcappelle roads. Beyond it there was still a gap, and the Germans were working round its flank. The whole 1st Canadian Brigade was in reserve, and it was impossible to use it at a moment's notice; but two of its battalions were in the brigade reserve of the 2nd and 3rd, and these were brought forward by midnight and flung into the breach. A battery of 4 7 guns, lent by a London Territorial division to support the French, was in the wood east of St. Julien. The gun teams were miles away. That wood had no name, but it deserved to be christened by the name of the troops who died in it. For through it the two Canadian battalions charged at midnight, and won the northern fringe. They recaptured the guns, but could not bring them away; but they destroyed parts of them before they fell again into German hands, when the line was forced back by artillery fire. Another counter-attack was attempted to ease the strain. Two further battalions of the 1st Canadian Brigade charged the German position in the gap. They carried the first German shelter trenches, and held them till relief came two days later.

A wilder battle has rarely been witnessed than the struggle of that April night. The British reserves at Ypres, shelled out of the town, marched to the sound of the firing, with the strange, sickly odour of the gas blowing down upon them. The roads were congested with the nightly supply trains for the troops in the Salient. All along our front the cannonade was severe, while the Canadian left, bent back almost at right angles, was struggling to entrench itself under cover of counter-attacks. In some cases they found French reserve trenches to occupy, but more often they had to dig themselves in where they were allowed. The right of the German assault was beyond the canal in several places, and bearing hard on the French remnants on the eastern bank. All was confusion, for no staff work was possible. To their eternal honour the 3rd Canadian Brigade did not break. Overwhelmed with superior numbers of men and guns, and sick to death with the poisoned fumes, they did what men could do to stem the tide. And all the while there was the yawning rent on their left which gave the enemy a clear way to Ypres. Strangely enough, he did not push his advantage. As in the First Battle of Ypres, he broke our line, but could do little in the breach.

Very early in the small hours of Friday morning, the 23rd, the first British reinforcements arrived in the gap. They came mostly from the 28th Division, which, as we have seen, was holding the line from east of Zonnebeke to the south-east corner of the Polygon Wood. The line was held by three companies of each battalion, with one in support, and the supporting companies were sent to reinforce the Canadians. This accounted for the strange mixture of units in the subsequent fighting. In addition they had in reserve the 2nd Buffs, the 8th Middlesex (Territorials), the 1st York and Lancaster, the 5th King's Own (Territorials), and the 2nd East Yorks. These five battalions, under the command of Colonel Geddes of the Buffs, took up position in the gap, and acted along with the battalions of the 1st Canadian Brigade, which had conducted the first counter-attack. This force varied from day to day—almost from hour to hour—in composition, and for convenience may be referred to as Geddes's Detachment. It picked up, as the fighting went on, some strange auxiliaries. Suddenly there were added to it two officers and 120 men of the Northumberland Fusiliers. They were the grenadier company of that battalion, who had been lent to Hill 60, and had already been eight days in the trenches. Bearded, weary, and hungry, this company, marching back to rejoin their division, fell in with Geddes's Detachment, and took their place in its firing line. That night the "Fighting Fifth" lived up to its fame.

On the morning of Friday, 23rd, the situation was as follows: The 27th Division was in its old position, as was the 28th, save that the latter was much depleted by the supports which it had dispatched westwards, and was strung out in its trenches like beads, one man to every twelve yards. The Canadian 2nd Brigade was intact, but the 3rd Brigade was bent back so as to cover St. Julien, whence the supporting Canadian battalions and Geddes's Detachment carried the line to the canal at Boesinghe. North of this the French held on to the east bank; but the Germans had crossed at various points, and had taken Lizerne and Het Sas, and were threatening Steenstraate. The British cavalry—General Allenby's three divisions and General Rimington's two Indian divisions—were being hurried up to support the French west of the canal. That day there was a severe artillery bombardment all along the front of the 28th Division, the Canadians, and Geddes's Detachment, especially from the heavy guns on the Passchendaele ridge. But the fighting was heaviest against the Canadian 3rd Brigade, which by now was in desperate straits. Its losses had been huge, and the survivors were still weak from the effects of the gas. No food could reach it for twenty-four hours, and then only bread and cheese. Holding a salient, it suffered fire from three sides, and by the evening was driven to a new line through St. Julien. One company of the Buffs sent up by Geddes to support it was altogether destroyed. There were gaps in all this front, and the Germans succeeded in working round the left of the 3rd Brigade, and even getting their machine guns behind it.

About three o'clock on the morning of Saturday, the 24th, a violent artillery cannonade began. At 3.30 there came the second great gas attack. The gas was pumped from cylinders, and, rising in a cloud, which at its maximum was seven feet high, it travelled in two minutes the distance between the lines. It was thickest close to the ground, and filled every cranny of the trenches. Our men had still no knowledge of it, and were provided with no prophylactics, but instinct taught some of them what to do. A wet handkerchief wrapped round the mouth gave a little relief, and it was best for a man to keep on his feet. It was fatal to run back, for in that case he followed the gas zone, and the exertion of rapid movement compelled deep breathing, and so drew the poison into the lungs. Its effect was to fill the lungs with fluid and produce acute bronchitis. Those smitten by it suffered horribly, gasping and struggling for breath, with blue, swollen faces, and eyes bursting from the head. It affected the sight, too, and produced temporary blindness. Even a thousand yards from the place of emission men were afflicted with violent sickness and giddiness. After that it dissipated itself, and only the blanched herbage marked its track. That day, the 24th, saw the height of the Canadians' battle. The much-tried 3rd Brigade, now gassed for the second time, could no longer keep its place. Its left fell back well to the south-west of St. Julien, gaps opened up in its front, and General Currie's 2nd Brigade was left in much the same position as that of the 3rd Brigade on Thursday evening. His left was compelled to swing south to conform ; but Colonel Lipsett's 8th Battalion, which held the pivoting point on the Grafenstafel ridge—the extreme north-eastern point of our salient—did not move an inch. Although heavily gassed, they stayed in their trenches for two days until they were relieved. The 3rd Brigade, temporarily forced back, presently recovered itself, and regained much of the lost ground.

About midday a German attack developed against the village of St. Julien and the section of our line immediately east of it. The 3rd Brigade was withdrawn some 700 yards to a new line south of the village and just north of the hamlet of Fortuin. The remnants of the 13th and 14th Battalions could not be withdrawn, and remained—a few hundred men—in the St. Julien line, fighting till far on in the night their hopeless battle with a gallantry which has shed eternal lustre on their motherland. Scarcely less fine was the stand of Colonel Lipsett's 8th Battalion at Grafenstafel. Though their left was in the air they never moved, and at the most critical moment held the vital point of the British front. Had the Grafenstafel position gone, the enemy would in an hour have pushed behind the 28th Division and the whole eastern section. Far on the west the French counter-attacked from the canal and made some progress ; but the Germans were still strong on the west bank, and took Steenstraate, though the Belgian artillery succeeded in destroying the bridge behind them. Meantime British battalions were being rushed up as fast as they could be collected. The 13th Brigade from the 5th Division took up position west of Geddes's Detachment, between the canal and the Pilkem road, and they were supported by the York and Durham Brigades of the Northumbrian Territorial Division, which had arrived from England only three days before. The 10th Brigade from the 4th Division was coming up to support the 3rd Canadian Brigade south of St. Julien. To reinforce the critical point at Grafenstafel the 8th Battalion of the Durham Light Infantry Brigade of the Northumbrian Division, and the 1st Hampshires from the 4th Division, took their place between the 8th Canadians and the left of the 28th Division. The Canadians were gradually being withdrawn ; the 3rd Brigade had already gone, and the Lahore Division and various battalions of the 4th were about to take over this part of the line.

But meantime an attempt was made to retake St. Julien. Early on the Sunday morning, 25th April, about 4.30, an attack was delivered by General Hull's 10th Brigade and two battalions of the York and Durham Brigade against the village. It was pushed up through the left centre of the Canadian remnant to the very edge of the houses, where it was checked by the numerous German machine guns. In the assault the 10th Brigade had desperate casualties, while the York and Durham battalions, which missed direction in the advance, lost 13 officers and 213 rank and file. On that day, so mixed was the fighting, General Hull had under him at one moment no less than fifteen battalions, as well as the whole artillery of the Canadian Division. Farther east the 8th Battalion of the Durham Light Infantry Brigade at Grafenstafel was heavily attacked with asphyxiating shells—less deadly than the gas, but for the moment incapacitating—and at 2 p.m. a German attack was launched against its two front companies. From 2 to 7 p m. they hung on, and then the pressure proved too great, and they fell back with heavy losses. Farther on, at the extreme eastern point of the front, the Germans made a resolute attempt with artillery and asphyxiating bombs on the line of the 28th Division at Broodseinde. The 85th Brigade, however, managed to hold its ground, and made many prisoners. The position on that Sunday night was that the British line from west to east was held by the 13th Brigade, part of the York and Durham Brigade, Geddes's Detachment, the 10th Brigade, more York and Durhams, the Lahore Division, the Hampshires, the 8th Battalion of the Durham Light Infantry Brigade, and the 28th Division Our front was intact on the east as far north as the Grafenstafel ridge, whence it ran in a generally western direction through Fortuin.

Monday, the 26th, was a day of constant and critical fighting, but we managed to get our reliefs in and take out the battalions which had been holding the pass since the terrible night of Thursday. The 3rd Canadian Brigade had retired on Saturday, and the 2nd followed on Sunday evening. But on the Monday the latter, now less than 1,000 strong, was ordered back to the line, which was still far too thin, and, to the credit of their discipline, the men went cheerfully. They had to take up position in daylight, and cross the zone of shell fire—no light task for those who had lived through the past shattering days. That night they were relieved, and on Thursday the whole division was withdrawn from the Ypres Salient, after such a week of fighting as has rarely fallen to the lot of British troops. Small wonder that a thrill of pride went through the Empire at the tale, and that Canada rejoiced in the midst of her sorrow. Most of the officers were Canadian born, and never was there finer regimental leading Three battalion commanders died; many of the brigade staff officers fell; from the 5th Battalion only ten officers survived, five from the 7th, seven from the 8th, eight from the 10th. Of the machine-gun men of the 13th Battalion thirteen were left out of fifty-eight, in the 7th Battalion only one. Consider what these men had to face. Attacked and outflanked by four divisions, stupefied by a poison of which they had never dreamed and which they did not understand, with no heavy artillery to support them, they endured till reinforcements came, and they did more than endure. After days and nights of tension they had the vitality to counter-attack. When called upon they cheerfully returned to the inferno they had left. If the Salient of Ypres will be for all time the classic battleground of Britain, that bloodstained segment between the Poelcappelle and Zonnebeke roads will remain the Thermopylæ of Canadian arms.

The Monday's fighting fell chiefly to the Northumbrian and Lahore Divisions, which had taken the Canadians' place. Let us glance at the several engagements along our front. The 13th Brigade on the left was not seriously troubled, nor was Geddes's Detachment, which that evening was broken up and the battalions returned to the 28th Division. Its gallant commander fell mortally wounded as he was leaving the trenches. At four in the morning the Germans attacked the two companies of the 8th Battalion of the Durham Light Infantry Brigade at Fortuin and enveloped them, so that they were compelled to fall back behind the Hannebeeke stream, from which in the evening they retired 400 yards to still another line. The other battalions of the brigade were ordered to advance to the Frezenberg ridge, so as to take the enemy in flank. They suffered heavily from shell fire, for the Germans were making a curtain behind us to prevent our receiving reinforcements. The Northumberland Brigade, under General Riddell, was ordered at 10.15 a.m. to move to Fortuin. Along with the Lahore Division they made an attack upon St. Julien. It was part of a general counter-attack by the Allies, which farther west led to the French retaking Lizerne and the trenches around Het Sas, and which did much to check the enemy's offensive and relieve the desperate pressure on our line. But the attack on St. Julien prospered ill. The Northumberland Brigade had had no time to reconnoitre the ground, it was held up by wire, and it received the worst of the shell fire. Its 6th Battalion managed to get 250 yards in advance of our front trenches, but could not hold the position. The brigadier, General Riddell, fell at 3 30, and the Brigade lost 42 officers and some 1,900 men. Daylight attacks of this kind were impossible in the face of an enemy so well provided with guns, and the Lahore Division fared no better. Most of its battalions never got up through the fire curtain to our trenches. The 40th Pathans, the famous " Forty Thieves " of Indian military history, were among the chief sufferers. Their colonel fell, and nearly all their British officers were killed or wounded. Farther east, at Grafenstafel, there was fierce fighting. The 85th Brigade kept their line intact, but on their left, in a wood between the ridge and the Passchendaele road, there was a fatal corner. By the evening they were compelled to give up the north-west section of the ridge, and our front was temporarily pierced at Broodseinde. That night we slightly altered our line. The 28th Division on the right held its old front from the south-east corner of the Polygon Wood to just north of Zonnebeke and the eastern edge of the Grafenstafel ridge. Then our front bent south-west along the left bank of the Hannebeeke stream to a point half a mile east of St. Julien. There it turned south to the Vamheule Farm on the Poelcappelle road. That farm our men christened Shelltrap, and it played a great part in the later fighting. Thence it ran to just west of the Langemarck road, where it joined the French. The British line from left to right was held by the 13th Brigade, from the French to Shelltrap Farm ; the 10th Brigade on to Fortuin ; the Northumbrian Division, and the 28th Division, which had now for the most part received back its battalions from the western and central sections. The Lahore Division was being withdrawn, and the 11th and 12th Brigades of the 4th Division were on their way up, and there were odd fragments of other divisions in the front. The patchwork nature of our line made staff work excessively difficult. Units and bits of units were brought up and used to strengthen weak places. We have seen the experience of the brigadier of the 10th Brigade on the 25th. General Prowse of the 11th Brigade a few days later found himself suddenly in command of twelve British battalions and three French.

We may pass over the next few days till the morning of Sunday, 2nd May. On the last day of April the 12th Brigade, under General Anley, took over the line held by the 13th Brigade on the extreme left of the British section. On its right was the 10th Brigade from Shelltrap Farm to Fortuin. Then came the 11th

Brigade, holding 5,000 yards on the right of the northern section. On the 29th it was badly shelled, and the London Rifle Brigade lost 170 men. Next day it had to face a German thrust from St. Julien, which the Territorials drove back with machine-gun fire. The 10th Brigade held the old French second trenches, very badly made and awkwardly placed, but it was their boast that they never lost a trench. Beyond it lay the 28th Division, holding 6,000 yards down to the Polygon Wood. It was obvious that the 4th Division was holding far too long a line, and General Bulfin, who was in charge of the operations, resolved to shorten the front. The extended Salient had always been a danger. Now that it had been broken on the north there was no reason for maintaining a position which was open to assault upon three sides. We held what was virtually an oblong, five miles long by about three broad, with ugly corners at Grafenstafel and the Polygon Wood. Accordingly preparations were made for a bold retirement which would make of the Salient an easy curve with its farthest point under three miles from the town. But first, on Sunday, 2nd May, we had to meet a new German attack. Gas and asphyxiating bombs were discharged both against the French on the Ypres Canal and the 4th Division east and west of Fortuin. The French were ready for it. Their 75-mm. guns mowed down the invaders, and the German position in that section was in no way improved. Against the British they fared little better. By this time our men had respirators—not yet of the best pattern—and they managed to let the gas blow past with little loss. The result was that the 4th Division, assisted by the 4th Hussars, who had come up as reinforcements from the 3rd Cavalry Brigade, succeeded in holding its ground.

On 3rd May the time came to shorten the line. The 12th Brigade on the left did not move; it was the pivot of the operation. Battalions were withdrawn piecemeal, and picked riflemen from each company were left to cover the retirement This withdrawal, in perfect order, in a very short time, and with no losses, was a most creditable piece of staff work. The task was begun as soon as the darkness fell. Every day of the fighting the wounded had been got in under cover of night, and in the cellars of Zonnebeke village operations had been performed by candle-light. That evening the wounded were evacuated, all but a small number of very bad cases whom it was impossible to move, and who were left behind in charge of two orderlies. The Royal Army Medical Corps had never done more brilliant work in all its brilliant history. The difficulty of such a withdrawal may be realized from the fact that at some places, such as Grafenstafel and Broodseinde, the Germans were within ten yards of our line. Not less than 780 wounded were removed from our front, and the retirement of the battalions was equally skilful. Not a single man was lost. The 85th Brigade had a difficult task, coming from the extreme north-eastern point of the Salient. The 11th, coming from Fortuin, had to move for nearly four miles down lines of parallel trenches. Most of the supplies and ammunition was removed, and what could not be carried was buried.

The new line ran from the French west of the Langemarck road by Shelltrap Farm, along the Frezenberg ridge, and then due south, including the Bellewaarde Lake and Hooge, and curving round to the Zillebeke ridge and Hill 60. The 27th Division held it from near the latter point up to the Menin road, the 28th along the Frezenberg ridge to just east of Shelltrap, and the 4th Division to the junction with the French. This line was at least three miles shorter than the old one, so it could be held with fewer troops, which gave a chance of rest to some of the brigades which had been most highly tried. The critical point was now the centre on the eastern front of the Salient, which ran from the Hannebeeke stream along the eastern face of the Frezenberg ridge. This ridge covered all the roads from Ypres by which supplies and reinforcements travelled, and if the Germans should carry it our position would be gravely prejudiced. It was a ridge just as Hill 60 was a hill—by courtesy only; for the eye could barely detect the gentle swell among the flat meadows.

For the next three days there was little more than a heavy shelling. At the south-western extremity of the Salient, Hill 60 was recaptured by a German gas attack on 5th May. Early on the morning of the 8th, about 5 30, there was an attack on the centre held by the 28th Division. The result of that day and of the next, Sunday the 9th, was that our line was pushed back west of the Frezenberg ridge till it ran east of the well-named hamlet of Verlorenhoek, on the Zonnebeke road.

On the following Wednesday, the 12th, certain changes were made on the front thus further drawn in. The 28th Division went into reserve. It had been fighting continuously since 22nd April, and its losses had been almost equal to those which the 7th Division had suffered in the First Battle of Ypres. Only one lieutenant-colonel was left, and most of its battalions were commanded by captains. Its place was now taken by a cavalry detachment, the 1st and 3rd Cavalry Divisions, under General De Lisle.* The line was now held from left to right by the 12th Brigade, the 11th Brigade, and a battalion from the 10th Brigade of the 4th Division to a point north-east of Verlorenhoek. Then came the 1st Cavalry Division up to the Roulers railway, and the 3rd Cavalry from the railway to the Bellewaarde Lake, whence the 27th Division continued the line to Hill 60. It was not a good line, for it had no natural advantages, and its trenches were to a large extent recently improvised.

The cavalry took up their ground on the evening of Wednesday, 12th May. The 1st Division line was held from left to right by the 1st and 2nd Brigades, with the newly formed 9th Brigade in reserve; that of the 3rd Division by the 6th and 7th Brigades, with the 8th Brigade in reserve. Early on the morning of Thursday, the 13th, a day of biting north winds and drenching rains, a terrific bombardment began against the cavalry front. The 2nd Brigade of the 1st Division was affected, but the brunt came on the 3rd Division. In a short space more than 800 shells fell on a line of little more than a mile. General David Campbell brought up the Royals from his brigade reserve, and the line of the 6th Brigade remained intact. Not so that of the 7th Brigade on the right. There the shelling was too desperate for man to endure, and the brigade fell back some hundreds of yards, making an ugly dent in our front, and leaving a gap between it and the right of the 6th Brigade. The 10th Hussars and the Blues were hurried up to fill the rent, and at 2.30 p.m. the whole 8th Brigade, under General Bulkeley-Johnson—the 10th, the Blues, and the Essex Yeomanry —made a counter-attack to recover the lost ground. That charge of dismounted cavalry was one of the great episodes of the battle. The cavalry advanced as if on parade, so magnificent was their discipline. The charge succeeded, for we took the lost ground; but it was beyond our power to hold it. The German heavy guns, exactly ranged, made the place a death-trap. By that evening this section of our line had fallen back in a sag between the Bellewaarde Lake and Verlorenhoek. For that day we paid a heavy price. In the 1st Division the 9th Lancers and 18th Hussars suffered much, and in the 3rd Division the Royals, the Blues, the

* Important changes had now been made in the high commands. Sir Horace Smith-Dorrien, who had acquitted himself brilliantly in a long series of actions from Le Cateau to La Bassée, had relinquished the command of the Second Army, and his place had been taken by Sir Herbert Plumer, the commander of the Fifth Corps. The Fifth Corps was now under Allenby, and he in turn had handed over the Cavalry Corps to Julian Byng, who had formerly commanded the 3rd Cavalry Division.

10th Hussars, and the three Yeomanry regiments were mere shadows of their former strength. As always in our battles, the toll of gallant officers was lamentably high. On the same day the infantry on our left were fiercely attacked, but contrived to hold their ground. The gallant stand of the London Rifle Brigade, a Territorial battalion, saved the right of the 4th Division. Farther on the left the 2nd Essex, the reserve battalion of the 12th Brigade, did no less brilliantly. Shelltrap Farm, between the Poelcappelle and Langemarck roads, had fallen into German hands. The Essex cleared it with the bayonet, and all that day the place was taken and retaken, but we held it in the evening.

Battles in this war did not usually end with a grand climax, but ebbed away in a series of lesser engagements. By this time our activity in the Festubert region and the vigorous thrust of the French towards Lens had compelled the Germans to move some of their heavy guns farther south. There remained, however, the deadly weapon of the gas, and before we close the tale we must record an instance of its use, the most desperate of all. After the 13th the 3rd Cavalry Division, which was now severely reduced, was withdrawn into reserve, and its place taken by the 2nd, under General Briggs. The early morning of Monday, the 24th, promised a perfect summer day, with a cloudless sky and a light north-easterly breeze. Just after dawn our front was bombarded with asphyxiating shells, and immediately afterwards gas was released from cylinders against the whole three miles of line from Shelltrap to the Bellewaarde Lake. The wind carried it south-westwards, so that it affected nearly five miles of front; the cloud in some places rose to forty feet, and for four and a half hours the emission continued. The chief sufferers were the infantry of the 4th Division on our left. Where the men were handy with their respirators they managed to hold their ground, and the cavalry on the whole suffered little. After the gas came a violent bombardment from north, north-east, and east. The chief attacks were in the vicinity of Shelltrap, against our front on the Roulers railway, and along the Menin road near Bellewaarde Lake; and in these areas we were forced back for some little distance. The three salients which the enemy had now established did not profit him much, and before the evening our counter-attacks had re-established most of the line except in two places near Shelltrap and the Menin road. This last stage of the battle was a triumph for the cavalry, and their splendid steadfastness saved the infantry on their left and right.

The Second Battle of Ypres was less critical than the first, for it was not fought to defeat any great strategical intention. It was an episode in the war of attrition, in which the Germans, by the use of heavy artillery and gas, caused us severe losses without gaining any special advantage of position. We still held the Ypres Salient—a diminished salient; but we had lost so heavily that, so far as attrition went, the balance of success was clearly with the enemy. On the other hand, the moral gain was ours. The Germans had a wonderful machine—a machine made up of great cannon firing unlimited quantities of high-explosive shells, an immense number of machine guns, and the devilry of the poisoned gas. We had no such mechanism to oppose to theirs, and our men were prevented from coming to grips. The Second Battle of Ypres was the first event which sharply brought home to the British people the inferiority of the machine which handicapped their man-power, and it led indirectly to that reconstruction of the Government with which we shall presently deal.

The moral gain was ours, because no battle in the war so convinced us of our superiority in manhood, and inspired our troops with a stronger optimism or a more stubborn determination. We learned that we had now a homogeneous army, in which it was hard to say that one part was better than another. The Territorials, infantry and cavalry, whether they had been out since November or had left home a few days before, held their ground in the most nerve-racking kind of conflict with the valour and discipline of veterans. The miners of South Wales and North England, the hinds and mechanics of the Scottish Lowlands, the shepherds and gillies of the Highlands, the clerks and shopboys of London and the provincial cities, were alike in their fighting value. They were led, and often brilliantly led, by men who a little time before had been merchants, and solicitors, and architects. One lean veteran had ten months before been a spruce clerk on the Stock Exchange, travelling to the City every morning in the sombre regimentals of his class. He looked now like a big-game hunter from Equatorial Africa. Another stern disciplinarian of a non-commissioned officer was a year ago a business man who cultivated tulips in his suburban garden. Now from him to Norwood was a far cry. A grimy private from whom the visitor asked the way answered in the familiar accents of Oxford. Two men fresh from battle, and full of keen professional interest, were once London shopwalkers. The change was most marked in the case of the Scots. The kilt as worn to-day has a somewhat formal and modern look, suggestive less of Rob Roy than of the Prince Consort. But mark that company of Camerons returning from a route march. The historic red tartans are ragged and faded, the bonnet has a jaunty air, the men have a long, loping stride. They might be their seventeenth-century forbears, slipping on a moonlight night through the Lochaber passes. Here is a battalion from the Borders. The ordinary Borderer in peace time looks like anybody else, but these men seem to have suddenly remembered their ancestry. They have the lean strength, the pale adventurous eye of the old Debateable Land.

I first saw Ypres from a little hill during the later stages of the battle. It was a brilliant spring day, and, when there was a lull in the bombardment and the sun lit up its white towers, it looked a gracious and delicate little city in its cincture of green. It was with a sharp shock of surprise that one realized that it was an illusion, that Ypres had become a shadow. A few days later, in a pause of the bombardment, I entered the town. The main street lay white and empty in the sun, and over all reigned a deathly stillness. There was not a human being to be seen in all its length, and the houses on each side were skeletons. Here the whole front had gone, and bedrooms with wrecked furniture were open to the light. There a 42-cm. shell had made a breach in the line, with raw edges of masonry on both sides, and a yawning pit below. In one room the carpet was spattered with plaster from the ceiling, but the furniture was unbroken. There was a buhl cabinet with china, red plush chairs, a piano, and a gramophone—the plenishing of the best parlour of a middle-class home. In another room was a sewing-machine, from which the owner had fled in the midst of a piece of work. Here was a novel with the reader's place marked. It was like a city visited by an earthquake which had caught the inhabitants unawares, and driven them shivering to a place of refuge. Through the gaps in the houses there were glimpses of greenery. A broken door admitted to a garden—a carefully tended garden, for the grass had once been trimly kept, and the owner had a taste in flowers. A little fountain still plashed in a stone basin. But in one corner an incendiary shell had fallen on the house, and in the heap of charred debris there were human remains. Most of the dead had been removed, but there were still bodies in out-of-the-way corners. Over all hung a sickening smell of decay, against which the lilacs and hawthorns were powerless. That garden was no place to tarry in.

The street led into the Place, where once stood the great Church of St. Martin and the Cloth Hall. Those who knew Ypres before the war remember especially the pleasant façade of shops on the south side, and the cluster of old Flemish buildings at the north-eastern corner. Of the southern side nothing remained but a file of gaunt gables. At the north-east corner, if a man crawled across the rubble, he could see the remnants of some beautiful old mantelpieces. Standing in the middle of the Place, one was oppressed by the utter silence, a silence which seemed to hush and blanket the eternal shelling in the Salient beyond. Some jackdaws were cawing from the ruins, and a painstaking starling was rebuilding its nest on a broken pinnacle. An old cow, a miserable object, was poking her head in the rubbish and sniffing curiously at a dead horse. Sound was a profanation in that tomb which had once been a city. The Cloth Hall had lost all its arcades and most of its front, and there were great rents everywhere. Its spire looked like a badly whittled stick, and the big gilt clock, with its hands irrevocably fixed, hung loose on a jet of stone. St. Martin's Church was a ruin, and its stately square tower was so nicked and dinted that it seemed as if a strong wind would topple it over. Inside the church was a weird sight. Most of the windows had gone, and the famous rose window in the southern transept lacked a segment. The side chapels were in ruins, the floor was deep in fallen stones, but the pillars still stood. A mass for the dead must have been in progress, for the altar was draped in black, but the altar stone was cracked across. The sacristy was full of vestments and candlesticks tumbled together in haste, and all were covered with yellow picric dust from the high explosives. In the graveyard behind there was a huge shell crater, fifty feet across and twenty feet deep, with human bones exposed in the sides. Before the main door stood a curious piece of irony. An empty pedestal proclaimed from its four sides the many virtues of a certain Belgian statesman who had been also mayor of Ypres. The worthy mayor was lying in the dust beside it, a fat man in a frock coat, with side-whiskers and a face like Bismarck.

Out in the sunlight there was the first sign of human life. A detachment of French Colonial *tirailleurs* entered from the north—brown, shadowy men in fantastic weather-stained uniforms. A vehicle stood at the cathedral door, and a lean and sad-faced priest was loading it with some of the church treasures—chalices, plate, embroidery. A Carmelite friar was prowling among the side alleys looking for the dead. It was like some *macabre* imagining of Victor Hugo.

Behind the optimism of the British people there had been growing up slowly a certain uneasiness about many aspects of the conduct of the war. There was no distrust of the generals in the field or the admirals on the sea; still less was there any weakening in warlike purpose. But it was gradually becoming apparent that the mechanism of national effort was faulty, and did insufficient justice to the resolution of the nation. Ever since the beginning of the year certain events had compelled thinking men to re-examine their views, and certain other events had produced in ordinary people that vague disquiet which ends in a clamour for change.

The Second Battle of Ypres, with its heavy casualties, did much to foster this feeling. No totals were issued at the time, but the endless lists of names published in the press did more to unnerve the public mind than any totals. In June the Prime Minister announced the casualties in the war by land up to 31st May as 258,069, of which 50,342 were dead, 153,980 wounded, and 53,747 missing. On 4th February the total had been 104,000, with about 10,000 dead. In four months, therefore, without any conspicuous success or any battle comparable to First Ypres, we had multiplied our losses by $2\frac{1}{2}$, and our dead by five. Then there was the Dardanelles affair. Much violent and ill-informed criticism in the press and a perpetual tattle in private life had convinced many people that a disaster was imminent, and the high hopes of the early spring changed to forebodings. Germany's submarine campaign was also a source not of depression but of irritation, and irritation soon issues in a demand for a more effective policy. Our losses were indeed trifling as compared with German forecasts. On 19th May it was three months since the great " blockade " had been instituted, and during that time we had lost fifty ships—one-sixth per cent. of those which had arrived at or left our ports. In the later weeks Germany had waged war against trawlers to improve her average, and in one week no less than seventeen trawlers and drifters were sunk. It was relatively a small loss, but it was a loss; it involved many valuable lives; and, above all, we had not succeeded in accounting for any considerable number of enemy submarines. Then on 7th May came the news of the sinking of an unarmed liner, the *Lusitania*, with nearly 1,500 souls. The news threw Germany into transports of delight, and roused in Britain and America a deep and abiding anger, of which anti-German riots in London and elsewhere were the smallest symptoms. It was universally felt that the war had taken on a new character. Henceforward for the least well-informed it was a strife à *outrance*, and the people began to look about them to make sure that nothing was left undone.

During these weeks, too, the limited number who turned their minds to economic problems were beginning to be seriously disquieted. We had conducted the war on a lavish scale, and clearly there had been much avoidable waste. The foolish doctrine that expenditure was a good thing in itself, since it increased the circulation of wealth, seemed to have captured the minds of those responsible for our outlay. It was clear that we must find out of our savings or our capital the better part of a thousand extra millions a year, if we were to provide the Government with money to meet their current war expenditure and pay other nations for our colossal purchases. It was already probable that the debit balance against us in our external indebtedness would be not less than £400,000,000 a year. This could only be reduced by the practice by all classes of a rigid economy; failing which, we should be obliged to export gold to balance the account, or see the exchange go heavily against us, and lose our premier position as the financial centre of the world. But few in authority emphasized the danger. We spoke and behaved as if our purse were bottomless.

More important, because more generally understood, was the shortage in munitions—in rifles, in machine guns, in heavy pieces, and especially in high-explosive shells. It is to the eternal credit of Lord Kitchener that from the start he saw the importance of providing and munitioning armies on the grand scale. But there were immense difficulties in the way, all of which sprang from one tap-root—the fact that the nation had not been methodically organized for war, and that so long as it remained unorganized we were fighting, whatever our spirit, with one hand tied up. Our voluntary recruiting, splendid in its enthusiasm, worked unfairly and wastefully. Skilled workers in vital industries had been allowed to go to the trenches, and others, who would have been good soldiers in the firing line, had been sent back to a work in which they had no particular skill. The compulsion of recruiting posters and public opinion was drastic, but it was unscientific. Many men in those days who still believed in voluntaryism as the system best suited to the British temper were driven to modify their views, and to accept a form of state compulsion as at any rate the proper measure for a crisis. A common basis of agreement between the different schools was found in the desire for some kind of national registration, which would enable the State to use to the best advantage any special powers it might assume. But for the moment the chief need seemed to be less men than munitions When France after the Battle of the Marne realized the nature of the future war and her lack of shells and heavy guns, she set to work at once to supply her deficiencies. Every factory which could be turned to the purpose was utilized; every scrap of talent in the nation was called upon; local committees were formed everywhere to organize the effort. She had one great advantage in her conscript system, which enabled her to produce munitions under military law and to bring back her skilled workers from the trenches and send the less useful to take their place. In Britain the need, not less great and far more difficult to meet, was not generally recognized till the February strikes brought the matter to a head. Mr. Lloyd George addressed himself to the problem with zeal and courage. He spoke the naked truth, though his candour was somewhat discounted by the official optimism of the press and his colleagues. He fastened upon drink as the chief cause of the evil, and announced a drastic policy of prohibition. Various eminent people proclaimed their intention of forgoing the use of alcohol during the war, but their example was not generally followed, and Mr. Lloyd George, under pressure of political opinion, was forced to whittle down his scheme into a device for a few new taxes, which presently were dropped as manifestly unworkable. Various expedients were tried and relinquished. After the British fashion a number of committees were appointed, which occupied the time of many able men, and succeeded in getting in their own way and in the way of willing manufacturers. The national effort was still being directed with something of the crudity of earnest amateurs

The War Office, indeed, had shown commendable industry. Faced with every kind of scientific and industrial hindrance, the Ordnance Department in May had arranged for the production in three days of the quantity of ammunition usually produced in a year. If 20 were taken as an index figure for September 1914, the shell supply by March 1915 had risen to 388. Many thousands of new firms had been added to the Government list, and it was Lord Kitchener himself who first pressed for the policy of dilution of labour. If we must acquit the War Office of inertia, we must equally acquit it of obtuseness as to the Army's specific requirements. That before August 1914 the obvious lesson of the Balkan War had not been learned and provision made to equip field guns with high explosives as well as shrapnel, must be set down to the blame of the then Chief of the Imperial General Staff. At the outset of the fighting it was only the strong representations of the Ordnance Department at home that induced the British command in the field to permit a proportion of high-explosive shells. Early in November, when the need became clamorous, General Headquarters asked for 50 per cent shrapnel and 50 per cent. high-explosive, but a week later they asked that the percentage of the latter should be reduced to 25. When the command in the field spoke with so uncertain a voice it was difficult for the War Office to frame its plans ; and in any case there were insuperable technical difficulties in the way of switching factories instantaneously from one class of shell to the other. During those months the War Office laid the foundation of that great production which began to bear fruit in the autumn of 1915 and lasted till the spring of the following year, and the credit for which was unjustly given by the ordinary man to the new Ministry of Munitions.

But all its labours were inadequate, for demand continued to race ahead of supply. By 15th May 481,000 18-pounder shells should have been issued to the Army, instead of which it received less than one-tenth of that number. On 20th April the Prime Minister made a speech at Newcastle in which occurred this passage : " I saw a statement the other day that the operations of war, not only of our Army but of our Allies, were being crippled, or at any rate hampered, by our failure to provide the necessary ammunition. There is not a word of truth in that statement. I say there is not a word of truth in that statement, which is the more mischievous because, if it was believed, it is calculated to dishearten our troops, to discourage our Allies, and to stimulate the hopes and activities of our enemies." Mr. Asquith spoke at a delicate moment ; large operations were impending, and it was important not to allow the enemy to be encouraged or our Allies to be dispirited. Sir John French had assured Kitchener that he had all the ammunition he needed for his next forward movement, and the Secretary for War passed the information on to the Prime Minister before his speech.* Nevertheless Mr. Asquith was gravely

* It is needless here to enter into the controversy raised by Lord French in his *1914* Many of the statements are obviously so inaccurate, and the author seems to have changed his views with such mercurial speed, that this part of the book is worthless as evidence.

misinformed, for, though supplies might equal immediate needs on Sir John French's and Kitchener's calculation, in the larger sense there was a deplorable deficiency. Presently came dramatic proof of this truth. Two days after the Prime Minister's speech the struggle began in the Ypres Salient. We were almost without heavy artillery, and what we had was very short of shells. The Germans had a great number of heavy guns in action, and endless munitions. We beat off the attack in the end, but with a terrible sacrifice, and the lives of our soldiers were the price we paid for our deficiency in high explosives. Again, on Sunday, 9th May, we made an attack from Fromelles against the Aubers ridge. Our artillery preparation was necessarily inadequate, our men were held up by unbroken wire and parapets, and the result was failure and heavy losses. The lesson was writ too plain to be misread. We must pay either in shells or in human lives.

The public uneasiness was accompanied by the clamour of a section of the press, and this clamour continued to the end of the war. Certain popular newspapers presently took the part of the eighteenth-century mob, a part which would otherwise have remained unfilled, since the manhood of Britain was too busily engaged for agitation. Like the old mobs they were sincerely patriotic and imperfectly informed; they conceived violent admirations and violent dislikes; they were often sound in principle and wrong on the facts, sometimes correct on the facts and false in their deductions, rarely right in both, like the old mobs, too, when things went wrong they hunted perseveringly for scapegoats. They underestimated the complexity of government and hugely overrated their own infallibility; but on the whole they did little harm to the national cause, though often they wrought gross injustice on individuals. On this occasion they claimed that they compelled a change in Mr. Asquith's policy, and Sir John French has taken credit for himself inspiring the agitation to this end.

The claim can only be admitted with reservations. The press undoubtedly expedited the formation of the Ministry of Munitions by sharpening the popular anxiety about the shells and guns sent to the armies in France. Its attacks upon Lord Kitchener failed utterly, and established him more firmly in the confidence of his countrymen; and the changes in the Ministry, presently to be recounted, had little to do with newspaper criticism. Their principal cause was the very general feeling that a partisan Government was not the proper machinery with which to conduct a war. The Liberal Government had for years been sinking in esteem; its loudly proclaimed principles had come to seem to many vapid and jejune, and its adroit opportunism no longer impressed. In the stern realities of war what place was there for the gift of manipulating caucuses and making deft speeches? The one thing needful was high administrative talent, and this for long had been at a discount. What led a politician to fame had been skill in debate and rhetoric; even if he possessed executive gifts and did well by his department, he got less thanks for the work than for a hectic platform campaign which did service to his party. Now all these pleasing gifts were discounted. It was unfair to blame politicians for not possessing what they had never claimed to possess, for not cultivating a thankless administrative efficiency in a world where the prizes fell to him who could tinkle most loudly the party cymbal. But the nation had now become conscious that its Government did not represent the best available talent for the task, since too many of its members were irrelevant legacies from a world that had passed away.

Early in May a Unionist private member gave notice of a motion which was virtually one of no confidence. Mr. Bonar Law and the other Opposition leaders, reading rightly the temper of the people, interviewed the Prime Minister and demanded a reconstruction of the Ministry; and Mr. Asquith, also correctly diagnosing the situation, consented. He had no choice, for to let things remain as they were would have meant a speedy fall from power. There were other reasons why it was necessary to re-form the Government on a broader basis. Various members had made themselves highly unpopular by their speeches or deeds. With the injustice of those who have been grievously surprised, many laid the blame of the war upon Lord Haldane, merely because he had conspicuously laboured to prevent it. It was an ironic fate which vented popular chagrin upon the Minister who, of all others, had done most for the British army. If he was misled by Germany, he erred in company with almost the whole nation, and at any rate he had provided an Expeditionary Force, a General Staff, and a valuable Territorial levy. The root of his offending in the eyes of his critics was that he owed much to German literature and philosophy, and had had the generosity to acknowledge his debt. Mr. Churchill, too, was beginning to be widely distrusted, partly for the Antwerp venture, partly for the Dardanelles campaign, of which he was believed to be the chief begetter, and largely because of the atmosphere of hazard and irresponsibility with which his personality had come to be surrounded. His ardent spirit, his courage, and his quick, if not always judicial, intelligence predisposed him to take grave risks and afforded endless material for his enemies; for in easy-going ministerial circles he moved like a panther among seals. Lord Fisher, the First Sea Lord, had long been chafing at the blindness of the Government to the merits of his North Sea projects, and was thoroughly out of temper with the whole Dardanelles policy. On 15th May he resigned, and his resignation brought matters to a crisis. It was clear that in popular opinion Mr. Churchill was now impossible at the Admiralty. There were no alternatives before the Government except to go out of office or to reconstruct on a broader basis.

On 19th May the Prime Minister announced the formation of a National Ministry. It would have come with a better grace eight months earlier; but Ministers are human, and so long as things seem to be going well they are anxious to keep the credit for themselves. It is only responsibility, when it looks as if it may be heavy, that they are ready to share. Now that the smooth self-confidence of the early days had gone, they were anxious to make all parties liable for the conduct of the war, and this, rather than a resolve to mobilize the best talent in the country, seems to have been the immediate motive of the change. Sir Edward Grey and Lord Kitchener of course remained at their posts; in them the country had the fullest confidence. Mr. Churchill was given the Duchy of Lancaster, so that his great abilities were not lost to the Cabinet councils. The new Ministers were still untried in the conduct of war, but they were new, and the popular mind could therefore regard them hopefully. Lord Lansdowne brought to the common stock a unique administrative experience, Mr. Austen Chamberlain his financial knowledge, Mr. Bonar Law a reputation for business talents, and Lord Curzon a remarkable intelligence and untiring energy. By the appointment of Lord Robert Cecil to the Under-Secretaryship of Foreign Affairs the Ministry was strengthened by a man of first-rate ability and courage. Mr. Balfour, the greatest pure intellect which our time has seen in the profession of politics, went to the Admiralty.

The reconstruction of the Government awakened little interest among the people at large. The old political game was out of fashion, and the bitter cry of the wire-pullers passed unheeded. This popular apathy was unfortunate, for in a war of peoples the true centre of gravity is not in any naval or military command but in the civilian Cabinet at home. The one vital fact to most men was the creation of a new department, a Ministry of Munitions, which should take over all the responsibility for *matériel* which had fallen upon the Secretary for War, and should also assume some of the powers hitherto belonging to other departments. The selection of Mr. Lloyd George for the post was generally approved. His imagination, his zeal, and the seriousness with which he faced the war, had profoundly impressed his countrymen. He had not only the power of kindling enthusiasm by his eloquence, but he had the courage to speak plain truths to his quondam supporters. He did not despair of the republic, and he had the intellectual honesty to jettison old prejudices and look squarely at facts. As an administrator he was indeed of small account, touching little of detail that he did not confuse, but it was believed that he might inspire more competent hands and more orderly minds. The Coalition had also the useful result that it demobilized the respective caucuses and allowed criticism greater liberty. Henceforward there was no obligation upon a Liberal to spare the Ministry from party loyalty or a Unionist from motives of good taste. The Government was now the whole people's to applaud or censure.

A review of political accidents is apt to leave a false impression of the temper of a nation. At this juncture the British people were a little dashed in spirits, but there was no serious pessimism, and there was certainly no weakening. It was instructive to remember the history of the war with Napoleon, and to reflect how many of the best brains then in England were out of sympathy with the national cause. In this struggle we had no Fox or Sheridan to lavish praise upon the enemy and lament in secret a British victory. The working classes and their official spokesmen were most earnest and practical in their determination to carry the war to the end, and many a man who had imagined that he was a cosmopolitan discovered that he was a patriot. Such slender opposition as there was came from that class whom we call intellectuals because of the limitations of their intellect. There were the honest opponents of all war, who imagined that by saying that a thing was horrible often enough and loud enough they could get rid of it. Paradoxical *littérateurs* secured a brief moment in the limelight by foolish utterances. There were protests from men who, physically unwholesome, felt that pain was the worst of all evils, and from those who, having no creed or faith, and staking everything upon the present world, regarded loss of life as the ultimate calamity. One or two amiable sentimentalists proclaimed that we must not humiliate Germany, apparently under the delusion that you may make of a barbarian a good citizen if you avoid hurting his feelings. A few political *déclassés* attempted to redeem their insignificance by venting their spite on their country. But the opposition was as feeble as in Burke's famous metaphor: " Because half a dozen grasshoppers under a fern make the field ring with their importunate chink, whilst thousands of great cattle, reposed beneath the shadow of the British oak, chew the cud and are silent, pray do not imagine that those who make the noise are the only inhabitants of the field ; that, of course, they are many in number ; or that, after all, they are other than the little, shrivelled, meagre, hopping, though loud and troublesome, insects of the hour."

CHAPTER XXVIII.

THE ALLIED WESTERN OFFENSIVE IN THE SUMMER OF 1915.

April 5–June 17.

Germany's Summer Strategy—The French in Alsace and Lorraine—The French Advance in Artois—The British Attack at Festubert—The Summer's Stagnation—The War in the Air.

By the end of March the German Command had reached two important conclusions: that their forces in the West, though considerably outnumbered by the enemy, were competent to hold that front against any Allied attack; and that an effort must be made at once to bring about a decision against Russia. The desperate position of Austria, and the likelihood that in the near future Italy and Rumania might be added to the roll of their antagonists, forced the necessity of an immediate concentration of effort in the East upon the mind not only of Hindenburg, who believed that the war could be won on that front, but of Falkenhayn, who considered the West to be the crucial theatre. The issue proved that Germany had judged more shrewdly than the Allied Staffs. She alone was fully awake to the precise nature of the war in its present phase. All through the winter, when Britain was speculating how long German stores of food and explosives would last, she had been busy preparing her armoury. She found substitutes for materials which she had formerly imported, and the whole talent of her chemists was drawn upon for the purpose. All the human strength of the nation, which was not in the field, was employed directly or indirectly to make munitions. Women and girls and old men took their places in the armament factories. Early in the year Falkenhayn satisfied himself that for the next twelve months he would have no anxiety on this score. When we remember that she supplied 900 miles of front (with some assistance from Austria) in the East, more than 500 miles in the West, and equipped Turkey for the Dardanelles campaign, and that her use of shells was five or six times more lavish than that of her opponents, we may get some notion of the magnitude of the national effort. It was more impressive in its way than the muster of her great armies in August. She had created a machine with which she believed she could destroy one enemy and in the meantime keep the other at a distance. Her losses had been heavy, for she was tied to a military theory which demanded a lavish sacrifice of men; but apart from that she was saving of life. She believed that her machine could keep the enemy at long range on the West till such time as she could turn and deal with him. She had no illusions about the Allied offensive, or, if she had, it was in the direction of under-estimating it. She knew, or thought she knew, that no weight of men could break her front till the Allies had created a machine as strong as her own. She therefore disregarded the West, and swung the bulk of her new strength and the chief weight of her artillery against Russia—the unreadiest of her foes—leaving in France and Flanders only sufficient weight of men and guns to hold the line in a long-range contest.

It was a bold decision, for she took many risks. But its boldness must not be exaggerated. Her force in the West, though numerically smaller than the Allied armies, was better equipped with artillery and far better provided with shells. It contained a high proportion of seasoned regulars, and the fresh divisions which she now formed were a skilful blending of old and new, of experienced and fresh battalions. The fourteen new divisions now in training behind the Western front were the pick of the German army. They were strictly " divisions of assault," a spearhead to be used where the chief danger threatened. One disadvantage, indeed, was beginning to show itself. She had lost terribly in her officer class—perhaps half its effectives; and since that class was also a caste, it was difficult to fill the gaps without a violent break with her whole service tradition. But the gaps must be filled, and accordingly there appeared a new type of officer, created, so to speak, for the war only, an officer on probation, and with limited privileges. Now the German officer had his drawbacks, but for the purposes of the German theory of war he was highly efficient. His vigour, his ruthlessness, his mechanical perfection, his professional zeal, were all invaluable. The new type might be a better and abler man, but he did not fit in so well with the machine, and where the machine is everything no part of it can safely be out of gear.

An Allied offensive in the spring and summer had been decided upon as early as November 1914. Its primary reason was to be found in the psychology of the French nation. They had shattered the first German plan at the Marne and the second in Flanders, and yet much of the soil of France was in the hand of the invader. No high-spirited people could sit down to a slow defensive war while such an outrage continued. Joffre was as inevitably driven to an offensive by the temper of his countrymen as the British navy would have been compelled by popular opinion to bring to battle any enemy fleet that ventured out to the high seas. On the military side it was essential that an attempt should be made to relieve the pressure on Russia, and to assure Italy, when she entered the alliance, of the vigour and resolution of her colleagues. It was true that the new armies of Britain were not ready, and that the munitionment everywhere fell short of what was required. But both Joffre and Sir John French believed that, even so, they had the power to break the enemy front and force a retirement. They conceived that what had been done on a small scale at Neuve Chapelle could be repeated at more vital points with deadly consequences. They gravely under-estimated their enemy as regarded his discipline, his tenacity, and the power of his artillery; they had not grasped the strength of a defence in depth or realized of what slender value were small breaches in his line and at what a high price to themselves they would be effected. The result was a series of costly and futile attacks which continued through the summer, attacks based on a mistaken principle, delivered on various sections of a long front, but radically unco-ordinated. They did nothing to relieve the distress of Russia, and Germany was able to repel them without departing by a hairbreadth from the plan of campaign she had devised in March—a remarkable achievement for which she deserved the utmost credit, and a conspicuous example of the value of a unified over a disjointed command.

The main attack was preceded by various lesser enterprises undertaken by Dubail's group on the right wing.* In Alsace there was bound to be continual bickering on the crests and in the passes, and in March and April there was a prolonged struggle for Hart-

* The front was now under three group commands—Dubail from Verdun to Belfort, Castelnau from Verdun to Compiègne, and Foch from Compiègne to the North Sea There had been various changes in the army commands, Pétain succeeded Castelnau with the Seventh Army, Putz succeeded D'Urbal with the Eighth Army, and D'Urbal took over the Tenth from Maud'huy, who went to the First Army in the Vosges.

mannsweilerkopf, that spur of the Molkenrain *massif* which dominates the junction of the Ill and the Thur. The summit was lost, taken, and lost again, till the little peak became a comic feature in official communiqués. There was also a steady pressure, mainly by the Chasseurs Alpins, down the upper reaches of the Fecht, towards Metzeral, in the effort to reach Colmar and the lateral railway which served the German front in the Alsatian plains. More important than this hill-fighting was the attempt made during April to cut off the St. Mihiel salient. Dubail's aim was not to attack the wedge at its point, where the guns of the Camp des Romains made a strong defence possible, but to squeeze it thin by pressing in the sides, and ultimately dominating the communications of the St. Mihiel apex. At the beginning of April the north-western side of the German salient ran from Etain in the north by Fresnes across the Les Eparges heights, then by Lamorville and Spada to St. Mihiel. The south-eastern side ran from St. Mihiel by the Camp des Romains, the Bois d'Ailly, Apremont, Boudonville, Regniéville, to the Moselle, three miles north of Pont-à-Mousson. Obviously the important point was the Les Eparges plateau, which commanded much of the northern interior of the salient, and the possession of which was the preliminary to an attack upon the vital position of Vigneulles. Operations during February and March had given the French the village of Les Eparges and part of the north-western slopes, but they were still a long way from the crest, and their advance was terribly exposed, since every movement was obvious to the enemy on the upper ground. The great attack on the position began on 5th April, about four o'clock in the afternoon. It was raining heavily, and the whole hillside was one mass of mud seamed by the channels of swollen springs. A considerable piece of ground was won, but when the Germans counter-attacked early next morning the French were unable to maintain their position. For three days there was severe fighting, which culminated on the evening of 9th April in the winning of the crest of the ridge.

For a moment it seemed that the St. Mihiel salient would presently be squeezed so thin that it would cease to be, and that the line of Strantz's army would fall back to those uplands west of Metz which contained the fields of Mars-la-Tour and Gravelotte. To the world it appeared that this was the first step in a great movement into Lorraine which would strike a deadly blow against the German left. The soldiers of France were eager to meet the enemy on that very ground where, forty-five years before, Bazaine and

MacMahon had led them to defeat. Moreover, to outside observers, it looked as if the southern front offered the best chance for that manœuvre battle which was impossible in the congested north. But if such a policy was ever entertained, it was abandoned by the beginning of May. The seriousness of the movement against Russia had by that time revealed itself. Something must be done to relieve the fierce pressure upon our Eastern Allies, and it must be attempted in the theatre which promised the speediest results. A movement upon Lorraine and Alsace, however successful, would be slow. It would entail the attack of great fortresses, and it would not strike at any vital communications. At the best it would threaten the hill country of Baden and Würtemberg, an area far removed from the heart of Germany. It was incumbent upon Joffre to develop a strategy which would distract the enemy from the Eastern front by putting some more vital interest in jeopardy. One section was marked out above all others for such a venture. If the Tenth Army in Artois could advance over the plain of the Scheldt towards Douai and Valenciennes, the communications of the whole of the German front from Lille to Soissons would be in instant peril, and a wholesale retreat would be imperative. Elsewhere a blow might be struck at the local communications of one army, but here a blow was possible against the lines of supply of three armies. The history of the Allied summer offensive is, therefore, the history of the thrust of the French towards Lens and of the British towards Lille. The centre of interest passes from the armies of Dubail to the armies of Foch.

To follow the fighting in Artois we must note with care the nature of the country between Arras and La Bassée. The downs which bound on the south the valley of the Scarpe are continued on the north by a low tableland which falls in long ridges to the valley of the Lys and the flat country around Lens. This chalky plateau is full of hollows, most of which have their hamlets. Its highest part is known as the ridge of Nôtre-Dame de Lorette, which runs west and east, and is scored by many ravines. In the glen south of it lay the village of Ablain St. Nazaire, and across the next ridge the village of Carency. Then came a broad hollow, with the Bois de Berthonval in the centre, till the ground rose again at Mont St. Eloi. North of the Lorette ridge was the plain of the Lys. East of it the ground sloped in spurs of an easy gradient to the trough where ran the main road from Béthune to Arras, with the villages of Souchez and La Targette on the wayside. Farther east it rose again to the low heights of Vimy, beyond which ran the

Arras-Lens road. The country was in type like an outlying part of the Santerre—hedgeless fields cut by many white roads, with endless possibilities of defence in the ravines and villages. The Lorette ridge was a bare scarp, but its sides were patched with coppices which clustered thickly in the gullies.

At the beginning of May the German lines in this area formed a sharp salient. They extended from east of Loos, across the Lens-Béthune road, east of Aix-Noulette, and reached the Lorette plateau well to the west of its highest spur, where stood the Chapel of Our Lady. They covered Ablain, which was the extreme point of the salient, and Carency. They then curved sharply back east of the Bois de Berthonval, covering La Targette and the Béthune-Arras road. This last section of their front was known by the French as the White Works, because of the colour of the parapets cut from the chalk. The village of Ecurie was inside their line, which thereafter fell back to the east of Arras. The meaning of this salient was the protection of Lens, which was the key of the upper plain of the Scheldt, and the flat country towards Douai and Valenciennes. Once they were driven off the high ground, their hold on Lens would be endangered, and the railway which ran behind this front would be useless. During the early months of the year the French had been nibbling at the positions on the Lorette plateau, and had won considerable ground. During the first week of May a huge weight of artillery was concentrated, not less than 1,100 guns of different types, and Foch, the commander of the army group, took personal charge of the operations. The German force opposed was certainly outnumbered by the French, and probably outgunned; but it had the advantage of holding one of the strongest positions on either the Western or Eastern front. We may describe its line as consisting of a number of almost impregnable fortresses, armed with machine guns, and linked together by an intricate system of trenches. Between Ablain and Lens there were at least five series of trench lines prepared, each with its *fortins*, which would enfilade an enemy advance.

On Sunday, 9th May, in clear weather, the French began their artillery preparation, in the section between La Targette and Carency. That bombardment was the most wonderful yet seen in Western Europe, and may be compared with the attack which Mackensen was at the same time conducting in Galicia. It ate up the countryside for miles. Parapets and entanglements were blown to pieces, and all that remained was a ploughed land and fragments of wire and humanity. For hours the great guns spoke with the rapidity of maxims, and more than 300,000 shells were fired in the course of the day. About ten in the morning the infantry were let loose. On the right they took what remained of La Targette, and with it the vital cross-roads. East of it, in the hollow below the Vimy heights, lay the village of Neuville St. Vaast, with its big church. By noon the French had taken the west part of it, and by three o'clock they were attacking the church. The whole place bristled with machine guns, and the battle was waged from house to house and from cellar to cellar. Farther north, the centre moved from the trenches in the Bois de Berthonval, and swept like a flood over what had once been the White Works. They poured on beyond the Arras-Béthune road, and in an hour and a half had won more than two and a half miles—the most conspicuous advance made in the West since the war of trenches began. Like Jeb Stuart's troopers in Virginia, they plucked sprigs of lilac and hawthorn and stuck them in their caps as they surged onward. Had the whole line been able to conform to the pace of the centre, Lens might have fallen in a day. But meanwhile the left was battling hard for Carency. Here progress was slower, owing to the endless ravines and nooks of hill. The first movement carried it into the outskirts of the village, whence it pushed east, and cut the road from Carency to Souchez. The siege of Carency had begun, for the only communication of the German garrison was now with Ablain and the north. When darkness fell the French had, on a front of five miles, carried three German trench lines.

Next day, the 10th, the battle spread farther north. After a hard fight the French carried all the German entrenchments across the Loos-Béthune road. Farther south they attacked the fortified chapel of Notre-Dame de Lorette, and captured the trenches south of it, which connected with Ablain and Souchez. On the right they took the cemetery of Neuville St. Vaast, and repulsed the German reserves which came up in motor cars from Lens and Douai. All this was preparatory to the great assault of the following day. That day, the 11th, saw the beginning of the end of Carency. The ruins of the town, into which 20,000 shells had fallen, were surrounded on west, south, and east. It was slow and desperate work, for the Germans had turned every available place into a *fortin*, and each had to be separately carried. On Wednesday, the 12th, about 5.30 in the afternoon, the German remnants in Carency surrendered. That same day the summit of Notre-Dame de Lorette fell, with its fort and chapel, and, late in the afternoon, Ablain, now in flames, followed suit, though one or two strongholds still held out. The whole of the high ground west of Souchez was now in French hands, with the exception of a few German strong points on its eastern ridges.

On Thursday, 13th May, the weather changed to a north wind and drenching rain. The French attack was now mainly directed on Souchez, Angres, and Neuville St. Vaast. The situation was peculiar. In a sense the German line had been broken. In the direction of the Vimy heights all the trenches had been carried, and the way seemed open for a passage. What had happened was that instead of bending back when attacked and maintaining its cohesion, the German front had become a series of isolated forts, like drops of mercury spilled on a table. The most notable of these were the sugar refinery at Souchez, the cemetery at Ablain, the White Road on one of the Lorette spurs, the eastern part of Neuville St. Vaast, and especially the place called the Labyrinth, between Neuville and Ecurie, where the Germans had constructed an extraordinary network of trenches and redoubts in the angle between two roads. These *fortins* were manned by numerous machine guns, in some cases worked only by officers. They were so placed that it was difficult for long-range fire to destroy them, and until they were cleared out any advance was enfiladed. The battle, therefore, resolved itself into a series of isolated actions against forts. On 21st May the White Road was taken, on 29th May the Ablain position fell, on the 31st the Souchez refinery was captured, though it changed hands several times before it finally fell to the French. Eight days later Neuville St. Vaast was wholly in their hands. But as one *fortin* fell another revealed itself. The Labyrinth especially was a difficult business, where the fighting was desperate and continuous, and a day's progress had to be reckoned in feet. There the German burrows were sometimes fifty feet deep, and the struggle went on in underground galleries by the light of electric torches and flares—a miners' warfare like Marlborough's siege of Tournai.

By the end of May the French Battle of Artois had virtually closed. It had been a triumph for the fighting quality of the French infantry, and not less of the French gunners. But as a strategic movement it had failed. Much ground had been won at a terrible cost, but the enemy still held the ridges that commanded Lens. The marvellous artillery preparation had flattened and sterilized the landscape, but it had not overcome the enemy defence in depth. Strangely enough, even so good a soldier as Foch did not make the true deduction, and the underestimate of the German defence system was to continue for the better part of three years.

The British advance in May in the Festubert region was intended mainly as an auxiliary to the French effort in Artois. It was designed in the first place to detain the German forces opposite in position, and to prevent reinforcements in men and guns being sent south to Lens. But it had also a positive if subsidiary purpose. If successful, it would win the Aubers ridge, for the sake of which we had fought Neuve Chapelle, and so threaten Lille and La Bassée, and if the French got to Lens we should be in a position to conform effectively to their advance.

The first movement took place on the morning of Sunday, 9th May, and the section selected was that between Festubert and Bois Grenier. On the right, part of the 1st Corps and the Indian Corps advanced from the Rue du Bois in the direction of that old battleground, the southern end of the Bois du Biez. But the main attack was delivered by the 8th Division, from Rouges Bancs, on the upper course of the river Des Layes, towards Fromelles and the northern part of the Aubers ridge. The artillery preparation which preceded it was inadequate, and our men came up against unbroken wire and parapets. Some ground was won, but the gains could not be held, and by the evening we had made little progress. The next advance was on the morning of Sunday, 16th May, and the ground chosen was that immediately east of Festubert, where the German front showed a pronounced salient. The Battle of Festubert, as it may well be called, would in other wars, looking at the casualties and the numbers engaged, have been a major action, but in this campaign is ranked only as an episode—one link in the long-drawn chain of the Allied attack. Our artillery preparation began late on the Saturday night, assisted by three groups of French 75-mm. guns, and just after dawn the infantry advanced. The movement was entrusted to two brigades of the 7th Division, and part of the 2nd Division and the Indian Corps. The latter attacked on the left near Richebourg l'Avoué; the 20th Brigade moved from the Rue du Bois south-eastward; while the 22nd Brigade on the right advanced to the south-east of Festubert against the Rue d'Ouvert. The left of the movement was held up by a tangle of fortified farms. The 2nd Division captured two lines of trenches, but the Indian Corps found progress impossible. The centre, advancing from the Rue du Bois, made good progress till it was checked by a severe flanking fire. Reinforcements

enabled it to proceed, and it reached a point to the north-west of La Quinque Rue. The most successful operation was that of our right, the 22nd Brigade, which advanced for more than a mile. The German trenches at this point were curiously complicated, and we reached what was their main communication trench near the Rue d'Ouvert. The country was dead flat and seamed with watercourses, and it was not easy to find the points indicated by our air reconnaissance. The enemy attempted to make a barrage of fire behind us, so that it was a perilous business to get up reserves of men and ammunition.

Rain fell on the following day, and this and the marshy character of the ground to some extent nullified the effect of the German cannonade, for shells often sank into the earth without bursting. For three days we fought for the German communication trench, and endeavoured to disentangle our left from the network of German *fortins*. On the Monday evening a second advance was made on the right, this time by means of the 21st Brigade. In this fight the farthest point was reached by the 4th Cameron Highlanders, a Territorial battalion recruited largely from Skye and the Outer Islands. Their advance began at 7.30 p.m., and presently they found themselves faced by a deep ditch which could not be jumped. It was Sedgemoor over again; the appearance of an unexpected stream threw out a whole movement. Many of the men swam it, and one company reached the farthest German communication trench. Here its flanks were in the air; it had no bombs; reinforcements could not reach it; while the Germans were closing in on both sides and "watering" the whole hinterland with their fire. In the small hours a retirement was ordered—no light task, for the parapet was high, and there were no communication trenches (since the trench was itself a communication trench). The battalion was reduced to half its strength when, worn-out and mud-covered, it regained the British position.

By this time it was clear that the operation could not succeed. Ground had been won, but we were still far short of any real strategic point, and the losses had been out of all proportion to the gains. The fighting continued up till the 26th May, on which day Sir John French ordered Haig to curtail the artillery attacks and consolidate his position. The British Commander-in-Chief thus summed up the results: "Since 16th May the First Army has pierced the enemy's line on a total front of four miles. The entire first-line system of trenches has been captured on a front of 3,200 yards, and on the remaining portion the first and second lines of trenches are in our possession." This epitome is the best comment on the Allies' failure.

Meanwhile, as May passed into June, there came news from the East of unvarying calamity. The first counter-movement in the West on Russia's behalf had done little to aid her ; was it not the duty of France and Britain to attempt another ? Their civilian peoples looked for it ; the soldiers on the Western front expected it daily. The Russian press asked what the Allies were doing, and we may believe that the heroic armies of Russia turned their eyes wearily westward in the hope that France and Britain would soon reap the fruit of their sacrifice.

There were two reasons against such a step—one of policy and one of fact. In a boy's game, when one member of a side is hard pressed, it is right for others of his side to attempt a counter-pressure on their opponents. That is the ritual of all sports where the players are organized in teams. But the game of war is played under grimmer rules. Its object is victory at any cost ; and it may be necessary to permit the continued and desperate harassing of one section, perhaps even its destruction, in order to secure the greater end. Thermopylæ was fought by Leonidas and his Spartans for reasons of sound strategy. Had the Greeks refused the sacrifice and made an abortive attempt at relief, they would have been crushed somewhere on the Locrian coast, and the world would not have heard of Salamis and Platæa. Hence the time when one ally is hard pressed may be the time for the others to hold their hands. If the enemy is triumphant in one section he will be able to send relief to another section which is in difficulties. Provided the ally who receives the onslaught is really capable of supporting it, it may be wiser to let the enemy expend his strength in that quarter. It is a cold-blooded policy, but it may be justified by the higher interests of the whole alliance. The time for the armies not yet attacked to hurl themselves into the fray may be not when the enemy is succeeding elsewhere, but when he is failing, when he has exhausted his impetus, and is beginning to yield to counter-attacks. For then the wedges will be driven in on both sides of the tree, and its fall will be the speedier.

Such was the strategic justification, on the value of which opinion may reasonably differ. But there was a reason of fact for the apparent supineness in the West, an argument to which there was no answer. The Allies were not able to make a really effective diversion. Although their numbers were greater than the Germans, they were still behind them in machine guns, heavy pieces, and stores of shell. Against an enemy so firmly entrenched and so amply equipped mere numbers availed little. The advance of the Allies at Festubert and in Artois had convinced them of two facts. One was that to hurl infantry against German entrenchments without a very complete artillery preparation was a senseless waste of life. The other was that it did little good to pierce the enemy's line on a narrow front. To drive in a thin wedge meant no more than that a dangerous salient was thereby created, and Ypres had disillusioned them on the subject of salients. Even to break the hostile line for five miles, as in Artois, was not enough. Mackensen on the Donajetz had shattered a front of forty miles, and they needed some space like that if they were to manoeuvre in the gap. A rent on a great scale would prevent the enemy concentrating his artillery in a sufficient number of *fortins* to bar their advance. It would be a wound which he could not staunch in time. To achieve it they required a far greater artillery machine. It need not be more powerful than the enemy's; it need not be as powerful; but it must be powerful enough to permit of a concentration on a front not of half a dozen miles, like their past efforts, but of twenty, thirty, forty. Until they possessed this complement their diversions could achieve nothing of substance to themselves or their Eastern Allies. Could they have torn a wide rent in the Western front, pushed their cavalry through, and harried vital communications, then indeed they might have brought great armies hurrying back from the Vistula. But to drive in tiny wedges could have no effect on the death-grapple in the East, any more than to beat a bull-dog with a light cane will make him slacken his grip. To attempt an abortive offensive would be to play Germany's game. She wished the Western Allies to keep hurling themselves against her artillery bulwarks, and break themselves in the process, for she believed that thereby they would weaken and lose heart. The path of wisdom for the Allies was identical in both East and West. It was their business to avoid exposing themselves to the full blast of the German machine till they had secured a machine of their own. They must retire, or fight a holding and delaying battle. The long sword of the Allies was not ready, and they had to keep their armies intact till it came.

The story of this summer in the West is, therefore, a chronicle of small things—small attacks followed by small counter-attacks, or local struggles for strong points where a week's advance was measured in yards. There was fighting in the Ypres Salient and at

Givenchy. In Artois the movement against Lens degenerated into a nightmare of subterranean struggles in the Labyrinth, which for horror can be paralleled only from the sack of some mediæval city. There were minor affairs around Les Eparges and in the Vosges. In the Argonne at the end of June the Imperial Crown Prince attacked the French lines between Vienne and Varennes, and won and lost a hillock called La Fille Morte. It was the winter's stalemate repeated, but the balance of the war of attrition was not now in the Allies' favour. Little ground was lost, but little was won, and the list of casualties, French and British, advanced ominously for a period which showed no major action. The enemy machine was taking its toll.

The line had become on both sides a series of elaborate fortifications. It was a far cry from the rough and shallow shelter trenches in which the autumn battles had been fought to the intricate network which now spread from the North Sea to the Vosges. Along the Yser, though the floods had shrunk, enough water remained to constitute a formidable defence. There the low-lying positions were made as comfortable as possible by ingenious schemes of drainage and timbering, in which the Belgian soldiers were adepts. There, and in the Ypres Salient, the trenches could never be of the best. They could not be made deep enough because of the watery subsoil, and resort was had to parapets, which were too good a target for artillery fire. From Ypres to Armentières the autumn fighting had left the Germans with the better positions on higher ground, but the British trenches there had been brought to a wonderful pitch of excellence. In the Festubert and La Bassée region, and still more in Artois, the several Allied advances had reduced the front trenches to something like the autumn improvisations, but there was now a strong system of reserve positions. From Arras to Compiègne in the light soil of the Santerre and the Oise valley the conditions were favourable, though there were one or two horrible places, such as La Boisselle, near Albert, where the French front ran through a graveyard. On the Aisne the Germans had the better ground, and the peculiar chalky soil made trench life uncomfortable. Things were better in northern Champagne, while in the Argonne, the Woëvre, and the Vosges the thick woods allowed of the establishment of forest colonies, where men could walk upright and lead a rational life. Three-fourths of the whole front were probably unassailable except by a great artillery concentration. The remainder was in that fluid condition which a war of attrition involves. But everywhere—as distinguished from the state of affairs in autumn—there was on both sides a series of prepared alternative positions.

Trench fighting had now reached the rank of a special science. The armies had evolved in nine months a code of defensive warfare which implied a multitude of strange apparatus. There were more than a dozen varieties of bombs, which experience had shown were the only weapons for clearing out a trench network. There were machines for hurling these not unlike the Roman ballista. The different species of shells in use would have puzzled an artillery expert a year before. Provision had been made to counteract poison gas and liquid fire, and respirator drill was now a recognized part of the army's routine. Every kind of entanglement which human ingenuity could suggest appeared in the ground before the trenches. The intricacy of the science meant a very hive of activity behind the lines. Any one journeying from the base to the first line might well be amazed at the immense and complex mechanism of modern armies. At first it seemed like a gigantic business concern, a sort of magnified American " combine." Fifty miles off we were manufacturing on a colossal scale, and men were suffering from industrial ailments as they suffered in dangerous trades at home. There were more mechanics than in Sheffield, more dock labourers than in Newcastle. But all the mechanism resembled a series of pyramids which tapered to a point as they neared the front. Behind were the great general hospitals and convalescent homes; then came the clearing hospitals; then the main dressing stations; and last of all, the advanced and regimental dressing stations, where mechanism failed. Behind were the huge transport depôts and repairing shops, the daily trains to railhead, the supply columns; and last, the hand-carts to carry ammunition to the firing line. Behind were the railways and the mechanical transport, but at the end a man had only his two legs. Behind were the workshops of the Flying Corps and the squadron and flight stations; but at the end of the chain was the solitary aeroplane coasting over the German lines, and depending upon the skill and nerve of one man. Though all modern science had gone to the making of the war, at the end, in spite of every artificial aid, it became elementary, akin in many respects to the days of bows and arrows.

The communication trench was the link between the busy hinterland and the firing line, and no science could make that other than rudimentary. A hump of ground was as vital to the scientific modern soldier as to the belligerent cave-man. There were all varieties of communication trenches. In some fortunate places they were not required. If the trenches lined a thick wood, a man could reach them by strolling through the trees. Sometimes they took their start from what had been a village cellar, or they suddenly came into being behind a hedge a mile or two from the fighting line. In some cases the front trenches could be reached easily by daylight; in others it was a risky enterprise; in one or two parts it was impossible. The immediate hinterland was the object of the enemy's shelling, and he showed great skill in picking out the points which relieving battalions or supply convoys must pass at a fixed time. Except in an attack, the trenches were safe and salubrious places compared to the road up to them.

Things had changed since the winter, when the weather had turned the best-constructed trenches into icy morasses. What had been a sodden field was now a clover meadow, and the tattered brown woods were leafy and green. It was extraordinary what a change the coming of spring wrought in the spirits of the men. The Indians, who had believed that the sun was lost for good, became new beings in April. The foreignness seemed to be stripped from war for the soldier who looked out on corn and poppies in no way different from those in English fields; who watched larks rising in the open ground between the opposing lines, and heard of an evening the nightingales in the pauses of the machine guns. When there was no attack, life in the trenches in summer was not uncomfortable. There was plenty of good food, relief was frequent, and the dry weather allowed the trenches and dug-outs to be made clean and tidy. The men, who in the winter had been perpetually wet, ragged, and dirty, were now smart and well-clad. They took to cultivating little gardens and ornamenting their burrows. The graveyards behind the lines, tended by British and French alike, were now flower-decked and orderly. As the summer went on the heat gave little trouble. Exposure by day and night burned the men brick red, but the northern sun had no terrors for those who had largely fought under tropical skies. Flies became a nuisance, for Flanders is a land of stagnant pools, and billets were apt to be surrounded by moats which bred swarms of insects. Yet there was little sickness, and probably never in history has so great a concourse of men fought in a healthier campaigning ground. The summer months, which in the Dardanelles were sheer purgatory, were in Western Europe pleasant and equable. The hinterland was worse than the trenches, for there the ceaseless traffic smothered the countryside in dust.

All the old British battalions of the line and most of the Territorials had had heavy losses, so they were largely composed of new drafts, and their officers were mostly young. In May one famous battalion, which won great honour at First Ypres, had, besides its colonel, only one officer who had seen more than a year's service. Yet for the ordinary purposes of the trenches it would be hard to say that the units were inferior now to what they had been in October. This new phase of the fighting was especially made for youth. It was a subaltern's war. Young men with six months' experience were as efficient for trench warfare as veterans of several campaigns. They had all the knowledge that was relevant, since the conditions were so novel that every man had to learn them from the beginning, and they were young and keen and cheerful to boot. Never had what we may call the " public school " qualities been more at a premium. High spirits, the power of keeping men up to their business and infecting them with keenness, good humour, and good temper, were the essentials demanded; and boys fresh from school had these gifts to perfection. Their temperament was attuned to that of the British soldier, and the result was that perfect confidence which is the glory of an army. The routine of trench work was varied with many bold enterprises of reconnaissance and destruction, undertaken with something of the light-heartedness of the schoolboy.

Spring and summer brought easier conditions for the air services of the belligerent Powers; but the comparative stagnation in the Western theatre, where the service had been most highly developed, prevented any conspicuous action by this arm. The work of the winter in reconnaissance and destruction went on, and the story was rather of individual feats than of any great concerted activity. The importance of the air had revealed itself, and all the combatants were busied with new construction. In Britain we turned out a great number of new machines. We experimented with larger types, and we perfected the different varieties of aerial bomb. The Advisory Committee on Aeronautics, containing some of the chief scientists of the day, solved various difficult problems, and saw to it that theory kept pace with practice. We added largely to the number of our airmen. At the beginning of the war we had only the Central Flying School, capable of training at one time twenty pupils; by midsummer we had eleven such schools, able to train upwards of two hundred. The enemy airplanes began to improve in speed and handiness, but where Germany advanced an inch we advanced an ell. Admirable as was the air work of all the

Allies, the British service, under its Director-General, Sir David Henderson, had reached by midsummer a height of efficiency which was not exceeded by any other branch of the Army or Navy.

To a student of military affairs it seemed amazing that a department only a few years old, and with less than one year's experience of actual war, should have attained so soon to so complete an efficiency and so splendid a tradition. Perhaps it was the continuous demand upon nerve and intelligence. Young men gathered from all quarters and all professions became in a little while of one type. They had the same quiet voices, the same gravity, the same dulled eyes, with that strange look in them that a man gets from peering into infinite space. The air, like the deep sea, seemed to create its own gentility, and no service had ever a more perfect breeding. Its tradition, less than a year old, was as high and stiff as that of any historic regiment. Self-advertising at this stage did not exist. In the military wing, at any rate, no names were mentioned; any achievement went to the credit of the corps, not of the aviator, unless the aviator were killed. Its members spoke of their profession with a curious mixture of technical wisdom and boyish adventure. The flying men made one family, and their *esprit de corps* was as great as that of a battleship. To spend some time at their headquarters at the front was an experience which no one could forget, so complete were the unity and loyalty and keenness of every man and officer. To be with them of an evening when they waited for the return of their friends, identifying from far off the thresh of the different propellers, was to realize the warm camaraderie born of a constant facing of danger. In the air service neither body nor mind dared for one second to be stagnant, and character responded to this noble stimulus.

The summer was punctuated with Zeppelin raids, which vied with the submarine exploits in their fascination for the German public. With its curious grandiosity of mind, that public chose to see in the sudden descent of the mighty engine of destruction out of the heavens a sign of the supernatural prowess of their race. A great mystery was made of the business in the hope of exciting among the civilian population of the Allies a dread commensurate with German confidence. In this Germany was disappointed. The French and British peoples took the danger with calmness. It was a war risk, unpleasant in its character, but very clearly limited in its scope. There was a moment in Britain when the peril was over-estimated; there were also moments when it was unduly minimized; but for the most part the thing was regarded with calm good sense. There were four types of German airship in use—the Zeppelin, the Schütte-Lanz, the Parseval, and the military ship known as the "M" type—but the term Zeppelin was used popularly to cover them all. During the war Germany went on building at the rate of about one a month, a rate which more than made up for losses. Her chief difficulty was the supply of trained crews, for her reserves at the beginning of the campaign were speedily absorbed. The eastern and south-eastern coasts and the capital itself were in England the main objects of the German raids. During the first year of war seventy-one civilian adults and eighteen children were killed; and 189 civilian adults and thirty-one children injured. No soldier or sailor was killed, and only on one occasion was any damage inflicted which could be described as of the smallest military importance. The principal French centres assailed were Calais and Paris, and there, too, the victims were few. No military or naval depôt was damaged. Little shops and the cottages of the working classes alone bore the brunt of the enemy's fury. It was very different with the Allied air work. The yellow smoke of burning chemical factories and the glare of blazing Zeppelin sheds attested the fruitfulness of their enterprises. The truth was that the boasted Zeppelin proved an unhandy instrument of war. Its blows were directed blindly and at random. This was not to say that it might not achieve a surprising result, but that achievement would be more by accident than design.

It had been foreseen that the true weapon against such raids was the airplane itself. A fight between a Zeppelin and an airplane had been long looked forward to as, sooner or later, inevitable, and the Allied aircraft had instructions to engage a German airship whenever it appeared. It was not till the morning of 7th June that such a duel took place. About 3 a.m. Flight-Sub-Lieutenant R. A. J. Warneford, an officer of the British Naval Air Service, discovered a Zeppelin between Ghent and Brussels. He was flying in a very light monoplane, and managed to rise above the airship, which was moving at a height of about 6,000 feet. Descending to a distance of about 50 feet, he dropped six bombs, the last of which burst the envelope, and caused the whole ship to explode in a mass of flame. The force of the explosion turned the monoplane upside down, but the skill and presence of mind of the airman enabled him to right it. He was compelled to descend in the enemy's country, but was able to re-start his engine and return safely to his base. The Zeppelin fell in a blazing mass to the ground, and was destroyed with all its crew. The hero of this brilliant exploit had only received his flying certificate a few months before. It would be hard to overpraise the courage and devotion which inspired such an attack, or the nerve and fortitude which enabled him to return safely. Flight-Sub-Lieutenant Warneford's name became at once a household word in France and Britain, and he was most deservedly awarded the Victoria Cross and the Cross of the Legion of Honour. His career was destined to be as short as it had been splendid, for on 17th June he was accidentally killed while flying in the aerodrome at Versailles.

CHAPTER XXIX.

THE RUSSIAN RETREAT FROM THE DONAJETZ.

April 28–June 21, 1915.

Russia's Position in April—Hindenburg's Plan—Mackensen attacks—Retreat of the Russian Armies—The Loss of Przemysl and Lemberg—The Russian Position at Midsummer.

IN April popular opinion in Western Europe looked with confidence to the Eastern front, where Russia seemed to be winning her way to a position which would give her a starting-place for her great summer offensive. It was certain that she had abundance of trained men, and it was believed that there was sufficient equipment to double the force which had held the long winter lines. There was some division of opinion, indeed, as to where the offensive would fall. One school held that the old route by Cracow to the Oder promised the best results; another considered that, having won fifty miles and more of the Carpathian watershed, and in many places dominated the southern debouchments of the passes, she would sweep down upon the Hungarian plains and strike a blow which would detach Hungary from her alliance and render her no more a German granary. There was little evidence to decide between the rival views, for to clear the crest of the Carpathians was a necessary preliminary both for an advance to Cracow and a descent upon Hungary. But on the main point there was no difference of opinion. Russia would speedily assume a vigorous and sustained offensive, the great offensive of the Allied summer strategy.

What actually happened was one of the most dramatic reversals of fortune which the campaigns revealed. So far from being the attacker, Russia became the attacked. In a second, as it seemed, the centre of gravity was changed, and the main strength of Germany descended upon her in an avalanche not less deadly than the great swing from the Sambre and Meuse in the first months of war. Under this assault the Russian offensive disappeared like smoke. Cracow and the Hungarian cornlands were alike forgotten, the gains of nine months vanished, and the whole fortitude of the nation was centred on a desperate effort to save its southern armies from destruction. But if the disaster came as a sharp surprise to the civilians of the Allies, it had not been unexpected by their General Staffs. For some months it had been becoming clear that Russia might be a giant in strength but that she was a giant in fetters. Her numbers could not be armed or transported with any speed. She was desperately short of every form of artillery and every kind of ammunition. As against the German 12-inch gun she had nothing bigger than half that calibre.* The nature of her government and her economic system made it impossible for her to supply her needs in time. On her nine hundred miles of front there were a dozen danger-points for a resolute enemy.

The release of Selivanov's army of Przemysl enabled Ivanov to strengthen the front which opposed Linsingen, and to weight the blow of Brussilov's right wing against the Uzsok and Lupkow passes. But it was not possible for Russia to use her army of Przemysl as Oyama had used Nogi's army of Port Arthur, which decided the Battle of Mukden by its unexpected offensive on the Japanese left. In a struggle for mountain passes the theatre is necessarily circumscribed, and the number of men employed is strictly determined by the slender communications and narrow approaches. Ivanov wisely held most of Selivanov's force in reserve, and the day was approaching when there was need of the ultimate reserve in man and rifle. Przemysl fell on 22nd March. On the 25th the Russian position was well south of the Dukla near Bartfeld, just short of the crest of the range at the Lupkow and the Uzsok, and then among the foothills till the Bukovina was reached, where on that day they crossed the Pruth. By the end of March the last Austrian position on the Lupkow had fallen to them, and they were pressing hard against the village of Uzsok, to the east of the pass of that name. Here they were aiming at the spurs of the hills running from the glens of the upper Dniester, which would command the Austrian right defending the pass. All through the first week of April the regions south of the Dukla and Lupkow and north of the Uzsok were the centre of severe fighting. The last of the winter storms was raging, and from the Dukla to the Bukovina there was snow to the thighs in all the higher glens. By the middle of the month the crest of the range

* The details may be read in Gurko's *Russia in 1914–17*, chap. x.

for seventy miles was Russia's, but the Uzsok still maintained its stubborn defence. Brussilov, while continuing his frontal attack, pushed on with his right wing south of the watershed, and tried to work his way to the rear of the Uzsok position from the Laborcz and Ung valleys. The important junction of Eperies south of the range was rendered useless to the enemy, and the Austrians took some steps to clear the inhabitants from the Ung valley. Brussilov was now within two or three days' march of the Hungarian plains.

From the 17th to the 20th April the Austrian offensive suddenly revived, and there was a vigorous counter-attack against Brussilov's left flank in the vicinity of Stryj. The cause was the arrival of German reinforcements. By the 22nd the attack had failed, and the Russians in turn were pressing on the Bukovina border. The last fortnight of the month saw one of those sudden thaws which Poland and Galicia know well. The high valleys became impassable, for the melting snow had brimmed every torrent. Fighting, therefore, was perforce confined to the foothills, and on 25th April another Austrian counter-attack developed all along the line from Koziova to the Delatyn Pass, and lasted for the better part of a week. Linsingen's army appeared to be aiming at the Stryj-Stanislau railway, and observers in the West assumed that this was the last desperate effort of Austria to save the Carpathian line, and with it the Hungarian lowlands. A further portion of the Przemysl army was hurried to this section, which was precisely what the Austrians desired.

During April, too, there had been a curious activity on the extreme north of the Eastern front. On 17th March a Russian detachment had occupied the East Prussian town of Memel, and had held it till the 21st, when they retired before a German relieving force. On the 25th the Germans retaliated by bombarding the villages of the Courland coast by means of their Baltic squadron, and sending a body of East Prussian Landsturm, under Prince Joachim, across the frontier, which captured Turoggen, north of the Niemen. On the last day of March Libau was heavily shelled by the German fleet, and during April troops from Lauenstein's command made some progress on the line of the Dubissa, and presently a cavalry brigade entered Libau. The West read in this northern activity and the counter-attack towards Stryj the same lesson. Both were attempts to relieve the pressure on the Carpathian line, which threatened at any moment to collapse and uncover Hungary. The West was wrong; they were feints to mislead Russia. For in the very region which was confidently expected to be the scene of the great offensive that should give her Cracow, a mighty blow was preparing which was to wring all Galicia from her hands.

Rarely has a secret been better kept, for even Austrian Headquarters were not informed till the middle of April. No accurate details were known till the blow had fallen, but curiously enough the possibility had been widely canvassed for weeks, and very generally dismissed. The first hint came about 4th April, when fighting was reported on Dmitrieff's right on the Biala. Small attacks were undertaken there, in order that when the great movement began it should not at first be recognized for what it was, but assumed to be merely a continuation of the sporadic assaults of the past. On 6th April came a story that a German corps had been sent from Flanders by way of Munich to the Carpathians, and that Austria was withdrawing troops from Tyrol for the same purpose. On 13th April large bodies of German troops were reported to be passing through Czestochova. Then, from the 17th onward, came the attacks on Brussilov's left in the Stryj neighbourhood, and all the rumours seemed adequately explained. The enemy had been making a last effort to keep the invaders north of the mountains. On the 23rd the Russian newspapers discussed frankly the appearance of new German armies round Cracow. From the 24th for several days there was an almost complete absence of news. The German censorship had suddenly been drawn tight, for the bolt was ready to launch.

From the fall of Przemysl onward Germany had been busy behind her frontiers. Her Landsturm might go raiding with Prince Joachim, and her Bavarians battle under Linsingen for the passes, but these were only the fringes of a mighty effort. Three-fourths of the winter's accumulation of shell were brought to Cracow and carried out by night to the Donajetz line. Guns of every calibre came from everywhere on the Eastern and Western fronts and from Essen and Pilsen and Budapest, and in one section alone of about twenty miles along the Biala over 1,000 pieces were placed in position. Train after train kept bringing material and pontoons, and all the supplies of the engineers, for the land before them was a land of rivers. New hospital stations and new depôts for food and munitions were prepared close behind the front; a new telegraph network was established; great bands of cattle were driven up to their pens under cover of darkness. And then came the troops—from the East and the West fronts, and new levies from Austria and Hungary and Germany—all silently getting into place in a great hive of energy from the Nida to the Carpathians. Meanwhile Dmitrieff, in the Donajetz lines half a mile off, inspected his trenches and conducted his minor attacks and counter-attacks without an inkling of what was brewing. German organization had put forth a supreme effort. The world had never seen a greater concentration of men and guns more swiftly or more silently achieved.

How came Russia to be caught napping? The question is easier to ask than to answer. There were rumours in the West during March and April that the next German thrust would be eastward from Cracow. The activity in Germany, the troop trains passing up the Oder valley, might be directed to this end; but, on the other hand, they might not. They might pass through the Gap of Moravia, to the south side of the Carpathians, to reinforce Boehm-Ermolli, or Linsingen, or Pflanzer-Baltin. This possibility of a double interpretation for a movement which was known, at any rate in part, to the Russian Staff was exactly what Germany had counted on. That was why the counter-attack upon Stryj was undertaken. Up to the very eve of the great blow Russia's eyes looked south for the enemy rather than west.

At the same time it was anticipated that a blow might be struck against the Donajetz, but the Grand Duke Nicholas had no notion of the strength in which it would be delivered. Like every other Allied commander, he was ignorant of the gigantic artillery strength which it had been Germany's winter work to accumulate. He expected no more than the ordinary attack of the Austrian I. Army, a little reinforced, perhaps, by German troops, which Dmitrieff had for four months beaten off with ease. The Donajetz position, with the river big from melting snows, was believed to be impregnable. So, indeed, it was to any ordinary attack. Dmitrieff had dug himself in securely since that day in December when he first took up the ground. Unfortunately, confident in the strength of his defence, he had neglected to create second and third lines to which in an emergency he could retire. Behind him was a series of rivers—the Wisloka, the Wislok,* and the San. The first would give a good straight river line covering the main western passes which Brussilov held. But if he were forced from the Wisloka, there was no river in the rear to afford complete cover to his front, and the situation of Brussilov in the mountains would be dangerously compromised. Dmitrieff, a brilliant and audacious leader in a

* The Wisloka and the Wislok are identical names in Polish, but for clearness a different spelling has been adopted.

manœuvre battle, showed himself too little prescient and cautious in a war of positions.

In the last week of April there had been no change in the Russian commands, except in the northern army group, where General Russki, whose health had suffered gravely from the winter campaign, gave place on Easter Day to General Alexeiev, who had commanded the little army in the Bukovina. Alexeiev had begun his military career in the Turkish war of 1877, and had been Chief of the General Staff in the Kiev command. In the south, in Ivanov's group, Evert commanded the army on the Nida, Dmitrieff that on the Donajetz and the Biala, Brussilov and Tcherbatchev the armies of the Carpathians, and Lechitski the forces in the Bukovina. Ivanov's aim was to clear the passes and the southern foothills of the mountains, after which a movement south into Hungary or west towards Cracow could be undertaken at his discretion. The spring had brought him new troops, as yet ill-equipped, and especially lacking in heavy artillery. He may have considered that until he was better supplied with shells the valley warfare of the Carpathians was more suited to his forces than an attack upon the entrenchments of Cracow.

During April there had been a very complete readjustment of the commands and forces of the Teutonic League from the Nida to the Sereth. Until then Woyrsch had been on the Pilitza, the Archduke Joseph on the Nida, Boehm-Ermolli on the Donajetz, Boroevitch and Linsingen in the Central Carpathians, and Pflanzer-Baltin in the Bukovina. Now the group between the upper Vistula and the mountains was placed under direct German control, Hindenburg's former lieutenant, Mackensen, taking up the work of group commander.* Woyrsch and the Archduke Joseph still commanded north of the Upper Vistula. Then, tightly packed in the narrows between the river and the hills, came the Austrian IV. Army and the new German XI. Army. The Austrian III. and II. Armies faced Brussilov's right in the Carpathians, Linsingen was opposite Koziova and the road to Stryj, while to the east the Austrian VII. Army held the front towards the Sereth. These, with one exception, were the armies of the previous month, with the commands slightly rearranged. The exception was Mackensen's force on the left centre, which was the operative part of the whole machine.

Mackensen's group was probably the strongest which Ger-

* Mackensen surrendered his old command, the IX. Army, to Prince Leopold of Bavaria.

many had ever mustered under one general. The XI. Army consisted of eight German and two Austrian infantry divisions, and one division of cavalry, and the Austrian IV. Army had five Austrian infantry divisions and one German, and one of cavalry. Most of the German divisions were seasoned troops brought from the Western front. But more important than its infantry strength was its gigantic munitionment, for the heavy batteries numbered not less than 1,500 guns. Mackensen, soon to be made a field-marshal for his services, was one of the ablest of the German generals. A Saxon by birth, he had risen, like Kluck, by sheer merit to high command. He had been responsible for the great offensive of November which had given Germany western Poland, and had gravely threatened Warsaw. Germany had never played her traditional game to more brilliant effect than in the movement which we have now to relate. It was more dramatic than her great sweep on Paris in August, for then she was working in the heyday of her first enthusiasm; whereas now she was stemming a hostile tide after long months of drawn battles. There was no degeneracy in the fighting quality of a Power which could thus belie the expectation of the world, and out of set-backs and checks snatch the materials for a sounding triumph.

The elements of Mackensen's plan were simple, like the elements of all great strategy. The main fact was that, for all her success, Russia's southern position was not a good one. She was holding the southern side of a salient, and so was virtually enveloped; only the mountain barrier of the Carpathians and the weakness of the Austrian armies prevented her from suffering the usual effects of envelopment. Now in such a position a strong blow does not merely dint a line; it may compel a wholesale retreat of remote parts of the front. Russia's communications were the main railway through Przemysl and Lemberg, and the southern line which followed the foothills by Jaslo, Sanok, and Stryj. A thrust from the Bukovina which recaptured Lemberg would mean the retreat of the whole Russian front in western Galicia. A blow from the central passes which reached Jaroslav would cut off Dmitrieff on the Donajetz and the bulk of Brussilov's army. Finally, a thrust from the Donajetz which succeeded would uncover the Galician outlets of the passes which Russia held, and drive Brussilov back from the watershed. Obviously the first and second of these plans, if they could be compassed, would be the most fruitful. But Germany's trump card was her mass of artillery, and this could not be handled with precision among the wooded glens of the Bukovina or the strait valleys of the Central Carpathians. The place for it was the rolling plateau of Galicia. Accordingly the thrust was made from the Donajetz.

The ultimate aim was clear. If the German guns were numerous enough and fully supplied with ammunition, there would be no rest for the Russian armies till they were outside the zone of good Austrian railways, and back among the indifferent communications beyond their own frontier. It was a mathematical calculation. A certain weight of shell would make any position untenable. This meant that Przemysl and Lemberg would be retaken and handed back to Austria as a proof of the potency of her ally. It meant that the valuable oil-fields of Galicia would once again be in German hands. It meant that the Hungarian cornlands would be safe, and Count Tisza would be appeased. It meant that the coquetries of Rumania with the Allies would be summarily ended. She would no longer be disposed to attack Austria, and, if she had the disposition, she would not have the power. These were political ends, important, but still secondary. The main purpose was military—not the reoccupation of territory, but the crippling of Russia's field armies. If Mackensen could drive Ivanov from Galicia, a time would come when the Russian front would have to fall back everywhere to conform. The ultimate position would be south-west of the railway from Rovno by Cholm, Lublin, and Ivangorod to Warsaw, which would provide it with lateral communications. If that position were broken, then Warsaw must fall, and the whole front retire behind the Polish Triangle. This would mean that the armies of the north, based on Petrograd and Moscow, and the armies of the south, based on Kiev, were in danger of being separated by that triangle of lake and swamp called the Marshes of Pinsk or of the Pripet, over which lay no communications for large masses of modern troops. If that happened, then Alexeiev and Ivanov would be out of touch. It was not the capture of Warsaw that would damage Russia's position, but this isolation of her army groups. No offensive would be possible for months if such a fate were hers. The German high command had at the moment no desire to risk the fate of Charles XII. and Napoleon, and embark on a serious invasion of Russia. Enough for them to put the Russian armies temporarily out of action.

The plan was bold and sagacious, but it had one drawback. It demanded nothing short of complete success. If the Russian forces could be driven over their border, and so split up that concentrated action was impossible for many months, then indeed a great thing would have been gained, and half a million men might be spared to reinforce the Western front. But it was not enough merely to drive them from Galicia. It would be a costly process, and even though the Russians lost more heavily, they could afford it the better. Somewhere in the not very distant future lurked for Germany the spectre of shortage of men, and, if she wasted her manhood in costly methods of war for the sake of anything but the most decisive successes, her case would be evil. A new trench line on the eastern Galician frontier would be no real change in the situation. It would be more difficult to hold, for her lines of communication would be several hundred miles longer, and as the result of her efforts she would have fewer men with which to hold it. Russia would still be permitted a dangerous offensive. Therefore it was incumbent upon Mackensen to carry out the whole of his plan. Nothing less would suffice. A partial success, however splendid it might appear, would be a failure, for it would leave him weaker and in a worse position than when he started.

On the morning of Wednesday, 28th April, the Austro-German front lay along the left bank of the Donajetz to its junction with the Biala; then along the left bank of the Biala to the foothills of the Carpathians, where it crossed to the right bank in the vicinity of Ropa. Its communications were good, for it had for its left the Vistula, for its centre the main railway from Cracow, and for its right the line which runs through Novo Sandek to the junction at Grybow, on the Biala. The possession of Tarnow, then held by Dmitrieff, would give it a valuable cross line up the Biala valley.

On the 28th the action began with an advance of Mackensen's right on the upper Biala towards Gorlice. The place was skilfully chosen, for it had already been the object of some minor attacks, and the additional pressure did not at first reveal the importance of the movement. It is a vital advantage for a general not only to keep his concentration secret, but to get the actual fighting begun before the enemy realizes what it means. Further, a success here would outflank Dmitrieff's position, and would threaten the rear of Brussilov's right wing, now well south of the Dukla Pass. For two days the attack progressed, positions were won, and Dmitrieff was compelled to weaken his front in order to support his left.

Then on Saturday, 1st May, the great batteries were loosed.

The centre of the attack was now the village of Ciezkovice, half-way between Grybow and Tarnow. Under cover of a prodigious artillery fire bridges were pushed across the Biala, and Ciezkovice was taken. Its oil tanks were presently in flames, and soon it was a heap of smouldering ruins. Hundreds of guns were unmasked northward along the valley, and the Russian position was simply blown out of existence. Over 700,000 shells were said to have been hurled into the Russian trenches. It was Neuve Chapelle over again, and a greater than Neuve Chapelle. The Russians had no artillery powerful enough to check the awful storm. Taken by surprise, they made what fight they could, but the bravest of men cannot continue in trenches which have ceased to exist. Meanwhile the force which had crossed at Ciezkovice acted in conjunction with the advance from Ropa, took Gorlice, and turned the whole of Dmitrieff's front. On Sunday, 2nd May, the defence collapsed. Masses of the enemy had forced the Donajetz-Biala line at various points, and by that afternoon the Russians were retreating twenty miles to the line of the Wisloka. Mackensen had won an indisputable victory. The retreat to the Wisloka was not far from a rout, and Dmitrieff paid the penalty in guns and men for not having prepared a series of alternative positions. Especially in the south the Russians fared ill. The troops in the Carpathian foothills extricated themselves only with heavy losses. The Wisloka was a river and no more; no entrenchments had been made ready; and the guns which had driven in the Donajetz line would have little difficulty in annihilating one so conspicuously weaker.

But by this time the Russians had recovered from their first surprise, and they made a wonderful stand on the Wisloka. Reinforcements had been hurried up, including General Irmanov's famous Caucasian Corps from the Bzura front. The Caucasians defied the artillery storm and got to grips with the enemy. But in spite of more than mortal courage, the case was hopeless. For five days—from Sunday, 2nd May, to Friday, 7th May—the Russians clung to their shallow trenches on its eastern bank. Mackensen delivered his main attack against the railway crossing at Jaslo, and forced it early on the morning of the 7th. Had the Wisloka been held the Dukla might still have been saved, but when it went the troops in the hills were in deadly danger. They fell back in something of a rout, and Mackensen's right gave them no rest. Their goal was the upper glen of the Wislok, and the Germans followed along the two railways which branched eastward from Jaslo.

By the Saturday evening the enemy had won the Wislok, crossing by the railway bridge east of Rymanov, and lower down at the sharp bend of the river near Frysztak. Only the Russian right succeeded in making a stand. It ran from Dembica, on the Cracow-Jaroslav line, to the Vistula, a few miles west of the point where it receives the Wisloka. Evert's army on the north shore had meantime fallen back from the Nida to the Czarna, to conform with the southern retirement.

The forcing of the upper Wislok had in effect broken the Russian line. For a moment it looked as if Mackensen were about to roll up the two halves and effect a second Sedan. But the Russians were now alive to the German purpose, and had devised a strategy to meet the danger. At all costs they must prevent a disaster to their left, so they pushed out strong forces from Sanok, on the upper San, to stem the enemy's tide, which was surging now beyond the upper Wislok. This temporary check enabled Brussilov's army, after much desperate fighting during the Sunday and Monday, to extricate itself from the Carpathian foothills. The troops from south of the Dukla and Lupkow passes had a long way to travel, and the Germans naturally made many prisoners. At the same time Ivanov's right centre was compelled to fall back from the Wisloka to the lower Wislok.

Next day, Tuesday, 11th May, the retirement to the San began. The Russian left was already across its upper waters, and by the Wednesday evening the bulk of the line lay just west of the lower San as far as Przemysl and then south across the broken country to the upper Dniester, whence it was continued to the old Koziova position, which was still intact. During the two following days the San was crossed, except in its extreme lower course, and the front ran from Przemysl northward along the right bank of the river. That was on the evening of Friday, 14th May. The latter part of the retirement was managed with great skill and in good order. The bridge-head at Jaroslav was held till troops and guns were safely across, in spite of all Mackensen's efforts to turn the retreat into a rout. In a fortnight the army of Dmitrieff had fallen back eighty-five miles, and had lost heavily in prisoners and in material—losses exceeded by Brussilov's troops, who had to cut their way out of the hills. In some cases a corps lost three-fourths of its strength. But both armies were still in being. Ivanov's southern front had not been broken.

The Russian alignment along the San marked the end of the

first stage of the great German offensive in the East. That stage had within itself two phases. There was first the overwhelming thrust and the huddled Russian retreat till the Wislok was reached. They stayed not upon the order of their going, outnumbered as they were, and blasted and scorched by the fiercest artillery bombardment which the world had seen. In such circumstances the stand for five days on the Wisloka, which enabled the guns to get away and saved Brussilov from destruction, must rank as a surprising feat of arms. Like the brother of Æschylus, who at Salamis grappled a Persian ship, and when his hands were cut off clung by his teeth, thereby earning immortal fame among his countrymen, the Russians in their uttermost peril showed all the silent fortitude of their race. Their rearguards held the pass till the army could make good its escape. Not less fine was the dash of Brussilov's troops through the Carpathian foothills. They fought their way to safety as Bulgakov's remnant had fought in February through the Augustovo forests. Their losses were terrible, but it was still an army that assembled on the Wislok.

From the Wislok onward the case was changed. The Grand Duke Nicholas had mastered the facts of the situation. It was idle to hope to withstand Mackensen's onslaught. That terrific phalanx of men in close formation, preceded by a thunderstorm of shell, could only be countered by a machine of the same quality, and that Russia did not possess. The German Staff was right. The laws of mathematics apply universally, and this was a mathematical calculation. Russia must give way before the blast. But the most elaborate accumulation of war material will some day be expended, and a phalanx is the weaker for every thrust. It was Russia's business to exhaust the great machine by drawing it out to full stretch, though hundreds of miles of territory should be sacrificed in the process. The danger was from Mackensen. If we may judge by the stand of the Russian right, the army of the Archduke Joseph had not proved over formidable; and it is obvious that the III. and II. Austrian Armies had blundered, or Brussilov, caught between two fires, would never have been able to bring away most of his forces. Before Mackensen retreat must be the only course, but it must be retreat in close contact with the enemy, drawing his fire, exhausting his munitions, and depleting his ranks. It could not be such a retreat as lured on Charles XII. and Napoleon, but one in which the Austro-German troops had to fight for every mile and halt again and again on bloody battlefields. From the Wislok onwards the Grand Duke

Nicholas had the reins tight in his hands. His object was to save the most for Russia at the greatest cost to the enemy.

But he made no mistake about the German strength. His policy involved a retreat not of miles and days, but of leagues and weeks. Behind Ivanov's line lay Przemysl, for whose capture ten weeks before all the bells in Russia had rung, and Lemberg, which had been the first spoil of Russian arms. Two hundred miles north was the great city of Warsaw, for which Germany had thrice striven in vain. Such a retreat as the Grand Duke contemplated might give all three to German hands, and one at least was doomed when his armies fell back on the San. But it had always been a trait of his nation that it sat loose in its territorial affections. The words which Kutusov, in Tolstoy's *War and Peace*, speaks to his council on the question of the sacrifice of Moscow, had always been the creed of Russia's generals.* No province or ancient city was to be weighed for a moment against the safety of the armies of Russia. The Grand Duke was aware that Mackensen must succeed fully or not at all, and he knew that success did not mean the occupation of territory. Though the Russian armies were to be forced back to the Bug and the Sereth, and Warsaw, Lemberg, and Przemysl were to be prize of the conqueror, yet if these armies were still intact the adventure had failed.

It was now the morning of Friday, 14th May. The Russian right was being pushed towards the Vistula, but was still in the neighbourhood of Opatov. Their right centre was west of the lower San, their centre east of the river had looped forward so as to cover Przemysl, their left centre was along the upper Dniester, while their left was conducting a counter-offensive in the district between the Dniester and the Pruth. The Russian wings were having some success, but the main movement was in the centre, where Mackensen's phalanx was slowly coming once again into action. It travelled leisurely, for with the best communications in the world you cannot move a multitude of heavy pieces and a great weight of shells with the speed of infantry. It had for its passage the two good railways of Western Galicia, and along the highroads light rails had been laid to facilitate its transport. May

* "The ancient and holy capital of Russia! Allow me to remind your Excellency that the phrase conveys absolutely no meaning to Russian hearts. . . . It is simply a military problem, to be stated as follows: Since the safety of the country depends on the army, is it more advantageous to risk its destruction and the loss of Moscow by fighting a pitched battle, or to withdraw without resistance and leave the city to its fate? . . . In virtue of the power placed in my hands by the Czar and my country, I command that we shall retreat."

on the Eastern front was a month of constant rain, and rivers and floods clogged the mobility of the great machine. Once again the Russians drew some assistance from the weather.

What are we to understand by a " phalanx " as used in this supreme German thrust? To the minds of most people the word brings the picture of a compact oblong of men, packed like sardines, and gaining their effect by the sheer weight of human bodies. If they elaborate the idea they still think of the phalanx of Pyrrhus or Alexander, or the dense infantry masses of mediæval battles. But the whole conception is erroneous in modern war. The Germans believed in massed attacks, but the density of their order was relative to the British practice, and had always in view the conditions laid down by modern weapons. A mass is a good target, and its striking power is at any one moment only the striking power of the men in its front rank. Mackensen would seem to have launched his infantry in successive lines, perhaps a score of yards apart. In each line the men were in what we should regard as close order, probably one man to the yard, which would appear to be the limit of density compatible with free individual movement. This formation had the moral effect of weight: each man felt that he was closely supported to left and right and behind. We must therefore think of Mackensen's tactics as a series of efforts by lines of men in close order, and not the impulsive power of a serried mass. Such tactics, according to the orthodox view, would not prevail against well-disciplined and well-entrenched infantry. The experiment was tried at Mons and at Ypres, and failed. But Mackensen calculated upon the disintegrating effect of his artillery bombardments. It was not an attack of massed infantry upon infantry in position, but of fresh troops against a dazed and broken foe. The phalanx was destined to perform the work usually assigned to cavalry—to complete an action by disintegrating the last remnants of the defence. On this theory Mackensen's tactics were sound, but the artillery preparation beforehand had to be sufficient. Otherwise, if anything was left to the defence, the attack lost terribly. In this advance there were places where the bombardment was incomplete, and the German infantry came upon trench lines still held and machine-gun positions, and went down like corn before the scythe.

It was Ivanov's aim to check the enemy till such time as Przemysl could be cleared of supplies and armament. His method was a holding battle on his centre and a vigorous counter-thrust on his wings. Let us look first at the battles on the flanks.

Evert's army, the right wing of the Russian command, had been compelled by the retirement of the centre to fall back from the Nida towards the Vistula. It was opposed by Woyrsch's command and the Austrian I. Army, which had not the fighting value of Mackensen's centre, and its retreat was determined by the strategical necessity of conforming, rather than by superior pressure. It retired behind Kielce, which gave the enemy the railway junction and the branch line to Ostrovietz. It will be remembered that in the first assault on Warsaw this line had played a great part, since from Ostrovietz a good road led to the easiest crossing of the middle Vistula at Josefov. On Friday, 14th May, the Russian right was well in front of Ostrovietz, and ran through the town of Opatov to the Vistula, west of its confluence with the San. Evert resolved to attempt a counter-attack which would both check the dangerous move on Josefov and, if fortune favoured, do something to relieve the pressure on the centre. The Austro-German advance guard was progressing comfortably under the impression that the Russians would not make a stand till the Vistula was reached, when, on the morning of Saturday, 15th May, Evert suddenly struck. His blow was aimed at both flanks of the advance, while his Cossacks fetched a wide circuit and fell upon the communications. The result was that, in a three days' battle, the enemy was checked, and fell back to west of Ivaniska, where he received reinforcements which enabled him to make a stand. This action was fought largely with the bayonet, and since the enemy was caught in the open, the traditional Russian pre-eminence in this arm had full play. The troops just south of Evert along the San, infected by the activity on their right, delivered a fierce attack, which drove back the Archduke Joseph to the town of Tarnobrzeg, on the Vistula. Here the action was stayed, rather because of Ivanov's general orders than because the Russian energy was exhausted. With his right wing much depleted for supports to his centre, he had not the troops to attempt a true enveloping action on a flank.

On the extreme Russian left, on the frontiers of the Bukovina, the Austrian VII. Army had been gradually pushing back the Ninth Army of Lechitski. Pflanzer-Baltin had a position which on his left was about half-way between Nadworna and the important junction of Stanislau. His right centre was on the lower Dniester, holding the railway crossing of Zalestchiki. On 9th May the Russians struck at this extended front, which can scarcely have been less than a hundred miles long, and in five days' fighting cleared him from the Dniester line. By Saturday, the 15th, his left was back on the Pruth, and Nadworna was in Russian hands. The Russians, too, were on the south side of the Pruth at Sniatyn, and they had cut the railway between Austria and the Bukovina. They were threatening, but had not taken, the towns of Kolomea and Czernovitz.

It was a considerable success. They had driven back the enemy in some places as much as thirty miles, and had for the moment checked a movement which might have cut one of their communications with southern Russia. On a different kind of front these two rapid and effective blows at the wings would have compelled a halt in the centre. But in the situation of the Galician armies they had only a local effect. The Russian right, as we have seen, was too weak to attempt an enveloping movement or the cutting of Mackensen's and the Archduke Joseph's communications. The Russian left, though it drove the enemy back to the hills, could incommode Pflanzer-Baltin only, and not the whole Austro-German command. To strike at the main enemy communications it would have to advance over the passes into the Hungarian plains, and for this it had not the men or munitions. The Carpathian barrier had the effect of making the central enemy advance singularly insensitive to what happened on its right wing. We may, therefore, regard Russia's two counter-attacks as merely efforts to gain time. The centre of gravity was still on the San, where Mackensen's success would render nugatory the losses of the flanks.

The Battle of the San began on Saturday, 15th May, and must rank as one of the major conflicts of the retreat. It is important to note the Austro-German dispositions, and the direction of the converging attacks. On the left the Archduke Joseph was operating against the lower San, from the Vistula up to the neighbourhood of Jaroslav. The Russians held the left bank close to the stream from Jaroslav down to Sieniawa, and from that point ran well to the west till the Vistula was reached at Tarnobrzeg. From Jaroslav they followed the San in front of Przemysl, bent round in a shallow salient to the railway junction of Dobromil, and then ran east by Sambor, Drohobycz, and Stryj, covering the upper waters of the Dniester. Against the section Jaroslav-Przemysl Mackensen's phalanx was advancing on a narrow front, with the corps of Boroevitch supporting its right. The Austrian III. Army, having crossed the Dukla and Lupkow passes, was moving against the re-entrant of the salient, just south of Przemysl; and the II. Army was aiming at the railway between Dobromil and Sambor. Linsingen, having at last forced the Koziova position, was moving upon Stryj and the line of the Dniester, with his right flung out in the direction of Halicz, where contact was attained with the extreme right, under Pflanzer-Baltin.

About midnight on Saturday Jaroslav fell. The Russian rearguard was driven from the low heights west of the town, but it had fought a delaying action sufficient to ensure the passage of the San for the rest of the Russian centre. All Sunday the Archduke Joseph battled for the San crossings, and on Monday 100,000 men had forded the river at several places. Next day, Tuesday, he had taken Sieniawa, and the Russian right was two miles back from the eastern bank, astride the tributary stream of the Lubaczowka. Here it made a new stand. It would appear that Mackensen's phalanx had not yet come up into line, for during these days there was no strong attack upon Przemysl from the west. It was otherwise with the re-entrant on the south. On Saturday, the 15th, Marwitz captured the railway junctions of Dobromil and Sambor, and pushed northward against the Przemysl lines. This attack was clearly most dangerous, for an advance of a few more miles would give the enemy control of the main line between Przemysl and Lemberg, and cut off the troops in the city. The hazard of such a position, as we have already seen, is not the apex of the salient, but the angles at which it joins the main front. At Ypres in October the most deadly German attacks were on Bixschoote in the north and the Klein Zillebeke ridge in the south. At Lodz in November the German salient was almost destroyed by the Russian pressure on the two sides of its base. The chief danger, therefore, came at the moment from the Austrian III. and II. Armies. Farther east Linsingen was attacking Stryj and the Dniester line.

Przemysl, after its capture by Selivanov on 22nd March, had not been put in a state of defence. Inside the place were a number of guns captured from the Austrians, a quantity of supplies, and a good deal of rolling stock, which had accumulated in the great junction. Such materials cannot be removed in a few hours, and it was Russia's aim to hold Przemysl long enough to permit her to get them clear away by the Lemberg railway. Ivanov was well aware of the danger of the salient, and had no sentimental desire to hold the fortress. All he asked for was a week or so to complete its evacuation. From the 20th of May till Wednesday, the 2nd of June, the work of clearance went on, while Mackensen hammered at the western forts and the river line as far as Jaroslav, and

Boroevitch attempted to force the southern re-entrant, or at any rate get the Lemberg railway under his fire. Marwitz, on his right, made no progress, being held up by the impassable marshes of the Dniester between Drohobycz and Komarno. Mackensen succeeded in crossing the San at Radymno, just below its junction with the little river Wisnia, a success which made the neck of the Przemysl salient no more than twelve miles across. But meantime the Russian right pushed the Archduke Joseph out of Sieniawa and Lezachow, forced him in some places back across the San, and threatened the flank of Mackensen's position at Radymno. The consequence was that what might have been a most dangerous attack upon the northern re-entrant was for the moment foiled. It was clear that Mackensen had weakened the armies on both sides of him for the attack upon the salient itself.

The days of Przemysl were now numbered. The Austro-German lines were pressing in on three sides, and during the last two days of May the outer defences began to crumble. By the evening of Monday, 31st May, Bavarian infantry had carried the northern forts, and on the Tuesday afternoon the southern forts were evacuated. At 3.30 on the morning of Wednesday, 2nd June, Mackensen entered the city. The Russians had held it a little over two months. Germany was enabled to hand back to her ally her chief fortress, and thereby greatly strengthen Austria's loyalty to the alliance. But it is needless to rate the exploit too high. The recapture of Przemysl was without military significance except as an incident in the Russian retreat. No booty to speak of fell into Austro-German hands. The rolling stock, the stores, and most of the captured guns had gone eastward, and only a few useless pieces remained to be magnified in German communiqués into an arsenal of artillery.

We can now see something of the method of the great German advance. Mackensen's phalanx travelled slowly. The wings pushed out beyond the centre, and against them the Russians fought delaying actions with some success. But so soon as the heavy guns arrived retreat became necessary, and only the fortifications of Przemysl enabled the Russian centre to make so long a stand. It was this slowness of the phalanx which enabled Przemysl to be evacuated with little loss. One result of the method was a constant shifting of the main centre of operations. Now it was Jaroslav, now the southern re-entrant, now the western front of the salient, and, after Przemysl's fall, it travelled many miles to the south. While the great machine was getting in order for a further movement, it fell to another army to take the next step in the offensive.

It was the turn of Linsingen. Stryj fell to him on Tuesday, 1st June, after an attack in which a division of the Prussian Guard played the main part. The place was important as a railway centre, and Brussilov seems to have held on too long, for he lost some guns and several thousand prisoners. The fall of Przemysl a day later compelled an alteration in the Russian front. It now ran west of the lower San, crossing to the east bank below Radymno, and following the valley of the Wisnia, west of Mosciska, till it reached the Dniester, west of the great marshes. After that its line was the cañon of the Dniester till it dipped south by Stanislau and Nadworna to the Pruth. On Monday, 7th June, Linsingen forced the crossing of the Dniester at Zuravno, and occupied the high ground north of the river. The place was the key to the river line. The Stryj, descending from the Carpathians and passing the town of that name, enters the Dniester at Zydaczow, a village which marks the eastern end of the main Dniester marshes. To cross there meant that an army had to ford both the Stryj and the Dniester, which run for a short way parallel before they join. East of Zydaczow is a lesser belt of marsh, and then comes Zurawno, with firm land on both sides, an easy ford, and good roads from railhead. Linsingen chose his front well, forced a passage, and got the bulk of his army across. Count Bothmer commanded the main advance, and succeeded in taking the northern heights and advancing some way into the forests towards the railway from Stryj to Tarnopol. He was now little more than forty miles as the crow flies from Lemberg.

On 8th June Brussilov turned and caught him. It was the story so familiar in these campaigns, a repetition of what happened at Augustovo in September and at Kazimirjev in October. The German machine got too far from its railways, its guns and ammunition travelled too slowly by the bad country roads, and the more mobile Russians caught it at a disadvantage. Bothmer, in a three days' battle, was flung back across the Dniester with heavy loss. But this success could have no influence upon the general situation. About the same time Pflanzer-Baltin began to move in the east, and he had against him a force much depleted to supply reinforcements for the centre. Linsingen's right forced a crossing of the Dniester at Zaleszky above Halicz; Pflanzer-Baltin pushed Lechitski from the Pruth to the Dniester, took Stanislau, and near Czernovitz forced the entire Russian left back to the Russian frontier. Meanwhile Mackensen's phalanx was again moving, this time in a north-easterly direction. He cleared the Russians from the San between Sieniawa and Jaroslav, and, pivoting on Sieniawa, swung round his right towards Mosciska. In this advance he took many prisoners, for the sudden change of direction made the Russian retirement difficult. At first the line of the Lubaczowka was held, and thence by Mosciska to the Dniester. But here there could be no continuance. On 14th June Marwitz captured Mosciska, and the whole Russian centre began to retire on the famous Grodek positions. Evert was now back from Opatov and Ostrovietz, and approaching the left bank of the Vistula, the right centre was on the San and the Tanev, the centre among the Grodek ponds, and Brussilov and Lechitski along the Dniester as far as the frontier.

The Grodek position was a line of shallow, swampy lakes, in all some fifteen miles long. Few roads crossed the tangle, and the place was impregnable to most armies. It was the district where the Russian commanders anticipated that Auffenberg would make a stand after the capture of Lemberg in September. But such a position, if it cannot be forced, can be turned, and Ivanov was unable to hold it now for the same reason as Auffenberg in the autumn. Then Russki had turned it on the north, and now Mackensen followed the same strategy. Lemberg was doomed as soon as the phalanx forced the Sieniawa–Jaroslav line, and swung its right towards Mosciska. Moving along the Jaroslav–Rava Russka railway, it was certain, unless checked, to outflank the Lemberg defence on the north. Boroevitch advanced against Grodek, Linsingen and Pflanzer-Baltin battled for the Dniester crossings, but the operative part of the movement was that of the great phalanx, advancing steadily north-east across the Lubaczowka, in a country where there could be no real defence short of the valley of the Bug.

By the 16th the army of the Archduke Joseph had compelled a Russian retreat from the east bank of the lower San, and was already, in part, inside the borders of Russian Poland, with its right nearing Tarnogrod. Mackensen was moving on a broad front towards Rava Russka, while Boroevitch advanced directly upon the Grodek position. The evacuation of Lemberg had begun, and thousands of passports were issued for Russia. On the 17th Mackensen's right was in the town of Javorov. On the 19th his advance guard was very near Rava Russka, the scene of the Russian victory in September, and Linsingen had forced the crossing of the Dniester at Nizniov. On Sunday, the 20th, there was a fierce battle for Rava Russka, and by the evening the Russians had been driven north of the road and railway which connected the town with Lemberg by way of Zolkiev. Late that evening Rava Russka and Zolkiev were in Mackensen's hands.

The key of Lemberg had been won, and the Grodek position was turned. That night the Russians fell back in good order from the Grodek lakes, and at the same time Brussilov evacuated the ground he had held south of the Dniester between the marshes and the mouth of the Stryj. The upper Dniester position was obviously untenable, and Halicz was now the western limit of the Russian stand on that river. The centre fell back east of Lemberg to a line between the upper waters of the Bug and the Gnila Lipa, the very position which Dmitrieff had stormed before the capture of the city in September. The way to Lemberg was open, and on the afternoon of Tuesday, 22nd June, the IV. Army of Boehm-Ermolli entered without opposition. It was a proud moment for the Austrian general, to whom Germany gave the privilege of first entry. After nine months the capital of Galicia was once more in Austrian hands. Lemberg was worth a score of Przemysls both in sentimental and practical value. It controlled a network of lines, and was the last post of a civilized railway system before the Russian frontier was reached with its two barren routes of communication. The Power which held Lemberg held a strong fortress against any invasion from the east, for it had six lines whereby to bring up supports to one at the disposal of the invader. With the fall of Lemberg the reconquest of Galicia was complete.

If we take the 21st day of June as a viewpoint, we find Ivanov's forces in the following position. Evert was back near the west bank of the middle Vistula, running from west of Radom to the junction of the Vistula and the San. The Russian line ran along the east bank of the San and the north bank of the Tanev, and thence south of Zamosc to the valley of the Bug. It left the Bug at Kamionka, and continued due south by Przemyslany and down the Gnila Lipa to Halicz, on the Dniester, whence it followed that river to the Russian frontier. In the seven weeks of fighting it had suffered heavy losses. Dmitrieff's original army of the Donajetz had been much shattered, as had also been Brussilov's wing; but before the San was reached both forces had been renewed by some of the picked corps from Alexeiev's northern command. We may, therefore, regard the armies which lay in position on 21st June as weary, depleted, but still unbroken forces. Ever since the San the retreat had been premeditated.

With the fall of Lemberg the second great stage begins of the Austro-German offensive. The thrust had succeeded brilliantly up to a point, but Mackensen's problem was not the clearing of territory, but a culminating blow at the heart of the Russian position. Let us be clear as to what this signified. We have seen already the nature of the Polish salient, the wedge of Russian territory thrust out between Galicia and East Prussia. But there was an inner salient, which was the vital one. Warsaw was at its apex, and the northern side was the railway running by Bialystok and Grodno to Petrograd; the southern was the line by Ivangorod, Lublin, Cholm, Kovel, and Rovno to Kiev. If the northern or southern line were cut Warsaw must fall; if both were pierced, then the whole Russian force must fall back behind the Polish Triangle, and not improbably behind the marshes of Pripet. The capture of Lemberg was only an incident in Mackensen's sudden swing to the north-east; his main object was an attack upon the Warsaw–Kiev line. Accordingly, Ivanov in his retreat saw to it that the railway was covered. He was still not closer to it at any point than fifty miles, and it provided him with what Mackensen now lacked, a good line of lateral communication.

Meanwhile there had been activity at other parts of the Eastern front. In the middle of May the Germans were in strength on the Dubissa, twenty miles from Kovno. Libau had fallen to them on 9th May, they had reached the Windawa, and throughout May and early June they made steady progress in the Courland province. They attacked north of Przasnysz towards the Narev line, and on 6th June they made a violent but ineffective gas assault upon the Rawka position. These attacks were part of a persistent pressure along the whole front to prevent Russia reinforcing her harassed southern command. But the time was drawing nigh when the assault on the southern side of the Polish salient was to be balanced by a no less fierce assault on the north. The crisis was not yet, and before the armies of Russia still lay a long season of peril and heart-searching and suffering. In her extremity her behaviour commanded the admiration of the world. She had been equable in success, and she was no less calm and resolute in misfortune. She was like that English worthy of whom Fuller wrote: "Had one seen him returning from a victory, he would by his silence have suspected that he had lost the day; and had he beheld him in retreat, he would have collected him a conqueror by the cheerfulness of his spirit."

CHAPTER XXX.

THE BEGINNING OF ITALY'S CAMPAIGN.
April 26–August 21, 1915.

Sonnino's Diplomacy—The Treaty of London—Italy declares War on Austria—Italy's Strategic Position—The First Engagements on the Frontiers—The Beginning of the Isonzo Campaign—Italy declares War on Turkey.

In an earlier chapter we glanced at the political situation in Italy during the first months of war. The country seemed to the foreign observer almost equally divided between the two parties who bore the names of Interventionists and Neutralists. The latter class was composed of the extreme clericals, who distrusted France and Russia on religious grounds, a small aristocratic section who saw in Germany a bulwark against socialism, the extreme socialists who followed a pacificist and anti-national tradition, and a great body of ordinary middle-class people who asked only for a quiet life. Much of the capital employed in the development of North Italy was German; the banking system was largely in German hands; and at first it seemed as if the commercial interests of the country would be strongly ranged on the side of neutrality. To the prudent Italian his land seemed but ill-prepared for war. She was still a young nation, imperfectly integrated: she had neither coal nor iron; for much of her food and shipping she depended on foreign states; she had no great accumulations of capital, and the burden of her taxation even in peace was severe. Against this stood the potent tradition of the Risorgimento, a national antipathy to the Teutonic character, and a popular revulsion against the barbarism and arrogance of Germany's creed.

The situation was complicated by what seemed a parliamentary stalemate. In March 1914 Antonio Salandra had succeeded Giovanni Giolitti as Premier. He was believed to have favoured war from the start; but his Foreign Secretary, the Marquis di San Giuliano, had leanings towards Germany, and this fact was instrumental in maintaining neutrality. In December San Giuliano died, and was succeeded in office by Baron Sidney Sonnino, in whose ancestry there were Jewish and British elements. Sonnino had been twice Premier, and had done much by his upright and straightforward methods to purify public life and to restore the economic prosperity of his country. In accomplishments and character he was one of the most remarkable figures in the public life of Europe. Renowned as a scholar, a philosopher, and a financier, he despised the common arts of the politician, and his cold exterior and stiffness of manner, the result of his detestation of popularity-hunting, caused him to be easily outstripped by his rivals in the ordinary parliamentary game. His was the type of mind and temperament which is realized and fully valued only at a time of national crisis. On the other side stood Giolitti, four times Premier, and the most powerful political influence in Italy. Of the 508 members of the Chamber of Deputies three-fifths were believed to be his followers. Though he supported Salandra, it looked as if he held the Ministry in the hollow of his hand. Enthusiasm was foreign to his nature; he was an opportunist, and not without reason, like the majority of his countrymen. He desired certain gains for his nation, but preferred bargaining to war.

Sonnino's appearance at the Foreign Office meant the beginning of a long and intricate diplomatic duel, in which the Italian Minister conducted his case with remarkable skill and discretion. Early in December he took his stand upon the terms of the Triple Alliance, especially Article VII.* That clause, he reminded Count Berchtold, the Austro-Hungarian Foreign Minister, bound Austria not to occupy any Balkan territory without a previous agreement with Italy, and without adequately compensating her. Italy had the deepest interest in preserving the integrity and inde-

* " Austria-Hungary and Italy, who have solely in view the maintenance, as far as possible, of the territorial *status quo* in the East, engage themselves to use their influence to prevent all territorial changes which might be disadvantageous to the one or the other of the Powers signatory of the present Treaty. To this end they will give reciprocally all information calculated to enlighten each other concerning their own intentions and those of other Powers Should, however, the case arise that, in the course of events, the maintenance of the *status quo* in the territory of the Balkans or of the Ottoman coasts and islands in the Adriatic or the Ægean Seas becomes impossible, and that, either in consequence of the action of a third Power or for any other reason, Austria-Hungary or Italy should be obliged to change the *status quo* for their part by a temporary or permanent occupation, such occupation would only take place after previous agreement between the two Powers, which would have to be based upon the principle of a reciprocal compensation for all territorial or other advantages that either of them might acquire over and above the existing *status quo*, and would have to satisfy the interests and rightful claims of both parties."

pendence of Serbia : Austria had invaded Serbia, and so disturbed the whole political gravity of the Balkans ; compensation was due to Italy, and he invited Austria to discuss its terms. Count Berchtold replied that Italy could have no grievance, because the Austrian occupation of Serbian territory was "neither temporary nor permanent, but momentary." Upon this Sonnino reminded him that in April 1912 Austria had protested against the Italian bombardment of the Dardanelles, and had prohibited even the use of searchlights against the Turkish coast. She had declared that such acts were an infringement of Article VII., and threatened that " if the Italian Government desired to regain its liberty of action the Austro-Hungarian Government would do the same."

The diplomatic honours at this point lay with Sonnino. Prince Bulow, the German ex-Chancellor, was hurried to Rome, and a complex game of intrigue began. The aim of the Austrian diplomatists was to play for time, but Sonnino pinned them to the question—" What compensations are you prepared to offer for a breach of the Triple Alliance which you are obliged to admit ? " Austria was willing enough to offer these from other people's territory, but this Italy declined to consider. Germany now took a hand. Her offers of Corsica, Savoy, Tunis, Malta were smilingly put aside. Prince Wedel, who was at Vienna, then pressed Austria to surrender the Trentino, and Bülow at Rome urged Sonnino not to ask for Trieste. Meanwhile Italy was putting her army on a war basis, and throughout the winter bought large quantities of military stores. In February 1915 the Chamber met, and the dullness of the sittings led to a general opinion that Bülow had succeeded. In March rumours of intervention revived with the activity of the Allied fleets in the Dardanelles. Italians in America began to close their German accounts, and many Germans in Italy made preparations for departure.

On 9th March Baron Burian, who had succeeded Count Berchtold, under pressure from Germany accepted the principle that compensation must be made from Austrian territory. Sonnino replied that the negotiations must take place at once, and must be between Italy and Austria, without any German intervention. Bülow tried threats, and drew tragic pictures of the consequences to Italy of a war with the Teutonic League ; but on 20th March he informed Sonnino that he had been authorized to guarantee in the name of Germany the execution of any agreement that might be concluded between Vienna and Rome. This touched the heart of the matter. Italy had insisted that the transference of any territories agreed upon must be made at once.* Austria demurred, and Germany offered to back her bills. But Sonnino very naturally asked what good the guarantee would be if the Teutonic League were defeated. He might have added that, after recent experience of Germany's public honour, it would be no more than a scrap of paper in the event of her victory.

April was devoted by Austria and Germany to manœuvring for position. The Chamber had been adjourned till 12th May, and Germany tried to intimidate Italy by spreading rumours of an impending separate peace between herself and Russia. Sonnino replied by setting forth his demands in the shape of a draft treaty, under which the Trentino and several Dalmatian islands would have become Italy's, and the Istrian coast and Trieste would have been occupied by her, pending their constitution after the war as an autonomous state. These proposals were declined by Vienna on 16th April. On 26th April the secret Treaty of London was signed by Italy, France, Russia, and Britain.† By this pact the Allies undertook to pay Italy a far higher price than anything which the Teutonic League could offer. The urgency of their need is shown by this extraordinary document, which not only divided the bear's skin before the bear was killed, but jettisoned many of the traditional

---

* The concessions which Austria was willing to make were, according to the German Imperial Chancellor, as follows :—

1. The part of Tyrol inhabited by Italians to be ceded to Italy.
2. Likewise the western bank of the Isonzo in so far as the population is purely Italian, and the town of Gradisca.
3. Trieste to be made an Imperial free city, receiving an administration ensuring an Italian character to the city, and to have an Italian university.
4. The recognition of Italian sovereignty over Avlona and the sphere of interests belonging thereto.
5. Austria-Hungary declares her political disinterestedness regarding Albania.
6. The national interests of Italian nationals in Austria-Hungary to be particularly respected.
7. Austria-Hungary grants an amnesty for political or military criminals who are natives of the ceded territories.
8. The further wishes of Italy regarding general questions to be assured of every consideration.
9. Austria-Hungary, after the conclusion of the agreement, to give a solemn declaration concerning the concessions.
10. Mixed committees for the regulation of details of the concessions to be appointed.
11. After the conclusion of the agreement, Austro-Hungarian soldiers, natives of the occupied territories, shall not further participate in the war.

It should be noted that these concessions differed materially from and were substantially larger than those offered by Vienna (see Italian Green Book, 1915). The conduct of the negotiations was in Germany's hands, and the above represented the extreme terms which she was confident that she could coerce Austria into granting.

† The treaty would have been signed earlier but for the opposition of Russia. See Kitchener's telegram to the Grand Duke Nicholas, *Life*, III., p. 349 n.

prejudices of the signatories and not a few of the sound principles of European policy. In return for Italy's assistance she was promised the Trentino, southern Tyrol up to the Brenner, Trieste, Istria up to the Quarnero, the province of Dalmatia and most of the Adriatic islands, and the Gulf of Valona; in the Ægean the Dodecanese; in the event of a partition of Turkey a share equal to that of each of the other Allies in the Mediterranean basin; a share in any war indemnity corresponding to the magnitude of her efforts and sacrifices; compensation in Africa for any enlargement of the colonial possessions of France and Britain at the expense of Germany; and an immediate loan of fifty million sterling to be floated in London. Italy was to break with the Teutonic League within one month after the signature of the pact. On 3rd May Sonnino denounced the Triple Alliance, and it was decreed that no member of the Government must for the present leave Rome.

Then came a political crisis. An important section of Giolitti's followers began an agitation for accepting the Austro-German terms, and the attitude of their leader was doubtful. It was possible that he might turn out the Government and become Premier with an anti-war policy. On 13th May Salandra placed his resignation in the King's hands, on the ground that his Ministry did not possess "that unanimous assent of the constitutional parties regarding its international policy which the gravity of the situation demands." He was already beaten in the Chamber, for Giolitti had more than 300 deputies behind him. But the Chamber did not represent the nation; or rather it represented the nation on the cautious, cynical, and material side, which is only one phase of the Italian temper. Suddenly the discussion was transferred from Parliament to the people, and the essential idealism of Italy blazed forth and consumed the prudential webs. The intellect of the land, as represented by Croce and D'Annunzio, Fogazzaro, Ferrero and Marconi, had already ranged itself on the Allied side. The sinking of the *Lusitania* had aroused the wrath of a race which has no love for deliberate cruelty. Above all, the ordinary man felt that to bargain with Austria was to put his land in perpetual tutelage to an ancestral enemy. He realized that Italy's nationality was not yet complete, and that if she sacrificed thus her political independence the consummation of the work of Cavour, Garibaldi, and Mazzini would be for ever impossible. The citizens of every Italian town went down soberly into their market-places crying death to Giolitti. D'Annunzio, whom the world had known as a hot-house poet, became suddenly a second Rienzi. His marvellous speeches, as perfect in form as any oration of Cicero, summoned his countrymen to a conception of Italy's future far other than that expounded by the worldly-wise. "No, we are not, and we will not be a museum, an inn, a village summer resort, a sky painted with Prussian-blue for international honeymoon couples, a delightful market for buying and selling, fraud and barter." Before the popular whirlwind of those "days of May" the Neutralists cowered and broke. Salandra's resignation was refused by the King, and he returned to office; Bülow hastened beyond the Alps, and Giolitti retired to his estate in Piedmont.

On 20th May the Chamber, by 407 votes to 74, passed a bill conferring full powers on the Government in the event of war. On the 22nd a general mobilization was ordered. On the 23rd Italy declared war upon Austria.* Baron von Macchio in Rome was handed his passports, and the Duke of Avarna was recalled from Vienna. That day the first shots were fired by the frontier guards in the north.

The Italian Foreign Minister's brilliant handling of the negotiations had put Italy technically in the right. She went to war on grounds fully justified by the public law of Europe. But the discussions were in reality academic, for the dominating reasons lay elsewhere. Where would Italy have been had Germany triumphed? Supposing she had got the territory she had asked for, how long would she have kept it in face of a victorious Germany, which would regard these concessions as having been forced from her under duress? And if she had relied on Germany's bond, she had some reason to doubt the strength of a pledge given by a Power whose declared international ethics were anarchy. These were considerations which were of supreme importance even to those who took the most mercantile view of national interests. In all Sonnino's dialectical finesse there was a certain unreality, for he aimed at making not a bargain but a breach. He exacted, it is true, a high price for his final decision, but in the case of a poor and ill-equipped country it may well be argued that it was the duty of a statesman thus to safeguard her interests. Italy's allegiance was of immense market value. Had she joined her colleagues of the Triplice in August 1914 there would have been no Battle of the Marne, for, as Bismarck once said, an Italian bugler posted on the French frontier would immobilize four of France's army corps.

* The following day was popularly regarded as the opening of the war—that *Ventiquattro Maggio* which will remain a marked day in Italian annals.

When she joined the Allies in May she menaced the flank of Austria-Hungary. And let it be remembered that the making of war was in the last resort the work of the plain citizen, who had never heard of the Treaty of London.

She had amply vindicated herself in the eyes of the world. So far from coming to the succour of the victor, she had joined the Allies when their prospects were darkening. As she marched to the Isonzo, Mackensen was driving the Russians to the San ; and at Ypres, in the West, the British had suffered grievously. The Dardanelles expedition had not succeeded, and to the eyes of most men its prospects were cloudy. We cannot judge the temper of a nation by its formal diplomacy or by its parliamentary debates, and in Italy as war opened there flamed up a popular enthusiasm which had very little care for material rewards. The Irredentist tradition was less one of territorial enlargement than of racial liberation. The nation desired to wipe out the memories of Custozza and Lissa and of the darker days before, but they also fought in the cause of European liberty. It was such a crusade as Mazzini would have sanctioned, that wise idealist who wrote: " War is a fact, and will be a fact for some time to come, and, though dreadful in itself, is very often the only way of helping Right against brutal Force." In the spirit of Garibaldi and his Thousand, Italy entered upon her latest war of liberation, as in the ancient days when the streets of her cities heard the war-cry: "*Popolo: Popolo · muoiano i tiranni.*"

A parallel might be drawn between the antecedents of the Italian kingdom and those of the modern German Empire. Both in their present form were less than half a century old. Both had been built up round the nucleus of a long-descended monarchy, and the House of Savoy had curious points of kinship with the House of Hohenzollern. Its rulers ascended from being Counts of Savoy to being Kings of Sardinia and then Kings of Italy, as the Hohenzollerns were first Electors of Brandenburg, then Kings of Prussia, and then German Emperors. William II. of Germany and Victor Emmanuel III. of Italy were each the third of their line to hold their high positions. But the military strength of the two states had not developed on the same lines. Italy's problem since 1870 had been one of peculiar difficulty. Her creation as a kingdom had left her with an unsatisfactory northern frontier. The additions of Lombardy and Venetia to the dominions of Savoy had been acquired less by overmastering victories in the field than by the diplomatic difficulties in which Austria at the moment found herself. The French victories in 1859 were discounted by the Emperor Napoleon's divided aims, and Venetia was ceded because of the Prussian victory at Sadowa, though Austria had been successful in her Italian campaign. In this acquisition, therefore, Italy exhausted her purchase; the situation was too delicate to insist upon that rectification of boundaries which would have made them secure. All the Alpine passes and all the crossings of the Isonzo were left in Austrian hands. Accordingly she could not be otherwise than anxious about the north. Again, her population was from the military point of view curiously heterogeneous. Districts differed in their military value as widely as Sparta differed from Corinth. These circumstances—the overwhelming strategic importance of the north and the mixed character of the recruits—made it impossible to follow the German plan of an army on a territorial basis. A regiment was recruited from all parts of the country, but on mobilization reservists joined that regiment which happened to be quartered in their district. In time of war, therefore, about half of those serving had no previous connection with the units in which they served.

Service was universal and compulsory, and the liability began at the age of twenty, and lasted for nineteen years. Recruits were divided into three classes. The first formed the first line; the second were also regulars, but with unlimited leave; while the third passed into the Territorial militia. The second class—corresponding to the German Ersatz Reserve—received a few months' annual training for eight years, and then passed into the Mobile Militia and the Territorial Militia. The third class received only thirty days' annual training. The first class—the first line of the regular army—served for two years with the colours, six in the Reserve, four in the Mobile Militia, and the remaining seven in the Territorial Militia. The unit of organization was the army corps, which consisted normally of two divisions. Each division comprised two brigades of infantry and a regiment—five batteries—of field artillery. A brigade contained two regiments, and a regiment three battalions. The peace establishment showed twelve army corps, half of which had their stations near the northern frontier. A cavalry division consisted of two brigades of two regiments each, and two batteries of horse artillery; there were twenty-nine cavalry regiments on the peace establishment. The light infantry was the Bersaglieri, corresponding to the French Chasseurs and the German Jägers. A regiment of four Bersaglieri battalions—three of infantry and one of cyclists—was part of each army corps. Two other formations must be noted. The six battalions of the Carabinieri were a force of military police, selected from the regular army The Alpini—twenty-six battalions of the first line, organized in eight regiments, with thirty-six batteries of mountain artillery—were special frontier troops for the defence of the northern borders. The line regiments suffered to some extent from the best men being taken for the picked corps of Bersaglieri and Alpini.

The peace strength of the army of Italy in the year before the war was approximately 15,000 officers and 290,000 other ranks. On mobilization a division of Mobile Militia was added to each corps, bringing up its strength to 37,000 men and 134 guns. The war strength was approximately 700,000 in the first line—that is, from the two classes of the regular army—and 320,000 in the Mobile Militia, with a reserve of something over 2,000,000 in the Territorial Militia. Italy's field force might, therefore, be reckoned at something over 1,000,000 trained men. Her field artillery was armed with a 75-mm gun, and she had a large number of batteries of Krupp howitzers, and a siege train of very high calibre.

The Italian Commander-in-Chief was King Victor Emmanuel, a monarch whose gallantry and straightforward simplicity had won him a high degree of popular confidence. The Chief of the General Staff and the Generalissimo in the field was General Count Luigi Cadorna, a native of Pallanza, and a man of sixty-five at the outbreak of war. He was the son of that Rafaele Cadorna who, in September 1870, led the Italian army into Papal territory and blew in the Porta Pia. He had served on his father's staff during that expedition, had commanded the 10th Bersaglieri, had been a corps commander at Genoa, and had succeeded General Pollio in 1914 as Chief of the General Staff. He had won fame throughout Europe as a writer on military science, and he had a unique knowledge of the terrain of the coming war. As Hindenburg had studied the East Prussian bogs, so had Cadorna mastered the intricacies of Italy's northern frontier.

A word must be added on the Italian navy, which now took over from France the task of holding Austria in the Adriatic. It contained four Dreadnoughts, and two more were on the verge of completion. These ships were all armed with 12-inch guns. It possessed also ten pre-Dreadnought battleships and a number of older vessels. Its armoured cruisers were none of them faster than 22 knots, but it contained three very fast light cruisers, as well as twenty submarines, a large number of torpedo boats, and forty destroyers. At the lowest computation it showed a considerable superiority over the fleet of Austria-Hungary. The Admiral-in-Chief was the first cousin of the King, the Duke of the Abruzzi—perhaps, after the Grand Duke Nicholas and King Albert of Belgium, the most brilliant member of any reigning house in the world. A man of forty-two, he had won fame as an explorer, a mountaineer, and a scientific geographer. He had shown extraordinary skill in organizing expeditions in the most difficult latitudes from Alaskan and Himalayan snows to the mountain jungles of Ruwenzori, and in the Tripoli War had commanded with distinction a division of the Italian fleet.

The strategic position of Italy was disadvantageous. The strategy of Cadorna was determined perforce by hard geographical facts, and it is necessary to examine the configuration of the Italian-Austrian frontier. Its length of about 480 miles fell naturally into three parts—the re-entrant angle of the Trentino; the great wall of the Dolomites, the Carnic and the Julian Alps; and the space on the east between the main Alpine chain and the Adriatic. The Trentino forms a salient the sides of which are mountain buttresses. It is drained towards the south by the Adige and the Sarca, which flows into Lake Garda. An enemy attempting its conquest must advance principally by the Adige valley, and would presently find himself confronted with the strongly fortified town of Trent, which in the Middle Ages so long defied the attacks of Venice. If Trent were safely passed, he would struggle for long in a wilderness of lateral valleys, and would still have to force the main ridge of the chain at the Brenner. Now, a salient may be a cause of weakness in war, as Russia found in western Poland, for it is open to assault on both flanks. But the containing walls of the Trentino make flank attacks all but impossible. On the western side, high up in the hills, is the Stelvio Pass, leading from the upper Adige to the vale of the Adda. Over this pass in 1797 an Austrian detachment had crossed, but this was the only record of its passage by troops.[*] It is the loftiest carriage pass in the Alps, more than 9,000 feet high, and even if a modern army could win its strait defiles it would find itself in a lateral valley, with many difficulties before it ere it reached Bozen and the main road to the north. Going south, we find the Tonale Pass, south of the Ortler *massif*, which

[*] Dessolles' passage in March 1799 was made by the adjacent Wurmser Joch, 800 feet lower, which leads into Swiss territory.

carries the road from the Noce to the Oglio ; but for a great army that was little better. Close to Lake Garda is the road pass of Cornelle, too narrow in its debouchments for any considerable force. On the eastern side of the salient the conditions were still worse for invasion. The railway from Venice to Innsbruck crosses the Valsugana at Tezze, but the Brenta valley which it traverses gives a difficult road to Trent. Farther north the road-pass from Caprile to Campitello leads into the defiles of the Dwarf King's Rose-garden—a possible passage, for these passes of the western Dolomites are bare and open, but one useless for an invader, since the road bends away to Bozen, and there is no route north to the Pusterthal. The salient of the Trentino was a fine offensive and defensive position for those who held it. It was a hollow headland of mountain jutting into the plains, and it was hard for the plain-dwellers to pierce its rim. The deep hollow of the Lake of Garda was no real opening in the barrier. The breach, so far from weakening the defence, was in reality a source of strength, for it compelled an attack from the Italian plain to be made on divergent lines from different bases, east and west of the lake.

The second part is a shallow arc of sheer rampart—the Dolomite and Carnic ranges. The main pass is that of Ampezzo, where the great highroad known as the Strada d'Allemagna runs from Belluno to Toblach through the heart of the white limestone crags at an altitude of little over 5,000 feet. But between Cortina and Toblach it makes a sharp detour westward to circumvent the mass of Cristallo, and that part is a defile commanded by a hundred danger points. The adjacent passes of Misurina and Monte Croce are no better, and as we go east the Val d'Inferno and the Plocken are little more than bridle paths. The main pass in the chain is that which leads from the valley of the Fella by Pontebba to the upper streams of the Drave. It carries the railway from Venice to Vienna, and its highest point is only 2,615 feet. It was the old highroad of invasion from the north ; but, though the easiest of the great routes, it was still narrow and difficult, a gate which a modern army should with ease be able to close and hold. South-east of it among the buttresses of the Julian Alps there was no pass of any military value.

The third section of the frontier, destined to be the main theatre of the war—the low ground between Cividale and the sea—was not the natural avenue of movement which small-scale maps suggested. It is a narrow front, less than twenty miles wide, and behind it is the line of the river Isonzo, with hills along its eastern bank. The upper part of the stream above Salcano is a ravine; then come six miles of plain in front of Gorizia; then the hills begin again and sweep round to the sea-coast by Monfalcone. The value of such a position for the defence was obvious. A strong field force with a full complement of artillery could make of the Isonzo a front as impregnable as any river line in Europe.

For a modern army the natural strength of a position is not enough; there must be adequate lateral communications In this respect Italy had the advantage, for she had the elaborate railway system of her northern plains behind her, while Austria had only the restricted railways of mountain valleys. The main Italian line ran from Verona by Vicenza and Treviso to Udine. It sent off numerous branches up to the base of the hills—from Verona up the Adige, from Vicenza to Torrebelvicino, from Cittadella to the Valsugana, from Treviso up the Piave to Belluno, from Udine to Pontebba, and from Udine to Cividale. It was backed by a coast railway, and between the two there were many connecting branches. Austria possessed a railway system running round the whole half-moon of frontier, but it had few feeders, for the hill valleys in which it lay made branches difficult. From west to east it ran from the point of the Trentino salient by Trent and Bozen to Franzenfeste, then east along the Pusterthal by Lienz and Spital to Villach. It then bent back from the frontier, ran down the upper Save, rounded the *massif* of Monte Nero, and descended to Gorizia, where it connected by two routes with Trieste. This encircling line was well fed from its main bases, like Innsbruck, Salzburg, Vienna, and Trieste, but it sent off very few branches to the edge of the frontier. One ran from Trent to the Valsugana; after that there was nothing for 150 miles till Tarvis was reached, when the Pontebba line began. Branches went west from Gorizia to Udine, and from Monfalcone to San Giorgio, and these four were the only feeders on the Austrian side of the border. This paucity of branch lines meant that any Austrian offensive must concentrate at certain definite places—Trent, Tarvis, and Gorizia. It meant conversely that an Italian offensive must aim at the same points and at one more. This was Franzenfeste, the junction of the Pusterthal line with that which runs from Innsbruck to Trent. If that point could be taken the communications of the whole of the Trentino salient would be cut. Unfortunately for Italy, this nodal point of Franzenfeste was just the one which it was hardest to reach, for south and east of it stretched the whole complex

R. Inn
Innsbruck
Landeck
Blanke
Nauders
Soiden
Sterzing
Brixen
Klausen
S Leonhard
Franzensfeste
Meran
Lana
Bozen
R. Adige
Fondo
Caldaro
Egna
Cavalese
R. Avisio
Salerno
Mezzolombardo
Cembra
Lavis
Trento
Pergine
Borgo
Pinzolo
Tione
Stenico
Vezzano
Riva
Arco
Mori
Rovereto
Ala
Bormio
Poschiavo
Grosotto
Tirano
Edolo
Breno
Lovere
Pisogne
Salo
Lago di Garda
Caprino
Garda
Bardolino
Brescia
Lonato
Castiglione
Peschiera
VERONA
Villa Franca di Verona
Goito
Mantua
Cremona
Piadena
Ostiglia
Legnago
Montagliana
Cologna
Lonigo
Vicenza
Schio
Thiene
Bassano
Valstagna
Asiago
Montebelluna
Castelfranco
Cittadella
Treviso
Mestre
VENICE
PADUA
Dolo
Mirano
Este
Conselve
Chioggia
R. Adige
Cavarzere
Rovigo
Adria
Lendinara
Barbarano
Piove di Sacco
Pontelongo
Bagnoli
Feltre
Fonzaso
Belluno
Mel
Longarone
Agordo
Moena
Cortina
Cadore
Pieve
Auronzo
Sexten
Toblach
Brunneck
Puster Thal
Welsberg
Innichen
Lienz
Drauburg
R. Drave
Ampezzo
Tolmezzo
Gemona
Maniago
Spilimbergo
S Daniele
Aviano
Vittoria
Sacile
Pordenone
Codroipo
Conegliano
Valdobbiadene
Oderzo
Portogruaro
Dona di Piave
Gulf of Venice
ADRIATIC
Reference
Land over 9 000 feet shown
Scale

system of the Dolomites. The long space without branch lines was as awkward for the one offensive as for the other. What seemed a lengthy and precarious line of communication was in reality defended by an almost insuperable mountain wall.

The military history of that frontier during the past century was an exposition of the difficulties which Italy was now called upon to face. In 1797 Napoleon, having overrun Northern Italy the year before, resolved to force Austria to sue for peace by a threat against Vienna. He marched what we would now call a small army into Carinthia, where the country was open and defenceless. Austria had no adequate force with which to oppose him, and an armistice was concluded when he reached Klagenfurt. It was an easy victory, but the point to note is that he did not dare to cross the eastern frontier till he had pushed forward an army as strong as his own from Verona to Trent to protect his rear and his communications. The campaign of 1866 showed the strength of the Trentino position. In that year the Austrian commander, General Kuhn, left only small detachments to guard the passes, and kept his main force at Trent, which he made the pivot of his defence. He easily defeated the Garibaldian columns which attacked on both sides of the Lake of Garda and by the Tonale Pass. The main Italian advance was made from Padua up the Brenta valley, and this was not seriously opposed till it was near the watershed. There Kuhn was waiting with his reserves; but the action was never fought, since the first shots had scarcely been fired when news came that an armistice had been signed at Vienna. But it was the general verdict at the time that if the forces had been engaged, Kuhn would have held his own From the first he had been greatly outnumbered, but, thanks to his central position, he was always able to secure a local superiority against attacks made from widely divergent points. At that time, it must be remembered, the passes were not fortified, for the reason that Venetia had been Austrian territory for half a century, and the Trentino border was not a state frontier. Trent, too, was then an open town. Now the conditions were more favourable for the defence. An Italian army attacking the Trentino would have to fight its way up narrow valleys, all of which converged upon Trent, the central fortress. The defence would, therefore, be able to mass its reserves for a counter-attack against one line of advance after another, and need not strike till the invaders had already suffered heavily in breaking down the advanced fortifications of the passes.

The problem before Cadorna was, therefore, by no means

simple. Austria had her hands full in the Carpathians, and it was unlikely that she would be able to take that swift offensive for which her frontier had been designed. It was a sovereign chance for an Italian forward movement, and the direction of that movement was not in doubt. It must be mainly towards Trieste, the Istrian peninsula, and the wooded hills of Styria which sweep to Vienna. There Austria was most vulnerable, and there lay a terrain where modern armies could manœuvre. But the configuration of the frontier made it impossible for a commander to direct all his forces upon one section. The whole northern border must be watched and held, else Austria from the Trentino salient might cut his communications and take him in the rear. Accordingly he resolved to attack at all the salient points—towards Trent, across the Dolomite passes against the Pusterthal railway, at the Pontebba Pass, across the Julian buttresses in order to threaten the Tarvis-Gorizia line. Such a series of movements would keep the enemy busy and prevent any flanking strategy. And meantime with his chief army he would strike at the Isonzo and the road to Trieste.

Undoubtedly there was a chance of a swift and crushing attack, but to succeed such an attack must be made at once and be of the nature of a surprise, before Austria could use the natural strength of her frontier against it. But Italy suffered from two grave drawbacks. Her army was not yet ready for war, and her mobilization was slow; and the dangers of the great northern salient compelled her to dissipate her efforts over too large a front. At first her hopes ran high. She remembered what Napoleon had done with 60,000 men; with 600,000 might she not speedily repeat the triumph of Leoben?* But a rapid and decisive advance was difficult, since any attack towards the Isonzo had its flank turned by the configuration of the frontier, and it seemed necessary to have strong forces along the whole line from the Trentino to the Julian Alps. Cadorna assembled on the Isonzo his Third Army (six divisions of infantry and three of cavalry), and the Second Army (eight divisions). North of this he had the Carnic detachment of twenty-nine battalions, and in the Dolomites his Fourth Army of six divisions. In the Trentino salient was the First Army of five divisions, and he had ten divisions of infantry and one of cavalry in reserve. His plan was an

* See Capello's *Note di Guerra*, Vol. I. (1920). Austria's first intention was to inveigle the Italians into the eastern hills and concentrate her forces in the valleys of Villach-Klagenfurt and Laibach. This plan was vetoed by Germany as too dangerous, and she defended the frontier crests. Falkenhayn's *General Headquarters*, pp. 91–92.

offensive on the Isonzo and a defensive on all other fronts, but the defensive must be in itself an attack, since positions for a secure defence had first to be won. It would have been wiser had he either taken greater risks and gambled more boldly in the Isonzo section, or been content to move at first slowly on all fronts and wait till a sustained effort was possible. As it was the chance of surprise was lost, and Austria was able to maintain her defence without seriously weakening her armies in Galicia and Poland.

War began on 24th May, and the first serious blow was struck by the enemy. This was a well-organized raid on the Adriatic coast, the object of which was to delay the Italian concentration by damaging vital points on the coast railway from Brindisi to the north. The attack began a little after four on the morning of Monday, 24th May, and was carried out by a squadron from Pola made up of two battleships, four cruisers, and some eighteen destroyers, strongly supported by aircraft. The line, which ran along the Adriatic shore, was at many points much exposed to attack from the water. Ancona station, for example, was on the high ground outside the town, and most of the river bridges were within sight of the sea. The assault extended from Brindisi to Venice, and at the latter place airmen threw bombs into the Arsenal and attacked the oil-tanks and the balloon sheds on the Lida. In the Western press the movement was interpreted only as a barbarous attempt to send St. Mark's the way of Rheims and Louvain; but it was in reality a serious military operation. In the north the cruiser *Novara*, with a flotilla of destroyers, attacked Porto Corsini, north of Ravenna, in the hope of wrecking the Italian torpedo-boat base. The destroyers were driven off, and one was seriously damaged. Farther south the cruiser *St. George* bombarded the railway station and bridges at Rimini. In the centre the battleship *Zrinyi* attacked Sinigaglia, and claimed to have wrecked the railway station and railway bridge and part of the railway line, while south of Ancona the battleship *Radetzky* wrecked the bridge over the Potenza River. In the south the cruisers *Helgoland* and *Admiral Spaun*, assisted by destroyers, attacked in the neighbourhood of Manfredonia and Viesti. They shelled a railway bridge, a railway station, and several signal stations, and did some damage to the coast towns. It was all over before 6 a.m., and the squadron sailed back to Pola in safety. The Italian fleet seems to have been taken by surprise, and the marauders were unmolested. It was a well-conceived and well-executed enterprise, and achieved much of its purpose.

On the same day, 24th May, the Austrians blew up two bridges in the Adige valley, thereby revealing their plan of campaign. They were resolved to stand on the defensive at the outset in the strong positions which fortune had given them. They would hold the crests of the passes along the frontier of the Trentino and the line of the Carnic Alps. On the Isonzo front they would abandon all the country west of the river line, and make their stand on a fortified line well to the east, which only touched the Isonzo at Gorizia, where they held a bridgehead on the western bank. Their best troops were busy in Galicia, and they had only Landsturm and a few reserve divisions wherewith to meet the army of Italy. Their aim was to risk nothing till Mackensen had finished his Galician enterprise and first-line troops could be spared for this frontier.

The slowness of the Italian mobilization meant that till the close of May the actions were only affairs of covering troops, and little ground was won except that which the Austrians voluntarily yielded. On the evening of the 24th the eastern force was well inside Austrian territory, its left pushed forward to Caporetto on the Isonzo just under Monte Nero, its centre looking down on Gorizia from the high ground between the Idria and the Isonzo, and its right between Cormons and Terzo. On the extreme right, among the islands of the coast, the Italian destroyers were busy. In the following week and onward till the end of the month the record was one of slow and cautious advance. It was a wet season, and the Isonzo, fed from the hills, floods easily, thereby making operations difficult when the enemy had destroyed the bridges. The Italian left about Caporetto was reinforced, preparatory to an attack on the height of Monte Nero. Italian aviators persistently bombarded Monfalcone and the railway between Gorizia and Trieste, in order to cut off supplies and reinforcements for the troops on the river line, while destroyers shelled the Monfalcone shipyards, and the coast town of Grado was taken. By the end of May the Isonzo had been reached, but had not been crossed, by the Italian army. In the central section of the frontier there was much scattered fighting, and the Italians succeeded in occupying several of the passes. On the 24th the Val d'Inferno pass at the head of the Degano valley was carried by a bayonet attack. More important was the capture, on the 30th, of Cortina, on the great Strada d'Allemagna. The place was not more than fifteen miles as the crow flies from the Franzenfeste-Villach railway, but in these fifteen miles were included the highest peaks of the Dolomites, and the road—one of the finest in Europe—ran through a cañon which gave every advantage to the defence. The Trentino fighting began also on the 24th. Detachments on that day pushed forward to the frontier on both sides of the Lake of Garda ; up the Chiese valley to Caffaro, which is just on the border under the guns of the Italian fort of Rocca d'Anfo ; and up the Oglio valley to the Tonale Pass. Troops moved along the Italian ridge of Monte Baldo, east of Lake Garda, towards the Austrian summit of Monte Altissimo. On the east side of the salient in the Brenta valley an advance began, and on the 27th it had reached a point five miles from Borgo. On the same day the frontier town of Ala, on the Adige, was captured, and by the end of the month the Italians held the high ground on the south which commanded the forts of Rovereto. So far the successes, though small, had been continuous. Trent was girdled by a number of lesser fortresses commanding the converging routes. Such was Rovereto on the Adige ; such were Lardaro on an upper feeder of the Chiese, Levico on the Brenta, and the important fort of Riva at the head of Lake Garda. The closing in upon these outworks by the Italian armies meant that daily the offensive power of the enemy in the salient was declining. He no longer held the rim of the cup from which he could descend at will upon the plains.

Meanwhile the Third and Second Armies were battling in the difficult country which looked towards Trieste. The Isonzo cuts its way southwards through the butt of the Julian Alps in a deep gorge which ends sharply north of the town of Gorizia. Gorizia lies in a pocket of the hills, with the uplands protecting it in a semi-circle on the north. West of the Isonzo, dominating the bridge-head and the road and railway to Gradisca and Udine, is the spur of Podgora, which also commands Gorizia itself. South of the town stretch some four miles of level plain, till on the east bank of the river rises the extraordinary plateau which Italians call the Carso and Austrians the Karst, and which rolls east and west behind Trieste, and south almost to the sea. The Carso is a low, wind-swept tableland, strewn with limestone boulders, seamed with deep fissures, and covered with rough scrub and great masses of scree. North of Gorizia the Julian Alps rise towards the stony uplands of the Krn or Monte Nero. A tributary, the Baca, enters the Isonzo on the eastern bank a little south of the town of Tolmino, and up its difficult valley and through the great Wochein tunnel runs the railway to Villach and Vienna. The difficulties of such a country for the offensive are too obvious to need explanation. The only passage through the uplands was the strip of land beside the sea, far too narrow for an army to travel. The flat land south of Gorizia was not really a gap, for the hills closed in a mile or two east of the town. The ridges of Monte Nero, the gorge of the upper Isonzo, and the plateau of the Carso offered secure positions for any defence.

Since the main object of Cadorna was Trieste, it was desirable to cut, if possible, the communications of that city with its bases of supply. The navy of Italy could ensure that nothing entered it by sea. Trieste was served by two chief lines—one running by Gorizia and the Wochein tunnel to Villach, the other by St. Peter's to Laibach. The first had two branches which united at Gorizia —one by the coast and Monfalcone, the other running direct across the Carso plateau. The second received a branch from Pola, and at St. Peter's the main line from Fiume. To isolate Gorizia it was not enough to cut the Villach line north of it, or the Monfalcone line south of it. The Carso line in the east must also be cut, and that involved a considerable advance across the plateau. To isolate Trieste was still more difficult. The cutting of the Gorizia line would deprive it of its best and shortest connection with Vienna; but there would still remain the Laibach line, which would only be effectively cut if the junction at St Peter's were captured What looked like open country to a casual student of the map was therefore in its character an intricate and difficult natural fortress. The Carso, in particular, was a position which might be compared with the Labyrinth in Artois, save that it owed its chief strength to nature rather than to man. A swift advance was out of the question. So soon as the first chance of surprise had been lost, Cadorna's task must be to reduce the position by the capture of its chief details.

Gorizia was the key of the Austrian front. So long as it was held it blocked any real advance across the Carso, since it threatened an attack on the flank, and, till the Carso railway was cut, could be munitioned direct from Trieste. The Austrians held not only the town but the bridgehead on the west bank of the Isonzo, and the spur of Podgora which commanded that bridgehead. The Italian armies advanced against this front in three sections. One, consisting largely of Alpine troops, moved against Tolmino and the heights of Monte Nero Its immediate task was to cut the Vienna line north of Gorizia, and to protect the left of the main advance against reinforcements coming from the direction of Villach. The centre moved directly against Gorizia itself, and especially against the Austrian position on the Podgora spur. The right wing advanced on Monfalcone, to cut the coast railway and begin the assault on the Carso plateau All three movements were fortunate in their communications. The Italian left had the railway to Cividale, and the roads beyond over the Starasella Pass and the other saddles of the Julian range. The centre had the Udine-Gorizia railway. The right wing had the San Giorgio-Monfalcone line.

By 1st June the Italians had occupied the greater part of the west bank of the Isonzo with little opposition. The Austrians had chosen their line, and were not concerned to defend the indefensible. The weather in early June was heavy rain, and those who know the quick flooding of the torrents which descend from the Julian Alps can realize how slow must be an advance under such conditions. The Italian mobilization was not yet complete, and the fighting fell chiefly to the screen of troops on the flanks. The left wing was beyond the Isonzo, and fighting its way among the shale and boulders of Monte Nero, where the Austrian artillery had strong positions. The navy and the air service were active, and Monfalcone was under constant bombardment.

On the 7th an advance in force began all along the front. The left wing continued its struggle for the Monte Nero slopes. Bridgeheads were established along the middle Isonzo south of Gorizia, and large bodies of cavalry crossed at various points, and began the work of entrenching on the eastern bank. On 9th June Monfalcone fell without trouble It was scarcely defended, for it lay outside the zone which the Austrians had marked for their defence. This meant that one of the loops of the Gorizia-Trieste railway was cut, but the Carso branch still remained. Next day the centre made a great effort east of Gradisca and Sagrado, but the river line proved far stronger than had been believed. So did Tolmino, which was now under the fire of Italian guns. The only success was won that night at Plava, north of Gorizia, where a surprise attack carried the place, and so menaced the railway from Gorizia to Vienna. The floods were the main obstacles on the lower course of the river, and the Austrians added to these by breaking the banks of the Monfalcone canal. Had it been possible during these days to push forward in full strength, Trieste would have fallen, for the Austrian armies were still slender. But the weather and the incompleteness of the Italian mobilization made the advance partial and ineffective.

Austrian troops were beginning to arrive from the Galician

front. Some portion of the Tyrolese Corps was brought to the lines in the mountains. Regiments of Southern Slavs, who had no love for Italy, were sent to the Isonzo, and so spared the difficult task of fighting against their Russian kinsmen. Lastly, there came at least one division of Hungarians, who, apart from the Tyrolese, represented the finest fighting material in the Austrian ranks. The chance of an easy victory was slipping from Italy's hands. Cadorna was discovering the strength of the Austrian artillery, which seems to have been admirably placed. All along the western fringe of the Carso, and especially on the Podgora spur which commanded Gorizia, were ramifications of trench lines, protected by elaborate entanglements and *fortins*, and with the glacis heavily wired. The Austrian Staff had not forgotten the lesson of Galicia.

On 15th June the first Italian attack was made on the Podgora position. Next day the Alpini on the left wing carried the important position of Monte Nero, climbing the rocks by night, attacking at dawn, and taking many prisoners. But the conquest of these spurs of the mountains did not greatly advance the purpose of the campaign. No guns of great calibre could follow them, and Tolmino, where Dante is rumoured to have written part of his great poem, could, with its fortress artillery, defy the posts on the heights. On the 17th the Villach-Gorizia line near Plava was definitely cut. That fight for Plava was a spirited performance. The village lay in the bottom of the ravine beside the swift river, with precipitous wooded hills on either side. The bridge had been destroyed ; but the Italians with a great effort constructed pontoons during the night, and at dawn on the 17th began their attack. The defence had 12-inch guns, and entrenchments surrounded by deep networks of wire. By the evening the Italians had carried the first line with the bayonet, and stood firm all night against counter-attacks Next day they routed the enemy, taking many prisoners, and occupied the heights on the eastern bank of the stream.

In the following week there were repeated counter-attacks at Plava and on Monte Nero, where the Italian Alpini were engaged with their fellow-mountaineers of Tyrol. By the 25th some ground north of Plava was won, and, what was more important, a beginning was made with the advance on the Carso, the edge of the plateau being gained between Sagrado and Monfalcone ; while from Cormons the Podgora position and the Gorizia bridgehead were bombarded. The month of June closed in storms, with thick fog in the mountains, which interfered with artillery work, and deluges of rain in the flats. By this time the inundations of the lower Isonzo were being mastered, for the Italian engineers, working under the enemy's fire, succeeded in damming the opening of the Monfalcone canal. On the 28th the bridgehead of Castelnuovo, on the east bank of the river, was carried by a bayonet attack. This gave Cadorna two important bridgeheads—Plava was the other—inside the Austrian zone of defence. Monfalcone, though on the east bank, was outside the zone, and Caporetto and Gradisca were on the wrong side. On the last day of June there was a great artillery bombardment, but a general infantry attack on the centre failed to achieve any results. The position was now that Cadorna's left wing was strongly posted, but in the nature of things could not do much against Tolmino; his centre was facing the great entrenched camp of Gorizia; while his right was on the edge of the Carso, and had advanced its flank as far as Duino, on the Monfalcone-Trieste railway. The Gorizia line had been cut north and south of the town, and only the Carso line remained to link the fortress with Trieste. The first rush had failed, but preliminary positions had been won from which to initiate a new struggle for the plateau and the Gorizia defences.

That struggle began on 2nd July. It was an attack on a broad front, not less than twenty-five miles, and it was aimed directly at Gorizia. The left was to occupy the heights east of Plava and then swing round through the Ternovanerwald against the defences of Gorizia in the north, and east round the village of San Gabriele and San Daniele. The centre was directed against the Podgora spur and the Gorizia bridgehead, while the right, which had already won the western and south-western edges of the Carso, was to move against the northern part of that plateau which takes its name from the village of Doberdo. The chief operative movement was that of the right wing, for, if the Doberdo upland were carried, the Trieste railway would be cut and Gorizia must fall. The forces on Monte Nero might be regarded as an outlying defence of the left flank of the advance.

The long and confused fighting which began on 2nd July, and which ebbed away into an artillery duel about the middle of August, is properly to be considered as one action, which may be called the First Battle of the Isonzo. The details may be briefly summarized. On 3rd July the centre attacked fiercely the Podgora position, and next day, after a lengthy bombardment, the right pushed some way into the Carso. On the 5th the centre and right—four corps strong—were again in action, and slowly advanced their lines. The Italians—now less than twenty miles from Trieste—had brought some of their heavy guns up to the edge of the plateau, and for a few days there was a continuous bombardment and counter-bombardment. On Monday, the 19th, the right made a successful attack, carrying several lines of trenches. Next day the centre, after a desperate fight, carried a considerable section of the Podgora spur, though the Austrians still held the eastern end overlooking Gorizia. Meanwhile the left had been heavily engaged in the Plava neighbourhood. Four brigades were hurled against the wooded heights east of the river, and for two days fought their way from ledge to ledge. The Hungarians who opposed them, being plainsmen unaccustomed to mountain warfare, yielded at first before the attack of the Alpini, but fought resolutely on the upper heights. The Italian batteries from the other side of the river plastered the hillside with shell, till the mountain flared to heaven like a volcano. A Dalmatian regiment was brought up from the Austrian reserves, and, concealed in rifts and gullies, their fire flung back three times the charge of the Piedmontese. Then came a period of utter weariness, and for twenty-four hours both sides rested. Next day three new Italian brigades were brought up, and King Victor Emmanuel himself was present to encourage his troops. The final assault carried the heights, the last ground being won by a close-quarters struggle with the bayonet. This Plava battle was terribly costly to both sides, and the Italian commander was seriously wounded in the closing stage.

The action was renewed along the whole front on 22nd July. That day the Italian right captured the crest of San Michele, which dominated most of the Doberdo plateau. Before evening a violent cross fire drove them off the actual ridge, but they maintained their position just below it. Cadorna was now engaged with the enemy's second line of defence, and he found it stronger than the first line. To add to his difficulties, further reinforcements arrived in the early days of August, for the fall of Warsaw had enabled the enemy to dispense with some of his troops. By the middle of August the First Battle of the Isonzo had virtually ceased.

The result was less than the valour of Italy deserved. Much ground had been won, but no vital position had been carried. Gorizia was intact, and Trieste was no nearer its fall than in the first weeks of the campaign. The line of the Isonzo had been carried, except the loop west of Gorizia. The western and southern portions of the Carso were in Italian hands, including the important vantage points of Sei Busi, San Martino, and San Michele. The Plava heights had been won, but it was difficult to advance from them; the western part of the Podgora spur was in Italian hands, but not the critical eastern section. Gorizia was invested on three sides, but no one of its vital outworks had been taken. Cadorna was discovering a truth which had been burned in upon the minds of the armies in Western Europe—that a first line may be carried, but that the real difficulties only begin with the second line. Provided the enemy has his communications intact, and has a country behind him well adapted by nature to defence, a withdrawal may only mean the accession of fresh strength. The Austrian Staff deserved credit for the handling of this section of the campaign. They chose their ground with skill, defending only what was defensible, and allowed the enemy to break his teeth against positions which were short of their vital lines. The Italian plan was sound, the Italian fighting was beyond praise for its courage and resolution; but once again was proved the enormous strength of the defence in modern war, provided that its artillery equipment be adequate. The result of the three months' campaign was a check, and since the offensive was with Italy the Austrian command was justified in claiming the honours.

The campaign in the high mountains was primarily a war of defence. Italy must safeguard her flanks and rear before she could push on with confidence beyond the Isonzo, and such offensive purpose as she had was subsidiary to the main effort against Trieste. We have seen that the mountain battle-ground fell into three clearly marked areas—the salient of the Trentino, the passes of the Dolomites, and the passes of the Carnic Alps. Very early in June she had won the crest of the ridge in the two latter theatres, and developed a slow offensive against the Pusterthal railway. In the Trentino the problem of defence was more intricate. It was not enough to win the rim of the salient. She must push her front well inland towards the nodal points of the converging valleys. By August this task had been largely accomplished, and she could look forward with composure to the winter, since she held the keys of the mountain gates.

The details of the Carnic fighting convey little save to experts in its confused topography. Early in June the Italians had crossed the frontier at the railway pass of the Fella, and the Austrian fort of Malborghetto was under their guns. At the same time an attack was made on the right by way of the Predil Pass against Plezzo, and the mule paths over the range on the left were occupied by parties of Alpini. No effective crossing of the range was, however, achieved, and the important railway junction of Tarvis was not in danger. In the western Carnic Alps the main struggle centred round the pass of Monte Croce Carnico. A fortnight after the outbreak of war the Alpini had driven the Austrians from the dominating position to the east of the pass. They then took the Zellenkoffel to the west, and in successive weeks captured the summits of Pal Grande, Freikoffel, and Pal Piccolo. This gave the pass to Italian hands; but the Austrians, supported by their artillery on the northern hills, clung to the farther slopes. The Italians blasted paths and gun positions out of the solid rock, and secured their position; but, beyond repulsing Austrian counter-attacks, they found themselves unable to do much during the summer. As an example of the dash of the Alpini, the capture of the Freikoffel may be cited. The summit was taken by ten volunteers, who climbed the sheer southern wall of the peak in the darkness before the summer dawn.

Farther west, in the Dolomite region, the attack was pressed hard, for the objective was very near. Cortina having been captured on 30th May, the Italians moved westwards towards the Falzarego Pass, which leads to Bozen, and north towards the Pusterthal railway. The former advance may be regarded merely as a flank guard, but the latter was a serious effort conducted with great skill and audacity. From the Ampezzo valley there are two main routes to the railway. One is the Strada d'Allemagna from Cortina under the precipices of Tofana to Schluderbach and Toblach, and another goes by the Sexten valley to Innichen. Between the two lies a third from Misurina by the Val Popena, which joins the first route at Schluderbach. There are other paths for cragsmen, but these are the only roads for guns and transport. By the middle of August the Italians had crossed the watershed, and were only a few miles from the Pusterthal railway. Casual students of the map daily anticipated that that line must be cut. But the difficulties of the Dolomite advance were not to be measured in yards and miles. The debouchment at Toblach was a narrow opening among precipitous crags. All the routes led through defiles, where an advance could only be secured by the capture of the neighbouring heights. This the Alpini brilliantly performed. They scaled the shining white cliffs of Tofana and Cristallo, and brought their mountain guns to vantage points which cleared the passes for some distance before them. The Austrians, with the assistance of their forts, fought delaying actions in the narrows, and their detachments skirmished on the heights. In this stage of the business the Italians had a clear advantage, but the real defence of the Pusterthal had not begun. It is the first rule in mountain warfare that to control a pass you must control its debouchments. In the Pusterthal, with its excellent railway, reserves were waiting to greet the heads of any columns that passed the defiles. With a broad valley and a railway behind it the defence could concentrate where it pleased. The Italians, on the other hand, could not support each other, for each column moved in its own groove, and their only lateral communications were far behind in the easier country of the foothills. The Alpini, who could see from above Schluderbach the rock gate which led to Toblach almost within range of their field guns, were in reality as far from their objective as if a province had intervened. Italy had made good her defence on the northern heights, but the conditions were still ominously against a true offensive.

The Trentino campaign aimed only at the security of the Lombard plains. By the end of May the Italians had the passes, and were moving by three main routes—by the Adige valley against Rovereto, and by the Val Sugana and the Val Giudicaria against Trent. Farther north, on the western side of the salient, they were holding the watershed in the vicinity of the Tonale and Stelvio passes. The movement on Trent and Rovereto was slow and difficult, owing to the necessity of mastering in detail the surrounding heights and to the immense strength of the Austrian fortifications, hewn, as they often were, out of the living rock. The main interest of the summer months was the curious campaign on the western ridges, where fighting became a business of small detachments widely separated by precipitous ravines and snow-clad peaks. Those who have mountaineered in the Adamello and Ortler groups know the strait, steep valleys, with meadows in the bottoms and woods of fir and pine on the lower slopes, and above them the stony heights studded with green alps, and over all the snows and glaciers of the summits. In such country there was room for only small bodies of troops, and the raising of guns to the lofty ridges was a toil which only the hardiest mountain-bred soldiers could accomplish. The Austrians, mountain-bred also, were not an enemy to be despised, and many desperate encounters took place among screes and rock terraces—campaigning only to be paralleled by the exploits of the Gurkhas in the Lhasa expedition. It was a type of mountain warfare far more arduous than the campaign among the low saddles of the Carpathians.

By the middle of August the eagle's feathers of the Alpini were seen on all the vantage grounds from the Stelvio to Lake Garda.

A chain of posts lined the heights, passing through the snows of the Ortler summit and the high mountain huts of the Adamello. In these eyries, often at a height of more than 10,000 feet, entrenchments and entanglements were created, guns were put in position, and the strange spectacle was seen of barbed wire among the crevasses of the glaciers. Mountaineers know the peculiar gifts of the best Italian guides — their inexhaustible resource, their inspired audacity, and their unwearying zest for difficulties. The same qualities were present in the work of Italy's mountain soldiers. Feats of physical endurance, which involved long days of unbelievable toil, were varied by expeditions whose keynote was boyish adventure. One party of Alpini blew up a power-station in a gorge which supplied the forts of Rovereto. Others made night attacks which involved wonderful feats of cragsmanship, dropping from the skies at midnight upon an unsuspecting enemy. This clean warfare on the old simple lines suited the genius of Northern Italy, and it abundantly achieved its purpose. If the Adige valleys were still in Austrian hands, the plains of Lombardy were none the less safe from the invader.

The naval war during those months showed no action of importance. The Austrian battle fleet lay snug in Pola, and only its submarines and smaller craft ventured into the northern Adriatic. The Italian fleet in June cruised along the Dalmatian coast, and destroyed the wireless stations on the islands of Lissa and Cuzzola. On 7th July Italy proclaimed a blockade of the Austrian and Albanian coasts, warning off vessels of all flags from the Adriatic. Early on the morning of the 18th a substantial loss was sustained, the old Italian cruiser *Giuseppe Garibaldi* being sunk off Cattaro by an Austrian submarine, with the loss of one hundred lives. On the 23rd some Austrian destroyers bombarded Ortona and the coast railway. Two days later the Italians occupied the Dalmatian island of Pelagosa, and a French destroyer blew up the submarine and airplane supply station on the island of Laogosta. These incidents had little importance, belonging only to the outer fringe of naval activity. The Italian losses to the end of July were two cruisers, a submarine, and a destroyer. The situation in the Adriatic was in miniature the same as that in the North Sea—the Allied Fleet had the mastery, and moved at its pleasure, subject to the menace of submarines and occasional abortive raids of the enemy's lighter vessels from Cattaro. The much-indented Illyrian coast had, since the days of Virgil, been a hostile sheltering ground too good for the ease of the Adriatic.

The relations between Italy and the Teutonic League were still at this stage curiously vague. She was definitely at war with Austria only—a war supported by the full weight of racial aversion and traditional grievances. But she had not declared war against Germany, though diplomatic relations between the two Powers were suspended. Germany had for forty years been engaged in building up great commercial interests in Italy, and she had no desire to lose her financial control of some of the chief Italian industries. It may be added that the fire of resentment against German ideals did not burn so fiercely in Italian hearts as among the other Allies. The popular repugnance to *Deutschtum* went rather to increase the hatred felt for the traditional enemy of Vienna than to pillory the dimly realized plotters of Berlin. But with the third member of the Teutonic League Italy had a long-standing quarrel. The war with Turkey, which broke out in October 1911, ended a year later with the Treaty of Lausanne. But under that treaty Turkey did not recognize formally the Italian occupation of Tripoli and Cyrenaica; she ignored it, and set herself to put every possible difficulty in Italy's way. Italian prisoners of war were not released; the Ottoman troops in Libya remained under their old officers and flag. Enver continued sporadic hostilities during the closing months of 1912, and Aziz Bey did not leave the country till June 1913. After that, Turkish officers, specially trained by Enver, continued to drift back to Tripoli and Cyrenaica, and encourage the recalcitrant Arab bands. When the great war broke out, the *jehad* was preached as much against the Italians in Libya as against the French in Morocco and the British in Egypt. By the summer of 1915 Italy's North African possessions were in a state of profound confusion and unrest, and not unnaturally she blamed Turkey for the situation. Her diplomatic protests had been treated with the more than Oriental apathy of Constantinople.

There was another and a very real grievance. The liberty of Italian subjects within the Ottoman Empire itself had recently been grossly interfered with. Italian citizens had not been allowed to depart from various ports in Asia Minor. Turkey anticipated a declaration of war, and behaved as if it had already come. On 3rd August the Italian Ambassador in Constantinople addressed a Note to the Porte demanding among other things that Italians should be allowed to depart freely from Beirut, Smyrna, Mersina, Alexandretta, Haifa, and Jaffa, and that local authorities in the interior should give up their opposition to the movement of Italian subjects to the coast and provide facilities for their voyage. This

Note was in form an ultimatum, and forty-eight hours were granted for its consideration. The Grand Vizier accepted all the demands within the time specified, but he did nothing more. On the 9th news arrived that the Turkish authorities had revoked their consent to the departure of Italians at Beirut and Mersina. On Saturday, 21st August, Italy's patience was exhausted, and she formally declared war.

CHAPTER XXXI.

THE FIRST YEAR OF WAR: A RETROSPECT.
June 28, 1914-June 28, 1915.

The Military Result—Germany's Calculations—Her Strength and Weakness—The Position of the Allies—The British Problem of Men and Munitions—British Finance—The Allies' Lack of Central Direction—The Neutral States—The Naval Position—The Leaders.

It is desirable in the chronicle of a campaign to halt now and then and look backwards over the path we have travelled. It may be a help to a true perspective if we attempt a summary and an estimate of the doings of the year of war, which we may reasonably date from that Sunday, the 28th of June, when the heir to the Austrian throne was murdered at Serajevo.

The military results of the year must have seemed to any man, casting up the account on paper at some distance from the atmosphere of strife, an indisputable German triumph. Belgium, all but a small western fraction, lay captive, and was in process of Germanization. The rich industrial district of Lille, and all northeastern France between the Oise and the Meuse, were occupied by her troops. She had battered down with ease the northern fortresses. She had driven a wedge across the upper Meuse. The Woëvre was in her hands. Her battle front was only thirty miles from the gates of Paris. To set against this, the Allies had penetrated German territory for a small distance in Alsace, but Alsace was not Germany in the sense that Picardy was France. Again, she held her conquests with a line of trenches which for eight months the Allies had endeavoured in vain to break. She had the high ground from Ypres to La Bassée; she had the crest of the Falaises de Champagne; and even positions which seemed precarious, like the St. Mihiel salient, had proved so far impregnable. In August 1914 she had defeated the Allies in a series of great battles; and though thereafter her progress had been less notable, it was difficult to point to any counterbalancing Allied gain. It was true that her first plan had shipwrecked at the Marne, and her second on the bastion of Ypres; but she had made a third, and the third had prospered. She was holding the Western front with fewer men than her opponents, and she was holding it securely. The much-vaunted efforts of Champagne, Les Eparges, Artois, Neuve Chapelle, and Festubert had made only inconsiderable dints in her battle line. She had reaped the full benefit from the territory she had occupied. Belgium and north-eastern France had been bled white in her interests, and she was using their wealth and industrial organization to forge new weapons against her foes. The situation in the West, an impartial observer might have decided, was wholly advantageous to Germany. There she could keep off the enemy with her left hand while she struck with her right elsewhere.

But if German eyes could turn westward with a modest comfort on that 28th day of June, they looked eastward with something like exultation. There, surely, the age of miracles had dawned. The early disasters in East Prussia had been gloriously atoned for at Tannenberg. Hindenburg, after one failure, had secured western Poland. Austria had blundered at the start and lost the better part of Galicia, and for some months there had been anxious hearts in the Oder valley. But since the opening of the New Year all failures had been redeemed. East Prussia was inviolate, and German armies were hammering at the gates of Riga. Galicia had been won back, its great oil-fields had been regained, and the menace to the cornlands of Hungary had gone. Further, with immense slaughter, the armies of Russia had been driven inside their own frontiers; the Warsaw triangle was being assailed, Warsaw seemed doomed, and it looked as if all Poland would soon be in German hands. Even if Germany was granted no Sedan in the East, she had broken the Russian offensive for a year, and would presently be free to use half her Eastern armies to compel a decision in the West. Her colleagues had not distinguished themselves; but in the grip of the German machine even Austrian and Turk could march to victory. The threat from Italy did not disturb her; she knew the strength of the Austro-Italian frontier. The Allies were committed to an impossible enterprise at Gallipoli, where even success, in her eyes, would not atone for their desperate losses. She noted with approval that the Balkan States still maintained their uneasy neutrality. After her victories of the summer there would be small inducement for Rumania, Bulgaria, and Greece to pledge their fortunes to a drooping cause. Even if they lost their heads, it would matter little. Germany had a supreme contempt for subsidiary operations. When she had crippled Russia, and broken France and Britain, she could deal at her leisure with any foolish Balkan princeling.

The naval position was less satisfactory. It was true that Germany's fleet was still intact in the sanctuary of the Heligoland Bight, but it was a weapon that might rust for want of use. The Allied navies had swept her mercantile shipping from the seas of the world. Her coasts were blockaded, and her breaches of international law had compelled Britain to rewrite the maritime code and to bear hard upon those neutrals in whom she had trusted. She had no ships of war anywhere except in her home waters, and the occasions on which she had tried conclusions with Britain had not ended prosperously. Her submarines had, indeed, done marvels, but they were fruitless marvels. They had sent to the bottom a large number of Allied and neutral merchantmen, and had exasperated her enemies; but they had not seriously interfered with the sea-borne Allied commerce, and they had done nothing to relieve the blockade of Germany. No doubt they had destroyed several Allied ships of war, and they had driven the big battleships from the Dardanelles; but thoughtful people in Germany were beginning to look with some disfavour on the submarine worship of which Tirpitz was the hierophant. It was daring and brilliant; but it had not weakened the Allied navies or interfered with their operations, and it was raising ugly difficulties with America. On the general question of the rival Grand Fleets there was little difference of opinion. The war must be decided on land, and the victor there would impose his own terms as to the future of the seas. The British fleet had destroyed Germany's overseas trade, and there its activity ceased. If, in spite of it, Germany could obtain the requisite supplies, then the boasted naval predominance of Britain came to nothing. She would give Britain no occasion for a Trafalgar, and all the battleships on earth could not interfere with the decision on the Vistula or the Oise.

Her economic position, which some months earlier had occasioned much searching of heart, had now been more clearly determined. Germany could still, through the complaisance of her enemies, receive certain foreign supplies, such as cotton, and for the rest she could make shift with her own productions. The Teutonic League was virtually self-supporting. All the mechanical skill of her engineers, all the learning and ingenuity of her chemists, were utilized. Her industrial life down to the smallest fraction was mobilized for war. Substitutes were invented for former imports, food supplies were organized and doled out under Government supervision, and the machinery of her recent commercial expansion was switched on to the making of munitions. She was confident that she could maintain a far greater output than the Allies for a long enough period to ensure victory. As for her finances, she was living upon the certainty of that victory. Her internal credit, which was all that was needed, would last out the war. If she were beaten, then, indeed, she would be bankrupt on a colossal scale ; but defeat did not enter into her calculations.

The position of the Teutonic League and Turkey, its ally, was gloomy enough outside Europe. The Turks, though they were doing well under German supervision in the Dardanelles, had been beaten in the Caucasus and in Mesopotamia, and their invasion of Egypt had ended in a fiasco. In the Far East the great German fortress of Tsing-tau, on which millions had been spent—her one foothold on the continent of Asia—had fallen to Japan. Her Pacific possessions had melted away like a mirage. In Africa the dreams of Wissmann and Nachtigal were vanishing. Togoland was a British colony. The vital parts of the Cameroons were in British and French hands, and its German garrison had been forced far up into the inhospitable hinterland. In East Africa she was holding her own ; but she could get no reinforcements there, and it could be only a question of time till her enemies pressed in the sides of the quadrilateral. In South Africa, on which she had counted, the situation was sheer farce. The rebellion had been a flash in the pan ; Botha had overrun and conquered German South-West territory ; and the land which she had looked upon as a likely ally was preparing to send an expeditionary force to France. But she might well comfort herself with the reflection that the ultimate fate of those outland possessions would follow the decision of the European conflict, and she did not doubt what that decision would be.

Such a summary would have represented the view of an impartial outsider on June 28, 1915, and, a little more highly coloured, that of the average thinking German. On the whole—the conclusion would have been—the honours of the first year of war lay with Germany But those who sought to judge the situation rightly were compelled to look beyond the bare facts to the policies of which they were the consequence. An outlook may seem roseate enough to everybody except the man who bears the responsibility. Mere successes do not signify much unless they represent stages in the realization of the central purpose. How far had Germany achieved her desires? Were the victories she had won bringing her nearer to that kind of result which alone would serve her need?

Her first plan of campaign had presumed a speedy decision. The Allies in the West were to be crushed by the Day of Sedan; and then, with France prostrate under her heel, she could turn eastwards and compel Russia to sue for peace. That dream of a battle without a morrow had died on the day in September when her great armies recoiled to the Aisne plateau. Then had come a new plan. The second offensive was to seize the Channel ports, move on Paris from its northern side, terrorize Britain, and compel a settlement before winter had fully come. That scheme, too, had to be relinquished when, in the first week of November, the most crushing odds had failed to force the West Flanders gate. Thereupon, with admirable courage and amazing vitality, Germany adopted a third course. She consented in the West, and presently in the East also, to a war of attrition which went directly against her interests, for it wore down the one thing she could not replace —her numbers of men. But meanwhile she was busy piling up a weight of munitions which far exceeded the total complement of the Allies. The exact point of this policy should be noted. It would enable her to hold her front, and even to take the offensive, with far fewer men than her enemies. With its aid she could, though outnumbered, hold the front in the West, while she could destroy the Russian lines. It nullified not only the superior numbers of the Allies, but their peculiar fighting qualities. She could destroy them from a distance, as an undersized mechanic in an airplane might with bombs annihilate a regiment of heroes. She had grasped with extraordinary precision the exact bearing of modern science upon modern warfare. If we are to do justice to Germany's achievement, we must realize that this policy was the reverse of that with which she started. She began with an attempt to break her foes in manœuvre battles. When that failed, she calmly and methodically revised her calculations, and adopted a new, difficult, and laborious scheme, which required immense efforts to set it in working order. That is the essence of a performance whose magnitude it is folly to decry.

This new plan of war involved a revision of her national purpose. The dream of sweeping like a new Timour over East and West, and dictating terms in a halo of glory, was promptly relinquished. She saw herself condemned to a slow war which would give her enemies the chance of increasing their strength, of making that effort which she had made years before the first shots were fired. She resolved to turn the odds against her to her advantage. Russia and Britain might add millions to their first levies, and multiply their war supplies by twenty, but the business would be slow, for the Allies had not patiently organized themselves for war. If she could hold her own for two years, rifts would appear in the Allied lute. Their populations, faced with unfamiliar problems involving novel sacrifices, would grow restive. Criticism would flourish, ministries and governments would fall into discredit, and half their efforts would be dissipated in idle quarrels. There was a chance, too, of serious differences arising between the Allied governments. One Power would carp at the supineness of another; recriminations would follow, and then a diversion of energy. Germany hoped for much from the old difficulties that confront an alliance of equals. Her own allies would give her little trouble, for they were not equals, and she was carrying their burden as well as her own Britain was the most dangerous enemy, because of her wealth and her man-power. But the longest purse will some day empty itself, and Germany noted with pleasure that Britain, who had to finance much of the Allied preparations, was conducting her expenditure with a wastefulness which must soon impoverish even her deep coffers. As for the British levies, however numerous and sturdy they might be, she comforted herself with the reflection that the British Staff had in the past been trained to handle only small forces, and would in all likelihood find the ordering of millions beyond its power. Her aim was no longer a sweeping conquest, but a draw which would leave her in possession of certain vantage points. This "white peace" would find her much depleted in men and money, but with a resounding fame as by far the greatest military power in history. Then would follow some years of recuperation, and in due time a second and successful stroke for the dominion of the world.

These calculations were not ill founded, and on the 28th day of June 1915 might well have seemed to impartial observers a just forecast. It is always hard to estimate fairly the achievement of an enemy. Our judgment is apt to follow our inclination till the moment of panic comes, when it follows our fears. In Germany was seen for the first time in history a great nation organized for war down to the humblest detail. No atom of national energy was dissipated in irrelevancies; every channel was tributary to one main purpose. The very faults of Prussianism in peace—its narrowness, its officialdom, its contempt for individual freedom—became assets in strife. If Germany fell it would be no fault of hers, for she had done all that mortal could do to deserve success. But while it was right to estimate her achievement high, it was easy to put it too high. The machine had taken long years to create. If you have a docile people and a centralized and autocratic Government, and bend all your energies to the preparation for conquest, then you will create a far more efficient machine than your enemy, who has no thought of conquest and only a hazy notion of defence. In a struggle such as this the only side which could be fully prepared was the side which had always contemplated war. The perfection of German methods stood out in relief as contrasted with the unprofessional ways of the Allies rather than because of its intrinsic virtues, though these were great.

In an earlier chapter we have discussed some of Germany's preparations. A few had grossly failed, and had defeated their own end. For nearly half a century her teachers had been endeavouring to get Europe to accept an idea of the Teutonic race as God's chosen people. Racial generalities are not an exact science, and this crusade led to some sad nonsense. But it made many converts. Historians in Britain and America fell victims to it, and decried for its sake the Slav and the Latin, and even in Italian schools under German influence there was an attempt to inculcate the worship of *Deutschtum*.* The first whiff of grapeshot scattered these whimsies, and the laborious efforts of the pedants— outside Germany—went for nothing. So, too, with the attempt on the part of the German governing class to infect the world with a new morality. The Nietzschean doctrine of force, which in peace time was poisoning the springs of the world's thought, suddenly lost its appeal when war began. It lost its appeal even in

* One factor in this odd propaganda was *The Foundations of the Nineteenth Century*, by Mr Houston Stewart Chamberlain, an Englishman who had become a German citizen and had married a daughter of Wagner. This work, written with ability and occasionally with real historical insight, was an attempt to prove that all that is valuable in our modern civilization is the work of the Teutonic genius. For this purpose the author boldly annexed Leonardo and Dante as Teutons. A spurious originality can always be got by writing history up to a fanciful thesis, and one effort of this kind is usually followed by an equally successful effort from the opposite standpoint. If you write a history of the world to prove that progress is the work of red-haired men, somebody else will show as convincingly that it is the work of the black-haired. The pendant to Mr. Chamberlain's book appeared in 1912, *Die Juden und das Wirtschaftsleben*, the work of the Berlin professor, Werner Sombart. It showed that modern civilization was mainly the creation of the Jew, and claimed as Jews—among others—Columbus, and the Scotsman, John Law of Lauriston.

Germany. The prophets of the new morality tumbled over each other to prove that they were still devotees of the old Britain was blamed for actions which, if true, would have been precisely those which Treitschke and Bernhardi had recommended to their countrymen; and the latter teacher was compelled to explain that he had been misunderstood, and had always been on the side of the old-fashioned angels. The German people were made to believe that they had Right on their side—copy-book, Scriptural Right—and they died confident in the same cause for which the Allies fought, and which to the fashionable German moralists had been as foolishness.

The weakness of Germany, it was already obvious, lay in her profound political ineptitude. Her preparation for war, except that part of it which was the military machine, was not only ineffective, it was directly subversive of her interests. Her one political success was that she convinced her own people that she was the aggrieved, not the aggressor; but it was not clear that this persuasion would last. At midsummer 1915 the *Burgfriede* was not what it had been in the preceding September. In December Liebknecht had been alone among the Social Democrats in opposing the war credits; by June the "minority" group included men like Ledebour and Haase, and the official organ, the *Vorwärts*, had gone into opposition.* As for foreign peoples, whether neutral or Allied, she had utterly failed to understand their temper or appreciate its practical significance. She had created and was blunderingly increasing an antagonism which could not be measured merely by the Allied fleets and armies. Her leaders might persuade their obedient people that they stood for truth and righteousness, but to the eyes of the world their writings, their speeches, and above all their deeds, remained damning evidence to the contrary. There lay the chink in the shining German armour. No conquest in history has ever endured unless the conquerors brought to the conquered substantial benefits. The Romans gave law and security, Charlemagne gave peace, even the Turkish dominion in the late Middle Ages brought some order and comfort for the plain man. Still more true was it of the modern world, where education had disposed the majority of men to a critical habit. For Germany to win, she had to persuade not only neutrals but belligerents that an endless and terrible war was more dreadful than her victory. She had persuaded the world of the opposite. To

* The growth of the opposition may be followed in E. Bevan's *German Social Democracy during the War* (1918).

three-fourths of mankind no price seemed too great to pay for her failure. Even those who retained some kindliness for the rank and file of the German nation were being driven to the conviction that its only hope of ultimate salvation was to endure a crushing defeat. Germany was playing now for a one-sided peace, but to win any kind of peace you must convince your opponents that the prospect is at least tolerable. She had by her conduct of the war and by her avowed purpose convinced the Allies that it was of all prospects the most intolerable. This indisputable truth, of which she seemed to have no inkling, vitiated all her plans. She had nothing to offer to the world as the price of acquiescence. She stood glaringly bankrupt in all that the better instinct of our mortal nature desires. The tragedy of Germany was far deeper than the tragedies of Poland and Belgium.

The position of the Allies on 28th June has already been sketched by implication in the preceding pages. There was no slackening of resolution, but to the ordinary man there was a very real dashing of hope. In Britain especially, where the contest had been entered upon in a spirit of exuberant optimism, the truth about the German machine had been slow to dawn upon the popular mind. We had sacrificed so much, we had raised and lost so many men, and now it seemed as if the effort had been fruitless. The talk about "organization," which political mentors used, perplexed and frightened the nation. To some timid souls it seemed Prussianism under another name. Could we beat our enemy only by adopting what we had been led to regard as that enemy's vices? And even those who desired to make the ultimate sacrifice did not know how to set about it. We clung to old constitutional watchwords about the " freedom of the individual," and attempted the ancient impossibility of crossing an unbridged river dryshod. The lack of any conspicuous national leadership intensified the confusion. The British people are not slow to recognize facts when they are once pointed out, but the recognition of facts is the rarest of virtues among politicians, who are accustomed to a particular game, and object to any tampering with the rules and counters. In a democracy such as ours the mass of the people are quicker to learn and wiser in the result than their professional leaders, who, accustomed to wait for a popular "cry" and "mandate," are rarely capable of that thinking and doing in advance which is the true function of leadership. But for opinion to percolate up from below takes time, and in the urgency of a crisis there is sore need of statesmen to initiate and lead. A democracy is rarely fortunate in its normal governors. That is why in the hour of need it is apt to seek a dictator.

The British people during a season of military set-backs had two difficulties to face which their Allies did not share. Both sprang from their previous lack of interest in military questions. A prosperous business man will rarely take his adversary to the law courts. He will prefer to compromise even at some loss to his own pocket, for litigation is a waste of time and may give an undesirable publicity. It is the same with commercial nations like Britain and, in a far greater degree, the United States. They will always prefer, except in the very last extremity, to pay Danegeld rather than fight the Danes, and if they have to fight they regard their wealth as their principal asset. But conceive the case of a business man who has unwillingly gone to law, announcing that if money can do it he will crush his opponent. Conceive the position of such a man when he suddenly finds that the litigation will deplete his balance, and that he may have great difficulty in paying the fees of the eminent counsel on whom he has set his heart. Yet about midsummer that was not unlike Britain's position. She realized as in a blinding flash the enormous outlay to which she was committed, and understood that even her vast resources would be strained to meet it. A second source of discouragement was the extreme popular ignorance of the conditions of war. In every campaign there are critical, and even desperate, moments, times of black uncertainty, obstacles which seem at the time insuperable. It is unnecessary to refer to the position of the North during the first two years of the American Civil War. Take even so small and simple a campaign as the Sudan War of 1898. The situation after the seizure of Berber, the chance of a night attack before Omdurman, and the position of Macdonald's brigade during the actual battle, were all matters to cause grave uneasiness to those in authority. In the ordinary campaign such anxious hours are experienced only by the commander-in-chief and his staff. The public knows nothing of them till long afterwards, when detailed histories are published. But in a war like the present, in spite of the paucity of official information, the movements were on so gigantic a scale that they stood out like large type. Every man understood when Paris or Warsaw was in peril, when the Allies failed, and when the Germans succeeded. Moreover, the movements were so long drawn out that instead of critical hours, as in other campaigns, they involved critical weeks. In France the ordinary educated man had the rudiments of military knowledge which the average Briton lacked. He was aware that war has its ups and downs, that what seem gigantic losses may have little influence on the ultimate decision, and that what looks like a glowing success is often the prelude to failure. In Britain we did not know these things, civilians having rarely interested themselves in the science of war, and consequently the inevitable mischances of the campaign presented themselves to us in darker colours than the truth.

Since in a real sense Britain was the linchpin of the Allies, and since her problem was peculiarly difficult, because her geographical position and her history had endowed her with certain stiff and unyielding beliefs and certain not very malleable forms of government which made new departures slow, her domestic history at this moment was part of the main march of the history of the war. In the beginning of June the new Coalition Government was getting into working order. The country was alive to the need for an unprecedented effort, an effort which involved not only the provision of fresh resources but the organization and economizing of those which already existed. There was no question any longer of awakening the ordinary man. He was almost too much awake, and was inclined to be impatient even of the necessary preliminaries of reform. But both he and his leaders found it hard to reach that clarity of mind and that capacity for sacrifice without reservation which were inspired elsewhere by the stringent lessons of direct suffering. For a little our racial energy tended to go round in a whirlpool rather than to find a clear outlet.

The question of national service, hotly canvassed in those days, suffered from this general confusion. Those who had always preached it were inclined to put their case too high, and argue that its acceptance a year ago would have prevented war—a proposition something more than disputable. Others were content to dub it unnecessary, because of the excellent response to Lord Kitchener's appeal for recruits for the new armies. To such it was answered that our recruiting had been unscientific, unfair in its incidence, and most costly; that the so-called voluntary system was neither truly voluntary nor much of a system; that the whole nation and not merely the fighting part of it required to be organized; and that national service in the true sense meant that every citizen must be at the disposal of the State. In a phrase of Mr. Lloyd George's, the trench-lines were not only in France and Gallipoli, but in every factory and workshop, every town and village in Britain; and trench-fighting meant being under orders.

A great crisis calls for the sacrifice not only of time and money and life, but of principles—those political principles which, being themselves deductions from facts, are rightly jettisoned when facts alter. It would be unfair to underrate the reality of this last sacrifice. Trade Unions were required to give up temporarily rules and regulations for which they had fought hard for half a century. Others were asked to relinquish doctrines of voluntaryism and individualism which were in the warp and woof of their minds. But it may fairly be said that the great bulk of the British nation was prepared to make any sacrifice of which the necessity was clearly proved. The number of those who sincerely believed in voluntaryism at any cost was probably small and insignificant in quality. They had no moral justification, for it is not ethically nobler to pay men to fight for you than to fight yourself. They were true doctrinaires who for the sake of an adjunct of liberty would have sacrificed liberty itself. Prussia, when confronted by Napoleon, declined to fight for her own interests, but she was presently compelled to fight for the interests of her conqueror. The extreme voluntaryist, like the wife of Master-Builder Solness in Ibsen's play, could think only of the safety of his dolls when the house was burning.

Obviously the matter had gone beyond the sphere of argument. Pleas for or against national service of the kind familiar before the war were no longer relevant. Nor did newspaper propaganda help towards a solution. Those who had always advocated the reform lay under suspicion of desiring to use a national emergency to further their pet scheme. The strong argument against it lay in the fact that the Government had not declared it necessary, and clearly only the Government were in possession of information which allowed them to decide on the necessity. It was not a question of the inherent desirability of national service, but of whether or not the immediate situation made it imperative. The difficulties of the Government were no doubt very great. They could not be certain that they had judged the popular temper correctly, and, assuming that the objections to compulsion were widespread, then its benefits might be too dearly bought at the cost of national disunion. Trade Union leaders who agreed to suspend Union rules found that they had no power to bind their followers, the whole discipline of the Unions having woefully declined since the passing of the Trades Disputes Act. Here, again, to grasp the nettle boldly would have been the wisest course. The State, if it speaks with a resolute voice, has an authority which no minor organization can possess. But as yet the Government gave no clear lead to popular opinion. It was obvious from their actions that they were converts to a certain measure of compulsion, and the speeches of many Ministers seemed to be arguments in favour of the general principle. Now in a crisis there must be leadership; and if a sharp change in national habits and modes of thought is necessary, that leadership must be bold and confident. The previous Government had not hesitated at compulsion for purposes of social reform, even unpopular compulsion, as in the case of the Insurance Act. But for some reason compulsion which might involve in certain cases service in the field seemed to many different in kind from any compulsion which they had hitherto practised.

The matter was beset with difficulties—of detail as well as of principle, and the result was that, after our traditional fashion, we compromised and dealt with the question piecemeal. The doctrine which statesmen were never tired of preaching, and popular leaders apparently accepted—that the whole nation must be organized in a great effort and everybody put at the disposal of the State—was not given effect to. What our Government toyed with was a form of industrial compulsion. With that we thought we were familiar; we thought that it would be accepted without serious opposition, especially on the part of those classes whose creed was semi-socialism, and who had clamorously announced their opposition to military conscription. It was a strange, topsy-turvy procedure, destined to break down at the first trial National service for everybody without exception was, assuming the necessity to be established, a comprehensible and a genuinely democratic principle, but industrial compulsion was neither more nor less than a vicious type of class legislation. The people at large were probably willing enough to respond to any call. They were less attached to shibboleths than their nominal leaders, and would have done the bidding of any man who spoke clearly and with authority. That clear voice did not sound, and in its absence we tended to approach the question by shy and timid curves. The first tentative towards national service was the passing of a Bill for a national register. This was introduced by Mr. Walter Long on 29th June, and became law on 15th July, in spite of the jeremiads of a few members of Parliament. The Bill for the creation of a Munitions Department was passed on 9th June, and it was made clear that the new department was a temporary expedient, to last only during the war. An Order in Council defined the Minister's duties as " to examine into and organize the sources of supply and the labour available for the supply of any kind of munitions of war, the supply of which is in whole or in part undertaken by him, and by that means, as far as possible, to ensure such supply of munitions for the present war as may be required by the Army Council and the Admiralty, or may otherwise be found necessary." * It was a supply department to meet estimates and requisitions provided by the military and naval authorities. It took over from the Army Council most of the functions of the Master-General of the Ordnance, the control of Woolwich Arsenal, the Government small-arms factories and similar establishments, and it was endowed also with a large field of discretionary activity.

Mr. Lloyd George set to work at once. He visited the chief provincial cities to inquire at first hand into local conditions, and he made many stirring speeches in order to rouse the ordinary workman to a sense of the gravity of the position. The problem he had to face was not materially altered from that to which a startled Government had awakened in the early spring. To put it briefly, Germany alone of the belligerents had shown herself to be *industrially* organized for war. By Government assistance she had kept not only the regular armament works but a vast number of civilian factories, which could be adapted for the purpose, in a state of constant activity and efficiency. Again, she had for some time shared with America the supply of machine-tools for the world, and this enabled her to improvise new factories. Moreover, the cessation of her foreign trade turned her whole energies to the making of war material. Her manufacturers had no option in the matter; their only market was their own Government. Economic loss proved, not for the first time in history, to be a military gain. In Britain the system and position were the precise opposite. Government establishments had been decreased, and many private firms who, in the past, had made armaments had grown disheartened and dropped the business. The Admiralty side was different; there steady Government orders and a large amount of foreign business had maintained both public and private yards at full strength. But when it came to improvising military stores we found our machinery lamentably short. The Government began by trusting to the chief armament-makers, who in

* The Minister had power to deal not only with armaments in the narrower sense, but with any form of production connected with the war—such as clothing, boots, jam, tinned foods, railways, huts, etc.

their turn endeavoured to find sub-contractors throughout the country. But, since our private industries had not been organized with a view to adaptability, the business of increasing production proved too slow. There was much cut-throat competition for labour; there was a universal shortage of machine-tools, which could not be improvised; and with the best will in the world both Government and manufacturers found the situation beyond them. The process of industrial organization, it was realized, must be drastic and wholesale, and it must begin at the beginning.

The Munitions Act—introduced on 23rd June and passed into law on 2nd July—was an attempt to put our whole industrial system on a war basis. It was framed after much consultation with Trade Union leaders and employers of labour, and it aimed at applying a moderate degree of compulsion to all industries concerned directly or indirectly with the supply of war material, to replacing in certain cases private management by Government control, and to collecting and employing the large amount of administrative and inventive talent which had been placed at the disposal of the nation. Arbitration was made compulsory in all trade disputes, with whatever subject they might be concerned. A difference had to be reported to the Board of Trade, which would refer it for settlement to an arbitration court or some other tribunal. Strikes and lock-outs were forbidden unless a month had elapsed and the Board of Trade had not intervened. Primarily this rule referred only to munition works, but the Minister of Munitions was empowered to apply it by proclamation to other industries. The coal miners and the cotton operatives objected, and it was agreed that, if machinery existed for settling disputes without stoppage of work, this should stand without Government interference. However, in the last resort, the right of State interference even in these industries could be exercised. The Minister of Munitions, if he thought it necessary for the successful prosecution of the war, could declare any works " a controlled establishment." * This step involved four important consequences. In the first place, employers' profits were limited. The owner was permitted to take out of the gross profits the net profits plus one-fifth, the rest to go to the State. Net profits were to be ascertained by taking the average net profits " during two corresponding periods completed just before the outbreak of war." A small

* Up to 6th August, 356 establishments had been declared " controlled "—a very small proportion of the total engaged in war contracts. The machine-tool makers were taken over *en bloc*.

committee was appointed to decide difficult questions about depreciation and such like matters, and the Minister had power, if the arrangement worked unfairly in any case, to submit the question to referees. In the second place, Trade Union rules, and all rules, practices, and customs not having the force of law were to be suspended, if they tended to restrict production and employment.* This was for the period of the war only, and was in no way to prejudice the future position of the workmen. It was understood that wages would not be affected by the introduction of semi-skilled or female labour. Disputes under this head were to be decided by the Board of Trade or arbitrators appointed by it. In the third place—in order to prevent a sudden and arbitrary decline in earnings—no changes in wages were to be made without the consent of the Minister or an arbitration tribunal. Finally, the Minister was empowered to make special regulations to which all employees in a controlled establishment must submit. The weak part of the Act was its penalty clauses. Small fines, which might be deducted from wages, were imposed for breaches of its provisions, the maximum being £5 per man per day. Penalties were to be imposed by a munitions tribunal, which, besides a president, would be composed equally of representatives of Labour and Capital. To prevent idle competition, employers were forbidden to give work to a man who had recently worked at munitions, unless six weeks had elapsed since he left his prior employment, or he held a certificate from his last employer or from a munitions tribunal.

Mr. Lloyd George announced various co-ordinate activities. The country was divided for munitions purposes into ten areas, each controlled by a committee of local business men. Efforts were to be made to bring back skilled workers from the front and from the new armies still training at home. The Munitions Department, with its headquarters close to the War Office, was organized with the usual paraphernalia of a Government office. At first there was some confusion as to its *personnel*. Mr. Lloyd George was himself too busy with speech-making and ministerial work to be a possible administrative head. The services of many of the

---

* The way had been prepared for this step so far as the Trade Union leaders were concerned. On 17th–19th March there was a conference between the Government and the representatives of thirty-five labour organizations. An agreement was reached that for the period of the war " the relaxation of the present trade practices is imperative, and that each union be recommended to take into favourable consideration such changes in working conditions or trade customs as may be necessary with a view to accelerating the output of war munitions or equipments."

ablest business men in Britain were available, but there was grave danger at the start that knowledge and earnestness would be wasted owing to the lack of a co-ordinating authority at the top. A sub-department for inventions—an admirable scheme—was presently organized, and did good service. Less successful was the plan for a Mobile Munitions Brigade to be recruited voluntarily among the workers. After an elaborate advertising campaign, involving much expenditure of public funds, some 100,000 volunteers were enrolled, but an enormous proportion of these were already employed on war business, and could not be spared. A few thousands at the most were the result of the enterprise.

The new department entered upon its task with abundant energy. But in the nature of things results must be slow. It was the labour of Hercules to improvise a gigantic system of State socialism under the name of "controlled establishments," and to combine in the service of the State the scientific and industrial talent of the people. The Munitions Act, for all its merits, gave an inadequate weapon to the hand of the Government. It had begun at the wrong end. By introducing compulsion only for one class it provided no sanction for the enforcing of such compulsion. Its penal clauses were futile. Fines were no remedy against the resistance of a mass of men, and since under the Trades Disputes Act the Union funds were inviolate, any large body of strikers could set the Government at defiance.

Proof was not slow in coming. On 1st April the Miners' Federation of South Wales and Monmouth had handed in notices to terminate the existing wages agreement within three months, and to negotiate another. The Board of Trade attempted to make terms, and offered certain proposals into which we need not enter. It was one of the old disputes, so familiar in peace time, between Labour and Capital for the division of the spoils. On 12th July the delegates met at Cardiff, and rejected the Board of Trade proposals. Their executive advised them to continue at work under day-to-day contracts, pending further negotiations, but they refused to accept anything less than their original proposals, and resolved to stop the collieries on 15th July unless their demands were conceded. The miners, at their own request, had been excluded from the Munitions Act, but their leaders had undertaken that there would be no strikes or stoppages during the war. Unfortunately, however, their official leaders had small authority, and the men were led by self-elected extremists. On 13th July the Government by proclamation extended the Munitions Act to the South Wales coal area. This made it an offence to leave work, and enjoined the reference of the dispute to arbitration. That same day the Miners' Federation of Great Britain advised the men to work from day to day, and the colliery owners put themselves wholly at the Government's disposal. Next day the executive again tried to persuade the miners to keep to their work pending a settlement. The advice was not taken, and on the following day, the 15th, 200,000 men went on strike. That day the delegates had met at Cardiff, and by a majority refused to countermand the strike—an act which constituted a defiance of the Royal Proclamation of 13th July, and an open challenge to the nation.

The Government proceeded to set up, in terms of the Act, a munitions tribunal for South Wales and Monmouth. On the 16th, Mr. Runciman, the President of the Board of Trade, saw the executive, but found them powerless. That day several furnaces were damped down. The situation had reached a deadlock. How could the Government fine or imprison 200,000 men? Their Act had broken down under its first trial. Many of the miners —especially the older men—felt the shame of the situation acutely, but they were bound by loyalty to their fellows and by the net which agitators had woven round them. On the 19th the position was grave indeed. That day Mr. Lloyd George went to Cardiff, accompanied by two other Ministers, Mr. Runciman and Mr. Arthur Henderson, and met the executive. Next morning terms of settlement were arranged, which the delegates accepted, and the men returned to work. These terms were in substance the granting of the men's demands. An emotional meeting, at which Mr. Lloyd George spoke with great seriousness and frankness, showed the tension of everybody's nerves and the relief of the miners at being extricated from a position where they were fast earning the contempt of their fellow-countrymen. It was an ugly episode, which did little credit to any one concerned in it. The stoppage of labour meant the reduction of our daily coal output by 200,000 tons, at a time when every ton was needed. It had the worst effect upon public opinion among our Allies, and it exasperated our sorely tried troops in the field. A settlement was only reached by the submission of the Government—submission to men to whom, collectively and individually, attached the guilt of treason. The blame must fall impartially on both sides—on the Government for not having anticipated what obviously must happen and preventing it in time, on the men for sinking their patriotism and good sense in a selfish trade squabble. The main lesson of the incident was the folly of half measures and irrational compromises. Compulsion applied piecemeal to one class could neither be enforced nor defended.

The question of finance, since the easy confidence of the winter had gone, began to weigh heavily on the Government by the end of May. We were waging war on an extravagant scale as compared with France, and still more with Germany. This was partly due to the fact that we had to improvise so much, for things done in a hurry are always expensive. It was due still more to our voluntary system of recruiting, which meant that we had to offer terms high enough to attract men from the labour market, and that, owing to our inability to select our material, we had to take often the costliest type of recruit. A few figures will make this clear. We needed a great number of motor-drivers for our mechanical transport, and to attract these we paid six shillings a day, and a lavish allowance for dependents. Germany secured as many as she needed at something below the ordinary wage rate of peace time. The German allowance for a wife was 9s. a month from May to October, and a minimum of 12s. per month for the rest of the year. Her rate for each child and dependent was a minimum of 6s. monthly. The British allowance for a wife alone began by being 7s. 7d. per week; it was raised in October to 12s. 6d. per week; and in March 1915 to 17s. 6d. Higher rates were paid to the families of non-commissioned officers and to those resident in the London area. Since our system was unselective, we took a large number of married men with families. The patriotism of such recruits was admirable, but from the point of view of the national finances it would have been better if their places had been taken by unmarried men. Again, the Government continued civil expenditure which may have been justifiable enough in times of peace, but was no better than waste in war. Further, rich men were allowed to make very large profits out of material directly or indirectly connected with the war, profits which meant a loss to the public purse.

Had that purse been bottomless this extravagance might have been defended; but it was becoming painfully clear that our financial resources had strict limits. We were already expending some 1,000 millions a year on the actual conduct of the war, and our national revenue fell short by some £80,000 of the mere interest on this outlay. In such a crisis, whether in public or private life, there are three means of remedy—to reduce expenditure, to increase income, or to do both together. Obviously our military expenditure could not be seriously reduced, for the lavish scale we had instituted at the beginning must be maintained more or less unchanged to the end. The saving could only be in our civil expenditure. Hence arose the need for universal thrift—economy not only in civil government but in every detail of the private life of each citizen. Normally our imports from foreign countries were paid for by our exports, by freights, and by the interest on the securities of those countries held in British hands. In time of war our exports were curtailed, our freights yielded less, and, on the other hand, from certain foreign countries we increased our imports under the head of munitions. If the balance of trade was not to go fatally against us, it was essential to reduce our normal imports. This could only be done by a rigorous economy which decreased the consumption of imported goods—not only articles of luxury, but staples like meat and grain. Our actual expenditure under all heads must be diminished, and so far as possible British-produced substitutes found for the necessaries of life. The thrift campaign was inaugurated by some of the chief authorities in British finance, and warmly seconded by the Government. Excellent and most practical instructions were issued to householders as to how to avoid waste and how to exclude foreign goods from their daily bill. There was reason to believe that this crusade made a genuine appeal to many thousands of homes. Men and women who were unable to serve their country otherwise welcomed the chance of this humble but invaluable service.

The problem of increasing the national revenue was faced with courage and good sense. A loan on a colossal scale was necessary, and that could only come out of the savings of our countrymen. In November 1914 we had issued a loan of £350,000,000, at a discount of 5 per cent., and carrying $3\frac{1}{2}$ per cent. interest. It was resolved in June 1915 that another loan should be raised, since it was impracticable to sell our foreign securities, and the method of renewable Treasury bills was inconvenient, and did not bring in the general public. It was further decided that the new loan should be issued at par, and that every effort should be made to popularize it with the humblest investor. It is the multitude of small subscriptions by which a national loan succeeds, just as it is the manufacturer of some cheap article of universal use who makes the largest fortune. The new loan was to be of an indefinite amount, and it was to carry $4\frac{1}{2}$ per cent. interest—a wonderful change from twenty years before, when Consols at $2\frac{3}{4}$ per cent.

stood at 112¾.* Subscribers of £100 and its multiples applied through the Bank of England; but vouchers for 5s., 10s., and £1 were purchasable at any money order office in the country, and these vouchers carried 5 per cent. interest. Everything was made easy for the small investor. A vast " publicity " campaign advertised him of the benefits of the scheme. When his scrip vouchers reached £5 or any multiple, he could exchange them for a stock certificate, and he received a bonus on the exchange. War Loan stock bought through the Post Office or a savings bank could be sold at any time through the same means at the current market price, and scrip vouchers would be accepted as the equivalent of cash in making deposits. The whole loan was redeemable at par in 1925 at the discretion of the State, and was compulsorily redeemable in 1945. A new and interesting departure was the opportunity given to holders of the Three-and-a-half loan of November 1914, of Consols, and of other Government securities, to convert into the new loan. The motive of the concession was to increase subscriptions to the new loan, for the aforesaid holders could only convert by also taking up stock in the latter.

The high rate of interest, the right of conversion, the privileges given to small investors, the widespread " publicity," and the turning of the national mind at the moment to questions of thrift combined to make the loan a conspicuous success. The lists closed on 10th July, and on that day the amount subscribed through the Bank of England was £570,000,000, and through the Post Office £24,000,000. It was far the greatest loan ever raised—greater by £144,000,000 than that which Germany claimed to have floated at a higher rate of interest and accompanied by many dubious financial expedients. The finance of the British loan was wholly sound and straightforward. For the first time in our history we attempted what many economists had long urged—the popularization and retail sale of a premier Government security. The only doubt entertained was as to whether we were not raising too large a proportion of our funds by loan, and thereby placing an undue burden on posterity. Though increases in taxation had been made, the amount thereby contributed was a very small fraction of the total. It had not been so in our earlier wars. The eight years' War of the Austrian Succession cost us more than £43,000,000; of this nearly a third was paid out of revenue. The

* It was a cheap loan, however, compared with those raised during the Napoleonic wars, which were issued at a heavy discount and accompanied by an extravagant system of bonuses. It has been estimated that during that war, on the average, for every £100 received, £169 of debt was created.

Seven Years' War cost £82,000,000, and a quarter came from revenue. It is true that the American War was financed mainly by loans, but in the great struggle with Napoleon fully 47 per cent. was raised by taxation—an amazing effort, which was possible only because of the rise at the same time of British industrialism. Even so the burden left by that war was sufficiently crushing, and for six or seven years after Waterloo the economic health of Britain was in a parlous state. Nearly half the cost of the Crimean War was met out of revenue. To meet our new liabilities increased taxation had given us in June no more than £65,000,000 a year. A deputation from the City of London, which about this time met the Prime Minister, urged among other things the taxation of imported articles and a wholesale revision of the income tax, so as to relieve the arbitrariness of its incidence, and reach the wages of the prosperous workman. As things stood the middle classes were bearing a disproportionate burden. If the taxation of imports tended to check their flow, that, as we have seen, was in itself a desirable end. If, on the contrary, they still came in, their taxation would give us revenue.

No survey of British effort would be complete without a reference to the work done by voluntary bodies and by individuals in the thousand and one paths of charity which the war revealed. The British Red Cross Society, the Order of St. John of Jerusalem, and the Voluntary Aid Detachments provided a nursing organization which could not be paralleled in the world. Private hospitals were sent to Serbia, where they grappled with the insoluble problem of an army ill supplied with medical comforts and scourged by deadly epidemics, and lost many devoted members of their staffs. Nurses and ambulances went to the French, Russian, and Belgian fronts, and the civilian population of France and Belgium were cared for by special organizations. The immense business of dealing with the refugee Belgian population was skilfully handled, and they were temporarily absorbed into the social life of Britain, while with the assistance of a commission of neutrals food supplies were sent to Belgium itself. Large sums were raised for the relief of distress in Poland and for a dozen other charitable purposes. Happily there was little immediate distress in Britain, and the energies of her people could be devoted to war purposes and the succour of the invaded lands. Our own troops were amply supplied with the small luxuries and comforts which are not included in rations. Scarcely a household in the Empire but did its part. The remotest cottages in the Highlands, the loneliest farms in

Alberta and Queensland, were connected by strange threads with the far-away theatres of war. During these months women began to appear in many novel employments. As ticket-collectors, tram-conductors, car-drivers, bill-posters, postmen, and in a score of other tasks, they released men for the fighting line. Never had the women of Britain shown to finer advantage. Of all who were compelled to remain at home, they were the chief sufferers, for they had given sons and brothers, husbands and lovers, to the field of danger. From the beginning they realized the gravity of the struggle. The women's movement of recent years had given to a large class a special organization and discipline, which was turned to admirable purpose. The leaders of that movement in the press and on the platform did a great work in rousing the nation, and none dealt more trenchantly with counsels of supineness and peace. The women of Britain asked only for the chance of service, and when the munitions difficulty revealed itself they were foremost in offering their work. What had happened in Germany and France was beginning to take place in Britain. The barriers of sex were falling, like the barriers of class, before the trumpet call of the national need.

The most signal weakness which the first year had revealed in the Alliance was its lack of central direction. We have seen what Germany did with her unequally yoked allies, putting precision into the Turks and homogeneity into the Austrian legions, and turning every economic advantage of her colleagues to the profit of the whole. France, Russia, Italy, and Britain, though in spirit more united than the Teutonic League, had by midsummer still failed to pool their assets scientifically, and to make full use of their advantages of position. The buying of war stores by the different Powers was still often at cross purposes. Events proved that the different strategic plans had not been perfectly harmonized, and that the vital matter of munitions was not treated as one problem, concerning not Russia and Britain as individuals, but the whole Allied front. It is true that much had been done by conferences to make the financing of the war uniform; but even in this sphere Germany would have carried the policy further. She would have devised that which Pitt appealed for in the House of Commons in 1783, " a complete economic system adapted to the new features of the situation." Had France, Russia, Italy, Britain, Japan, Belgium, and Serbia formed themselves into an economic league to control all matters of international commerce, a formidable weapon would have been prepared against their enemies and a powerful lever to influence the policy of hesitating neutrals.

The main asset of the Allies was their unity of purpose and singleness of heart. They had agreed to make peace as one Power, and they were wholly resolved to make no peace which should be indecisive. When Charles XII. of Sweden was faced, at the age of eighteen, with an attack by three armies, he told his council: " I have resolved never to engage in an unjust war, but, on the other hand, never to conclude a just one but by the ruin of my foes." In such a spirit all the Allies now faced the future. Their situation was stronger than could be gathered from a map of rival positions. Every day was adding to the numbers of their armies. They were moving towards the construction of a machine as strong as the German—gropingly and slowly, it is true, but steadily. Time was still on their side. No one of their armies had been destroyed Their losses, great as they were, had been made good More and more, in the eyes not only of soldiers but of politicians and peoples, it was clear that Germany would be defeated only by the destruction of her field armies, and that all her gains of territory were irrelevant except in so far as they postponed that purpose. Hence the conquests which exhilarated Berlin were borne by the Allies— even by those at whose expense they had been made—with a certain robust philosophy. A lion is the less dangerous to an African village when it has gorged itself upon a portion of the herds. What Germany had fondly counted upon had not come to pass. They were working harmoniously, in spite of the strenuous efforts of their enemy to stir up strife. Certain German sympathizers in Britain attempted to set labour and capital by the ears ; their cousins in France whispered to the French people how infamous it was that Britons should be going on strike in such a crisis, and insisted on the shortness of the British line ; while others in Russia, helped by the dregs of the Baltic-German bureaucracy, quoted certain unfortunate witticisms of French generals, pointed to the stagnation in the West, and observed that France would resist no doubt to the last drop of blood, but that that blood would be Russian. On the surface it looked as if the field for mischief-making were clear. But three things combined to make the seeds of strife sown by Germany fall upon unreceptive ground The first was the gravity of the crisis and the intense antagonism which Germany had inspired. Men engaged in what they believe to be a holy war are the less inclined to be captious about their colleagues.

The second was the goodwill between the Allied armies brought about by the sincere admiration felt by each for the performance of the others. The memories of the Marne and Ypres and Le Cateau, of Rava Russka, Augustovo, and Przasnysz, were the best preventives of a carping spirit. Most important of all, each of the Allies was profoundly conscious of its shortcomings, and was more disposed to criticize its own unpreparedness than that of its neighbours. Each was busy setting its own house in order.

This modesty, admirable in itself, might, if carried too far, have conduced to those evil results on which Germany counted. She cunningly hoped that a spirit of doubt and disquiet would go abroad among the Allies, and lead to the fall of ministers and the dismissal of generals. In Britain, where, since the popular voice was most easily audible, criticism might have been most expected, we sinned, on the whole, little in this respect. Indeed, under the influence of Lincoln's warning against " swapping horses in the middle of the stream," we were inclined to be almost too tolerant of proved administrative incompetence and too chary of even well-informed and patriotic criticism. It is a mistake to change horses in the middle of the ford ; but if the horse can only lie down, change is necessary to avoid drowning. The fact that competent critics were patriotically silent left the necessary task of public watchfulness to men who had small authority in the nation.

The position of neutral states on that 28th of June was still obscure. Italy had joined the Allies, but the Balkan nations— the only ones remaining in Europe whose decision from a military point of view was vital—were still perplexed by contradictory interests In Greece, though M. Venizelos had won a victory at the polls, he was not yet in office, and his country was uncommitted. Bulgaria had come to a railway agreement with Turkey, but had as yet taken no overt step to join the Teutonic League. Rumania, though undoubtedly influenced by Italy's decision, was still keeping an anxious eye on Bulgaria. She did her best to preserve a strict aloofness, and refused to allow officially the passage of war munitions to Turkey through her territory.

The United States, whose markets provided the Allies with war materials, was finding her position one of great and growing difficulty. President Wilson's policy, though expressed by him in an academic phraseology which seemed curiously inept in such a crisis, was based upon a judicial view of American interests.* The pitfalls which beset her path were not fairly estimated by European observers. But Germany seemed determined to make neutrality impossible. The sinking of the *Lusitania* drew a strong Note from the American Government, a Note which brought about the resignation of the Foreign Secretary, Mr. Bryan, who had spent his life in a world of emotional verbiage. To this protest on behalf of neutrals against the barbarity of her submarine practices, Germany replied defiantly. In the middle of July Mr. Lansing, Mr. Bryan's successor, presented what would have been regarded by the older diplomacy as an ultimatum. He laid down three principles: that the high seas are free to neutral ships; that this freedom can only be interfered with after the character and cargo of the ship has been ascertained; and that the lives of non-combatants can only be lawfully endangered if the vessel seeks to escape after summons or attempts resistance. A repetition of the breaches of these principles of which Germany had been guilty would, said the Note, be regarded as an unfriendly act. Germany, through her press, replied with an arrogant disdain; and a few days after the receipt of the Note her submarines sank an American steamer off the Orkney Islands. The atmosphere was electric, but what with another Power would have meant an immediate declaration of war did not necessarily involve such a consequence in the case of the United States. Her diplomatists had never regarded "terms of art" in the European way, and the phrase "unfriendly act," which elsewhere was the wording of an ultimatum, was with her only a strong type of protest.

The relations with Britain were also, in spite of very real goodwill on both sides, moving to an *impasse*. In March, it will be remembered, the British Government declared a blockade of Germany—a blockade which, since it could not be made fully effective, was not in accord with the accepted principles of international law. It decreed the seizure and confiscation of non-contraband goods of German origin, ownership, or destination carried in neutral ships to neutral ports, though Britain did not propose to apply the rule with any technical rigour. This practice involved a considerable breach of the recognized code of maritime law, a breach which Britain justified by the exceptional

---

* "Any question of war involves not only a question of right, not only a question of justice, but also a question of expediency. Before any Government goes to war it ought to be convinced, not only that it has just cause for war, but that there is something which renders war its duty; a duty compounded of two considerations —the first what the country may owe to others; the second what she owes to herself."—Canning: *Speech on the Spanish Question*, 1823.

character of the circumstances and by the international anarchism of Germany, and defended on the precedent of the novel methods adopted by America during her Civil War. The rival views were fully stated in the correspondence which passed during July between Sir Edward Grey and the American Ambassador in London. There was a great deal to be said for the British contention ; there was much to be said for the American counterplea. But obviously so grave a matter could not depend only on the argumentation of international lawyers and the Foreign Offices which employed them. The plain facts were that America was seriously affected by British policy in perhaps her most vital interest—her cotton export. She saw her trade with enemy countries and to some extent with neutral countries hampered, and this on a plea which was manifestly at variance with accepted international practice. It did not convince the Southern planter to be told that the North in the Civil War also had done something in the way of rewriting international law. America was on strong ground, and she knew it, and she pressed her claims with much force during the summer months. It was gradually becoming apparent that the British plan, though reasonable enough in itself, would have to be modified.

Cotton was the chief difficulty, and three steps were pressed upon the Government as a solution. The first was to declare cotton contraband. It was clear that it was a most vital munition of war, since it was practically essential to the manufacture of nitro-cellulose, the basis of most modern propellent charges. It was perfectly true that to declare cotton contraband would have given us no weapon to restrict its import to Germany beyond what we had at present, though we should have been able not only to stop but to confiscate cargoes. But, combined with the doctrine of continuous voyage, it would have given us an authority which America could recognize. She herself had made cotton contraband in her Civil War, and on the facts it was now a military munition like sulphur and saltpetre in former days. In the second place, it was suggested that neutral states might be put on rations, and that we might permit only a certain amount of cotton to be consigned to them, based on their average consumption for the three years before the war. Finally there was a proposal to purchase that portion of the American cotton crop which was normally exported to the enemy countries, and to hold it till after the war. The importance of the question was as great as its intricacy. On 28th June it was the foremost problem that we had to face in connection with our policy towards neutrals, and, since America was the munitioning ground of all the Allies, it vitally affected the whole Allied cause. The wheels of diplomacy move slowly, and the months passed without a solution. Happily the goodwill of the majority of the American people, and the genuine anxiety of Ministers on both sides of the Atlantic to reach an agreement, prevented the controversy reaching the stage of crisis.

In reviewing a year of war we look naturally to see what new military doctrines had justified themselves, what novel methods in tactics and strategy had appeared in the various theatres. We find nothing revolutionary, nothing at variance with the accepted practices of war. One German principle had been clearly justified, but by those who had reflected on the subject it had never been seriously denied. That doctrine was the crushing effect of artillery both against forts and field positions. The German practice of massed infantry attacks had nothing in itself to recommend it; when it succeeded it was only because of the artillery preparation which preceded it. It was less a device deliberately selected than a *concessio propter infirmitatem*, necessary to armies which had to absorb into their ranks, as the war went on, much inferior fighting material. Even as regards artillery the special German merit was not the tactical handling of it, but the ample supply. Heavy field pieces and machine guns in great quantities involve certain tactics, as inevitably as the length of reach of a boxer determines his method. The supreme achievement of the German Staff was that they saw precisely the part modern science could be made to play in modern warfare, and that they kept their eyes resolutely fixed on it. Since they were organized for war not only militarily but industrially, they could concentrate as a nation upon a single purpose in a way impossible to the freer civic organisms of their opponents. Germany made use of all her assets; her blow was weighted with her full national strength—that, in a sentence, was the gist of her excellence.

The Allies might claim that their theories of war had on the whole been justified whenever it had been possible to apply them. The attack in open order, and their high standard of individual rifle fire, provided good results wherever the enemy's guns allowed fighting at close quarters. Man for man, the average Frenchman, Russian, and Briton had demonstrated his equality with, if not his superiority to, the German soldier. It was not a question of courage, for the bravery of the German ranks could not be overpraised, but rather of dash, fortitude, stamina, and that indefinable thing which we may call temperamental predominance. This was conspicuously proved in bayonet work, in bomb-throwing, and especially in most daring and successful aerial reconnaissance. Wherever individual qualities were demanded there the Allies were conspicuous. Our fighting machine, too, so far as it concerned the human element, was at least as good as the German. It was only in material, in the scientific aids to war, that we were excelled, and then only in one class of weapon, which, however, happened to be the most vital.

The naval position was wholly in favour of the Allies. In all the seas of the world German merchantmen and German ships of war had disappeared. In the north-eastern corner of the Adriatic, Italy held the Austrian fleet; in the Ægean, the British and French fleets were operating against the Dardanelles. The sole German success, the Battle of Coronel, had been promptly redeemed by von Spee's destruction at the Falkland Islands. The German High Sea Fleet lay behind the shelter of the Frisian Islands. The Battle of the Bight of Heligoland showed that Britain could carry the war inside German territorial waters, and the one serious German raid had been checked and defeated in the battle of 24th January. The boasted German submarine campaign had effected nothing of a military purpose, except the withdrawal of the larger British battleships from the Dardanelles. Up to a date early in July it had sunk 98 British merchantmen—or 195 if we include trawlers—30 Allied ships, and less than 50 neutrals, and had thereby raised international difficulties for Germany which far outbalanced these trivial successes. The British losses by submarines were only about $1\frac{1}{4}$ per cent. of our total shipping, and the new risk did not raise insurance rates or affect in the slightest degree the nerve of our merchant seamen. The boasts of Count Reventlow were conclusively answered by Mr. Balfour in a letter to an American correspondent—a letter which stated with admirable clearness and justice the achievements of the British navy. He pointed out that in the past year it had performed all the functions of a fleet in war: it had driven the enemy's commerce from the sea, and protected its own; it had rendered the enemy's fleet impotent; it had made the sea transport of enemy troops impossible; it had transported its own troops at will; it had secured their supplies, and could, when necessary, assist in their operations.

The British Grand Fleet during the year was, like the country of the proverb, happy in that it had no history. Without any of the great battleships firing a shot it had fulfilled its task. Its potent inaction was not idleness. It was ready and anxious to meet its opponent as soon as he ventured forth. But till that day came it held the seas and waited, as Nelson's fleet for two years before Trafalgar watched the coasts of the enemy. How great a strain this duty involved is beyond a civilian's estimate. Day and night the great ships kept the sea, in the stormy winter months steaming without lights in black darkness, with the perpetual menace of mines and submarines around them. They were hidden from the nation's gaze No achievements filled the papers. There was nothing to relieve the tedium of their toil or key the spirit of their men to that high pitch which is the reward of war. In months of danger and heavy labour they had to endure something worse than the monotony of peace. Yet the Grand Fleet kept its health unimpaired, its nerves steady, its eagerness unabated. Such a moral achievement was not the least of the triumphs of the year, for he that ruleth his spirit is better than he that taketh a city.

A great war usually throws up a great soldier or statesman, but not necessarily at the beginning. England at various times in her history had been long in travail before she had produced a man Her Civil War was well advanced before it saw the advent of Cromwell and Montrose. The French Revolution was four years old before the star of Napoleon rose above the horizon, and the men who led the armies of France during those years were none of them in the first rank. Britain had to wait fourteen years for the coming of Wellington. The American Civil War was an exception, for almost from the start two leaders of the highest genius, Lee and Jackson, sprang full panoplied into fame, like Athene from the brain of Zeus. But the case of the North restored the rule. Lincoln had to work through a long succession of inferior generals, McClellan, McDowell, Burnside, Pope, Banks, and Hooker, before he found in Grant a competent soldier able to use effectively the vast resources of the Union. Unless a war is originated by a genius like Alexander or Charles XII., there must generally be a long interregnum till the nation finds the leader who possesses that " stellar and undiminishable " something which is greatness. How long had the Punic War to wait for Scipio, or the Roman Revolution for Julius Cæsar?

In modern warfare it would seem that the period of waiting must be longer, for modern warfare sunk the individual in the machine. Just as industrialism tended to turn the craftsman into a mere machine-tender, so the latest developments of war transformed the soldier into a kind of operative. Till the other day we were accustomed to speak of " fighting races "—of men like the tribesmen of the Indian frontier, or the Boers—whose life had given them a natural hardihood, an eye for country, quick senses, and great bodily endurance, and to contrast with them the products of urban civilization who were born with none of these gifts. But it looked as if we must revise our views. Our new war machine abolished, or at any rate greatly modified, the distinction between martial and non-martial peoples. The ideal soldier appeared to be the skilled mechanic, who won his fortitude partly from a high discipline and partly from confidence in his machine The noble savage with the spear had fallen before the lesser physique of civilization armed with a rifle. Now it would seem that the soldier, trained in the various branches of the military art, and full of valour and self-reliance, must yield to the pallid operative who could handle at a distance the levers and bolts of a great gun. In the same way modern warfare gave small chance for individual generalship. Surprises, night marches, ingenious feints were seldom possible. The conditions were rigidly prescribed, and could rarely be dominated and altered by the most fertile mind. The general had also become a machine-tender. The brains—the genius, if you will—were to be found in the construction of the machine, for its use was more or less a mechanical task. Some men would be more skilled in it than others, but the highest skill was not the same thing as generalship in the old sense. A Marlborough, a Cæsar, even a Napoleon, would beat ineffectual wings against the new barriers.

All this was true, and those who declaimed during this stage of the campaign against the absence of genius in generalship forgot that generalship, like other arts, needs the proper occasion. Supply will scarcely be forthcoming if the demand is nil. In former days war was three-fourths an art and one-fourth a science. Now it was at least three-fourths science, and the human element was circumscribed. . . . Yes, but not wholly, and not in the last resort. For a machine is not immortal. It may break down through internal weakness, or because it is confronted with a machine of equal strength. When that day came war would become an art once more, and individual generalship and individual fighting quality would recover their old pre-eminence.

The first year of the war revealed no superlative distinction in statesmanship in any of the belligerent countries. Statesmen of the higher type may be roughly divided into builders and governors. Since Napoleon the world had seen two constructive brains of the first order—Bismarck and Cavour,* and one governing mind not less great, that of Abraham Lincoln. The second decade of the twentieth century saw several men alive in Europe who seemed to have the essentials of the higher statesmanship. M. Venizelos, for example, had the talent of his famous countryman for making a small town into a great city, and under his lead a new Greece was emerging. But there were as yet few outstanding figures, though many of great respectability. Russia still suffered from her bureaucratic system, largely German in origin, which stifled true nationalism, and since the death of Stolypin she had had no political leader of the first quality. In Britain our system, as we have seen in an earlier chapter, discouraged administrative efficiency, and administrators cannot be easily improvised. Men of proved executive ability—such as some of our Imperial administrators—were too remote from common politics to be readily made use of. But the lack was most glaring in Germany. Bethmann-Hollweg, Jagow, and Helfferich were very ordinary folk; but they still wore the giant's mantle which had descended from the great days of Bismarck, and for a time it covered their insufficiencies. Perhaps the two strongest personalities in Europe were the Italian, Sonnino, and the Hungarian, Tisza. Both were men a little cold and rigid in temperament, but both had the steeliest kind of resolution. They saw their path clearly, and walked in it with undeviating steps.

A constructive statesman of the Bismarck type was scarcely needed in this crisis. Far-reaching policies had to be put aside for the moment, and Europe must live in the hour. But a governing statesman—the mind which can maintain its purpose undivided, which is an inspirer of fortitude in others, which in hectic moments keeps its judgment, and which has that potent and pervasive effect on the temper of a whole people which is what we mean by political genius—that, indeed, was clamorously required Such a one as Lincoln would, perhaps, have best filled the part. But by midsummer of 1915 there was no sign of a new Lincoln in any belligerent land.

It is not often that a country possesses at one and the same

* Cecil Rhodes was of the same type, but he wrought on a smaller scale and in the face of far fewer difficulties. I am speaking here of the statesman as man of action Statesmen who contented themselves with ventilating or inventing political dogmas were as common as peas.

time great soldiers and great civilian ministers. More often a Marlborough fights under the direction of a Godolphin, and rarely does a Chatham find a Wolfe and a Clive to do his bidding. The absence of great statesmen was not, however, atoned for by the presence of commanding figures in the field. By 28th June the new Napoleon had not come, not even perhaps a new Moltke. In military circles in Germany before 1914 the high commanders were frankly discussed. One heard often the names of Eichhorn, Einem, and Kluck; occasionally of Mackensen; and very especially of Falkenhayn, the Prussian Minister of War. In assessing German personalities we must remember that the machine was far greater than the individual. The praise belonged rather to those who had perfected the machine than to those who worked it. Hindenburg was for Germany the discovery of the first year of war, and by September he had become a popular idol. But it was difficult to detect in his handling of the campaign any transcendent military genius. He inspired enthusiasm among his troops, but the plans were not his, but those of the machine behind him, worked out by his brilliant Chief of Staff, Ludendorff, whose reputation was still confined to a narrow circle. Hindenburg's sledge-hammer blows at different parts of the Russian front were really predetermined by the nature of his weapon. For the rest, Germany produced a number of highly competent army commanders, of whom Mackensen was the most successful. If they could not be said to reach the first rank, it would be none the less foolish to underrate their work. To handle the machine might not demand great genius, but it required a high degree of expert training and a very cool head.

On the side of the Allies two figures still overtopped all others —General Joffre and the Grand Duke Nicholas. They were in a sense national dictators, possessing the confidence of their respective nations; and, since their wills could override all other wills, in them was focussed the government of France and Russia. They were men of a large simplicity; and each, in spite of very real intellectual limitations, had a gift for disentangling the essential from the less essential; for disregarding side-issues, and seeing losses in their true perspective. Above all, they had stout hearts. Both generalissimos were fortunate in having brilliant subordinates. The army group commanders—Alexeiev and Ivanov, Foch, Castelnau, and Dubail—had certainly no superiors in the German forces. The great figure of Foch was still imperfectly revealed to the world; but in failure and disappointment he was learning his trade, and preparing himself for the day when he should be called upon to control the war. In the British forces, though so far the high command had not had occasion to prove itself in major operations with armies on the grand scale, the reputations of Sir William Robertson and Sir Douglas Haig had conspicuously increased. One British soldier had by midsummer won a unique position Botha was so far the one clear conqueror, and in his difficult campaign he had shown not only true political wisdom but a high degree of technical military skill.

But the year which ended on 28th June had revealed a war less of the high commands than of subordinate leaders. Trench fighting and the importance of artillery combined to annul all major strategy, and put the main burden on the brigadiers, the battalion and company commanders, and even on the subalterns. There were many chances for individual gallantry, but few and rare were the occasions when officers, from subalterns to generals, could earn distinction by initiative or special military knowledge. In the stalemate in the West war was reduced to very primitive elements, and the *débâcle* in the East submerged human skill under a shower of shell. Such was the inevitable result of modern scientific war in its early phases. But there were compensations, and that very science, which depressed the human factor, contrived in its extreme developments to make it the more conspicuous. For a sphere where courage and brains found full scope we must look to the most expert warfare of all—the work of the submarine and airplane. There the possession of one kind of machine took a man out of the grip of the Machine, and set him adventuring in a free world, as in the old days of war. The doings of Max Horton, Holbrook, Boyle, Naismith, and Weddigen under the sea, and of Rhodes-Moorhouse, Warneford, and Garros in the air, ranked with the most brilliant individual enterprises of earlier campaigns.

CHAPTER XXXII.

THE ASIAN AND AFRICAN CAMPAIGNS.

October 1914–July 9, 1915.

Transcaucasia—The Mesopotamian Campaign—The Capture of Nasiriyeh and Kut—The Cameroons—The War in German South-West Africa—The Surrender of the Enemy.

THE outland campaigns during the spring and summer of 1915, with the exception of the Gallipoli expedition, were almost uniformly successful, but their success had as yet no bearing upon the main battlefield. In one, the German South-West African, victory was complete; in another, the Mesopotamian, the hard-won triumph of a small army was beginning to divert the minds of the British and Indian Governments from the duties of sound strategy. But this was for the future, and the chief interest of those extra-European wars lay in the proof of how closely knit was the modern world, and how the greater political problems had annihilated space and surmounted those barriers which nature had set up to demarcate peoples. While some of the Allies fought in the frozen bogs of Masurenland or among the deep snows of the Caucasus, others were engaged in scorching deserts or fever-haunted swamps. Britons in the Flanders trenches found their chief enemy in rain and floods; Britons in South-West Africa valued water more highly than gold. There was no extreme of cold and heat that on the same day was not endured by some part of the Allied forces. The campaign embraced all climates, landscapes, privations, pests, and terrors.

Let us look first at the Asian theatre. In Transcaucasia there is little to recount. The defeat at Sarikamish had broken utterly the cohesion of the Turkish army, and the Russian troops were engaged during the subsequent weeks in driving the remnants across the frontier. The chief sweeping movement was down the Choruk valley, whither, it will be remembered, the 1st Turkish Corps had retired after the disaster at Ardahan. One Russian column moved from Ardahan through the passes, while another, supported by vessels of the Black Sea Fleet, operated along the coast from Batum. By the end of March the whole frontier region was empty of the enemy. Farther south from Sarikamish there were a number of insignificant conflicts. Turkish stragglers united with the local professionals to form banditti, and this necessitated the kind of campaign familiar on our Indian frontier. Villages, the strongholds of the enemy, had to be cleared, and the brigands driven to the snowy hills. In all this there was no serious Turkish defensive, and presently the Turkish and Persian borders were as quiet as they were ever likely to be in a world-wide upheaval. The Russian commander made no attempt to advance to Erzerum, for Russia's object was merely to hold the gate. The vital blow at Turkey must come from another quarter.

In the Persian Gulf area the British force was at the beginning of the year securely entrenched on both sides of the Tigris at Kurna and Mezera, a strong position commanding the highway to the sea. The situation, however, was not without its anxieties. In spite of Turkey's rebuffs in Transcaucasia and her diversions towards the Suez Canal, she had sufficient troops left in the Bagdad command to outnumber gravely the small British army of one division on the Shatt-el-Arab. Early in January 1915 it was discovered that the Turks were occupying a strong position on the banks of a canal some eight miles north of Mezera, and on 20th January a reconnaissance was organized to ascertain their strength and dispositions. Supported by gunboats from the Tigris we shelled their camp, and drove them back with considerable casualties. In February a further brigade arrived from India. The enemy next appeared near Ahwaz, on the Karun River, the scene of an engagement between Sir James Outram and the Persians during the short war of 1857. There we had placed a small garrison to protect the pipe line of the Anglo-Persian Oil Company. West of Ahwaz a Turkish force of three regiments and a number of Arab tribesmen were reported, and on 3rd March we made an attempt to reconnoitre this position. The enemy was discovered in strength, the small British expedition was in imminent danger of being cut off, and retirement was not effected without heavy fighting. The sight of the red and white flags of the Arabs, whom we had hoped for as allies in breaking the Turkish rule, was disquieting, and it presently appeared that the enemy was clustering in strength round our whole area of occupation. On the day following the operations near Ahwaz, our cavalry, reconnoitring towards Nakaila, twenty-five miles north-west of Basra, had a sharp encounter with mounted Turks. Another brigade was demanded from India, and presently a second division—the 12th—was constituted in the Mesopotamian army.

A word must be said at this point on the Indian military system. For some years before the war there had been in India a strong movement towards economy, and one result had been a reduction of the military establishments. The number of divisions available for immediate mobilization was reduced from nine to seven, the number of field guns to the division was cut down, and of heavy pieces there were none. This economy was felt nowhere more strongly than in the medical establishments; their standard had always been below that of the British army, and now even that modest standard was suffered to decline. No provision had been made for India's co-operation with the Home Government in the event of war. Sir Douglas Haig, when Chief of the Indian Staff in 1911, had endeavoured to remedy this, and prepared a memorandum to deal with such a contingency, but he could not obtain the approval of the Viceroy, Lord Hardinge. On the outbreak of hostilities India was therefore unready, and a series of peremptory requests from Britain for immediate help—in France, Egypt, East Africa, Mesopotamia—had to be met out of depleted resources and by means of a most imperfect organization. Moreover, there was a perpetual difficulty as to which was the governing authority, whether the British War Office or the Indian Commander-in-Chief, London or Simla, the British Cabinet or the Indian Viceroy. In such circumstances it was not easy to equip expeditionary forces at all, it was inevitable that the subsidiary services should be faulty, and it was not improbable that owing to the overlapping authorities the place of the operations in the main strategy of the war would be imperfectly considered.

On 9th April Lieutenant-General Sir John Nixon arrived at Basra and took command of the Mesopotamian corps, which contained the 6th Division, under General Townshend, and the 12th Division, under General Gorringe. In Nixon's instructions from the Indian Commander-in-Chief was one significant sentence. He was asked to submit plans for "effective occupation of the Basra vilayet," and for "a subsequent advance on Bagdad." Now the policy of Britain in Mesopotamia had hitherto been purely defensive, and marked by almost excessive caution. The occupation of the Basra vilayet, which extended to within a few miles of Kut and included both Nasiriyeh and Amara, might have been justified as a necessary precaution for the defence of Basra, the delta, and the pipe line; but an advance to Bagdad involved a bold offensive and a wholly different strategic plan. Yet here we had the Indian Government, which was directly responsible for the supply and organization of the troops, already turning its eyes to ambitious objectives.

Nixon's arrival synchronized with a comprehensive Turkish attack. Three places—Kurna, Ahwaz, and Shaiba, a few miles west of Basra—were selected for the assault. On 11th and 12th April Kurna was bombarded at long range, but beyond the destruction by a floating mine of one of the Tigris bridges, no damage was done, and the attack was not pressed home. The bombardment of Ahwaz was no more effective, and nothing was seen of the enemy but clouds of horsemen. Kurna and Ahwaz were only feints, and the real blow was directed against Shaiba and the possession of Basra. The action began on 12th April, and lasted for three days, and the invading forces were mainly regulars of the Bagdad Corps. The British position around Basra was protected on the east by the river, so the Turkish assault was directed from north, west, and south. Early in the morning, under cover of a heavy artillery preparation, the Turkish infantry advanced from three sides, and when their gun fire slackened, set to work to dig themselves in. The attack was resumed in the afternoon from the south, where we succeeded in beating it back. During the night there was a steady fire from rifles and machine guns, and in the morning we found the Turks in possession of some houses and rising ground to the north of us, from which it was imperative that we should oust them. Our advance was completely successful, and a simultaneous counter-attack by the Turks from the west was easily repulsed, with the loss of several hundred prisoners.

That afternoon a new concentration of Turkish troops was observed to the south, where a strong position had been entrenched at Barjisiyah, some four miles from the British lines. On the morning of 14th April we moved in force against these entrenchments, which contained the bulk of the enemy army. We carried their advanced position, and in the afternoon swept them from their main trenches in spite of a heavy machine-gun and rifle fire. A final charge with the bayonet put the whole force to flight. As usually happened, the routed Turks were set upon by their former Arab allies, who completed what the British had begun. This victory meant the end of a serious Turkish offensive for the moment. The Turkish general fell back to Nakaila, but he could not stay there, and we occupied the place on the 17th. By the 20th the enemy was more than a hundred miles from Basra. On the river twelve of his boats were either captured or sunk. April is the season of floods in Mesopotamia, and our pursuit was much impeded by the swollen waters. The reconnoitring parties whom we dispatched found no sign of the enemy in all the countryside except abandoned positions and derelict stores.

During May Gorringe was sent to Ahwaz and the Karun river to shepherd the Turkish forces there towards Bisaitun, while Townshend was to proceed north of the river to Amara, the seat of the provincial Turkish administration, in the hope that he would reach the place before the Turks retiring in front of Gorringe, and so cut off their retreat. The joint operation was carried out with complete success. Of orthodox water transport there was little, but every kind of craft was brought into requisition, gunboats were improvised, and on 3rd June Amara yielded to an advance party of twenty-two soldiers and sailors. Two days later the Turkish division which Gorringe was driving before him arrived, its vanguard was captured, and the rest dispersed in a flight to the north.

Basra is seventy miles from the sea, Kurna fifty miles from Basra, and Amara ninety miles up the Tigris from Kurna. To secure the vilayet, Nixon resolved that he must reach Kut, 150 miles up river from Amara. There was risk in the attempt, for at each step he was dragging a lengthening chain of communications, the medical equipment was scarcely adequate for a single division, and there was no hope of receiving the additional transport asked for before the middle of the following year. The difficulties of the land were very great. The floods, which began in February, created huge lagoons on both sides of the river, and as these shrank there remained isolated meres and large areas of swamp. Old irrigation canals, often deep and wide, ran out from the river, and complicated the problem of transport. The power of the sun in the summer months was not the least of our trials. At dawn it might be 110° F., and in the afternoon well over 120°, and the baked sands retained the heat so that night brought little coolness. Shade there was none. A blinding glare was reflected from yellow earth and blue water. But Nixon possessed for the operations men who had served an apprenticeship to the Indian heats, and he considered that the advance to Kut was within his power, as it was certainly within his instructions. The possession of Amara, whence ran the direct road to Ahwaz, secured his right flank and the pipe line. The possession of Kut would give him a natural halting-place, and also safeguard his left wing, for from the Tigris at that point ran the Shatt-el-Hai to the Euphrates at Nasiriyeh, which gave a chance for an attack on the British left rear.

The first step must be the occupation of Nasiriyeh, and thither early in July Gorringe marched with the 12th Division from Kurna. All the country between the two rivers was flood and marsh, through which ran many old channels, and the expedition forced its way to the Euphrates by way of the Hamar Lake. That amphibious journey, now wading, now embarked in boats, now making portages —through a maze of creeks and lagoons and thick date groves under a pitiless sky and amid swarms of flies—must rank as one of the most uncomfortable ever undertaken by British troops. We found the entrance to the main stream of the Euphrates mined and barricaded, but we succeeded in dislodging the enemy from the river bank and forcing him back upon Nasiriyeh. On 24th July we drove in the main Turkish position in front of that town. The Turks were astride the river, and had prepared strong entrenchments defended with barbed wire. By eleven o'clock they were broken, and our gunboats pushed on and shelled Nasiriyeh, while the main enemy force retreated twenty-five miles in the direction of Kut. Next morning we occupied the town, which as the old capital of the Mustafik tribe of Arabs had a political importance in addition to its strategical situation. The vital junction of the Shatt-el-Hai and the Euphrates was in our hands.

Kut remained, and early in August Nixon gave orders for an advance by Townshend's 6th Division up the Tigris. Along that river of endless twists and turnings the progress of troops must be slow. Riverine marshes had to be crossed or circumvented, and canals had to be bridged. The enemy offered no serious opposition. He was content to wait for us some seven miles downstream from Kut, on a front extending on both sides of the Tigris for a distance of about six miles. His troops were nearly 10,000 men, regulars of the Bagdad Corps, and he had the usual motley following of mounted Arab tribesmen, whose conduct depended upon which way the battle went. On 14th September Townshend reached Sheikh Saad, and on the 15th he had forced the strong Turkish position at Abu Rumanneh. On the 28th he was in action with the main enemy force at Kut. The Turkish left, cleverly

THE MESOPOTAMIAN CAMPAIGN.

posted between two marshes, was turned by an enveloping movement, and their centre at the same time was broken by a frontal attack. At dawn on the 29th the sun rising through the haze of the riverside revealed an empty battlefield. The enemy had retired by road and river towards Bagdad. Our cavalry were loosed, and entered Kut, a native town of some 6,000 inhabitants, with a large trade in grain and liquorice. They pushed on over the solid plain, for between Kut and Bagdad the marshes cease, while our gunboats led the pursuit upstream, followed by Townshend with an infantry brigade in steamers. One of our airplanes succeeded in dropping bombs on the rearguard of the Turkish flotilla. The pursuit continued for fifty miles as far as Aziziyeh. The result of the day was very large captures of prisoners, two thousand and more, representing nearly a quarter of the Turkish command.

The taking of Kut marked the limit of a defensive campaign in Mesopotamia. The labours of the arduous summer months had been amply successful. "I do not think," said Mr. Asquith in the following November, "that in the whole course of the war there has been a series of operations more carefully contrived, more brilliantly conducted, and with a better prospect of final success." The tribute was deserved, but it was not wholly accurate. The campaign had not been carefully contrived; it had been a magnificent gamble against odds, and audacity had won. Now its purpose had been achieved, the whole Basra vilayet was ours, and every reason of prudence was in favour of calling a halt. But it is one of the penalties of a dashing success that it awakens a rash spirit in its promoters, and the defensive was presently to slip into the offensive. Memories of the reconquest of the Sudan began to recur to men in authority. There there had been the same advance simultaneously by land and water, the same strip of green between deserts on either side, the same desire to put a limit to the advance, the same eternal shifting of the limit a little farther on. The Sudan wars did not stop till Khartum fell, and it looked as if the Mesopotamia campaign must lead sooner or later to an assault on Bagdad. For through that city ran the channel of German communications with the Indian frontier. Its possession, too, by the Turks meant that the ancient capital and one of the most sacred cities of Islam was under Germany's influence. More than Constantinople it cast its spell over the Moslem world. The golden minarets of the great Shiah tombs, which catch from far off on the plain the traveller's eye, had a compelling sanctity greater than St. Sophia. Moreover, of all the Turkish possessions it was knit least closely to the centre on the Bosphorus. Till the coming of Midhat Pasha the Bagdad vilayet had been almost independent. The inhabitants looked on the speech and faith and learning of Stamboul as bastard, and preserved a vigorous provincialism. For the orthodox Turk, whether soldier or civilian, to be sent to Bagdad was to be sent into exile. Of all Turkey's provinces it seemed that Mesopotamia was the most easily detachable. Should the general situation clamour for some dramatic or romantic success the lure of Bagdad might prove too strong for British discretion.

The African theatre of war during the first half of 1915 had little of interest except in the extreme south-west, where Botha was slowly and patiently forcing his way to the German capital. In Egypt, after the fiasco of the Canal attack in February, there were only affairs of outposts, till on 22nd March another attempt was made to reach the Canal. An enemy force, mainly infantry with guns, but including a few cavalry squadrons, was located near El Kubri, in the neighbourhood of Suez. Shots were exchanged, and the Turks retired to a point eight miles from the Canal. Next day the British, under Lieutenant-General Sir George Younghusband, fell upon their camp and drove them seventy miles inside the desert. These, however, were minor incidents: it was clear that the Turkish army destined for the invasion of the Canal was thoroughly impotent and disheartened; and Egypt was used as a base for our Dardanelles operations without any anxiety as to its eastern frontiers.

In October 1914 we left the Germans in the Cameroons reduced to defensive warfare in a difficult hinterland. The Allies were not slow to push their advantage. Presently two columns of the Anglo-French force, under Brigadier-General Dobell, were moving along the two lines of railway which run from Duala to the interior. Edea, a point on the railway and the Sanaga River some fifty miles from Duala, was the first object of attack, and it was arranged that it should be assailed both by parties moving on the railway and by parties ascending the river in boats. The march was difficult, moving through dense forests and much harassed by snipers; but there was no resistance in the town itself, which was occupied on 26th October. The enemy retired to Yaunde, a station far up on the interior plateau. Six weeks later the Germans made an effort to regain Edea, but were beaten back with a loss of twenty Europeans and fifty-four natives. There followed an Allied advance in three columns against Yaunde, in which we fought two little battles on 27th and 28th January 1915, and seized the post of Bersona. Colonel Mayer with a French detachment crossed the river Kele, and a British column a little farther north took the bridge of Ngua. Meanwhile north of Duala, on the other railway line, good progress had been made. During December we seized Nkongsamba and Baré, the latter a station six miles north of the railhead, and this gave us the whole of the northern line.

In the early spring, therefore, we held both the railways running up from the coast, and columns were entering the country from north, east, and south, from Nigeria and the Chad territory and French Equatoria. The main forces of the enemy were believed to be on the head-waters of the Benue in the high country around Ngaundere. But there were other forces, notably one which operated near the coast just beyond the railheads of the two lines, and there were a number of fortified posts in the southern district towards the French Equatorial border. Hence the campaign resolved itself into several distinct expeditions, directed to the "rounding up" of the various sections of the enemy. The railways had to be closely watched, for on them depended the existence of our central army. The rainy season soon began, and the dripping savannahs and the dank forests were as formidable a barrier as German machine guns. In May the main Allied force under General Dobell was operating along the two railway lines. A French column under Colonel Mayer, starting from Edea, captured Eseka on 11th May, after some difficult forest fighting, where the Germans showed great skill in entrenching themselves at the river crossings. A fortnight later, on 29th May, the same column had transferred itself to the northern railway, and driven the enemy from Njok to the north-west of that line. Late in the same month the southern columns fought actions at Monso and Besam, and on 25th June occupied the important post of Lome. The French had now taken practically all the country in the south up to their old boundary. The torrential rains of July impeded further movements on this side, and the centre of interest shifted to the higher country towards the Nigerian border.

The first British incursions from Nigeria had been unhappily fated, our men with considerable losses having been driven from Garua and Nsanakong. In April the post of Gurin inside the Nigerian border was attacked by German troops from the Garua garrison, but the little fort held out for seven hours, and finally beat off the enemy. Next day the Yola column arrived at Gurin, having marched sixty-two miles in twenty-two hours. This column, under Colonel F. H. G. Cunliffe, composed of men of the West African Frontier Force, marched upon Garua, and prepared to reduce the position. It was assisted by a French column which had moved westward from the north-eastern border. On 11th June Garua surrendered unconditionally. This cleared the northern part of the colony except for one small German post which occupied a hill at Mora. The Allied columns then swept south, and on 29th June occupied Ngaundere, the most important German station in the central Cameroons. The enemy retreated south-west towards Tibati, while the Allies followed, and on 11th June consolidated their position by taking the post of Tingr, 3,700 feet up on the plateau, and some seventy miles south-west of Ngaundere. The German forces had now been penned into the comparatively small area of hilly country between Tibati and the head-waters of the Sanaga River. On all four sides the Allied columns were closing in upon them.

In East Africa, the failure in November at Tanga was repeated in January 1915 at Jassin, a small advanced post which was held inside German territory north of the former town. On 18th January the place was attacked by a strong enemy force, and next day the little garrison surrendered. This disaster compelled a withdrawal of our outlying posts in that region, and the Germans were justified in claiming that their East African territory was completely free from the enemy, while they occupied several posts inside the British borders. On 26th February we announced that from midnight on the 28th the 300 miles of the coast of German East Africa would be blockaded, four days being allowed for the departure of neutral vessels. In April Major-General M. J. Tighe, of the Indian Army, was appointed to the command of the British East African forces. The summer campaign was mainly concerned with small expeditions on the shores of Victoria Nyanza and on the borders of Nyassaland and North-Eastern Rhodesia. But the early days of July saw the end of the German cruiser, the *Königsberg*. Ever since the close of October she had been sheltering some distance up the Rufiji River, in a place too shallow for the ordinary ship to approach. When we discovered her we sank a collier at the mouth of the river, and so prevented her escape to open sea. Early in June Vice-Admiral King Hall, Commander-in-Chief of the Cape station, brought out two river monitors, the *Severn* and the *Mersey*. Our aircraft located the exact position of the *Königsberg*, which was surrounded by dense jungle and forest. On the morning of

6th July the monitors entered the river and opened fire. The crew of the *Königsberg* had made their position a strong one by means of shore batteries which commanded the windings of the river, and look-out towers with wireless apparatus, which gave them the range of any vessel attacking. Owing to the thick jungle a direct sight of the enemy was impossible, and we had to work by indirect fire with airplanes spotting for the guns. The attack was resumed on 11th July, when the vessel was completely destroyed, largely as a result of the brilliant work of our airmen. The fate of this German cruiser, marooned for months far from the fresh seas among rotting swamps and jungles, is surely one of the strangest in the history of naval war.

When Botha declared war against German South-West Africa it was generally believed that his campaign would not be concluded before the great struggle in Europe had reached a decision. The strength of the Germans, and their ample provision of artillery, the immense distances to be covered, and the difficulties of attaining a decisive result in a country so strongly fortified by nature, inclined most men to the belief that the war would soon resolve itself into a stalemate and a siege. Such a view underrated the energy and the skill of the South African generals. So soon as the rebellion within Union territories had been finally crushed, Botha set himself to carry out an admirable strategical plan against the German defence. But, first, the last embers of the rebellion had to be extinguished. Moving along the Orange River, a body under Maritz and Kemp gained two small successes, surprising two posts held by the 8th Mounted Rifles. The arrival of reinforcements obliged them to abandon their prisoners and hastily retire. On January 12, 1915, Raman's Drift was retaken by Colonel Bouwer, which gave the Union force the entire line of the Orange, and penned the hostile remnants into the angle formed by the river and the German frontier. On 24th January the rebels, dispirited and half starving, made their last sally. Led by Maritz and Kemp, and about 1,200 strong, they attacked Van Deventer at Upington, but they were easily repulsed. Next day the end came. The leaders offered to surrender unconditionally. On 3rd February Kemp and his commando—43 officers and 486 men, including the prophet Van Rensburg—surrendered at Upington, and some of Maritz's band followed suit at Kakamas. Maritz himself was not among them. Knowing that for him there would be no mercy, he fled back to German territory.

The position in January, when the main campaign against South-West Africa began, was as follows: We held Walfisch Bay and its surroundings, and on 14th January we seized without trouble the adjoining German port of Swakopmund, the terminus of the line to Windhoek and of the line to Tsumab and Grootfontein, in the north of the colony. We had held since September Luderitz Bay (or Angra Pequeña)—the terminus of the southern line which ran to Windhoek by Keetmanshoop. Our capture of Schuit Drift and Raman's Drift gave us the fords of the Orange. We therefore held all the gates of the German colony, and our command of the sea made us free to use them. Botha's plan of campaign was an enveloping movement against Windhoek, and the forces at his disposal were divided into two main armies. The Northern, under his own command, was to move from Swakopmund as a base along the railway to Windhoek. The Southern, under General Smuts, was divided into three separate columns. The first, under Sir Duncan Mackenzie, was directed to move east along the railway from Luderitz Bay. The second, under Van Deventer, was to move north along the line running from Warmbad to Keetmanshoop; while the third, under Colonel Berrange, was to start from Kimberley, and, crossing Bechuanaland, invade the colony from the east. All three columns were to concentrate at Keetmanshoop, whence, under Smuts, they would move northwards to join Botha. The plan was skilfully devised, for, if successful, it meant the shepherding of the German forces away from modern communications into the desert country of the eastern frontier, where the waterless sands of the Kalahari barred all escape.

Let us follow first the doings of the Northern army. During January the various bases were well provisioned, and from Swakopmund a railway was laid along the coast to Walfisch Bay, and sea walls built to facilitate landing. Botha reached Swakopmund on 9th February, and on the 22nd his army began to move. At first its progress was slow. Two German posts were seized without loss, and then nearly a month was spent in reconnoitring the enemy's strength and preparing an advanced base. On 19th March the business of clearing the railway was taken in hand. That evening two mounted brigades left our post of Husab. The left column of the second brigade, under Colonel Celliers, had orders to cut the railway line between Jakalswater and Sphinx, and then, having hampered the movements of any reinforcements coming from Windhoek, to attack Jakalswater itself. The right column, under Colonel Alberts, was to seize Pforte, another station on the line. The first brigade, commanded by Colonel Brits, and accompanied by Botha himself, was to attack Riet, an important point south of the railway, while the Bloemhof commando, operating on its flank, was directed to seize the hill of Schwarze Kopje. The attack was timed for dawn on the 20th. Celliers, having cut the line and captured a train laden with supplies, moved against the German position at Jakalswater. There, however, he found the enemy strongly entrenched, and his attack failed in its main object, though it prevented assistance being sent to Pforte. At the latter place Alberts was wholly successful, and that afternoon received the surrender of the garrison—210 men and four guns. The main objective of the movement, however, was Riet, where the German position was very strong. Its right rested on the Swakop stream, its left on the foothills of the Langer Heinrichberg, while its guns, skilfully placed, commanded the main road and the river. In our attack the gunners of the Transvaal Horse Artillery did admirable work, and so stoutly was it pressed that by the evening the enemy was driven out in disorder. The completeness of our success was marred only by the failure of the Bloemhof commando to reach its allotted place on the Schwarze Kopje, which would have enabled us to cut off the enemy's retreat. During April the advance proceeded steadily. Colonel Skinner with the Kimberley regiment protected the railway behind us, and our control of the Tsumab line as far as Trek-kopje prevented any serious operations against our left flank and rear. In the first days of May Botha with the main army was at Kubas, and on the 5th, after a march of thirty-five miles, the junction of Karibib was reached and occupied. Another twenty miles took the army to Johann Albrechtshohe, and a further ten to Wilhelmsthal. South of the railway ran the main road between Windhoek and the coast, and along this, too, our troops advanced. By this time all serious resistance was over for the Northern army.

We turn now to the doings of General Smuts's army in the south The heaviest task fell to Van Deventer, moving north from the Orange. He came into touch with the enemy at Nakob, and early in March he occupied Ukamas and other posts in that region. Ten miles north of Ukamas he seized the German camp at Nabas, with large quantities of stores, and thirty miles on occupied Platbeen. On 3rd April his left wing occupied the railway terminus of Warmbad, and in the following week he penetrated nearly a hundred miles north of it. On 11th April Smuts met Van Deventer at Kalkfontein, and arranged to drive the enemy out of the Karas Mountains, which gave them an awkward position on the flanks of our advance. The movement was made in three columns and was completely successful, the mountains were cleared, and on 17th April Van Deventer entered Seeheim, the junction of the lines from Warmbad and from Luderitz Bay. The Germans abandoned the place in such haste that they had no time to destroy the bridge across the Great Fish River. Colonel Berrange's column, which entered the colony from the east, had by 19th March reached the borders, and was in the neighbourhood of Rietfontein.* On 1st April he captured an entrenched position at Hasuur, fifteen miles from the latter town. From there he fought his way westward, with constant skirmishes, to his appointed meeting-place with Van Deventer. The two forces met a little to the east of Keetmanshoop, in the third week of April. The combined column then advanced on Keetmanshoop, which surrendered without fighting on 20th April. The place, which is 170 miles from Warmbad and 195 miles from Luderitz Bay, was the business capital of German Namaqualand, and its possession was highly advantageous. Smuts made it his headquarters, and waited there for Mackenzie's force, which was moving inwards from Luderitz Bay.

Mackenzie had to begin by clearing the immediate neighbourhood of Luderitz Bay. Presently he seized Garub, seventy miles up the line, and advanced towards the hills which mark the end of the coastal desert. He occupied Aus, twenty miles farther on, where the Germans held a strongly fortified pass, from which they retired without a blow. At Aus Mackenzie's column was clear of the worst desert region. He left the railway, took Bethany, and struck north-east in the direction of Gibeon, a station on the line between Keetmanshoop and Windhoek. Entering Beersheba without opposition, he reached the railway on 24th April at Aritetis, a small station seventy miles north of Keetmanshoop and forty south of Gibeon. Mackenzie was now co-operating directly with the main movement of Smuts from Keetmanshoop, and the retreating Germans were between the two forces. Van Deventer

---

* His transport problem was the most difficult of all. From Kimberley to Kuruman (140 miles) the transport was by donkeys, and after that by oxen. The whole line of communications was about 600 miles, and we may guess at the difficulties of the 400 odd miles served by oxen only, including one stretch of 111 miles without a drop of water. Ox transport could not, of course, keep up with the columns, so the army was fed by a fleet of motor cars operating from the end of the line. At times the gap which the cars filled was over 40 miles. The whole affair was a very remarkable transport feat. After Berrange joined Van Deventer and Mackenzie, the eastern route was closed, and the whole Southern army was then supplied from Luderitz Bay.

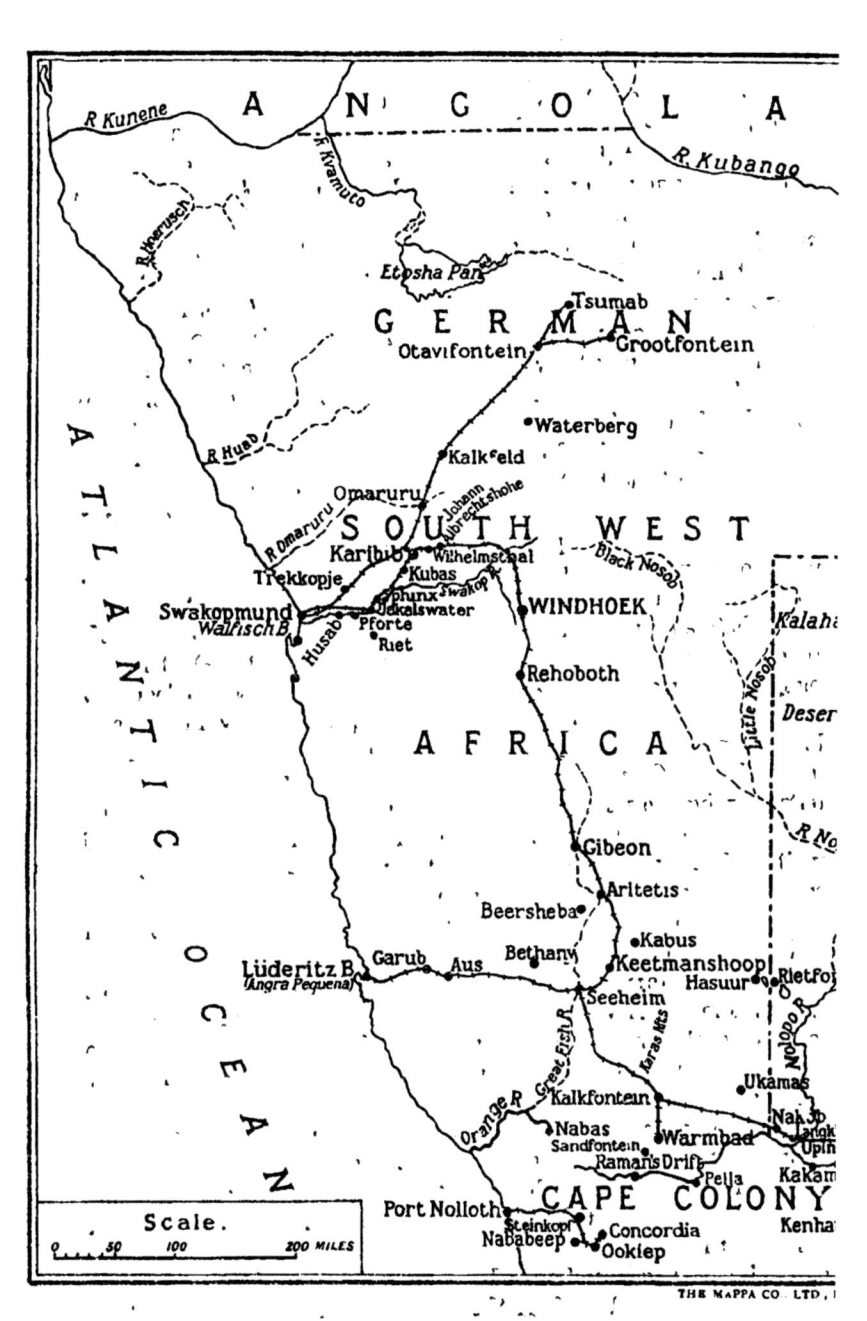

THE CAMPAIGN IN SOUTH-WEST AFRICA.

pushing from the south, came into touch with the enemy at Kabus, and after an indecisive engagement the Germans succeeded in reaching Gibeon, whence, as Mackenzie learned, they proposed to reach Windhoek by train. He sent out a small party to cut the line north of Gibeon, while the 9th Mounted Brigade went forward to engage the enemy. At first the Germans were successful, but on 28th April our main force came up and inflicted on them a serious defeat. We took their two field guns, most of their transport, and some 200 prisoners, and released our own men who had fallen into their hands. We pursued them for twenty miles, and only the rocky and difficult country prevented their complete annihilation.

The circle of steel was now closing in upon Windhoek. By the 1st of May all the German colony south of Gibeon was in British hands, and Botha was threatening the capital from the west. On 10th May he was informed that Windhoek was prepared to surrender. With a small escort he reached the place, where he was met by the burgomaster, and terms of capitulation were arranged, and on the 12th at noon his army entered the town. In it were 3,000 Europeans and 12,000 natives. The German troops had withdrawn to Grootfontein, in the north-east of the colony, which, it was declared, was now the capital. The wireless station was found intact, and with its capture Germany had lost all her stations outside Europe. After the entry of the troops under General Myburgh, a proclamation by Botha was read in Dutch, English, and German, which placed the conquered territories under martial law, and drew attention to the futility of further resistance.

The German forces at Grootfontein had a position in which they could not hope to stand, and from which there was no obvious retreat. The war had now resolved itself into a "rounding-up" expedition, and some of the Union forces could be dispensed with. Accordingly, in May, Smuts sent home a considerable part of his southern command. A few small actions were fought to the east of the capital by Colonel Mentz and General Manie Botha, when a considerable number of prisoners were taken, with few British casualties. Early in June the advance began up the northern line. The station of Omaruru was occupied, eighty miles from Windhoek, and a few days later Botha was at Kalkfeld. The first objective was the junction of Otavifontein, where the northern railway forks, one branch going north to Tsumab and the other north-east to Grootfontein. Against this position the Union forces advanced in three columns. To the left went General Manie Botha with the Mounted Free State Brigade. To the right General

Lukin marched with the 6th Mounted Brigade, composed of the South African Mounted Rifles. In the centre, along the railway line, moved Botha and the Headquarters Staff. Otavifontein was taken on the morning of 2nd July, with few British casualties. The chief part was played by General Manie Botha, who in sixteen hours marched forty-two miles without a halt through the most difficult bush country. Lukin's flanking column covered forty-eight miles in twenty hours under the same conditions.

The fight at Otavifontein was the last serious German stand. The Union forces now moved towards Tsumab, Colonel Myburgh on the right advancing between the two railway lines, and General Brits making a big westerly detour towards the great Etosha Pan. Brits's aim was to prevent the enemy retreating over the Angola borders. His detour involved a march of 200 miles, and it effected its purpose. Meanwhile Myburgh's force, which was the operative part, moved laboriously over the sandy Waterberg plateau, where the mid-winter cold was bitter, and on 4th July came into contact with a force of 500 Germans, about sixteen miles south of Tsumab. The Germans made only a slight resistance, and left many prisoners in our hands. The end was now in sight. Dr. Seitz, the German Governor, opened communications with Botha. At two o'clock on the morning of 9th July an unconditional surrender was agreed to. Botha could afford to be generous, for his conquest was complete. The numbers surrendering were officially reported as 204 officers and 3,293 of other ranks, while 37 field guns and 22 machine guns were captured. About 1,500 Germans were already prisoners in our hands. Three hundred thousand square miles of territory had been conquered at a less cost than that of a minor action in the European theatre. British and Dutch had fought side by side with equal valour. The Boer commandos, with no particular uniforms and the loosest formation, showed all their old skill in desert campaigning. General Smuts's words were justified: " Not only is this success a notable military achievement, and a remarkable triumph over very great physical climatic and geographical difficulties. It is more than that, in that it marks in a manner which history will record for all time the first achievement of the united South African nation, in which both races have combined all their best and most virile characteristics, and have lent themselves resolutely, often at the cost of much personal sacrifice, to overcome extraordinary difficulties and dangers in order to attain an important national object."

CHAPTER XXXIII.

THE ABANDONMENT OF WARSAW.
June 22–August 5, 1915.

Germany exploits her Success—The Crushing of the Warsaw Salient—The Advance of Mackensen and Linsingen—The Advance of Gallwitz—Comparison with Napoleon's Invasion—Prince Leopold enters Warsaw.

On the 1st day of July, when Lemberg had fallen, the Emperor met Hindenburg, Ludendorff, and Falkenhayn at Posen. The scene of the meeting was the new and staring royal castle, built in the heavy modern German style that aped the Roman, which frowns over the sluggish Warta and the ancient Polish city. The plans discussed were as grandiose as the environment. We can picture the Emperor, his spirits high at Mackensen's success, and his fancy inflamed with dreams of an entry into Warsaw as conqueror and deliverer, declaring that the moment had come for that annihilating blow which would establish for ever the dominance of German arms. The conditions were, indeed, fortunate for an army that possessed so mighty an engine of artillery and prided itself on its desperate impulse in attack. The weakness of the whole Russian position in Poland had now revealed itself. It was a salient, and a precarious salient. It depended upon the integrity of the two long railway lines which connected Warsaw with Petrograd, Moscow, and Kiev. In front of each of these lines lay the enemy—from Mlawa to Shavli in the north, from Sandomirz to the Dniester in the south. At the apex stood Warsaw, the capital of Russian Poland, and the key of the Vistula. The German armies were already pressing northward against the southern line. It was now Hindenburg's business to balance this movement by a descent from East Prussia upon the northern sector. Mathematical calculations would again be vindicated. What had happened on the Donajetz, the Wisloka, and the San would happen on the Narev, the Niemen, and the Bug. Once the railways were cut Warsaw would fall, the troops in the point of the salient would be isolated, and it would be strange if they could extricate themselves from such a trap.

But Hindenburg and Ludendorff aimed at more than the conquest of a capital or a river line or the occupation of a few more thousand square miles of Polish ground. Their business was to shatter the Russian armies. To this end they fell back upon the favourite German enveloping strategy. The army of the Niemen had overrun Courland as far as the Windawa, and was within measurable distance of Riga. If this force struck strongly it might hack its way south, master Kovno and Vilna, and cut the Petrograd line far to the eastward. Then the Russians in the salient would be taken both in flank and rear. Squeezed between the enemy on north and south, the Bug would be no halting-place, nor would any stand be possible in the Pripet marshes. A greater Sedan would follow, and the remnants that escaped to the line of the Beresina would be but a fraction of the force which in April had looked for a triumphant summer. The scheme was not overconfident. Germany had behind her all the advantages of speedy transport. Her shell supplies were still enormous, she had lost few guns, and the gaps in her ranks had been filled up from the reserves. Reinforcements were necessary for the great movement, and they could be got by drafts from the still stagnant Western front. The Austro-Hungarian armies were, indeed, fatigued and demoralized, but the operative part of the new plan would be Germany's, and her victorious troops were still far from the limit of their strength. The forces which faced Russia after Lemberg were more formidable than those which had begun the advance in the early days of May.

This plan was undoubtedly a sound one, and was the only means by which that decisive military victory could be won for which Ludendorff longed. So far Germany had done brilliantly, but she had not shattered Russia's strength in the field. To cut off the Polish salient and master Warsaw would not bring about that result. But to bite in far behind from the northern flank, where alone there was freedom of movement, would prevent a repetition of the Galician retreat, and compel a wholesale surrender not of territory but of armies. Had Russia been the only enemy, Hindenburg and Ludendorff would beyond cavil have been right. But Falkenhayn differed, and he won his way. He believed that in a month or two the Western front would flare up into fierce life; therefore he dared not borrow too much from it, and soon, he anticipated, he would be forced to lend. To strike at once for Kovno and Vilna was too ambitious a project for Germany's frugal resources, and might well lead to a second Marne. He resolved to be content with a limited objective—to bend the armies of the south northward and the armies of the north southward, and so put an end for good to the Polish salient.

Certain adjustments were accordingly made in the German line of battle. Beginning from the left, the Niemen Army (Otto von Below) was to move steadily in Courland against an enemy weakened by the transfer of troops to the south; the X. Army (Eichhorn), the VIII. Army (Scholtz), and the new XII. Army (Gallwitz) were to press down on the line of the Bobr and the Narev; the IX. Army (Prince Leopold of Bavaria) at the point of the salient would make no serious attack, for it would be confronted with the outer defences of Warsaw. South of it Woyrsch would attempt the crossing of the Vistula. To the right of Woyrsch considerable changes were made. The Austro-Hungarian I. Army was moved east to the neighbourhood of Sokal, and the order was now—Woyrsch: the Austro-Hungarian IV. Army; the German XI. Army; the new Bug Army (Linsingen), formed out of the XI.; the Austro-Hungarian I., III., and II. Armies; the Southern Army (now under Bothmer); and the Austro-Hungarian VII. Army (Pflanzer-Baltin). The two main striking forces were Gallwitz in the north, and Mackensen and Linsingen in the south.

The Grand Duke Nicholas was aware of the enemy's strategy. He read clearly the meaning of the strange activity in the north. So far as he could he kept his armies at full strength. Their losses in men could be replaced, but rifles and machine guns could not be improvised, nor could all the courage and goodwill in the world provide in a few weeks an adequate accumulation of shells. The immediate danger was the Ivangorod-Lublin-Cholm railway, against which moved Mackensen's phalanx. Radko Dmitrieff had handed over the Third Army to General Lesch, who had formerly had a corps in that command. For the rest the *personnel* was unchanged, save that Russki, now happily recovered, was given the Army of Petrograd, which might soon be called upon to defend the Russian capital.

Let us look first at the campaign in the south, where Mackensen, with Woyrsch on his left, and Linsingen on his right, faced the armies of Evert and Lesch. On 22nd June Lemberg had fallen to Boehm-Ermolli. Whilst that army pressed on towards the line of the upper Bug, and the Southern Army fought for the Dniester crossings about Halicz, and Pflanzer-Baltin threatened the line of that river eastward to the frontier, the armies of Mackensen moved steadily northward. His objective on the left was Krasnik and Lublin, on the right Zamosc, Cholm, and Kovel. The Austrian IV. Army had already left the railways behind it, and was moving through a country of plains, forests, and bad country roads, a country generally flat, but rising near Krasnik to inconspicuous uplands. The XI. Army, when it left the railheads north of Rava Russka, had the same country before it, but it had to face also the considerable marshes around the upper stream of the Wieprz. The summer was wet, and the tangled levels, now scorched with the hot winds of the Polish plain, now drenched with torrential rains, made the movement of the great phalanx slow and painful. At first sight it would seem that the easier plan would have been to strike at the railway east of Kovel, where it would be nearer the Galician railheads. But to do that involved getting the difficult valley of the Bug between it and the Austrians, and so separating the two parts of Mackensen's striking force. At first the two armies met with little opposition. Small rearguard actions were fought by the Russians at Tomasov, but the main forces of Lesch and Evert were thirty miles away. By the end of June the Austrians were north of the woods which bound the Tanev watershed, and had their centre on the tolerable road, embanked above the reach of floods, which runs by Krasnik to Lublin. The XI. Army was approaching the antiquated fortress of Zamosc, a place served by no railway, and had before it the main road to Cholm by Zamosc and Krasnostav. By 2nd July the Austrians were in Krasnik, and Zamosc had fallen without trouble

But that evening the situation changed, for Mackensen was now in touch with the main Russian defence. Its position was about half-way between the Galician railheads and the vital Russian lateral railway. At Krasnik the chief road or causeway to Lublin starts, and it was the aim of the Russians to prevent the Austrians debouching on it. The village stands on a little stream, the Wisnitza, which flows west to the Vistula. To the east of it the Bistritza rises in some high ground, and runs north by Lublin to the Wieprz, having its course just to the east of the highroad. At first the Russians succeeded in holding the bank of the Wisnitza north of the village, but on Sunday, 4th July, the Austrian right managed to turn the Russian front by way of the hamlet of Bychava, east of the Bistritza, and the Russians fell back to a position on the Lublin road some three miles north of Krasnik. At the same time the XI. Army found itself checked about half-way between Zamosc and Krasnostav in the angle formed by the Wieprz and its tributary, the Wolitza. The position was suitable to the defence, for the front of about seven miles was protected from envelopment on its flank by the two streams, which flowed in marshy hollows across which artillery could not easily move. On 7th July the German advance came to a standstill, and resolved itself into an artillery duel. Presently the Austrians at Krasnik were engaged in a serious action. The battle began on the morning of Monday, the 5th, and ended in a considerable defeat on the evening of Friday, the 9th. The two enemy armies, aiming at the railway, were separated by the valley of the Wieprz, and consequently were unable to co-operate in their movements. On the evening of Sunday, the 4th, the Austrians lay with their left at Urzedow on the rising ground north of the Wisnitza, their centre on the Lublin road, and their right at Bychava, on the slopes east of the Bistritza—a front some eighteen miles long. On the Monday morning the Russians struck at the Austrian centre, drove it in, took the wayside hamlet of Wilkolaz, and cleared the enemy's left wing out of Urzedow. The next four days of attack and counter-attack led to the retreat of the Austrians, an average of two miles on a front of eighteen. The Russians carried Bychava village, and the hamlet of Bistritza on the stream of that name, and forced the whole enemy line back to the slopes just north of Krasnik, with the loss of some thousands of prisoners, a very large number of machine guns, and heavy casualties in dead and wounded. On the 9th the Austrian IV. Army was in this position, with its right centre on the small elevated triangle between the two sources of the Bistritza—the place called Hill 218 in the survey maps. Here it was secure, but its advance had been checked, and was to remain checked, as was that of the XI. Army, for a week. The vital Russian railway was safe for the moment.

Let us look at what had been happening meantime to the flanking German armies. Evert, whose opponent was Woyrsch, had on 22nd June been astride the Vistula. The advance of the Austrian IV. Army compelled him to retire his left, and the rest of his line slowly followed suit. By the end of June he was well back from Opatov, on the line Zawichrost–Ozorov–Sienno, and that night Zawichrost, on the Vistula, was relinquished. His right fell back down the valley of the Kamienna, fighting stubborn rearguard actions on both sides of the stream. Presently the river crossing at Josefov—celebrated during the first assault upon Warsaw—had gone, and early in July, before the battle of Krasnik, Evert's line ran sharply back from Radom, crossed the Vistula below the mouth of the Kamienna, and covered the Ivangorod–Lublin railway.

The right wing of the Austro-German advance was in the nature of a flank-guard to protect the main movement of the Archduke Joseph and Mackensen. One army was directed towards the upper Bug from Kamionka to Sokal, one moved against the Gnila Lipa and especially against Halicz, while Pflanzer-Baltin operated upon the lower Dniester as far as the frontier. By 24th June the Dniester was crossed west of Halicz; on the 28th Halicz was captured, which turned the Russian lines on the Gnila Lipa; while on the same day the Austrian II. Army was approaching Kamionka, where the Lemberg–Kiev railway crosses the Bug. For some days there was heavy fighting on the Gnila Lipa, as the Russian rearguard held off the pursuit to enable Lechitski to retire in good order. On the night of 3rd July the whole Russian front in this sector was back on the Zlota Lipa, a tributary of the Dniester, some twenty miles to the eastward. Meanwhile Brussilov, farther north, held the upper Bug, and frustrated Austrian attempts to cross that river at Sokal and Kamionka. By 10th July there was a lull in this part of the front corresponding to the check of the main attack upon Cholm and Lublin.

The precedent of the Japanese strategy at Mukden may now have been in Hindenburg's memory, when Oyama struck not simultaneously but successively in different places. If the effect of each blow is not lost, if each attacking force retains the positions won and engages a portion of the enemy's reserves, then each new blow has the effect of a surprise, for the line assailed cannot be easily reinforced, and the result is a general and cumulative disorder. The Grand Duke Nicholas was not caught unawares, but he was compelled to strain his resources to their uttermost to meet the danger. A number of minor incidents had shown him the direction of the wind. Through the last days of June skirmishes in the Shavli area went on. On 6th July Eichhorn's X. Army woke into activity, and carried a position west of the road from Suwalki to Kalvaria. On 8th July there was fighting at Stegna, north-east of Przasnysz. About the same time there was a German movement on the Bzura which won some trenches near Goumin, and lost them on 9th July. On 12th July there was much activity on the Bobr, and the long-suffering fortress of Ossovietz was again bombarded. On 15th July there came more ominous news. The Germans in Courland were pressing hard on the Windawa and Wenta rivers, the whole

THE FIGHT FOR THE NAREV.

Niemen front was engaged, and the Russians were resisting an attack in force just south of Przasnysz. Przasnysz had fallen to the Germans the day before. It was the first muttering of what soon became a tempest.

The great onslaught involved every army on the front, from the Baltic to the Bukovina; but for the moment the vital attacks were against the two lateral railways. Elsewhere we have considered the Narev terrain, where in February Hindenburg had fought and failed. Its valley, from its junction with the Bobr, runs south-west till it joins the Bug at Sierok, fifteen miles from Novo Georgievsk. It is heavily wooded, marshy in parts, but in several places diversified with sand ridges. Thirty or forty miles south of it ran the great Warsaw–Petrograd railway, sending off several branches to the north which met at Ostrolenka. The main river crossings at Sierok, Pultusk, Rozhan, Ostrolenka, and Lomza were fortified. The Narev line represented the screen of the Petrograd railway. If it could be forced, that railway must soon be mastered by the enemy. The attack began on 14th July, when Gallwitz, with five corps, moved on both sides of Przasnysz. He had behind him the admirable East Prussian railway system, and to serve his right flank the line from Mlawa to Novo Georgievsk. On his left moved the army of Scholtz, connecting with Eichhorn. The Russians, falling back from Przasnysz, took up a prepared position running from Czechanov to Krasnosielce, in the Orzyc valley. Here they were attacked on the 15th, but their rearguards managed to hold the line for two days while the main forces fell back towards the Narev. In this way the salient was curtailed, and the drawing in of the northern side necessitated the withdrawal of the point. About the 18th the famous lines of the Rawka and Bzura were relinquished—voluntarily, for there was small pressure there—and the Russian force covering Warsaw on the west retired fourteen miles to the Blonie lines, some fifteen miles from the city.

During the next week the Russians fell back, fighting stubbornly, on the Narev. By the 20th they were mostly on its southern bank, but held all the bridgeheads on the northern shore. The river fortressess were coming under the fire of the German heavy guns, and their outworks were crumbling. There were sorties from Novo Georgievsk, but they had little effect. On the night of the 23rd Gallwitz won certain crossings of the Narev. The chief was just opposite the mouth of the Orzyc, between Pultusk and Rozhan. Farther east a passage was won between Ostrolenka and Lomza, where the ground on the south side is free from marshes.

By Sunday, the 25th, no further ground had been won on the south bank, but Gallwitz's right was on the Bug between Sierok and Novo Georgievsk. Though he had not yet won the river line on a broad front, he was within twenty miles of Warsaw and the Petrograd railway.

Meanwhile the battle had been resumed on the southern sector. On 16th July the Austrians attacked the Russians on the Krasnik-Lublin road, but after many assaults failed to carry the Wilkolaz position. The same day the XI. Army made a great effort against Krasnostav. As we have seen, its centre lay in the angle between the Wieprz and the Wolitza, the Russian lines crossing the narrower end. During the week it had bridged the marshy streams on its flanks, and was able to dispose its artillery on a broad front and use its superior numbers for envelopment. It pushed its left across the Wieprz towards the village of Pilaskowice, and flung its right across the Wolitza, while the centre—where were the heaviest guns —forced a passage along the Cholm road. Before such weight of men and guns Lesch's force was compelled to give way, and fighting desperate rearguard actions with the bayonet, fell back behind Krasnostav. On the morning of Sunday, the 18th, Mackensen had won that town and the village of Pilaskowice, and was within ten miles of the vital railway.

The skies had darkened for Russia along the whole front. Before Warsaw, where the enemy's strength was lowest, the Blonie line was still held, but the events to south and north were speedily making it a position of danger. For in those days Woyrsch's army began to drive Evert from the whole left bank of the Vistula. The advance of Mackensen was bound very shortly to make Ivangorod untenable, and the shortening of the Bzura front turned the flank of the Radom position. On the 19th Evert's centre was driven east of Itza on the Itzanka river, Woyrsch's cavalry were on the Radom-Ivangorod railway, and Radom had fallen. Presently Sienno fell, and on the 21st Woyrsch's advanced guard seized the Vistula bridgehead at Nova Alexandria. On the 22nd the Russian right was driven into Ivangorod, which was thus assailed at once from south and west. The Russians holding the Austrian IV. Army at Wilkolaz now found themselves outflanked by Woyrsch on the right and Mackensen on the left, and were compelled to fall back nearer Lublin. Far in the north there loomed a peril more remote but not less deadly. On the 14th the left of Otto von Below's Niemen army had crossed the Windawa near Kurschany, and was sweeping round towards Tukkum, the half-way

house between Windau and Riga, while his centre was in front of Shavli, with the great guns of the East Prussian fortresses in support. Tukkum and Windau fell on 20th July, and the advance on Mitau began, while the centre was now east of Shavli. Farther south, on the Dubissa, the Russian line was forced, and Eichhorn's left wing advanced on Kovno. The factories and depots at Riga began to move their goods and plant to the interior. Otto von Below was within twenty miles of Riga, and Eichhorn within sixty of Vilna.

Such was the situation on Saturday, 24th July. It was sufficiently desperate, for Russia had drawn all the spears to her breast. The enemy was close up on the railway salient—fifteen miles from the apex, ten miles from the southern side, no more than twenty from the northern. The fortified line of the Narev was pierced, though not yet wholly broken. In these days the Grand Duke Nicholas had been called upon to make one of the most momentous decisions in the history of his country. The great Polish triangle of fortresses, the base of Russia's frontier defence—Novo Georgievsk, Ivangorod, Brest Litovsk—was still intact. Should he endeavour, with the aid of these works, to hold the triangle, and with it Warsaw ? Or should he sacrifice Poland and its capital, with all that it held of military and political significance, and fall back to the east, as Peter the Great and Kutusov had done before him ? The second course was far the harder. To extricate great armies from a narrowing salient along three railways, two of which might any day become impossible, in the face of an enemy so amply equipped, might well seem to demand a miracle for success. It meant that his wearied troops must hold for a space of weeks the sides of the salient while the front retired. The easy and fatal path would have been to trust the fortresses, and hold out in the triangle, in that hope of some sudden gift of fortune with which even strong men sometimes flatter their souls. He chose the path of difficulty and of sound strategy. Kutusov's view was his ; it was not land or cities that mattered, but the armies of Russia. He trusted his men to perform the impossible. Some day out of the East these armies would return, to win back more than they had sacrificed. Somewhere, on the line of the Bug, or, if necessary, on the Dnieper, a position would be found in which to await the preparation of the machine that would redress the balance.

On 15th July the resolution was taken to abandon Warsaw, and with it the rest of Russian Poland.

There is a tale that Alexeiev, then Chief of Staff to Ivanov, differed from his colleagues in the preceding August when the Austrian armies crossed the southern border of Poland. They saw the weakness of the enemy's position, and were resolved to give effect to that strategic plan which in a fortnight gave them the victories of Lemberg and Rava Russka. But Alexeiev, it is said, took a larger view. He counselled retreat, and still retreat, behind the Pripet marshes, away into the heart of the country. Let us inflame our opponents by means of easy successes, he said, and they will follow blindly, and then, when winter comes, we shall not beat them, we shall destroy them. His advice was not taken. Had it been, who shall say how the campaign would have evolved? Hypothetics is a bastard science, which should be shunned by the historian. But the legend is interesting as revealing in an extreme form the deepest instinct of Russian strategy. The determining factor had never been Peter or Kutusov, or the Grand Duke Nicholas, but General Russia. It was an echo of the policy which gave them Poltava and Krasny and the Beresina, and which five hundred years before the birth of Christ had baffled the army of Darius. "The Scythians," wrote Herodotus, "in regard to one of the greatest of human matters, have struck out a plan cleverer than any I know. In other respects I do not admire them, but they have contrived this great object, that no invader of their country shall ever escape out of it or shall ever be able to find out and overtake them unless they themselves choose."

But the precedents of 1709 and 1812 were no accurate guide to the happenings of to-day. Let us look more closely into the matter, and consider exactly what causes led to Napoleon's failure, and whether or not they were still operative. On such an inquiry must depend our view of the wisdom of the Grand Duke's strategy.

The main lines of the 1812 expedition are familiar. By the third week of June in that year Napoleon had massed 400,000 men and 1,000 guns on a front roughly defined by the great bend of the Niemen, which has its centre at Kovno. He began the crossing of the river on 24th June, and presently the Grande Armée was swallowed up in the silence of the northern forests. On the 28th he occupied Vilna, and on 23rd July reached Vitebsk. Here, as the readers of Ségur will remember, he fell into a mood of indecision, and paced restlessly up and down the rainy street. He found his supply system working badly, and sickness and poor food had done much to reduce his forces. Accordingly he told his marshals that the campaign of 1812 was over. He proposed to go into cantonments on a line running north and south through Vitebsk, covered by Murat's cavalry divisions. During the winter Poland and Lithuania would be reorganized, and supplies collected on the Vitebsk front, and from this advanced base the operations for the campaign of 1813 would begin. The plan was sound, and had it been persisted in the course of history would have been different. But on 8th August the Russians made a surprise attack on Murat's centre. Napoleon counter-attacked, and set the whole Grande Armée in motion, believing that his enemy was about to give him the chance of fighting a decisive battle. He moved on Smolensk, and entered it on 18th August. Once there he was captivated by the notion of a dash for Moscow. His hope was that, if he could beat the Russians in a great battle and occupy their ancient capital, Alexander would be willing to make peace, as he had done after the disaster of Friedland. Accordingly, Napoleon found himself committed to a march on Moscow in the late summer, which could only be a desperate race against time.

The decision sealed his fate. His army began to vanish long before he reached the capital. At Borodino he had little more than 130,000 men in line. He entered Moscow with less than 100,000. Three-fourths of the Grande Armée had gone. The rest of the great tale is tragedy. We know from Ségur the strange scene on the Sparrow Hills, where Napoleon waited for the capitulation of the Russian nobles which never came. Then followed the entry into a sepulchre of a city, then the great fire, and then, on 13th October, the first frost of winter and the beginning of the retreat. The country rose behind the invaders, and cold and famine hastened like avengers of blood on their trail. Presently the Grande Armée was only 40,000; soon it was only 24,000. The Beresina was reached, where the Emperor fell into a stupor, and murmured "Poltava." Eighteen thousand broken men crossed the Niemen, where a few months before the Emperor had whistled "*Malbrouck s'en va-t-en guerre;*" and Ney, as the story goes, staggered into Dumas' bivouac crying, "Je suis l'arrière-garde de la Grande Armée." Malbrouck had gone to the wars and had returned, but when he entered Warsaw by sledge he had left his empire behind him.

The *débâcle* of 1812 was due mainly to the impossibility of obtaining adequate supplies. It was that rather than the winter weather which destroyed the Grande Armée, for it is too often forgotten that that army had ceased to be an efficient force before it reached Moscow. What was Napoleon's method of supply?

In the seventeenth century the small armies of the day lived largely on the country they occupied. Their system was one of inadequate magazines and transport lines, supplemented by a general levying of contributions and extensive plunder. The army of Gustavus Adolphus fought in alliance with Prussia, but it took Prussia fifty years to recover from its exactions. This system proved as inadequate as it was demoralizing. In the eighteenth century, accordingly, armies were munitioned by the help of contractors, who formed magazines at the base and the advanced bases, and brought up supplies to the front by horse and water transport. This was the regular system, and it was supplemented not by levying contributions, but by purchasing supplies locally, and paying for them out of the travelling military chest. The eighteenth century was probably the time when, speaking broadly, armies inflicted the least hardships on the districts in which they operated.* The French Republican levies broke from the system, and Napoleon followed them. The new plan was to make war support itself. They levied money contributions on the cities they occupied, and still larger contributions in kind. This practice secured far greater freedom and rapidity of movement for moderately large forces operating on a broad front. If supplies for men and horses could be found on the ground, it was no longer necessary for the units to depend on the wagon-trains coming slowly up from the base. But when Napoleon began to advance from the Niemen the conditions were such that living off the country was impossible. Wood and water were the only things that could be furnished locally. The district, poor at the best, was swept clear of everything, not only because the Russians deliberately destroyed supplies but also because, as they retired, they ate up all that was locally available. Napoleon had to depend upon the old system of magazines, which in May and June were collected on the Niemen front. But to send forward supplies was a difficult business. The roads were atrocious, wagons and horses were constantly breaking down, the quantity of transport required was enormous, and grew daily as the lines of operations extended. The very life of the Grande Armée depended on the continuous double stream of wagons coming up loaded from the Niemen front, and returning empty for further supplies. The problem proved too great. In that realm of Chaos and old Night, where roads were tracks and rain turned the land

* The fashion was carried sometimes to a farcical excess. In 1806 the Prussian army, which still followed the eighteenth-century practice, found itself occasionally starving in the midst of ripe cornfields, or shivering beside piles of cut timber, because the commissaries had not closed the bargain for corn and firewood.

into a morass, the whole commissariat went to pieces, and victories only meant starvation.

Clearly the situation in this respect was very different in 1915 from what it had been in 1812. The German soldiers at Windau were eating bread baked and fresh meat packed in Berlin the day before. Railways were being built a mile behind the advancing forces, thousands of motor wagons were ready to supplement them, and, if necessary, an asphalted road fifty miles long could be constructed in two days. The German base on the Niemen would not consist of magazines filled up during a few weeks by collecting food and forage from Poland and East Prussia. They had behind them a railway system which enabled them to draw continuously on all the resources of Central Europe. The magazines would merely represent the temporary accumulation at the railheads, and every day would bring in more. If the Russians destroyed local supplies it would matter little. The German armies would live on their railways and their motor transport.

The view was sound, but it was not all the truth Modern science had indeed removed one of the worst of Napoleon's difficulties. The precedent of 1812 was no basis for a precise forecast, but certain rock facts remained. Russia was still a country of infinite distances. The heart of the land was the people, and no capital or province. Human energy is limited, and all the railways on earth could not make a campaign in hostile territory a hundred miles from the frontiers as easy as one fought just outside them. As the German line of communications lengthened out it must grow weaker and more vulnerable, for though the relation of distance to time had changed, it still remained a fixed proportion; supplies would still take twice as long to travel four hundred miles as to travel two hundred. Moreover, as the German army advanced eastward the front would tend to broaden and the lines grow thinner. A space of some hundreds of miles proved fatal to Napoleon; that space might now need to be multiplied by ten or twenty, but space, if ample enough, would sooner or later dissipate the fiercest energy.

In two respects the situation was more fortunate for Russia than in 1812. Then she was still without the self-consciousness of a nation. The Poles and Lithuanians were all on the French side. Vilna celebrated Napoleon's birthday; Minsk greeted the troops of Davoust with music and flowers; at Mogilev there was mass in the cathedral for the Emperor's well-being. Even in Russia proper the people were confused, for a few years before their Tsar had been in alliance with the French. They were ignorant of the doings in the West, and were for long puzzled to understand the meaning of the invasion. Nor was there any fierce hostility felt then or later to Napoleon himself, such as flourished at the time in Britain. Pushkin's words represented the judgment of many classes: " All hail! He pointed out a great destiny to the Russian people, and from the gloom of his banishment bequeathed to the world lasting freedom!" The feeling of the ordinary Russian was bewilderment and pity rather than wrath. When a priest of Smolensk, on his way to a dying parishioner, met the Emperor tramping moodily in the icy slush, he pressed on him the sacrament, because he seemed the greatest of human sufferers. But in 1915 the slow consciousness of Russia had partially awakened. She knew the war for a struggle not of armies and dynasties, but of peoples and of ideals. Civilization had laid its hand on her since 1812. Her great spaces were pierced with roads and railways, and cornlands lay where had once been wood and marsh. The Germans were advancing in an easier country, but the century which had improved the face of the land had given a new cohesion and force to the human resistance.

Again, the armed strength of Russia, both absolutely and relatively, was far greater than in 1812. Napoleon, it should be remembered, thought first of dividing and breaking the Russian armies. The occupation of Moscow was only a secondary matter, a quasi-political move forced on him by his inability to get really to grips with his foe. " Bagration and Barclay will not see each other again," he had said confidently when he crossed the Niemen, believing that he had driven a wedge between the armies of the north and of the south. He was wrong, for on 3rd August the two armies joined hands at Smolensk, and thereafter their cohesion was never broken. But the united Russian forces were not formidable; at Borodino they numbered little over 103,000, and on that bloody day they lost some 58,000 killed and wounded, including twenty-two generals. They had no commanders of genius, certainly no one comparable to Napoleon. The troops which the Grand Duke Nicholas led in 1915 yielded to their foe in few things but equipment. Once again, as in 1812, the aim of the invader must be the destruction of the armies. If these could retreat without grave loss into their infinite hinterland the enterprise of Hindenburg might shipwreck as grievously as Napoleon's.

With such considerations the Allies in the West comforted themselves as they watched the spectacle of the Russian disasters.

They were reasonable and weighty arguments, but they suffered from one doubtful proviso. Germany might fail, but in her failure she might bring down the whole edifice of Russian society. Even if armies are not broken in front, their sufferings may so react upon the people at large that treasons come into being which destroy them from behind. The nation was still unwieldy and inorganic, and it was not easy to be confident that so imperfect a mechanism of government could withstand so fiery a trial. Hopeful signs there were: Guchkov, the Octobrist leader, had been made Minister of Munitions; the Duma seemed to be asserting itself as the popular mouthpiece, and the ally of the Third Duma, General Polivanov, had become Minister of War. But the uncertainty remained. Germany might not succeed in her immediate purpose of destruction, and yet, blindly and unwittingly, might sow for Russia the seeds of a more terrible downfall.

The last days of July in Warsaw saw a strange sight. The great factories with their plant migrated eastward. While homeless peasants from the neighbouring country thronged into the city, the normal inhabitants, to the number of nearly half a million, sought refuge in Russia, travelling by the northern line within sound of the guns on the Narev. All goods which could be useful to the coming enemy were removed, and what could not be taken was burned. The Praga and Alexander bridges were thronged with convoys carrying gold from the banks, archives from the State departments, and sacred relics and ikons from the churches. The crops were destroyed in the surrounding fields, when no man could be found to reap them. A migration of hackney carriages began, carrying families on the thousand-mile road to Moscow. The newspapers announced the evacuation, and then appeared no more; their linotype machines and founts of type were carried off, and all the copper fittings which could be found in the city. Only Poles remained, and the very poorest of the Ghetto

The civil evacuation was carried out with extraordinary efficiency and speed. But the real task was the withdrawal of the troops from the western lines. The railway to Brest Litovsk was reserved for military trains, and about 24th July the Blonie forces began to fall back gradually to the suburbs of the city. If the army in the front of the salient was to get clear away the sides must be held, and especially that northern side where, on the Narev and Bug, the enemy was only some twenty miles distant. The holding battle fought there during the last week of July was one of the finer episodes of the retirement. Heavy reinforcements were brought against the Narev, and Gallwitz and Scholtz attacked fiercely on 26th July and the subsequent days, but they were unable to break the Russian resistance. Farther south, where the position was for the moment less critical, the enemy won several notable successes. On the 28th Woyrsch succeeded in crossing the Vistula between Warsaw and Ivangorod at several points south of the mouth of the Pilitza. Ivangorod was now untenable, and very wisely it was resolved not to defend the great fortress. Evert's army fell back north-eastward, keeping in touch with the army defending Warsaw. Next day Mackensen at last pierced the southern railway. His left wing, thrust forward between Lublin and Cholm, cut the line at the station of Biskupice, and dominated a section east of that place, while his right advanced north-east of Krasnostav to a point five miles south of the line. The following day Lesch fell back from the railway to a position well to the north, and Lublin and Cholm were in German hands.

Feverishly the work of evacuation went on, and the flanking forces were able either to hold the enemy or to make his progress slow. By 4th August the moment had come for the point of the salient to yield. The stores and guns had all gone eastward, and, while the flanking army of the Narev still held, it was high time for the centre to fall back. On the evening of 4th August the Russians retired without difficulty from the Blonie lines, and began to move through the city. For the past days German aircraft had been dropping bombs on Warsaw, and the great guns had set the western suburbs on fire. By midnight the last troops were filing over the bridges, fighting rearguard actions with the pursuing cavalry. At three o'clock on the morning of 5th August, there was a sound of heavy explosions. The three Vistula bridges had been blown up. Two hours later the German cavalry, the advance guard of Prince Leopold's army, entered the city.

The Emperor did not fulfil the expectations of his opponents. He made no spectacular entry into the Polish capital. On the last day of July he had issued a manifesto to mark the anniversary of the beginning of war. It was a curious document, an illustration of the attitude of the German people as reflected in the mind of their Emperor, that faithful mirror of popular opinion. In it he repeated the story that an innocent Germany had been attacked by a jealous coalition which had been preparing for a decade, but " the dykes which she erected in an anticipation that she would once more have to defend what she gained in 1870 have defied the highest tide in the world's history"; and he summoned his people to a new covenant with the Omnipotence Who had so amply blessed their arms. On the news of the crowning mercy of Warsaw he permitted himself one modest outburst, and in a telegram to the Queen of Greece gave rein to his exultation. "My destructive sword," he said, "has crushed the Russians. They will need six months to recover. In a short time I will announce new victories won by my brave soldiers, who have shown themselves invincible in battle against nearly the whole world. The war drama is now coming to a close." He had some cause for his pride. The Christmas gift, the birthday gift, had failed; but Warsaw had now come to him as an anniversary memento, a token that the first year of war had ended in a German triumph.

The privilege of entering Warsaw as a conqueror was left to Prince Leopold of Bavaria, an old gentleman of seventy, who had never before commanded anywhere but at manœuvres. He had married the eldest daughter of the Emperor of Austria, and his selection was due to a desire to placate Austrian sentiment, and reveal to the world the conquest as due to the valour of both nations. Prince Leopold was no Attila, and he had only a remnant to deal with. He took hostages after the German fashion, and after the same fashion issued a proclamation announcing that he waged war against troops and not against peaceful citizens, and inviting the people "to trust to the German sense of justice." As he rode with his suite in the evening through the Sigismund Square on his way to the Palace he saw a glow on the eastern horizon. It was the ominous sight which Napoleon had seen—the skies reddened with the flames of crops and villages as the armies of Russia fell back before the invader.

CHAPTER XXXIV.

GALLIPOLI: THE BATTLES FOR KRITHIA.
April 29–July 31, 1915.

The Attack of 6th May—The Australasian Corps at Sari Bair—The Battle of 4th June—The Withdrawal of the larger Warships—Kitchener's Difficulties—The Action of 21st June—The Action of 12th July—Arrival of British Reinforcements.

WE left the Allied forces, after the first movement against Krithia on 28th April, extended on a line running from a point on the Gulf of Saros, three miles north-east of Capa Tekke, to a point one mile north of Eski Hissarlik, whence it bent back a little to the shore of the Dardanelles. For the next months the story of the campaign is concerned with a slow and desperate struggle for Krithia and the Achi Baba heights, which were the first steps towards the conquest of the peninsula. Before we enter upon the details of that struggle it may be well to glance at the problem of the Turkish communications, for it had a direct bearing upon the Allied strategy of the campaign. Liman von Sanders had on the peninsula not less than 70,000 men and a lavish provision of artillery, and he had another 20,000 close at hand. To feed his troops and supply his guns he needed ample communications, and these could not be found in the narrow road from Rodosto across the Bulair isthmus, a road bad at the best, and now commanded by the fire of the Allied ships in the Gulf of Saros. His true communications lay by water down the Sea of Marmora to the ports of Gallipoli and Maidos If this water transport should be hampered, the only remaining plan was to bring his reserves and supplies along the Asiatic coast to Chanak, and have them ferried over in the darkness of the night. This was a practicable route, but slow and circuitous If he wished for free and speedy transport he must keep the Sea of Marmora inviolate. It was the object of the Allies

SECOND BATTLE FOR KRITHIA.

to make that sea impossible, and the only means at their disposal was the submarine Several brilliant enterprises by British submarine commanders carried the war into the Marmora and up to the wharves of Constantinople. The result was that the Sea of Marmora was no longer regarded as safe, and the Turkish supplies began to travel by the Asiatic shore and the ferries of the Narrows. This involved a certain dislocation and delay which were of inestimable service to the Allied troops which faced the formidable batteries of Achi Baba and Kilid Bahr.

The first advance on Krithia, on 28th April, came short of success because of the weakness and weariness of the attacking force, worn out with the desperate struggle of the landing. The failure of the landing at Y Beach, which was within a mile of Krithia, prevented Sir Ian Hamilton from undertaking an enveloping movement, and forced him to a frontal assault. Through no fault of his the battle in the butt-end of the peninsula had ossified into an affair of parallel fronts, for the Anzac forces were too precariously situated to turn the enemy defence in flank. Yet it is clear that at this stage, had reserves been present, Krithia and Achi Baba could have been carried by a direct frontal attack. The tragedy of Gallipoli was that when reinforcements came they were invariably too late, and the situation had so changed, that what could have been achieved by their aid a fortnight before was now impossible.

On 30th April two further battalions of the Royal Naval Division disembarked, and next day came the 29th Brigade of Indian infantry. The first days of May saw various Turkish attacks which failed, and Allied counterstrokes which were brought to an end by barbed wire and machine guns. Already the casualty list for the British alone was some 14,000, and the Fusilier Brigade of the 29th Division had lost 68 out of its 104 officers, and more than half of its men. Sir Ian Hamilton could now count upon only about 33,000 rifles, of which some 5,000 were British regulars. He resolved to strike again at Krithia, and the new attempt was made on the morning of Thursday, 6th May. The assaulting troops were the 29th Division (reinforced by a Lancashire Territorial Brigade and the 29th Indian Brigade) on the left, and the French on the right, supported by part of the Naval Division. Two Anzac brigades had been brought down from Gaba Tepe to act as a general reserve. The plan of attack was for the left and centre to occupy the Krithia ridge, while the French should assault the high ground on the right across the valley of the Kereves Dere—the small stream which enters the Dardanelles just beyond Eski Hissarlik. The French guns opened fire from the neighbourhood of Sedd-el-Bahr about eleven in the morning, aiming at the southern spur of Achi Baba and the broken ground in front of it towards the Krithia road. At the same time the battleships in the Straits plastered the upper slopes of Achi Baba and the Turkish trenches in the Kereves valley. After half an hour of artillery preparation the French infantry attacked in open order, but as they reached the top of the slope overlooking the Kereves Dere they came suddenly upon Turkish trenches skilfully concealed behind the crest. Part of the Naval Brigade was sent forward to reinforce them, but they too fell in with concealed Turkish trenches. Again and again through the afternoon the Allied right struggled to advance, but the place was too strong, and about 5.30 p.m. the fighting died away. The result of the day was that the French had pushed forward a mile, and had dug themselves in on the slopes above the Kereves Dere, but had failed to carry the Turkish trenches on the reverse slope or the redoubt at the top of the valley. That night the Turks counter-attacked between 10 p.m. and 2 a.m., but the French held their ground. The 29th Division on the left had also advanced a few hundred yards with heavy casualties.

Next day, 7th May, about ten o'clock, the ships began a bombardment of the Turkish right on Achi Baba. They directed special attention to the ground at the head of the ravine leading to Beach Y. A quarter of an hour later the British left and centre attacked, the 87th and 88th Brigades towards the slopes between Krithia and the sea, and the Naval Brigades in the centre towards Krithia village. They carried the front Turkish trenches, but the second line held them up, and their supports were heavily shelled by Turkish guns from the heights. Meantime the French on the right had lain quiet till noon. Then they began an elaborate bombardment, and at 3 p.m., supported by part of the Naval Division, attacked over the same ground as the day before. During the afternoon they made some progress, but about 5 p.m. their advanced infantry was caught on the slopes by such a hail of shrapnel that the line wavered and broke. The Turks counter-attacked and took the French trenches on the crest. D'Amade flung in his reserves, and after an hour's severe fighting they recovered the lost ground, and held it till nightfall under a heavy fire. During the afternoon the British had done little. Shortly after five our infantry advanced, and about six attempted to carry the hill between Krithia and the sea. It proved too strong, but as a result of the day we had entrenched our front within 800 yards of Krithia. It was desperately costly fighting. Our artillery fire seemed to have no effect upon the enemy, who had trench lines cunningly hidden over the whole position.

Next day, 8th May, the battle was renewed at ten o'clock. Again the ships in the Gulf of Saros bombarded the Turkish right and the ground behind it, and after half an hour's " preparation " the British left and left centre attacked. The 87th and 88th Brigades gained further ground in the broken bush country between Krithia and the sea. The 86th Brigade and the Australian and New Zealand supports were then pushed in to strengthen the line. Nothing happened on the right of our front, and during the afternoon there was a lull. We were reorganizing our forces, with a view to a last attempt upon Krithia village. At 5.15 p.m. all the available ships and the shore batteries united in a terrific bombardment. The Turkish position appeared to be smothered in flame and smoke, and not an enemy gun spoke. But once again we were to learn the strength of scientifically prepared entrenchments. At 5.30 our advance began, and no sooner did we move than the Turks opened fire along the whole front with artillery, machine guns, and rifles. On the left we moved a little way towards Krithia, but soon reached our limit. The French on the right carried the first Turkish trenches, and there stuck fast. Confused fighting continued till 7.30 p.m., when night put an end to the battle. The result of the three days' struggle was that our front had been advanced over a thousand yards, but we had not touched the enemy's main position. We realized its unique strength, and all idea of rushing it was abandoned.

Meantime the Australasian corps at Sari Bair was persistently attacked during the battles of 6th-8th May; but, though they had lent part of their forces to the Krithia front, they held their ground at all points. It was this flanking force which the Turks especially feared, and they spent the first fortnight of the month in ringing it in with elaborate defences. The Australian line lay in a semicircle, with the enemy's trenches close up to it—in some places as near as twenty yards—except in that part adjoining the shore where the ships' guns kept him off. A wide hollow, which our men called Shrapnel Valley, divided the position into two sections, and on the northern section the Turkish trenches were on much higher ground than ours. On the night of 18th May Liman von Sanders brought fresh troops from Constantinople, and drew off part of his Krithia garrison. About midnight a heavy fire from rifle and machine guns broke out against the Australian trenches, and at various points attacks were made which crumbled before our defence. At 5 a.m. on the 19th the Turkish artillery began, and all morning the enemy attempted to rush our lines. The cool and steady shooting of the Australians kept him at bay, and by eleven o'clock the battle died down. It was one of the most costly of the enemy reverses, and the Turkish losses were believed to be not less than 7,000 men.

On the main front in the south various changes had taken place. The whole of the 42nd East Lancashire (Territorial) Division, under General Douglas, had landed, and had replaced the 29th Division in the line. The 29th, 42nd, and Royal Naval Division had been formed into the 8th Corps, under General Hunter-Weston, General De Lisle replacing him in command of the 29th. A second French Division had arrived under General Bailloud. On the night of the 12th the Gurkhas of the 29th Indian Brigade, under cover of a cannonade from the water, rushed the bluffs above Beach Y with few casualties. For the rest of the month the battle languished, while Sir Ian Hamilton was slowly wringing drafts out of the Government at home. All his units had taken the field short of establishment, and he found it impossible to keep them at anything like a normal strength. Some of the divisions were already only divisions in name. His position had become one of tragic difficulty. He could not sit still at Helles under the perpetual bombardment from Achi Baba. The heats of summer were increasing, and in that crowded heel of land his position would soon be one of intense discomfort and danger. A new attempt must be made on Krithia.

The third action was fought on 4th June. Sir Ian Hamilton had, apart from the French, 17,000 bayonets for the attack and 7,000 in reserve. His dispositions ran: on the left the 29th Division, with the 29th Indian Brigade: on the left centre the 42nd Division; on the right centre the Royal Naval Division; and on the right the 2nd and 1st French Divisions. After a "preparation" by all the shore batteries and ships' guns, the advance began at noon. The Indian Brigade at first made good progress, and captured two lines of trenches. Unfortunately, on their right a part of the 29th Division had found itself faced with a heavy wire entanglement which our artillery had not cut. This checked their progress, and the Indians were compelled by enfilading fire to retire to their original line. The rest of the 29th Division captured a redoubt and two trench lines beyond it, and advanced the front by 300 yards. The 42nd Division in the centre captured three lines of trenches, and advanced 600 yards, but they were too far beyond the rest for comfort, and after holding an advanced captured trench for a day and a night, had to fall back to the second trench. The Naval Division progressed for 300 yards, taking a redoubt and a line of trenches, but was obliged to yield its gains owing to the position on its right. There the French, charging with desperate gallantry, retook for the fourth time the redoubt of "Le Haricot," but were driven out of it by shell fire. The fruits of this third attempt on Achi Baba were an advance of at the most 400 yards on a front of three miles, and the occupation of two lines of Turkish trenches. The Allied casualties were heavy, and the affair cannot be regarded otherwise than as a costly reverse.

It was after the battle of 4th June that the need for large reinforcements became too urgent to be denied. After five weeks' struggle, in which the fighting had been as desperate as any in the war, we had not yet touched the outer Turkish position. The German engineers had turned the ground to brilliant defensive uses, and even when long lengths of trenches were carried by our infantry attacks, there remained redoubts, like the *fortins* on the Western front, to make a general advance impossible. It may be questioned whether a more abundant supply of high explosives would have greatly altered the case. Our bombardments had been lavish enough, but they had scarcely touched the enemy. The Gallipoli campaign had revealed itself as a slow and deadly frontal attack, in which yard by yard we should have to fight our way across the ridges. Such warfare was costly beyond all reckoning. Up to 31st May (that is, covering the landing and the first two attempts on Krithia) the casualties in the Dardanelles—exclusive of the French—reached a total of 38,636, of whom 1,722 were officers. The battle losses for the three years of the South African War were only 38,156.

Meantime things were going no less ill on the water. The Allied Fleets had shared in every land attack, and the *Goeben*, on the Turkish side, from farther up the Straits, took part in at least one engagement. These large vessels, stationary or moving very slowly along the coasts, were a superb target for under-water assault, and presently news came that some of the large ocean-going German submarines, which had been commissioned early in the year, were on their way to the Mediterranean. About the middle of May one was reported near Malta, and there were many spots on the long indented Anatolian coast where they could find a base.

This possibility gave much anxiety to the Allied admirals. Meantime, on the night of 12th May, a Turkish destroyer performed a singularly bold feat on its own account. It found the old British battleship, the *Goliath*,* protecting the French flank just inside the Straits, sunk it by torpedo fire, with a loss of the captain, 19 officers, and 500 men, and managed to return safely. Such an exploit was only possible under cover of darkness, and the risk of it did not interfere with the daylight operations of the fleet. But presently a far more formidable foe arrived, a foe whose presence made naval support—so far at least as concerned the great battleships—a very doubtful and costly undertaking.

About midday on 26th May the *Triumph* was moving slowly up the northern shore of the peninsula in support of the Australasian troops. Apparently her nets were out, and there were destroyers close at hand. A torpedo from a German submarine tore through the nets, struck the vessel amidships, and sank her in nine minutes. Here was an incident to give serious thought. The enemy in broad daylight, in water full of shipping, had broken through all our safeguards, and destroyed a battleship. The hunt for the submarine was vigorously conducted, but nothing was heard of it till next day, when the *Majestic*, steaming very close to the shore, was sunk in the same fashion. The Allied Fleets, compelled by the necessities of gunnery to move slowly, were obviously at the mercy of an enemy under water. From this date, therefore, the larger vessels began to withdraw. The *Queen Elizabeth* returned home, and there remained only a few of the older battleships, a number of cruisers, French and British, like the *Euryalus, Minerva, Talbot, Phaeton, Amethyst,* and *Kleber;* and a flotilla of destroyers, including the *Scorpion, Wolverine, Pincher, Renard,* and *Chelmer.* In addition we had some of the monitors which had operated in October off the Flanders coast—a type of vessel whose shallow draught made it most suitable for coast bombardment and less vulnerable to submarine attack.

In the old historical novels the hero, when he was not to be observed wending his way on horseback up a mountain path in the twilight, was generally found holding a narrow staircase against uncounted foes. To the Turks had fallen the favourite romantic situation. We had chosen to attack them in one of the strongest natural fortresses in the world. The convex arc of the Achi Baba heights might have been created for a modern defence. Not a yard of it was dead ground; every foot was exposed to bombard-

* Built in 1900: 12,950 tons, 19 knots, four 12-in. and twelve 6-in. guns.

ment from the well-placed guns and the concentric trench lines. With a base a few miles square, we attempted by frontal fighting to win a step now and then of the staircase. It is true that the Australasian Corps had secured a position on the enemy's right rear; but that, too, was a step of a staircase, and our overseas troops clung precariously to the edge of the cliffs. Every detail of our position was under fire, and there was no safe hinterland for wounded and reserves except that to be gained by an embarkation and a voyage. The wounded had to go to Alexandria and Malta, and munitions, food, and water had to travel many leagues of sea. Drinking water had to be brought from Egypt, or further. The position is best described in Sir Ian Hamilton's words: "The country is broken, mountainous, arid, and void of supplies; the water found in the areas occupied by our forces is quite inadequate for their needs; the only practicable beaches are small, cramped breaks in impracticable lines of cliffs; with the wind in certain quarters no sort of landing is possible; the wastage, by bombardment and wreckage, of lighters and small craft has led to crisis after crisis in our carrying capacity; whilst over every single beach plays fitfully throughout each day a devastating shell-fire at medium ranges." Such a position would have been grave against a feeble opponent. But the Turk was no despicable foe. He had long before at Plevna proved himself a great master of defensive war. He was aided by the best German military skill and the latest German science. He was holding the gate of his sacred capital against the infidel—a gate, like the bridge of Horatius, where a thousand might be stopped by three; but his numbers were greater then ours. He was like a posse of mailed men on the summit of a narrow stairway, with every advantage of ground, weapon, and forewarning.

In June the political and strategic importance of the Dardanelles expedition had been amply manifested. What had not been dreamed of in April had come to pass. The determined attack upon Russia could not yet be balanced by a counter-offensive in the West, and the Dardanelles was the only terrain where the Allies could directly aid the hard-pressed armies of the Tsar. They were striking a blow to free the Russian left flank, to secure a passage for munitions to the Black Sea ports, and to win for Christendom and Russia the cradle of the Orthodox Church and the capital of that Eastern Roman Empire to which Russia asserted a claim of heirship. The value of the enterprise on Russian public opinion cannot be overstated. Strategically, too, there was much to be said in its defence. The Allies could not win the war within reasonable time without the help of the Russian armies, and anything which conduced to their aid was a contribution to the whole Allied cause. Besides, Germany had given the East a special significance. It was clear that, as a great land power, she was turning her eyes more and more to those vast continental tracts of Eastern Europe and Western Asia where sea-power was meaningless. Her victory there might threaten India and Egypt, points as vital to the British Empire as Verdun and Belfort were vital to France.

Ever since the first weeks of May the Dardanelles situation had weighed heavily on the mind of the British Government. The hope of an easy success had gone, and Kitchener was faced with a task of which he had not counted the cost—of which indeed the cost was beyond his means. Sir Ian Hamilton needed more troops, more ammunition, more transport, and it was hard to see how his needs could be met without failing in our duty to the Western Front and to France. The Russian corps at Odessa had become a phantom, and there was no chance of help in that quarter. Yet we had gone too far to break off the operations, and any retreat would involve a certain loss of credit and a probable loss of men. On 17th May, Sir Ian Hamilton, questioned by Kitchener, had put his requirements at two fresh army corps. Then came the confusion incidental to the formation of the Coalition Government, and the War Council was enlarged by the addition of Unionist members and changed its name to the Dardanelles Committee. Withdrawal was impossible; it seemed equally impossible to provide the strength necessary for an immediate decision; accordingly it was resolved on 7th June to continue operations with such reinforcements as could be spared, so as to distract the Turks and keep the door open to Balkan intervention. Three divisions of the New Army not allotted to France would be sent out and two Territorial divisions, and all five would arrive before the end of July. With such an accession of strength in prospect, Sir Ian Hamilton could prepare his plans.

Meantime he was about to receive a reinforcement which had been promised him in the early days of the campaign—the 52nd (Scottish Lowland Territorial) Division, under Major-General Egerton. There had been some changes in the commands. Major-General Bridges, commanding the Australian Division, had been killed, and his successor was Major-General H. B. Walker. D'Amade's health had broken down, and he had been replaced by General Gouraud. Gouraud, one of the youngest and most brilliant of French corps commanders, had earned the name of the "Lion of the Argonne" from his winter's work in that forest campaign with a corps of Sarrail's Third Army. In Sir Ian Hamilton's phrase, " a happy mixture of daring in danger and of calm in crisis " made him an ideal leader for the French Colonials. No one who ever met Gouraud was likely to forget him. His grave and splendid presence, the fire in his dark eyes, the lofty resolution in every line and gesture, gave him the air of some great paladin of France who had held the marches with Roland and Oliver.

In the battle of 4th June we had advanced in the centre from 200 to 400 yards on a front of three miles. Our left wing had moved only a little way forward, and the French on the extreme right were still held up by the ravine of the Kereves Dere. The front was now in the form of a semicircle, with the horns flung well back, and our next business was to straighten it. The time for bold and sweeping efforts had gone by. There had been a moment on 28th April when Krithia and the Achi Baba heights had been at our mercy; but, as the Turkish defence consolidated itself, all that remained for us was a slow war of " nibbling " and attrition. Surprise was out of the question. In Sir Ian Hamilton's words : " The enemy was as much in possession of my numbers and dispositions as I was in possession of their first line of defence ; the opposing fortified fronts stretched parallel from sea to straits ; there was little space left now, either at Achi Baba or at Gaba Tepe, for tactics which would fling flesh and blood battalions against lines of unbroken barbed wire Advance must more and more tend to take the shape of concentrated attacks on small sections of the enemy's line after full artillery preparation. Siege warfare was soon bound to supersede manœuvre battles in the open Consolidation and fortification of our front, improvement of approaches, selection of machine-gun emplacements, and scientific grouping of our artillery under a centralized control must erelong form the tactical basis of our plans " These words were written of the situation after 11th May, but they applied with equal force to the position on 5th June.

During the first fortnight of June there were frequent Turkish attacks, directed to regain the trenches lost on the 4th. On 21st June a beginning was made with the straightening of the Allied front. The most critical position was that of the French corps on the right, which was still held up south of the Kereves Dere. At 1.30 in the morning a great bombardment began. All the south-eastern shoulder of Achi Baba was plastered with heavy shells, and the 75-mm. field guns played incessantly on the slopes of the ravine. Then came the infantry rush. The 2nd French Division, on the left, made good progress. By midday it had captured the first two lines of the Turkish position, and taken the much-contested Haricot Redoubt, with its tangle of wire and deep-cut trenches and machine-gun *fortins*. They were across the ravine, when they found that their right flank was in the air. For the 1st Division, between them and the Straits, though it had kept line in the first onslaught, had been driven back by counter-attacks. Twice the division advanced, and twice it was compelled to retire. At a quarter to three in the afternoon there was some risk that all the gains of the 2nd Division would be lost. General Gouraud accordingly issued the order that in the five hours of daylight that remained the right of the advance must at all costs succeed. British artillery was brought up, and every gun that could be massed poured shells on the Turkish lines, while the *St. Louis* in the Straits kept the Asiatic batteries quiet. At six o'clock the last assault was delivered, and the position carried. Turkish reinforcements coming up were spotted by an airplane, caught by the 75's in the open, and destroyed. By nightfall the French had won 600 yards of Turkish trenches, and the whole Allied right wing was well beyond the Kereves ravine.

The right wing having advanced, it remained to bring on the left. That left ran from the Krithia road, crossed the ravine called the Saghir Dere, about half-way between its head and its mouth, and rested on the high ground above the Gulf of Saros. The Saghir Dere—known to us as Gully Ravine—was one of those desolate and arid water-courses common in Gallipoli and on the Anatolian coast. At the sea end its sides were 200 feet high, clothed for the most part with a light scrub, but with open patches of yellow clay. A small stream, generally dry, trickled down it, and there were a few springs. Towards its head it grew shallower, and finally died away in the Krithia plateau. The north end was held strongly by the Turks, who had entrenched themselves on the top of the banks on both sides, and had fortified a small redoubt, which we called the Boomerang Fort, in front of their position. The Allied plan was to pivot upon a point in our front about a mile from the sea, and to swing forward our left wing until its outer flank had advanced 1,000 yards. This meant that the distance to be covered decreased as the pivoting point was neared. The extreme left had to carry five Turkish trenches, the left centre no more than two The forces to which the task was entrusted were, from right to left, the 156th

Brigade of the 52nd Division, the 29th Division, and the 29th Indian Brigade. The movement was in the charge of General Hunter-Weston. On the morning of 28th June the wind blew steadily from the west. At 10.20 a.m. the bombardment began with high-explosive shells, and columns of dust hid Achi Baba. The French lent some of their big trench mortars, and the cruiser *Talbot* and the destroyers *Wolverine* and *Scorpion* from the sea enfiladed the trenches of the Turkish right. Our field guns, firing shrapnel, succeeded effectually in cutting the enemy's wire. At 10.20 the bombardment increased, every Allied piece firing in conjunction. At 10.45 our infantry rose from the trenches. The attack was wholly successful. In an hour and a half we had won all we had aimed at except a small section of trench near the pivoting point. Most of Gully Ravine was in our hands, and our left wing, instead of facing north-east, now faced due east, and was considerably less than a mile from Krithia.

In the last days of June there was fighting all round the peninsula. At Sari Bair at 1.30 on the morning of the 30th a Turkish column advanced with bayonets and bombs against Godley's division. It never came to the shock, for it was completely broken by the musketry and machine-gun fire of the 7th and 8th Light Horse. By two o'clock the enemy were routed, and many fell in the withdrawal. On the Australian left they had come up against a well-concealed sap ahead of our main line, and the dead lay in swathes before it. At 3 a.m. they tried again. A small party came over the parapets in front of Quinn's Post, and died to a man. The main threat against the left and left centre was similarly broken up by rifle and gun fire. On the Allied right, too, there was heavy fighting. On the night of the 29th the Turks attempted a surprise attack along the shore of the straits, but the movement was discovered by the searchlights of the *Wolverine* and brought to a standstill. The van of the attack was not stopped till it was some forty yards from our trenches. At 6.30 on the morning of the 30th the French moved forward, and in less than an hour had carried the fortified network known as the Quadrilateral, east of the head of the Kereves Dere. The Infanterie Coloniale carried seven lines of trenches, and their leading companies for a moment were in danger of being cut off. They held, however, to the ground they had won, and by the afternoon had beaten off all counter-attacks and consolidated their position. This advance, taken in conjunction with the advance of the Allied left on the 28th, straightened out the dangerous bulge in our front. One serious loss marred the success of the day. General Gouraud was blown over a wall by an 8-in. shell, while visiting the sick and wounded on V Beach. The wound, which later involved the amputation of his right arm, compelled him to return home and relinquish the command of the French Corps to Bailloud. These violent Turkish assaults resulted in nothing but the needless loss of many brave men. Liman had instructed his troops to act strictly on the defensive, and not to attempt to recover lost ground. But Enver, arriving during the fight, on the 28th, reversed the policy and ordered counter-attacks along the whole front.

On 12th July the Allies made their last attempt at a frontal attack on the Krithia position. The first movement was made by the Allied right and right centre, the French Corps, and the 52nd Division. Our bombardment began at dawn, and thereafter our infantry carried the first two lines of Turkish trenches. Some of the Scots Territorials indeed went farther, for the objectives set by the High Command were not always accurate, and continued till they were checked by our own barrage. The bombardment continued all day, and at 4 p.m. a special cannonade was delivered on the enemy positions in the upper ravines of the Kereves Dere, where they ran into the face of Achi Baba. On the right, overlooking a ravine, the Turks had a great rectangular redoubt, bristling with machine guns. At 5 our guns lengthened and attacked the ground where the Turkish reserves might be looked for, while a warship bombarded the observation station on the top of Achi Baba with 12-inch shells. Then the Scots surged forward against the redoubt, and carried it with the bayonet. By nightfall 400 yards of ground had been gained. It was a considerable advance, which brought us very near to Krithia. But the heights of Achi Baba were as far off as ever.

The discomforts of the life in the peninsula grew as the summer advanced and the heat waxed greater. The whole of our position was honeycombed with trenches and dug-outs like a colony of sand martins in the bank of a river. There was no shade from nature, for the copses were only scrub. The sun beat down pitilessly on the acres of rock and gravel, and was reflected from the blue waters around. Our men were very close together, and the whole earth soon became tainted in spite of all our care. Sunstroke cases were few, for the sun of Gallipoli is not the sun of India; but fevers and dysentery began to take their toll. The scarcity of water, the difficult journeys for the sick down communication trenches and cliff roads, and the long voyage before hospital was reached, intensified our discomfort. And everywhere fell a plague of flies. Men who had fought in South Africa remembered the curse of the fly on the veld; but the South African scourge was feeble compared to the clouds which hung over the baked peninsula. Remember there was no movement or chance of movement. The troops had to sit still in their stifling trenches, and every acre of that butt-end of Gallipoli was searched by the enemy's fire. Under such conditions—no movement, grave losses, grave discomforts—it was a marvel that we maintained so high a spirit and so steady a cheerfulness. Men returned to the habits of their first parents. Khaki "shorts," a shirt, and a sun-helmet formed the only wear of even exalted generals. The Australians and New Zealanders especially, perched in their eyrie at Sari Bair, showed a noble disregard of apparel. These troops, embracing in their ranks every class and condition, had shown themselves superb fighting men. There was a perpetual competition for the posts of danger, and money was offered freely for the right to a place in some hot corner. Their easy discipline knew none of the usual military conventions; but it was real enough, and got through the work required. They had the finest average of physique in any of the belligerent armies —those lean, great-limbed men, without an ounce of soft flesh on their bodies. In the midsummer heats they were burned to a dull brick-red, for they fought almost naked. Coats, shirts, boots, and putties disappeared in succession, their trousers shrank into "shorts," as they toiled in the dust of the trenches till the hour of relief came, and they could wash in the shrapnel-dotted Ægean. The oversea nations of the Empire had won great honour—the South Africans among the deserts of German territory, the Canadians in the sickly meadows of the Ypres Salient. Not less glorious was the record of the Australians in a land as sunburnt as their own.

The three summer months had been among the most costly in our military history. Out of some six British divisions we had lost by the end of May over 38,000 men. By the end of June the total was over 42,000; by the end of July it was nearly 50,000, of whom 8,000 were killed, 30,000 wounded, and 11,000 missing. The French losses were on a similar scale, and the naval losses must be added to the total casualties of the expedition. All the divisions had suffered, and, to the people of the Scottish Lowlands especially, the word Dardanelles came to bear the fateful meaning which Flodden bore for their ancestors. The results gained were not proportionate to this huge wastage—an advance of two miles on our left and one on our right. But not even at Ypres had our troops shown a more dauntless courage, a more complete devotion, or a more stubborn resolution. In a letter taken from a dead Turk was found this sentence: "These British are the finest fighters in the world. We have chosen the wrong friends." No kind of warfare involves a sterner trial for the human spirit than the slow sapping towards a fortress, when there is no obvious advance, no chance of the swift excitement of a manœuvre battle. Not less splendid was the performance of the French Corps. Under Gouraud the newest recruits had fought like heroes, and had shown the Turks that *furia francese* which centuries before had carried the walls of Jerusalem. "Shall not thou and I," said King Harry in the play to the Princess Katharine, "between Saint Denis and Saint George, compound a boy, half-French, half-English, that shall go to Constantinople and take the Turk by the beard?" The first half of Shakespeare's prophecy had come true. Saint Denis and Saint George fought in unison, but the beard of the Soldan was still unplucked. In this rivalry of gallant men the enemy was not outdone. The Turks fought with all their old patient steadfastness. They advanced to hopeless assaults, and died in hundreds in the open; they clung to ruined trenches when the Allied steel was upon them; but the stolid Anatolian peasants did not waver. To them the war was Kismet, and they obeyed orders uncomplainingly.

By the end of July the complete stalemate had compelled Sir Ian Hamilton to revise his strategy. A certain daring Englishman, who knew Turkey well, contrived to be taken blindfold one night into the enemy's trenches, and for several hours talked to the Turkish officers. He was told on parting: "Some day you may take Constantinople, but Achi Baba—never." This was rapidly becoming the view of those responsible for the expedition. The promised reinforcements were arriving during July at Egypt and Lemnos. To fling these into the congested butt of the peninsula was clearly folly. Had a quarter of the new 50,000 been present on 28th April we should by this time have been in Constantinople. Had a third been there in May or a half in June we should have won Achi Baba. That road was now barred, but another might be found, and Sir Ian Hamilton examined in turn the possibilities of Enos and Bulair and of the Asiatic coast. He found good reason for rejecting each terrain, and decided that he would use his new reserves in an attempt to break out from the Anzac position, and so turn the enemy in flank and rear. The new landing would be at Gaba Tepe and Suvla Bay.

CHAPTER XXXV.

THE STRAINING OF AMERICA'S PATIENCE.

America's Temper—Reasons for her Hostility to Germany—The Difficulties of immediate Intervention—President Wilson—German Activities in America—Dr. Dumba.

It is necessary at this stage to turn from the narrative of the campaigns in the Old World and consider the difficulties which confronted the greatest of neutral Powers, the Republic of the United States. A man who is engaged in a life-and-death struggle is inclined to resent the detachment of a friend, even though that friend has not shared in the cause of quarrel. Analogies from private life are too readily and too loosely applied to the affairs of nations, and surprise and irritation are engendered which seem baseless on a dispassionate survey of the facts. During August the neutrality of America became from various causes a razor-edge on which it seemed impossible for any government to continue to walk. The case for and against intervention was habitually overstated by the press of both continents, and in Britain especially there was a tendency to underestimate the difficulty of President Wilson's problem. America, even as a neutral, was called on to play so large a part in the war, and her attitude was so vital to the ultimate issue, that it will be well to examine with some care the intricacies of her position after the first year of conflict.

The temper of her people at that time and the reasoned convictions of her leaders were preponderatingly hostile to the German cause. The large Teutonic admixture in her population had not played the part which German publicists had forecast. In 1910 the foreign-born elements numbered $13\frac{1}{2}$ millions out of a total of 92 millions. There were just over $2\frac{1}{2}$ million Germans, nearly $1\frac{1}{4}$ million Austrians, and half a million Hungarians. The Irish, who numbered well over $1\frac{1}{4}$ million, had lost something of their hatred of Britain, save for a few fanatical organizations, and the bulk of them, even if they had little love for England, had less for Germany. The German-Americans, a thrifty, industrious, and law-abiding element, tended far more than most immigrants to be speedily absorbed, and to take on the native American characteristics. They had never played a large part in public life, and had developed no distinctive race stock. The younger generation was as a rule distinguishable only by its enthusiastic Americanism. Hence, except for recent immigrants, there were few bearers of German names who felt any real kinship with German ideals and interests. There was certainly no racial tradition strong enough to stand out against the very real anti-German feeling which soon predominated.

The origin of this feeling must be sought in a number of converging lines of development. The first was the historic kindness for France as an ancient ally, and the growing sense of community with Britain. The latter phenomenon deserves some explanation. In the past there had been endless misunderstandings, for a common tradition held with a difference may be the most potent of disruptive forces. The American Revolution, and still more the War of 1812, had left the seeds of bitterness. Britain's part during the Civil War did not improve matters, for the best-intentioned neutrality in such a struggle must be a provocation to criticism. American history-writing in those days was an elementary business—the simple virtues of the republican set against the scowling infamies of the monarchist. But as America advanced in power and wealth her outlook broadened. She became more critical, and discovered a truer perspective. Her scholars and thinkers were less inclined to the worship of mere words, and no longer found republicanism the source of all the virtues. Her social reformers discovered that a republic might be an oligarchy and a monarchy a democracy. As she moved towards a truer national culture of her own, she began to realize her debt to the Old World, above all to those islands from which she had inherited language, literature, law, and a thousand habits of thought. The touch of superciliousness which had marred the British attitude towards her through much of the nineteenth century disappeared on a closer understanding, and the whole-hearted admiration of modern Englishmen for her great personalities like Lee and Lincoln awakened an equal interest in contemporary British movements. American flamboyance was a defence against British patronage, and the two tended to decline together. As America took her place in the larger life of the world, she developed a new appreciation of that old land which had been battling with world-problems for four hundred years. She discovered, somewhat to her surprise, that in the last resort she had the same way of looking at the major matters of life as her cousin across the seas.

The recognition of what an American writer has called " like-mindedness " did not mean that the two peoples would always see eye to eye in everyday matters. There was a great deal of foolish talk about kinship by British writers and statesmen which was in defiance of the proved facts of history. Blood relationship and common standards do not prevent members of a family from moments of acute exasperation with each other. But in those ultimate crises which now and then confront nations and families, " like-mindedness " awakens all the subconscious instincts and dormant memories, and makes apparent the strong common structure below the surface differences. Even the most critical and contumacious households are likely in emergencies to show a solid front to the world.

A second reason was to be found in the American philosophy of politics. The United States has produced many learned publicists, but we shall not find her popular political philosophy in their admirable works. That philosophy, like all popular creeds, was crude and naïve, but it was universally held, and impregnated the habits of thought of the ordinary man to an extent which was probably not to be paralleled from any other people. Its keynote was liberty—an unanalysed term which degenerated often into a mere catchword, but which represented a very deep and abiding instinct. It was the old English instinct expounded with a new accent. Usually stated in the high-coloured Jeffersonian style, it was interpreted in practice with Alexander Hamilton's wary good sense. A man should be allowed to live his life in the greatest freedom compatible with the enjoyment of the same right by his fellows. The State had no doubt rights against the individual, but the individual had most vital rights against the State. It was for this freedom, construed in different senses, that both sides had fought in the Civil War. It was this worship of the individual which made America the stoniest soil on the globe for communist propaganda. It was this instinct which was responsible for much slackness and corruption and anarchy in her administration, since no half-truth can be safely worshipped. Hence the bureaucratic state, such as Prussia, was of all forms of government the most repellent to American minds. And this right of the individual to live freely was a right, too, of nations, however humble. Cæsarism, as well as bureaucracy, was anathema

Another item in the creed was a profound belief in law, an inheritance from English progenitors. The nation which had produced Story and Marshall, which lived by a written constitution, which had created the Supreme Court, which had fought a great war on the construction of a clause in an old document, which had had to forgo direct taxation because of a phrase in its charter of government, and which submitted time and again to serious administrative embarrassment rather than shake loose a single legal fetter —such a nation was not likely to have much sympathy with Germany's view that " reasons of State " might override any law, and that international law in especial was only a pious make-believe to keep the world quiet while the strong man armed. Laws might be broken in a fit of wrong-headedness or weakness, but that law should be deliberately contemned seemed to her an outrage on civilization.

Lastly, into her philosophy of the State she read the ordinary ethical code of Christianity. She believed in old-fashioned conservative right and wrong. The ethical anarchism which set special individuals or nations above Christian morals seemed to her at once blasphemous and silly. She had few subtleties in her national soul. Good was good and evil was evil, and no rhetoric or hair-splitting would make them otherwise. The strong Puritan strain at the back of her mixed ancestry was conspicuous in her public professions. Her practice might limp behind her creed, but at any rate she would never blaspheme the light. Such an attitude was not hypocrisy; it was fidelity to a profound conviction.

A third reason for fighting shy of Germany was to be found in that humanitarianism which is part of the American character. There is no reason to question the reality of this attribute. Monstrously cruel in its results as was much of her civilization, it was never so consciously or deliberately. She could not be brutal, since brutality implies premeditation. The nation was tender-hearted, with a great pity for weakness and suffering. Her desperate Civil War was waged on both sides with a singular chivalry. The German outrage on Belgium and the long series of infamies proved against the armies of the Emperor revolted America in her inmost soul. The detestation was increased when it presently became clear that these barbarities were calculated and were part of a carefully-thought-out system She might forgive the lapses of passion, but never the outrages of copybook desperadoes

A fourth cause was the pacificism to which as a national ideal she had long been committed. Her Civil War, one of the bloodiest in history, had involved the death of a million men, and had destroyed the best of her race stocks. The memory of that holocaust had inspired her with an intense hatred of war. Standing outside the ordinary diplomatic entanglements of the world, she had not brought herself to envisage an armed struggle between nations as an eternal contingency. Moreover, as a commercial people, she saw the economic loss and folly of warfare, and for long she had striven to give effect to her views and to lead the nations into the pleasant paths of conference and arbitration. The elements of militarism in her daily life were few. Her army was small, and as a profession made little appeal to her youth. Her navy was unknown to most of the inhabitants of her vast territories. Expenditure even upon defence seemed to her waste, for she had no urgent menace before her. Her love of abstractions and of high-sounding phrases made peace a favourite counter in her popular oratory. In this attitude there were, no doubt, unworthy elements. There was something of the pedant who generalizes from an exceptional case. There was much of the prosperous rich man who repudiates whatever has no immediate cash value. There was a touch, too, of self-righteousness, which is not the quality that exalteth a nation. Vapourings such as Mr. Bryan's were the product of a mind drunk with its ample rhetoric. But behind all these pacificist follies America had a sober conviction which did credit alike to her head and her heart. She had a vision of a wiser and not less virile world where " the glories of our blood and state " would be independent of the sword. To such an idealism the creed of the new children of Odin seemed the last and fatalest heresy.

Last, but not least, among these causes we must rank the incredible blindness of German diplomacy. Intensely conscious of her nationality, America found certain elements in her population treated by German agents as if they were still subjects of the Emperor—which, indeed, according to the German naturalization laws, many of them were. Proud of her independence and her position in the world, she had to submit to alternate threats and cajoleries, and to an insufferable patronage. Count Bernstorff and his coadjutors were masters in the art of blundering. There were weak points in the case of the Allies from an American point of view, which an adroit man might have used to advantage. There were features in the British conduct of the naval war which might easily have been turned into an irritant to inflame the quick American sense of legality. But Germany flung away lavishly the cards which the gods had given her. The Allies had no need of an advocate: Germany herself was the chief pleader in their case.

The consequence was that from the outset of the war the intelligence and the popular feeling of America had been against the Teutonic cause. A few political or legal theorists admired the German system; a few sociologists had an affection for the German municipal régime; a sprinkling of scientists looked up to German scholarship; some of the army officers professed esteem for the German army; one or two great financial houses could not forget their German affinities; and a considerable proportion of German-Americans made no secret of their sympathies. But these elements, though loudly vocal and well supported by a subsidized press, were a mere fraction of the American people. Some even of the leading German-Americans were favourable to the Allied cause. And the ablest statements of that cause came from the pens of men who, in the eyes of their countrymen, were the most representative and authoritative Americans.

It may be asked—it was a stock question at the time in France and Britain—why, since America's convictions were thus clear, she did not range herself forthwith with the Allies. When inquiry was made as to what it was proposed that America should do, the reply was that on behalf of international honour and public morals she should have declared war upon Germany, or that at any rate she should have called her to task. Both came to the same thing; for a protest, to which Germany would have given a summary answer, would, if strongly supported, have meant war. What reasonable ground was there for holding that it was America's duty, apart from direct provocation, to enter the struggle on the Allies' side. The matter is important, for on it depends our estimate of American conduct. We are dealing at present with the early stages of the war, before Germany's submarine policy had created a definite cause of offence.

Now it should never be forgotten that a nation, in making the momentous decision for or against an armed conflict, is guided not by sympathies but by interests. A statesman is bound to consider the enduring interests of his country, and not the passing moods of popular sentiment. He may for this reason have to fight an unpopular war, or to insist upon an unpopular peace. It may be the highest unwisdom, because the feelings of his countrymen are moved on a particular issue, such as the misfortune of a dynasty, or the harsh treatment of a little state, to go crusading on its behalf. It is not his business to act as *censor morum* to the world at large, or as the knight-errant of distressed peoples. His duty is to consider the good of his own realm. Occasionally he may be forced by popular clamour to take up arms lest his country be rent internally. But, save in this extreme instance, his path is clear. The steady light of policy, and not the marsh-fires of sentiment, must be his guiding star.

In the case of America it might well be argued that her deepest interests would be malignly affected by Germany's success. But to set against this we must remember that the conflict in the Old World appeared to American observers to be at least evenly matched, and that they did not seriously believe that Germany would win in the long run. Had the odds in favour of the Central Powers been greater, American policy might have shaped itself differently from the beginning. Again, it was clear that American sympathy with the Allies, while sincere in itself, was by no means so intense as to force the hand of a politic statesman. Advocates for immediate intervention, such as Mr. Roosevelt, based their argument rather on sentiment than on policy, and that sentiment was still far short of a passion. America as a whole was anxious that the Allies should be victorious, but she did not consider it her duty to take up cudgels in a quarrel which at first only remotely concerned her. Her statesmen believed with much reason that neutrality was for her the path of interest, and by no means inconsistent with honour. The popular temper was slightly different, but not different enough to set up a dangerous antagonism to these counsels of peace.

President Wilson, therefore, played a discreet and aloof part, and he was supported in it by the great majority of his countrymen. America realized what many of her critics failed to understand, that an active participation in the conflict was the only alternative to complete neutrality, and she did not see her way to so bold a step. She knew little about the actual quarrel, for the average American was profoundly ignorant of foreign affairs. She remembered Washington's warning against European engagements,[*] and Jefferson's famous watchword, " Peace, commerce, and honest friendship with all nations, entangling alliances with none." Her cherished Monroe Doctrine was the charter of her

[*] " Europe has a set of primary interests, which to us have none or very remote relations. Hence she must be engaged in frequent controversies, the causes of which are essentially foreign to our concerns."

detachment. At the Hague Conferences of 1899 and 1907 she had formally restated her "traditional policy of not intruding upon, interfering with, or entangling herself in the political questions or policy or internal administration of any foreign state," and she had become a party to the Algeciras Treaty with the same reservation. A decade earlier she had appeared to assume the duties of a World Power, but her experience in the Philippines had caused a reaction against this nascent imperialism, and her recent relations with Mexico had sickened her of foreign adventures.

These reasons decided public opinion, and, since in America public opinion is the true sovereign, President Wilson was loyal to his master. The President of the United States has in theory more absolute executive powers than any ruler in the world But he is bound to an unseen chariot wheel. He dare not outrun the wishes of the majority of the citizens. His pace is as fast as theirs, but no faster, or he courts a fall. A true democracy is a docile follower of a leader whom it has once trusted. But an incomplete democracy, such as America, demands not a leader but a fellow-wayfarer who can act as spokesman. Hence it was idle to talk of President Wilson's policy as if it were the conclusions and deeds of an individual. It was his business to interpret the opinion of America at large, and there is no reason to believe that he erred in this duty. A vital and magnetic personality like Mr. Roosevelt could, indeed, create opinion on his own account, and initiate novel departures. But Mr. Roosevelt was not the orthodox Presidential type. Mr. Wilson was far more in the true line of succession from the founders of the republic. He was a man of wide and liberal ideas, and a deeply-read student of history and politics. Probably no modern ruler has ever brought to his task a stronger equipment of theoretical knowledge. Though a Democrat, he did not follow the Jeffersonian tradition, and his best-known political work revealed him as an enthusiast for the new American imperialism. His political career before his election showed that he possessed courage and initiative. In those days he described him· self as " a conservative with a move on," a phrase which may be taken as a summary of the central public opinion of both America and Britain. His detractors called him academic, but the term was an unwilling tribute to the judicial quality of his mind. Having decided that the temper and the interests of his country were on the side of neutrality, he balanced the scales with a meticulous precision. That in itself was no slight achievement in the midst of a universal hurricane of war.

His mistake, and that of his friends, was that they were apt in their public utterances to base their policy on the wrong grounds, and to spoil their case with irrelevant rhetoric. America's conduct was founded on self-interest and on nothing else. She looked to present and future advantages, as she was justified in doing. No man is bound to be a crusader, and no nation is called upon to be quixotic. But when the President, in an unfortunate phrase, declared that America was " too proud to fight," and when others, with half the world suffering for the eternal principles of right and wrong, announced that American neutrality was a triumph in the cause of human progress, it had an ugly air of cant. Common sense is an excellent thing in its way, but it is not heroic. The successful merchant becomes an offence when he masquerades as a paladin.

The American attitude was a godsend to Germany, but the latter had not the wit to appreciate her blessings. The difficulty arose over the Allied command of the sea. American markets were open to all the belligerents to purchase munitions of war, but only the Allies could take delivery. Germany protested that this one-sided commerce was a breach of neutrality, which it certainly was not, and received on this point a very clear answer from the President. Then she set herself with immense industry to hamper the Allied purchases by fomenting internal trouble in the United States. Presently came the British blockade, and her reply to it by submarine warfare. The indiscriminating nature of the latter campaign was certain to bring about trouble with neutrals, but Germany presumed upon American disinclination for war. She believed that she had the measure of Washington, and that if she spoke fair words she could escape the consequences of her own offences, and, if fortune smiled, even provoke a breach with Britain. She trusted Count Bernstorff and his merry men to organize German sympathizers across the Atlantic, and use the western and the southern states to balance the eastern. Meanwhile her submarines would pursue their business unchecked. If America suffered she would apologize—and a little later do it again.

The sinking of the *Lusitania*, when over a hundred of her citizens lost their lives, first awoke America to the nature of Germany's game. It led to the retirement of that clumsy diplomatist, Herr Dernburg, who at the request of the American Government returned to his fatherland on 13th June. In an earlier chapter we have considered President Wilson's Notes to Berlin, and the evasive answers they received. The Note of 21st July was in the nature of an ultimatum. It declared that American citizens were within their rights in travelling wherever they wished on the high seas, and that the American Government would take the necessary steps to protect these rights. Germany was not slow to put this resolution to the proof. At half-past nine on the morning of Thursday, 19th August, the White Star liner *Arabic*, which had left Liverpool for New York the afternoon before, was torpedoed and sunk off Cape Clear without warning by a German submarine. The loss of life was small, as the vessel remained afloat for ten minutes, and there was time to lower the boats. But the indignation in America at this outrage was great, for twenty-six Americans were among the passengers. The first German excuses were that the *Arabic* was a British ship going out for a cargo of war materials, and carrying on board gold to pay for them; that the vessel had been mined, not torpedoed; and that in the alternative, if torpedoed, it was because she had tried to ram the submarine after notice had been given her to stop. This curiously inconsistent defence was disproved in every detail by the officials of the shipping company, and by the affidavits of American survivors. The wrath of the American people was so unmistakable that Count Bernstorff thought it well to trim. He implored Washington to wait for the official report, adding the usual diplomatic assurance about his Government's regret if American lives had been lost. Eight days later he informed Mr. Lansing that full satisfaction would be given to America for the sinking of the *Arabic*, while Jagow announced that before that event Germany had adopted a policy designed to settle the whole submarine problem.

What this policy was appeared on 1st September, when Count Bernstorff handed Mr. Lansing a written pledge. "I beg to inform you," it ran, "that my instructions concerning our answer to your last *Lusitania* Note contain the following passage: 'Liners will not be sunk by submarines without warning, and without ensuring the safety of the lives of non-combatants, provided that the liners do not try to escape or offer resistance.' Although I know that you do not wish to discuss the *Lusitania* question until the *Arabic* incident has been definitely and satisfactorily settled, I desire to inform you of the above, because this policy was decided upon by my Government before the *Arabic* incident occurred." This undertaking obviously fell far short of America's requirements. It ignored Mr. Lansing's assertion of the rights of neutrals bound on lawful errands in ships of belligerent nationality to be preserved in life and limb, for no submarine was able to ensure their preservation. It could drive them into the boats before torpedoing the vessel, but small boats in mid-ocean may be a slender basis of security. There were cases during the war of one being without food and water for four days before being picked up, and of consequent deaths from exposure. Again, it applied only to passenger liners and not to ordinary merchant ships. Further, a submarine could sight a liner before a liner could see a submarine, and the field was wide for bogus charges of attempted escape. Yet in spite of its ambiguity and insufficiency, the undertaking was received in America with a pæan of triumph over Mr. Lansing's diplomacy, and eulogies of Count Bernstorff's moderation. That a hard-headed race should have shown such enthusiasm over a dubious promise showed the intense disinclination of the American people for war, and President Wilson's success in interpreting the feelings of his countrymen.

The truth was that at this time the star of Tirpitz was obscured. Germany found that her submarines were mysteriously disappearing, and that the value of the whole campaign was scarcely worth the price. Quick to seize a momentary advantage, Count Bernstorff used the new temper of America to angle for the support of the peace sentimentalists. His agents in the press and elsewhere hinted not obscurely that the Emperor wished to settle the submarine controversy in order to get the help of the United States in bringing the war to a close. This was indeed Germany's main desire at the moment, and, while her arms were triumphant in Russia, she hoped for a peace on her own terms. But in the midst of this atmosphere of brotherhood, when righteousness and peace in the shape of the German Embassy and the American Foreign Office kissed mutually, there fell a thunderbolt. About half-past eight on the night of Saturday, 4th September, the Allan liner *Hesperian* was torpedoed without warning, 130 miles west of Queenstown. The vessel did not sink immediately, and was towed towards port, but foundered at seven o'clock on the morning of Monday, the 6th. There was a small loss of life, but among the crew were two American citizens. The incident played havoc with the new harmony. It was clear to America that whatever the Government of Berlin might say, and whatever instructions might be given, submarine commanders would go on their old path, and would invent some excuse or other to cover their actions. The irritation was increased by the official Note on the subject of the *Arabic*, which was handed to the Ambassador in Berlin on

7th September. In it an unbelievable tale was told of a deliberate attack by the liner on the submarine, and it was announced that, even if the commander had made a mistake, Germany could not recognize any duty of compensation. In the event of no agreement being reached, she offered to submit the matter to the Hague Tribunal. This Note the American Government refused to accept.

It was now becoming apparent that no undertaking by Germany had any real significance, since in each case she would allege some special circumstance which took it out of the general rule she had agreed to observe. While the reaction from the premature rejoicing of the first days of September was in full swing, American patience received the hardest trial of all. It was bad enough to have Germany playing fast and loose with the lives of American citizens on the high seas, but it was worse to find her tampering with domestic affairs within America itself. For months there had been rumours of sinister underground activities directed from the German Embassy in Washington. Passports had been falsified—a work in which the naval and military attachés, Boy-Ed and von Papen, were the prime movers. The methods of the Black Hand were adopted. There were dynamite outrages in Canada and incendiary fires in various factories throughout the Union German money was lavished in subsidizing a portion of the American press, and in distributing pro-German literature. During August the *New York World* published documentary evidence to prove the establishment of a German press bureau under the pretence of an impartial agency for the supply of news. It showed that Count Bernstorff had an income of some £400,000 a week for propagandist purposes. It proved also that German emissaries were engaged in engineering strikes in American munition works, and that German agents were urging the Imperial Chancellor to prevent the dispatch of goods purchased in Germany by United States manufacturers in order that the blame might be put upon the British blockade. This constituted a gross interference with internal American affairs, which not even the most pacific people would be likely to tolerate. But matters reached a head on 6th September, when the Dumba case was made public.

This business, for all its seriousness, belonged so much to the world of pure comedy that it affords a welcome relief to the grimmer chronicle of war. On 30th August the steamer *Rotterdam* touched at Falmouth In it was an American journalist, Archibald by name, whose aim in life seems to have been the acquiring of minor foreign decorations. The night before his departure from New York this agreeable cosmopolitan had dined with the German and Austrian Ambassadors, and, as an aspirant for the Iron Cross, had been entrusted with some highly confidential messages. He was also given a number of letters of introduction, including one to Kuhlmann at the Hague, and in a covering letter Count Bernstorff expressed his pleasure that he was once more returning to Europe " after having promoted our interests out here in such a zealous and successful manner." In another letter von Papen wrote of him as "a strictly impartial journalist." This pose was, of course, necessary for the success of the former activities. In the Archibald budget seized by the British authorities there were documents bearing the signatures of Count Bernstorff, Dr. Dumba, and von Papen. Count Bernstorff's principal contribution was a copy of his memorandum to Mr. Lansing of 10th June, in which he dealt with the charges of American newspapers that Germany was negotiating for the purchase of factories and war material in the United States. These charges he categorically denied. There was also a memorandum from the same hand, dated 18th August, in which he faced the difficult problem raised by the *New York World's* disclosures. On the 31st of July Dr. Albert, the Financial Adviser to the German Embassy, had lost his portfolio in the New York Elevated Railway, stolen from him, he declared, by the spies of the British Secret Service. This portfolio came, as we have seen, into the hands of the *New York World*, and for a week or so made sensational reading for the students of American journalism. Count Bernstorff accordingly felt himself obliged to offer to the American Government a "short statement concerning the facts." He did not disclaim any longer the German attempt to obtain control of American munition factories, or to purchase their output. He declared, indeed, that nothing of the sort had as yet been achieved, but he asserted—with some reason—Germany's right to do it if she had the money for the purpose. That Germany had ever tried to stir up strikes or "take part in a plot against the economic peace " of America he resolutely denied. He denied also that there was anything improper in the very modest press campaign which Germany had conducted. So much for the Ambassador. Unfortunately, his wholly correct sentiments were not shared by his colleagues and underlings. Dumba and von Papen ingenuously toppled down the tall tower of ambassadorial decorum.

Dumba, the Austro-Hungarian Ambassador, was one of those

stormy petrels of diplomacy who have often found shelter in the dovecotes of the Ballplatz. A Macedonian by birth, the world first heard of him as an *agent-provocateur* in the Balkans. He was a walker in tortuous ways, with a front of brass and an elastic conscience. The Archibald portfolio contained three of his dispatches to the Foreign Minister at Vienna. The first was not published. The second contained a very full description of the efforts he had made to stir up unrest among the munition workers. This was dated 20th August, two days after Count Bernstorff had sent his official denial to Mr. Lansing. "It is my impression," wrote Dumba, " that we can disorganize and hold up for months, if not entirely prevent, the manufacture of munitions in Bethlehem and the Middle West, which, in the opinion of the German military attaché, is of great importance, and amply outweighs the comparatively small expenditure of money involved." In the next sentence he revealed himself as a social reformer. " Even if the strikes do not come off, it is probable that we should extort more favourable conditions of labour for our poor down-trodden fellow-countrymen. In Bethlehem these white slaves are now working for twelve hours a day and seven days a week! All weak persons succumb and become consumptives." Dumba was a provident soul, and was resolved, if the secret came out, to pose as a philanthropist. Then he proceeded to implicate the German Embassy. "So far as German workmen are found among the skilled hands, a means of leaving will be provided immediately for them. Besides this, a private German registry office has been established, which provides employment for persons who have voluntarily given up their places, and it is already working well." He enlarged on the details. He explained what the local Hungarian, Slovak, and German press was doing, and how its activities could be increased. It may be noticed in passing that this was a libel on the Slovaks in America, who had shown themselves throughout on the side of the Allies. One passage revealed the main lines of the plot. " To Bethlehem must be sent as many reliable Hungarian and German workmen as I can lay my hands on, who will join the factories and begin their work in secret among their fellow-workmen. For this purpose I have my men turners in steel-work. We must send an organizer who, in the interests of the Union, will begin the business in his own way. We must also send so-called 'soap-box' orators, who will know how to start a useful agitation. We shall want money for popular meetings, and possibly for organizing picnics. In general, the same applies to the

Middle West. I am thinking of Pittsburg and Cleveland in the first instance."

The third Dumba dispatch was a long rigmarole about the best ways of inflaming the anger of American importers against Britain. There was also a letter in which the *New York World* disclosures were discussed. "Count Bernstorff," we were told, " took up the position that these slanders required no answer, and had the happy inspiration to refuse any explanation. He is in no way compromised." As we know, Count Bernstorff did explain the whole matter to Mr. Lansing, and had the happy inspiration to deny the charge of fomenting strikes. Dumba, who knew the truth, went on to console himself and his employers with the reflection, " there is no evidence to support the main charge." That evidence, by the favour of Archibald, the world possessed on 6th September.

Von Papen's contributions were the most curious of all. One referred to the ordinary small talk of the espionage business. One, addressed to the German Ministry of War, revealed the fact that German agents had bought up large amounts of war material, and had great difficulty in knowing what to do with them. It was proposed, among other things, to dump a quantity of toluol on the Norwegian Government. But the most interesting document was a private letter which is worth quoting in full :—

" We have great need of being bucked up, as they say here. Since Sunday a new storm has been raging against us—and because of what ? I'm sending you a few cuttings from the newspapers that will amuse you. Unfortunately they stole a fat portfolio from our good Albert in the Elevated (English Secret Service, of course !), of which the principal contents have been published. You can imagine the sensation among the Americans ! Unfortunately there were some very important things from my report among them, such as the buying up of liquid chlorine and about the Bridgeport Projectile Company, as well as documents regarding the buying up of phenol (from which explosives are made), and the acquisition of the Wrights' aeroplane patent. But things like that must occur. I send you Albert's reply for you to see how we protect ourselves. We composed the document together yesterday. It seems quite likely that we shall meet again soon. The sinking of the *Adriatic* [sic] may well be the last straw. I hope in our interest that the danger will blow over. How splendid on the Eastern front ! I always say to these idiotic Yankees they had better hold their tongues—it's better to look at all this heroism full of admiration. My friends in the army are quite different in this way."

No nation, not even the most pacific, likes to be called idiotic. The Archibald disclosures coming on the top of the unsatisfactory reply about the sinking of the *Arabic*, and the more recent *Hesperian* incident, left an ugly impression on the public mind of America. The Austrian Embassy was revealed as a nest of insolent intriguers. The German ambassador was shown writing pompous disclaimers to Mr. Lansing with his tongue in his cheek, while his satellites of the von Papen type were busy at the very activities which he denied. The whole German attitude towards the United States was now blindingly clear. " These good and naïve Americans," said the German Government, " live on a diet of windy words. Let us flatter their bent and give them plenty of this inexpensive provender, and we need not deviate one inch from the course we have set ourselves. They are determined not to fight, and will seize on any shadow of an excuse to keep out of the quarrel."

This conclusion, though it had much surface justification, was a complete misreading of the American temper. We need not blame the Teutonic ambassadors too much. The private correspondence of most embassies, if published unexpectedly, would make sensational reading for the countries concerned. " The most malicious democrat," wrote Bismarck on one occasion, " can have no idea what nullity and charlatanry are concealed in diplomacy." But we may be grateful that a fortunate chance let in the light on a colossal humbug. America was wounded in her *amour propre*, and was compelled to take firm action. Washington demanded that Dumba should be recalled, on the ground that he had been guilty of a violation of diplomatic propriety. Vienna hesitated and quibbled, and Dumba was thereupon handed his passports. By the middle of September the reputation of the German Embassy had fallen like speculative stocks in a financial crisis. The chance of floating an Allied loan, which had not been rosy during the summer, and in the beginning of September had looked black indeed, had by the middle of the month suddenly become hopeful. The Government objection had been the risk of stirring up bad feeling between the heterogeneous elements in the American people, but Count Bernstorff and his friends had nullified that argument. Their ill-advised intrigues had spilt the fat into the fire, and made a decorous neutrality impossible.

CHAPTER XXXVI.

GALLIPOLI: THE NEW LANDING.
August 6-27, 1915.

The New Plan—Suvla Bay and its Neighbourhood—The New British Divisions—The Preliminary Attack at Cape Helles—The Anzac Advance on Koja Chemen—The Landing at Suvla—Its Failure.

By the end of July preparations had been made for a final effort against the Gallipoli defences. Three divisions of the New Army and two Territorial Divisions had arrived in the Eastern Mediterranean, and a mounted Division had been for some months in Egypt. The submarine menace had sent the monsters of the British Fleet back to home waters or to the shelter of protected harbours, and during the summer only the destroyers, a few light cruisers, and an occasional battleship were seen off the shores of the peninsula. But in July new craft arrived, specially constructed to meet the case. A strange type of monitor, with a freeboard almost flush with the water, and looking more like a Chinese pagoda than a ship, suddenly appeared in the northern Ægean. They were of different sizes, the smaller being little more than floating gun-platforms; but they were admirably suited for their purpose. Even the little ones, with a crew of seventy, could fling 100 lbs. of high explosive twelve miles, and they feared submarines no more than a gull fears a swordfish. There were also cruisers protected by lateral protuberances, which our men knew as "blister ships," and motor lighters, profanely called "beetles," for landing purposes. The preliminaries of the new assault on the naval side were prepared.

The plan which Sir Ian Hamilton had evolved was bold and ingenious. To understand it we must note the features of the peninsula north of the Anzac position. The Australians held, as we have seen, the edge of the plateau at the top of the long ravines which run to the coast. Eastwards the land rises in the uplands of Sari Bair, till about a mile and a half north-east of the position the culminating point of the system is reached in the peak 305, nearly 1,000 feet high, called by the Turks Koja Chemen. On all sides the ground slopes away from the crest, which is distant some four miles as the crow flies from the waters of the Straits, and five from Maidos and the Narrows. North and west a jumble of ridges falls towards the Gulf of Saros—ridges wildly broken and confused, sometimes bare scree and clay, sometimes matted with scrub and separated by dry and tortuous nullahs. From a point on the shore of the Gulf of Saros south of the Fisherman's Hut a fairly well-marked ridge, called Walker's Ridge in the lower part, runs up to the Koja Chemen summit. On this there are various points which were to become only too famous, notably Chunuk Bair, nearly 900 feet high, and Q, or Nameless Peak, between it and Hill 305. North of this is a watercourse called the Sazli Beit Dere, and a little farther north the Chailak Dere. Separating the two is a long spur which leaves the parent *massif* just west of Chunuk Bair. Its upper part was called by our men Rhododendron Ridge, and the under features nearer the coast were known as Big and Little Table Tops. North of Chailak Dere is another ridge, with the feature known as Bauchop's Hill. Still farther north is a wide watercourse, the Aghyl Dere, which near its head splits into two forks, both descending from Hill 305. From the Fisherman's Hut the flat ground between the hills and the sea widens northwards, as the coast sweeps towards the cape called Nebrunessi. Beyond is the half-moon of Suvla or Anafarta Bay, two miles wide, enclosed between Nebrunessi and the cape of Suvla Burnu, the north-western extremity of the Gallipoli Peninsula

The hinterland of Suvla Bay is curious. It consists of a rectangle of hills lying north of the Azmak Dere watercourse, and connected towards the east with the outflankers of the Koja Chemen system. The north side, lining the coast, is the ridge of Karakol Dagh, over 400 feet high. The south side, lining the Azmak Dere, and breaking down into flats, two miles from the coast, is a blunt range, rising as high as 500 feet, of which the westerly part is called Yilghin Burnu, and was to become noted later as Chocolate Hill. The eastern side of the rectangle is a rocky crest, rising in one part to nearly 900 feet, and falling shorewards in two well-marked terraces. Between the three sides of hill, from the eastern terraces to the sea, the ground is nearly flat. Along the edge of Suvla Bay

The Salt Lake, Suvla Bay
From a painting by Norman Wilkinson

runs a narrow causeway of sand, and immediately behind it lies a large salt lake, in summer partly dried up, but always liable to be converted by rain into an impassable swamp. Eastward of it the hills and flats are patched with farms and scrub, mostly dwarf oaks, and on the edge of the terraces the scrub grows into something like woodland. Everywhere the plain is cracked with futile watercourses. Two villages are points in the hinterland—Kuchuk (or Little) Anafarta on the slopes at the south-eastern angle of the enclosing hills, and Biyuk (or Big) Anafarta two miles south across the watercourse of the Azmak Dere, and just under the northern spurs of Koja Chemen. The road connecting the two runs southwards to Boghali Kalessi on the Straits.

In the beginning of August the Fast of Ramadan was drawing to its close, and for a little there had been something like stagnation in the opposing lines. Sir Ian Hamilton, aware that the Turks were massing forces for a new attack, was resolved to anticipate them. The plan he adopted involved four separate movements. In the first place, a feint was to be made at the head of the Gulf of Saros, as if to take in flank and rear the Bulair lines. Next, a strong offensive would be assumed by the troops in the Cape Helles region against their old objective, Achi Baba. These two movements would be read by the Turks as the main British offensive and its covering feint, and it was hoped would lead them to send their reserves to Krithia. But in the meantime the Anzac Corps was to advance with its left, and attempt to gain the heights of Koja Chemen and the seaward ridges. It was impossible to attack eastward, for on that side the enemy was well prepared; but if Birdwood could strike out to the north-east, and then wheel to his right, he would assail Sari Bair on its steep north-western slopes, where no attack was expected. Simultaneously, a great new landing would be made at Suvla Bay, where it was believed the Turks would be wholly unprepared. Suvla Bay had the advantage that it was well sheltered from the prevailing winds, and afforded a submarine-proof base. If the Anafarta hills could be taken, and the right of the new landing force linked up with the left of the Australasians, the British would hold the central crest of the spine of upland which runs through the western end of the peninsula. Such gains would enable them to cut the communications of the Turks in the butt-end, the one land route to Maidos would be commanded, and the way would be prepared for an action in open country, when the grim Turkish fortifications of the Pasha Dagh would be taken in flank and in reverse. If the undertaking attained the most reasonable success, the western end of the peninsula would be ours, and the European defences of the Narrows would be won.

The plan was bold, but entirely legitimate, and its details were worked out with great care by Sir Ian Hamilton and his Staff. The element of surprise could be rightly counted upon. Some of the operations would be difficult, but no single one seemed beyond the capacity of British troops. He had the necessary force to make the attempt, and considerable reserves behind his first attack. The plan was indeed one of the few strategic devices showing any originality and imaginative breadth which the Allies evolved during the first two years of the war. But at the same time it was attended by many risks. The chief danger lay in the fact that all the movements were so closely interdependent. Exact timing was imperative, since three separate forces were employed, and for this was needed not only a good Headquarters plan, but the most assiduous Staff supervision from hour to hour. But the staffs of the new divisions were still raw to their task, and their first employment in the field was to be in a surprise landing and intricate night movements. Moreover, the troops engaged must be of uniform capacity, for the failure of any one unit would jeopardize the success of the whole. A defect in divisional leading or in the stamina of one brigade would nullify the most splendid victories of other parts of the line. Such a risk is inevitable in any elaborate movement, but in this case it was accentuated by the fact that a considerable portion of the attacking force was wholly untried. The three new divisions destined for the attempt had never before been in action. One, the 13th, had indeed had a few weeks' experience on the Helles front, but the others were novices in war. It will be seen that Sir Ian Hamilton had devised an intricate scheme for which he had at his disposal somewhat raw material. He chose to take the risk in the hope that the new divisions would show the same aptitude as the 42nd and the 52nd. Indeed, unless he were to forgo the chance, he had no alternative, for to move his seasoned troops from Helles to Suvla would have cast an impossible burden upon the Navy and the transport services.

The 13th (Western) division of the New Army, under Major-General F. C. Shaw, began to arrive at Helles in the first half of July. The 11th (Northern) Division, under Major-General Hammersley, appeared in the second half of the month, one brigade going to Helles and two to Imbros. At the end of July came the 10th (Irish) Division under Lieut.-General Sir Bryan Mahon, part of it going to Mitylene in Lesbos, and part to Mudros. The two Territorial Divisions—the 53rd Welsh (Major-General F. S. Inglefield) and the 54th East Anglian (Major-General the Hon. J. E Lindley) were not due till 10th August. A new army corps, the 9th, was constituted from the 10th, 11th, and 13th Divisions, under the command of Lieut.-General Sir Frederick Stopford Sir Ian Hamilton had no say in the appointment of the commanders ; he had asked for Sir Julian Byng and Sir Henry Rawlinson for the new corps, but was refused, and could only acquiesce in Kitchener's nominations. Sir Frederick Stopford was a man of over sixty, and though a distinguished Staff officer had never held high command in the field. General Inglefield was also over sixty. General Hammersley was in poor health, and had recently had a serious breakdown. The choice of commanders obviously increased the unknown risks of the Suvla enterprise, for they were as unproved in this form of war as the troops they led. According to Sir Ian Hamilton's plan, Birdwood, for his attack on Sari Bair, was to have his two Anzac divisions, together with the new 13th Division, the 29th Brigade of the 10th Division, and the 29th Indian Brigade. Stopford, at Suvla, would have the remaining brigades of the 10th Division, the 11th Division, and presently the 53rd and 54th Territorial Divisions. For the total operation there would be— at Helles, 23,000 British and 17,000 French infantry ; at Anzac, 37,000 ; at Suvla, 30,000. The Turkish forces now on the peninsula were probably not less than a dozen divisions. It was a weak point in the British plan that so large a proportion had to be maintained at Helles, the least vital part of the battlefield, because of a threatened Turkish attack which might ruin at the outset all our preparations.

Let us consider first the preliminaries to the main assault. On the afternoon of Friday, 6th August, the 8th Corps at Cape Helles made a general attack upon the Turkish position at Achi Baba. The brunt of the fighting fell to the 29th Division, holding the left of the line, and the East Lancashire Territorials of the 42nd Division on their right. In the early afternoon the 88th Brigade, after an artillery preparation, attacked across open ground against a section of the enemy's front which had defied all our previous assaults. The attack was boldly delivered, but failed to win its objective, and there were many losses among the leading battalions. The Lancashire Territorials were also heavily engaged east of the Krithia road, and advanced the line at one point 200 yards. The Turkish line had been reinforced by two fresh divisions, and their offensive had only been anticipated by an hour or two. Consequently next morning we had to face a counter-attack, which we repelled, and which was followed by an advance of the 125th and 129th Brigades. For the two days following the struggle raged, principally in the centre round the vineyard west of the Krithia road. This engagement was intended as a holding battle, and as such it must be regarded as successful. It distracted the attention of the Turks for the moment from the main theatre farther north, and induced them to send the bulk of their new reserves to Achi Baba.

We pass to the desperate struggle in the area of the Anzac Corps, in many ways the most desperate and the most brilliant which Gallipoli had yet seen. The operation, of which the details had been left to Birdwood, was arranged in two parts. An attack was first to be made by troops of the Australian Division on the right against the Lone Pine Plateau, a position which commanded one of the main sources of the Turkish water supply. It was in essence a feint to cover the movements of General Godley's forces on the left, which were to move up the coast and deliver a converging assault with two columns against the heights of Koja Chemen. The Australians began the attack at five in the afternoon of the 6th, when the action at Cape Helles had well started, and the troops employed were the 1st Infantry Brigade, the men of New South Wales, under Brigadier-General Smyth. The Turkish trenches at the Lone Pine were enormously strong, and had been roofed in with great logs as a cover against shrapnel. After half an hour's bombardment by the artillery and the ships' guns, the Australians—every man with a white band on his sleeve—raced across the open, and in a few minutes were upon the enemy's position. Then began a deadly struggle for the roofed trenches, while the Turkish artillery and machine guns played upon the exposed attack. No cover was to be had, for the shell of the position had to be broken before the men could get into the entrenchments. An observer has described that strange contest. " Some fired down into the loopholes ; some, who happened to find small gaps in the line of head-cover in front of them, jumped down there and began to work into the dark shelters under the head-cover where the Turks were ; others went on over the first trench, and even over the second trench, and into communication trenches which had no head-cover over them, and through which the Turks were fleeing. Others noticed that in the solid roof in front of them, near the edge where the loopholes were, there were manholes left at intervals, apparently to allow the listening patrols to creep through at night. They were just large enough to allow a man to wriggle through, and that was enough for the 1st Brigade. They wriggled down into them, feet foremost, as a burglar might into a skylight " In a quarter of an hour the first Turkish line had been carried, and before the summer night fell the Lone Pine position had been won. The victors had to maintain their ground for the next few days, until 12th August, against violent counter-attacks, and this they achieved with a stubbornness as conspicuous as the fury of their assault. The action was fruitful, for it drew all the local Turkish reserves to meet it, and as a feat of arms it cannot be overpraised. In Sir Ian Hamilton's words, " One weak Australian brigade, numbering at the outset but 2,000 rifles, and supported only by two weak battalions, carried the work under the eyes of a whole enemy division, and maintained their grip upon it like a vice during six days' successive counter-attacks." The high gallantry of the performance may be realized from the fact that of the nine Victoria Crosses awarded for the August battles at Gallipoli seven went to the conquerors of Lone Pine.

Meantime the Anzac left wing had begun to move in the first darkness of that night of the 6th. General Godley's force consisted of the New Zealand and Australian Division, less the 1st and 3rd Light Horse Brigades, the 13th Division of the New Army, less five battalions, and General Cox's 29th Indian Infantry Brigade. The 29th Brigade of the 10th Division and the 38th Brigade of the 13th Division were held in reserve. The plan was to divide the force into right and left covering columns and right and left columns of assault. The right covering column, under General Russell, was to seize the Table Tops, and the position between the Sazli Beit Dere and the Chailak Dere ravines. The left covering column, under General Travers, was directed to occupy the hill called Damakjelik Bair, north of the Aghyl Dere nullah. The right column of assault, under General Johnston, was to move up the ravines against the Chunuk Bair ridge, and the left column of assault, under General Cox, to work up the Aghyl Dere against the summit peak, Hill 305.

At 9 30 p m. General Russell's column, including the New Zealand Mounted Rifle Brigade, the Otago Mounted Rifles, and the Maori contingent, moved along the coast as pioneers to clear the foothills. A destroyer bombarded as usual the Turkish trenches, and the occupants took cover ; but to their amazement, when the firing ceased, they found the New Zealand bayonets upon them.

The Auckland and Wellington Mounted Rifles on the right cleared the Little and Big Table Tops, which are the lowest points on the ridge between the Sazli Beit Dere and the Chailak Dere, while the Otago and Canterbury Regiments swung farther north to occupy the ridge named Bauchop's Hill. The work was done in silence, and, as in all night attacks, there was some confusion. Men lost their way in the darkness, for the foothills were a maze of broken ridges and indeterminate gullies. Soon the Turks were alive to the movement, and their fire sputtered over the whole hillside. By dawn much had been won, including the two Table Tops and part of Bauchop's Hill, where the officer who gave the place his name had fallen. Meanwhile General Travers's column, which included part of the 40th Brigade of the 13th Division, the 4th South Wales Borderers, and the 5th Wiltshires, pushed up the coast and attacked Damakjelik Bair. By 1.30 in the morning the whole place was carried, a fine piece of work for the New Army. The way was now prepared for the columns of assault.

On Saturday, the 7th, at dawn, the main operation began. Before we consider the attack of the left wing on Koja Chemen, we must glance at the supporting movement in the centre, designed to engage part of the enemy's strength. Very early in the morning, part of the 3rd Australian Light Horse Brigade advanced from their trenches on Walker's Ridge, while part of the 1st Light Horse Brigade attacked on the right from Quinn's Post at the head of Shrapnel Valley, where they were supported by a detachment of the Welsh Fusiliers. The attack of those magnificent troopers, unequalled both in physique and in courage, had never a chance of succeeding. Line after line left the parapets, to be met with a storm of fire in which no mortal could live. For a moment, but only for a moment, the flag of the Light Horse fluttered from a corner of the Turkish position, where a few desperate adventurers had carried it, but presently it had gone. The affair was over in a quarter of an hour, and must stand as one of the most heroic and forlorn of the episodes of the campaign. Of the 450 men who attacked from Walker's Ridge, less than 100 came back, and of the 300 at Quinn's Post no more than 13. Yet the sacrifice was not in vain. It pinned down to their trenches the Turkish centre for many hours, for the enemy believed that such amazing valour must be the prelude to a great concerted attack.

We must now follow the fortunes of Godley's two columns of assault. Johnston's column, on the right, consisting of the New Zealand Infantry Brigade, was ordered to advance up the gullies on each side of the Table Tops ridge against the summit of Chunuk Bair. On the left, Cox's column, made up of the 4th Australian Brigade and the 29th Indian Infantry Brigade, was to make a circuit to the north, and move up the Aghyl Dere against the northern flanks of Koja Chemen.

It was a day of blistering heat, one of the hottest yet experienced in that torrid summer. All night the troops had been on the road, and the force on the left of the attack had to fetch a long and weary circuit. The New Zealanders on the right at first made good progress. Advancing up the Chailak Dere and the Sazli Beit Dere, they carried the hogs-back called Rhododendron Ridge, which joins the main *massif* just west of Chunuk Bair. That was at ten o'clock in the morning, when the Australians and Indians on the left should have been well up the Aghyl Dere ready to take the defences of Chunuk Bair in flank. But there was at first no sign of the left wing. It had been held up by the difficult country in the lower reaches of the Aghyl Dere, and where the ravine forks had split into two, the Australians going up the left-hand gully and the Indians the right. The 10th Gurkhas on the extreme right managed to get into touch with Johnston's forces, but by this time the men of both columns were exhausted, and were forced to call a halt. Later in the day the New Zealanders reconnoitred the main ridge, and prepared for the great offensive on the morrow. Meantime the enemy, now aware of what was happening, had hurried his 4th Division to Chunuk Bair, and shortly after dawn had reinforced the detachments on the main ridge.

At dawn on the 8th, Johnston's New Zealanders, supported by two battalions from the 13th Division, the Maori contingent, and the Auckland Mounted Rifles, attacked from Rhododendron Ridge, and after a hard struggle carried the crest of Chunuk Bair at the south-western end. The losses were heavy, as may be judged from the case of the Wellington battalion, which had been 700 strong on the 6th and was now reduced to 53. Of the 7th Gloucesters Sir Ian Hamilton wrote: " Every single officer, company sergeant-major, or company quartermaster-sergeant, was either killed or wounded, and the battalion by midday consisted of small groups of men commanded by junior non-commissioned officers or privates. Chapter and verse may be quoted for the view that the rank and file of an army cannot long endure the strain of close hand-to-hand fighting unless they are given confidence by the example of good officers. Yet here is at least one instance where a battalion of the New Army fought right on, from midday till

But the enemy pouring solidly down the slopes, offered a superb target for our gunners. A stream of high explosive and shrapnel burst from our land batteries and the ships' guns. In the Indian section ten machine guns caught the Turks in flank at short range. The attack could not retire, for fresh men kept sweeping over the crest and driving the wedge forward to its destruction. Soon it slackened, then broke, and with fierce hand-to-hand fighting among the scrub we began to win back the lost ground. By midday the danger was over. It had been grave indeed, for the last two battalions of the Anzac general reserve had been sent up in support. Of one party of 5,000 Turks who had swarmed over the crest but 500 returned. That afternoon the fighting ceased from the sheer exhaustion of both sides. We had leisure to reconstruct our line, which now ran from the top of Rhododendron Ridge north-east to a position among the spurs of the Aghyl Dere.

Two days later, on 12th August, Godley at last obtained touch with the right wing of the Suvla Bay force at a place called Susuk Kuyu, on the Azmak Dere, a little west of its junction with the Asma Dere. The Anzac advance had been a most glorious but a most costly enterprise. By the evening of 10th August the casualties had reached 12,000, including a very large proportion of officers. Let Godley speak for the quality of the men. " I cannot close my report without placing on record my unbounded admiration of the work performed, and the gallantry displayed, by the troops and their leaders during the severe fighting involved in these operations. Though the Australian, New Zealand, and Indian units had been confined to trench duty in a cramped space for some four months, and though the troops of the New Armies had only just landed from a sea voyage, and many of them had not been previously under fire, I do not believe that any troops in the world could have accomplished more "

We turn now to the fortunes of the Suvla landing. The force under Stopford consisted, as we have seen, of two divisions of the New Army—the 10th, less one brigade, and the 11th, with two Territorial Divisions, the 53rd and 54th, to follow. The 10th Division had no artillery with it, and the 11th Division a single brigade, from which only one battery was available for the first day's fighting. All day of the 6th the 11th Division was busy embarking at Kephalos Bay, in Imbros, each man being given rations and water for two days. When the transports set sail after dusk it was to a destination unknown to all save the Staff. About 9.30 p.m. the ships, showing no lights, entered the little bay of Suvla, four miles north of the main Anzac position. The night was dark, for the moon did not rise till two o'clock. The Turks had no inkling of our plan. That day we had made a pretence of landing at Karachali, at the head of the Gulf of Saros, on the coast road from Enos to Bulair. That day, too, the attack at Cape Helles and Lone Pine had begun, and the enemy's attention was diverted to the extreme ends of his front. As the transports crept northwards the New Zealanders, on the dark shore to starboard, were already moving along their saps, and before the landing was well begun, the firing had started where the Mounted Brigades were clearing the foothills. But at Suvla there was no sign of life, till searchlights from the Anafarta slopes, in their periodic sweeping of the horizon, discovered the strange flotilla, and an intermittent rifle fire broke out upon the beach.

Three landing places had been selected—A, inside the bay north of the Salt Lake, and B and C, south-west of it. All night long the work of disembarkation went on. The 32nd and 33rd Brigades landed at C, and the 34th at A. Opposite B and C was a little hill called Lala Baba, held by the enemy. It was readily carried with the bayonet, and for the rest of the night our only trouble was from scattered snipers in the scrub. The 34th Brigade had some difficulties at A with a Turkish outpost on Hill 10, but with the assistance of the 32nd Brigade they pushed northward and carried the ridge of the Karakol Dagh. At dawn on the 7th the 11th Division was ashore, and held both sides of the bay and the neck of land between them. At daybreak six battalions of the 10th Division arrived in the bay from Mitylene. It was Stopford's intention to use the 10th Division on his left, but since the experience of the 34th Brigade had shown that the shallows at A were awkward, it was landed at C, and marched slowly northwards along the coast. Presently the remaining three battalions of the Division arrived from Mudros along with Sir Bryan Mahon.

It was now necessary to deploy into the plain and take up a broad front east of the Salt Lake. The earliest light brought the Turkish artillery into action. At first our men heard only the guns of the New Zealanders, now far up on the slopes of Chunuk Bair. Then suddenly a storm of shrapnel broke on the beaches, which burst too high to do much damage, while the ordinary shells buried themselves in the sand. The 10th Division, in good order, moved along the causeway to the north end of the lake, while a field battery which we had established on Lala Baba provided a useful support. At the same time the cruisers, monitors, and destroyers in the bay made good practice against the Turkish batteries on the heights. By two o'clock, with few casualties, the two divisions—the 10th for the most part on the right instead of on the left—held a line east of the lake running from the Karakol Dagh to near the butt-end of the ridge called Yilghın Burnu. So far the operation, though slow, had been conducted without serious hitch.

It was imperative to push on if we were to get the benefit of surprise. But as the afternoon advanced, little progress was made. The intermingling of the 10th and 11th Divisions had resulted in a general confusion. It was very hot, and the troops were weary and tormented with an unbearable thirst, most of the men having emptied their water-bottles by eight o'clock that morning. At 4 p m. there came a thunderstorm and a heavy shower of rain, which cleared the air, and at five we managed to advance our front a little under a violent shelling from the guns on Anafarta Ridge. Late that night our right won a real success, for two battalions of the 11th Division succeeded in carrying the position of Yilghin Burnu—which we called Chocolate Hill after its scrub had caught fire and been reduced to a barren desolation. This, and the parallel position of Keretch Tepe Sirt in the north, where Sir Bryan Mahon made a spirited attack, safeguarded our flanks; and, in the event of our advance on the morrow succeeding, would allow us to link up with the left of the Anzac Corps on the Azmak Dere.

Next day, Sunday, the 8th, the day on which the New Zealanders won Chunuk Bair, was the critical stage at Suvla. We had a strength of some 25,000 men. The Turks on the Anafarta heights were, at the start, weak in numbers—no more than 4,000— and an attack resolutely pushed forward must have carried the position. East of Salt Lake there lay a wide stretch of flat, sandy plain. Beyond this was a strip 2,000 yards deep of tillage, scrub, and woodland, and little farms stretching to the edge of the slopes. To the south-east there was a gap in the hills, where stood the village of Kuchuk Anafarta in a dark clump of cypresses. The plan of the Turkish commander was to hold his trenches on the heights very thinly, while he pushed forward a screen of riflemen into the cover of the patches of scrub. This screen was brilliantly handled, and from its mobility and invisibility seems to have given our men the impression that they were facing a huge enemy force. Meanwhile the Turkish guns in the rear bombarded our lines and supports, and searched every road leading from the beaches. And enemy supports were on the road, the 12th Division hastening to Kuchuk

Anafarta and the 7th to Biyuk Anafarta. All through that unlucky day we made sporadic attempts to advance, losing heavily in the process and gaining little ground. A whole British corps was held up by a screen of sharpshooters, well backed by artillery. The troops were new, and lacked that self-reliance and individual initiative which is necessary in open-order fighting in a difficult country, while there was undoubtedly a lack of purpose and resolution in their leadership. The close secrecy in which the whole operation had been veiled prevented the battalion officers from understanding the extreme necessity of speed. General Stopford was not satisfied with his artillery support, and the water arrangements had broken down; but he did not sufficiently recognize the vital importance of an infantry advance at all costs when it is a question of making good a landing in hostile territory. In Sir Ian Hamilton's words, " The very existence of the force, its water supply, its facilities for munitions and supplies, its power to reinforce, must absolutely depend on the infantry being able instantly to make good sufficient ground without the aid of the artillery other than can be supplied for the purpose by *floating* batteries. . . . Driving power was required, and even a certain ruthlessness, to brush aside pleas for a respite for tired troops. The one fatal error was inertia. And inertia prevailed."

On Monday, the 9th, our chance had almost vanished. The heart had gone out of the attack, and we were settling down to a war of positions. Sir Ian Hamilton had arrived the night before from Imbros, and had striven to inspire the corps and divisional commanders with the spirit of the offensive. In his full and candid report, he has described the situation. The general commanding the 11th Division declared himself unable to make a night attack. The Commander-in-Chief insisted, but units had been fatally mixed up, and nothing could be done. Early on the morning of the 9th an attack was indeed attempted by the 32nd Brigade, a gallant endeavour to carry the main Anafarta ridge, and one company actually won the crest. But the effort had been made too late, for the Turkish defence was already thickening. Our difficulties were increased by an event which happened at midday. A strong wind was blowing from the north, and either by shell-fire or by Turkish design the scrub on Hill 70 was set ablaze. From that place, henceforth christened Burnt Hill, the tongues of flame leaping with the wind swept across our front, and drove us back. The incident suspended all serious operations for the day. Next day, the 10th, the opportunity had gone for good, for the enemy was now amply reinforced. The 33rd Brigade attacked at dawn on Hill 100, which the Turks called Ismail Oglu Tepe. Some of the men reached the summit, but could not hold it. The 53rd Territorial Division had now arrived, and the 54th followed next day. On the 10th the 53rd attacked the main Anafarta ridge, but failed to reach it. That day Birdwood had also failed at Hill Q and Chunuk Bair, and Sir Ian Hamilton's great design had been defeated.

Something was done, indeed, to consolidate our front, which now ran from the Azmak Dere across Chocolate Hill to the 10th Division on the left. In the latter area we pushed forward a little on the Keretch Tepe Sirt, and presently had a continuous trench-line across the plain. On the 12th the 163rd Brigade on our left centre won some ground, and there the 1/5 Norfolks, under Colonel Sir H Beauchamp, charged so gallantly that their colonel with 16 officers and 250 men disappeared for ever in the forest. On that day, as we have seen, the right of the Suvla force obtained touch with the men of Anzac on the Azmak Dere. On the 15th Stopford relinquished the command of the 9th Corps, and was succeeded by Sir Julian Byng.

For the next ten days the Suvla operations languished. But it was necessary to gain elbow room, and Sir Ian Hamilton was forced to continue the offensive. For that purpose he brought to the scene of action the veteran 29th Division, temporarily commanded by General Marshall. To it was added the 2nd Mounted Division of Yeomanry, under Major-General Peyton, and the whole force was put under the direction of General De Lisle. The objective was the encircling hills behind the Suvla plain, extending from Hill 70, now in the possession of the Turks, to Hill 100. By this time all the advantage of surprise had gone, and the enemy position was held in equal or superior force. The only tactics left to us were those of a frontal assault The attack of the 29th Division was entrusted to the 86th and 87th Brigades ; the 88th Brigade, which had been seriously depleted by the Cape Helles fighting of 6th August, being held in reserve. At three o'clock in the afternoon of the 21st a great bombardment was opened on the ridges. The enemy's guns replied, and soon the remainder of the scrub on Chocolate Hill was blazing, and our right was enveloped in a fog of smoke. Unfortunately there was also a natural mist which discomfited our gunners. We had reckoned on the Turks being blinded by the afternoon sun, which should at the same time show up their positions ; whereas the opposite was the

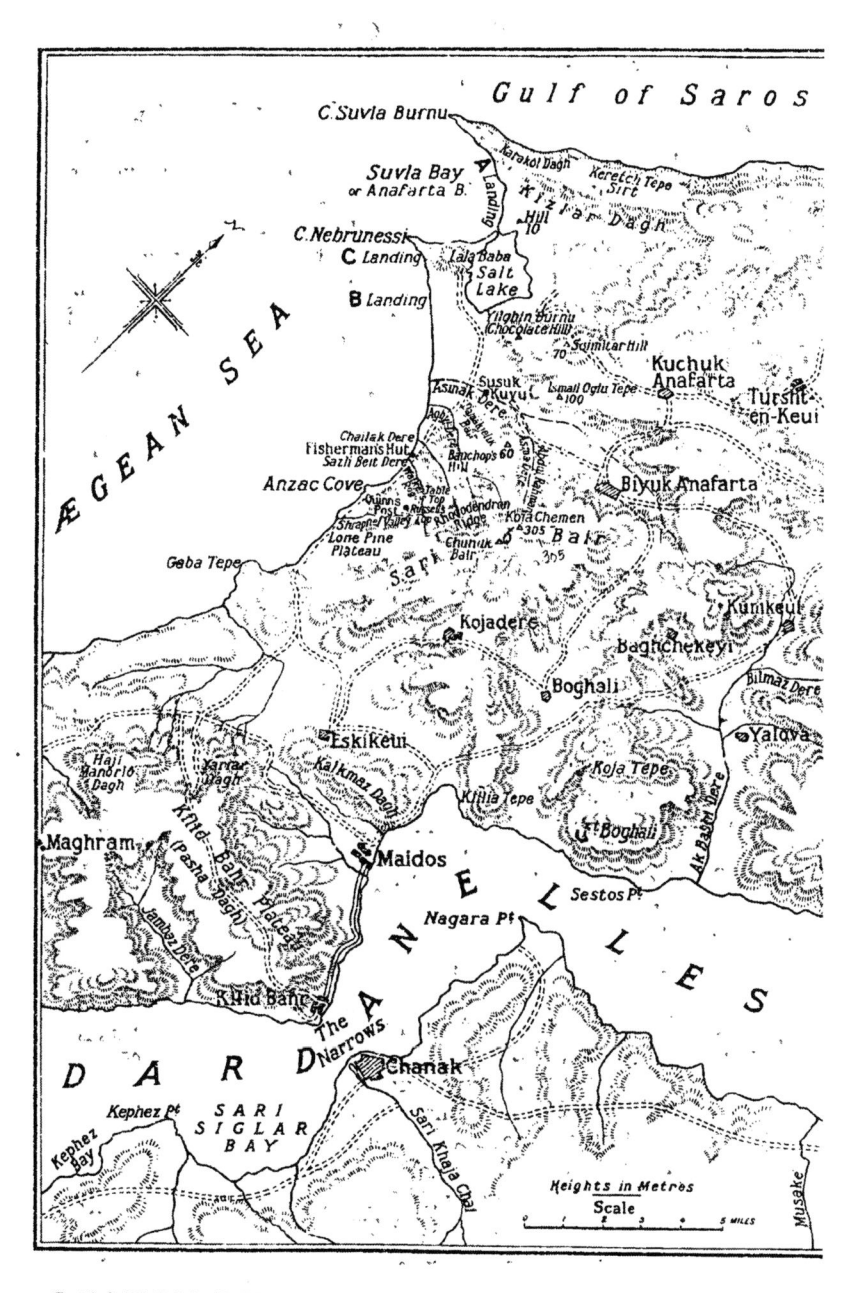

GALLIPOLI PENINSULA: ANZAC AND SUVLA AREAS.

case. At 3.30 the 87th Brigade advanced against Hill 70, and the 86th against Hill 100; while on their right the 11th Division moved against the trenches in front of it, with orders, if successful, to swing northwards and assault Hill 100 from the south The 87th Brigade at first made good progress, but the shell-fire from behind Hill 100 was too strong, and the Turkish machine guns held it back in the last hundred yards. Meanwhile the 86th Brigade made repeated and most gallant attacks on Hill 100, but their efforts were fruitless. The New Army division on the right was held fast in the flats, and could do nothing in the way of a flanking attack.

About five o'clock the Mounted Division was ordered into action. They had been held in reserve below the knoll of Lala Baba, and now advanced across the open in perfect order under a devastating rain of Turkish shrapnel. For two miles they moved forward, as if on parade, and formed up below the 87th Brigade between Hill 70 and Hill 100. Sir Ian Hamilton has described the scene. " Such superb martial spectacles are rare in modern war. . . . Here, for a mile and a half, there was nothing to conceal a mouse, much less some of the most stalwart soldiers England has ever sent from her shores. Despite the critical events in other parts of the field, I could hardly take my glasses from the Yeomen. . . . Here and there a shell would take toll of a cluster ; there they lay ; there was no straggling ; the others moved steadily on ; not a man was there who hung back or hurried." As the darkness was falling, the Yeomanry rose from their cover and charged the hill. Lord Longford's 2nd (South Midland) Brigade, consisting of the Bucks, Berks, and Dorset regiments, led the assault ; and the watchers in the plains saw the troopers near the crest, reach it, and then disappear as the first ranks leaped into the Turkish trenches. It was a fine feat of arms, and a great shout went up that Hill 100 was won. In the gathering dark, made thicker by the smoke from the burning scrub, it was difficult to tell the result ; but the perpetual patter of rifles and machine-gun fire showed that the conquest would be hard to maintain. As it happened, the Yeomen had only won an underfeature ; the Turks still held the crest, whence their machine guns enfiladed the troops below. During the night it became clear that we could not hold the position, and by daylight we had fallen back upon our old lines. The final effort against Anafarta had failed. The one gleam of success that day was on the Azmak Dere, where the left of the Anzac Corps effected a lodgment on Hill 60, and enabled our front to be fully established. On the 27th Hill 60 was finally won.

It is not easy to see how the second Suvla attack could have succeeded. It was another of those desperate frontal assaults of which, in the Helles region, we had already learned the futility. The Turk entrenched on his hills was not to be driven out by the finest infantry in the world. But no failure can detract from the merits of the performance of the 29th and the Mounted Divisions. The Yeomanry suffered terribly. Two brigadiers fell, and more than one regiment was almost destroyed. Once again, as on 13th May at Ypres, the English yeomen had shown " the mettle of their pasture." Had the troops used on the 21st been used on 7th August, the Anafarta heights must have been won.

The August fighting was the most costly part of the Dardanelles campaign. For the first three weeks of the month the casualties were close on 40,000, of which at least 30,000 were incurred between 6th and 10th August. It was an intensity of loss greater than the First and Second Battles of Ypres, and, considering the numbers engaged, greater than the advance at Loos in the following month. It was, moreover, a fruitless sacrifice, for nothing material was gained. We had extended the length of our battle-front by six miles, and we had advanced it on the left of the Anzac Corps by winning a mile or so of the Koja Chemen ridges. But we were no nearer to a decision. Our new line commanded no part of the enemy's communications, and it was in no way easier to hold. We had secured a little more room in the Anzac zone, and that may be taken as the sum of our practical achievement.

The enterprise, at once so gallant and so tragic, was an example of a brilliant and not impracticable scheme which miscarries owing to mistakes in detail. It may be doubted, indeed, whether its success would have given an immediate decision to the Gallipoli campaign, for it was a far cry from Sari Bair to Pasha Dagh and Achi Baba, and the enemy in the latter positions could still have drawn supports across the Narrows from Asia till such time as Maidos fell. But it would have prepared the way for the capture of Maidos, would have struck a deadly blow against the Turkish land communications, and would have brought victory within a measurable survey. It was of necessity a complex plan, demanding a simultaneous success at more than one point, and it made the severest demands on the troops employed. In fixing the hours by which certain key points should have been won Sir Ian Hamilton drew heavy drafts on the valour of his men, and those drafts at Sari Bair were nobly honoured. But splendid achievements in one quarter were not enough, and the scheme was doomed by the disaster of a single part. It is possible to detect what may seem on review minor blunders, but the secret of failure is to be found in the overestimate of the capacities of the Suvla forces. It is true that their task was not to be named for difficulty with the problem of Sari Bair, but it was too great for their strength, and in allotting it to untried generals, staffs, and men, Sir Ian Hamilton indubitably erred ; though his error is intelligible, when we remember how the original force at Helles had acquitted itself against all odds. He was entitled to hope for something from fortune, but fortune averted her face. It is clear, too, that the Suvla failure was only in small part due to the rawness of the New Army troops, for the men of the 13th Division on Sari Bair behaved like veterans. It was rather due to the inertness of old, tired, or sick commanders, and to the bungling of ill-trained staffs. At the same time it is unjust too harshly to condemn these staffs and generals. They were men of a good record, who found the work too great for them—a common circumstance in war, and one which no foresight can wholly prevent. But on Suvla the adventure, when it had all but succeeded,* shipwrecked. The heroic performance of Birdwood's men on the ridges of Koja Chemen was nullified by the bareness of their left flank, and by the fact that they were face to face with an enemy in no way weakened by the attack to the north. The check to Stopford's corps on that torrid Saturday in the Suvla flats was the undoing of a great enterprise.

* Liman von Sanders has admitted that even after the Suvla failure he was very near the end of his tether, and that if a further landing had been made in the Gulf of Saros he would have had no men to meet it.—*Fünf Jahre Türkei*, 1920.

CHAPTER XXXVII.

THE GREAT RUSSIAN RETREAT.

August 5–September 30, 1915.

The essential Russian Weakness—Germany's Next Step—The Russian Armies' Retreat to the Bug—The Fall of Kovno and Novo Georgievsk—The Fall of Brest Litovsk—The Fall of Grodno—The Retreat from the Vilna Salient—The first Russian Counter-strokes—Political Changes.

THE fall of Warsaw consummated a process which began in the early days of May—the awakening of Russia to the full gravity of the war. From the start the nation had been united. The campaign had been a popular one beyond any in her history. It had been recognized by every class as a struggle not only for national existence, but for the essential ideals of civilization and humanity. But the magnitude of the contest had not revealed itself. Her conquest of Galicia, her firm defence of the Warsaw front, and her bold ventures across the Carpathians had obliterated the memory of the first weeks when her unpreparedness had weighed heavily on her High Command. The extraordinary fighting quality of her soldiers had made her forget how small a part individual valour plays in the first stage of a modern war. Russia had grown overconfident, and that confidence had almost been her undoing.

Looking back in August at the course of events since April it was easy to discover her mistakes. In the first place, she had been holding an impossibly long line for her numbers of men and guns, and her Carpathian advance had made it daily longer and more vulnerable. The Russian front was not the continuous series of entrenchments which existed in the West. There were long gaps in it, the junctions of the different armies offered points of serious weakness; and in many parts it was terribly thin. Take Dmitrieff's Army on the Donajetz. In April one corps was holding a front of forty-five miles, one division held eight miles, one regiment, about 4,000 strong, held nearly five. It was believed that in case of attack, reinforcements could be readily brought up; but the communications were bad, and little was done to improve them. Proposals to bring out skilled workmen from England were toyed with and shelved. No attempt was made to double the single line from Lemberg to Jaroslav, the chief feeder of the Donajetz front; nor was the railway bridge at Przemysl repaired after the capture of that city, so as to make available a direct double route from Lemberg to Tarnow. The result was that the Russian army suffered from lack of mobility. Troops could not be brought up quickly to the threatened point, and each unit was in effect left alone to repel any attack that might be made on it. The enemy in an advance could by means of his admirable railways weaken remote parts of his front to strengthen the operative part, but the same tactics were not open to the defence. Hence Russia lost the advantage of holding the interior lines. Though the enemy had to operate against a convex front, he had far greater powers of local concentration.

Again, the personal ascendancy which the Russian soldier had established on the southern front led to an undue depreciation of his opponents. During the long halt on the Donajetz the Austrians kept up an incessant bombardment; but this did little harm, for they never followed it up by an infantry assault, and consequently a large proportion of the Russian troops could be withdrawn from the trenches attacked. This state of affairs led also to a certain slackness of intelligence work, and the sense of security which it induced prevented alternative positions being prepared. It may well be questioned, however, whether the existence of such positions would have made much difference in the *débâcle* of May. The best trenches in the world would have been useless against the German artillery, especially if, as frequently happened, they could only be manned by unarmed soldiers at a distance of twenty yards from each other.

This brings us to the essential Russian weakness in equipment. Her total of heavy guns was far lower than the enemy's, and her lack of railways prevented her recalling readily those which had been sent to other parts of the front. Her field artillery, excellent in pattern and efficient in its gunnery, was poorly supplied with shells; and at various times in the course of retreat its munitions gave out altogether, and it made no attempt to cope with the fire of the enemy. The Russians were terribly short also in machine guns, having at the most one to the enemy's four. As the retreat continued, even their musketry fire was in danger of starvation. Many of the new recruits took their places in the firing line without rifles, and captured rifles, preserved as souvenirs, were collected from the Red Cross detachments and wherever they could be found. Men had to wait in the trenches under heavy fire till they could get arms from wounded comrades. In one army a whole division had to face an attack without a single rifle, and the field artillery of that army was limited to two shells a day. When Irmanov's 3rd Caucasians fought their great battle at Jaslo, their general at one moment was compelled to refrain from a counter-attack because he had only twenty rounds of rifle ammunition per man. In the words of a Russian private: "We had only one weapon, the living breast of the soldier." Even an army of veterans in circumstances like these might have looked for annihilation. At any rate its retreat, by all human calculation, should have been a rout and a confusion. The amazing fact was that there was no rout; that this force, which had lost the better part of a million men in prisoners alone, which was short of every munition of war, held the enemy firm, and after the first week fell back at its own pace, with stubborn rearguard actions and many successful counter-advances. Observers who took part in the retreat bore witness to the absence of panic, and, indeed, of any signs of excitement. Corps like the 3rd Caucasians, which had been reduced to a fragment, still planned and executed bold measures of reprisal. The fibre of the Russian soldier seemed a thing beyond the power of mortal calamity to weaken. He might perish in millions, but the survivors took up the weapons of the dead and cheerfully continued.

But the effect on the Russian people—the relatives of the dead and missing in a thousand cities and a myriad villages—was tremendous, the more tremendous in that it wrought as slowly as the thawing of the ice in spring. There was as yet no weakening, but everywhere there was perplexity and confusion. In the circles of government the honest men laboured to purge the administration of its infinite corruption; many reputations were dimmed, suspicion fell upon the highest quarters, gossip was busy with all its tongues. The determination of the great people behind the bureaucrats was strong; and when in July, before the fall of Warsaw, Germany made overtures for peace, she was haughtily repulsed. The convening of the Imperial Duma on 1st August was a wise step, for the Duma, along with the Army, was the only representative of the whole nation, and it met to renew its oath of resolution. The war had already been prolific of eloquence, but men were a little weary of words and the old stimulants were losing their power. But there are certain speeches which have the quality of deeds. Such had been the fiery orations of Chatham and Gambetta, the homely good sense of Cromwell, the noble simplicity of Washington, the grave elevation of Lincoln. Such, now, was the address of Rodzianko, the Duma's President. His words moved his hearers to a strange exaltation, and rang throughout the land from the Dnieper to the Pacific. He drew a picture of the army— "the living sword of our native land, menacing the foe, but humble before God." He reviewed the events of the year, and spoke words of comfort to the patriots of Poland. The war, he said, was no longer a duel of armies but of peoples, and victory could only be won if civilians and soldiers alike wrought for the common purpose. "Our duty—sparing neither strength nor time nor means—is to set to work without delay. Let each one give his labour into the treasury of popular might. Let those who are rich, let those who are able, contribute to the common welfare. The Army and the Fleet have set each of us an example of duty dauntlessly fulfilled. They have done all that man may do; our turn has come." For victory, he pointed out, a change of spirit was needful in the Government, and the change must involve a new trust in the people.

The occupation of Warsaw compelled Falkenhayn to decide the difficult problem of his future objective. Two courses were open to him. One was to entrench himself upon the ground he had won, and make the Niemen, the Narev, and the Vistula the front of the central and northern armies. The line of the rivers in German hands could be made of a strength which would defy any Russian counter-advances for many a day. Warsaw, the magazine and depot of the Grand Duke's forces, was in his hands; and though it is easy to overrate the importance of any single city, yet the possession of Warsaw conferred great and obvious advantages. Such a position would paralyze Russian efforts for the immediate future. It would enable him to weaken his armies without danger, and send great contingents westwards. And it would give his troops, weary with three months' incessant fighting, the opportunity to rest and recruit. This plan had been in the mind of the German Staff during the winter; but the successes of the summer had widened their outlook, and they had come to cherish more spacious projects. The efforts required to win Warsaw had made the Vistula almost impossible as a halting-ground. The Archduke Joseph and Mackensen were already north of the Lublin railway ; the right wing was pushed almost to the Sereth ; while in the far north Eichhorn was well east of the Niemen, and Below, south of Riga, had pressed forward in a deep salient towards Dvinsk. To be content with a defensive line on the rivers meant the sacrifice of these substantial gains, and the holding of a long concave front. It was desirable to straighten out the position by advancing the centre.

But the chance of a crushing, perhaps a decisive, offensive was what dominated Hindenburg's mind. The Russian armies were clearly in a perilous case. With Warsaw fallen, the southern railway cut, and the Narev line crumbling, it seemed beyond human power to extricate the centre from the narrow apex of the salient. Meanwhile, in the north, Below and Eichhorn were almost within striking distance of the Petrograd railway ; and, once this was cut in the neighbourhood of Dvinsk and Vilna, the whole Russian front must split into isolated and unrelated groups. It was a sovereign chance to compel a field battle, in which more than one of the armies of Russia should find destruction. Between Riga and Petrograd lay three hundred miles of forest and meres, served by one railroad. The same distance separated Tarnopol and Kiev, though the country there was better suited for the movements of great armies. In a few weeks the autumn rains would begin, and in two months the first snows of winter. The time was too short to reach Petrograd or Kiev, even had these been the gains that promised most. The Grand Duke Nicholas might yield them both and fall farther back into the heart of the country, and Russia would still be unconquered. But let her armies be beaten in detail in the next month, and Russia would indeed be vanquished. She was already in an almost hopeless position, with no great base near, with slender communications, with her ranks terribly depleted, and with her old insufficiency of equipment unrelieved. The fruit was almost within the German grasp. One great effort, as forecast by the Kaiser in his telegram to the Queen of Greece, must bring about that decisive victory, so far unknown in the war, which would put the defeated side out of action.

On the desirableness of this end there was no difference of opinion, but there was a serious conflict between Hindenburg and Falkenhayn as to the means. The former sought to make sure of a settlement with Russia even at the cost of a hazard to every other battle-front. He wished to strengthen his left, and strike towards Vilna with the northern force. The latter was resolved to fight on the basis of limited liability. He did not believe in any case that Hindenburg's plan was certain to succeed. "One cannot hope," he told him, "to strike a comprehensive and deadly blow by means of an encircling movement at an enemy who is numerically stronger, who will stick at no sacrifice of territory or position, and in addition has the expanse of Russia behind him." Moreover, he was much occupied elsewhere. The entry of Bulgaria as an ally was all but arranged, and that would entail sending troops to Serbia. The French and British offensive in the West was only a few weeks distant. He still hoped for a Russian *débâcle*, but it must be achieved by the adroit handling of the existing armies, and not by a large and combined operation. Even if the Grand Duke escaped from the trap, the German position would be greatly improved by an advance. It would give them Brest Litovsk, the last of the Polish fortresses. It would give them the marshes of the Pripet as a great piece of dead ground in their line. It would still further disintegrate the Russian forces, till they fell from an extended front into groups, from groups to armies, and from armies to disjointed corps. Further, there was a position which could be held for the winter, and which offered greater security than even the river line of the Vistula. There was a lateral railway running south from Riga by way of Dvinsk and Vilna to Rovno. If this were held, and the Austrian right wing stood firm on the Dniester, a winter front would be gained shorter than the old one by four hundred miles, and with communications certainly no worse than those of western Poland. Again, such a line would give Germany complete possession not only of Russian Poland, but of all the territory which Polish nationalism had ever claimed. Now, the unity of the Polish race had always been the central ideal of Polish patriots. Since the war began the wisest brains among them had been loyal to Russia, believing that only Russia could give them once more a racial and territorial solidarity. But with Galicia and Russian Poland, as well as Posen, in German hands, the allegiance of the Poles would be sorely tried. Germany alone, it might then appear, could implement her promises and give reality to their aspirations. Besides, there was the vast Jewish residuum of the Polish population, without national tradition, which might be trusted to worship the rising sun.

Fortune seemed to smile happily on the German purpose on that day when Prince Leopold entered Warsaw. Russia had one pressing duty before her—to extricate her armies and refuse at all costs to be driven into a field battle. Her first business was to get her troops out of the Warsaw salient. That meant that while her centre fought constant rearguard actions against Prince Leopold's advance, her right centre must check Gallwitz and Scholtz on the Narev, and her left centre the advance of Woyrsch towards Lukow, till such time as she had fallen back east of Siedlice. She had left the great fortress of Novo Georgievsk to hinder the use of the Vistula for German supplies, in the hope that it would hold out for at least a month. In that event the loss of its large garrison and its many guns would be justified. Once the apex of the salient was clear, the retirement would be on Brest Litovsk ; and to enable her to effect this in good order, the northern fortress of Ossovietz and Kovno must resist till, at any rate, the end of August. Otherwise, in the difficult country around the Bobr and the upper Niemen, there was a chance of more than one corps being cut off. It was already clear that the upper and middle Bug could not be held long against the thrust of Mackensen. Behind Brest Litovsk lay the marshes of the Pripet, and to withdraw through that area meant a stiff holding battle around Brest, for the withdrawal would be slow and intricate.

Russia had thus two great perils immediately before her. One of her armies or army groups might be enveloped, especially on the right flank, where Below and Eichhorn had already driven in deep salients. Or the onslaughts of the German centre, aided by Mackensen's drive north-eastwards, might force her to fight west of the Pripet marshes. If an army has narrow and congested communications behind it, and the enemy presses hard, it may be compelled against its will to accept battle. The extraordinary difficulties of Russia's position must be understood if we are to do justice to the magnitude of her achievement. Let us look first at her immediate task—the retirement from Warsaw to the Bug.

Ivangorod had fallen on 4th August. To defend it would have been folly, for it was wholly surrounded, and it commanded no vital route of communication. The guns and munitions were removed by the railway to Lukow, and only the husk was left for the conqueror. The rearguards of the Russian centre were still in Praga, the Warsaw suburb east of the Vistula ; but by Monday, 9th August, they were driven out, and Prince Leopold could begin the bridging of the river. In spite of the ruin of the bridges both there and at Ivangorod, the Germans were not slow to find a means of crossing. Using the big thousand-ton barges, which were the staple of the Vistula navigation, they constructed pontoons, over which they ran their railways. The main advance of Prince Leopold beyond the Vistula began on 10th August. It was stubbornly opposed, and made slow progress. The Russian resistance in this section was wholly conditioned by what was happening on the flanks. They dared not delay one hour longer than the time permitted them to escape from the pressure of Gallwitz on the north and Woyrsch on the south. Had there been no such coercion, Prince Leopold might have been held up indefinitely, for his army was the weakest in the German dispositions. But the thing had become almost a mathematical problem. So soon as Gallwitz and Woyrsch reached certain points, the Russian centre must break off the action and retire to a position which would allow them to evade outflanking.

The tactical handling of the Russian centre was skilful, even brilliant. The gravest peril came from the Narev front, where the Russian remnants were working as if to a time schedule. Gallwitz, it will be remembered, had first crossed the river on the 26th of July, after crushing the resistance of the fortified bridgeheads at Pultusk and Rozhan. He was held in the wooded country between the Bug and the Narev, and was not able to force the crossing on a broad front. On 9th August Novo Georgievsk was completely isolated, and Gallwitz's right wing took Sierok and Zegrje, at the junction of the Bug and the Narev. On the 10th Scholtz stormed Lomza, and next day Gallwitz, moving east between the Bug and the Narev, had won a very dangerous position, no less than the junction where the central line to Ostrolenka joins the main Warsaw–Petrograd railway, a few miles from where the latter crosses the Bug. This meant that the whole Russian front on the Narev and Bug west of this point must give way. They had destroyed the Bug railway bridge, and fallen back, apparently in good order, by the Bialystok railway, and by the lateral Malkin–Siedlice railway, which was still in Russian hands. On the south Woyrsch had joined hands with Mackensen on 10th August. Moving northeast, he took the railway junction of Lukow two days later. By that time the Russian centre was in Siedlice, ready for a further retreat as the enemy flanks closed in.

On the 12th Gallwitz was at Zambrovo, south-east of Lomza, an important junction of five roads. His right wing was at Andrychov, just north of the Petrograd line. Siedlice and the lateral railway were clearly no longer tenable, especially as Scholtz, on Gallwitz's left, had crossed the Narev at its junction with the Bobr and was threatening Bialystok. On the 13th the Russian centre fell back from Siedlice and Sokolov into the profound forests which stretch towards the Bug. The worst peril was over, for the narrows of the salient had been cleared. It remained to hold the ground in front of Brest Litovsk till the flanks could straighten themselves into line with the centre.

That centre by the 14th was at Losice, some twenty miles east of Siedlice, with its right on the railway running north-east from Siedlice and its left on the Lukow–Brest railway. There for the moment it was safe, but to north and south the position was precarious; for next day Mackensen, pushing north along the Cholm–Brest line, took Vlodava on the Bug, and Woyrsch was advancing along both sides of the Lukow–Brest lines. In the north the left wing of Gallwitz's army had forced the crossing of the river Nurzec, which enters the Bug about fifteen miles west of the place where that river is crossed by the main Petrograd railway. Next day Prince Leopold's left crossed the Bug at Drohiczyn, which brought it in touch with Gallwitz's right, while its centre took Biala on the Krzna River, and Mackensen from the south moved down the Bug from Vlodava. Already the enemy was within twenty miles of the fortress of Brest. It was time for the Russian centre to fall back on Brest, and for the High Command to decide whether that stronghold should be surrendered or defended.

It is probable that the Grand Duke's first intention was to hold Brest and the line of the upper Bug. The railway from Brest to Bialystok would give good lateral communication behind the fronts, though by the 15th this line was already endangered by Mackensen's advance from Vlodava, which gave the Germans the mastery of the Bug above the fortress, as well as the southern part of the lateral line. But the essential condition of the maintenance of the position was the Russian control of the upper Niemen and especially of the fortress of Kovno. There Napoleon had crossed the river, and there ran the main line from East Prussia to Vilna. Ossovietz would be a point in this front, which would run roughly from Brest north by Bielsk and Ossovietz to the Niemen. But if Kovno fell it was untenable, for that would give Eichhorn a chance of a flanking movement which might threaten the right of the Russian centre, and might even cut it off for good from the armies in Courland.

The importance of Kovno was even greater in relation to the situation on the Russian right. Tukkum and Mitau had fallen to the army of Below, whose clouds of cavalry were now scouring the valley of the Aa. He was well east of Shavli by the end of July, and by 12th August was at Poniebitz, moving towards

Dvinsk by the Libau–Dvinsk railway. That day the Russian right made a strong counter-attack upon Below's centre, and another attack checked his left wing on the Aa. But if Kovno fell, various awkward consequences would ensue. The Niemen below the town was already in German hands. Kovno, Olita, and Grodno were the three fortresses of the upper Niemen, and the first in the present situation was the most vital. Its loss would imperil the other two ; it would make the position of the Russian armies on the Bobr an acute salient ; it would give the enemy a direct route to Vilna and the Petrograd line. Above all, it would place the Germans in rear of the Russian position on the Sventa, which enters the Niemen on the right bank a little below the town.

Kovno, an old city with a flourishing trade in grain and timber, was defended by eighteen forts, five on the east safeguarding the Niemen, four on the north protecting the Vilna bridge, and nine on the south and west. The Russians had no time, any more than at Ivangorod and Brest, to defend it by those earthworks in a wide perimeter which were the salvation of Verdun. The end of July saw Eichhorn's X. Army close on Kovno from the west, and on the day that Warsaw was abandoned the bombardment began. For twelve days a concentration of heavy artillery rained shells on the fortifications, while the infantry struggled for the outworks. The factories were stripped of machinery, and the Government records sent east, for soon it began to appear that the 16-inch guns of the East Prussian fortresses must speedily make an end of the defence. It was urgent that the place should be held till the latest moment for the security of the rest of the Russian line, and for twelve desperate days the garrison stuck to their post. On Sunday, 15th August, the end was very near. The German 40th Corps under Litzmann carried a small fort at the south-west corner, and pushed through the gap thus created. The forts by this time were in ruins, and on the night of Tuesday, the 17th, the heroic garrison was overwhelmed. The eastern works resisted to the last, and a portion of their defenders got away. The Germans claimed 20,000 prisoners and over 200 guns. When a forlorn hope is destroyed there is little chance of saving men and artillery.

The fall of Kovno—unexpectedly, for it was counted upon for a long resistance [*]—revived the peril which for a moment seemed to have passed by. It allowed Eichhorn to transport his army across the Niemen and to outflank the Russians on the Sventa, and it

[*] Its commandant, General Grigoriev, was tried by court-martial and sentenced to fifteen years' imprisonment for his " insufficient measures of defence."

put the Bobr armies and the force holding Ossovietz in a position of the gravest danger. A retirement on the right centre was necessary to avoid envelopment, and no less urgent was a retirement in the centre. For on the 18th Gallwitz cut the Brest-Bialystok railway at Bielsk, thereby isolating Brest on the north. That same day Prince Leopold crossed the Bug at Mielnik, east of his previous crossing at Drohiczyn, and thus secured for a line of advance and supply the railway which ran north-east from Siedlice, and traversed the Bug between these two crossing points. Farther south Mackensen was east of the Bug, north of Vlodava, and moving to cut the Brest–Moscow railway behind the fortress. Prince Leopold's right was that evening attacking the western forts of Brest itself.

Next day came a fresh and unexpected blow. The siege of Novo Georgievsk had been entrusted to Beseler, the conqueror of Antwerp, who for many months had disappeared from the war bulletins. The Russian Staff assumed a lengthy defence, and a consequent hold-up to German communications. But the great cannon which had battered down Liége and Namur carried Novo Georgievsk in something under three weeks. Eighty thousand of the garrison were taken, and over 700 guns, most of which had first been rendered useless. The cyphers and maps were carried into Russia by a brilliant feat of airwork. Beseler was rewarded by being put in charge of the administration of Poland.

Brest alone remained now of the Polish Triangle, and it was very clear that Brest was no continuing city. The first Russian line of retreat had been planned as on a front from Riga through Kovno, Grodno, Bialystok, to the upper Bug. But Kovno had fallen, and Mackensen had turned the river line in the south. A further retreat was needed, and once more the duty revived of extricating the weaker and most critical part by desperate holding battles. But the task was now of a somewhat different nature. The worst salient had been cleared, and the problem concerned itself with the manœuvring of armies so as to avoid envelopment while moving through exceptionally arduous country. For behind the Russian centre lay the great marshes of the Pripet, which must divide the front into sharply defined groups.

While Russia grappled with the urgencies of her land retirement there came a sudden threat on the north from the sea. In March a German squadron of battleships and torpedo-craft had shelled the coast villages of Courland. In the early days of June there had been fighting around Gothland and the Gulf of Riga, in

ACTION IN THE GULF OF RIGA.

which the Russians lost the mine-layer *Yenesei* and the Germans the transport *Hindenburg* and a destroyer. Russian torpedo boats engaged German cruisers off Windau on 30th June, and there was an action off Gothland on 2nd July. These activities forewarned the Russian Baltic Fleet, under Admiral Kannin, that at any moment an attempt might be made to assist the armies by a landing of troops on the Riga shore. Such a landing, if successful, would have turned the Russian right and led at once to the fall of Riga. But, for the landing to be possible, the mastery of the sea must be secured. It was Germany's business first of all to sink or blockade the Russian fleet. Till that was done any landing was the height of rashness, more especially since her object was not to gain a port but to establish an advanced base for her extreme left, and such a base involved a secure and continuous passage for her transports from Königsberg and Danzig.

On Sunday, 10th August, an attack was made on a large scale. A German fleet, consisting of nine of the older battleships, twelve cruisers, and a destroyer flotilla, attempted to force the southern channel which leads to the Gulf of Riga. The attempt was defeated, mainly by the Russian submarines and smaller craft. But on 16th August it was renewed with determination. The opening of the Gulf is defended by a group of islands, of which Oesel is the largest, with the smaller islets of Dago, Mohn, and Wormso stretching to the north-east. The chief entrance, the only one practicable for ships of heavy draught, lies between Oesel and the mainland, but there is another east of Mohn through the northern archipelago. Riga, on the mouth of the Dvina, lies at the southern end of the Gulf; and on a bay on the eastern shore, about halfway as the crow flies between Riga and Reval, is the little port of Pernau. On 16th August the German fleet engaged the Russian at the mouth of both channels. The attack was repulsed; but next day a thick fog settled on the water, and the enemy was able to sweep the mines from the entrance. The Russian light craft retired into the Gulf, while the larger units remained outside, since in such weather a general action was impossible. The Germans moved in, apparently under the impression that the Russians had withdrawn from the Gulf altogether. On the 19th they began their preparation for a landing at Pernau, a port chosen because it was unfortified, and was on the road to Petrograd. Four very large flat-bottomed barges laden with troops moved inshore, and on the 20th attempted to land. The conditions were favourable only on the assumption that there was no enemy craft near, for the shoal water forbade the ships in support to approach the shore. It was the opportunity of the Russian light craft, and quickly they seized it. The whole landing force was captured or destroyed.

Meantime the Russian fleet had joined battle throughout the length of the Gulf. The heaviest fighting was in Mohn Sound, where the retreating German vessels were caught by the Russian destroyers. One old gunboat, the *Sivoutch*, engaged a German cruiser which was escorting the torpedo craft. The action began at a range of about 1,200 yards. "The *Sivoutch*," said the Russian Admiralty report, "wrapped in flames, and on fire fore and aft, continued to answer shot for shot until she went down, having previously sunk an enemy torpedo boat." It was the only serious Russian casualty. Eight German destroyers and two cruisers were either sunk or put out of action, a submarine was driven ashore, and it seems probable that an auxiliary cruiser was also destroyed. On the 21st the Germans had evacuated the Gulf.

In the three weeks which ended on that day the German centre in the East had advanced a hundred miles. The forts of Warsaw, Ivangorod, Novo Georgievsk, and Kovno had fallen. Eichhorn was menacing Grodno; Gallwitz had isolated Brest on the north; Prince Leopold was close on the western walls of that fortress; and Mackensen was east of the Bug, and threatening to take the place in the rear. It was no small achievement for twenty days, but it was not the success for which Germany had hoped. The Russian armies had extricated themselves from impossible salients along intricate corridors with comparatively few losses. Falkenhayn's mind was now less set upon a decisive field victory than on the attainment of an impregnable winter line with a lateral railway behind it. The immediate German objective on 21st August may be set down as—Riga, the Dvina valley, Dvinsk, Vilna, the Volhynian fortresses Lutsk, Dubno, and Rovno, and all the country west of, up to, and a little beyond the Riga-Rovno line. The matter pressed, for winter was coming. Germany was embarking on what she hoped would be the final stage of the campaign two months later than Napoleon had crossed the Niemen. The Russian position, though full of difficulties, was better than a month before. Their line was nearly straight, save for a salient at Ossovietz, and the great sag on their right, where Below approached the Dvina. Their problem was to prevent Mackensen from getting to the rear of Brest Litovsk before Evert's centre was clear, to hold firm on their right, and to make a permanent stand west of the Dvinsk-Vilna-Rovno railway. Ossovietz and Bialystok clearly must go, and Grodno must hold out just long enough to enable the forces there to fall back on Vilna by the main Petrograd line. If one danger exceeded another when all were so great, it was the menace to the crossings of the Dvina. If Dvinsk were taken in flank, the retreat of the right wing would be gravely compromised.

After the fall of Kovno the Russian armies fell back by the railway towards Vilna, and on the 22nd made a stand at Koshedary to enable the Vilna stores to be removed. On that day Bialystok was still in their hands, and all the Petrograd railway beyond it, so that the forces at Ossovietz had still their path of retreat clear. But Gallwitz held Bielsk to the south, and there was no easy communication between the Army of the Niemen and the Army of Brest. The latter fortress was now invested on three sides, and its evacuation was the immediate problem of Evert's centre. Beseler, the siege expert, having reduced Novo Georgievsk, was now bringing his guns against the western works of Brest. Next day, the 23rd, Ossovietz fell. The fort had held out since the previous autumn against repeated German attacks. It owed its strength to the fact that, except at the road and railway crossing, swamps stretched on both sides of the Bobr, and it was difficult to find positions for heavy artillery.* In the end it did not fall to assault, but was abandoned by its garrison. With Bialystok and Grodno threatened, it had become an indefensible salient. The same day Tykocin was stormed, and a thousand prisoners taken; Eichhorn's right wing south of Kovno was approaching Olita, which but for Grodno was the only Niemen fortress left; and the Russian troops west of the Niemen in the eastern section of the Augustovo woods were beginning to find their position untenable. Meanwhile the German front was closing in to the north of Brest, and the whole of Prince Leopold's left wing was across the Bialystok-Brest railway. Mackensen, farther south, had driven in the Russian rearguards on the Bug at Vlodava, and was pursuing them through the marsh country to the east. That country was the beginning of the great Pripet marshes, the source of the Pripet River being in the swamps southeast of Vlodava, only a few miles from the right bank of the Bug.

On 25th August Brest Litovsk fell. It had held out long enough to enable Evert to get away with guns and supplies, and only a little corn remained for the victors. With Brest went the last fort of the Polish Triangle. Evert's armies were now well into the

* The position was chosen by Skobelev. The first forts were built in 1883, and reconstructed in 1910, with the experience gained in Port Arthur as a guide. The forts occupied a series of low, thickly wooded hills.

tangle of the Pripet marshes, with Mackensen following on the south, and on the north Prince Leopold's group fighting their way through the great forest of Bieloviezsk, the last sanctuary left to the ancient European bison. Evert had escaped without envelopment or being forced into a battle. He had the main Moscow railway to assist his retreat, and for his right wing the line and highroad from Brest to Minsk. His pursuers were held up by rearguard actions in the wooded fringes of the marshes, while the main body moved leisurely eastwards. On the 26th the situation grew more threatening in the north. The Augustovo troops began their retreat, and not an hour too soon, for the Germans were close on Olita. That day Bialystok fell at last to Scholtz, and Below's centre was in action on the Sventa River in the direction of Dvinsk. The movement warned the Russians that a bid was being made for the Petrograd railway north of Vilna. Next day, the 27th, Olita was evacuated, for it was hopelessly outflanked. Lying half-way between Kovno and Grodno, it marked an important ford of the Niemen, and though barely reckoned a fortress in the days before the war, it had been entrenched ever since Hindenburg's threat against the river line in the preceding autumn. With Bialystok and Olita gone, Grodno was rapidly becoming the point of a salient, and all the Petrograd line south-east of Vilna was in hourly peril. All Government papers, stores, and factory equipment were being hastily moved out of Dvinsk and Vilna.

On 28th August Below began his attack on the line of the Dvina. In all the valley of that river, from Riga upwards, there was no crossing till the little town of Friedrichstadt was reached, some fifty miles from the coast. Below it great stretches of marshy forest line the left bank of the stream, and no road followed its course on that side. On the other side, where the ground was harder, there was the main Riga–Vilna railway. At Friedrichstadt, which lay on the left bank, a road reached the riverside, and five miles south of it was a single-line railway. So long as the Russians held Friedrichstadt they controlled the only practicable crossing of the Dvina between Riga and Jacobstadt, and they protected the communications of the port with Dvinsk and Vilna. When Below moved on Friedrichstadt he aimed, not at isolating Riga, for there was still the northern line to Petrograd, but at cutting it off from the Russian armies to the south. That same day there was a kindred movement on the extreme German right. We left Pflanzer-Baltin on the Dniester; Bothmer near Brzezany; Boehm-Ermolli from Zloczow northwards towards Brody, and a large cavalry force under Puhallo on his left. All four armies had behind them excellent communications in the Lemberg railways. For the past fortnight Ivanov's southern command had been little harassed, and, since the campaign in the north was going well, the Austrians resolved to advance in the south, clear the environs of Lemberg, and begin the attack on the Volhynian forts. Puhallo flung his cavalry across the river Styr and moved towards Lutsk, while Bothmer and Pflanzer-Baltin pushed the Russians from their position on the Zlota Lipa. The movement, if successful, would force Ivanov back into difficult country, and cut him off effectually from Evert in the north.

That day, too, Evert himself was being harried east of Brest. Mackensen was well into the marsh country between the rivers Pripet and Mukhovatz, and his cavalry were at Samary, on the road from Kovel to Kobrin. The summer had been comparatively dry, and these western marshes were not impracticable. Prince Leopold was meantime pushing through the forest of Bieloviezsk, slowly and with constant fighting, for it was vital that he should not reach the Brest–Minsk railway till Evert had retreated far enough to get lateral communications by the line which ran east of Pinsk between Vilna and Rovno. By that day the Germans had nearly passed the forest belt, and fought an action just inside its eastern borders. Meanwhile Scholtz was closing in on Grodno; while Eichhorn on a broad front was moving on Vilna, and Below hammered at Friedrichstadt and the Dvina line.

It was clear that Grodno must be relinquished, or the Russian right centre would be surrounded. The Augustovo troops had been withdrawn east of the Niemen, and during those days there was an immense eastward movement between the main Petrograd railway and the Pripet marshes. Troops, baggage trains, and civilian fugitives filled all the roads and choked the two lines still available. These were the railway through Lida and Polotsk, a single line, and the double Brest–Minsk railway. The main Petrograd line by Vilna could scarcely be used, for Vilna itself was in danger. On 30th August Pflanzer-Baltin had reached the Strypa, and Puhallo was close on Lutsk. But Ivanov had the matter in hand. He strengthened his wings, and counter-attacked strongly with his left, checking the advance of the German right. Stubborn fighting continued at Friedrichstadt, on the Dvina; Eichhorn was close on the west front of Grodno; Prince Leopold was nearing Pruzany, on the road from Brest to Slonim; and Mackensen was at Kobrin, on the railway thirty miles east of Brest. But the real menace was against Vilna, where Hindenburg was making his chief effort. If this great nodal point of roads and railways could be taken swiftly there might be a general *débâcle* of all the Russian right centre in the Grodno salient. The German plan was for an advance along the north bank of the Vilia River, while Scholtz, as soon as Grodno fell, was directed to move in support on the southern bank. The Russians met the thrust with a great concentration. Every man who could be brought out of reserve, or spared from other parts of the line, was hurried to Vilna, and an entrenched position was taken up through Meiszagola, fifteen miles north-west of the town, on the road to Vilkomir. Here developed on the second day of September one of the few pitched battles of the retreat.

The last day of August saw Ivanov vigorously counter-attacking on the Russian left around Zloczow. But next day Lutsk fell to Boehm-Ermolli's left wing, and Bothmer had a success on the upper Strypa, near Zborov. That same day Eichhorn was close on Orany, a junction on the Grodno–Vilna railway, and the last hour of Grodno had struck. On 1st September the western works of the place, on the left bank of the Niemen, were carried by Scholtz, and the Russians evacuated that section. Beseler's siege artillery was present, but the place was not stormed but gradually evacuated. It was Eichhorn's threat to Orany which made the Grodno salient untenable. The 2nd of September was the official date of the fall of the town, but fighting continued in its eastern environs for a day later during the Russian withdrawal, and on that day there was a bold counter-attack, Russian troops re-entering the place and taking eight machine guns and 150 prisoners. By the morning of the 4th the Germans held Grodno, but their booty was small. They claimed only six fortress guns, which showed the completeness with which the Russians had cleared it, and some 2,000 prisoners—the rearguard which in such a retirement is inevitably doomed to capture. Meantime, on the southern wing there were severe attacks and counter-attacks. The Austrians had crossed the Styr on a broad front, Brody had fallen, Bothmer was pushing his opponents towards the Sereth, and Pflanzer-Baltin was across the lower Strypa. This was on 2nd September. Next day Ivanov struck back on the Styr, but his extreme left yielded further ground.

On the Dvina there had been a desperate struggle for the Friedrichstadt crossing. Below had issued a special order to his troops: " After the brilliant campaign on the Russian front, and the occupation of many cities and fortresses in Poland and Lithuania, you must make one more effort to force the Dvina and seize Riga. There you will rest during the autumn and winter, in order to march on Petrograd in the spring." On the night of 2nd September the Russians, who held the left bank of the river below Friedrichstadt, made a gallant assault on Below's flank But on the morning of the 3rd the Germans attacked the position at the bridgehead with incendiary shells, and forced the Russians back to the east side. Below had cleared the left bank for a space of ten miles, but he had not won the bridgehead for his attack on the Riga–Dvinsk railway.

There come moments in a campaign when the high tide of an advance appears to be reached and the ebb begins. At the time it is imperceptible to the combatants of both sides, but the turn has come, the summit has been passed. On 4th September the Russian generalissimo, looking to the condition of his front, after four of the most tempestuous months that ever mortal armies endured, might have detected a slight clearing of the skies. The desperate salients had gone. The line was nearly straight. The wings were hard pressed, but could still resist. The centre was too deep in the Pripet marshes for easy capture. In front of Vilna a fierce battle was in progress, but it was a battle of choice rather than compulsion The Russian armies now were not struggling for dear life, but for a strategical purpose. Retreat was everywhere open to them if they chose that course. When they halted and gave battle it was because they had decided to halt, to defeat some cherished German plan. The retirement which at one moment had seemed endless now showed itself as a thing with clear limits. The great armies of Russia were in substance safe. If they could hold the Riga–Rovno line and the Dvinsk railway against the enemy, they might yet wrest from him the initiative and make him rue the day when he crossed the Vistula. One of these mysterious waves of confidence, which men feel but will not express lest they offend the gods, passed through the anxious souls of the Russian High Command. Those who had braced themselves for the last endurance now dared to hope.

At that moment the Emperor of Russia put himself at the head of his soldiers. On the morning of Sunday, 5th September, the Tsar signed an Army Order announcing that he had taken supreme command.

" To-day I have taken supreme command of all the forces of the sea and land armies operating in the theatre of war. With firm faith in the clemency of God, with unshakable assurance in final victory, we shall fulfill our sacred duty to defend our country to the last. We will not dishonour the Russian land "

The Grand Duke Nicholas had for more than a year borne perhaps the heaviest burden yet carried by any single man in the campaign. He had been called on to make vital decisions involving immense sacrifices. He had purged his armies of many unworthy elements, and had inspired them with a complete confidence in their leader. A commander-in-chief of forces so huge leans much on his staff, and individual group and army commanders have a wide discretion. But however high we rate the work of Ivanov and Russki, Alexeiev and Evert, it is certain that the talents of the generalissimo were great, and the sobriety of his judgment and the tenacity of his will were more valuable, perhaps, in that first phase of war than strategical ingenuity and wide military knowledge. But no man can command continuously for a year without growing very weary. The health of the Grand Duke had never been good, and it had suffered from the harassments of the summer. Moreover, there arrives a day in all campaigns when some relief to the higher command may be of real military value. A new mind applied to the same problems may work more shrewdly and expeditiously. But the determining cause of the change was the resolve of the Tsar to take the command himself. Clearly there could not be two royal princes at the head of the armies of Russia. The Tsar as generalissimo must have as his Chief of Staff the ablest master of the profession of arms that could be found, and it is no disparagement of the Grand Duke Nicholas to say that as a professional soldier, and especially as a staff officer, he did not rank with the best of the group commanders.

The Tsar in taking command followed the example of Peter the Great and his predecessors in the hour of national crisis. Many of his advisers, including Rodzianko, opposed the step as too great a hazard for the dynasty. Others at court urged it not because of its political value, but because of their jealousy of the Grand Duke. There was a web of intrigue woven on both sides, but on the part of the Tsar himself the decision was based solely on a sense of duty. It was a sign to his people that Russia would not waver— an answer to Germany's overtures for a separate peace. At the moment when, by all the calculations of Berlin, Russia should have been embittered against her allies, broken in spirit, and ready to approach her conqueror in suppliant tones, her monarch himself took up arms, and summoned the nation to rally behind the majesty of his office. The Grand Duke succeeded Woronzov-Dashkov as Viceroy of the Caucasus, a post which would give him a much-needed rest, and which, as the campaigns progressed, would afford a great field for military activity. He took with him to Tiflis General Januschkevitch, and the duties of Chief of the General Staff developed upon Alexeiev, who surrendered to Evert the group command of the armies of the West. A man of the people, and a soldier from his earliest youth, Alexeiev had revealed himself as a master of the traditional Russian strategy, and to him must be attributed the chief successes of the great retreat. Shy and taciturn in manner, a scholar in his profession, a man of quick judgment and high powers of administration, as a staff officer he had at the moment few rivals in the world.

In early September the German front in the East changed its character. It was no longer a single front devoted to one great combined operation, but relapsed into two groups, the Germans in the north and the Austrians in the south, each with its separate objective. Nine divisions were taken from the armies of Prince Leopold and Mackensen for Serbia and France, and presently Mackensen himself departed to the Danube, leaving to Linsingen what remained of his old command. The Austrians sought only a good winter position, but Hindenburg still hoped with the northern force to achieve a substantive victory and destroy a portion of the Russian field strength. The policy of his campaign since May had been the creation and destruction of salients, and the Russian problem had been to hold the sides of a salient till the troops in the apex could fall back to a point at which the front would be approximately straight. The plan did not appear in the first movement from the Donajetz, but the case of Lemberg was a perfect instance. There Mackensen struck from the north-west and Boehm-Ermolli from the south-west, and only by a miracle of steadfastness was the salient saved. When Lemberg had fallen, the strategy was repeated on a larger scale, its object being the great salient of Poland, of which the sides were the Warsaw-Petrograd line in the north and the Warsaw-Kiev line in the south. It succeeded in the last days of July, when the Narev line was forced, and the Archduke Joseph and Mackensen crossed the Lublin-Cholm railway. The Russian front then broke up into a number of lesser salients, of which the most dangerous was that with Warsaw as its apex and the line of the middle Bug as its base. By the third week of August this had been safely evacuated—the greatest tactical performance of the whole retreat. There remained still four salients or possibilities of salients at Riga, Kovno, Grodno, and Brest Litovsk. The first was saved by the failure of Germany to make a landing at Pernau, or, more accurately, by her failure to account for the Russian Baltic Fleet. Riga was not threatened on the north, and Below's operations resolved themselves into an enveloping movement on the south. The Kovno salient was shallow, and was readily evacuated. But Grodno and Brest remained points of danger, more especially the former, since its fall would enable the enemy to concentrate his efforts on creating and destroying the inevitable salient which must presently be formed with Vilna as its apex. The troops from Vilna must retire by the railway to Minsk, and this line was also the way of retreat for the troops farther south, just north of the Pripet swamps. If the salient were prematurely cut, the whole of the Russian right centre would be menaced, and not improbably driven down in confusion to the slender communications of the marsh country.

In considering the fighting of September, the last stage of the retreat, we are concerned chiefly with the battles around Vilna. But before we reach that point we must note the retreat from Grodno, the subsidiary salient which offered the immediate point of danger. The German strategy attacked Grodno and Vilna together, but it was necessary for the Russians to extricate themselves from the first danger before they could offer any concentrated resistance to the second. If the situation was less grave than in the Warsaw salient in the first days of August, it was strategically far more complex, since it involved a withdrawal from two adjacent salients, the four sides of which had to be simultaneously guarded.

The Grodno salient was roughly defined by the upper Niemen and its tributary the Meretchanka, on which stands the town of Orany. This district is a maze of lakes and forests, which offered many opportunities for rearguard fighting. Inside the salient, following its sides, were two railways—the main line from Grodno north-eastwards to Petrograd by Orany and Vilna, and a southern line by the junction of Mosty, which connected at Lida with the great lateral system Riga–Vilna–Rovno, and was continued to join the railway from Vilna to Minsk. The retreat of the Russians was covered by rearguards towards Grodno, and by a screen of troops delaying the German advance across the main Grodno–Petrograd railway. Clearly, this latter line had to be held as long as possible, for a German advance across it would cut in on the flank of the retirement. The first ten days of September were wet and cold, and the rivers overflowed and turned the swamps into meres. The weather gave some slight advantage to the Russians in the Grodno salient, since there were no railways moving from the sides into the interior by which the enemy could advance. Gallwitz attacked Mosty from the south-west, and Scholtz, moving by the line from Olita, attacked Orany, as the first stage in an advance on Lida. By 8th September Mosty had not fallen, and in the north the line of the Meretchanka had not been cleared, while the Russian rearguards were still resisting on the line Ozery-Skidel in the centre of the salient. The stand on the flanks had served its purpose, for, when Skidel fell on the 12th, the whole Russian front had fallen back to a line from Mosty north to Orany, covering the vital junction of Lida. The salient had been cleared, and if we concede the Germans their claim of 4,000 prisoners it was not too high a price to pay for its evacuation. The situation at Grodno on 3rd September had been only less anxious than Przemysl on 20th May or the Warsaw salient on 8th August. In ten days the danger had passed, and the line had been straightened.

We turn to Vilna, where Hindenburg's main strategical plan was now maturing. It was fixed for 9th September, a combined movement of the XII., VIII., and X. Armies. The Russians lay astride the Kovno–Vilna railway behind Koshedary, across the river Vilia, and along the Sventa River towards Vilkomir, while southwards they touched Orany, and held the Petrograd line towards Grodno. Immediately after the fall of Grodno Eichhorn made a frontal attack upon the Russian position west of Vilna, and in particular upon a sag in it between the Vilia and the Sventa Rivers, on the low downs three miles north-west of the hamlet of Meiszagola. This point, marked Hill 154 on the map, was the position of danger not only for Vilna but for the whole Vilia line and the railways to Petrograd and Minsk, and accordingly the Russians strengthened it by bringing up two divisions of the Imperial Guard. Eichhorn, while driving in the centre just west of Vilna by a great artillery bombardment, made his chief effort on his flanks. From the 2nd onward he was fiercely engaged at Hill 154. The Russian trenches were carried by the weight of German artillery, and for days the Germans held them against counter-attacks. On the 12th they advanced, and after cutting their way through the Russian Guard, stormed the village of Meiszagola, and drove the Russians back towards the Vilia. Meanwhile great masses of German cavalry swept round by Vilkomir and Kurkl, and, threading the marshes by way of the railway from Shavli to Sventsiany, threatened the lines of retreat of the

Vilna troops. Scholtz, on the southern side of the salient, was pressing beyond Mosty and Skidel, and moving on Lida, which place was being bombarded by German Zeppelins. The result of the Battle of Meiszagola on the 12th compelled the Russians to fall back across the Vilia, and presently the German cavalry had cut the Petrograd line at the station of Pobrodzie, some twenty-two miles from Vilna. On Monday, 13th September, it was plain that Vilna must fall. Most of the stores had been evacuated long before, and it remained to release the troops by a corridor which daily grew narrower.

The Grodno salient was clear, and Alexeiev was able to concentrate all his attention on the Vilna problem. Suddenly, on Wednesday, the 15th, he was faced with a new and startling development. At that moment Eichhorn's troops were enveloping the city in the form of a horse-shoe, running from west of Lida through Orany, Novo Troki, Meiszagola, to Pobrodzie. But on the 15th the German cavalry masses swept up the Vilia River towards the town of Vileika, which lies on the branch line running north from Molodetchna junction. Vidzy fell to them next day, and on Friday, the 17th, they occupied Vileika. The Russian front had long ceased to be continuous, and there was a gap between the armies operating in front of Dvinsk and those now falling back from the Vilna salient. Through this gap was thrust the horn of the cavalry. At the same time the right of the horse-shoe closed in, and on that day was half-way between Orany and the Lida–Vilna line. Vilna was being enclosed in a buckle, of which the ends were oriented not north and south but east and west. The clasp was the line from the river Lebeida, south-west of Lida, to just north of Molodetchna junction—a distance of some eighty miles.

The forces in the Vilna salient had only one good line of retirement—the railway to Minsk passing through Molodetchna—besides the great causeway some distance to the south. The southern railway by Lida was still open, but a retirement by it would be in the wrong direction, and would lead to a congestion with the troops falling eastwards before Gallwitz and Scholtz. The Germans were all but in possession of the Minsk railway, and were drawing very near to the Lida line. Vilna was no longer tenable, and on Saturday, 18th September, the old Lithuanian capital fell. The Germans found it empty of stores and guns. All had gone eastwards towards Minsk, and the troops were falling back by the Minsk line and the great causeway. The evacuation was not an hour too soon, for presently Gallwitz's cavalry cut the Lida railway. To protect their retreat it was necessary to fight a series of holding battles on the right flank. The salvation of the Russians lay in the fact that the van of the enemy were cavalry, without infantry or heavy artillery supports. All along a line north of the Minsk railway, between Vilna and Molodetchna, the invaders met with a stubborn resistance. The Russian rearguards fought desperately in front of Michelski, Smorgon, and Molodetchna, and by a heroic effort Vidzy, which the enemy had held for four days, was retaken on the 20th. Yet on that day the situation was something more than critical. The gap available for retreat had shrunk to little more than fifty miles. The Lida railway had gone, and the Minsk railway was in constant danger. Only the great causeway was clear, but a single road is no avenue for an army. Besides, if Molodetchna were taken, the Uhlans would in an hour or two be astride the causeway.

Then suddenly the situation was eased. Partly the German thrust was weakening from pure exhaustion. Partly their closely massed armies were getting in each other's way. The shortening of their front and the concentration against a salient meant overcrowding in a country where roads were few, and to this we may attribute the slowness of the advance by Gallwitz and Scholtz. It is clear, too, that the munitionment of the Russian armies had improved. Reserves had arrived; there was no longer any serious scarcity of shell; and the supply of small arms, though still inadequate, was largely increased. On the evening of 20th September the retreating troops were thirty miles from Vilna, and the Minsk railway still held. The right wing of the retirement fought the enemy at the crossings of the upper Vilia, and on the 21st drove him out of Lebedovo, west of Molodetchna, and retook Smorgon with the bayonet, making large captures of machine guns. The northern horn of the horse-shoe suddenly began to break. For some days there was heavy fighting around Vileika, and a German counter-offensive to the east. But by the end of the month Vileika had been cleared, and the Russian line had straightened itself so as to run through Smorgon, due south to Novo Grodek. The anxious Russian Headquarters at Mogilev breathed freely again. A salient had been evacuated only less critical and not less difficult than the salient of Warsaw in the first days of the German advance east of the Vistula. It was a performance requiring brilliant staff work and the most steady courage and resolution on the part of the troops. How great was that steadfastness may be realized from one incident in the struggle. In the victory at Meiszagola, where the Russian troops were blown out of the trenches by artillery, the German captures were 5,000 prisoners—but only one gun.

It may well be asked why Hindenburg's plan miscarried, for it began with all the advantages in its favour. The Germans had greater mobility in all that concerns routes of transport and transport appliances, and so could obtain at any point local superiority. Their munitionment was many times better than that of the Russians. They had the mechanical devices—limitless motor transport, skilled gangs of road-makers—to remedy the pathlessness of the country. The campaign was no longer one of hammering at entrenched lines. The only entrenchments now on both sides were rough shelter trenches. The Russian front was not continuous, but a group of armies, and these armies had been shaken loose from all fortified bases. It seemed a sovereign chance for Germany to put into effect her outflanking and enveloping strategy, and to turn her strategic pursuit into a series of decisive actions. Napoleon's success after Jena might well be repeated. Why, then, did all the battles of the salients fail of being a German victory ? Why, save for two days in the retreat from Vilna, were her armies never within sight of success ?

Much must be set down to the tenacity and skill of the Russian resistance. For that no praise can be too high, and a closer study of the details increases our admiration for the achievement. But there were contributory faults on the German side. As her armies rolled eastwards they began to lose their initial advantage. Large numbers were absorbed, like the French in the Peninsula, in garrison duties and in guarding lines of communication. The country was hostile, and security must be fought for. The remainder lost in elasticity, the greatest misfortune of all. Partly they were very tired, for many units had been advancing since May, and, though they had occupied great tracts of land, they had never received that inspiration which comes from inflicting indubitable defeats on the enemy in the field. Again, they were clogged by their very strength. Under the best of circumstances their great guns and their large supply trains must travel slowly. Hence, while any section of the Russian front could be driven in, the fruits of the resulting salients could not be reaped. Before their bases could be cut, the Russians had slipped out of the noose and straightened their line. True elasticity could be found only in the cavalry, and the mounted arm by itself was not enough. It may be doubted

if German cavalry reached the same level as the other branches of her service. In the wars of Frederick the Great they had been the best in Europe, and at Rossbach had performed one of the classic cavalry exploits of history. They had failed in the Napoleonic wars; they had one or two fine feats to their credit in the war of 1870 *; but in the present war they had shown themselves feeble in shock tactics, and of little value as mounted infantry. Had the cloud of horsemen who swung round the Russian right at Vileika on 15th September been supported by infantry, the long-sought decision might have been reached. Even had they been trained to mounted infantry work and trench fighting, like British cavalry, they might have compromised the Russian retreat.† As it was, they were checked, held, and finally routed. Speed was necessary if Germany wished to win a second Ulm, but her great machine could not be hurried. It could strike a hammer-blow, but not at the spot and at the moment that the blow was most deadly. It could create many salients, but it could not compel a rout. Her method of war seemed to have been designed for elderly group commanders, highly trained, aided by a superb equipment, but without the fires of genius or youth.

We turn to the lesser salient—that formed by the retreat of the Russian centre from Brest Litovsk. We left Mackensen's army—now under Linsingen—marching north-east to cut off their retirement, and Prince Leopold just leaving the forest of Bieloviezsk in his advance against the Brest–Minsk railway. On 5th September the latter had forced a defile of the marshes north of Pruzany, through which ran the road from Brest to Slonim, while his cavalry had reached the Brest–Minsk line at Kartuzskaia Bereza. The right of the Russian centre accordingly fell back towards the Zelianka River, a tributary of the Niemen, where it was in touch with the left of the retreating Grodno army. Meanwhile, by the 7th, Linsingen had reached the Pinsk railway, about thirty-four miles from Pinsk and seventy from Brest. His progress in the early days of September must have reached an average of four or five miles a day. That western fringe of the Pripet

---

* For example, at Mars-la-Tour, Vionville, and Loigny-Poupry.

† Von Morgen, who served on the Russian front, wrote: "The German cavalry . . . was always hampered by a certain dependence on the infantry. It always retired at night behind them. It ought to have been able to arrange for its own security. Its taste for enterprise against the enemy's rear and flanks was not great; and when as an exception it did show it, sufficient use was not made of fire, and it charged, though carbines would have been more effective."—*Meiner Truppen Heldenkämpfe*, 1920.

marshes in a dry season was not too difficult even for a modern army, as this rate of advance showed. But in the pursuit of the Russian centre the main risk came from Prince Leopold, who, moving in better country, with several roads and two railways to assist him, endeavoured to outflank the Russians on the north. Between Volkovysk and Slonim, in the mid valley of the Zelianka, was the ground chosen for the blow. He took Volkovysk on the 7th, and swung his right southwards against Rozany. Linsingen was now entering more difficult country, and though his centre moved steadily along the Pinsk railway, his wings were in trouble in the marshy upper valleys of the Pripet. On the 16th, after an action with the Russian rearguards east of Janovo, he occupied the town of Pinsk.

The Army of Brest had never been in serious danger, and Prince Leopold's efforts were now directed rather to the southerly envelopment of the Niemen armies retreating from Grodno. He swung his right flank beyond Slonim, and endeavoured to turn the Russians on the Shara, and take the junction of Baranovitchi, which would cut the immediate communications with Minsk for that section, isolate the Army of the Niemen from the Army of Brest, and give him a point on the coveted lateral Riga-Lemberg line. In this enterprise he failed conspicuously. After some hard fighting he was flung back from Baranovitchi, and by the end of the month was firmly held by the Russian right centre on a line running through Novo Grodek, and cutting the Brest-Moscow railway a little east of Pinsk.

The Russian front had once more been straightened, except for the curve westwards to Riga. This curve, however, was no longer a sag, since the bend of the line in front of Dvinsk was broad and shallow. The exact configuration was not unlike a hockey stick, with the head to the north. Below's operations against the Dvina line had progressed little during the month, and south of him there had been a Russian counter-offensive from Dvinsk against the northern flank of the great cavalry sweep which had for a moment put the Vilna army in peril. In the south of the front Ivanov had done more than hold his ground. He had struck so vigorously against the German right that he was in a fair way to free the Volhynian Triangle.

His main counter-stroke began on 7th September. As the German centre advanced towards Pinsk it became necessary to bring forward the right wing, which held the country south to the Rumanian border. The German aim, apart from the improved alignment to be gained by an advance of the right wing, was to get possession of the section of the lateral Riga–Lemberg railway between the junctions of Sarny and Rovno. From Kovel the main line to Kiev runs through Sarny, and another line to Kiev and Odessa passes through Rovno, sending off a southward branch to Lutsk. The lateral railway runs from Sarny by Rovno to Lemberg. If Rovno and Sarny could be taken, the whole Volhynian system would be in German hands, and a vital section of the lateral line would have been obtained for operations against the southern flank of the Russian centre. Farther south, the railways radiating south-eastwards from Lemberg furnished magnificent communications. The chief was the main line to Kiev and Odessa, which crossed the Sereth at Tarnopol junction, and from which a line ran down the east bank of that river towards Rumania, thereby providing another valuable link in lateral transport. The Dniester receives on its north bank a series of tributaries running roughly parallel with each other—from west to east the Gnila Lipa, the Zlota Lipa, the Strypa, and the Sereth. The events of the past two months had forced the Russian left, under Lechitski, from river line to river line, and on the 7th of September they were back on the west bank of the Sereth, with their flank on the Dniester. It was the last river position available to the defence.

On 7th September the right wing of Linsingen's army was moving towards Sarny junction, on the hard ground just south of the Pripet marshes. Boehm-Ermolli, with Puhallo's cavalry, was advancing from Lutsk and Dubno, both of which he held, against Rovno junction. Bothmer was threatening Tarnopol, and Pflanzer-Baltin was preparing for a great assault on the Sereth line and Tremblova. The Russian front had a deep sag in it southeast of Dubno, caused by Ivanov's advance the week before on the Styr, and the necessity of holding on to Tarnopol. That day Ivanov chose for a counter-attack. Part of Bothmer's force had been moved against Tarnopol, when it was surprised and broken by an assault of Brussilov's army. At the same moment a blow was delivered by Lechitski from Tremblova, farther south, against Pflanzer-Baltin. The enemy was taken unaware in both places, and in the two days' battle which followed lost the better part of an army corps. Linsingen, in the north, attempted to relieve the pressure by an assault on the 11th upon the line of the river Goryn, west of Sarny. He failed, and lost many prisoners. On that day the Russian left advanced from Tremblova, swept Pflanzer-Baltin from the banks of the Sereth, and drove him westwards across the watershed to the Strypa. There was a counter-attack next day, but on Monday, the 13th, the whole of Pflanzer-Baltin's force, as well as Bothmer's right, was back on the Strypa. Next day the Russians had cleared most of the eastern bank, and even won a few bridgeheads. Up in the north Linsingen and Boehm-Ermolli continued their efforts to win to Rovno and Sarny, but achieved nothing. In a week Ivanov had advanced his front in some places as much as twenty miles, and had accounted for at least 80,000 of the enemy's troops. In the last fortnight of the month he continued his pressure, directing his attention to the northern sector. Dubno was retaken, and on the 23rd his rearguards entered Lutsk, while his cavalry seem for a moment to have threatened Kovel itself. He had effected something very like a demoralization of the forces opposed to him. Reserves had to be brought down in haste from Prince Leopold, and it was found necessary to put the Austrian IV. Army and all the troops of the Dual Monarchy to the north of it under Linsingen's charge.

The end of September saw a very definite check in the triumphal German advance. Vilna and Grodno had fallen to them, but they had not made good the line of the Dvina. They possessed only a small section of the lateral railway system which they desired —that between a point south of Dvinsk and a point south of Lida. They had failed to cut off the troops in the Grodno and Vilna salients. Winter was almost upon them, and they had as yet found no suitable position for winter quarters, and must still struggle through the rains of autumn and the first snows before they could find a line of security. Above all, Russia had won time without the sacrifice of any armies. There is reason, indeed, to believe that in September the retreat was scarcely less costly to the German attack than to the Russian defence. Arms and supplies were coming in, sufficient to check the tide, if not yet enough to turn it.

Nevertheless no country can suffer as Russia suffered from May to September without a strong reaction. Army corps cannot be reduced to less than 1,500 bayonets without the nation asking questions. The myriads of homeless peasants pouring eastwards along every highway, the troops retiring from the front to the bases, the endless streams of wounded were a reminder of misfortunes which gave the most casual to think. The mere problem of relief was enough to strain the capacity of the country to the utmost. We have seen the consequences of the first Galician disasters, which led to the disgrace of the War Minister, who had prophesied smooth things, the appointment of Polivanov in his place, and of Guchkov as Minister of Munitions. But the purge of the bureaucracy was not yet sufficiently drastic At the meeting of the Duma in August astounding revelations were made as to the extent of subterranean German influence. It was alleged that various banks were under German control, and had endeavoured to "corner" certain commodities and hamper the manufacture of munitions; that many shares in armament works were owned by Skoda and manipulated by Krupp, and that in consequence the companies had dismissed workmen, or limited them to a five hours' day. Such revelations inspired a profound uneasiness among all classes of society. The Duma, when it met in August, was looked to for the expression of the national will.

But the Duma, as is the manner of popular assemblies, tended to dissipate its energies. It was given complete freedom of speech, and for a little seemed about to become at once a safety-valve for popular feeling and a new broom to sweep clean the bureaucratic chamber. A Progressive *bloc* was formed, under the presidency of M. Miliukov, comprising all the moderate and liberal elements in the Assembly. Its avowed purpose was, in the words of its declaration, "strict conformity of the Administration with the law for the removal of duality in civil and military operations, the dismissal of unworthy and incompetent administrators, and the adoption of a wise and tolerant policy in internal affairs, so as to remove racial, class, and religious differences." Unfortunately, the *bloc* began instantaneously to develop a left and a right wing. The right wished all the energies of the Duma to be devoted to administrative reform; while the left, under Miliukov, made the mistake of raising a controversial constitutional question, and asking that the Cabinet should be made responsible to the Duma. A blizzard is not the best moment for even the most reasonable scheme of redecorating and improving the comfort of a house. The Premier, M. Goremykin, secured the Emperor's assent to the prorogation of the Duma till November. It was indubitably a blunder, for the Duma was the only means of expression for the popular voice. The immediate result was a week of confusion and danger. There were serious riots in the cities, and strikes in the munition factories. The agitation was patriotic in intention on the part of most of the agitators; but it is more than likely that German *agents provocateurs* had a hand in its inception. The Emperor summoned the rival leaders to his tent in the field, and an understanding was arrived at.

Miliukov dropped his constitutional schemes, and all parties agreed to concentrate on practical administrative reforms. The period of prorogation was cut short, and the new Minister of the Interior was chosen directly from the Duma. This was M. Khvostov, a Moderate-Conservative deputy from Orel, whose anti-German vigour in the August session now gave him the office once held by Stolypin.

Meanwhile, as political strife died down and as the Russian armies drew clear of danger, news came which opened a new stage in the campaign. For on 25th September the long-expected offensive in the West had begun.

CHAPTER XXXVIII.

CHAMPAGNE AND LOOS.

September 23–October 2, 1915.

The Allied Line in the West—The Policy of the New Advance—The Great Bombardment—The Attack in Champagne—The French Attack in Artois—The British Subsidiary Attacks—The Battle of Loos—The Achievement of the 15th Division—Summary and Criticism.

I.

In September a man with a passion for discomfort and ample leisure might have walked in a continuous ditch from the North Sea to the Alps. Two trenches, from thirty to two hundred yards apart, represented the first lines of the opposing armies. Behind the British front there were second and third lines, and further positions at intervals in the rear. But the Germans had these, and something more. From the day when their High Command resolved to stand on the defensive in the West, they had expended immense ingenuity and labour in strengthening their position. The ramifications of their trenches were endless, and great redoubts, almost flush with the ground, consisting of a labyrinth of trenches and machine-gun stations, studded their front. In natural defensive areas, such as the mining districts of the Pas de Calais, every acre contained a fort. The German lines in the West were, in the fullest sense of the word, a fortress. The day of manœuvre battles had for the moment gone. There was no question of envelopment or outflanking, for there were no flanks to turn. The slow methods of fortress warfare—sap and mine, battery and assault—were all that remained to the offensive.

The past nine months had taught the Allies many lessons. They perceived the formidable nature of the enemy's defence. Though much inferior in numbers, his position and his weight of artillery made him impregnable to any ordinary attack. Guns must be met by guns of equal calibre and equal munitionment. Before infantry could advance, a section of the stronghold must be destroyed by bombardment. Further, it was clear that this destruction must be on a broad front. That was a moral which had been drawn in bitterness after the summer's campaign in Artois. To tear a rent no more than five miles wide meant that time was given for local reserves to come up and hold the gap, so that the enemy's front hardened like concrete before the advance. After the Donajetz the German plan in the East, as we have seen, had been to drive in the Russians in two adjacent sections, and then attempt to cut off the salient thus formed between them by striking inward at its re-entrant angles. That plan was, perhaps, the best in a country where the communications were precarious, and where the opposing front was not continuous. But in the West, where ample roads and railways lay behind every section, where there were no natural difficulties in the terrain, and where the whole front was a continuous fortress wall, it was argued that a single rent on a great scale would be the wiser plan. If the German position could be broken on a front of twenty miles, there would be no time for reserves to hasten up from the flanks and re-form the line. The fortress would be breached, and the assailants, manœuvring in the gap, might compel a general retreat.

It is important at this stage to grasp what exactly is meant by breaking an enemy front. Let us suppose that an artillery bombardment has destroyed the first position; the infantry advance, and are brought up against the second. The second position is more difficult for the guns to destroy, since it is, as a rule, outside direct observation, and can only be dealt with by indirect fire. This means that its bombardment is not likely to be so complete as the bombardment of the first, and the advancing infantry will be held up by patches of parapet and wire which have not been cut. Let us assume, however, that a large number of infantry get through the second position, and confront the third, and probably final, position. Here they will be able to do little, for presumably that position has not been touched by artillery at all. Therefore a halt must be called, and an artillery concentration directed against the third position. But before this can be done the second position must be fully cleared, for there are likely to be a good many points there still held by the enemy. Hence the operation cannot be a swift and continuous thing. There will be a great dash the first day; then a halt, while counter-attacks are being beaten off, and the enemy is being cleared out of points of vantage in his old second position. That takes time, but it must be done before the third position can be properly assaulted. If that assault, when it comes, is successful, and the final lines are carried with a sufficiently broad breach, then the enemy's front may be said to be pierced. The troops which get through have a more or less undefended hinterland to operate in. They can take in flank or in rear other parts of the enemy's front which have not been broken. Their cavalry can cut the main enemy communications. If we remember that the German Western front was very much the shape of a right-angled triangle, it will be obvious that any success of this kind would put a large part of their forces in dire peril. They would be compelled to fall back to positions ten or twenty miles in rear under an overwhelming pressure, and with a perpetual risk of being outflanked. Such a retreat must involve a great loss in prisoners and guns, and under certain circumstances might develop into a rout.

Such were the elements of the problem which faced the Allies in September. Success depended upon a full complement of artillery and shells, for the bombardment must be overwhelming and continuous. It depended not less upon superior numbers. In protracted operations there is always the risk that the enemy will fortify new lines behind those threatened, so that when his positions are broken, the attack is faced not with open country but with a new set of defences. To construct fortifications on the modern scale, however, demands either ample time or a great number of workmen The German man-power, as the Allies well knew, was wearing thin, and the whole of German strategy in the West was directed to holding their lines with fewer troops than their opponents. If after the first attack a constant pressure was maintained along the whole front, the reserves brought up must be used in the fighting line, and there would be no great surplus for the work of fortification. The Allied plan, therefore, fell into three stages— the destruction of one or more positions at the first attack ; the consolidation of the ground won in such a way as to prepare for the next blow, and to leave the enemy no leisure to strengthen his remoter defences ; the attack on the final position, and such movements thereafter as fortune might grant.

The plan which matured in September was for the Allies a change of policy. Foch and Sir John French had, indeed, early in the summer contemplated a great autumn offensive, but the battles in Artois had not augured well for its success. In July Joffre had decided to postpone any forward movement till the following spring. But the situation in Russia, where the German armies seemed to be getting into a position where they could neither force a conclusion nor break off the combat, suggested that the decision might well be revised, and the unexpected improvement in the supply of munitions strengthened the argument. In September there was for Britain a welcome change from the lean days of the early summer. In one branch of explosives alone the production was thirty times as great as it had been in the end of May. Over a thousand factories were now "controlled establishments," and these employed little short of a million workers. Many thousands of soldiers, who before the war had been skilled mechanics, had been released for munitions work. The purchase of supplies and men had been centralized and organized, every machine-tool factory in the United Kingdom was under Government control, and, in addition to the twenty national shell factories, eleven new Government projectile works had been established. The situation of France was even better. The hope expressed in the summer, that by October the full French complement of shells would be attained, seemed likely to be realized. The six thousand guns of different calibres which Germany possessed on the Western front were now equalled by the Allies, and the accumulation of shell from June to the end of August had risen to a gigantic figure. There was also a very clear superiority in numbers. By September Sir John French had nine divisions of the New Army in France, and some had been in training in the trenches since May. The Territorial battalions had been combined in divisions, and a separate division had been constituted from the Guards. Of the splendid human material of these new divisions there could be no question, and one of them, the 14th, had already proved its mettle in resisting a local enemy attack at Hooge on 30th July. But in spite of this apparent strength it is certain that the Allied Staffs, under the influence of the false deduction from Neuve Chapelle, misread the problem before them. They realized in theory that a break-through would be a protracted operation, but they did not guess how protracted it would be. The conception of a breach in a sea-wall still dominated their minds, and they underestimated the strength of the enemy system of defence in depth. Nor did they understand what meticulous perfection of staff work was needed for a series of assaults upon successive positions involving new bombardments and the bringing up of fresh reserves. Their preparation was in reality only for the first assault; beyond that it faded into vagueness and improvisation. It is probable, indeed, that, even if the full intricacy of the problem had been grasped, the Allies would not have been able to meet it. Months of training were still needed before their troops could become a weapon sufficiently edged and precise to pierce Germany's defence.

Champagne and the *secteur* of Castelnau was chosen as the scene of the main attack. The reason is obvious, if we consider the nature of the ground. The German front in the West formed a blunt salient with its apex at Compiègne, and the corner of northern Champagne and the Argonne was its re-entrant angle. A wedge driven in there would threaten the communications of all the southern side of the salient, and would threaten them at a point far from their railheads. If communications can be cut, the most effective blow will be that delivered most near to their base. A brief study of the map will reveal the main lines which might be imperilled. The first was the lateral line, Bazancourt–Grand Pré, which had been the object of the French attack in February. Beyond that was the great trunk line running from Rheims by Rethel to Mezières, and continued to Trèves by Sedan, Montmédy, and Luxembourg. Still farther north was the line from Mezières west to Hirson. Any blow which embarrassed these communications would cut the direct avenues of supplies from the central Rhine valley, and force the whole transport of the Western front into the northern railway system based on Maubeuge. If at the same time the Western front could be forced back, this congestion might involve disaster. Moreover, if the French advanced any distance in Champagne, there was a chance of penning the Crown Prince's army between that advance and the defences of Verdun. These, of course, were possibilities on the far horizon of the main objective. They could scarcely be realized in one effort, but they might be the result in which succeeding efforts should culminate.

Apart from its strategical importance, Champagne offered a terrain peculiarly suited to an attack of massed artillery and an infantry concentration. The rolling chalk downs and their shallow valleys were open and bare. In Flanders the entanglements of meadows, villages, and all the appurtenances of high cultivation made any advance a piecemeal business. In the Pas de Calais the coal-pits, mining hamlets, and numerous mineral railways produced a natural fortress. But in Champagne the only defences must be those hollowed out of the ground. The whole landscape was well fitted for artillery observation and air reconnaissance. Guns could be used to the best advantage, and infantry could reap to the full the fruits of a bombardment. There was something due also to sentiment and tradition. On those dull levels thrice in history had the freedom of France been won. Every Frenchman looked on the chalky downs about the Camp of Attila as a place of destiny for his country. It was as if a British fleet were fighting again in the waters off Cape Trafalgar.

But to support the grand attack there must be others. The salient must be assaulted on its northern side, and the place chosen was the sector between La Bassée and Arras. There the French had delivered their attack in May, clearing the ridge of Notre-Dame de Lorette, and winning a line from Souchez village to the trench network called the Labyrinth, between Neuville and Ecurie. An advance thence into the plain of the Scheldt towards Douai and Valenciennes would threaten the German lateral communications from Lille to Soissons. The immediate objective was Lens, and Lens is situated in the flats between two low swells of ground. South are the Vimy Heights, which d'Urbal had failed to carry in May, north lie the insignificant slopes around the village of Loos. An advance along the whole front might make Lens untenable, and prepare the way for a movement against Douai and Valenciennes, and even against Lille itself. It should be noted that, while the Artois movement had its immediate strategic objective, this did not rank on the same plane as the end sought in Champagne. The country was too difficult to look for any swift and sudden break in the line. It was conceived rather as a subsidiary operation to distract other parts of the German front, to prevent reliefs being sent south, and to induce some uncertainty in the minds of the enemy's Staff as to which was the main effort of the Allies.

Other subsidiary attacks were necessary for the same purpose, and these were entrusted to the British forces. The German front was weak in the areas of the projected assault. Einem had only seven and a half divisions on the thirty-mile front of his III. Army; the Bavarian Crown Prince had sixteen divisions on the fifty miles between Armentières and the south of Arras. The IV. Army from the sea to Armentières was in greater strength, and it was essential that Duke Albrecht's forces should not be used to support other parts of the front. To ensure this there must be a number of lesser attacks. If these succeeded, and ground was won, so much the better, but it was not essential that they should succeed. They were strictly holding battles, and it was enough if they distracted and occupied the attention of the enemy.

The early weeks of September saw perfect autumn weather,

with the clear cool days that an east wind brings. In the evening the smoke from the little fires of field refuse cloaked the country like a sea fog. Early in the month a general bombardment began along the whole Allied front. Its purpose was to serve as a screen behind which the preparations for attack could be made, and to puzzle the enemy as to which section of his line was chiefly threatened. It was violent in Lorraine, in Champagne, in Artois, and around Ypres, and it naturally elicited a counter-bombardment. But it was fitful, a demonstration rather than an attack, and though it did much damage it was not intended to be the real work of preparation. Much had to be done, also, to make ready the front for the advance. In some sections new trenches had to be dug in front of the old, fresh telephone wires had to be laid, and special bomb stores constructed. The Allied aircraft were busy, for it was important that no German machines should reconnoitre over our lines. In every week of September there were at least a score of fights in the air; in many cases the German airmen were brought down, and in every case they were driven back. In the third week there were twenty-seven fights over the British lines alone, and only one British machine suffered damage. Brilliant work was done, too, in reconnaissance, airmen remaining in many cases for over two hours at an altitude of 7,000 feet above enemy territory, subject to a constant bombardment. As the 25th of the month approached our airmen went farther afield, and bombed vital parts of the German railways. They burned Valenciennes station, derailed and blew up trains, and interfered ruthlessly with the enemy's communications. The "Taube" shrank from crossing that frontier of death, the Allied first line. In Champagne all the country about Châlons and Bar-le-Duc had been cleared of its civilian inhabitants, and had become a military zone where troops and guns moved by day and night behind the defences of the northern batteries. As it happened, the enemy was aware of our purpose, and guessed the chief areas of attack; it was only the exact hour of it that he could not determine.

On Thursday, 23rd September, the main bombardment began. From La Bassée to Arras, and along the Champagne front, hell was loosed from thousands of pieces. The German first position was being methodically destroyed yard by yard, while by indirect fire the howitzers were battering their second line. To such a storm there could be no reply, and the long German front seemed bereft of life. That night the wind changed to the south-west, and the morning of Friday, the 24th, dawned mild and wet, with a Scots mist settled on all the countryside. Any section of the front that day was a curious sight. All the roads were full of returning gun teams without their guns, and long files of ammunition wagons. Everywhere there was an atmosphere of stress and expectancy. Commanders knew only the orders for their own men, but there was that subconscious tension which heralds the coming of some great event. It was known to every one that for the first time the Allies were taking the offensive on the grand scale, and the minds of their troops were not yet dulled to hope.

About midnight the bombardment drew to a head. Every gun on the front was speaking, and speaking without rest. From thirty miles off it sounded like the roll of giant drums. Close to the front the sound was beyond description. In the misty night nothing was visible but the flashes from the guns or bursting shells. Modern battles are not pictures for the eye; they are assaults upon the ear, and that never-ending growl of artillery conveyed a grimmer impression to the brain than any spectacle. From the small hours of the morning, in a pandemonium of din, troops were moving into the communication trenches. The great masses just behind the front were beginning to percolate into the labyrinth of narrow ways which led to the first line. Between them and the skies was a canopy of flying projectiles, and when they could raise their heads they saw the dark, dripping night lit with splashes of fire. Dawn began to struggle through the gloom, and Saturday, 25th September, opened in a drizzle.

Suddenly the guns ceased. The instant quiet seemed death-like, and smote on the ear and brain with a shock like icy water. The troops crawling forward knew what it meant. The gunners were shifting range and lengthening their fuses. The first of the infantry were going over the parapets, and the battle had begun.

II.

At dawn on that Saturday morning the French lines in Champagne lay roughly east and west of the little town of Ville-sur-Tourbe. From the southern outskirts of Auberive—the Germans held the village—they ran east in undulating ground just north of the old Roman road, and enclosed the village of Souain. In this section the Germans faced them on a number of ridges, where were situated four famous redoubts—the Palatinate, the Magdeburg, the Tirpitz, and the Wilhelm II. From Souain the French position skirted the south end of the Bois Sabot, and cut the road from Perthes-les-Hurlus to Tahure, a little over two miles north of the former place. Here the German lines lay on a series of swells, the chief of which was Hill 170, with important redoubts at the Trou Bricot Mill and the spot called the Cabane. North-east of Souain, half-way on the road to Tahure, was the German work which the French called La Baraque. Going east, the French lay along the south end of the Bois Jaune Brûlé to just north of Massiges, cutting across the southern flank of Hill 171. This belt was part of the curious flat down known from its shape as the Hand of Massiges. Between the Perthes–Tahure road and the Hand of Massiges the Germans were strongly posted on a ridge—the Butte of Mesnil—which commanded the shallow valley of the river Dormoise. From Massiges the French position ran in an almost straight line to a point north of the town of Ville-sur-Tourbe, where it bent northwards by Servon to Binarville in the Argonne.

It is hard to present a bird's-eye picture of that strange countryside. It is a land of low chalky downs, without walls or hedges, separated by the shallow waters of little muddy streams. The downs are some 600 feet above the sea, but no more than 150 or 200 feet above the level of the valleys. New plantations of scrubby firs—sure proof of an impoverished soil—vary the monotony, but the shell-fire of months had ploughed them into ragged shadows, and in some cases left only a chaos of splinters. The country is the same northwards beyond the railway. It is the watershed of many inconsiderable waters—the Suippe and the Py flowing north-west, the Dormoise, the Alin, and the Tourbe going north-eastwards to the Aisne. As the Argonne is neared and the broad Servon valley the streams grow more limpid, and oaks and poplars replace the pines of the barrens. From almost any observation point the whole landscape lies clear to the eye. In the coarse chalk the great scars of trenches and earthworks showed up white among the rough grasses, so that under a blue sky the place had the air of an alkali desert. The German lines in Champagne were immensely strong, since the section was strategically so vital, and Einem had but few divisions to man it. Apart from the infinite ramification of the trenches, there were huge dug-outs, protected by timber and steel casings, capable of holding nearly a hundred men. There were several hundred miles of light trench railways. All the critical points were held by machine guns in concrete and steel casements, deeply buried in the earth. No part of the front showed such colossal industry in defence. It was one vast semi-subterranean encampment, fortified in every yard with the latest devices of science.

In the days before the 25th there was a feverish activity behind the French lines. The men had been carefully instructed, so that every platoon knew precisely its objective. Besides their ordinary equipment they were armed with trench knives for the desperate close-quarter fighting of which the summer's work at the Labyrinth had warned them. Shelters and assembly trenches had to be improvised for the advancing infantry, and in some places saps and tunnels had been run out towards the German lines, so that the first assault should spring suddenly from the earth. As the troops moved forward in their new horizon-blue and the steel helmets, which made them look like the pikemen of Gustavus, the big new Creusot howitzers, which the men christened "Les Vainqueurs," were speaking night and day. On the night of the 24th an extra ration of wine was issued, and the packed trenches waited with little sleep for the morning. At dawn they looked out on a grey and dismal world. A thin, fine rain was falling, and the wet chalk clung to boots and clothes. Yet those who had read history had a memory to console them. It was the weather of Valmy. One hundred and thirteen years before, in the same month, on those sodden downs, the guns of the Army of the Revolution had checked an invasion and turned homewards the most reputed troops in Europe, whose only trophy was dysentery from a debauch of Champagne grapes.*

The artillery for a little ceased fire, and men waited in an eerie quiet. Then, at a quarter past five, on a fifteen-mile front from Auberive to Massiges, the blue-grey waves surged from the trenches. At the same moment, at lengthened ranges, the guns flung their curtain of fire between the enemy and his supports.

The first or "outpost" German position had been devastated by the great bombardment. The Champagne-Pouilleuse has been compared to a frozen sea, and now the image was just, for whole acres of chalk had been churned by shell-fire into the likeness of surf and spume. Over this the French swept in their stride, under a hail of fire from the German batteries. Plunging through the

* Hence the song of Dumouriez's men :—
"Savez-vous la belle histoire
De ces fameux Prussiens ?
Ils marchaient à la victoire
Avec les Autrichiens ;
Au lieu de palme et de gloire
Ils ont cueilli des raisins."

THE FIRST DAY OF BATTLE.

debris of the first line, they left detachments to " clear up "—to ferret out prisoners from the deeper dug-outs, and take the machine guns which a few heroic survivors still tried to man. These machine guns took heavy toll of the attack, and the German artillery from far in the rear were " watering " the path of the advance. The road was marked by piles of blue-grey dead, but the impetus did not slacken. Slipping and stumbling among fragments of wire and the slimy chalk, now horribly marked with blood, the infantry crossed the support and reserve trenches of the first position. The French line before the charge had been fantastically configured, some trenches looking east, some north, some west. The German lines corresponded, so that there were many awkward corners to be rounded off. This explains why in some parts the assault went clear into the German second lines, and in others battled desperately with the first. There were moments of confusion, such as are inevitable in every great attack. Battalions were mixed up, and junior officers found themselves in command of brigades.

The most desperate fighting was on the left, where the Colonial Corps was engaged with the line of wooded hills between Auberive and Souain—the trenches around the lonely house called the Epine de Vedegranges and on Hill 150. On the extreme left the attack was held up after a kilometre, but on its right trench after trench was taken, the first position was cleared, and by midday the troops had reached the great line known as the Lubeck trench, which ran east to Hill 193. All through the dripping afternoon the struggle continued, and as the twilight fell it became possible for the French Staff to take stock of its winnings. On a front of fifteen miles the advance had been carried forward an average of two and a half miles. For every yard of front an unwounded prisoner had been taken, and nine guns for every mile. Let us follow the new position from left to right. Between Auberive and Souain the great redoubts of the Palatinate, Magdeburg, von Tirpitz, and Wilhelm II. had all fallen, and the French faced the Lubeck trench, the chief position in the second line. On the road from Souain to Tahure they had carried La Baraque, and were looking down on the farm of Navarin, which lay on the slopes towards the lateral railway. Eastwards they held Hill 193, but had not reached the German second line east of Navarin Farm, since the enemy still clung to the woods which they had christened Spandau and Kamerun. From this point eastwards the position was complicated. The French commanded but had not reached the village of Tahure, north of which lay the Butte of Tahure, defending the railway.

They had cleared and made great captures of men and guns in the Cabane, the mill of Trou Bricot, and on the slopes of Hill 170. North of Beausejour Farm the resistance had been stubborn, and no impression had been made on the Butte of Mesnil. But part of the Hand of Massiges had been carried, and the great shell-hole called the "Crater," and the right wing had won the farm called Maisons de Champagne, which stood on the edge of the shallow vale of the Dormoise. Practically the whole German first line had gone, and the French held parts of the second line, west of Navarin Farm, and east of Tahure.

The critical moment of the battle was still to come. It was essential to prevent the enemy consolidating his remoter defences and bringing up reserves, so the artillery was pushed forward, and all that night of 25th September the bombardment was resumed. Meantime the French dug themselves in in their advanced position, adjusted the captured trenches, and got their machine guns ready against counter-attacks. It was no light task bringing up batteries across that scarred and pitted battlefield, but the work was accomplished in the hours of darkness. On Sunday the left wing cleared all the summits of the downs from Auberive to Souain. The centre cleared the woods east of Souain, and joined up with the right of the left wing on Hill 193. The so-called "Camp of Sadowa," with great quantities of *matériel*, was taken. Hill 201, facing the Butte of Tahure, was captured by the evening, and a position won in the great Trench of the Vistula on the slopes in front of Tahure village. The northern slopes of the Hand of Massiges were cleared, perhaps the finest achievement of all, for the German commander had boasted that the place could be held by a washerwoman and two machine guns. Some progress was also made against the strong German lines on the Butte of Mesnil, which now formed a salient menaced from east to west. All along the front, by means of alternate artillery bombardments and bomb attacks, the line was advanced. But the enemy battle position was not pierced except in patches too small to be exploited.

For that day the Germans rushed up all available men to the point of danger. The first day they had held on desperately against odds, and when the strain continued on the morning of the 26th, Einem was hesitating on the brink of a withdrawal of his whole front. But that afternoon supports came—a division from Alsace, the 10th Corps which had just arrived from the East, and the reserves of Heeringen's VII. Army of the Aisne. They

were just in time, for the French in many places had won to the battery positions. Indeed the whole front was cracking, and but for a deluge of rain, which prevented the French artillery coming up with any speed, the German second position would have fallen.

Castelnau had begun the battle with thirty-four divisions at his disposal, and had not yet exhausted his impetus. The second great French effort was made on the 29th, and the place chosen was to the west of Navarin Farm, where the second position had already been pierced. Such an attack, so soon after the first, could not be delivered with the same vigour. Reconnaissances could not be so complete or the artillery concentration so strong. Yet for one moment the attempt seemed about to be crowned with success. It was rumoured at first that the last German position had been carried on a front of three divisions—say, five kilometres—and all along the Allied lines from Nieuport to Belfort there was a moment of wild anticipation. Men asked each other if the cavalry could go through at last and ride for the key-points of the railways. The rumour was false. The position had been breached, but on a front of less than a kilometre between the Lubeck trench and the coppice called the Chevron Wood. The gap was too narrow for use. The enemy's guns were moved behind it, and poured in a torrent of shell, and all that the French could do was to dig themselves shelter-trenches, and cling to the position under a heavy enfilading fire. With this action the main operations closed.

The Battle of Champagne was the greatest of the Allied attempts to break the enemy front by a single crashing blow. It was within limits a success, for the French took more guns and prisoners than Napoleon had taken at Jena or Austerlitz—150 of the one and 25,000 of the other—and therein it had its value for the *moral* of the nation. But it failed conspicuously in its chief purpose, and it showed no tactical ingenuity or strategic subtlety The Germans knew the French aim and the French methods; Castelnau knew with equal clearness the German modes of defence. The situation was that of the siege of a fortress—a straightforward trial of strength. Both sides were fairly matched, if we allow the intricacy of the German defences to balance the greater numbers of the French troops. In a struggle between forces approximately equal it is luck which turns the scale. A little extra good fortune—a weakening at a vital point, an unexpected celerity in the handling of guns, any one of those thousand chances which may happen in action—would have taken Castelnau through the German front.

He had the right to hope for such fortune, but it did not come. For a moment it looked as if the game were won, but the defence was too strong to fall at the first attack; the Allies must still sit down in front of the fort and prepare for the next assault. They had learned one lesson of the uttermost value—that fortune could not be trusted to favour an ambitious offensive, and that the crumbling of the defence demanded a more elaborate preparation and more patient tactics.

It is well to remember what such fighting meant for the men engaged in it—both attackers and attacked. In other battles there had been advances under desperate fire, but they had been short, and had been cheered by the hope of a rout and a pursuit. But this warfare involved an endless procession under the heaviest shelling known to history. When one trench was cleared another awaited, and there was no respite for a second from the tornado of the defence's fire. We praise the *élan* of the Napoleonic armies, but what degree of courage and vigour was needed to drive forward an assault which could not lead to the rout of the enemy, but only pave the way for another desperate attack, and still another? So too with the German defence, to which Falkenhayn's tribute is not too high.[*] We praise the discipline of those marvellous armies of the eighteenth century, with their inhuman steadiness under fire. There was Marlborough's attack on the Schellenberg, when he lost in one hour more than a third of his men, and the Guards had twelve officers down out of seventeen. There was the great attack by Cutts's left on Blenheim village, when Row led his men steadily up under the French volleys till he tapped the palisade with his sword. Most famous case of all, there was the advance of Cumberland's centre at Fontenoy, up to within fifty yards of the French guard, when Lord Charles Hay toasted the enemy, and the British looked coolly at a row of muzzles till the order came for their volley. Or, to take an instance from the end of the old régime, there were the Prussian infantry who, on the day of Jena, faced Lannes at the village of Vierzehnheiligen, and for two hours stood dressed in line volleying at sheltered enemies, because such were their orders. That discipline was equalled, nay surpassed, by the troops who pushed from trench to trench in the mire and rain of the Champagne battle, and by those who withstood them.

[*] *General Headquarters 1914-16* (Eng. trans.), p. 173.

III.

The attack in the north which was launched on the 25th of September was a movement subsidiary to the great effort in Champagne. While it was under the general direction of Foch, the details were left to two different commands—the French Tenth Army and the British First and Second Armies. There was a smaller concentration of men and guns than in the south, and inevitably there was less co-ordination in the parts. We may divide it into two main operations—d'Urbal's attack upon the Vimy Heights and the advance of the British First Army against the line La Bassée–Haisnes–Hulluch–Loos. Both had the same purpose—to isolate the railway junction of Lens and open the road into the plain of the Scheldt. In addition, four attacks were undertaken north of the La Bassée Canal—one by the British 2nd Division from Givenchy; one by the Indian Corps from Neuve Chapelle; one by the 3rd Corps from Bois Grenier; and one by the 5th Corps in the south of the Ypres Salient. These were secondary attacks, designed to distract the attention of certain parts of the German front; and the fact that the Artois attack was not the main movement of the Allies was partly responsible for certain misfortunes in the handling of the troops. For what happened was that by accident the British force did find a real weakness in one section of the German front, and, had it been a major operation and the plans laid accordingly, a comprehensive disaster might have overtaken the enemy in the north. But for this success they were not prepared. Reserves were not ready in time, or in sufficient strength. The lesser gain which they had anticipated was secured, the greater success slipped from hands unprepared to receive it. It was the kind of misfortune which is frequent in an assault upon a long front, and it was made almost inevitable by the fact that the British army formed a quasi-independent command. In spite of the closest and most cordial relations, operations controlled by two separate staffs, differing in quality and methods, are not likely to reach complete co-ordination or a uniform strength at every point.

In considering the complex fighting along a front of nearly fifty miles, it will be well to deal first with the doings of the French Tenth Army, which had a clear objective in a self-contained terrain; then to consider the various holding battles fought north of the La Bassée Canal; and lastly, to describe in some detail the great movement which captured Loos, and for a moment shook the whole German northern front.

D'Urbal's Tenth Army, which had been increased to eighteen divisions, on the morning of 25th September held a line from the British right at Grenay, past Aix Noulette, to the west side of Souchez village. Thence it ran just east of Neuville St. Vaast into that tangle of trenches between the roads from Arras to La Bassée and to Lens which was known as the Labyrinth. The old Labyrinth had been long ago in French hands; but since May it had extended itself, and some of the eastern trenches up to the Lens road were held by the Germans. The aim of the attack was the same as that of the battles of the early summer. East of Souchez a tiny river of the same name ran among meadows. On the west bank was a coppice called the Bois de Hache, and across the stream a little to the south a larger woodland, called the Wood of Givenchy. Just east of the trees lay the village of Givenchy-en-Gohelle, at the junction of several roads; and south and west were the slopes of the Vimy Heights. These were not high—the flat top was just over 400 feet—but they commanded Vimy station and the railway between Lens and Arras, and gave a prospect over rolling slopes away to the valley of the Scarpe. One other point must be noted. On the southern slope, looking over the Labyrinth, lay the village of Thelus. From Souchez to Thelus the Heights of Vimy stretched roughly in the shape of a half-moon.

The French bombardment had been heavy for three weeks. Early on the morning of 25th September it stopped. The Germans, expecting an infantry attack, manned what was left of their front trenches, but no infantry came. Instead, the French turned their 75's on the first line, and caused great slaughter. Once again the bombardment began, and the British troops, fighting at Loos, could see nothing in the south but a pall of smoke torn by flashes of fire. For some reason not yet clear the French infantry attack did not begin till one o'clock, seven hours after the British in the north had gone over their parapets. Seven mines were exploded at the same moment along the enemy's front, and under cover of the cloud of dust the French sprang from their trenches. The bombardment had done its work, but the position was still strong. There were three German lines west of the Souchez stream; and the remnants of the village, where no house was left standing, were held by machine guns in the cellars. The first trench was cleared, and on the French left the Germans were driven into the

little Bois de Hache. The second trench was in the wood, and this and the third line, on the west bank of the stream, were quickly taken. Then came a counter-attack, heralded by a heavy bombardment, and conducted by troops in close formation, armed with grenades. Far into the misty twilight the struggle went on, and just at the darkness the enemy was pushed back across the river. In front of Souchez the centre prospered less. The cemetery was taken, but no impression could be made on the village itself. On their right the French took the last trenches of the Labyrinth, and so cleared that death-trap. Night fell on an inconclusive battle. Much had been won, but the attack was still far from the Heights of Vimy.

Next morning the weather had cleared. A strong west wind and a bright sky attended the second phase of the contest. On that day the British in the north were being heavily counter-attacked, and since the enemy at the moment had insufficient reserves to meet two strong attacks on adjoining sectors at the same time, the French won considerable successes. On their right they gained a position north of Thelus, on the lower slopes of Vimy. On their left the chasseurs carried the line of the Souchez River, crossing the water by means of planks left by the Germans, under a devastating artillery fire. With the bayonet they took the German trench on the east bank, and charged into the Wood of Givenchy, now little more than a mass of splinters. Here there was heavy fighting, the chasseurs sheltering behind tree-stumps and in shell-holes, and bombing their way yard by yard. By the evening they had won the greater part of the wood, and were well up the north-west side of the Vimy slopes. That day, too, the centre carried Souchez village, and ferreted some 700 Germans out of the cellars.

On Monday, the 27th, the French were busy reorganizing and consolidating their front. On Tuesday, a cold, grey day, they began their final movement against the Heights. The Germans had received reinforcements, including divisions of the Guards which had just arrived from Russia. The French guns played on the slopes, and the French line fought its way foot by foot up the terraced and honeycombed hillside. But by Wednesday morning the Vimy Heights had not been won. The French position was well short of the crest, though the western slopes and most of the Givenchy Wood were in their hands. The situation to the north made it necessary to hold back for the present. The British line was very thin, and it had extended east of Loos in a deep salient beyond the French alignment, so that its right flank was to some extent in the air. Joffre accordingly requested Foch to strengthen the British front by taking over the south side of that salient. The 9th Corps was sent to Loos; and by the first days of October, French forces composed the pincers menacing Lens from north and south. The change, apart from the relief it afforded to the British front, was in itself desirable. If a "pinching" movement against Lens was to be undertaken, it was expedient that it should be under a single command.

In considering the various minor actions on the British front, we may begin with that fought in the Ypres Salient. The Hooge fighting of August had brought the British line on the south side of the Salient to a point west of the Bellewaarde Lake, then east of the shell-hole called the Crater, whence it ran south of the highroad into Sanctuary Wood, at the northern corner of which was a dangerous German *fortin*. The whole Ypres region was strongly held by the enemy. From there, if from anywhere, reinforcements could be sent south; and it was essential to detain the left wing of the Duke of Würtemberg's command. The British attack was entrusted to Allenby's 5th Corps, which for the purpose borrowed the 14th Division from the 6th Corps. All day on the 24th Ypres was heavily shelled; but Ypres was no longer the neck of the bottle: we had other ways of bringing up troops and supports to the Salient, and the bombardment of the ruined city did little harm. At four o'clock on the morning of the 25th we began our final bombardment of the Hooge trenches. At 4.30 we exploded a mine north of the road, and a few minutes later the attack was launched by the 3rd Division on the right and the 14th Division on the left. On the left we were attacking Bellewaarde Farm, and on our right moving towards the fortress in the north of Sanctuary Wood.

The Germans, except in the area of the exploded mine, were not taken by surprise. They had looked for an attack in the Salient, and the bombardment of their right wing on the coast by a squadron of the British fleet under Admiral Bacon seems to have convinced them that here the main British effort was to be made. When the assault began they hurried up reserves from their front farther south, thereby assisting the Allied purpose. But no forewarning enabled them to support the shock of the British infantry. Presently the whole of their first line gave way. Bellewaarde Farm and the ridge on which it stood were carried, and south of the Menin road we advanced for 600 yards.

But gains in the Ypres Salient were hard to hold. The big guns from the Passchendaele ridge and from the neighbourhood of Hill 60 on the south came into play against our new front. Moreover the Germans had a far greater artillery concentration behind their lines. The Bellewaarde ridge could not be maintained, and long before the evening our left was driven back to its old line. But south of the highway we clung to some of the ground we had won, and managed to consolidate our position. It may fairly be said that the thrust at Hooge fulfilled its purpose. We had occupied the attention of several German corps while greater matters were in progress in the south.

The second of the minor operations was that undertaken by Pulteney's 3rd Corps. Its front before and south-west of Armentières was held from left to right by the 27th Division, the 8th Division, and the 20th Division of the New Army. The attack in this section was made by the 8th Division, the division which had fought at Neuve Chapelle, and had attacked at Fromelles on the 9th of May. It moved from in front of Bois Grenier against the German trenches. The attack was timed to begin before dawn at 4.30 a.m. on the 25th, after the usual bombardment. The first charge went well, save at a point in the centre where a German searchlight revealed the movement, and one unit was held up by a deadly fire from machine guns. Except at this point the whole German first line was carried; and by six o'clock a large part of the second line was taken, when the guns lengthened their range and played on the enemy's third line. By this time the Germans were recovering from the first shock, and a strong counter-attack with bombs was delivered. Our advance had been uneven, and while the wings were far forward the German centre formed a wedge which exposed us to enfilading fire, and checked effective communication between our units. By three o'clock in the afternoon the action was closed, for it had abundantly achieved its object. Our troops were withdrawn in perfect order, and, thanks to the heroism of the stretcher-bearers, all our wounded were safely brought in. This affair was a model of what a holding battle should be—an advance not pushed beyond the possibility of an orderly retirement, but conducted with sufficient vigour to absorb the whole energies of the immediate enemy front.

The third operation, which took place just north of Neuve Chapelle, was less successful. At this time the Indian Corps held the line from Fauquissart through Neuve Chapelle to the neighbourhood of Festubert. It had on its left the 20th Division of the 3rd Corps, and it linked up on its right with the 2nd Division of the 1st Corps at Givenchy. The main movement on the 25th of September was to be that of its left, the Meerut Division, whose line ran roughly from a little east of Fauquissart to the place called the Duck's Bill, north-east of Neuve Chapelle village. In front of it lay the Moulin du Pietre, for which we had struggled fruitlessly on the second day of the Battle of Neuve Chapelle. A thousand yards beyond that point was the first swell of the Aubers ridge, the village of Aubers being about a mile and three-quarters from the British lines. At dawn there was an elaborate artillery bombardment on the section of attack. The Meerut Division loosed a cloud of gas, but in the mist and drizzle, with only a light wind behind it, the gas clung to the ground ; and when the Bareilly and Garhwal Brigades went over their parapets, they suffered from it in spite of their helmets.

The latter brigade came against uncut wire, but the former was brilliantly successful. In its first rush it took successive lines of German trenches, and pressed on towards the Aubers slopes. It did not follow the French practice of leaving clearing parties to occupy the captured positions, but, assuming that supports would follow and perform that task, it raced impetuously into the mist and disappeared from the ken of the British front. Then followed a strange situation. The Germans reoccupied the trenches in the rear of the attacking brigade, and bombed it from behind. There was no adequate support from our heavy artillery, most of its ammunition having been expended in the preliminary bombardment. In the foggy weather, made thicker by the fumes of gas and lyddite and asphyxiating shells, men lost their way, orders miscarried, and all morning there was a wild confusion. A German counter-attack drove in the line of the 20th Division on the left, and thereby exposed the flank of the attack. The Dehra Dun Brigade, the reserve of the Meerut Division, owing to the congested state of the communication trenches, could not get up in time. All day there was a curious stillness, broken only by intermittent firing from the Moulin du Pietre region. The attack had vanished, and the whole plan of operations had dissolved. Much of the blame must be attributed to the weather and the difficult conditions of the attack, but there must have been some defect in the co-ordination of the movement to make so wholesale a confusion possible. Meanwhile, the devoted brigades were fighting a hopeless battle inside the enemy's lines. Their impetus, which with adequate support might have carried the Aubers ridge, ebbed under the encircling counter-attacks. Nothing was left but to fight their way back. This they achieved with many casualties. The Bareilly Brigade came out 1,600 strong. Its two British battalions, the 2nd and 4th Black Watch, which had advanced with the pipes playing, were so reduced that they had to be amalgamated. The remnant of the 2nd Leicesters, one of the hardest-fighting units in the Army, did not return till the following day. A tribute should be paid to the splendid quality of the British battalions in the Indian Corps. In the battle of December 19-22, 1914, at Neuve Chapelle, and in the fierce struggle of 9th May, they had acquitted themselves like heroes, and again and again redeemed a lost situation. On 25th September they showed their old prowess, but on a fruitless field. The affair—whether by malign conditions or by a defect in leadership—had been too costly to rank as a legitimate holding battle.

The fourth of the minor actions was fought by troops of the 2nd Division, assisted by part of the 19th Division, in front and south of Givenchy. So far as terrain was concerned, it was the most vital, for the great thrust was being made south of La Bassée; and, if the movement on the north succeeded, La Bassée would be enclosed between two fires. But the Givenchy district, as we knew from bitter experience, with its brickfields and lines of railway and canal, was one of the strongest fortresses in the German front. In this fine action some advance was made, and part of the German first line was occupied; but since no reserves were available, our gains had to be relinquished before the evening. Yet the movement had effected its purpose. It had detained considerable German forces, which might otherwise have been used against the main armies to the south.

Apart from local failures, we may consider that the series of lesser actions on 25th September won a reasonable success. It should be remembered that in a large concerted movement the troops who have to fight containing battles have the most difficult task of all. They have none of the exhilaration of a great advance; they have usually but a small artillery support; their line may be none too strong. Their business is to hold the greatest possible number of the enemy, and it is generally a costly business. They are fighting for somebody else to win. The battalions in the main movement earn high honour, but let us not forget those others whose duty it is to stand and wait. They capture no great position, but without their aid no position would be captured.

IV.

We come now to the main British attack, which was directed against the German line from the La Bassée Canal to the slopes in front of Grenay. The elements of the ground were simple. The German front ran south from the rise of Auchy La Bassée over a flattish tract to the Vermelles-Hulluch road. Thence a long low swell runs southwards, on the west side of which the German lines continued just below the crest till the Béthune-Lens road was reached. South of that the British held the crown of the ridge to Grenay. Several points in the enemy front must be noted. A mile west of Haisnes stood a slag-heap marked on the map as Fosse 8, which lay about half a mile inside the German line, and commanded all the country to the south. South of that, and about a mile and a quarter west of Cité St. Elie, a great redoubt, the Hohenzollern, had been pushed out some five hundred yards in front of the line. It was connected with the main front by two trenches, known to our men as "Big Willie" and "Little Willie," and also with the defences of Fosse 8. South of this was another work, the Kaiser Wilhelm; and three-quarters of a mile northwest of Loos, on the summit of the ridge, was a strong fort, the Loos Road Redoubt, where a track from Vermelles crossed the downs. Just opposite Grenay stood a large slag-heap, called the Double Crassier. Behind the German front was a string of mining villages—Haisnes in the north, a mile and a half from La Bassée; Cité St. Elie, a mile south, on the Lens road; Hulluch, half a mile farther, and a little to the east, a village strung out along a little stream; Loos, two miles to the south-west, and about the same distance from Lens. Loos lies in a shallow hollow, and to the south-east rise further slopes, the highest point being marked on the map as Hill 70. From Hill 70 the ground falls away eastwards to the hamlet of Cité St. Auguste, about a mile from Lens, and virtually a suburb of that place. All these points were strongly fortified, and there were, besides, a number of other slag-heaps, pits, and natural features which lent themselves to defence. The most notable were the Quarries, half-way between the German front and Cité St. Elie; the Chalk Pit, three-quarters of a mile north-east of Loos; and the Pit No. 14 *bis*, between the Chalk Pit and Hill 70. The German reserve position was roughly just west of Loos, and west of the Quarries. The final position, so far as it had been located, ran from west of Cité St. Auguste northwards, behind the string of fortified villages, Hulluch and Benifontaine, Cité St. Elie and Haisnes.

The landscape, as seen from some one of the slag-heaps behind the British front, was curiously open. The opposing trench lines showed up clearly in the coarse chalk, and the country seemed a dead-flat plain, scarred with roads and studded with the head-gear of collieries and mean little red houses. But this openness was deceptive. Every acre was a possible fortress, and the low downs west of Loos screened at least half of the hinterland. Still, as compared with the Flanders battlefields, it was a clear terrain, where artillery could operate to some extent by direct observation, and where, in case of success, cavalry might be used. There was scarcely a tree to be seen except in the south, where several small coppices cloaked the north-eastern slopes of Hill 70. But for the collieries and slag-heaps the place had something of the air of the South African veld, coarse grasses and self-sown crops being scattered sparsely over the baked grey soil. The land was well drained, but two hundred years ago it was swampy, and even to-day after rain the mud might be formidable. It had been part of the field of Marlborough's Flanders campaign, and it was between Hulluch and Cuinchy that Villars, on June 14, 1709, began to construct the first section of the famous "Lines of La Bassée."

The disposition of the British forces was as follows: From Givenchy to the Vermelles-Hulluch road lay the 1st Corps, under Hubert Gough. The bulk of General Horne's 2nd Division on its left was engaged in the subsidiary attack from Givenchy. Opposite Fosse 8, in the centre, lay the 9th (Scottish) Division of the New Army, under Major-General George Thesiger. On the right, facing Cité St. Elie, was the famous 7th Division, under its old leader, General Capper. South of the Vermelles-Hulluch road lay Rawlinson's 4th Corps, now wholly changed in its constitution. On the left, facing Hulluch, was the 1st Division; not quite the old 1st Division which had fought at the Aisne and at Ypres, for the Guards battalions had gone, and Territorial battalions had been added. On its right lay the 15th (Scottish) Division of the New Army, under Major-General McCracken. It had been three months more or less in the trenches facing Loos, and had acquired a complete familiarity with the ground—an invaluable possession for an attacking force. On the right—the extreme right of Haig's First Army—was the 47th Territorial Division (the old 2nd London), under General Barter. The Londoners were now seasoned veterans, having been at the front for more than six months, and having greatly distinguished themselves in the May battles around Festubert. They lay in front of Grenay, facing the south end of Loos and the big slag-heap called the Double Crassier.

The German forces, heavily outnumbered, held a position which could hardly have been bettered. Fosse 8, and the rows of mining cottages clustered about its foot, the Hohenzollern Redoubt, the Loos Road and Lens Road Redoubts, and the Double Crassier—besides the endless points of vantage behind them—gave them excellent observation posts and ideal ground for machine guns. They believed that an attack, even if it carried the first fire trenches, would shipwreck grievously on the deadly labyrinth behind them. The Hohenzollern was a typical example of German skill and industry in this kind of fortification. It was shaped like a pear, with its broad end pointing northwards, and had a frontage of some five hundred yards. From the south end the trench called "Big Willie," and from the north end "Little Willie," ran back to the main line. The work was situated on a gentle rise, with before it a clear field of fire, every inch of which could be swept by the machine guns inside. From end to end ran a main trench, from which cross trenches radiated to the extremities, and each trench was studded with machine-gun emplacements.

At 6.30 on 25th September, when the great bombardment slackened, the 2nd Division found itself speedily checked in the desperate country south of the canal. On its right the 9th Division made for Fosse 8 and the Hohenzollern. The rise at Auchy La Bassée enfiladed its advance, and the 28th Brigade on the left had desperate fighting. They pushed beyond the Vermelles-La Bassée railway, and took the first line of the German trenches; but the position was too precarious to hold, and slowly during the day the Lowlanders were driven back. Meanwhile the 26th (Highland) Brigade had succeeded better with the Hohenzollern. Saps had been run up to within a short distance of "Little Willie," and the artillery bombardment had played havoc with the interior of the redoubt. It was taken, but not without heavy losses; and Fosse 8 was also captured after a violent struggle. The troops had to advance over a perfectly bare, shell-swept piece of ground; the machine guns on the Fosse played on them unmercifully; and, owing to the hold-up of the advance on their left, their flank was in the air. Yet by eight o'clock the leading troops were close on Haisnes, and British soldiers had actually entered the village. The 27th Brigade was brought up, and was employed to clear the maze of trenches and cottages to the east of Fosse 8; but it was eleven o'clock before it could reach the advanced front, and by that time the chance of the capture of Haisnes had gone. By midday this section of the British line had driven forward in a broad salient, capturing the chief works of the enemy. But its gains were precarious. Fosse 8 was cleared but not occupied in strength, for our reserves were scanty, and all the land between it and Haisnes was filled with isolated *fortins* and sections of trenches still held by the enemy's machine guns.

On the right of the 9th Division the 7th Division had made good progress. With no Fosse 8 or Hohenzollern to hold them back, they swept forward across the first German position. They reached the western side of the Quarries, where a sector of the German second line, strongly posted, held up that part of the advance. Their van entered the village of Cité St. Elie, and then pushed northwards, but by this time the weight of their attack was exhausted. The right brigade managed to reach the point where the Hulluch–Vermelles road crossed that from Lens to La Bassée. By midday the 1st Corps had, except on its extreme left, taken the whole German first line, and at three points had broken into the second. But it had used up all its reserves, and for the moment could do no more.

It was farther south, in the sector of the 4th Corps, that the advance reached its height. We have seen that the left south of the Vermelles–Hulluch road was held by the 1st Division. Its attack was made by two brigades, and the 1st Brigade on the left had a straight course. It swept forward for a mile and three-quarters, and early in the forenoon was in the outskirts of Hulluch, and up against the German last position. This charge was the more splendid, since its right was in the air. The 2nd Brigade, on the right, found themselves held by the German first position near the spot called Lone Tree, where the parapets and wire had been insufficiently destroyed by our bombardment. They had to lie pinned to the earth till afternoon, when it was found possible to send in the divisional reserves through the great rent torn by the 15th Division to the south. This brought them in on the flank of the German garrison, 700 strong, which was completely cut off and captured. The whole division was then able to advance and take position on the ground won by the 1st Brigade; but it was already many hours behind its time, and it could neither support the successes of the troops on its right, nor exploit those of its left brigade.

We now reach the brilliant advance made by the 15th and 47th Divisions, which resulted in the capture of Loos and—for a moment—the shaking of the whole German northern front. The Londoners, on the right, carried all before them. They had prepared assiduously for the day, working out the operations on a big model of the countryside, so that every battalion knew the lie of the land before it. Consequently, when one battalion lost all its officers, the men still carried out the plan with complete precision. As the French gunners watched the start, they were amazed to see one of the London Irish kick off a football from the parapet and dribble it across the thousand yards to the first German line They learned that day that the stolid British had their own *panache*. In half an hour the Double Crassier was won, and the Londoners were pushing on across the Lens–Béthune road, a veritable death-trap, every yard of which was dotted with shrapnel. Presently they had seized Loos Cemetery, and their left had swung into the outskirts of the village. The whole movement was admirably planned. A chalk pit south of Loos was taken, and the adjacent group of miners' cottages, so that the flank of the central advance was fully safeguarded Before eight o'clock they had joined hands with the Highlanders in the shattered streets beneath the twin Towers of Loos

The advance of the 15th Division deserves to be told in some detail, not only because it was the most conspicuous achievement during the first day of the battle, but because it was a type of the actions fought that day in various parts of our front. The plan was for the 44th Brigade to make the direct assault; the 46th Brigade, on the left, was to fetch a circuit and come in on the north side of the village; while the 45th Brigade was held in divisional reserve. The gas attack—the first made by Britain—was delivered about ten minutes to six. The wind was very light, and the cloud clung too close to the ground ; worse still, the breeze came from the south-west, and since Loos lay in a hollow, and a wind, as every stalker knows, is apt to eddy down a hollow, the gas blew back to some extent on the 46th Brigade on the left. The cloud was greeted with a fusillade of rifle and machine-gun fire, but as it passed over the enemy trenches the fire slackened. At 6.30 the whistles blew, and the Highlanders scrambled up the steps and were over the parapet.

Our own wire had all been cut during the night, and the

dark tartans of the Black Watch and Seaforths raced over No Man's Land and flung themselves on the German lines. The trenches were filled with German dead; but from the deepest dug-outs a gallant remnant, who had survived the bombardment, brought up machine guns and turned them on the advancing infantry. But nothing stayed the rush of the Scots. By five minutes past seven the whole of the German first position, several trenches deep, was in their hands, and the battalions swept across the 800 yards intervening between the crest of the ridge and Loos. In that sinister mist, reeking of powder and gas and blood, the fury of battle possessed the souls of men who a year before had been sober, law-abiding civilians. Singing, cheering, and shouting mad encouragements, the Highlanders went down the slope. In front of Loos was the German reserve line. The entanglements there had been largely destroyed by indirect fire, but patches remained unbroken, and these were cut by the Black Watch under heavy shelling. They lost severely, and the ground was terribly carpeted with their dead. But the brigade did not waver. It carried the reserve position, and at twenty minutes to eight, an hour and ten minutes after they had left their trenches, the Highlanders were surging through the streets of Loos.

South-west of the church stood the tall twin towers, the headgear of a colliery connected by a bridge, which our men called the Tower Bridge or the Crystal Palace, and which they believed had been constructed by the Germans before the war as an observation station. It was visible on a clear day from as far off as the Hill of Cassel, and from our old trenches the tops showed foreshortened over the downs, like the masts of a ship seen at a great distance at sea. The village itself consisted of four rambling streets, surrounded by many small gardens and enclosures. The clearing of Loos did not take long. The 47th Division was in its southern outskirts, firmly holding the flank, and the 46th Brigade of Scots Lowlanders was closing in on the north. Meantime the Highlanders bombed the enemy out of the houses and cellars. Before nine o'clock all resistance was at an end, the battalion headquarters had advanced, and Loos was in our hands.

But the Highlanders were not content. Their orders had been not only to take Loos, but to occupy the rising ground to the east —the broad down marked in the map as Hill 70. But the original plan had allowed for the attack to proceed beyond Hill 70, should circumstances be favourable, and though this had been modified on the eve of battle, the change had not been explained to all the troops, and the leading battalions were in doubt about their final objective. The rise begins just outside the village, and the crest of the flat top is about a mile from the church. The 46th Brigade was closing in on the slopes from the north, and the remnants of the 44th Brigade advanced up the western side. The fire from the defence for a moment gave them pause, and the German infantry came out of their trenches as if to counterattack. The sight spurred the Highlanders to a great effort. They streamed up the hill like hounds, with all battalion formation gone, the green tartans of the Gordons and the red of the Camerons mingled in one resistless wave. All the time they were under enfilading fire from south and north, but with the bayonet they went through the defence, and at nine o'clock were on the summit of the hill.

On the top, just below the northern crest, was a strong redoubt, destined to become famous in the succeeding days. The garrison surrendered—they seem scarcely to have resisted—but the Highlanders did not wait to secure the place. They streamed onward down the eastern side—now only a few hundreds strong—losing direction as they went, so that instead of making for Cité St. Auguste they swung south-east towards Cité St. Laurent, the fortified northern suburb of Lens. The attack had now passed outside the legitimate operations of war, and had reached a district which was a nest of fortifications. The Germans had a great array of machine guns on a small slope outside the village, and they were busy installing others on the railway embankment north-east of Lens. The Highlanders formed a mad salient, with no supports on south or north. The captured garrison had manned the crest of Hill 70, and assailed them with reverse fire; while from Cité St. Auguste, from near Pit No. 14 *bis* and the Keep to the north-west, from the environs of Lens and from the unbroken positions south-east of Loos, came a converging bombardment. The last stage of the Highland onslaught had been magnificent, but it had not been war, for there were no reserves to follow them. Had the supports been there, had their flanks been more secure, the enemy's northern front must have been pierced. In less than three hours the heroic brigade had advanced nearly four miles, and had passed beyond all but the last German trench line. Lens seemed already fallen, the enemy was feverishly getting away his heavy guns, and for one moment the fate of Lille and the plain of Douai trembled in the balance.

Between nine and ten a senior officer of the division took

command on the hill, now strewn with the remnants of the 44th and 46th Brigades, and endeavoured to recall the van of the advance, which was lost in the fog and smoke of the eastern slopes, and to entrench himself on the summit. The redoubt was out of our hands, and the line taken ran just under the crest on the west, and was continued north of Loos by the 46th Brigade. To retire the van was no light task. In the midst of encircling fire it was a forlorn hope, and few returned to the British lines on the hill. All down the slopes towards Lens lay the tartans, Gordon and Black Watch, Seaforth and Cameron, like the drift left on the shore when the tide has ebbed. By midday our line was consolidated with the help of the first troops of the 45th Brigade, the divisional reserve.

It is necessary at this point to consider what provision had been made by Sir John French for supports. A modern battle is won by the superiority of numbers at the proper place and moment. The day has gone when a handful of men, like Cortes' adventurers, may conquer a kingdom. To pierce an enemy's lines by a frontal attack is a question of reserves. The great successes in this type of operation, such as Sheridan's at Chattanooga and Longstreet's at Chickamauga, were won by the presence at the proper moment of adequate supports; the failures—Meade at Fredericksburg, Pickett at Gettysburg, Grant at Spottsylvania—by their absence. The principal British reserves were General Haking's new 11th Corps, consisting of the Guards Division, under Lord Cavan, and the 21st and 24th Divisions of the New Army. These troops Sir John French kept under his own hand, since our operations, according to his statement, were on so long a front and he did not know where the need might be greatest. There was the further difficulty that the French advance on Souchez was delayed, and it might be necessary to send troops to support our right flank. On the night before the battle the two New Army divisions were on the line Beuvry-Nœux-les-Mines—about five miles at the nearest point from our old firing line. The Guards Division that night was at Lillers, thirteen miles as the crow flies from the front and nearly twenty from the Loos area. Farther north, the 28th Division had been drawn out of the line of the 2nd Corps, and taken to Bailleul to be ready to move when orders came. The whole of General Fanshawe's Cavalry Corps, less one division, was in general reserve some twenty miles back; while General Rimington's Indian Cavalry was at Doullens ready to co-operate with the French cavalry in exploiting any infantry success. The 3rd Cavalry Division was just behind the line of the 4th Corps. The position on the eve of the battle was, therefore, that Haig had no reserves under his control except the 3rd Cava'ry Division. The 11th Corps, the 28th Division, and the rest of the cavalry were in Sir John French's hands.

At 9.30 a.m., when Loos had fallen and the Highlanders were in front of Cité St. Laurent, the Commander-in-Chief placed the 21st and 24th Divisions at Haig's disposal. At the moment they were about eight miles from the new front, and the route of their advance would be difficult as soon as the German counter-attack began. There were thus no reserves immediately available for the hard-pressed first line except the extra brigade kept in hand in each division. During the afternoon of the 25th these were brought up, and at the same time the Germans massed their supports. Till the darkening counter-attacks continued in a drizzle of rain, which broke towards twilight into a flight of rainbows and a stormy sunset. Our hold on Fosse 8 was getting desperately precarious, while east of Loos the 46th Brigade was driven from Pit 14 *bis*, and the position on Hill 70 was gravely threatened.

Meanwhile, through the rain and the darkness, the two divisions of the 11th Corps were marching towards the firing line in order to relieve the 1st and 15th Divisions of the 4th Corps. They were new troops, some of whom had landed in France only a few days earlier. They had been reviewed by Sir John French, who was impressed by their fine physique and their soldierly bearing, qualities which might well be nullified by lack of actual fighting experience. These men had never been " entered " to this kind of warfare, they had never been under fire, and they were destined to take their place in the front of one of the severest actions of the campaign. It was a trial too high for the finest material in the world. To add to their difficulties, the 21st Division was taken up to the trenches over exposed ground, where they were heavily shelled. Their transport, including their water-carts and copper cookers, was knocked to pieces; and when, early on the Sunday morning, they advanced to relieve the brigades of the 15th Division, they were in no condition to endure a prolonged strain.

That night German counter-attacks were frequent against our new front. The 7th Division at the Quarries were driven out of their trenches, but for the most part our line stood firm. Sunday, the 26th, dawned clear and bright. All that day fighting was severe against the line of the 1st and 4th Corps, but in the afternoon the 7th Division managed to advance and regain the ground lost at the Quarries. The new 24th Division attacked with one Brigade in the gap between Hulluch and the Loos Chalk Pit, and pushed forward most gallantly to the German last position in front of Vendin le Vieil. Their advance was carried too far, and in the afternoon they were compelled to fall back, with heavy losses, to their original line. For that afternoon a British attack had been projected against the redoubt on Hill 70, but it was anticipated by the enemy. Early in the forenoon he flung his reserves against our front, and the troops of the 21st Division, who had been for hours without food or water, were driven in. They thrice attempted to rally, but by that time their cohesion was gone. This lost us the Chalk Pit north-east of Loos and the advanced ground towards Hulluch, and caused our line to bend sharply back from Hill 70 to the Loos–La Bassée road. On Hill 70 itself we lost some trenches, and our hold on the place was in jeopardy.

It was a critical moment, for there were no reserves at hand. At six o'clock on the previous evening the Guards Division had arrived at Nœux-les-Mines, and on the Sunday morning Sir John French placed them at the disposal of Haig. They were then eight miles distant, and were not hurried, for they were intended to be used in the next stage of the advance. But the fate of the two new Divisions upset all our plans. The 44th and 46th Brigades of the 15th Division, which had been taken out, were sent back to hold the reserve trenches, and a dismounted brigade of the 3rd Cavalry Division—the 6th, under General David Campbell—was flung into Loos to form a garrison. To the 45th Brigade of the 15th Division was given the task of retaking the lost ground on Hill 70. They advanced most gallantly to the attack, but found themselves faced by strong German reserves, and under a severe converging shell-fire. All that day and the succeeding night the situation was desperate. The 45th Brigade and two companies of the 9th Gordons were for long the only troops holding the first lines. Had the Germans attacked in greater force we must have been driven out of Loos. The 3rd Dragoon Guards came up at nightfall and occupied the trenches east of the village, and they and the Highlanders clung on during the darkness under a constant enfilading fire from Pit 14 *bis*. It was not till after midday on the Monday that the Guards Division took over the front and the 15th Division was relieved. Its losses were heavy—over 6,000 for the two days' fighting—but it had earned a reputation second to none in the British forces. A year ago its men had followed civilian trades, and now they ranked in courage and discipline and every military virtue with the veterans of our army. The farthest rush of the Highland Brigade was, no doubt, a blunder, a magnificent but a barren feat of courage. And yet that madness contained the seeds of future success. It had in it the rudiments of "infiltration," the tactics by which storm troops found weak places in a front and filtered through. Behind them there was now no tactical plan, no certainty of supports; there was no prophetic eye among us to see what was implied in their exploit, and we set it down as a glorious failure. Three years later, when we had learned what the enemy could teach us, the same method was applied by a master hand to break in turn each of the German defences.

Monday, the 27th, was a day of cold rain and misty distances. The 28th Division had now been given to Haig, and was destined to reinforce the sorely tried 1st Corps. It had been brought down from Bailleul, but before it could come up Fosse 8 had slipped from our hands. The brigades which had made the advance on the Saturday had returned to the firing line, but under pressure of counter-attacks they were slowly forced back till our front coincided with the eastern part of the Hohenzollern. The Germans held both ends of the main communication trench, and gradually bombed our men out of the centre, while the recapture of the Fosse meant that we were terribly enfiladed by machine-gun fire. The German counter-attack was a well-managed affair, their artillery acting in perfect co-operation with their infantry. But the great event of the day was the advance in the afternoon of the Guards Division in the area of the 4th Corps. The line on the Monday morning ran from a point between Hulluch and the Loos–La Bassée road, dipping back to that highway and continuing round the north-east end of Loos, to the western slopes of Hill 70. Nearly three-quarters of a mile of ground had been lost on the left and centre during the Sunday, and it was the business of the Guards to win it back. It was the first time in the war that they had taken the field as a division, and great things were expected of them. These hopes were not disappointed. Two brigades of the Guards held the old first-line German trenches, the 1st on the left in front of Hulluch, and the 2nd to the north of Loos. The 3rd Brigade was for the moment in reserve behind

the ridge west of Loos. The business of the 1st Brigade was to advance and straighten the left of that section, so that it should run parallel with the Lens–La Bassée road. The 2nd was directed against the Chalk Pit and Pit 14 *bis*, since the enemy possession of these points made Hill 70 untenable; and immediately on their success the 3rd Brigade was to advance through Loos and attack the summit of Hill 70. The 1st Brigade succeeded in its task almost at once, and during the subsequent fighting it safeguarded the brigade on its right from any enveloping movement.

The 2nd Brigade was placed on the western slope of the shallow valley through which runs the Loos–Hulluch road. It looked across to the Chalk Pit, about three-quarters of a mile away, which lay in the north end of a small spinney. South stood Pit 14 *bis*, a large colliery and a tall chimney, with beside it a red house and a fortified "Keep." Behind it, on the east, was a tattered wood, the Bois Hugo, which, though badly thinned by our artillery fire, still gave cover to machine guns. At 4 p.m., after a sustained artillery bombardment, the attack began. The left battalions had at first an easy task, and took the spinney with few losses. But the right battalions fronting Pit 14 *bis* had a difficult time. When they had passed the Hulluch–Loos road, and begun to ascend the opposite slope, they were deluged with shrapnel, and had to face a furious machine-gun fire from the Bois Hugo. They won Pit 14 *bis*, but the enfilading fire was too severe, and the line in the evening did not extend beyond the south side of the spinney, though the Chalk Pit was firmly in our hands.

Meanwhile the 3rd Brigade had advanced against Hill 70. The ground had been well reconnoitred, and it was obvious that so soon as they crossed the ridge west of Loos they would come under a heavy bombardment. Accordingly the men were deployed in artillery formation. Once on the ridge the shrapnel tornado burst on them, but the Guards advanced with all the steadiness of parade. It was Fontenoy over again, and the wearied infantry and cavalrymen who had been holding the front cheered wildly as the ordered line of the Guards swept inexorably into Loos. Once through the town they had to face a storm of gas shells. When they gained the crest of Hill 70, and were outlined against the sky, they were greeted by a fierce bombardment, and by machine-gun fire from the redoubt. Realizing that the line on the crest was too good a target for the enemy, the brigade entrenched itself about 100 yards to the west of it. Here it had the 3rd Cavalry Brigade on its right; but its left was in the air, since there was a gap in the front between the Hill and Pit 14 *bis*. Next day, Tuesday, the 28th, the 2nd Brigade renewed the assault on Pit 14 *bis*. The place was important, for, being situated on the northern slopes of Hill 70, so long as it was in German hands it enfiladed our whole position east of Loos. At 3.45 in the afternoon it was attacked from the south end of the Chalk Pit, while our guns were turned on the Bois Hugo. Once again the enemy's machine-gun fire proved deadly, and, though a small party managed to reach Pit 14 *bis*, the place could not be held. We fell back in the evening to the Chalk Pit and the spinney, thus connecting with the 3rd Brigade east of Loos.

The main phase of the battle was now drawing to a close. The enemy during the 29th and 30th shelled our line heavily, while we in turn laboured to consolidate our positions and to replace by reserves the more weary of our front-line divisions. All round the Hohenzollern there was constant fighting, where, with heavy losses, the Germans won small sections of trenches. Our line from north to south ran roughly from the Vermelles–La Bassée railway, west of Fosse 8, just east of the Hohenzollern, through the Quarries, east of the Chalk Pit, west of Pit 14 *bis*, and along the western slopes of Hill 70, a hundred yards short of the crest. South of Loos we curved back in a sharp salient towards Grenay. By the 2nd day of October the readjustment of the front was complete. The French 9th Corps had taken over the line on the right from our original point of junction with d'Urbal's command to the north slopes of Hill 70, including the village of Loos. The 47th Division was moved farther north, and they and the 12th Division of the New Army under Major-General Wing completed the relief of the 4th Corps. The 1st Corps had received the 28th Division as supports, and the Guards Division was under orders to move to that part of the front which included the Hohenzollern. The 46th Territorial Division (the old South Midland) was moving south to take its place with the Guards and the 12th Division in the 11th Corps.

On the last day of September Sir John French issued an order to his troops setting forth the details of the action. Lord Kitchener in his congratulatory telegram described it as a "substantial" success, and that is perhaps the truest epithet. On a front of 6,500 yards we had everywhere carried the enemy's first line, and we had broken into his second line in many places. We had captured over 3,000 enemy rank and file and over 50 officers. We had taken 26 field guns and 40 machine guns, besides great quantities of other war material. A substantial success it was beyond doubt, the most substantial the British army had seen since trench warfare began. Our artillery had shown a brilliant competence, our subsidiary services had been good, and Sir John French in his dispatch paid a well-deserved tribute to the work of the Royal Engineers. Above all, our battalion fighting had been magnificent. Where battalions failed, the cause was not to be found in any defect of the human material.

Yet the exhilaration of victory, the sense that at last we were advancing, was tempered by a profound disappointment. We had had a great chance of which we had failed to take full advantage. Most of the results of surprise and of initial impetus had been lost during that tragic interregnum from Saturday at midday till noon on Monday, when a few weary and broken brigades clung heroically to an impossible front. There had been somewhere a colossal blundering. It is now clear that the whole offensive was in itself premature and mistaken, but such mistakes are inevitable for mortals who lack the gift of prophecy. But there are criticisms to be made on the British share which do not concern the major strategy. There were no reserves available for the main attack during the whole of the first day, and no adequate reserves till the third day; not till the Highlanders had taken Hill 70 were two reserve divisions placed at Haig's disposal; these divisions were untried troops, who bent under the strain; the Guards came into action on the afternoon of the third day, when the Germans had had ample time to consolidate their defences and bring up their supports. Had reasonable reinforcements been available for the 1st Corps on the morning of Saturday, the 25th, it is probable that Fosse 8 would have been won beyond fear of loss, and that Haisnes and Cité St. Elie would have remained in our hands. Had like reserves been ready for the 4th Corps it is at least possible that Lens would have fallen, that our cavalry would have penetrated the German front into the plain of Douai and the Scheldt, and that presently Lille might have been at our mercy.

It may be asked in the first place why our reserves were so scanty. There were only the three divisions of the 11th Corps and the cavalry behind the lines. Two more divisions were procured—the 12th and the 28th—by withdrawals later from our northern front. But we had, all told, nearly a million men in France and Flanders. On the front of the new Third Army not a shot was fired during the battle. Was it not possible to mass stronger reserves, even at the expense of leaving our line in places a little thinner? We knew that the French in their great concentration had large portions of their front dangerously depleted, but these risks must be taken in any offensive. That so few reserves were brought up argued a certain lack of prescience in the British plan. In the second place, the historian must inquire as to the quality of the reserves actually used. Two new divisions, unbroken to modern war, unfamiliar with trench fighting, and never hardened to that nerve-shattering experience, a great bombardment, were scarcely the material to use in the second stage of a great thrust. The physical fitness of the men was no justification; it could only serve to increase the regret that good stuff should have been wasted. Lastly, even had the reserves used been unexceptionable in quality and numbers, there was a strange delay in sending them up Some light is afforded in a sentence in the Commander-in-Chief's dispatch, where he explains that his troops were operating on a long line, and that it was desirable to keep the reserves at first under his own hand. Now, in a defensive action such a course would have been right. The general does not know where the enemy's main attack will be delivered, and must keep his reserves ready to bring forward at the point most gravely threatened. That has been a maxim of war since the days of Alexander. But the same precaution is needless in an offensive. For there the initiative is in the hands of the attacking side; its commander knows where he is going to make his great effort, and where he will merely fight containing actions. Admittedly the main British thrust was on the line La Bassée–Loos, and the four engagements fought farther north were only holding battles, where no reserves were required, since a permanent advance was not contemplated. Only in the First Army's area could reserves have been possibly used. But, since the earliest of these reserves were not available for Haig till the initial thrust was over, and at the time were at least eight miles from the scene of action, they could not be put to their proper use of strengthening and continuing the impetus of the first assault.

It is hard to avoid the conclusion that the superb drive and devotion of the troops of attack were frittered away by a certain fumbling and confusion in the mind of Headquarters. They anticipated some sort of success—or otherwise why was the cavalry massed in reserve?—but they had not considered fully the ways and means of it. They took the Germans by surprise, but were themselves caught unawares. They succeeded better than they had hoped, and were not ready to use the gifts of fortune. Of all the British actions in the war Loos was the one which did least credit to the High Command.

One result of the battle was that criticism of the British staff work, which had been rife during the summer, rose to a pitch which demanded the attention of the nation. During the operations which began on 25th September, as during Neuve Chapelle, Festubert, Ypres, and Hooge, there were doubtless instances of staff mismanagement. It would be hard to find a great battle in history which was free from them. Friction between the Staff and the battalions is as old as human warfare. Overwrought regimental officers are apt to regard the Staff as a Capua of ease and leisure, and to forget that the burden of the men behind the fighting line may be greater than that of the battalions in the trenches. As regards its Staff, the British army was in a special difficulty. The admirable Staff which belonged to our original Expeditionary Force had had to be multiplied many times, and the brain of the Army is precisely that which it is least easy to improvise. Again, at their best, our staff officers had not been trained to handle large masses of men after the fashion of our Allies and opponents. On this subject many wild things were said, single instances of failure were magnified into a general breakdown, and critics, both military and civilian, forgot that no human Staff is infallible, and that even Berthier and his colleagues had their lapses.* But there was this much of truth in the complaint : we were somewhat inclined to underrate in practice the importance of the quality of a Staff, and to regard it as a residuum instead of a picked body. Men were occasionally given staff appointments not because they were fitted for such duties, but because they were unfitted for others. We possessed many staff officers of conspicuous ability, but in certain directions our lack of selection allowed the average of competence to decline. The raising of this question, flagrantly unjust

* For example, the elaborate orders for crossing the Danube from the island of Lobau to Wagram sent Davoust and Oudinot to the wrong bridges. In the march from the Channel to Ulm the orders involved an entanglement between Davoust's and Soult's corps. Berthier told Murat to be in force at two different places at once (October 13, 1805), and Davoust was ordered to concentrate at two different places (October 1806) In 1806 Murat replaced Berthier in command of the army at Wurzburg, but Berthier was not told, and for a few days both issued orders Bernadotte's instructions, which he obeyed, kept him away from Jena and Auerstadt ; so would have Ney's, but he disobeyed them. It was the indifferent staff work of the French which largely led to their defeat at Salamanca. Ney's staff work in the Russian campaign was as bad as possible. Endless instances of the same thing may be found in the American Civil War—for example, Hooker's Staff at Chancellorsville and Longstreet's at Gettysburg—but the American Staffs were, of course, mainly non-professional. The Napoleonic orders were diffuse and complicated because, as Napoleon explained at St. Helena, many of his marshals did not understand what was in his mind. Efficient staff work in the modern sense really dates from Moltke.

though most of the charges were, had one good result. It compelled the nation to realize the vital importance of the thinking side of the Army, and the necessity, if we were to win the war, of seeking diligently and at all costs for capacity.*

The British losses up to the 1st day of October were in the neighbourhood of 45,000 men—almost as great as the losses of both North and South together at Gettysburg, or at the Wilderness. Among them were three brilliant divisional commanders. Major-General Sir Thompson Capper, commanding the 7th Division, was wounded in the advance of Sunday, the 26th, and died on the following morning. He had led his division at the First Battle of Ypres and at Festubert; he was dedicated, if ever man was, to his country, and brought to battle both the skill of the professional soldier and the ardour of the visionary. On the Monday Major-General George Thesiger fell in an heroic attempt to hold Fosse 8. The commander of the 9th Division was one of the ablest soldiers whom the Rifle Brigade, that nursery of military talent, had given to the Army. On 2nd October fell Major-General F. D. Wing, commanding the 12th Division. Up to that date twenty-eight battalion commanders had died in the battle. An attack tells heavily upon officers, but in no earlier action of the campaign was the death-rate among senior officers so high. With the appearance of the new divisions in action our losses began to take on a new character. They affected all classes in the nation, and brought mourning to many households who in the past had little dreamed that any son of theirs would find a soldier's death. Men of distinction, too, in civilian life, scholars, politicians, captains of industry, were among the slain. It was the first battle which taught our people that the union of classes and temperaments in a common effort is a partnership not only in service but in sacrifice.

* " Take any army of the nineteenth century, famous for the excellence of its grand tactics—viz. Napoleon's army of 1805-6-7; Wellington's army of 1813-14; Lee's army of 1864-1865; Grant's, Sherman's, and Johnston's armies of the same period; Moltke's army of 1870: the Staff of each one of them had been welded by years of experience and by the teaching of a great soldier into a magnificent instrument of war. They were not composed only of administrative officers, concerned with supply, organization, quartering, and discipline, but of tacticians and strategists of no mean order Combinations in war too often ' gang agley ' from the neglect of some trifling precaution, some vagueness or omission in orders; and in the excitement of battle, and of approaching battle, when arrangements have to be made, possibly on the spur of the moment, for the co-operation of large bodies, unless he has been so trained that the measures necessary to ensure simultaneous and harmonious action occur to him instinctively, it is an exceedingly easy matter, even for an able and experienced soldier, to make the most deplorable mistakes."—Colonel G. F. R. Henderson: *The Science of War*, p. 69.

CHAPTER XXXIX.

THE BALKAN LABYRINTH

The various Balkan States—Geography and History of the Peninsula—The Treaty of Berlin—The Balkan League—The First and Second Balkan Wars—Bulgaria's Discontent—King Ferdinand—Greece and Venizelos—Failure of Allied Diplomacy.

AT this stage of our chronicle it is necessary to attempt a sketch of the main features of that Balkan problem which for nearly a century had perplexed the statesmen of Europe. It was the land of surprises, where nationalities had no recognized boundaries. It lacked the contours of modern civilization, that which elsewhere was moulded to use being there left sharp and ragged. On the outbreak of the Great War the peninsula was at first dismissed as negligible, and its recent struggles regarded as no more than the quarrels of kites and crows. But as the tide of the campaign moved eastwards, as the guns sounded in the Ægean and Russia fell back from Poland, men woke with a start to the importance which those barren hills might acquire in the later stages of the contest. That importance Germany had not forgotten while the Allies slumbered. To understand it we must consider the determining factors in the labyrinthine Balkan politics.

The immediate strategic significance of the peninsula was obvious. Serbia, Bulgaria, and Rumania stood between the Teutonic League and its Turkish ally. While the two latter remained neutral Germany could not easily munition or reinforce the armies holding the gate of Constantinople. Should either or both take up arms against her, there was a possibility of an attack on the exposed Teutonic right flank or an addition to the fighting strength of the Allies in Gallipoli which might overbear Turkish resistance. The Balkan races were for the most part military peoples—those hard-bitten upland dwellers who, from the beginning of time, have made good soldiers. Accustomed to hardships, they could fight with a slender commissariat, and they had the bravery of those not accustomed to overvalue human life. If united, they could put into the field an army equivalent to that of a first-class Power, and, even without Serbia, their fighting strength stood at a million bayonets. Again, the Balkans were a fine field for diplomatic activity, for they represented the incalculable. Each state was still in a fluid condition. Each looked to extend its borders, for each owned many "nationals" outside its territorial limits. The Serb race was widely spread over Bosnia and Herzegovina and Austria-Hungary; there were Bulgarians in Rumania, and the partition of Macedonia by the Treaty of Bucharest did not correspond to nationalities. Each state had, therefore, its Alsace-Lorraine to which it turned jealous eyes. Moreover, while each state had nominally a constitutional government and believed itself a democracy, each, owing to the comparatively recent date of its emancipation from Turkish bondage, was liable to the rule of a camarilla, an army, or a dynasty. Excepting Serbia and Montenegro, all had alien royal houses. Rumania had a Catholic Hohenzollern on the throne, Bulgaria a Coburg, Greece a prince of the house of Schleswig-Holstein. History has shown that such conditions offer a unique chance for tortuous diplomacy.

To understand the Balkan situation a short survey is necessary of the topography and the history of the peninsula. It is a knot of mountains, with no great valleys and no natural geographical centre round which settled and civilized conditions of life could gather. Its peoples owed their nationalities primarily to race and historical accidents, rather than to geographical compulsion such as destined Britain and Italy to be nations. They were for long refugees in the uplands, and as mountain dwellers they continued to look down upon the plains of Thrace and Hungary. But the country was not a barrier but a thoroughfare, for through it lay the road from central Europe to the Ægean and Constantinople. It was the nature of these alleys of traffic which determined the development of the Balkan states so soon as their independence was secured.

The old Roman roads are the best guide to the natural possibilities of movement. The greatest, the Via Egnatia, ran from Durazzo on the Adriatic by Monastir and Salonika to Constantinople. Another ran from Belgrade by Nish and Sofia to the Bosphorus; a third from Skutari to Nish, and on to the Danube; a fourth from Monastir to the Danube by way of Sofia; a fifth from

Salonika by Uskub and Novi Bazar to Serajevo. Looked at geographically, there are two great gaps in this mountain system. One lies between the main Balkan and the Rhodope ranges, to-day the route of the trunk railway from the West to Constantinople. The second is the gap of Macedonia, a much-encumbered gap, but nevertheless a true alley between the Rhodope and the western mountains, through which by way of the Vardar, Ibar, and the western Morava valleys a way could be found to the Save and the upper Danube. Of this alley Kavala was now the eastern gate, as Philippi had been in ancient days. It is this alley-country, Macedonia, which has been littered with fragments of all the Balkan races, and which throughout history has been the storm-centre of the Balkans. " In this narrow belt, bounded westwards by the cruel karst hills, eastwards by the wooded, pasture-bearing central uplands, open widely at both ends, all but blocked at the sides—within this belt is concentrated most of the drama and most of the tragedy of the peninsula. Whether we think of the wistful Serb, with memories of past glories; the Bulgar, looking down from his upland boundary to his compatriots in the storm-swept plains below; the Greek, with his trader's instinct, pushing inland from the seaports of the coast; the Albanian, sweeping down from his mountains in brigand's raid, or creeping onward in peaceful agricultural penetration; or, again, of Teuton and Hungarian in the north; of Italian, watching the gaps of the coastal mountains; of the cynical Turk, still finding peasants to work for him in the midst of the pervading tumult—with whatever party our interests and our sympathies lie, we have to remember that here, in this alley-way, which we, quite inappropriately, still call Macedonia, in this gap between western mountains and central land mass, lies the key to the history of the whole peninsula." *

Such a geographical position had decisive effects on the ambitions of the several states. Greece, with a population of seafarers and coast-dwellers, stood outside the main problem; her natural extension was towards the islands of the Ægean and the coast of Asia Minor. Bulgaria, stretching out to the sea, looked naturally southwards. Her two main rivers, the Maritza and the Struma, flowed to the Ægean, and national expansion tends to follow the river valleys. Her small Black Sea coast-line was insufficient; the Marmora was blocked by Turkey; and at their best, Black Sea and Marmora were not open to the world like the Ægean. Serbia, too, looked southwards. She was landlocked, and had no

* Marion E. Newbigin : *Geographical Aspects of Balkan Problems*, p. 9.

outlet for her commerce save through the lands of strictly protectionist neighbours. Her natural road was to Salonika, but if this failed she had an alternative. A route to the Adriatic was possible, which should debouch, like the Via Egnatia, at Durazzo, on the flats of coastal Albania. Such an outlet, while more difficult than that to the Ægean, offered greater advantages, for it brought the markets of southern and western Europe within easier reach.

Macedonia therefore, both its coast and its hinterland, was certain sooner or later to become an acute problem for Serbia and Bulgaria, and in a lesser degree for Greece, and this purely on geographical grounds. It represented for the upland principalities the simplest path to the sea. If Serbia sought the Ægean she must have south-east Macedonia; if the Adriatic, she must control the northern districts. For Bulgaria to reach the Ægean meant the possession of eastern Macedonia, since the inhospitable Thracian coast offered no good harbours. Moreover, to both Serb and Bulgar Macedonia was *irredenta* in the full meaning of the Italian term. There, under foreign rule, dwelt many thousands of the compatriots and co-religionists of both. An alleyway full of unemancipated kinsmen, which to both states was the pivot upon which their racial ambitions moved, meant, so soon as they attained national stability, a contest first with Turkey and then, in all likelihood, with each other. The configuration of the earth's surface has been the ultimate cause of most of the quarrels of mankind.

If Balkan geography determined the general character of the problems, Balkan history had decided the special form in which they were presented to the modern world. "History," in M. Sorel's famous phrase, "never stops short." The fruits of forgotten deeds remain as a living legacy for the future. Under the Roman Empire the peninsula had become latinized and settled, and great trunk roads led from the Illyrian coast to the trans-Danube territories and the shores of the Bosphorus. But in the fourth and fifth centuries after Christ the Slavs swept down from the north, and absorbed the ancient Greek, Thracian, and Illyrian races, or drove them into the hills or the islands of the Ægean At the close of the seventh century the Bulgars appeared, a Turanian race akin to the Finns, whose home was the country between the Urals and the Volga. Then followed fleeting Bulgarian empires, when the horse-tail standards reached the gates of Byzantium. In the fourteenth century the Serbs rose to power, and for a short time dominated the peninsula. Next came the Turks. The Bulgarians fell before the conquerors in 1366, and in 1389 the Serbians were vanquished at Kossovo—that fatal "Field of Blackbirds," in memory of which a black patch was worn till the other day in the caps of the Montenegrins. Constantinople was taken in 1453, and with the defeat of the Albanians under Skanderbeg in 1466 the peninsula was in Ottoman hands.

For three hundred and fifty years this dominion was unshaken. The armies of the Crescent used the Balkans as the thoroughfare along which they marched to their campaigns on the plains of Hungary. The conquered peoples lived in their little villages in the hills, and had no traffic with the conqueror. The Turk did not try to assimilate his subject races; he was too proud and too indolent to proselytize on a serious scale, and he left them their language, religion, and customs with an easy toleration. Accordingly, when his rule grew feeble, there was a nucleus of nationality left to reassert itself. Greece, with the aid of France, Russia, and Britain, became independent in 1829. Serbia, under the first Karageorge, raised the standard of revolt in 1804, and by 1820 had won a spectral autonomy as a tributary state. The Danubian principalities of Moldavia and Wallachia had long had an uneasy separate life, and by 1859 they had become united under the name of Rumania. Bulgaria alone remained in complete subjection till 1876, when a rising broke out which was put down by Turkey with the barbarities which Western Europe came to know as the "Bulgarian atrocities." This event, and the previous declaration of war against Turkey by Serbia, led to Russia's participation in the struggle, and the outbreak of the Russo-Turkish War in April 1877.

In that war the Bulgarian contingent fought gallantly with Gourko in the Balkans, and the Rumanians, under Prince Charles, contributed much to the success of the Russian arms. On March 3, 1878, when Russia was approaching Constantinople, the Treaty of San Stefano was signed, under which Rumania was to surrender to Russia her portion of Bessarabia, and receive in return the Dobrudja territory, south of the mouth of the Danube. Bulgaria was constituted an autonomous state, with boundaries which fulfilled her wildest dreams, and which included every detached fragment of the Bulgarian race and something more. Her borders ran from the Black Sea to the Albanian hills, and from the Danube to the Ægean, and included the port of Kavala on the Ægean and most of Macedonia. This arrangement was not allowed to stand, since the Powers of Europe suspected that the new state might become a Russian dependency. By the Treaty of Berlin, signed on 13th July of that year, Bulgaria was given only the land between the Balkan range and the Danube, and the country south of the Balkans was created into the autonomous province of Eastern Rumelia. Serbia was given Nish, and Greece Thessaly; Bessarabia went to Russia; Rumania retained the Dobrudja; and Bosnia and Herzegovina were put under Austrian administration. Turkey was left with Macedonia, Albania, and Thrace on the continent of Europe, though she remained the suzerain of Bulgaria, Eastern Rumelia, Bosnia, and Herzegovina.

The modern history of the Balkans dates from the Treaty of Berlin. It is not an edifying record, being concerned chiefly with the quarrels of the separate states, and their indecision as to which of the Great Powers might most profitably be cultivated. The chief international importance is to be found in the record of Bulgaria. In 1879 the Assembly of the young state elected as sovereign Prince Alexander of Battenberg, who identified himself completely with Bulgarian national aspirations. In defiance of the Powers, he brought about a union with Eastern Rumelia in 1885. This led to a quarrel with Russia, and the withdrawal of all Russian officers from the Bulgarian army. Serbia chose the moment to declare war, but was decisively defeated by Prince Alexander at Slivnitza on 19th November. Russia attempted to abduct the Prince; but a counter-revolution, organized by Stambolov, the President of the Assembly, restored him. Unfortunately he now made a false move by offering to resign his crown into Russian hands, and was compelled to abdicate and leave the country on September 8, 1886. In 1887 Prince Ferdinand of Saxe-Coburg-Gotha was elected to the vacant throne; and the history of the following twenty years was made up of the rivalries of the Russian party and the anti-Russians, who adhered to the policy of Stambolov and attempted to reach an understanding with Turkey. War with the Porte was brought very near at times by Turkish barbarities among the Bulgarian population of Macedonia—barbarities which no doubt occurred, but which were at least equalled by the doings of the *komitadjis*. In 1908 the Austrian annexation of Bosnia and Herzegovina inspired Prince Ferdinand to declare Bulgaria an independent kingdom. The matter was settled by the payment of an indemnity, for which Russia advanced the funds.

This brings us to the eve of the Balkan Wars, and we may summarize the situation thus. Bulgaria owed gratitude to Russia

for her action in 1877 and 1908, and as the consistent protector of Slav nationalities; but the Stambolovists had a grudge against her for her treatment of Prince Alexander, and were inclined to look rather to Austria as a patron. Serbia had a general reliance on Russia, and had many scores to settle with Austria, partly on account of her treatment of the Southern Slavs under her sway, partly because of the Bosnian annexation, and partly because of old tariff wars as to the passage of Serbian live-stock beyond the borders. Rumania had a grudge against Russia because of Bessarabia, and a grudge against Austria because of the Rumanian districts of Transylvania. Greece had little love for Russia because of the Russian hankerings for Constantinople. All four Powers, too, were deeply suspicious of the Austro-German *Drang nach Osten*, the covetous eye cast on the shores of the Ægean and the road thither, which might put an end to their national existence. Bulgaria was suspected by Greece because of the old ecclesiastical quarrel between the Patriarchate and the Exarchate, and the strife of the rival *komitadjis* in Macedonia—a suspicion which she returned with interest. Bulgaria, too, looked askance on Serbia because of the unprovoked war of 1885, and on Rumania because of the Dobrudja and its Bulgarian population. The only bond which could unite these jealous little nations was a common grievance against Turkey; for in Macedonia, under the rule of the Porte, Serbs, Bulgars, Greeks, and Vlachs suffered indiscriminately.

An alliance between such disparate peoples might well have seemed impossible, even under the spur of the Macedonian grievance. A Balkan League had been tried in the past, and had failed. The Serbian Ristitch, fifty years ago, had advocated the scheme; there were discussions on the subject after the Russo-Turkish War, and King Charles of Rumania and Prince Alexander of Bulgaria approved it; in 1891 the Greek statesman Tricoupis attempted to form an alliance, but was met by the opposition of Bulgaria under Stambolov. Six years later Bulgaria herself revived the proposal. To the most sanguine idealist the stubborn particularism and the secular antagonisms of the states might well have seemed an insuperable bar. The one common ground —hatred of Turkey—might unite them for a little, but presently interests would diverge, and alliance give place to conflict.

This, as it happened, was the course of events. In the spring of 1912 a league was formed for the purpose of driving Turkey out of Europe. Its moving spirit was M. Venizelos, and he was assisted by M. Gueshov, the Bulgarian Premier, by the Serbian M. Pasitch, and not least by the *Times* correspondent in the Balkans, Mr. J. D. Bourchier. It was agreed that any territory conquered should be held in trust until the allies arranged for its partition. But a special treaty was made in February between Serbia and Bulgaria, under which it was arranged that northwest Macedonia—that is, Novi Bazar and the Prizrend and Prishtina districts—should go to Serbia unreservedly; that in the same way Bulgaria should have the south and south-eastern parts, notably Monastir and Ochrida, and that the zone between, comprising the Uskub territory, should be submitted to the arbitration of Russia.

The story of the First Balkan War need not be recounted here. The Bulgarian armies marched into Thrace, defeated the Turks decisively at Lule Burgas, invested Adrianople, and were only checked by the Chatalja lines. Greece drove the enemy northwards beyond Salonika, and Serbia cleared northern Macedonia and won the brilliant victory of Kumanovo. There was an armistice in December 1912, and an abortive conference held thereafter in London. Hostilities were resumed: Adrianople at last fell on March 26, 1913, to the Bulgarians, and on 5th March Jannina had surrendered to the Greeks. Meantime, in the previous December, Serbia had reached the Adriatic at Durazzo, and in April the Montenegrins took Skutari.

It was now that the real trouble began. The Triple Alliance categorically refused to allow Serbia and Montenegro a share of the Adriatic coast. This was the natural outlet on the sea for Serbia, the direction in which her ambitions had always tended. But since the road was closed to her there, she declared that she must find compensation elsewhere, and that her arrangement with Bulgaria, which had been founded on the assumption of an Adriatic port, no longer held good. Bulgaria stuck to the letter of the treaty, which had not mentioned the Adriatic. Serbia was willing to meet Bulgaria and to accept arbitration, provided that the whole allocation of territory was arbitrated on, and not merely the Uskub districts as formerly arranged. The Treaty of London, signed on 30th May, deprived Turkey of all her European possessions north and west of the Enos–Midia line. But the allocation of the conquered land among the victors was postponed by the outbreak of a new war. For a moment there seemed a chance of peace when Russia invited Serbia and Bulgaria to Petrograd. Serbia accepted, but Bulgaria insisted on laying down conditions about the limits of arbitration. Her intransigence was generally attributed to the influence of King Ferdinand ; it was certainly not approved by her civilian ministers or by the people at large.

The Second Balkan War broke out in the beginning of July 1913. The Greeks and Serbians had occupied land on the frontiers of the territory which Bulgaria held, and the latter state took the initiative in hostilities. In a week Bulgaria found herself attacked on four sides. The Turks, disregarding the Treaty of London, retook Adrianople and advanced to the old Bulgarian frontier. Greece and Serbia pressed in from south and west. Rumania, hastening to fish in troubled waters, annexed a further slice of the Dobrudja, which included Silistria and a population of a quarter of a million Bulgarians, and without striking a blow marched her armies to within fifteen miles of Sofia.

Bulgaria had no alternative but unconditional surrender. On 10th August the Treaty of Bucharest was signed by the Balkan States, and a separate treaty was signed later at Constantinople between Bulgaria and Turkey. As a result of two sanguinary wars, and losses of at least 100,000, Bulgaria gained only a strip of Thrace, a fraction of Macedonia, and the open roadstead of Dedeagatch. The place was useless to her, for Turkey, by regaining Adrianople, controlled the only railway from Bulgaria to the Ægean. Moreover, she lost to Rumania a slice of her north-eastern territory. Serbia gained all central and northern Macedonia, including Uskub, Ochrida, and Monastir, and Greece received most of the rest. The Greek gains included not only Salonika, which was a legitimate object of Greek ambition, but the port of Kavala, which was Bulgaria's natural outlet. The Balkan League had ended by producing a hostility the more deeply felt because it could not be expressed in deeds : a hostility compared to which the old quarrels had been friendship itself. In Sir Edward Grey's words, "The war began as a war of liberation. It became rapidly a war of conquest. It ended in being a war of extermination." The beaten intriguers at Constantinople, Berlin, and Vienna had builded better than they knew.

Such was the situation a year before the outbreak of the European contest. Let us take the different states in turn. Greece alone was satisfied, for she had won most with least effort, and in her winnings had gained something more than her economic needs warranted. Her true line of expansion was, as a maritime people, towards the islands and the Anatolian coast. Even if we grant that the great port of Salonika was justly hers, the addition of Kavala was beyond her due. But towards Bulgaria she felt a jealousy and bitterness which made her unwilling to surrender an acre. Ecclesiastical quarrels in the past; the brigandage in which the scum of both countries had indulged for years in Macedonia; and above all, the fear lest Bulgaria, with her industrious population, might beat the Greeks in the race for numbers and wealth, shut her eyes to the desirability for Balkan development of a peace founded upon a just allocation of territory Rumania stood somewhat aloof. She had got what she wanted, and did not intend to give it back; but she suspected Bulgaria, as a man suspects another whom he has not treated quite fairly.

Serbia had gained some of her desires, but had missed the vital one—an outlet to the sea—though she had certain running powers on the Salonika railway, and had been granted a shadowy permission to construct a line through Albania. In the scramble after the Balkan War she had on the whole behaved with the most dignity. In her argument with Bulgaria on the question of the secret treaty she was probably in the right; for her main object had always been to secure free exports, and the prohibition by the Powers of access to Durazzo meant, if she surrendered central Macedonia to Bulgaria while Greece held the north Ægean coast, that two protectionist states would intervene between her and the sea. It was clearly a case for the revision of any agreement, since the conditions had so materially altered. But the fact remained that she had not won her salt-water outlet, and she had acquired in her new Macedonian territory districts largely peopled by Bulgars, whom not even the familiar Balkan methods of proselytizing were likely to turn into good Serbians. The little state was under the guidance of a sane and politic statesman, M. Pasitch. She was a true democracy, full of valour, confidence, and no small military experience, having within a century fought Turkey four times and Bulgaria twice, and including among her citizens men who had seen five campaigns. After many dynastic troubles she had, in the grandson of Black George the Swineherd, a popular monarch. Her people, the Latins of the Balkans, fond of song and story, and thrilling to heroic traditions, were beginning to envisage with some sobriety the kind of future which was their due. Her wisest brains were thinking less of the East than of the West and South-west, of that Adriatic port which must some day be theirs, and of the championship of the Southern Slavs—Serbs, Montenegrins, Bosnians, Herzegovinans, Dalmatians,

Croats, Slavonians, and Slovenes—most of them now the uneasy subjects of the Dual Monarchy. Serbia in 1914 stood to the Southern Slavs as Piedmont in the Italian Risorgimento stood to Italy.

Bulgaria was left sullen and dissatisfied, with her pride deeply hurt and the glory won at Lule Burgas sadly tarnished. She had staked all on a throw of the dice, and had lost. She had taken the first step in hostilities against her former allies, and in the summer campaign of 1913 had violated many of the decencies of war. But she considered, with some justice, that her punishment was disproportionate to her offence. The war for which she had sacrificed so much had left her in an impossible position. She possessed no part of that district of Macedonia which was inhabited chiefly by Bulgars. The great route by the Struma valley which debouches at Kavala was in the hands of Greece, who already had ports enough and to spare. The route to the Ægean by the Maritza valley was cut by the Turkish reoccupation of Adrianople. Finally, in the north-east she had suffered the sorest grievance of all. The Treaty of Berlin had left Bulgaria the south-west corner of the Dobrudja plateau, including the town of Silistria on the Danube. Rumania at the time had protested against this, since the railway from Bucharest to the chief Rumanian port of Constanza crossed the river by the only bridge between Belgrade and the sea, at a point only twenty-two miles from the Bulgarian border. She had been told in reply that Bulgaria was not a military state, and constituted no danger; but after the Bulgarian exploits in the Balkan War she demanded some rectification of this frontier, and carried her point. The result was that Bulgaria not only lost a piece of territory essentially Bulgarian in character, but, instead of gaining new outlets on the coast, lost two Black Sea ports, Kavarna and Baltchik, which she had held for thirty years. The Bulgarian people are the least emotional of Balkan races. They have been called the Scots of the peninsula, and, like the men of North Britain, are shrewd, cautious, and industrious. The losses of 1913 were precisely of the kind which they would feel most deeply. No talk of Slav brotherhood could blind them to the fact that they had lost very definite practical advantages to which they had long looked forward, and which they believed they were entitled to claim. This prosaic and tangible grievance, rankling in the minds of such a race, was more explosive material than any whimsies about wounded honour.

By the summer of 1914 it was pretty clearly recognized by the wisest heads in the Balkans and by the statesmen of the Triple Entente that the Treaty of Bucharest had been a blunder, and could not last. No state—except Greece, who had gained most —really accepted it as final. The aim of Germany and Austria, as of Turkey before them, was to keep the Balkans in a state of ferment and disunion. It was Austria that inspired the ill-omened Second Balkan War. Cut-throat warfare among the little nations was the best prelude to that movement to the Bosphorus of which Berlin and Vienna dreamed, and which would put a speedy ending to the chaos of nationalities. The Triple Entente, on the other hand, could secure its interests only by the peace and unity of the several states, and to win this end there must be a redivision of territory.

It was easy to suggest schemes for a fairer division, but it was difficult to see where the motive power was to come from to force their acceptance. Observers in the West were accustomed to fix on some particular state and idealize it—Greece because of the tradition of Hellas, Bulgaria because of its sufferings, Serbia because of its warlike prowess. Few westerners who dabbled in those uneasy politics seemed able to avoid a truculent partisanship and a complete loss of perspective; and the " Balkanate " Englishman became as conspicuous a feature of the early twentieth century as the Italianate Englishman had been of the sixteenth. But the world was apt to forget that these were peasant states, nations of small cultivators but lately emancipated; that in such states there is apt to be much of the cunning and parochialism of the peasant; and that to ask them for broad views on world politics, more especially when such views demanded some sacrifice of present advantage, was like seeking grapes from thistles. Some strong persuasive influence from without was necessary before union could grow out of such sturdy differences.

Into this confusion of struggling interests fell the thunderbolt of the Great War.

Serbia's part alone was beyond doubt. The fates had placed her, like Uriah the Hittite, in the forefront of the battle. Rumania was torn between rival affections. King Charles, to whom she owed much, was a Hohenzollern; German money had built up most of her industries; in Germany and Austria she found her chief markets; she had not forgotten Russia's snatching of Bessarabia. On the other hand, if she looked to the west, she saw three million citizens of her blood in Transylvania under the Magyar yoke. On the south lay Bulgaria, watchful and unappeased. Clearly, whatever her sympathies, Rumania could not enter the war unless a prior understanding with Bulgaria were arrived at. Greece had nothing to gain from the Teutonic Alliance, and much to lose; but she, too, was obliged to keep an eye on Bulgaria's movements. Bulgaria had a court and king whose Teutonic sympathies were pronounced; but her people and her most conspicuous statesmen, such as M. Gueshov, inclined to the Allies. Yet not unnaturally she was suspicious and hesitating. She must be sure of her "rights," whatever way she moved. The urgent need from the Allies' point of view was a new Balkan League which could promulgate a common policy for all the states, since each was so busily engaged watching her neighbour that she had no eyes for the clouds gathering in the West. Such a League would have been the more justified since, if the Central Empires won, the danger would not menace one state alone, but the very existence of Balkan nationality.

At this point two personalities enter the tale. Topography and history will not by themselves wholly account for a problem; the human element plays its part; and the quality of the actors determines the climax of the drama. The first was Eleutherios Venizelos, the Prime Minister of Greece. No one who first saw that modest figure and grave scholar's face could have guessed at the strange career or the dauntless will-power of the man. He had been the leader of the Cretan rebels, and had held his own in the mountains in a life where the hand keeps the head. Called suddenly to deal with the military revolution in Athens in 1910, he had quelled faction, won over the court, and reformed the constitution by sheer dominance of character and mind. He feared nothing —neither the bullets of his enemies nor the reproaches of his followers. A democrat in policy, he could, if necessary, defy the populace and control it. As he told M. Take Jonescu, "I have always spoken to my fellow-countrymen the truth and the whole truth, and I have always been quite prepared to lay down my power without regret." His broad, sane idealism worked soberly in a world of facts. He had founded the Balkan League; he had striven to prevent the second war, and to modify the vindictive Treaty of Bucharest. He saw what was implied in a Teutonic victory, and, like a true nationalist, wrought for the enduring good of his nation and not for a temporary gain. Before the war his policy had been that of the Triple Entente, and from the first day of hostilities he took his stand on the Allies' side.

Far different was the second figure, Ferdinand of Bulgaria. As a character in fiction, if truly drawn, he would have amused the world, but would have been condemned on the ground of his manifest improbability. From the day when, twenty-eight years before, he had been selected—*faute de mieux*—by Stambolov to fill the throne which Prince Alexander had vacated, his career had been half comic melodrama and half romance. His mother, Princess Clementine, the daughter of Louis Philippe, and, according to Gladstone, the cleverest woman in Europe, had kept him secure in his early days in that uneasy seat. His treatment of Stambolov revealed his coldness of heart, but his quick assumption of Bulgarian nationalism proved his accuracy of judgment. He was like a parody of a Bourbon king in his tastes and manners. His hobbies were many—farming, gardening, ornithology, clothes, jewels; and in his youth he had dabbled in the sciences, and had written a book on his travels in Brazil. His court was ridiculously ostentatious, so that the frugal Bulgarians stared and pondered. Physical courage had been denied him, and he would babble to all and sundry about his fears and disappointments. Surely the strangest monarch for a taciturn and martial people!

But there was a method behind all this vanity and affectation. Ferdinand had a shrewd eye for his own safety and well-being, and, since his fate was bound up with Bulgaria's, he deserved well of his land. He gave it prosperity and international importance. He interpreted the saying "*Après moi le déluge*" in a different sense from its author, and was resolved that if the deluge were to come it should follow him, for he would be leading it. Fears of assassination made him determine to be the figurehead of the national advance, whithersoever it tended. M. de Kallay, the Governor of Bosnia, who knew him well, was reported to have put his dominant characteristics in the form of a parable. "We are here on the first floor. If I tell you that assassins are waiting for you with loaded pistols at the door of my room, and advise you to jump from the window at the risk of breaking your neck, you will hesitate; but if you see a cart laden with straw passing under your window you will jump. So will Ferdinand, but not till he sees the cart coming." The Balkan League gave him the chance of fighting Turkey in comparative safety; but Austria proved an inadequate cart in the Second Balkan War, and he had a heavy fall. In the Great War he waited patiently for the straw till he believed he had found it. Vanity was his main trait, and for all his timidity he had the occasional boldness of the vain man.

He knew also how to work on the vanity of others, believing, like de Tocqueville, that "with the vanity of man you do most good business." He was an incomparable sentimentalist. To one visitor he would deplore his fate as the leader of an ungrateful nation, in constant danger because of his virtues. To another he would pose as the lover of peace in the midst of strife. "I am like a blind man," he would say, "running about with a lighted torch among haystacks. Whichever way I turn, I must set something on fire." Ambassadors of rival groups would be dismissed with dignified tears, and bidden to take an old man's blessing with them. Some ingenuous souls were deceived; the more wary underrated him, and set him down as a *farceur*, which was probably the exact impression which he desired to produce. A fool's cap has before this covered a very shrewd and persistent brain. About the shrewdness of Ferdinand there was no question, and it was to this quality that he owed his hold upon his people. A monarch of such a state must be either braver or more cunning than those over whom he rules. Ferdinand had no courage to speak of, but his cunning was immense, and very generally respected by his subjects. They had had their hero in Prince Alexander, and had not greatly profited thereby; now they were inclined to pin their faith to the *politique*.

The course of Balkan diplomacy since the war has already been touched upon in earlier chapters, but the main events may here be summarized. By the beginning of 1915 there was little doubt but that Rumania's sympathies were preponderantly on the Allied side, and statesmen such as M. Take Jonescu prophesied her speedy entrance into the war. In January M. Ghenadiev, the ex-Foreign Minister of Bulgaria, was at Rome, and it was generally believed that an agreement had been arrived at between Bulgaria and Rumania. The Rumanian army, half a million strong, and one of the best equipped in Europe, was in a state of preparedness. During the early spring negotiations went on with Russia to determine Rumania's reward for intervention. At that period, with Russia in the Carpathian passes, the chance of an effective strategic blow by Rumania was good, but suddenly there came a hitch in the arrangements. Petrograd hesitated on one point which Bucharest regarded as vital, and nothing was done during March and April. By the time that matters were arranged the situation had changed. Russia had suffered her *débâcle* on the Donajetz, and the easiest road for Rumanian participation was now blocked. The little state was in a difficult position, with the Teutonic League triumphant on her northern border, and Bulgaria, on the south, once more plunged in the mire of indecision. She could do nothing but keep her army in readiness and wait.

The attitude of Greece was from the start benevolent to the Allied interests. In the second month of the war M. Venizelos intimated to France and Britain that, should the necessity arise, they might count on the certain assistance of his country. In January 1915 he realized that that necessity might be near, and on the 11th of the month addressed to his king a letter which so admirably states the obligations of Greece arising both from honour and national interest that some sentences may be quoted :—

"Until to-day our policy simply consisted in the preservation of neutrality, in so far at least as our treaty obligations with Serbia did not oblige us to depart therefrom. But we are called upon to participate in the war, no longer in order to fulfil simply moral obligations, but in view of compensations, which if realized will create a great and powerful Greece, such as not even the boldest optimist could have imagined only a few years back.

"If we allow Serbia to be crushed to-day by another Austro-German invasion, we have no security whatever that the Austro-German armies will stop short in front of our Macedonian frontiers, and that they will not be tempted as a matter of course to come down as far as Salonika. But even if this danger is averted, and we admit that Austria, being satisfied with a crushing military defeat of Serbia, will not wish to establish herself in Macedonia, can we doubt that Bulgaria, at the invitation of Austria, will advance and occupy Serbian Macedonia ? And if that were to happen, what would be our position ? We should then be obliged to hasten to the aid of Serbia unless we wished to incur the dishonour of disregarding our treaty obligations. Even if we were to remain indifferent to our moral debasement and impassive, we should by so doing have to submit to the disturbance of the Balkan equilibrium in favour of Bulgaria, who, thus strengthened, would either now or some time hence be in a position to attack us, when we should be entirely without either a friend or an ally. If, on the other hand, we had then to help Serbia in order to fulfil the duty incumbent on us, we should do so in far more unfavourable circumstances than if we went to her assistance now, because Serbia would already be crushed, and in consequence our aid would be of no, or at best of little, avail. Moreover, by rejecting now the overtures of the Powers of the Triple Entente, we should, even in the event of victory, secure no tangible compensation for the support we should have lent."

He saw that a new Balkan League was necessary, and to secure Bulgaria's adherence he was prepared to agree to a drastic revision of the Treaty of Bucharest. We have already seen the consequences of the Greek Premier's policy. The Dardanelles scheme failed to attract the support of the Greek General Staff; and King Constantine, relying on this circumstance, and swayed by his German relationship, insisted upon neutrality, and brought about M. Venizelos's resignation. An appeal to the people restored him to power, and by the middle of August he was again in possession of the reins of government. But no step was taken, for Bulgaria was being wooed by the Allies with concessions wrung with difficulty from Greece and Serbia.

Bulgaria, so it seemed in the early part of the year, might be won for the Allies if her price were paid. Serbia was slow to relinquish any part of Macedonia, more especially after the December Battle of the Ridges had freed her for the moment from Austrian invasion. The Greek people—but not M. Venizelos—were also loth to surrender Kavala. The compensating gains to them, it should be remembered, such as a slice of Asia Minor, were only for the future, whereas Bulgaria insisted upon a bird in the hand. We have seen that in September 1914 Bulgaria had signed a secret treaty with Austria, pledging herself not to enter into any alliance against her, but this was unknown to the statesmen of the Entente. But some anxiety was caused by the payment, in February 1915, by a German bank of a second instalment of the loan concluded in Berlin the year before, and men asked if it was likely that the money had been transferred without some substantial guarantee. In March there were Cabinet difficulties, and the Premier, M. Radoslavov, found it necessary to reassure the world that Bulgarian policy was one of strict and loyal neutrality. The attempts to cut the Salonika line by Bulgarian bands looked ugly; but it was assumed that they were only raids of the lawless Bulgarian *komitadjis*, for whom, in Dr. Johnson's phrase, patriotism was the last refuge of the scoundrel. But in May came Mackensen's Galician advance, and from that date it is clear that the opinions of King Ferdinand and his camarilla hardened in favour of the Central Empires. The Russian retreat and the Allied stalemate in the Dardanelles convinced them that victory would lie with the Teutonic League. On 29th May the Allies made a definite proposal to Bulgaria, and throughout the summer Serbia and Greece were brought into line, the representations to M. Pasitch on 4th August by all the Allies being the last step in the negotiations. M. Radoslavov on 20th July, and again on 12th August, declared that Bulgaria was prepared to enter the war as soon as she received guarantees as to her very modest national requirements. Serbia retorted that, on the contrary, Bulgaria was making difficulties because she did not want to move. About the same time there were rumours of a coming German assault upon Serbia which would clear up the Balkan situation by compelling each neutral state to a decision.

Serbia was right. While M. Radoslavov was protesting his honest neutrality, and King Ferdinand was weeping on the necks of the Allied diplomatists, Bulgaria's decision had been taken. In July the final negotiations began with the Teutonic League, under the auspices of Prince von Hohenlohe-Langenburg; at the end of August a Bulgarian representative visited German Headquarters; and on 6th September a convention was signed at Pless by Conrad von Hoetzendorff and Falkenhayn Within thirty-five days Bulgaria, Germany, and Austria were to march together. The Teutonic League paid Bulgaria her price, and something more. In return for intervention on their side, she was to be given Serbian Macedonia and Serbia east of the Morava, and if Rumania or Greece attacked her or her allies she was to receive in addition all the territories ceded to these states under the Treaty of Bucharest This momentous act, which was to have a far-reaching influence on the war, was not the work of the whole Bulgarian people, probably not of the majority. It was concealed from M. Gueshov and the Opposition, and from many of the chiefs of the army. The peasants, who still held to Russia, as their fathers had done in 1877, were not consulted. If John Bright was right, and the nation in every country dwells in its cottages, the treaty had no national sanction

The Allied diplomacy had failed, more especially that of Britain, which had been entrusted with most of the work. We had begun by refusing to take the Balkans seriously, and ended by passing from apathy to hustle. Two policies might have been followed, each in itself reasonable. Balkan unity might have been secured in the first half-year of war by putting sufficient pressure upon both Serbia and Greece. Neither was in a position to withstand the resolute representations of the Allies. Or Bulgaria might have been isolated, and Greece, Serbia, and Rumania brought forthwith into active alliance. As it was, by urging concessions ineffectually, we did not satisfy Bulgaria, and we made difficulties for the leaders of the other states. That lack of a clear and considered policy which produced the Gallipoli landing was responsible no less for the treaty of 6th September. The Balkan States, like many of a more advanced civilization, could be won only by straight and resolute dealing, backed by an adequate force of arms.

CHAPTER XL.

BULGARIA ENTERS THE WAR.
September 19–October 15, 1915.

Bulgaria's Alliance with Germany—Mackensen's Army—The Intrigues at Sofia—The Position of Greece—The Allies send Troops to Salonika.

AFTER the victories of Plataea and Mycale, as may be read in the ninth book of Herodotus, an Athenian expedition sailed to the Dardanelles and laid siege to the town of Sestos, which was in Persian hands. The place was the strongest position in the peninsula, and during the hot summer months it resisted stoutly. Autumn came, and the Athenians began to murmur, but their leader Xanthippus declared that there could be no return till Athens recalled her army or Sestos fell. Then one morning the enemy disappeared. The garrison had been in desperate straits for supplies, the Persian Artayctes drew off his men by night, and the gates of Sestos were opened to the conquerors. Such was one result of the strife between Europe and Asia at the sea-gates of the Marmora. But if the story of Herodotus offered a good omen for the Gallipoli adventure of the Allies in 1915, there was another tale of an overseas expedition told by a greater historian which could not but recur to men's minds. Sixty-two years after Xanthippus took Sestos, Nicias the Athenian led a mighty expedition to the siege of Syracuse. It was largely inspired by Alcibiades, a brilliant but erratic politician. It was conducted by the chief naval Power of the day and the chief protagonist of democracy. Its ablest soldier, Lamachus, found his plans overridden by instructions from home. The Syracusans had formidable defences, but they must have fallen, had they not been aided by Sparta, then the chief Power by land and the exponent of oligarchical government. On the part of Athens it was an amphibious expedition, involving a landing of an expeditionary force in co-operation with a great fleet. At first various small victories were gained, but soon the besiegers became the besieged, and the campaign dragged aimlessly on till that tragic autumn when Nicias and Demosthenes laid down their arms and the flower of the youth of Athens perished in the quarries. This, wrote Thucydides, was the greatest disaster that ever befell a Greek army. "For being altogether vanquished at all points, and having suffered in great degree every affliction, they were destroyed, as the saying is, with utter destruction, both army and navy and everything; and only a few out of many returned home."

The Syracusan expedition was the death-blow of the Athenian Empire. It was easy to make of it a parable, putting modern names for those of Nicias and Alcibiades, Lamachus and Gylippus, Athens and Sparta, and find a score of striking parallels. Such historical apologues, whether they cheer or depress, are to be sparingly used, since the data they provide are too loose for a fruitful deduction. But by the end of September it was clear to observers in the West that our position in the Eastern Mediterranean, never strategically good, was about to be complicated by that very event which we had hoped to frustrate. The Turks, depleted in men, and with their stock of munitions running low, were soon to receive dangerous reinforcements. Gylippus had come to the aid of the Syracusans.

By 22nd September the evacuation of the Vilna salient was complete, and the great German effort to force a decision in that quarter had failed. Ivanov's counter-offensive in the south had already developed, and the army of Pflanzer-Baltin was being pushed back from the Sereth. It was Germany's supreme merit that when she was foiled in one direction she struck quickly in another. The Great General Staff had always a number of alternate plans prepared in every detail, and when one miscarried another was taken from its pigeon-hole. Many reasons now combined to make a campaign in south-eastern Europe desirable. Turkey was hard pressed for munitions, and could not use her man-power to the full unless she received equipment from her allies. More, there was a risk that, unless she received substantial help without delay, the elements in Ottoman life which had no heart for the war and detested the German dominance might assert themselves against Enver and his camarilla. Again, the conquest of the road to Constantinople would release for Germany supplies of food, cotton, and metals, and, conceivably, of men. Bulgaria was already committed to the Teutonic League, and Bulgaria could put at least 300,000 trained soldiers in the field. The local situation was promising. Twelve British divisions were held up in the Gallipoli peninsula, where they could neither advance nor easily retreat. The Serbian army was depleted in numbers, and had no store of supplies to see them through a fresh campaign. With Bulgaria friendly, only a little effort would free the Danube route to Constantinople, and a further thrust would give Germany the Ottoman railway. With that in her hands, firmly guarded by the southern wall of mountains against attacks from the Ægean, Germany, if need be, could rest content for the winter. The difficulties of Greece and Rumania, great at the best of times, would be many times multiplied by the situation thus created. Whatever their sympathies or their fears, with the Central Powers driving a solid wedge towards the Bosphorus, with the Serbians pushed into the inhospitable Albanian hills, with the Western Allies held fast in Gallipoli, and with Russia unable to do more than maintain her long front from the Dniester to the Gulf of Riga, there would be small temptation for either to leave the path of neutrality.

But behind the Balkan expedition there was a shrewder purpose than the mere defence and comfort of a flank. The German plan which sought a speedy decision had long ago gone to pieces. She was compelled to keep her main armies on the Western and Eastern fronts, and on both she was already much inferior in numbers of equipped men. A decision in the true sense could only be got on these main fronts, and if the Allies concentrated their efforts there it was not likely that the result could be long delayed. Her aim was, therefore, to draw off her enemy's strength to a remote and irrelevant terrain. She knew our passion for divergent operations. Fears for India and Egypt would, she argued, cause us to forget the essentials of strategy. Already we had given hostages to fortune by locking up our troops in Gallipoli. With a little trouble she might induce us to divert to the Balkans many of the new divisions which were destined for France and Flanders, and even to strip our Western front of troops already there. She observed with approval that British statesmen talked rhetorically of the Near East, as the nerve centre of the War, and she was ready to indulge the curious fancy.*

The adventure was entrusted to Mackensen, the most successful soldier of the summer. Reports began to arrive in the West, chiefly from Bucharest, as early as the middle of August, that some

* See Ludendorff: *War Memories* (Eng. trans.) I., pp. 173-4.

kind of concentration was going on north of the Danube. Goods traffic between Rumania and Austro-Hungary was suspended. Units began to disappear from the Russian front, to the confusion of Russian staff officers, who could not fathom the reason for corps going suddenly into reserve. The Army of the Balkans was being formed, and before the end of August six divisions had gone southward. The fierce battles of early September for a little held up further reinforcements, but by the middle of the month a mass of troops was assembling north of the Danube and the Save. They included a new XI. German army of seven divisions under Gallwitz, who was succeeded by von Fabeck in command of the XII. army; and the III. Austro-Hungarian army under von Kövess, of four divisions, reinforced by a German corps of three divisions. Western Serbia was neglected, because the troops in Bosnia, weakened by drafts for the Isonzo front, were not equal to an offensive, though an Austrian detachment watched the banks of the Drina. The main forces were disposed opposite Belgrade, and along the Danube towards the Bulgarian frontier. On the 19th of September, about two in the afternoon, the first enemy batteries opened against the Serbian capital.

Before entering upon the details of the campaign, it is necessary to consider the events which brought in Bulgaria on the Teutonic side. We were not aware at the time of the secret negotiations which began in July, but by the end of August there was ample ground for suspicion. Peripatetic German agents—Prince Hohenlohe-Langenburg in July, Duke John of Mecklenburg and Dr. von Rosenburg in August—were being welcomed at Sofia. In September Liman von Sanders paid a visit from Constantinople. But for some reason the Allied Governments were loth to trust the evidence of their experts. They had talked themselves into believing that Bulgarian interests must be hostile to the Powers which meditated a *Drang nach Osten*, and on the face of it there were specious reasons for this belief. They received all rumours, therefore, with incredulity, and, in spite of Serbia's warnings, continued to cultivate the goodwill of Sofia, and believe the protestations of King Ferdinand.

The Bulgarian military system had for its working unit a strong division of sixteen battalions, or about 24,000 men. There were nominally fifteen divisions, ten of the first line and five of the second; but two new divisions of volunteers had been raised from the districts acquired in Macedonia and Thrace, bringing the field army up to about 300,000 rifles. Bulgaria was weak in reserves, for behind this force she had only a Territorial reserve of some 20,000, and the recruits of the 1916 class—all told, about 60,000 men. She could thus mobilize approximately 360,000 men, much the same strength as she had raised for the war of 1912-13. Her infantry—the first line at all events—was of excellent quality, and she possessed a General Staff of the most approved German pattern. Her weakness lay in her artillery. To each of her fifteen divisions nine batteries of field guns and one of 4.7-inch howitzers were attached, too small a complement for modern war. There was reason to believe that not all her field-batteries were of the quick-firing type, and in any case they were of two separate patterns—Creusot "75's," and the Krupp "77's," which she had captured from the Turks in the Thracian campaign. This lack of uniformity of type was conspicuous also in her heavy pieces. The Bulgarian army was therefore a force which might be to some extent handicapped if engaged in open country with a well-equipped enemy, but which, owing to its veteran character, was well fitted for warfare in a blind and pathless mountain region.

This is not the place to tell the full tale of the intrigues of Sofia during the summer—the currents and cross-currents which pulled the ship of state hither and thither, and finally swept it towards the cataract. Only a few events stood out clear to the world in the mist of rumour which hung over the Balkans during September. Some time between the 14th and 20th of the month it was known that a treaty had been signed between Bulgaria and Turkey. It purported to be no more than the settlement of the Dedeagatch railway question, of which we had heard in July, when the German intentions towards Serbia were already patent. Bulgaria's secret was well kept, but on 21st September, M. Venizelos, the Greek Premier, who believed that his country, owing to the terms of her alliance with Serbia, must enter the fray, asked France and Britain for 150,000 troops. Two days later the Bulgarian mobilization began. On the 24th the Western Allies acceded to M. Venizelos's request, and that same day Greece began to mobilize, the order having been signed by the King at four o'clock the afternoon before. On the 25th Bulgaria, following the precedent of Turkey in the previous November, issued an explanation of her mobilization. She declared she had no aggressive intentions, and mobilized, like Holland and Switzerland, only to defend her rights and independence. Her position, she said, was that of armed neutrality. That same evening came the news that Bulgarian cavalry were massing on the Serbian borders. Rumania, much agitated by the new situation, announced that as yet she would take no decisive step. Her army was already mobilized, and her troops remained concentrated on her frontiers. The Greek mobilization was calculated to produce a strength little less than Bulgaria's. In 1912 the Greek army had consisted of four weak divisions; in 1913 it had risen to ten divisions; and after peace it remained at eleven divisions. The new war strength was six corps, each of three divisions, giving a total of about 240,000 men, with half that number in reserve. Each division—numbering about 12,500 rifles—had eight field or mountain batteries, and in many cases a heavy battery as well, giving an average of three pieces per thousand as compared with the Bulgarian two per thousand. The whole of the Greek artillery was composed of modern quick-firing Creusot guns.

Meanwhile there were protests from within Bulgaria against the obvious trend of her action. A deputation of ex-Ministers—M. Gueshov, M. Danev, M. Zanov, the leader of the Radical Democrats, M. Malinov, the chief of the Democratic party, and M. Stambuliski, the leader of the Agrarians—sought an interview with the King. King Ferdinand, it may be believed, heard some plain speaking that day. M. Malinov demanded the immediate convocation of Parliament, since the country at large was opposed to any adventure in Germany's company. He warned his sovereign that the enterprise would be more disastrous for Bulgaria than the Second Balkan War. The Agrarian leader, a peasant by origin, was frankness itself. "This policy," he said, "will lead to fresh disasters, and will ruin not only our country, but your dynasty, and may cost you your head." King Ferdinand endeavoured to turn the conversation on to autumn crops, and dismissed his mentors.

The skies were darkening over Serbia, but there were still gleams of light. Mackensen was not yet advancing, and neither Save nor Danube was crossed. It was believed that Greece would be true to her alliance, and that the Western Allies were sending adequate reinforcements. The main danger was Bulgaria, for a sudden attack on flank would gravely compromise the situation, and might cut off the Serbian army from its communications with Greece and the Allies on the seaboard. On 27th September, accordingly, Serbia informed the British Government that she considered it wise to attack Bulgaria before the mobilization there was complete. Beyond doubt it was the correct military policy, for the Bulgarian menace was the most deadly, and if Serbia fought on a front running north and south she would be in a favourable position to join hands with any reinforcements sent by her Allies. Except that a formal declaration of war was lacking, there could be no doubt about Bulgaria's intentions. If Serbia delayed, Bulgaria would strike the first blow. The Serbian mobilization was complete, the Austro-Germans were not yet across the rivers, and the true centre of gravity was the eastern front. In the event of failure she could retire upon Salonika, but if Bulgaria once got round her flank she would be driven into the difficult Albanian hinterland and cut off from her friends. But the British Government discouraged Serbia's plan, declaring that the diplomatic and political arguments were against it. Apparently at that late hour we still cherished the vain hope that Bulgaria might stay her hand. It was a fatal decision. It compromised Serbia's plan of campaign, and could only have been justified if the Western Allies were in the position to fight the campaign on their own account and protect Serbia with ample armies. But this assistance, as we shall see, the Allies were not in the position to afford in time. We crowned our diplomatic failure of the summer by a grave error in military judgment.

Next day, 28th September, the British Foreign Minister made an important statement in the House of Commons. As Sir Edward Grey's words led to much future controversy, they deserve to be quoted in full.

"My official information from the Bulgarian Government is that they have taken up a position of armed neutrality to defend their rights and independence, and that they have no aggressive intentions whatever against Bulgaria's neighbours. It would, perhaps, be well that I should, with the leave of the House, explain quite shortly our view of the Balkan situation. Not only is there no hostility in this country to Bulgaria, but there is traditionally a warm feeling of sympathy for the Bulgarian people. As long, therefore, as Bulgaria does not side with the enemies of Great Britain and her Allies there can be no question of British influence or forces being used in a sense hostile to Bulgarian interests; and, as long as the Bulgarian attitude is unaggressive, there should be no disturbance of friendly relations. If, on the other hand, the Bulgarian mobilization were to result in Bulgaria assuming an aggressive attitude on the side of our enemies, we are prepared to give to our friends in the Balkans all the support in our power in the manner that would be most welcome to them, in concert with our Allies, without reserve and without qualification."

This statement left something to be desired in fullness; but as expounded by Sir Edward Grey in a later debate on 2nd November it was sufficiently clear, and it cannot have been misunderstood by

Serbia. It was based on the promise, made along with France, to M. Venizelos to send 150,000 men to Salonika to enable Greece to fulfil her treaty obligations. The words " without reserve and without qualification " referred to the fact that so long as there had been a hope of Balkan unity the Allied Powers had urged upon Greece and Serbia certain territorial concessions to Bulgaria. But if Bulgaria joined the Teutonic League, then all question of concessions disappeared, and the help that the Allies would be prepared to give to Greece and Serbia would be granted without qualification or reserve.

On 25th September the Greek Parliament met. M. Venizelos explained that mobilization was a necessary precaution, and declared that in certain contingencies Greece was bound by treaty to assist Serbia, though he sincerely hoped that the *casus foederis* would not arise. A bill was introduced for a loan of six million sterling, and M. Gounaris, on behalf of the Opposition, tendered his support to the Government. On 1st October word came that many German officers were at Sofia in consultation with the Bulgarian Staff. This piece of news, which was no novelty, seems to have convinced the Allied Governments at last of Bulgaria's intentions. That evening the British Foreign Office issued a statement announcing the fact, recalling the precedent of Turkey the year before, and declaring that the situation must now be regarded as " of the utmost gravity." Next day, M. Venizelos formally protested against the projected Allied landing at Salonika. It was the kind of protest which diplomacy demands from territorial sovereigns, and was intended by the Greek Prime Minister to be regarded as an assertion of sovereignty for the purpose of record rather than as a warning or a threat. Russia now took up the tale. On the afternoon of 4th October the Russian Minister at Sofia, M. Savinski, handed to M. Radoslavov a note of grave warning against " fratricidal aggression against a Slav and allied people." To this Bulgaria replied at 2.40 p.m. the next day. The reply was unsatisfactory, and the Russian Minister notified M. Radoslavov that diplomatic relations were at an end, a step in which he was presently followed by his French and British colleagues.

From this day, 5th October, we may date Bulgaria's formal entrance into the war. She took some pains to justify her course in a long official pamphlet, of which she distributed copies broadcast throughout her towns and villages. It is a curious document. Russia, she declared, was fighting for Constantinople and the Dardanelles; France for Alsace-Lorraine; Britain to ruin Germany; Italy, Serbia, and Montenegro for plunder. The Teutonic Alliance, on the other hand, fought only to maintain the *status quo*, and to ensure peace and progress for the world. Neutrality in the early stages had been advisable. " Neutrality has enabled us to bring the military and material preparedness of our army to such a pitch as has never before been reached." The document then embarked on economics. Bulgaria's trade interests were inseparably bound up with Turkey, Germany, and Austria-Hungary. Germany had lent Bulgaria money after the Treaty of Bucharest, and would in future give her financial support. She would be faced with economic collapse unless she took the part of the Central Powers. Serbia was discussed in a strain of extreme malevolence. She was the eternal enemy, and, since she was Russia's darling, Russian and Bulgarian policy must stand in conflict. The Western Allies had offered no real advantages. They had demanded that Bulgaria should place her army unreservedly at their disposal in order to take Constantinople and hand it over to Russia; in return she was to receive some paltry territories in Thrace, and some vague compensations in Macedonia—these latter only on the understanding that Serbia got all she wanted from Austria. The rewards for adhering to the Teutonic League were not specified, but official rumour had long been busy expounding their magnificence. These appeals were skilful enough, being directed purely to immediate self-interest and to the very real soreness against Serbia, and they proved that King Ferdinand and his advisers were by no means certain of the temper of the country, which still looked to Russia as her traditional ally. The effect in Russia of this treason to the Slav cause on the part of a nation for which she had fought many battles was to arouse a bitter and sorrowful resentment. Radko Dmitrieff returned to King Ferdinand his Bulgarian orders and renounced his allegiance. A fortnight later, on 19th October, an Imperial Manifesto issued in Petrograd denounced the treachery.

Meanwhile the Allied troops brought from Gallipoli were arriving at Salonika. The landing began on 3rd October, and on 7th October two divisions were on shore. The force was under the command of General Sarrail, formerly in charge of the French Third Army, and was officially known as the Armée d'Orient. Sarrail had come to loggerheads with Joffre, and the new post was invented to remove him to a sphere of more distant usefulness than the Western Front. The Greek commandant made a formal protest, and then directed the harbour officials to assist in arranging the landing. Greek officers took charge of the Salonika railway, and displaced the former German and Austrian employees of the company.

On Monday, 4th October, M. Venizelos made a speech in the Greek Chamber. He explained that in his view Greece's engagements to Serbia under her treaty of alliance, as well as the vital interests of the country, imposed on her the duty of going to Serbia's aid without awaiting a declaration of war by the Central Powers. If Bulgaria were suffered to win it would be farewell to Greece's hopes of the future. "I can only say that I should feel profound regret if, in the performance of my duty in safeguarding the vital interests of the country, I should find myself brought into opposition with nations with whom I have no direct quarrel. The danger of conflict is great, but we shall none the less fulfil the obligations imposed on us by our treaty of alliance." These manly and honourable words were the last which M. Venizelos was destined to utter as head of the Greek Government. They could have only one meaning—that the Greek army in concert with the Allies at Salonika, would take the field at once against Bulgaria on Serbia's behalf. But next morning the Prime Minister was summoned to the Palace, and told by King Constantine that his policy had not the royal sanction. That afternoon in the Chamber he announced his resignation, to the surprise of his countrymen and the consternation of the Allies. M. Zaimis, the Governor of the National Bank, was entrusted with the task of forming a Cabinet. The new Ministry proclaimed its policy as the maintenance, as long as events permitted, of a state of armed neutrality, but a neutrality, so far as concerned the Western Allies, "to be characterized by the most complete and sincere benevolence." Of this benevolence the tacit sanction given to the Salonika landing might be regarded as a proof.

Events now moved swiftly. On 7th October Mackensen forced the line of the rivers, and on Saturday, 9th October, Belgrade fell to Kövess. Two Bulgarian armies, the I. under General Bojadieff, and the II. under General Todorov,* were on the Serbian frontier. Turkish troops were moving over the Thracian borders, and around Dedeagatch. On Monday, the 11th, the Bulgarian advanced guards crossed the marches, and next day the Government of Sofia formally declared war upon Serbia. On 15th October Britain declared war upon Bulgaria. The situation at

* In the First Balkan War he had commanded the 7th Bulgarian Division, which marched on Salonika, and so was now employed in the terrain of his earlier operations.

this date was that more than 200,000 Austro-Germans under Mackensen were pressing southwards from the Save and the Danube against the Serbian front; a quarter of a million Bulgarians were moving westwards against Serbia's exposed right flank; far to the south 13,000 French and British troops were in the vicinity of Salonika; while Greece and Rumania, fully mobilized, were watching their frontiers and waiting upon fortune. The curtain had rung up on the tragic drama of Serbia.

Such is the summary of the events which preceded the new Balkan campaign. Two questions deserve further consideration —the attitude of Greece and the policy of the Western Allies. It is the duty of the historian to look behind the facile condemnations and criticisms of the man in the street, and attempt to envisage the difficulties which faced the Governments concerned. That most of these difficulties were due to prior blunders did not make them the easier to surmount. Men of the most undoubted honour and goodwill may find themselves faced by a puzzle to which there is literally no solution, a quandary from which there is no outlet except by way of some kind of disaster.

The dominant motive in Greek policy was fear. On a broad survey of the situation there was no answer to the arguments adduced by M. Venizelos in his speech in the Chamber on 10th October after his retirement. He declared his conviction that war between Greece and Bulgaria was inevitable in the near future. If to-day Greece allowed Serbia to be crushed, in three years' time she herself would fall an easy prey. He pointed out, too, the results of a Teutonic victory. It would mean the eradication of the Hellenic element in Turkey, however loud the German assurances to the contrary, and it would be the end of Greece's hopes of expansion on the Ægean littoral. Indeed, it would in all likelihood be the end of Greek nationality altogether. Every reason of policy was in favour of Greece's active adherence to the cause of the Allies. There was, further, the obligation to Serbia under the Treaty of 1913, but when on 11th October Serbia formally asked Greece for the help for which that treaty provided she was refused. The Greek argument [*] was that since Serbia had shown herself willing to concede certain tracts of Macedonia to Bulgaria, the purpose for which the treaty was made had disappeared, and that in any case the treaty referred only to an

[*] See M. Zaimis's statement of 29th September 1915, published in the *Greek White Book*, 1917.

attack on Serbia by Bulgaria, and not to an invasion by other Powers. These were obviously quibbles, and that they should have been used by the Greek Government showed the strength of its determination to cling to neutrality. The motive of that determination was fear. The King, himself allied by marriage with the Emperor, was oppressed by the evidence of German power. The General Staff had seen the futile result of the summer campaign in the Dardanelles. It had witnessed Russia being driven from post to pillar, while the French and British armies were held in the West. Had the Western offensive of 25th September been pushed to an indisputable victory things would have been different, but that advance seemed now to have reached its limit. Greece knew the strength of Bulgaria's fighting force; she knew the weakness of the Serbian remnant, and she could not tell what reinforcements Mackensen might yet bring to the Balkans. Besides, there were Turkish reserves who, equipped by Germany, could threaten her north-eastern marches. She saw her army of at the most 350,000 faced by enemies who might presently be twice or three times that number. Serbia, with less than 200,000 men, was strategically so placed that she must soon be put out of action. As for the Western Allies, they were committed to send 150,000 men, but that contingent would not turn the balance in her favour. She had acquired a not unjustifiable distrust of Allied strategy and leadership; it was useless to attempt to bribe her with Cyprus or promises of Turkish territory; before those gifts could materialize the enemy must be conquered, and the provision for his conquest was not apparent. Her only course, she argued, was to remain neutral, and wait upon events. She did not fear the vindictiveness of the Allies, should they be victorious; but she considered that the Teutonic League, if it won the campaign, would exact from her the uttermost vengeance if she had taken action against it.

These were not exalted or very far-sighted considerations, but they determined the decision of her Government, sorely perplexed about the future. They were not the views of the greatest Greek, M. Venizelos, but probably they were the views of the majority of the Greek people. For, as has already been pointed out, it was idle to expect from the little Balkan States any prescient or continuous policy. Like all lately-born peasant democracies, they tended to cultivate the immediate advantage, and to be obsessed by the immediate peril.

The question of Allied policy falls under two heads—the diplomacy before the crisis, and the military plan when diplomacy had failed. In any criticism it is fair to remember the extraordinary difficulties which faced the Foreign Offices of France and Britain. Since May the successes, the definite, tangible successes, had been all on the German side. They could point to nothing to set off against the triumphant sweep from the Donajetz to the Sereth, from the Vistula to the Dvina. In dealing with hesitating neutrals they were heavily handicapped. It was like a game of bridge in which a player has never in his hand a card which can take a trick. Again, in the case of the Balkan States, there was this special difficulty—that each state was at heart as jealous of its neighbour and prospective ally as of the Power which we sought to persuade them was the common enemy. Undoubtedly, before the Russian *débâcle* began, Bulgaria might have been brought in on the Allied side. Had Serbia been willing, say, in April 1915, to cede to Bulgaria with immediate occupation the disputed territory in Macedonia, Bulgaria would have been won over. But this Serbia obstinately refused to do; in reply to their appeals the Allies were told that the Serbians would sooner fight the Bulgarians than the Austrians; so the blame for some part of Serbia's misfortunes must rest on her own shoulders. When she proved amenable to persuasion it was already too late. Russia had suffered her disaster, and the glamour of German prowess had fallen upon Sofia.

It may fairly be said, therefore, that the Allied diplomacy was confronted with a most intricate problem. It is easy to be wise after the event; but, looking back over the course of twelve months, it would seem that its solution, though hard, was not impossible. The importance of the Balkans was recognized too late, and a strong and consistent policy was not adopted in time. It is difficult not to believe that prior to 1st May Bulgaria could have been won, if the Allies had insisted clearly upon certain concessions from Serbia and Greece. They had the power to insist if they had had the will. After that date they failed to recognize that Bulgaria was lost, and persisted up to 1st October in efforts at conciliation which were doomed to failure. From May onward there was only one argument which could prevail upon King Ferdinand, and that was fear. Since we could not make Bulgaria our ally she must be isolated. Had we in July, when there was already evidence of Bulgarian intentions, sent to Salonika the six divisions which went later to Gallipoli, it is more than likely that Bulgaria would have yielded, and, at the worst, we should have been able to attach Greece to our side and give Serbia adequate assistance in the hour of invasion. We underrated the importance of the Balkans from the first. History will record that our difficulties were great, but that they were surmountable, and that they were not surmounted.

The question of military policy raises once again the old subject of divergent operations. Our preoccupation with the Gallipoli campaign blinded our eyes to what was happening farther west on the mainland, and fettered our hands. Had we been able to place a force of 300,000 men at Salonika early in September we should have been in a position to help Serbia effectually, and wage a campaign with some chance of success. That chance had gone utterly by 6th October. Why, then, was the expedition persisted in? It was idle to talk about our prestige in the East. That could not be served by a second disaster on the Ægean shores. To achieve anything we must send at least three times our projected force, and that could be got only by depleting the Western front. There we had instituted an ambitious offensive, an offensive which to succeed must continue without intermission till the enemy's lines were broken. But if we took away sufficient troops to achieve anything in the Balkans, that offensive must be suspended ; and if we did not send an adequate force to the Near East it would be far wiser to send none. Moreover, it meant the establishment of a new and vulnerable line of sea communications at a time when we had no shipping to spare. It was the worst type of vicious circle. Every military consideration, therefore, pointed to the abstention from any further divergent adventures. Such in the end of September was the view of the French General Staff, and on 9th October the British General Staff drafted a memorandum against the Salonika expedition, since it was then too late to help Serbia. This led to Sir Edward Carson's resignation on 12th October, on the ground that we were not fulfilling our debt of honour. Next day M. Delcassé resigned for the opposite reason, believing that any expedition to the Balkans was indefensible. Of the two distinguished statesmen, M. Delcassé from a military point of view had the better argument. With far too few men, in a country where transport difficulties were great and demanded a complete re-equipment, we proposed to make a diversion on behalf of a gallant ally, whom no diversion could save. The true blow for the re-creation of Serbia could only be struck on the Western front.

But no war can be conducted solely by military science. There were reasons which made some effort on Serbia's behalf, however belated, a political necessity. We had promised assistance to that little nation, and every Serbian counted on our aid. Even if we were too late to save her, public honour seemed to demand that we should try. That, at any rate, was the view of the ordinary man in France and Britain, and in addition there were responsible statesmen in both countries who believed that French and British prestige in the Moslem world was at stake, and that, however disadvantageous the enterprise on purely military grounds, some kind of attempt must be made to check the German sweep to the Bosphorus. The latter view was rather a sentiment than a reasoned opinion; but the former—the point of honour—had real substance. An act of public disloyalty might be more damaging in the long run to the Allied cause than a rash adventure. A man who refrains from rushing to the help of a friend who is attacked in a street brawl is scarcely justified by the plea that he had followed the wiser course of going off to fetch the police. This view—to the credit of their hearts—soon obtained a great predominance among the Western Allies. In France and Britain there was much criticism—often bitter and unfair—of our diplomatic failure. The French Government became strong converts to the necessity of a Balkan expedition, and the French General Staff unwillingly followed suit.

In such circumstances it was inevitable that the correct military view must be overridden. The great Western offensive slackened, for, apart from the fact that divisions must be taken from that front, the mind of the High Command was compelled to divide its interests. The British 22nd, 27th, and 28th Divisions were dispatched to Salonika, and the Indian Corps to the Tigris. In the beginning of October the Allies were resolved to do something, but they had no very clear idea as to what that something should be. Few undertakings in history have been started in so complete a fog of indecision. The situation in the Near East, already sufficiently tangled, was to be complicated by a new sporadic effort, not undertaken as part of a considered plan, but the offspring of a sudden necessity.

CHAPTER XLI.

THE OVERRUNNING OF SERBIA.

September 19, 1915–January 25, 1916.

Serbia's Military Position—Mackensen's Problem—The Advance of Gallwitz and Kövess—Bulgaria's Flank Attack—Fall of Uskub—Fall of Nish—The Serbian Retreat to the Adriatic—The Allies in Salonika—The Austrian Conquest of Montenegro.

THE military situation which confronted Serbia in the second week of October was simplicity itself. There were no elements of hopeful doubt to relieve the darkness of her outlook. In modern war, unless the difference of quality is immense, it is numbers that win, and her numbers were few. Her great losses in the battles of 1914 had brought down her armed strength, allowing for the use of every available man, to less than 200,000, and her enemies already in the field could more than double her maximum. Moreover, her successes had impaired her defensive power. Thrice she had been invaded, and three times in heroic battles she had flung back the invader. But her country had been devastated, and she had been hard put to it to restore the common machinery of life. Then had come pestilence and famine, and throughout the spring of 1915 she had been fighting a sterner enemy than the Austrian. Her peasant soldiers had been compelled to return home to prevent their farms going out of cultivation, and throughout the summer she was singularly unprepared for a state at war with mighty neighbours. She was unable to take that offensive which is commonly the best method of defence, and was compelled perforce to put her trust in her Allies. The earlier invasions she had repelled unaided, but now she had to look beyond her borders for security. She was better munitioned than before the Battle of the Ridges; but in other military assets she was weaker. Her soldiers were very tired, and her generals were in the difficulty that, cognisant of great dangers, they simply could not frame an adequate plan to meet them. Her victories had given her a noble self-confidence; but her position forbade her to reap the fruits of it, and compelled her to rely on others.

To this weakness from the depletion and the disorganization of her armies was added the greater danger of a hopeless strategic quandary. Being a salient, she had the enemy on three sides of her. Her northern front of some 150 miles was held, by the decision of the British Government, by her main armies. Her eastern flank of nearly 300 miles marched through most of its length with Bulgaria. Her western flank for more than 100 miles adjoined unfriendly Bosnia; then for a little came the protection of Montenegro; but the southern part was bounded by Albania, which was at least potentially hostile. If the Serbian army were forced back in the north it could retire by the valleys of the Morava and the Vardar towards Salonika. By these valleys, which were followed by roads and railways, Serbia could receive supplies from the Allied base on the sea. If the only force was Mackensen's, she might well hope to stand on the ridges behind the northern plain, as she had stood nine months before, and hold the invader. But with Bulgaria on her flank the situation was wholly changed. The Bulgarian right, moving against the Timok valley, must sooner or later join hands with Mackensen, and force the Serbians south and west of the Constantinople railway. Such a position would be serious, but not desperate, for a stand might still be made on the hills of the upper Morava, and communication kept open with Salonika. But in the south the Bulgarian frontier came very close to the vital railway from the sea. Vrania was only twenty miles off. Strumnitza station was less, and the nodal point of Uskub was only fifty. It would be an easy task for the Bulgarian southern armies to cut the line. Once that happened there was no way of provisioning the Serbian forces except by the difficult hill paths of Albania and the Black Mountain. There was no way of retreat for them except into the wild recesses of the coastal ranges and the gorges of the Black and White Drin. Once such a retreat was compelled, Serbia would be overrun and the Serbian army put out of action.

The one desperate chance was that the Allies at Salonika might be able to turn the Bulgarian flank, and protect the railway at any rate as far as Uskub. That would allow of a stand on the line of the Ibar and the upper Morava. The Serbians were confident that this would happen. Indeed, in the early days of

October they looked for Allied assistance even on their northern front. At Nish the town was decorated, and the school children waited outside the station with bouquets to present to the coming reinforcements. But the Allies could not come. They were too few and too far away.

The Serbian campaign therefore falls into two sections wholly distinct and unrelated. The first is the expulsion from their native land of the Serbian army. The second is the contest of the Allied army of Salonika against the Bulgarian left wing for the hundred miles of line northward from the port, and their ultimate retirement to a fortified line near the sea. The stand of the Serbians, it may fairly be said, was in no material sense aided by the Franco-British operations. They fought their hopeless battle alone, and in that fact is to be found the failure of the Allied strategical plan.

I.

Mackensen's immediate objective was both strategically and tactically simple. The motive was to win a way to Constantinople, and two routes were possible—the Danube and the Ottoman railway. To secure the first it was necessary to cross the river on the front from Belgrade to Orsova close to the Rumanian frontier, and to master that narrow neck of north-eastern Serbia about forty miles wide between Milanovatz, on the Danube, and the mouth of the Timok. That would give him the whole length of the river now commanded by Serbia. The advantage of the river route was inadequately appreciated at the time in the West. Before the Ottoman railway could be used there must be a considerable amount of campaigning; the great bridge over the Save must be repaired, which had been blown up by the Serbians a year before; and bridges and embankments must be restored between Belgrade and the Bulgarian frontier. But to master the river was an easy task. Once Belgrade was taken the operations of the British Naval Mission would be at an end. As soon as the Serbians were driven from their position on the southern shore, the mines could be swept up, and there could be a clear waterway to the Bulgarian railheads connecting with the Constantinople line. On the northern bank there were a number of Austrian railheads, all provided with sidings, quays, and loading gear. For the river transport there were available flotillas of Austrian passenger steamers and tug-boats and thousands of barges. The Danube Steam Navigation Company alone could supply more than a hundred passenger steamers and over six hundred tugs. The concentration of Mackensen's army was largely effected by waterways, since a river convoy could load up wherever a railway touched the Danube or the Theiss. Again, the Danube was connected by excellent canals with the Elbe and the Rhine. In forwarding supplies by canal the slowness of transit, as compared to railways, was of little consequence once a steady stream of barges had been started. As much stuff as could be handled would be delivered each day at the farther end. It was possible for barges to be loaded at the great munition factories of the middle Rhine and pass through to the lower Danube without breaking bulk. While Mackensen was clearing the Serbian bank thousands of loaded freighters were accumulating between Semlin and Budapest, ready to go forward as soon as the river was open. There was the further gain in using the riverway that the convoys would not return empty, but would bring back to Austria and Germany supplies of Bulgarian and Rumanian meat and corn.

The second route to the Bosphorus would be slower to win. It involved the capture of Belgrade and the ridges to the south of it, and an advance to the south-east which would clear the Morava valley up to Nish and the tributary Nishava valley as far as the Bulgarian frontier. To secure both routes the German plan of campaign was one of converging attacks. On the south-west Albanian bands would threaten the Prishtina and Prizrend region on the Serbian left rear. On the west an Austrian force, operating from the Bosnian bases, would assault the line of the Drina. On the north were Mackensen's two armies. Gallwitz lay on the left from Orsova to a point opposite Semendria, and Kövess on the right, facing Belgrade and the lower Save. The eastern Serbian frontier was entrusted to the Bulgarians. Bojadieff's army covered the country from the mouth of the Timok to the Ottoman railway; Todorov's from that railway to the neighbourhood of Strumnitza. The Bulgarian attack had five main objectives. The extreme right was directed across the Timok to enable Gallwitz to clear the Danube. The right centre moved on Zaichar and the Timok, and was intended to follow the branch line to Parachin, on the Constantinople railway. The centre advanced on Pirot and Nish. The left centre moved from Kustendil against Vrania and Uskub—the most vital points in the Serbian communications. On the extreme left there was an advance from Strumnitza to cut the railway in the Vardar valley, the point at which during the past year Bulgarian bands on at least two occasions had made attempts on the line. The Bulgarian left and left centre had also the task of opposing any movement of the Allies from Salonika.

A plan which involved at least nine converging lines of attack demanded a very great numerical superiority and an enemy incapable of a dangerous offensive. These conditions were realized. General Putnik, the old Serbian field-marshal, could muster less than half the strength of his enemy. The poverty of Serbia's communications prevented him following the natural strategy of a defence on interior lines, and striking at one or more of the widely separated invaders. He was compelled to remain rigidly on the defensive, and on a partial defensive. His main forces were strung along the river front in the north—thin in the centre, where Belgrade was held by less than two divisions, but stronger on the wings, where a turning movement was feared. Mishitch commanded the First Army, as he had done in the December Battle of the Ridges, and held the angle of the Save and the Drina. On the right the Third Army, under Yourashitch, protected the valley of the Morava, and faced Gallwitz and the Bulgarian right. A small detachment lay at Ushitza to watch the menace from Bosnia against the left rear. On the eastern frontier there was a force facing the Timok valley, and protecting Nish was the Second Army, under Stepanovitch. It is obvious that such a disposition was in no way adequate to meet all the converging dangers. Serbia was compelled to leave the defence of the eastern frontier, which was threatened by far the most formidable foe, to her Allies, in the hope that they would be in time. If that hope failed, the most heroic stand in the north would be futile.

Life in Belgrade during the spring and summer had been curiously peaceful for a frontier city in time of war. Admiral Troubridge's Naval Mission with its armed launches did much destructive work at night against the Austrian monitors, issuing from the river quays as in old days the Illyrian pirate galleys issued from the screen of the Dalmatian Islands. The city was bombarded methodically at long range from the northern shore, but there seems to have been a clearly defined danger zone. Belgrade lies on a ridge which slopes up from the Save and the Danube, and, while in the riverside streets shells dropped and the houses were in ruins, in the upper thoroughfares life went on and the citizens took the air as usual. In those fantastic days it was possible for a visitor to dine at his hotel, drive in a cab to the quays, embark in a launch, spend the midnight hours in a spirited naval action, and return to his bed before morning.

On the afternoon of 19th September Kövess's batteries opened against Belgrade, and battle was joined all along the river line. At first the invaders made little progress, for their big guns had not yet come up and their infantry was not ready. But in the first days of October the situation changed. Bulgaria was mustering, the guns had arrived from Poland, and on 3rd October the first shots were fired in the real bombardment. It was such a "preparation" as had preceded the May onslaught on the Donajetz, or the September advance in the West. The Serbians had nothing of the same calibre with which to reply, and their positions on the south bank were slowly pounded into dust. Under cover of the guns both Gallwitz and Kövess attempted crossings—the former at Semendria, Ram, and Graditze; the latter at Shabatz, Obrenovatz, and especially at Ciglania Island, in the Save, just above Belgrade. Gallwitz was aiming at the Morava valley, Kövess at the capital.

On the 7th both Save and Danube were crossed, the latter at Belgrade itself. The immense weight of artillery fire made the city untenable, and on the 8th the Serbians began to evacuate it. During the day fierce fighting continued at the quays and the lower part of the town, but by the evening the Citadel and the royal palace had been taken. There was a desperate guerrilla struggle in some of the streets, and it was not till the morning of the 9th that Kövess had the whole place in his hands. He found little booty, except some old guns, for the pieces of the British Naval Mission were either destroyed or got away in time. His artillery had played havoc with the capital, and the German flag floated over a desolation. But it had been a calculated destruction, for the railway station was left intact.

On the left Mishitch, who had the best troops of the Serbian army under his command, managed to check any torrential crossing of the Save. At Shabatz, at Prograrska Island, and at Zabrej, he held the enemy for several days. But Gallwitz by this time had overcome the resistance of the Serbian right. He crossed at Semendria, at Ram, and near Graditze. Here, on the south bank, at the mouth of the valleys of the Mlava and Morava, for a little there were stubborn encounters. But the Serbians were gradually driven back to Pojarevatz, and on the 11th Berlin announced that one hundred miles of front from Shabatz to Graditze, on the south bank of the Save and Danube, had been won.

Next day Bulgaria formally entered the war, having waited till she was assured of Mackensen's ability to force the line of the rivers, and with that event Gallwitz's left wing in the neighbourhood of Orsova came into action. The Serbian position was now somewhat as follows :—Mishitch, on the left, was being forced slowly back from the Save towards the foothills of the Tser range, where a year before the Serbian army had made their first stand against the third Austrian invasion. His communications were bad, and he was in danger of having his flanks turned by the Austrian crossing of the Drina, and by the drive of Kövess's centre. The Serbian centre had fallen back from Belgrade to the foothills in the south, and had taken up position on the ridge called Avala, seven miles from the capital. The Serbian right, under Yourashitch, was being forced across the riverside plain from Semendria to Graditze, up the valleys of the Morava and the Mlava. For some days Mackensen moved slowly. It was not the lack of heavy artillery as had been the case two weeks before, because he had now his full complement of guns. It was in pursuance of a sound strategical plan. He must not press the Serbians too far south till Bulgaria had time to take them in flank and rear.

On the 12th Bojadieff attacked in two columns against Zaichar and Kniashevatz, while his right moved against Negotin in the lower Timok valley. At first the Serbian army of the Timok held the invaders, but two days later Pojarevatz fell to Gallwitz, and Bojadieff took the heights east of Kniashevatz. Next day Kövess drove the Serbian centre from the hills of Avala. On Sunday, the 17th, there was a concerted attack all along the eastern frontier. The day before the Salonika line had been cut by cavalry raiders at Vrania, and on the Sunday Todorov's centre from Kustendil captured Egri Palanka, while Bojadieff forced a crossing on the lower Timok. The enemy now commanded Vrania, and communications between Nish and Salonika were suspended. The last train which ran, conveying the property of the Serbian National Bank, passed through a battlefield, and arrived at the coast pockmarked with rifle bullets. Meanwhile Stepanovitch was being forced down the Nishava valley from Pirot by the Bulgarian centre. In the north Obrenovatz had fallen, and the line of the Save was clear for the invader.

Events now moved fast. The Allies were fighting their own battle in the south, which we shall presently consider. They were altogether cut off from the Serbians, though twenty miles north of them a Serbian detachment was falling back before the Bulgarian advance on Veles. In the week beginning Monday, the 18th, the chief effort was made by Todorov's II. Army. Veles, or Kuprulu, fell on the 20th, and on the 22nd, late in the afternoon, the Bulgarians entered Uskub, the nodal point of all the routes of southern Serbia. The advance was swift, for the simple reason that there was nothing to stop it. All the considerable Serbian armies were in the north, and the Allies from Salonika were too late to do more than check the extreme left of the Bulgarian movement. Had they been earlier on the scene, the long narrow gorge through which the railway ran north of Vrania might have given them a strong position in which to hold the enemy.

The loss of Uskub was a misfortune of the first magnitude. It cut off all communication between the Vardar and Morava valleys. It blocked the routes to Prilep and Monastir in the south, and the access to Kossovo and Novi Bazar in the north by the Katchanik Pass. The outlook for Serbia was black indeed, and she made a last despairing appeal to the Allies for aid. Throughout the land a mass of fugitives of every age and condition was fleeing distractedly by the few routes left open to the south-west. Nish was a beleaguered city. Food was scarce, and vehicles could hardly be obtained for love or money. By Tuesday, the 26th, disaster had followed disaster. On the Saturday Gallwitz's left had forced the passage of the Danube at Orsova, on the Rumanian border, the western opening of the defile known as the Iron Gate. The Germans crossed by the island below the town, and took the steep wooded heights on the southern shore which commanded all the bend of the river. That same day Negotin fell to Bojadieff's right, and the town of Prahovo, where the Bulgarians seized large quantities of supplies which had come up the river for the Serbians. These victories opened to Germany the Danube route to Constantinople. Gallwitz had also pushed some way up the Morava, and was in line with Kövess, who had occupied Valjevo. In the west the Austrians had forced the Drina at Vishegrad, and were threatening Ushitza. There was no chance of the Serbians retrieving their fortunes, as they had done a year before, by a stand on the ridges of Maljen and Suvobor. That position was already turned, with the Bulgarians pressing westward from Timok and Pirot. The line of the upper Timok still held, but it, too, was outflanked on south and west. The only route for withdrawal, if the army was to be saved, was by the long valley of the Ibar for their northern forces, and for the southern detachments by the ancient roads to the Adriatic from Prizrend and from Monastir.

But there was little time to lose, for the Austrians moving on Ushitza, and the Bulgarians pushing west from Vrania and Uskub, might cut at the roots of the salient. Moreover, the army of Stepanovitch, on the upper Timok, was in an ugly salient of its own.

On Tuesday, the 26th, the Austrians from Orsova and the Bulgarians from Prahovo joined hands, and the whole north-east corner of Serbia was in the enemy's possession. Next day Zaichar and Kniashevatz fell at last after a heroic defence, and the line of the Timok was gone. The main Serbian position now lay roughly through Kragujevatz, the arsenal, and Parachin, on the railway, and encircled Nish, with its right at Leskovatz. On the 28th Pirot fell, and Gallwitz, advancing up the Morava valley, made many prisoners. The Austro-Germans in their progress distinguished themselves by their brutality to the civilian population—brutality which had a direct military object. If they could produce a panic among the inhabitants, and cause a wholesale flight, the few roads would be encumbered with fleeing households, and the retreat of the Serbian army and guns would be hopelessly impeded. On Saturday, the 30th, Kragujevatz was taken. There was little left in it for the victors, only half a dozen old field pieces and some thousands of damaged rifles. We may now regard the Serbians as forming two forces. One, the remnant of the Armies of the North, lay from south of Kragujevatz to the north and east of Nish. The second and lesser was in the hills north of Monastir. The two were hopelessly isolated by the Bulgarian advance from Uskub towards Prishtina. The retirement of the first was by the hill roads and the Ibar valley into Montenegro, that of the second into the mountains of central Albania. Had they been faced by Germans alone with their heavy ordnance they would have had a reasonable chance of escape, for Mackensen had taken forty days to cover an average of forty miles; but in the Bulgarians they had opponents as skilled as themselves in marching and fighting in a mountain country. On the last day of October the main Serbian force was for a moment out of danger, for the Austrians seemed unable to advance towards Ushitza; but Stepanovitch's army defending Nish was in an acute and dangerous salient.

Stepanovitch won clear, but by the narrowest margin. The final attack on Nish began on 3rd November, and after three days of severe fighting, it fell on the 5th. The Serbians retired on Leskovatz, and north of Nish, half-way between Parachin and Zaichar, the Germans and the Bulgarians again joined hands. The Northern Army was now in full retreat, for the enemy had enclosed it in a half-moon, of which the horns were hourly bending inwards. There was no more fighting for Mishitch, Yourashitch, and Stepanovitch. The last action before the complete conquest of Serbia was fought by the small forces in the south in a despairing effort to stem the Bulgarian advance from Uskub upon Prizrend and Monastir. These battles of the passes were for King Peter's remnant the Kossovo of the campaign.

North-west of Uskub, crossing the low Katchanik Pass, a railway ran to Mitrovitza. Already the Serbian main army on the Ibar was getting desperately short of ammunition. They had shot away most of their supplies, and if any more were to reach them it must be from the south by way of Monastir, Prizrend, and Prishtina, for even if there had been stores at the Albanian ports the Albanian roads were too long and difficult. Moreover, if the Bulgarians advanced beyond the Katchanik and reached the railhead at Mitrovitza, there would be a good chance of enveloping and cutting off the army on the Ibar. If the retirement was to be made at all, it was necessary to hold the Katchanik till the latest possible moment. Five thousand men, the remnant of the Uskub garrison, in the last days of October made a stand on the hills at the Uskub end of the pass. The Serbians had their guns on the heights, and enough ammunition for a battle of several days. Three regiments had been sent down by Putnik from the north to act as reinforcements, and the order ran at all costs to hold the enemy. The Bulgarians advanced on a fifteen-mile front with a strength of two and a half divisions. They were in the form of a crescent, with their left in the plain of Tetovo, and their right across the Uskub–Mitrovitza line. At first the Serbian bombardment drove back the enemy several miles from his advanced position. On the third day their infantry attacked with the bayonet and bombs. All night the battle raged, and after a struggle of twelve hours the Bulgarian front was pierced by one division. But by that time the enemy had more than doubled his strength. He re-formed behind the gap, and the horns of his front began to envelop the small Serbian force. It was the situation of the Romans at Cannæ, and the Serbian centre was slowly driven back, till the peril on the flanks compelled a rapid retreat. Fighting desperately, and taking heavy toll of the enemy, they retired across the pass to join the retreating Army of the North. But their stand had given Putnik the respite he had sought, and before Mitrovitza was threatened the retreat was moving up the hill roads to the Montenegrin plain of Ipek.

The stand at the Babuna Pass was of a different kind. Its primary aim was to bar the way to Monastir, for once the Bulgarians were at Prilep the roads from Monastir northward would be shut to possible supplies. But it had also an offensive purpose. If the Allies could retake Veles, Uskub would be threatened, and the dangerous Bulgarian operations towards Mitrovitza would be checked. The Babuna Pass, a little over 2,000 feet high, is on the road from Uskub to Prilep. Some 5,000 Serbians held the heights commanding the northern approach, where in the first days of November they repulsed the assault of a Bulgarian division, and drove it back as far as Izvor, which is about a dozen miles on the road from Veles. But only an advanced guard of the enemy had been checked. Todorov's main force poured down from the Veles front, and presently the Serbian handful had the better part of four divisions before them. For a week and more the crest of the Babuna Pass was still held, but the failure of the Allies farther south, and the Bulgarian capture of the Mitrovitza line, made the position untenable. The Serbians fell back towards the Albanian borders, and the campaign, so far as that valiant army was concerned, was over. They had fought most gallantly a losing fight, in which they never for one moment could hope to succeed. They had lost greatly in guns and men, and it is not likely that more than 150,000 weary and famished warriors sought the shelter of the highlands. It was an army still in being, but only a shadow of that heroic force which a year ago had flung the Austrians across the Danube. Before the middle of November the paths which climb from the upper glens of the Vardar, the Morava, and the Ibar were littered with the bullock-carts of the transport and plodding soldiers, who halted now and then to take a last look behind them at their hills of home.

After the fall of Nish, Mackensen's interest in the campaign slackened. He had got what he set out to get—the Danube route and the Ottoman railway; he had put the Serbian army out of action; the campaign was now in Bulgarian hands, a campaign of long-cherished and bitter revenge. By the middle of November fighting had ceased through Serbia, save in the far south, where the Allied contingent was holding the gorge of the Vardar. The Serbian remnant was straining westward by every hill road which led to Montenegro and Albania. That strange migration was not only the retreat of an army but the flight of a people. The weaker and poorer fugitives were left behind in the foothills; but many women and children struggled on, cumbering the infrequent roads and suffering untold privations, till they reached the shores of the Adriatic. The campaigns had already shown great national dispersions—the flight from Belgium, the move of the Russian Poles eastward; and it had shown the retirement of mighty armies—from the Meuse to the Marne, from the Vistula to the Dvina. But no army in retreat and no people in flight had ever sought a city of refuge through so inhospitable a desert. The stony ridges of the coastal mountains were already deep in snow. The few roads were tracks which led over high passes and through narrow gorges beside flooded torrents. The Albanian tribes were eager to profit from the misery of the fugitives. If they sold food it was at a famine price, and they lay in wait, like the Spanish guerrillas in the Peninsula, to cut off stragglers. At the end of the journey was a barren sea-coast with few harbours, and between it and Italy lay the Adriatic, sown with enemy mines and searched by enemy submarines.

Mishitch's First Army and the detachment which had held Belgrade retreated by the upper glens of the Ibar to the little plain of Ipek, which is tucked away among the Montenegrin hills. Thence they made their way through the land of the Black Mountain to Skutari. Yourashitch's Third Army fell back upon Prishtina, whence they moved to Prizrend on the Albanian border. They then tramped down the White Drin to its junction with the Black, and while a portion followed the river to Skutari, the majority went south by the Black Drin to Dibra, and made their way by Struga to Elbasan, and so to Durazzo. Stepanovitch's Second Army followed much the same course, concentrating on Prizrend; and the Uskub garrison, after it had been driven from the Babuna Pass, moved straight by way of Ochrida upon Elbasan. The peculiar difficulty of the retreat for the southern armies lay in the fact that the Bulgarians, after the success at Katchanik and Babuna, had cut the route from Prizrend southward, and so forced the Serbians, in order to reach Elbasan, to make the journey on Albanian soil among the wild ravines of the Black Drin. Few of the guns got away. Many reached Ipek, where they were destroyed and abandoned, since the paths west of Prizrend were only for foot travellers lightly burdened. Every hour of the retirement was a nightmare. The hill roads were strewn with fainting and starving men, and the gorges of the two Drins found their solitude disturbed by other sounds than the angry rivers. Happily the conditions which made the retreat so hard imposed discretion upon the pursuit. The German armies took no part in the chase. They were busy repairing the Orient railway, and getting ready to enter the country of their new allies. But the Bulgarians pressed the pursuit hard, and, had the land been more practicable, and had they occupied Struga and Elbasan, they might have cut off at least one-half of the Serbian force. But the time was too short, and the Serbians were well on the way to Durazzo before the Bulgarian advanced guards had entered Albania.

One other piece of good fortune attended the retreat. Essad Pasha, who after many vicissitudes had made for himself a little Albanian kingdom after the flight of the ill-fated Prince of Wied, declared himself on the side of the Allies. He expelled all Austrian and Bulgarian subjects from the territories under his control, and gave to the Teutonic agents who appeared in December to stir up the northern tribes a taste of Albanian justice. He did his best to welcome the fugitives and assist the efforts of the British, French, and Italian missions to prepare for their reception. These efforts were made in the face of immense difficulties. Food was sent by Britain and France, and Italy provided the shipping. It was necessary to bring the Serbian remnant to Durazzo, and for this purpose jetties had to be built, rivers and marshes had to be bridged, and roads had to be repaired and constructed. Italian troops arrived at Durazzo from Avlona on 21st December, to provide a rallying point In one way and another nearly 130,000 men of the Serbian army were brought to the coast in safety. The civilian refugees went for the most part to southern Italy.

King Peter himself had a journey of strange vicissitudes. Travelling in a rude Macedonian cart he reached Prizrend with his troops, and then pressed on to Liuma, across the Albanian border. Thence he set out incognito, accompanied by three officers and four soldiers, and journeyed on muleback and horseback through the hills held by the Albanian Catholic tribes. After four days he reached Skutari, where he rested for a fortnight, and then continued along the coast by San Giovanni di Medua, Alessio, and Durazzo to Avlona. He crossed to Brindisi, and remained there six days unrecognized. Then he took ship to Salonika, and arrived there on New Year's Day, crippled with rheumatism and all but blind, but undefeated in spirit. His was a character with many flaws, but he shared the stubborn courage of his people. If his country was for the moment lost, he had sought the nearest camp of its future deliverers. " I believe in the liberty of Serbia," he said, " as I believe in God. It was the dream of my youth. It was for that I fought throughout manhood. It has become the faith of the twilight of my life. I live only to see Serbia free. I pray that God may let me live until the day of redemption of my people. On that day I am ready to die, if the Lord wills. I have struggled a great deal in my life, and am tired, bruised, and broken from it; but I will see—I shall see—this triumph. I shall not die before the victory of my country."

II.

The landing of the Allies at Salonika, which began on 5th October, was completed in three days, largely by the assistance of M. Diamantidis, the Greek Minister of Transport, whose co-operation was the last administrative act of M. Venizelos's Government. The French 2nd Division from Cape Helles arrived first, and encamped a mile and a half from the town. Then came the British, Sir Bryan Mahon's 10th (Irish) Division from Suvla. General Sarrail arrived on the 12th; but at this time the command at Salonika was not unified, the British and French forces being under their own generals. The French were the first-comers, and, apparently, the most ready for the field, so without delay they were moved up country. The aim of Sarrail was to make contact with the Serbian force in the Uskub neighbourhood before the Bulgarians completely outflanked and isolated it on the south. For this purpose he must secure the railway, if possible, as far as Veles. The line, a single grass-grown track which followed the windings of the Vardar, showed one point of especial danger. Ninety miles from Salonika, north of Strumnitza station, the Vardar flowed through a narrow gorge, called Demir Kapu, or the Iron Gate. At the mouth of the pass the railway crossed to the left bank of the river, and followed it on that side through the ravine, returning to the right bank where the valley widened out beyond the narrows. The Iron Gate thus involved two bridges, a tunnel a hundred yards long, and ten miles where there was no space to spare between the river, the railway, and the precipitous walls. If the Bulgarians seized this point all access from the south into central Macedonia was barred.

Bulgarian raiders had early in the month cut the railway at Strumnitza station, which was six miles from the frontier, and about twenty-five from the Bulgarian town of that name. On 19th October the French advanced guards reached the place, and drove out the enemy. Four days later, on 23rd October, the rest of the division began to arrive, and detachments were ferried across the swollen Vardar, and seized positions on the left bank. On 27th October the French occupied Krivolak without difficulty, and pushed posts farther up the line towards Gradsko. Sarrail now held a position from north of Krivolak to south of Strumnitza station, while the British 10th Division extended on the French right to Lake Doiran, to guard the flank against a Bulgarian attack from the Struma valley.

Across the Vardar from Krivolak rose a steep wall of mountain, called Kara Hodjali. The height commanded this whole section of the valley, and its possession by the enemy would make the railway useless. Accordingly it was resolved at all costs to occupy it at once. The Vardar was in roaring flood; there were no bridges, there was no time to get up pontoons; but there was an old ferry-boat by which with much labour a French detachment was ferried over. The enemy on the heights was only advanced guards, and without much trouble the French scaled the steeps and established themselves on the summit. Two days later the Bulgarians, recognizing the value of the point they had lost, attacked in force, and were only beaten off after a fight with grenades at close quarters. On 4th and 5th November they again attacked, but the position proved too strong, and they were reduced to entrenching themselves over against the French on the flat crest.

While the command of the Krivolak-Strumnitza section of the valley was being secured, the French had turned to the main object of their advance. Veles and Uskub were now held by the enemy, and he was pushing northwards over the Katchanik Pass, and southwards against the Serbians, who at the Babuna Pass guarded the road to Monastir. The Babuna Pass lies twenty-five miles due west of Krivolak, and the country between is rugged and difficult. The only road is one which runs from Krivolak to Prilep, by Negotin and Kavadar. The Tcherna, or Black River, deep and strong, which joins the Vardar between Gradsko and Krivolak, was spanned by a wooden bridge at Vozartzi, and a few miles farther on a similar bridge crossed the Rajetz torrent. North of the Rajetz, between it and the Babuna Pass, is a wild tangle of mountains, which rise in the peak called Archangel to a height of nearly 4,000 feet. Early in November, after the first Serbian success at the Babuna had been nullified by the arrival of Bulgarian reinforcements, and the defenders had been driven back to the crest of the pass itself, the French column from Krivolak attempted to join hands with them. On 5th November it carried the Vozartzi bridge, and attempted to escalade the heights. The Serbians at the Babuna were, as the crow flies, only ten miles distant. The French moved ten miles down the left bank of the Tcherna, and then, turning westward, pushed half-way up the slopes of Mount Archangel. But by this time the Bulgarian army was in great strength, and the French had behind them a difficult and precarious line of communication—a crazy wooden bridge, twenty miles of bad road, and a hundred miles of a single-line railway. The first attack failed. Meantime the Serbians had been driven from the Babuna Pass, and all hope of effecting a junction was at an end. The Bulgarians by a turning movement were threatening to cut the French off from the Vozartzi bridge, and pin them against the unfordable Tcherna. The French commander did the only thing possible in the circumstances. He fell back across the Tcherna, and took up a position in what was known as the "entrenched camp of Kavadar," in the triangle bounded by the Tcherna and the Vardar. In addition, he held a bridgehead at Vozartzi, and opposite Krivolak he occupied the heights of Kara Hodjali.

Such was the situation by the end of the second week of November. The Allies were now themselves upon the defensive, in greatly inferior numbers. The triangle of Kavadar was a good position so far as it went, but it had the drawback that its only internal means of transport was the single and very bad Krivolak-Vozartzi road. Moreover, its sole line of communication with the base at Salonika was exposed through a considerable part to the fire of the Bulgarian artillery, and if the enemy chose to advance against it in force he must compel a retreat. It could only be a matter of days till Todorov's II. Army, all Serbian resistance being at an end, turned its attention to enveloping the far-strung Allied front. Once Monastir was taken, the left flank could be easily turned, and the right flank at Lake Doiran reposed on no natural defence against a movement from the Struma. The Allied endeavour had come to nothing. It had brought no shadow of relief to Serbia,[*] and it had found itself in serious strategical difficulties. The task set Sarrail was hopeless from the start, as hopeless as the task before Putnik. Indeed, it may fairly be said that the constant expectation of Allied help had gravely compromised the Serbian resistance. We have seen that the refusal of the British and French Governments to approve of an attack upon

[*] Except in so far as Sarrail's operations delayed the occupation of the Katchanik and Babuna passes, and so permitted the retreat of the Uskub detachment.

Bulgaria meant that the chief Serbian effort was made on the wrong front. The fighting at Katchanik and the Babuna proved the prowess of Putnik's men; but they were never allowed to show it in a major action. Defence and then withdrawal were the order of the day, tactics little suited to the Serbian genius. It is probable that the Bulgarian conquest would have been far longer delayed, and might even have grievously miscarried, if Serbia had been allowed to follow her instincts and had relied upon her own mettle.

The war zone was now narrowed to the southern border of Serbia and the fifty miles of Greek territory between it and the port of Salonika. On 16th November the remnant of the Uskub garrison which had held the Babuna Pass retired on Prilep; on 2nd December they were forced back on Monastir, and evacuated that town on 5th December. To begin with, Monastir was administered by German officers, in order to avoid rousing the jealousy of Greece; but in a few days the farce was dropped, and it was handed over to the Bulgarians. The position of Todorov's armies made it dangerous for Sarrail to remain longer in the camp of Kavadar, and compelled him to retire to the Greek frontier. As early as 27th November the troops holding the bridgehead at Vozartzi, on the left bank of the Tcherna, were withdrawn to the right bank. On the 2nd of December, while a detachment feinted eastward from Kara Hodjali, the French drew in their lines from the Tcherna to the railway, and began their retreat. The passage of the Demir Kapu ravine was not attained without hard fighting. The railway and bridges were destroyed behind them, and by 10th December the French were clear of the gorge and in position along the little river Bojimia, which enters the Vardar from the east. On their right lay the British 10th Division, which had been protecting the right rear of the advance to Kavadar.

Meantime the British had been seriously engaged. They held the ground among the hills west and south of Lake Doiran, with their right crossing the railway which ran from Salonika by Dedeagatch to Adrianople. Todorov struck at them with his left wing, and on 6th December drove them out of their first trenches, and made retreat imperative. Next morning the attack was repeated, and slowly, at the rate of about two miles a day, they were pressed back from Lake Doiran towards the Vardar valley. We exacted a heavy penalty from the attack, and lost ourselves some 1,300 men, as well as eight guns, which in that rugged country

could not be moved in time. The Allies were now disposed from the mouth of the Bojimia south-eastward towards the village of Doiran. There was little time to waste if Sarrail was to avoid having his flanks turned, and by 12th December the French and the British had crossed the Greek frontier. The fourteen miles of the retreat had been completed methodically; transport and stores were got clean away, and no food-stuffs remained in the countryside for the enemy. Railways and roads were wrecked, and the frontier village of Ghevgeli was left in flames. Such a retreat, with casualties which scarcely exceeded 3,000, was a piece of unlooked-for good fortune, since Sarrail had ventured his force into as ugly a strategic country as could be conceived.

The Allies were now in position about thirty miles from the port, on a line running from Karasuli, on the Vardar and on the Nish railway, to Kilindir, on the Salonika–Dedeagatch railway. A branch railway connected the two points, and gave them lateral communication. It was a strong position, since it covered the main routes to Salonika, and could be reinforced at will. There were now in this theatre eight Allied divisions—three French, and the 10th, 22nd, 26th, 27th, and 28th British. Any invasion could be held up long enough to provide for the creation of a new Torres Vedras based on the sea. The enemy had his right wing, the Bulgarian I. Army, from Lake Ochrida through Monastir and along the Greek frontier; Gallwitz's XI. Army—two German and two and a half Bulgarian divisions—held the centre to the north of Lake Doiran, with the Bavarian Alpine Corps in reserve; Todorov with the Bulgarian II. Army lay to the east.

The retreat from Kavadar brought to a head the unsettled problems between Greece and the Allies. M. Skouloudis had succeeded M. Zaimis as Premier, and it was his opinion that any Allied troops which were driven across the Greek frontier must be disarmed and interned. On 23rd November France and Britain presented a Note to Greece, asking for assurances that this should not happen, and guaranteeing that all occupied territory would be restored and an indemnity paid for the use of it. The first Greek reply was vague, and a second Note on the 26th reiterated the demand. Meantime the Allies acted without waiting for an answer, and when the reply came, a fortnight later, it was a compliance. Most of the Greek troops were removed from Salonika, and the whole " zone of manœuvre," together with the roads and railways, was handed over to the Allies. Undoubtedly it was not an easy position for Greece, if she sought a correct neutrality, but it was the inevitable consequence of her acquiescence in the Allied landing. The Bulgarians waited on the frontier, but for the moment did not cross. Greece had announced with a certain voice that she would not permit her ancestral rivals to tread her soil; and caution was enjoined on Bulgaria by Germany, who did not desire at the moment to have a belligerent Greece on her hands.

The Allied statesmen had decided that Salonika should not be relinquished. Though the purpose for which its occupation had been designed had failed, there were insurmountable objections against letting it fall into German hands. It would provide a formidable submarine base in the Eastern Mediterranean. It would give Austria that Ægean port to which her tortuous policy had so long been directed. Accordingly preparations were made at once to defend it, as Verdun had been defended, by far-stretched lines. Salonika was, after Athens and Constantinople, the most famous city of south-eastern Europe. It had been the chief port of the kings of Macedon, and in its vicinity the fate of the Old World had been decided when Antony and Octavian defeated the murderers of Julius. Under the early emperors it was a free city, and the emporium of all the country between the Adriatic and the Marmora—the half-way house between Rome and Byzantium. It had seen many vicissitudes—the massacres by Theodosius, for which he did penance in Milan Cathedral; the sack by Berber pirates in the days of Leo the Wise; the capture by the Normans, with the short-lived rule of Boniface of Montferrat; the Turkish conquest under Murad the First; Venetian rule; the second Turkish dominion, which was destined to endure for centuries; the arrival of the Jews of the Sephardim from Spain, which was the key to its modern history; the inception of the Young Turk movement; the conquest by the Greeks in the Balkan War, and the murder in its streets of the Greek king.

In fortifying such a base it was necessary to find suitable points on the sea to form the flanks of the lines. Salonika lies at the head of the long gulf of the name, and, to prevent a turning movement of the enemy, a large tract of country had to be brought into the defended zone. West of the city is a swampy level extending to the mouth of the unfordable Vardar. Due north is a treeless plain rising to a range of hills, which are continued up the Vardar valley, but farther east sink into flats, where lie the two large lakes Langaza and Beshik. The trough which holds the lakes is continued in a wooded valley to the Gulf of Orphani. The country between the Vardar delta and the gulf was an admirable position for defence. At the Vardar end the deep and wide river with its salt marshes constituted a formidable barrier to envelopment, and any attack from Orphani was made difficult by the mouth of the Struma and the long Tahiros lake. Further, at Seres, at the north end of that lake, a portion of the Greek garrison of Salonika lay, thereby providing an awkward diplomatic obstacle to any Bulgarian attack. No narrower zone could give security. It was necessary to draw the Allied lines from the Vardar to the Gulf of Orphani, a distance of over sixty miles. Such a position included not only the immediate neighbourhood of the port, but the whole three-pronged peninsula of Chalcidice. The preparation of the lines and the communications behind them was pushed on with surprising speed. The now considerable numbers of the Allied troops, and the hosts of refugees which poured ceaselessly into the city, made labour plentiful. The French held the western section from the Vardar mouth to east of the Dedeagatch railway. The coast part of their line did not need to be defended by entrenchments; indeed, in the marshes trenches could not have been dug; the true defence lay in artillery fire. The lines bent back from the Vardar some ten miles above its mouth, and crossed the plain to the low ridges along the Dedeagatch railway. Here the position was very strong; the field of fire was perfect, and immense barbed wire entanglements cloaked all the possible points of attack. The British section included several parallel ridges of hills, and then the long trough of the lakes, which acted as a natural bulwark.

By Christmas Day the defence of Salonika was virtually complete. At the nearest point the lines ran ten miles from the city, following the analogy of Verdun, Dvinsk, and Riga. Castelnau, now chief of the French General Staff, visited the place on 20th December, and approved the plan. Sarrail's position was secure against anything but a repetition of Mackensen's combined October attack, but for a commander-in-chief it was no bed of roses. He had the Greek army on three sides of him, and, since he lay in what was technically neutral territory, he had to bow in many things to Greek authority. In the matter of requisitioning stores and buildings he was perpetually being thwarted. Moreover, he commanded a heterogeneous force, which looked for orders to its own governments as well as to the generalissimo. On 30th December he took one necessary step to ease his position. Salonika was a nest of spies, and the polyglot mob in the poorer quarters of the city offered dangerous material for the agitator to work upon. Accordingly, quietly and methodically, the German, Austrian, Bulgarian, and Turkish consuls and vice-consuls, with their staffs and families, were gathered in, and taken on board a French warship. Search at the various consulates revealed ample warrant for this drastic step. The Austrian consulate in especial was an arsenal of rifles and ammunition, stored for some sinister purpose. The measure was wholly correct and judicious. Military necessities were urgent, and it behoved Sarrail to see that he had no foes in his own household.

III.

The last act in this section of the Balkan campaign was played on the shores of the Adriatic. Early in December Italy had landed the better part of two divisions at Avlona, and, as we have seen, had pushed forward troops to Durazzo. Serbia having fallen, it remained for Austria to overrun the little kingdom of Montenegro, the last of the Balkan allies which still held the field. For this purpose she had her armies in Bosnia and Herzegovina, the troops which had taken Ushitza and were now on the eastern Montenegrin border, and the support of the Bulgarians on the Albanian frontier. By the end of the year the plain of Ipek was in her hands, and the towns of Plevlie and Bielopolie, and she was advancing up the Tara and the Lim, the upper streams of the Drina. More important, Mount Lovtchen, the fortified height up which the road to Cettinje climbs from the fiord of Cattaro, was being resolutely bombarded by warships in the gulf. If Lovtchen fell Cettinje must follow, and with the enemy pressing in from the east the days of the little kingdom were numbered.

Lovtchen fell on January 10, 1916, to an infantry attack supported by ships' fire. It had been held by a few thousand men, lamentably short of food, guns, and munitions. Three days later the Austrians entered Cettinje. The end of the Montenegrin resistance was a sordid tale. King Nicholas had played the part of certain Scottish lairds during the Jacobite risings: he had made interest in both camps, and while he himself was officially on the side of the Western Allies, his sons were in high favour at Vienna. Prince Peter, who was in command at Lovtchen, surrendered after a mere show of resistance. King Nicholas attempted to make a separate peace with Austria, but the terms were harsh, and on 19th January he thought it better to flee the country, announcing that he had resisted to the last The Montenegrin army, honest enough in its purpose, had been fatally compromised by its king, who had prevented it from joining in the Serbian retreat; and presently it was compelled to surrender *en masse*. If the Allies won, Nicholas would return; if the Central Powers, then his son would succeed; in either case he believed that he had secured his dynasty. On 23rd January the Austrians occupied Skutari, on the 25th, San Giovanni di Medua, and moved south against the Italian lines at Durazzo. The Teutonic League had secured a third little country to add to its trophies, and rouse the enthusiasm of those of its subjects who measured success in geographical terms.

Meantime, to guard against possible danger from Rumania and Russia, Austro-German forces had entered Bulgaria, and were watching the Danube line and preparing to resist any landing on the Black Sea coast. Germany was making haste to reap the fruits of her conquest. The Belgrade bridge and the Ottoman railway were being repaired, special rolling-stock was being sent out for the Constantinople journey, and time-tables were published for the through route from Berlin to Bagdad. The Emperor William himself visited Bulgaria in the beginning of the new year. At Nish on January 18, 1916, he hailed his ally as an illustrious War Lord, and praised " the sublime leaves of glory " which he had added to Bulgarian history. The grateful Ferdinand returned the compliment in doubtful Latin, greeting his guest as " *imperator gloriosus*," the redeemer of a stricken people. It was a strange piece of mock-heroic. Times had changed since, two years earlier, one of the official spokesmen of Prussianism had contemptuously dismissed the monarch of Bulgaria as a " hedge-king." The Emperor declared that he could expect no greater honour than to be honorary colonel of a Bulgarian regiment. It was the language of courtesy, but it had an ironical truth. Megalomania makes strange bed-fellows, and the tragedy-king, *grandiosus et gloriosus*, was reduced to hobnob with Pantaloon.

CHAPTER XLII.

GALLIPOLI: THE EVACUATION.
August 21, 1915–January 9, 1916.

Sir Ian Hamilton recalled—Sir Charles Monro's Report—Kitchener's Visit to Gallipoli—The Evacuation of Suvla and Anzac—The Evacuation of Helles—A Miraculous Exploit.

AFTER the second failure at Suvla on 21st August there could b. no question of a renewed offensive, though Sir Julian Byng was on his way out to take over the 9th Corps, and Major-General E. A. Fanshawe and Major-General Stanley Maude to take command of the 11th and 13th Divisions. In a telegram of 17th August Sir Ian Hamilton had declared that the Turks had 110,000 rifles on the peninsula as against his 95,000, and had asked for at least 50,000 men as reinforcements. But by 20th August the September attack in France had been agreed upon, and it was clear that no great number of troops could be sent to Gallipoli till that offensive was over. On 3rd September there came a ray of hope for the French Government, without consulting Joffre, offered t send four divisions for an attempt on the Asiatic side of the Darda nelles. The offer was presently withdrawn, and soon the positio of affairs in the Balkans radically changed the whole outlook. I became necessary to contemplate an expedition to Salonika, an on 21st September Kitchener asked Sir Ian Hamilton what forc he could spare for that area. On the 27th the French Governmen ordered Bailloud to get ready a French division for the purpose and next day Hamilton was instructed to concentrate two of hi divisions for transport to Salonika. This meant the end of th Gallipoli expedition, and the next step must be a withdrawal. On 11th October Hamilton was asked his opinion on this policy, and his reply showed that he regarded the scheme as unthinkable—politically and strategically wrong, and practically impossible. He was accordingly relieved of his command and brought home to report, and Sir Charles Monro, the commander of the Third Army in France, was appointed in his stead.

So ended what may well be ranked as the most tragic chapter of the British chronicle. The Allied policy was again in the melting-pot, and they were back in the position of the end of March, but faced with the results of failure and a far more intricate military problem. The blame—if the word can be fairly used in connection with honest endeavour in so speculative a business as war—lay with the Government which embarked on the scheme without counting the cost, and as the bills fell due were behindhand in their payments. The original scheme of the landing on the peninsula was open to criticism, but it would have succeeded had the necessary reserves been provided in time. Krithia could have been won in May, but as the days passed the Turkish defence was strengthened; soon Krithia did not involve Achi Baba, nor Achi Baba the Pasha Dagh, and what had originally been the keypoints of the citadel soon were no more than outworks. The August failure at Suvla and Anzac was not to be blamed upon the general strategy; it was the kind of disaster which must occur now and then to a nation which has to improvise armies and has no great area of choice among its generals. As for the Commander-in-Chief, while it is easy to find details in his handling of the problem which seem faulty in the light of after events, yet it is hard to point to any single error on his part which can be said to have been an essential cause of unsuccess. His hands were tied from the start, and under monstrous handicaps he fought his losing battle with resource, ardour, and resolution. " Si Pergama dextra defendi possent etiam hac defensa fuissent " might well be the epitaph on a heroic failure.

When a plan has failed and a campaign is brought to a standstill in one terrain it is common sense to try to break it off and employ the troops more fruitfully elsewhere. But it is not always easy to retrace one's steps. We had landed great forces in Gallipoli at a heavy cost; the question was—Could they be withdrawn without a far greater cost? This was obviously a matter for experts, and the experts differed. There were those who believed that to move the Allied forces from the peninsula would involve a higher casualty list than the April landings. There were others who maintained that with the support of the ships' guns only a comparatively small rearguard need be sacrificed. Many argued that to leave Gallipoli would be a fatal blow to our prestige in the East. Some maintained with much force that it was a case of Hobson's choice. Winter was coming, when contrary winds would make the task of supplying the Gallipoli lines extraordinarily difficult. The Turks were about to receive from Germany a great new munitionment, and in that case we must decide between abandoning our positions and being blown out of them. They did not minimize the difficulties of withdrawal, but they insisted upon the greater difficulties of remaining. On the purely military side, it was clear that if we were to fight a campaign in any part of the Balkans, and if speed was the essence of the undertaking, then the only troops which could be put in the field soon were those drawn from Gallipoli. But, on the other hand, it was urged that soldiers who had fought for months in cramped trench battles should not be forthwith used for a manœuvre campaign in an open country. They must be given an interval for rest and reorganization. Finally, there was a natural reluctance to leave the old battle-ground which had cost us so dear. This was especially felt by the Australian corps, who regarded the Gallipoli heights as sacred ground, the burial-place of their friends, which it was a point of honour to withhold from the enemy.

Such were a few of the difficulties to be faced in any decision. On 22nd October Sir Charles Monro left England to take command of the Mediterranean Expeditionary Force.* Monro had won a great reputation in the West, first in command of the 2nd Division, and then of the 1st Corps. He was a soldier somewhat after the Peninsular type, with admirable nerve, great sagacity and judgment, and the gift of inspiring confidence in all who served with him. No better man could have been found for this responsible and thankless task. A few days later Kitchener, at the request of the Cabinet, followed him, to judge for himself on the spot the situation in the Eastern Ægean. The Secretary for War was strongly prejudiced against withdrawal. He feared its effect on Britain's repute in the East; he was loth to relinquish any chance of joining hands with Russia, about whose social condition he alone of Western statesmen at the time had disquieting thoughts. Above all, he saw that a withdrawal from Gallipoli would release great forces for an attack on the Nile Valley. Was not Mackensen's group popularly known in Germany as the 'Army of Egypt'? He toyed with various alternatives, such as the scheme suggested by Commodore Roger Keyes and supported by

* He had two armies under him—the Gallipoli force commanded by Birdwood and the Salonika force commanded by Mahon.

Rear-Admiral Rosslyn Wemyss, who in November succeeded De Robeck, for another attempt to force the straits by ships, and one for a landing near Alexandretta. On 31st October Monro reported decisively in favour of evacuation, and of the three corps commanders, the ablest, Byng, was strongly of the same opinion. Kitchener visited the Gallipoli front, discussed the matter fully with the naval and military chiefs, and on 22nd November telegraphed to the Prime Minister that he considered evacuation inevitable. On 30th November he returned to London, offered his resignation, which was not accepted, and resumed his duties at the War Office.

On 7th December the British Government decided to evacuate the positions at Suvla and Anzac, but to retain Cape Helles. It was not an easy decision. It meant in the view of all concerned a considerable loss, and even those who took the optimistic side put that loss at not less than a division. Sir William Robertson considered the operation feasible, and not necessarily costly; but Sir Ian Hamilton put the certain losses at 50 per cent., and Gouraud at two divisions out of six. Lord Curzon, in two long and able memoranda fortified by much classical learning, drew a melancholy picture of chaos and death. Historical precedents were on the side of the doubters. An embarkation in the face of the enemy had always meant a stiff rearguard fight and many casualties. Corunna was a typical case. There we succeeded well, but in most instances the cost had been far greater. Take, for example, an almost forgotten episode in the Seven Years' War. In 1758 a British expedition attacked St. Malo. The troops disembarked six miles west of the town and tried to cross the Rance to the south of the place. This movement was prevented by the numbers of the enemy, and we fell back on the bay of St. Cast, where we re-embarked after heavy losses. It was the accepted military doctrine that re-embarkation without disaster was only possible after a victorious battle with the enemy, and that even then a considerable price must be paid for getting away. Even the more optimistic staff officers put the loss at 15 per cent., and provision was made at Mudros for 10,000 wounded.

While the Serbian army was in retreat to the Adriatic and the Allies at Salonika were slowly falling back to the coast zone, the campaign at Gallipoli had languished. Neither side had any inducement to a great attack. The Allies had shot their bolt and failed; the Turks were still awaiting the new munitionment which Germany's success in the Balkans had ensured to them. As

November wore on it became apparent that the enemy was getting bigger guns and an ampler supply of shells. New roads were being made, as we learned from prisoners, to facilitate the progress of the Krupp and Skoda monsters, and the six-inch batteries on the Asiatic shore became unpleasantly industrious in the bombardment of the Helles beaches. The Turkish possession of the high ground forming the spine of the peninsula gave excellent observation posts, and in the circumstances it was a miracle that their artillery did so little damage. But any increase in their batteries could not but be viewed by the Allied command with grave disquiet.

The weather of late autumn was mild and equable, but towards the end of November our men had a taste of an Ægean winter storm. On the 27th it rained without ceasing for twelve hours. The trenches became canals, the dug-outs cisterns, and every nullah held a raging torrent. Next day the wind shifted to the north, and there was a spell of bitter frost. This was followed by a snow blizzard, which recalled the worst days of the Crimea. " Frozen, buffeted by wind and sleet, with hardly a possibility of motion to keep the circulation alive, the men endured agonies. Sentries watching through the loopholes in the parapets were found dead at their posts when their turn came to be relieved, frozen solid, their stiff fingers still clutching the rifle in an iron-fast grip, the blackened face still leaning under its sackcloth curtain against the loophole." This weather bore especially hard on the Australian Corps, many of whom had never seen snow before, and who longed now for the dust and heat of the August battles. The force of the storm was felt chiefly at Suvla, where there were over 200 deaths from exposure. Over 10,000 sick were evacuated in the succeeding week as a further consequence.

The gale lasted three days, and was followed by a spell of mild weather which gave us leisure to repair the damage. But the experience was ominous; the Dardanelles winter had scarcely begun, and the worst storms might be looked for in the first months of the new year. Our troops were dependent for every necessary of life and war on seaborne supplies, and it became a question how our ships could keep the water if the gales were frequent. Without the aid of the warships we had no real answer to the Turkish bombardment, and without the transports and cargo-boats we should certainly starve. The publication of the Gallipoli casualties up to 11th December enabled the world to judge of the cost of the enterprise. In seven months over 25,000 officers and men had perished, over 75,000 were wounded, and over 12,000 missing—casualties nearly twice the number of the force which landed on 25th April. Sickness had been rife, and over 96,000 cases had been admitted to hospital. The chief causes were dysentery and para-typhoid, and the prevalent type of the former was one which demanded careful nursing and a long convalescence if it were not permanently to impair the constitution. A strange shadow had come to brood over the peninsula. "Everywhere," Mr. Masefield has written, "there was gaiety and courage and devoted brotherhood; but there was another thing, which brooded over all and struck right home to the heart. It was a tragical feeling, a taint or flavour in the mind, such as men often feel in hospital when many are dying, the sense that Death was at work there, that Death lived there, that Death wandered up and down there and fed on life."

On 8th December Sir Charles Monro issued orders for the evacuation of Suvla and Anzac. The difficulty of the problem was that it must be lengthy and must be piecemeal. It was not a question of shipping a division or two, but three army corps; it was impossible to move them all at once with our existing transports; there must be a gap between the operations, and this meant that of the later movements the enemy would be abundantly forewarned. Moreover, a protracted embarkation put us terribly at the mercy of the winter weather. Even a mild wind from the south or south-west raised such a ground-swell as to make communication with the beaches precarious. The problem fell into three parts: Suvla, Anzac, and Cape Helles. From Suvla the 10th Division had already gone to Salonika, as well as one French division from Cape Helles, and the 2nd Mounted Division had left for Egypt. But in each zone there remained a matter of three or more divisions to be moved. The whole thing was a gigantic gamble with fate, but every precaution was taken to lessen the odds. The plan, which was mainly the work of General Birdwood, was to remove the *matériel*, including the heavy guns, by instalments during a period of ten days, working only at night. A large portion of the troops would also be got off during these days, certain picked battalions being left to the last. New lines of trenches would be constructed to cover the embarkation points in case a rearguard action became necessary. Everything must be kept normal during the daylight—the usual artillery shelling and spurts of rifle-fire. Every morning before daybreak steps must be taken to hide the results of the night work. Any guns brought nearer the shore must be covered up so as to be unrecognizable by an enemy airplane. Success depended upon two things mainly—fine weather and secrecy. The first was the gift of the gods, and the second was attained by sheer bluff. It was a marvellous achievement, considering that every man in the British force had been talking for three weeks about the coming "rest camp." Its success may have been due partly to the curious apathy which at the moment had seized the Turks and made them disinclined for the offensive. The new big howitzers were arriving and settling down on their concrete emplacements; Enver proposed to wait till these could be used to blow the British off the peninsula. Unfortunately for him these pledges of German friendship arrived too late for the fair.

Before the end of November the battalions holding the firing lines were conscious of great nocturnal activity in their rear. Stores which had been accumulated at advanced bases were shifted nearer the coast, and at Suvla, especially on the two flanks, trenches and entanglements were being created which seemed irrelevant to any military purpose. From 8th December onward our men, night after night, watched the shrinking of their numbers. There was a generous rivalry as to who should stay to the last —a proof of spirit when we remember that every man believed that the rearguard was doomed to death or capture. Presently only those in the prime of physical strength were left; all the weak and sickly had gone to the transports, which nightly stole in and out the moonlit bays. Soon it became clear that the heavy batteries had also gone. To the ordinary observer in daylight they still appeared to be in position, but the guns in the emplacements were bogus. Then the field guns began to disappear, leaving only a sufficiency to keep up the daily pretence of bombardment. It was an eerie business for the last battalions as they heard their protecting guns rumbling shorewards in the darkness. The hospitals were all evacuated, and their stores moved to the beach. New breakwaters had been built there, and all night long there was a continuous procession of lighters and motor boats. Soon the horses and motor cars were also shipped, and by Friday, 17th December, very few guns were left. To the Turkish observers the piles of boxes on the beaches looked as if fresh supports had been landed, and we were preparing to hold the place indefinitely. These beaches were shelled all day, principally by the heavy howitzers behind the Anafarta ridge. But at night, fortunately for us, the shelling ceased.

SUNDAY, 19TH DECEMBER.

The weather was warm and clement, with light moist winds and a low-hanging screen of cloud. Coming in the midst of an Ægean winter it seemed to our men a direct interposition of Providence. It was like the land beyond the North Wind which Elizabethan mariners believed in, where he who pierced the outer crust of the Polar snows found a country of roses and eternal summer. No fisherman ever studied the weather signs more anxiously than did the British commanders during these days. Hearts sank when the wind looked like moving to the west. But the weather held, and, when the days consecrated to the final effort arrived, the wind was still favourable, the skies were clear, and the moon was approaching its full. Nature had joined the wild conspiracy.

On Saturday, 18th December, only picked battalions held the Suvla front. The final embarkation had been fixed for the two succeeding nights, and it was believed that if the first night was successful the whole enterprise would go through. Evening fell in a perfect calm. The sea was as still as a quarry-hole, and scarcely a breath of wind blew in the sky. Moreover, a light blue mist clothed all the plain of Suvla, and made a screen against the enemy observers, while a haze also shrouded the moon. At 6 p.m. the crews of the warships went to action stations, and in the darkness the transports stole into the bay. Not a shot was fired. In dead quiet, showing no lights, the transports moved in and out. Every unit found its proper place. By 1 a.m. on the morning of Sunday, the 19th, the bay lay empty in the moonlight.

That Sunday was one of the most curious in the war. Our lines lay to all appearance as they had been for the past four months, but they were only a blind. We kept up our usual fire, and received the Turkish answer, but had any body of the enemy chosen to attack they would have found the trenches held by a handful. There were 20,000 Turks on the Suvla and Anzac fronts, and 60,000 in immediate reserve. Had they known it, they had before them the grand opportunity of the campaign. But our warships plastered their front and they "watered" our routes of transport as methodically as they had done since the August battles. Lala Baba came in for a heavy bombardment, but there was no longer a gun on the little hill. An attack by our troops at Helles on that day distracted the enemy's mind from their immediate opponents. Night fell with the same halcyon weather. The transports—destroyers, trawlers, picket boats, every kind of craft—slipped once again into the bay, and before midnight the last guns had been got on board. At 1.30 a.m. on Monday morning the final embarkation of the troops began. Platoon by platoon they filed in perfect order down the communication trenches, a detachment occupying one of the new defensive positions till the other had passed. Strange receptions were provided for the first enemy who should enter the deserted trenches in the way of mines and traps and automatic bomb-throwers. There were messages left, too, congratulating "Johnnie Turk" on being a gallant fighter, and expressing hopes that we might meet him again under happier conditions. By 3.30 the last of the troops were on the beach, and long before the dawn broke all were aboard. One man had been hit by a bullet in the thigh: that was the only casualty.

The operations at Anzac were conducted on the same lines. The beaches at Suvla were five miles or so from the enemy, and open to his observation. At Anzac they were less than two miles in places, but concealed from view under the steep seaward bluffs. But the intricate Anzac lines, and the exceeding precariousness of many of the positions, made the movement of guns and troops far more difficult. Some of our gun positions there were on dizzy heights, down which a gun could only be brought part by part. This work was brilliantly performed. Half the guns and half the men of the New Zealand batteries disappeared in a single night. As at Suvla, only picked battalions were left to the end, and there was desperate rivalry as to who should be chosen to act as rearguard. On the Saturday night three-fifths of the entire force were got on board the transports. On Sunday night the rest left, with two men wounded as the total casualties. By 5.30 a.m. on Monday morning the last transports moved from the coast, leaving the warships to follow.

Then on the twelve miles of beach from Suvla Burnu to Gaba Tepe began one of the strangest spectacles of the campaign. All the pieces but four 18-pounders, two old 5-inch howitzers, one 4.7 naval gun, one anti-aircraft and two 3-pounder Hotchkiss guns had been removed, and these were rendered useless;* ammunition and the more valuable stores had been cleared, but there was a quantity of supplies, chiefly bully-beef, which was not worth the risk of human life. These were piled in great heaps on the shores and drenched with petrol. Before the last men left parties of Royal Engineers set them on fire. About 4 a.m. on the Monday morning the bonfires began, blazing most fiercely near Suvla

* These were at Anzac; every gun, vehicle, and animal was got away from Suvla.

Point. The Australians at Anzac about 3.30 had exploded a big mine on Russell's Top, and this called forth from the Turks an hour's rifle fire. As the beach fires blazed up the enemy, thinking that some disaster had befallen us, shelled the place to prevent our extinguishing the flames. The warships shelled back, and all along that broken coast great pharoses flamed to heaven, like giant beacon-fires in some strife of the Immortals. At 4.30 a.m. a motor lighter at Suvla, which had been wrecked some weeks before, was blown up, and added to the glare. Watchers on the Bulgarian coast, looking seaward, saw the peninsula wrapped in flames, as if its stony hills had become volcanoes vomiting fire. It was not till dawn that the Turkish guns ceased. Even then they did not know what had happened. They shelled the bonfires still blazing in the bright sunrise; they searched the solitudes of Lala Baba and Chocolate Hill with high explosives, and the British warships fired a final volley. Picket boats at Anzac and Suvla up to eight o'clock were still collecting a few stragglers from the beaches. By 9 a.m. it was all over, and the last warship steamed away from a coast which had been the grave of so many high hopes and gallant men.

We were just in time. That night the weather broke, and a furious gale blew from the south, which would have made all embarkation impossible. Rain fell in sheets and quenched the fires, and soon every trench at Suvla and Anzac was a torrent. Great seas washed away the landing-stages. The puzzled enemy sat still and waited. He saw that we had gone, but he distrusted the evidence of his eyes. History does not tell what fate befell the first Turks who penetrated our empty trenches, what heel first tried conclusions with the hidden mines, or with what feelings they viewed the parting Australian message left on Walker's Ridge—a gramophone with the disc set to " The Turkish Patrol."

The success, the amazing success, of the Suvla and Anzac evacuations made the position at Cape Helles the more difficult. Few observers in the West believed that there was any chance of a similar operation there. At the most they looked to see a new Torres Vedras fortified at the butt-end of the peninsula, where, with the help of the ships, the enemy might be held off till the situation cleared. It was true that Helles was ill placed for such a policy. It was too well commanded by the heights on the European and Asian shores, and it was doubtful how the Torres Vedras plan would work in the face of the big Austro-German howitzers, of which the departing Australians at Anzac had seen the first shots. But there seemed no other way. The first bluff had worked to admiration; but it is of the nature of bluff that it can scarcely be repeated against the same opponent. Moreover, the Turkish aerial reconnaissance had now become active over all our positions. Sunday, 19th December, the second last day of the Suvla and Anzac embarkation, saw a covering attack of the troops at Helles. At two in the afternoon the ships opened a bombardment of the enemy's front, which was soon taken up by all the land batteries, including those of the French, which had remained after most of their infantry had been withdrawn. Under this cover a brigade attacked up the Krithia nullah, and with some 250 casualties won 200 yards of trench, and left the Turks with an awkward salient to defend. After that came the storm, and then another spell of fine weather. The Turks did not press their advantage, though they now outnumbered the British by more than three to one. They did not occupy the old Anzac lines, and men from Cape Helles made excursions there, and brought back among other things some welcome cases of champagne. The enemy was still busy getting his new big guns in place, and did not dream that the Suvla and Anzac enterprise could be repeated.

On 20th December Monro telegraphed to Kitchener urging the evacuation of Helles, and on the 27th the Cabinet accepted his view, in which the naval authorities had now come to share. Towards the close of the month, in the first quarter of the new moon, guns and supplies and supernumerary troops were brought down to the beaches and quickly embarked. The French used S beach and the British used the famous landing-places of April. The French troops under General Brulard were now reduced to 4,000 men, and all except the gunners were embarked on the first night of January. On the last three days of the year the 52nd Division made a demonstration, and during the first days of 1916 there was a good deal of artillery fire along our depleted front. As at Suvla and Anzac, two nights had been allotted to the final evacuation, those of 7th and 8th January. New positions covering the landing-places were prepared, and an embarkation zone was created under the general commanding the 52nd Division, Major-General the Hon. H. A. Lawrence, who, having begun the war as a brigade-major of yeomanry, was to end it as Haig's Chief of Staff. There was no time to be lost, for all must be finished before the moon reached the full and while the fine weather held. An interesting device was used to mislead the Turk, who was, of course, on the lookout for an attempt at withdrawal. Our trenches would be perfectly silent for a day or two, but when the enemy made a reconnaissance they woke to aggressive life. The intention was to implant firmly in the Turkish mind the notion that quiet on our side did not mean that we had gone, in order that the real silence after the withdrawal might for a time pass undetected.

On Friday, 7th January, it looked for a moment as if a general action would have to be fought by way of farewell, a necessity which would have wrecked our carefully laid plans. From 1.30 to 3 o'clock in the afternoon all the front-line trenches held by the 13th and Royal Naval Divisions were continuously shelled, and the Turks opened a heavy musketry fire. At 4 they sprang two mines, and their parapets were manned with bayonets. But the infantry attack miscarried; only at one point did a charge come; and then a battalion of the Staffords beat back the enemy. Our losses were six officers and 158 men—casualties which had nothing to do with the evacuation proper.

Next day, Saturday the 8th, was calm and fine, the enemy was quiet, and all seemed in train for the final effort. But about four in the afternoon the weather changed. A strong south-westerly wind blew, which by 11 p.m. had increased to thirty-five miles an hour. This storm covered our retirement so far as the enemy was concerned, but it all but made it impossible. Hitherto, for example, our troops had been embarked in destroyers alongside the sunken ships at W beach, but the seas washed away the connecting piers, and lighters had to be used. At one beach, which felt the full force of the wind, shipment was impracticable, and the troops directed there had to march on to W beach. In one sense the weather was a blessing in disguise. An enemy submarine had been reported off Cape Helles at 9 p.m., but the seas made its efforts futile. By 2.30 a.m. on the morning of 9th January V and W beaches had been cleared, and by 3.30 the last troops were on board.

The Turks all night gave no sign. But when the transports had moved off, the stores left behind were fired simultaneously by time fuses. Instantly red lights burned along the enemy lines, and heavy shelling began on the beaches and our empty support trenches. Till sunrise the red lights burned and the bombardment continued. When the enemy learned the truth he made the best of the business, and proudly announced to the world that he had driven us from Sedd-el-Bahr, and that no Ally was left in the peninsula. He added that the retreat had been attended with

desperate losses, and that he had made great captures of guns.*
The claim was untrue. We blew up and left behind the ruins of
seventeen old worn-out pieces. Our total casualties amounted to
one man wounded.

The evacuation of Gallipoli was a triumph of staff work,
and of co-operation between the Army and the Fleet. To Sir
Charles Monro, to Generals Birdwood, Byng, and Davies, to
Admiral Wemyss, and not less to the divisional, brigade, and
battalion commanders, the highest praise is due for an achievement which, in the words of the Prime Minister, was " without
parallel in military or naval history." Nor must we forget the
splendid discipline and stamina of their men. The news was
received in France and Britain with incredulity, which speedily
changed to profound relief. To be sure, there was something
shamefaced in our pride. We were celebrating a failure and a
retreat. The gallantry of the wonderful April landings, the long
struggle for Krithia, the heroic Australasian attack on Sari Bair
had gone for nothing. We had spilled blood like water to win a
mile or two of land, and now we had relinquished all. Fifty
thousand Allied graves with their rude crosses passed under the
sway of the Crescent. But these melancholy reflections properly
belonged to the subject of the original Gallipoli adventure. Having
failed, we had succeeded in escaping the worst costs of failure.
We had brought off three army corps to be refitted and reorganized
for use in more hopeful theatres. We had defeated the calculations
of the enemy. We had stultified our pessimists and amazed even
the most optimistic. To frustrate the consequences of a disaster
is, as a military operation, usually more difficult than to win a
victory. There is less chance of the spirit of the offensive, for it
is a proof of the generosity of the human spirit that safety is less of
an incentive to effort than the hope of victory. A retreat, on the
confession of the greatest soldiers, is the most difficult task which
a general can be called on to undertake. The evacuation of
Gallipoli, in point of pure technical skill and soldierly resolution,
deserves to rank in the story of the campaigns with the retirement of Russia from the Vistula to the Dvina, and with that

* This story was repeated in the foolish production, *Der Kampf um den Orient*, by
one of Liman's staff officers. Liman himself considered the evacuation a remarkable
achievement (Callwell, *op. cit*, App. IV.), and this has been in general the view of German critics—cf. *Vossische Zeitung*, Jan. 21, 1916: " So long as wars exist, the British
evacuation of the Ari Burnu and Anafarta fronts will stand before the eyes of all
strategists of retreat as a hitherto quite unattained enterprise."

fateful retreat two years later on the Somme which was the prelude to victory.

We had upset all precedents. The impossible had been achieved by a series of incalculable chances. But for the two spells of fine weather and the unexplained preoccupation of the enemy the odds would have been crushingly against us. It is true that without a perfect organization and discipline we should not have been able to take advantage of our good fortune, but no human merit would have availed had the fates been unkind. It was an instructive lesson in the folly of dogmatism. In the spring of 1915 our ships had attempted to beat down the forts of the Dardanelles without the assistance of a land army. That effort failed, and it was condemned as contrary to all the lessons of history. The criticism was just; but those who claimed that precedents were not the whole of war were also justified. For in the evacuation of Gallipoli we saw an enterprise as flagrantly heterodox succeed. The "sporting chance" is not as a rule a desirable obsession for any commander. It is his business to use the accumulated experience of his predecessors, and to follow soberly the path of common prudence. But if some great end is to be won or some great misfortune avoided, there may come a day when it is his duty to defy precedents. For it should never be forgotten that the last hope, the desperate remedy, and the outside chance may win.

Across the ribbon of the Dardanelles, on the green plain of Troy, the most famous of the wars of the ancient world had been fought. The European shores had now become a no less classic ground of arms. If the banks of Scamander had seen men strive desperately with fate, so had the slopes of Achi Baba and the loud beaches of Helles. Had the fashion endured of linking the strife of mankind with the gods, what strange myth would not have sprung from the rescue of the British troops in the teeth of winter gales and uncertain seas! It would have been rumoured, as at Troy, that Poseidon had done battle for his children.

CHAPTER XLIII.

MESOPOTAMIA: THE BAGDAD EXPEDITION.

October 21-December 3, 1915.

The Turkish Massacres in Armenia—Trouble in Persia—The Question of an Advance to Bagdad—The Chief Responsibility for it—Townshend reaches Laj—The Battle of Ctesiphon—The Retreat to Kut.

MACKENSEN'S easy conquest of Serbia, the exhaustion of the Russian armies, and Britain's failure in Gallipoli, together with the ebbing of the Western offensive, may be said to mark the zenith of Germany's success in the campaign. She was now free to give her serious attention to that strategy in the Near and Middle East, of which the political consequences were very close to the heart of her statesmen. It was her task to clear and delimit the corridor which would unite under her sway Middle Europe with the Persian Gulf and even with her African possessions, and give her a land empire self-sustaining and unassailable by any sea-power. Her aim was simple and luminous, and her methods precisely calculated. She had freed Turkey from the menace of the West, and would soon be able to clear the eastern and southern Turkish borders of the enemy. But while that political purpose was never forgotten, the immediate duty was to use her favourable position to embarrass the strategy of the Allies.

The first business was Russia, whose Transcaucasian front was now in the charge of the Grand Duke Nicholas. The main armies of Alexeiev had been fought to a standstill, but it was imperative that Russia should not be permitted to use any other force to cripple Bulgaria by a landing on her flank or rear on the Black Sea coast, or to mass troops in Bessarabia which might bring in Rumania on the side of the Allies. Throughout the summer of 1915 there had been various minor battles, in especial a brilliant action in the beginning of May at Dilman, north-west of Lake

Urmia, and inside the borders of the Persian province of Azerbaijan, which Russia had been compelled to occupy. The better part of the 12th (Mosul) Corps, under Halil, attacked a weak Russian force, and after two days' heroic resistance on the Russian side the Turkish ammunition gave out, and Halil retired across the frontier with considerable losses. He was again in action later, and succeeded in reducing his army to a quarter of its strength. The battle of Dilman was opportune, for it prevented the Turks in Mesopotamia receiving reinforcements which might have checked the British advance, and turned the tide at Kut five months later.

The Turkish military failure on the Transcaucasian border was followed by one of the most wholesale and cold-blooded massacres in the distracted history of Armenia. That unhappy race, industrious and pacific, had long been the whipping-boy on which Constantinople had taken revenge for its defeats and fears. In the two years between 1895 and 1897 Abdul Hamid had destroyed little less than half a million. In 1909, the Young Turks, not to be outdone in this honourable activity, had instituted the Adana massacres. The atrocities which filled the first eight months of 1915 were carefully organized, and represented the fulfilment of a long-cherished policy. Their instigators were Enver and Talaat, ably seconded by other members of the Committee of Union and Progress. Now that Turkey was at war with the West, she need listen to no more pratings about humanity, what the Grand Vizier described as "nonsense about Armenian reforms." She could make a manly effort to extirpate a race she had always detested. She was in alliance with Germany, who had shown by her doings in Belgium that she possessed a robust conscience. Talaat was perfectly frank. "I am taking the necessary steps," he told the American Ambassador at Constantinople, "to make it impossible for the Armenians ever to utter the word autonomy during the next fifty years." He was as good as his word. In the early spring the irregular bands round Bayazid and Erzerum and on the Persian frontier slaughtered mercilessly, and drove the miserable remnants into Russian territory. From April onward the whole of eastern Anatolia, from Trebizond to Alexandretta, was the scene of systematic massacres. In a history such as this it is needless to dwell on a tale of horror which had no military significance, but a few instances will reveal the Turkish methods. At Angora, Bitlis, Mush, Diarbekr, at Trebizond and Van, at Urfa, even at distant Mosul, many thousands were butchered like sheep, partly by the gendarmerie, and partly by the mob. Women were violated, and they and their children sold to Turkish harems and houses of ill-fame. Hundreds of wretched creatures were driven into the deserts and mountains to perish miserably of starvation. In Urfa, where were interned many of the Allied residents arrested in Syria, we had the evidence of Occidental eyes for the most unheard-of barbarities. Talaat did not spare even the Armenian supporters of the Young Turk party. Aghmani, the leader of the Dashnakists, Haladjian, the ex-Minister of Public Works, the Deputies Vartkes and Zohrab, all disappeared, and though only Zohrab's fate can be traced, there was little doubt that they were put to death. Not always was the attack unresisted. Ten thousand Armenians were serving as volunteers with the Russian Army of the Caucasus, and they gave a good account of themselves at Van. At Shebin Karahissar, near Trebizond, 4,000 Armenians held back the Turkish troops for a fortnight, till reinforcements reached the enemy and all were put to the sword. The same thing happened west of Lake Van, where 15,000 Armenians banded together, and held out on the mountain tops. Near Antioch many of the Cilician Armenians withdrew to the hills, and made good their defence till they were rescued by a French cruiser. For the rest, about a quarter of a million refugees found haven in the Russian Caucasus, a few reached Bulgaria, and in one or two places the humanity of the local authorities gave them protection. But it was estimated that well over half a million perished, and great numbers of women and children were sold into slavery.

The protesting voices were few and ineffective. The Sheikh-ul-Islam resigned, and Ahmed Riza and Djavid declared their disagreement when it was too late. Only the Vali of Smyrna refused to be party to the crimes, and carried out his refusal by protecting the Armenians in his province. The Pope made remonstrances through the Latin Patriarch. The American Ambassador in Constantinople did his best, but his Austro-German colleagues declined to join him, declaring that they could not interfere in the internal affairs of Turkey, though they made a half-hearted protest, and asked the Grand Vizier for a written guarantee that they had had no connection with the massacres. Enver declared that his own experience as a revolutionary made him fear the revolutionary capacities of the Armenians. Talaat boasted that he had done more towards solving the Armenian problem in three weeks than Abdul Hamid had done in thirty years. Almost the last official act of the German Ambassador Wangenheim, who died in October of apoplexy, was a refusal to intervene; German publicists, like Naumann, supported this apathy as an unhappy necessity; and Turkey defended her policy on the ground that Armenians were rebels who deserved all they had received.*

The Turco-German pupils of Abdul Hamid were busy in another quarter In northern Persia they and their agents were carrying on what can only be described as a campaign of assassination. With wholesale bribery they tried to corrupt the Gendarmerie and the Persian officials. The strange spectacle was seen of the stout and elderly diplomatists of Turkey and Germany hurried about the land in the company of the sweepings of two nations. The German Minister, Prince Reuss XXXI., had won over to his side many of the Persian Ministers, a number of the local tribes, and the 6,000 men of the Gendarmerie, officered by Swedes, which had been established by Russia and Britain to police the country. There were numerous local risings, and the British civilians at Yezd and Shiraz were made prisoners. In the capital, Teheran, things presently rose to the pitch of crisis. In the second week of November a detachment of the Russian Army of the Caucasus moved upon that city. The German, Austrian, and Turkish *corps diplomatique* left on 14th November for the village of Shah Abdul Azim, on the Ispahan road, and strenuous efforts were made to induce the Shah to accompany them, and so put himself into German hands. Prince Firman Firma and one or two of his advisers resisted the proposal, and after much wavering the boy-king resolved to remain. It was a difficult decision, for he had no troops to rely on against the Gendarmerie and the Turkish irregulars, except the Persian Cossack Brigade, which remained true to its salt. Prince Reuss now showed his hand. He raised the standard of revolt, and with the 6,000 men of the Gendarmerie, a number of tribesmen, and at least 3,000 Turkish irregulars from Mesopotamia endeavoured to hold the key points, which would allow him to keep in touch with his friends on the Tigris. One was Kum, eighty miles south of Teheran, on the Ispahan road, which, being a telegraph junction, tapped all the communications with southern Persia. The other was Hamadan, near the ancient Ecbatana, two hundred miles from Teheran, on the Bagdad road. Prince Reuss divided his forces between these two places, and also held the pass which led to Hamadan from the north. By the end of November the Russians were in Teheran. One detachment marched south towards Kum, but

* Morgenthau's *Secrets of the Bosphorus* tells the story of the massacre from the standpoint of the American Ambassador.

the main force was at Kasvin, moving on Hamadan. On 9th December the rebels were routed at the Sultan Bulak Pass and forced back upon Hamadan. On the 11th Hamadan submitted, and on 17th December the Russians were pursuing the enemy through the mountains towards Kermanshah. Prince Reuss departed for Kermanshah to take counsel with the emissaries of von der Goltz. On the 25th the Persian Government fell, and Prince Firman Firma, a friend of the Allies, was appointed Premier. For a moment the air was cleared. But all Persia was in a ferment; the rebels who had been driven towards Kermanshah were in touch with the Turkish Army of Mesopotamia, and could call upon reserves which might gravely embarrass the far-flung Russian detachments. Germany had succeeded in one of her purposes. She had kindled a fire in the inflammable Middle East, and she was whistling for a wind to fan it.

These diversions were aimed alike at Russia and Britain. The main preoccupation of the latter was Egypt, to which Kitchener was about to direct the better part of the forces which would be evacuated from Gallipoli. What Bismarck had once called the "neck of the British Empire" invited attack from Germany, now that she was firmly posted at Constantinople with an open road behind her to Central Europe. But the way was long through Anatolia and Syria and across the desert, and the more urgent need was for support to Turkey in Mesopotamia, to stay the triumphant British ascent of the Tigris. German troops, guns, and staff officers were presently on their way from the Bosphorus to Mosul, and the veteran Marshal von der Goltz, who had for months been in Constantinople, was put in general charge of the Mesopotamian operations, a fitting post for one who had been the chief military instructor of modern Turkey. On 24th November he was in Aleppo, and at a banquet given in his honour announced that in the appointment of so old a man to so great a command he recognized the hand of God. "I hope that, with God's help, the sympathy of the Ottoman Empire and the friendliness of the whole people will enable me to achieve success, and that I shall be able to expel the enemy from Turkish soil." The counterstroke for Kut was preparing, and the small British force was about to embark upon a venture which placed it most fatally in the enemy's power.

When, at the end of September, the Turkish defence was broken at Kut, General Townshend was in the position in which many

British generals had found themselves since the days of Elizabeth. He commanded little more than a single division, and was outnumbered by the enemy's forces directly opposed to him, and vastly outnumbered by their potential levies. He was well over three hundred miles from his base on the sea. He had a river for his sole communications, and, after our amphibious fashion, was assisted by armed vessels from the water; but that river was full of shallows and mudbanks. All around him lay a country ill-suited for operations by white troops—sparsely-watered desert and reeking marsh, baked by the hottest of Asian suns, and brooded over by those manifold diseases which heat and desert soil engender. The local tribes were either treacherous or openly hostile, and might at any moment strike at his long, straggling connections with the coast. Before him, a hundred miles off by the short cut across the loop of the Tigris, lay one of the most famous cities of the world. That a little British army, wearied with ten months' incessant fighting, should advance to conquer a mighty province of a still powerful empire might well seem one of the rashest enterprises ever embarked upon by man. It was the war in the Sudan undertaken under far more difficult conditions, for the fall of Bagdad would not mean, like the fall of Khartum, the end of serious resistance, and no Sirdar had planned a Sudan railway to bring supplies and reserves more quickly than the route of the winding river. The Turkish army which had been beaten at Kut could be readily reinforced. The enemy had the Mosul Corps to draw upon; by the Tigris troops could be brought from Kurdistan; and from Damascus and Aleppo, by the caravan routes through the desert, reserves could be sent from the Army of Syria. Turkey had by no means used up all her supplies of men. The fronts in Gallipoli and Transcaucasia were stagnant, and the Allied embarrassments in the Balkans made any immediate pressure there unlikely. The British, on the other hand, could only add to their army by drafts from India or the Western front, a matter of weeks in one case and months in the other; and their river transport was grossly inadequate for any fresh force. In the face of a demoralized enemy a bold dash for the capital might succeed. But the Turks were not demoralized. If they had failed at Kut they had to all intents succeeded at Gallipoli, and by their side stood their German taskmasters to keep them to their business.

Moreover, Bagdad was no easy problem. The Tigris for some miles below the town loops itself into fantastic whorls, which meant that in many parts any land force, whose aim was speed, would be deprived of the co-operation of its flotilla. Again, some twenty miles below the city, the river Diala, entering the main stream on its left bank, provided a strong line of defence. Finally, Bagdad was an open city, and, even if won, would be hard to defend. In truth, it was an impossible halting-place. Once there, for the sake of security we should have been compelled to go on seventy-five miles to Samara, on the Tigris, the terminus of the railway from Bagdad. We should also be obliged to occupy Khanikin, where the Diala crosses the Persian frontier. From Samara it would soon be necessary to advance another hundred miles to Mosul. Indeed, there was no natural end, save exhaustion, to the progress which the need of security would impose on us. There was no attainable point where that security could be assured, for between the Tigris valley and the Russian front in Transcaucasia lay the wild mountains of Kurdistan. And all the while our communications would be lengthening crazily. At Bagdad we should be 573 miles by river from the Gulf, and between 300 and 400 by the shortest land route. We should be hopelessly out of touch with our sea-power. On every ground of strategy and common sense the advance was indefensible.

On the other hand, it was undeniable that the conquest of Bagdad would have great political advantages—if it could be achieved. The Allies were sadly in need of prestige, and its fall would be a make-weight to the German domination at Constantinople. So far, in Mesopotamia, miracles had been performed with a handful of troops, but the names of Kut and Nasiriyeh were not familiar in Europe. Bagdad, however, was known to all the world, and if the old city of the Caliphs fell to British arms, there would be a resounding success wherewith to balance our failure in the Ægean, and our much-tried diplomacy would have something to point to in its painful negotiations with suspicious neutrals. It would cut at their nodal point the principal routes of German communications with Persia and the Indian frontier. But even this success would not be final, for there would remain the great caravan routes of the northern Shammar desert, which followed the projected line of the Bagdad railway to Mosul, and thence to Rowanduz on the Persian frontier. Full success in our objective really demanded the control of the whole of northern Mesopotamia. Such a control might have been won, but it required an adequate force—at least two army corps fully equipped, and not one weary division.

The British Prime Minister, in his speech in the House of Commons on 2nd November, defined the objects of the Mesopotamia Expedition as " to secure the neutrality of the Arabs, to safeguard our interests in the Persian Gulf, to protect the oil-fields, and generally to maintain the authority of our Flag in the East." Of these aims the first may be dismissed as trivial. The Arab tribes of Mesopotamia were a much overrated folk, notable rather for low cunning than for military virtues. Their hostility and their friendship alike were worth little. The third we secured when we held Amara and the desert route to Ahwaz ; the second when we won Basra. The fourth was a vague aspiration which did not involve any specific military operations, but which did demand that we should not get ourselves into an impossible *cul-de-sac*. All the objects defined by Mr. Asquith were, in fact, realized when Townshend took Kut, and, by holding the northern end of the Shatt-el-Hai, prevented the enemy cutting his communications by a flank march. At Kut the extreme purpose of the original expedition was fulfilled. The advance to Bagdad was a new scheme involving a new policy.

The origin of this rash decision may be found in the report of the Mesopotamia Commission,* but from the tangled three-cornered correspondence it is not easy to fix the main responsibility. The Government of India from the start had had in mind an advance to Bagdad, and in March Nixon had been instructed to prepare a plan After Kut he considered that the enemy was broken and in retreat, and that Bagdad could be taken without difficulty. Mr. Austen Chamberlain, now Secretary of State for India, consulted the Viceroy, Lord Hardinge, and the latter's opinion, and that of Sir Beauchamp Duff, the Indian Commander-in-Chief, was against an advance, since no troops could be spared from India. But various members of the British Cabinet were bitten by the project, and on 4th October a special committee was appointed to consider its possibility. The General Staff at the War Office opposed the idea on the ground that, while the place might be taken by a *coup de main*, to hold it was impossible without larger forces and greatly improved transport. This, too, at the moment was the view of Sir Beauchamp Duff and the Viceroy. But the Cabinet pressed the matter, and Nixon gave it as his opinion that to occupy the city permanently he would require an additional division and one cavalry regiment, and a vastly increased river transport. Pressure was brought to bear on the Viceroy and Sir Beauchamp Duff—" We have great need of a striking

* Cd. 8610.

success in the East," the Secretary of State wrote on 21st October —and the Indian authorities consented, provided reinforcements were arranged. By the middle of October the consensus of opinion was that Nixon had a sufficient force to take Bagdad, but that to hold it he would require to be reinforced by at least two divisions. In the beginning of November, accordingly, an advance was ordered, and arrangements were made for reinforcements to be obtained from the Indian divisions then in France.

We are therefore presented with the spectacle of the British Cabinet eagerly desiring an advance on political grounds, Lord Kitchener and Lord Curzon, the two chief authorities on Eastern matters, alone dissenting. The military authorities in India and Britain agree, on the understanding that reinforcements are provided, and these reinforcements are arranged for. But the vital question was when they could arrive, and that depended upon transport; and it is strange that no attempt was made to clear up this matter. After Bagdad fell, any troops from India or Egypt would have to travel 500 miles from Basra to the front, and how was that to be accomplished with any reasonable speed? A telegram from Nixon was misconstrued as if it implied that the transport difficulties were over, but it is hard to see how any reasonable man could have made this interpretation in the face of Nixon's constant requests to India for more transport—requests which had not been fulfilled. On the ability to take Bagdad with the existing forces there was no doubt in Nixon's mind; Townshend, though he had grave misgivings, in substance agreed; and the home authorities naturally took this view as final. Undoubtedly Nixon was too sanguine, even on the information he possessed; for example, preparations were made at the base for the reception of only 500 seriously wounded. But Nixon and Townshend were not in possession of all the facts at the disposal of the Cabinet. They thought that they had only 9,000 Turks before them, who could make no stand before Bagdad; but the Secretary of State had informed the Viceroy on 31st October of a possible concentration of 60,000 Turks at Bagdad by January, and this vital information was never transmitted to Mesopotamia. The whole of the preliminaries to the Bagdad advance were a melancholy example of imperfect consideration and confused thinking due to hustle. The primary fact was that the Cabinet wanted a striking success on political grounds, and were not disposed to inquire too rigorously into details, and this spirit of haste infected also the Government of India. The root question, the chance of transporting the reinforcements rapidly to the fighting front, was never seriously considered. The generals on the spot were not unnaturally confident after their experiences of the summer, but they were not put in possession of facts known to the Home Government, and they were manœuvred into a position where it was very difficult for a soldier to decline the venture. No one of the authorities concerned can be exonerated from blame, but the chief responsibility for the Bagdad advance must rest with the British Cabinet.

In Mesopotamia Nixon had the Indian 12th and 6th Divisions —about 25,000 men. Townshend for the advance had the 6th Division, an extra infantry brigade, and two and a half regiments of cavalry—nominally a total of between 15,000 and 17,000; but he had only some 11,000 effectives, and the whole force was battle-worn and weary. But to cheer them they had a record of unbroken successes, for wherever and in whatever numbers they had found the enemy they had soundly beaten him. Since all the scanty transport was required for the carriage of supplies, the troops must make the hundred-mile journey to Bagdad on foot. In Mesopotamia the autumn days are bright and clear and the nights cool. It is the beginning of that bracing and clement winter which in sub-tropical deserts is the atonement for the arid summers—the best season of the year for an advance. At first there was no opposition, and presently the expedition was at Aziziyeh, half way to the capital. But unpleasant news had arrived—that Nur-ed-Din had concentrated at Laj, and that he had a prepared position at Ctesiphon, with 38 guns and 13,000 men to defend it. On 21st November we dislodged the enemy from Laj, and that evening moved against Ctesiphon. We were now some thirty miles from Bagdad.

At Ctesiphon the Euphrates and the Tigris approach within forty miles of each other. Such a position was obviously well chosen, for the Turks could bring reinforcements down the Euphrates from Aleppo and the Army of Syria. Had we been in sufficient force to send an expedition up that river, we should have won a double line of communications, and been able to adopt an enveloping strategy. But the enemy was perfectly familiar with our numbers, and knew that of such a movement there was no possible danger. Ctesiphon, the old Sassanid capital, had been the battle-ground of Romans and Parthians; but only the massive brick shell of the " Throne of Chosroes," rising above the squalid Turkish village, remained to tell of its former grandeur. Beyond the river lay the ruins of Seleucia, the old capital of the Seleucidæ, for at this point Parthia and Syria had faced each other across the

Tigris. The Turkish first position ran from the angle in the Tigris, with a second line about half a mile in the rear. The whole place had been strongly fortified according to the latest German fashion, and the wastes of old debris furnished admirable shelters for machine guns, of the same type as the redoubts on the Western front. The Turkish right wing was west of the Tigris, but their centre and left, comprising three-fourths of their army, were on the left bank.

On the evening of 21st November Townshend advanced from Laj. His force, as at Kut, was divided into three columns, and the tactical plan was almost the same. One column was to advance against the centre of the first Turkish position. A second column, under Delamain, was to envelop the left of that position; while a third was to make a wide detour, and come in on the left rear of the chief Turkish force, and co-operate with Delamain in driving them back towards the river. Behind the main Turkish position lay the village of Sulman Puk and the ruins of Ctesiphon. On the right flank of the second Turkish position was a bridge of boats across the Tigris, and it was towards this bridge that our right centre and right columns were directed. The cavalry was sent round to the left of the Turkish reserve trenches in order to hinder any retirement. The British troops marched seven miles in the bright moonlight, till they saw before them the ruins of Ctesiphon casting blue shadows on the yellow plain. Before dawn the centre column had dug itself in in front of the main enemy line, Delamain's right centre had done the same on the flank, and the right column had covered ten miles and taken ground well to the left rear of the enemy. The cavalry had wheeled to the northeast, and hung on the flank of the Turkish reserve trenches. Dawn broke, and the enemy was aware of our advent. We could see bodies of Turks moving northward, and our first idea was that they were relinquishing Ctesiphon and falling back on the Diala. The cavalry and the British right promptly attacked the flank of the retreat, which formed in line to meet us, and revealed itself as a force several times our strength. The Turks were now drawn up along two sides of a square, of which the northern side was their reserve trenches, the western the Tigris, the southern their main position, and the eastern the force with which our right and our cavalry were engaged.

About a quarter to nine on the 22nd the great attack began. Our centre moved against the main position, Delamain's right centre attacked at the junction of the eastern and southern sides, and the right and the cavalry assaulted the east side. The last, being greatly outnumbered, at first made no progress. Indeed they lost ground, and Delamain was compelled to detach some of his battalions to support them. At eleven he carried the angle, and about half-past one the centre, with Delamain's assistance, succeeded in piercing the main Turkish front. These successes gave us the first position ; but the Turks, assisted by their eastern flank, which defied our right and our cavalry, were able to retire in good order to their reserve lines. Our success so far had been brilliantly achieved, but there was to be no rout such as had followed the same tactics at Kut. Nur-ed-din had learned his lesson, and the real kernel of his position was the second line. At halfpast two in the afternoon we advanced against this second position. The eastern side of the former square was still intact, and our three columns drew together in an attempt to roll it up. But now we found out the true numbers of the enemy. Another division had joined him, and he counter-attacked with such force that he recovered the guns he had lost, and before evening had driven us back to his old first trenches. Delamain, however, managed to hold the village of Sulman Puk in advance of these lines. Both sides were utterly wearied, and about 11.30 p.m. the battle died away.

Next day fresh reinforcements arrived for the enemy, and all morning the two forces shelled each other. The Turkish attack came at three o'clock in the afternoon, and lasted till long after dark. It was now that they suffered their severest losses. Our men, being well entrenched, beat them back time and again, but all night long there were intermittent assaults. On the 24th they fell back to their second line, and that day was filled with bombardments and counter-bombardments. Our force was badly disorganized, so we spent the day in consolidating our ground, and next day we received by river some much-needed supplies. Our airplanes reported that reinforcements were still reaching the enemy. Townshend could clearly do nothing more. Our casualties were about a third of our force—some 4,500, with 800 killed, and the losses among officers and staff had been specially heavy. We had handled the enemy severely, but his strength was being replenished, and ours was waning. There was nothing for it but to fall back. We had won his first position and encamped on the battlefield, but we were very far from having broken his army.

At midnight on the 25th Townshend marched back to Laj.

The wounded went by river, and reached Kut on the 27th. All the 26th he halted at Laj to rest his men, and that evening retreated twenty-three miles over a villainous road to Aziziyeh. Four days later, on the 30th, he began to get news of the enemy. He had to halt to refloat some of the steamers which had grounded, and next morning he saw the smoke of the Turkish fires around him. The slowness of the enemy's pursuit was a proof of how severely he had suffered at Ctesiphon; for, had he been able to follow the trail at once, the whole British force must have perished. On the morning of 1st December the Turks attacked, but were beaten off with heavy losses, and, taking advantage of a successful counterstroke by the cavalry, Townshend marched on that day twenty miles to Shadi. On 2nd December the vanguard saw the solitary minaret of Kut on the desert skyline, and next day the main body of the force, which a month before had set out with high hopes, staggered into the little town. It had been a memorable feat of arms, but, as serious warfare, no more than a glorious folly.

Four days later, from north and east and west, the enemy closed in, and the siege of Kut had begun. Once again, as in the Nile Campaign, a beleaguered town far up an Eastern river was the centre of the anxious thought of our people.

CHAPTER XLIV.

THE SECOND WINTER IN THE EAST AND WEST.

The Fighting at Riga and Dvinsk—The Russian Attack on Czernovitz—The Aftermath of the Loos and Champagne Battles—The Winter Hardships—Sir John French surrenders his Command—His Qualities and Defects.

I.

GERMANY'S failure to cut off the Vilna salient marked the real end of the great summer offensive. When the German cavalry were flung back from the Polotsk railway, and the Russian right centre retook Vileika and Molodetchna, the immediate danger of a catastrophe in the field was averted. Presently came the offensive of the Russian Southern army, and on its heels the Allied advance in the West; Mackensen was already on the Danube; and consequently Hindenburg had to revise his plans. The old scheme of pushing in two adjacent sections of the enemy's front, creating a salient, and striking at its roots, had to be abandoned. Winter was approaching, and the marshes and forests of eastern Poland did not make for mobility even in the case of an army equipped with every device of modern science.

Hindenburg was compelled to turn his attention to the northern sector, the line of the Dvina from Riga to Dvinsk. The motive as expounded to his troops was to win a vantage-point from which to launch an attack on Petrograd in the spring; but nothing was further from the thoughts of the veteran Field-Marshal. His aim was safety and comparative comfort during the dreary business of the winter campaign. If he could gain the line of the Dvina he would free himself from the medley of bogs and forests in which the German left wing was now entangled. He would have a strong defensive position, which could be held with fewer men. For it was becoming very clear that the trans-

Vistula venture had not been an unmixed success. It had not won a decision, it had involved great losses, and it promised endless troubles unless a front could be obtained which offered some reasonable ease to the holders. The right wing in Galicia was clamouring for reinforcements, the need in the West for more men was already great and might soon become urgent, and the Balkan campaign was a gamble which involved unknown liabilities. Accordingly Hindenburg shifted his attack from his left centre to his left, and pushed against the Dvina—less as part of a calculated offensive than because he could not stay where he was, and Riga and Dvinsk, if they could be mastered, would appreciably improve his position.

At the beginning of October we must regard the German front in the East as made up of strong wings and a very weak centre. The line south of the Pripet was under the general charge of Austria, and was held from left to right by Linsingen's group, which was mainly German; Boehm-Ermolli's group, comprising the Austro-Hungarian IV., I., and II. Armies; Bothmer's Southern Army; and Pflanzer-Baltin's Austro-Hungarian VII. Army. Prince Leopold, with whom was Woyrsch, had the Army of the Centre. The left wing had been adjusted. The German XII. Army, now under Fabeck, lay from the Niemen to beyond the Lida–Molodetchna railway; then came Eichhorn's X. Army; then a group under Scholtz; and then towards the sea the Niemen army, now called the VIII., under Otto von Below.

Riga and Dvinsk as fortresses did not rank high. At the best their strength was far below that of Grodno, or Kovno, or Novo Georgievsk, or Ivangorod, which had crumbled before the German siege trains. The defences of the Dvina line lay in nature, not in art. The first of the Russian advantages was that their right flank rested on the sea. The second lay in the character of the country west of the Dvina. Through Dvinsk ran the great Petrograd line from Vilna by Sventsiany, and at the junction it received the line from Libau by Shavli, and the line from Riga, which followed the right bank of the Dvina. Three main roads also converged at Dvinsk: one from the north following the left bank of the Dvina, one from Novo Alexandrovsk in the south-west, and one from the south through the wide region of lakes and marshes which stretched towards the villages of Vidzy and Drisviaty. These roads and railways were carried on embankments and necks of hard ground through a country which was as generally impassable for guns and troops as the lake district of Masurenland. In the same way

Riga and the line of the Dvina south of it were defended by a tangle of natural difficulties. The river above the city is broad and studded with "matted rushy isles." Numerous small streams strain through the marshes, and enter it on the left bank. As if this were not enough, the considerable river Aa, with its tributaries the Eckau and the Misse, sweeps in a half-moon to the westward, and curls round along the coast till it reaches the Dvina delta, enclosing in its loop the Babit Lake with its reedy shores and three great areas of bogland. Through the middle of the half-moon ran the road and line from Mitau to Riga, and the line from Mitau to Dvinsk gave the attack a lateral railway. But this configuration limited the assault to certain well-defined routes. Riga could only be approached along the coast or by the Mitau line, which made possible an attack upon the river position where Dahlen island cuts the channel in two. Dvinsk must be attacked by one of the three roads leading from Illukst, from Novo Alexandrovsk, or through the lakes from Vidzy. The narrowness of these approaches greatly simplified the problem of the defenders. They knew the route of the enemy. They could not be outflanked. The situation was now different from that of August or September. Russki's Army of the North had to face a direct frontal assault along certain known and definite avenues. Below in August had tried to turn Riga and Dvinsk by cutting the Dvina line at Friedrichstadt. Eichhorn in September had hoped by swinging to the rear of Vilna to make Dvinsk the apex of a salient. Both plans had been foiled. The Russian front in the north was now straightened, and there was no alternative for Hindenburg but to attack in front and batter down the defence by sheer weight of guns and men.

Russki's defence of Dvinsk[*] was like Sarrail's defence of Verdun. He was determined that the great guns should not be brought too near, and he flung his lines west of the town in an arc, of which the radius was not less than twelve miles. The points Schlossberg, Novo Alexandrovsk, and Drisviaty may be taken as defining that sector. The first big attack was made on 25th September. The German airmen dropped bombs on Dvinsk, and the German artillery kept up for hours a hurricane of fire on the advanced Russian trenches. On the front due west some progress was made. After the artillery preparation, assisted by asphyxiating shells, the enemy infantry attacked in mass and pushed along the Novo

[*] The troops in this sector were the Fifth Army under Plehve, who was succeeded in December by Gourko.

Alexandrovsk road to within eight miles of the city. But Hindenburg was held on the more important routes—the road from the north, the railways from Mitau and Vilna, and the great road from the south. He failed to take Schlossberg, he was checked west of Lake Sventen and in the wide marshes beside the Vilna railway, and he was not allowed to approach the narrows between Lakes Drisviaty and Obole, through which ran the southern highroad. On the same day the Riga front was violently bombarded, and an attempt was made to advance along the coast road from Kemmern, between the Aa and the sea. It never had a chance of success. The Russian fleet with their guns swept the ribbon of hard land, and a comparatively small Russian force held the pass in the neighbourhood of Kemmern. This operation, however, must be regarded rather as a reconnaissance than as an action. Germany's main interest was still at Dvinsk.

On 3rd October Below made his next effort. The action may well be called the Battle of the Lakes, for in the Russian front these meres played the part of fortresses, and protected the flanks of the different sections. It was a series of thrusts, now at one point, now at another, supported by a great mass of heavy artillery. The centre, which moved along the Novo Alexandrovsk road, attempted to bring the city under howitzer fire at close range. On the left wing there was a strong thrust at Illukst, which took the ridge of Schlossberg and the ruins of Illukst, but failed to cross the little river of that name which flows to the Dvina. South of the Mitau line there was fighting north of Lake Sventen. On the right, on the line of the Lakes Demmen, Drisviaty, and Obole, there was a heavy artillery battle. The real danger was on the flanks, for if the Germans had been able to push south from Illukst, or north from Drisviaty, the defence would have been at the mercy of a cross fire. These flank attacks failed, and the German advance was confined to the movement along the Novo Alexandrovsk road, where the centre got no nearer the city than the hamlet of Medum, close to the lake of that name, and to an attempt along the Mitau railway. In these operations the German losses were considerable, and by the middle of October the army which had hoped to take Dvinsk in three days was no nearer its goal. Russia had learned the lesson of Verdun, and held Dvinsk with a field army flung far out from the city. Moreover, it was a better munitioned army. Though still short of rifles, it had ample stores of shells for the defence, and could check an attack otherwise than by the breasts of its soldiers. At Dvinsk was seen a portent of infinite encourage-

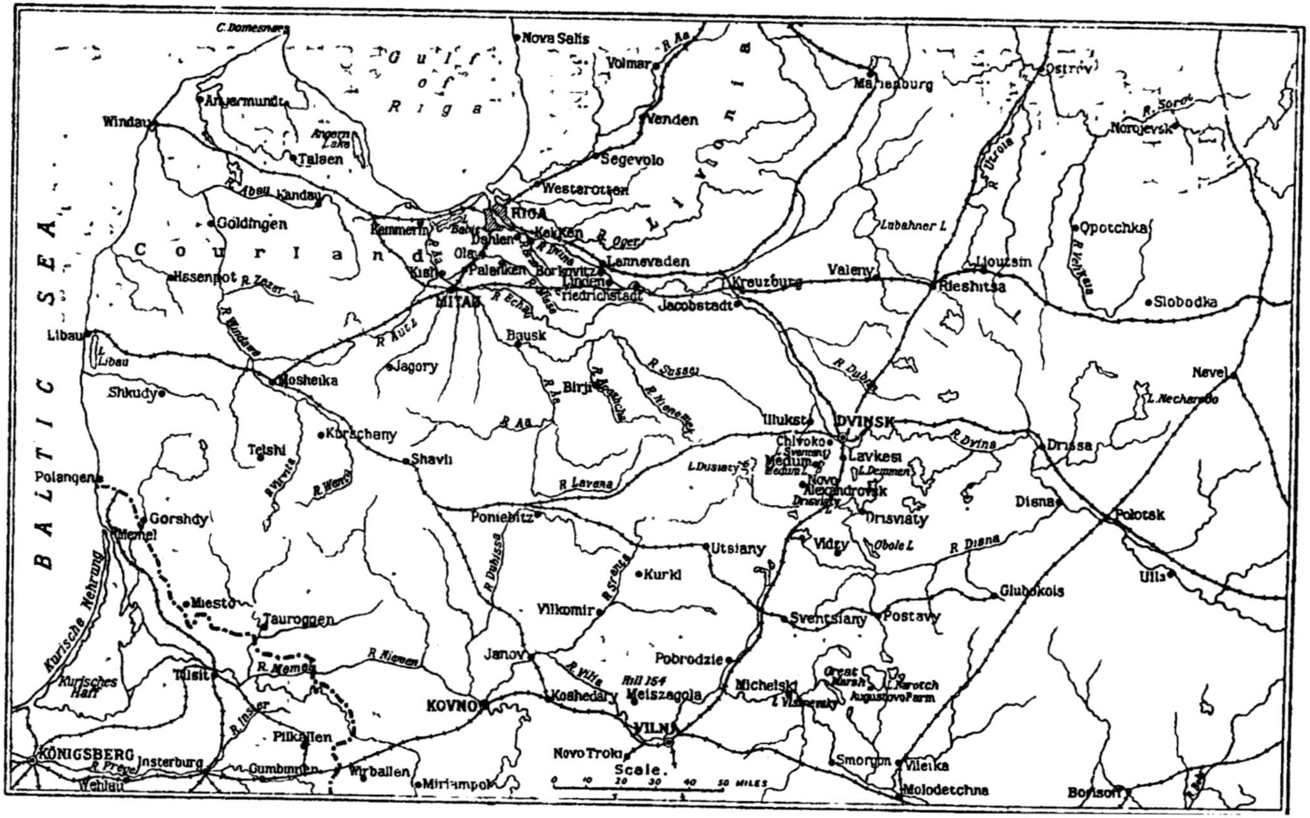
BALTIC SEA
Gulf of Riga
Courland
Livonia
Windau
Talsen
Goldingen
Libau
Shkudy
Polangen
Gorshdy
Memel
Telshi
Mosheika
Jagory
Shavli
MITAU
RIGA
Westerotten
Segevolo
Wenden
Volmar
Nova Salis
Lennevaden
Friedrichstadt
Jacobstadt
Kreuzburg
Bausk
Birji
Valeny
Rieshitsa
Slobodka
Opotchka
Norojevsk
Ostrov
Nevel
Drissa
Polotsk
Disna
Uils
Glubokois
DVINSK
Illukst
Lavkesi
Vidzy
Drisviaty
Utsiany
Kurki
Ponievitz
Vilkomir
Janov
KOVNO
Koshedary
Meiszagola
VILNA
Novo Troki
Pobrodzie
Sventsiany
Postavy
Michelski
Smorgon
Vileika
Molodetchna
Borisoff
KÖNIGSBERG
Insterburg
Wehlau
Tilsit
Pilkallen
Gumbinnen
Wirballen
Miriampol
Miesto
Tauroggen
Kurisches Haff
Kurische Nehrung
R. Niemen
R. Memel
R. Dvina
R. Disna
R. Dubissa
R. Aa
Scale.
0 10 20 30 40 50 MILES

ment for Russia, a thing not seen before in her campaign—German bombardments silenced by Russian guns, and infantry rushes checked and broken by fire alone.

By the third week of October the resistance in the Dvinsk section had convinced Hindenburg that here was no chance of that speedy success he desired. So, according to his custom, he shifted his main attack to another section, and struck hard at Riga. The Russian defence, as we have seen, followed roughly the half-circle of the rivers Aa and Eckau, the right resting on the sea in the vicinity of Kemmern, and the left on the Dvina. The German plan involved two lines of attack. One was from Mitau junction along the railway and road to Riga—a movement exactly parallel to the attack on Dvinsk from Novo Alexandrovsk. The other was an advance across the Dvina from a base on the railway Mitau-Friedrichstadt, so as to turn the defence of Riga in the south-east. The scheme was a classic one, for it had been Napoleon's favourite manœuvre—a turning movement, followed, when the enemy was nonplussed and distracted, by a sharp frontal assault. Six weeks before Below had won Friedrichstadt on the Dvina, but had not made a landing on the farther shore. Presently Linden was taken, also on the left bank, not far from Lennevaden. It was now the enemy's object to win points on the same bank nearer Riga. Already the railway from Riga to Dvinsk was under the fire of his big guns, which handicapped reserves in reaching the city. By 19th October he had taken Borkovitz, where a small affluent enters the Dvina, and by the 24th had pushed northwards to the vicinity of Kekken, which lies east of where the little river Brze enters the main stream opposite Dahlen island. He had now set the Russian command a difficult problem. He was only ten miles from Riga, and had one of its chief lines of communication under fire. If he intended to cross the river he had the choice of two good points, one near Borkovitz and one at Kekken. At both places islands split the broad stream into comparatively easy and narrow channels. At the same time Below pressed hard with his centre from Mitau. He crossed the Eckau, and his left wing crossed the Aa north of Mitau and took Kish. Soon Plehve was forced back from the lower Misse, and by the 22nd the enemy was at Olai, a place on the Mitau-Riga railway, only twelve miles from the city.

But the attack was now checked, and till the end of the month the Germans struggled fruitlessly to advance nearer Riga. On their extreme left they made one further attempt to move from

Kemmern along the strip of land between the Aa and the sea, failed signally, and gave up the enterprise. On the centre they found that Olai was the limit of their advance. The great belt of marsh north of the railway prevented a forward movement from Kish, and the line of the middle Misse was held in such strength that they failed to pierce it. One effort was made at Palanken, where there is a kind of causeway across the bogs. Some troops crossed the stream, but were made prisoners. In that country it was all but impossible to bring up sufficient guns to give the infantry proper artillery support. On the right at least six attempts were made to cross the Dvina. Kekken, at the mouth of the Brze, still resisted, but about the 28th of October the enemy managed to cross one channel of the Dvina and effect a lodgment on Dahlen island But he could not get his guns over in any strength, nor could he silence the concealed artillery on the eastern shore. He made a futile effort to cross the main channel, which was easily repulsed, and presently he was blown off the island itself. By the end of October the assaults on Dvinsk and Riga had come to nothing. The Germans were left with no better front on which to endure the rigours of the coming winter. Indeed, their position was the worse, for they were now entangled in the marshes of the Misse and the lakes west and south of Dvinsk.

The first stage of the war in the East had ended at the beginning of May with the check to the Russian movement on Cracow. The second most critical stage closed at the end of October with the definite stoppage of the torrential German invasion. The third stage was now beginning—the interregnum between defence and offence during which Russia was attempting to muster and organize her strength. No great blow could be struck till the spring, and then it must be no isolated attack, but part of a concerted advance by all the Allies. The winter might see local offensives, but they would be preparatory and partial, and not the great premeditated stroke. The events of October had done credit to Alexeiev, the new Chief of the General Staff, and had proved that the Russian army had recovered its strength, and maintained—what it had never lost—its confidence. For six months on a front of 700 miles blow after blow had been rained on it. Its one defect had been munitionment. That was now partially remedied; and if it had not yet the weapons for offence on the grand scale, it had enough for defence. It had learned, too, the lesson which had already been written across Manchuria in letters of blood, the prime lesson of modern war. In four words it may be defined as the importance of fire. On paper, indeed, it had been already learned. Every member of the Russian Staff would doubtless, if interrogated in July 1914, have given the most orthodox answers. But the true recognition, which involved the determination at all costs to provide an adequate fire, came only after months of disaster. Bold and martial races have a predisposition for shock action, an instinct for the hand-to-hand struggle. It is the fruit of self-confidence and courage. But the wise soldier knows that for "in-fighting" he must first get to close quarters, and that for this it is necessary to beat down the enemy's guns. A battle will always be won or lost at long range so long as the fire equipment of one force is less than the other. It was a lesson which the French learned by bitter experience in the Peninsula, when their advance was broken up before the point of shock by the steady volleys of the British infantry. Forgetfulness of this truth lost Austria Sadowa, and held Skobelev for long before the lines of Plevna. In South Africa it was the cause of Britain's initial disasters, and it was the main source of Russia's Manchurian defeats. To some extent all the Allies sinned in this respect, though their text-books enforced the doctrine. No better statement of it could be found than in the words of a distinguished French military critic : " In all times the struggle with cold steel has been the final phase, that which confirms the decision, the expulsion of the enemy from his position, and the conquest of the ground ; but in all times, likewise, *this final consummation has come to those who willed the means before willing the end.* Attack with pike, sword, or bayonet gives the last shock to the enemy's *moral;* but to shake the *moral* and put him at the mercy of shock action, the losses inflicted by bow and sling, by rifle and gun, are needed."* It was no less a soldier than Napoleon who wrote, " Battles to-day are decided by fire."

By the beginning of November the general features of the winter position were tolerably clear. Broadly speaking, both sides stood on the defensive. The Austro-Germans had reached a line which, though highly uncomfortable, was not unsafe. The character of the Dvina front made it fairly easy for Hindenburg to maintain himself, since the river, with its few well-defined crossings, was a bad base for a Russian attack. The assailant was strictly limited in his choice of routes, and the problem of the defence was thereby lightened. It was less like the holding of an ordinary river line than of a mountain wall, where the only gaps are the infrequent passes. Southwards, in the Pripet Marshes,

* Colonel Colin, *The Transformations of War* (Eng. trans.), p 56.

no Russian move was possible except on a broad front, and this the weather forbade. Farther south the Austrian lines lay along the Styr, which flows into the Pripet, and the Strypa, which joins the Dniester. On those two hundred miles the position of both sides was restless and ill-defined. The open country of the Podolian plateau gave opportunity even in winter for military movements, and there, if anywhere, lay the terrain for a winter campaign.

The Germans, after their fashion, made the best of their position. They dug formidable entrenchments, strengthened where possible with concrete and steel. Automatic rifles were served out to the troops, and they doubled their total of machine guns, making a nest of them in each section. Their heavy guns were mounted on concrete platforms on every knuckle of solid ground. Behind their front they improved their communications by building branch lines and doubling some of the existing railways, using for their new constructions the causeways which threaded the marshes. Much of the material so used seems to have been brought from Belgium, which, since before the war it had the greatest railway development to the square mile of any country in Europe, could spare material without missing it. Roads were improved for motor transport, and a great deal of bridge building was done all over the occupied area of Poland. So secure did the Germans feel in their possession, that engineering works on a big scale were begun, including a canal from the Vistula to the Warta, for which the Reichstag voted large appropriations. The unfortunate country was bled white by the conquerors. Its starving artisans were refused food so long as they remained in their native land, but were offered free transport to, and employment in, the industrial areas of Germany, since every Pole who became a munition worker released a German for the army. Further, conscript regiments were levied in Russian Poland, and an attempt was made to combine Poles from German, Austrian, and Russian territory into separate units.*

The tale of the November fighting is one of spurts of activity, chiefly in the northern sector, which presently died down to the complete stagnation which preceded the Christmas battles in the south. On the 10th there was a considerable action on the coast, and the Russians carried Kemmern and pushed the enemy in that quarter twenty miles west of Riga. There was also a ding-dong

* An interesting account of the immense activities which radiated from Headquarters at Kovno will be found in Ludendorff's *My War Memories*, I., pp 180-207.

struggle at Dahlen island, where neither side could claim victory. At Dvinsk the Russians counter-attacked in the first half of the month, and won the western shore of Lake Sventen. In the south there was a series of small engagements on the rivers which flow in parallel lines from the Podolian plateau to the Dniester. The Russian success of the autumn had rolled back Bothmer from the Sereth to west of the Strypa. These streams rise in a high, treeless tableland, and their early courses are through shallow troughs studded with ponds and marshes. Lower down they have cut cañons in the sandstone, which deepen as they flow southward till the walls are often 400 feet high before they join the Dniester. The November fighting was chiefly at the point where the one type of river valley ceased and the other began, and where, since neither swamps nor defiles impeded, a crossing was easiest. In all these engagements there was no great strategic purpose. It was the kind of encounter which is inevitable when two armies face each other, neither of which has formed a strong defensive line.

By the beginning of December the situation in the Balkans was such that it seemed to call for some great effort on the part of Russia if bad was not to become worse. The Allied forces at Salonika were shut in, awaiting attack. Before them was a Bulgarian army nearly twice their size, while on the lower Danube, watching Rumania, were Mackensen's divisions. If the main Austro-German right chose to make a great effort it might force its way into Bessarabia, with the result that Rumania would be caught as between pincers. In that event she would be forced, willy-nilly, to enter the campaign on the side of the Teutonic League. Germany had succeeded admirably in her game of bluff, of which engaging device we may detect two principal forms. The first is to announce your intentions, convince your adversary of your sincerity, and then refrain from carrying them out. That is the single bluff. The second and subtler is to announce your intentions, convince your adversary that you are lying, and then do precisely as you have announced. That is the double bluff. Germany had used it in her invasion of France through Belgium, which her staff had talked about for years. She had lately declared that she would take Salonika, drive the Allies into the sea, and invade Egypt. We suspected the double bluff, and sent armies to these theatres. In reality it was a most successful use of the single bluff. Germany was neither able nor willing to do one or the other, but she obtained what she wanted without crossing the Bosphorus or sending a single brigade to the Vardar. She was now free to use the threat of Mackensen to manœuvre Rumania into her fold.

From the late autumn Russia had been organizing a new army—the Seventh—at her Black Sea bases. Never in the course of the campaign, however hardly pressed she might be on her main front, did she shrink from any special effort which her Allies required. This army was put under the command of General Tcherbachev, formerly at the head of the Eleventh Army, and its first intention was a movement across the Danube against the Bulgarian rear. It was to anticipate this strategy that, after the Serbian *débâcle*, Mackensen's German divisions sat down to watch the river lines. It was hoped that, with this force to back her, Rumania would join the Allies; but Rumania, not without reason, declined. She preferred to follow the Fabian strategy which had served her so well in the Balkan War, since her northern frontier was far from safe. Without Rumania's consent an attack on Bulgaria was impossible, and Russia had to look to another sphere of action. The Bukovina, the gap between the Dniester and the Pruth, was the best alternative. If she attacked strongly in that quarter she would anticipate the Austro-German advance into Bessarabia, and she might attract some of the German divisions from the Balkans. If her advance succeeded, she would do much to calm Rumania's fears and ensure her future support. Further, any such move would explain to the enemy the meaning of the South Russian concentration, and attract his attention from her designs, which were now maturing, for a great attack in Transcaucasia. Lastly, there were rumours that the Austrians were contemplating an offensive against Italy, and with luck she might find their front weakened.

By the middle of December Ivanov had prepared his dispositions The new Seventh Army was on the middle and lower Styr against Bothmer, and the Ninth Army faced Pflanzer-Baltin in the Bukovina. Czernovitz, which had been in Austrian hands since the previous March, was the objective. Its capture would be the best protection of Rumania's northern frontier against the Austro-German menace. South lay the wild heights of the Eastern Carpathians, and by Czernovitz alone could a modern army sweep down on the plains of Moldavia, or work along the Pruth in an encircling movement. From Ivanov's point of view the ground between the Pruth and the Dniester offered an advance safeguarded on the flanks by formidable rivers, and free from any insuperable natural barrier. The Russian front in mid-December may be taken as running just west of the Bessarabia frontier. It lay between ten and fifteen miles from the city, and the ground between, save for the flats along the river, was filled with a range of oak-clad hills. On the eastern fringe of these uplands lay a chain of villages—Dobronoutz, Toporoutz, Bojan—which were held by the enemy. Ivanov's plan was to fight holding battles on his right wing and centre, to strike heavily against Czernovitz with the Ninth Army, and attempt an enveloping movement with the Seventh Army on the lower Strypa.

The first shots were fired on 24th December, and by the 27th the engagement was general along the front. The main attack was on the ridge between the villages of Toporoutz and Bojan. After a heavy artillery bombardment, Lechitski carried this on the evening of the 28th. Next day the holding battle developed on the Styr at the angle of Chartorysk. On Saturday, January 1, 1916, this attack was pressed on the bend of the river between the railway bridge of the Sarny-Kovel railway and Chartorysk, where the eastward curve of the Styr enabled the Russian guns to keep up a cross-fire on a front of seven miles. The Russians effected a passage and took Khriask, while farther south they cleared the east bank and took the village of Kolki. That same day the Seventh Army was in action on the Strypa. It was held at the bridgeheads of Buczacz, but its left wing managed to approach but not to take Usciezko, on the Dniester, thereby cutting the branch line from Czernovitz to Buczacz.

The whole enterprise had been political in origin, and much of the Seventh Army was only half-trained. Against Bothmer nothing was achieved, but Pflanzer-Baltin was at various moments in serious difficulties. Heavy snow had begun to fall, and by 15th January, in spite of desperate assaults, Czernovitz's ring of entrenchments was unbroken. The battle had lasted for twenty-two days, and some regiments on both sides had been continuously engaged for a fortnight. Strategically, Russia's Christmas offensive had not won its objective; but in its main purpose it had succeeded. It had eased the pressure in the Balkans, and it had prevented that Bessarabian advance which might have compelled Rumania to a disastrous decision. The mere fact that so soon after the great retreat so vigorous a counter-stroke should have been possible was a proof of the strong recuperative power of the Russian armies. In spite of the losses and trials of the year 1915, the situation seemed to most observers to be better at the end of it than at the beginning. Ivanov's attack was a local trial of strength, a sudden emergency measure, and no concerted offensive. Its cessation left the army and the nation without any sense of failure. The Minister of War, General Polivanov, while the battle was drawing to a close, spoke in a strain of high confidence. " Thanks to the mobilization of the great mass of men ordered some months ago, and the doubling of the number at our depots, we have now a permanent reserve of a million and a half young recruits, which will allow us to feed the various units without sending to the front men with insufficient military training. Behind the four Allies are the natural resources of the whole universe. Behind the armies of the Central Powers are only weakness and exhaustion." And the Emperor's Christmas address to the Knights of St. George once more advertised Russia's resolution to the world. " I will conclude no peace till we have chased the last foe from our soil. And I will make no peace save in unison with our Allies, to whom we are bound, not by paper treaties, but by affection and our common sacrifice."

II.

In the West, as in the East, the autumn saw the flickering out of great actions in a series of attacks and counter-attacks, which were directed only to establishing the line. This last grumbling of battle was chiefly found in Champagne and between Loos and La Bassée. On 3rd October the British lost all but the western rim of the Hohenzollern redoubt. On the 6th the French carried the Butte of Tahure, the farthest point reached in the Champagne advance, and improved their position west of Navarin Farm. On the 8th the Germans attacked on the front between the Hohenzollern and Hulluch, and against the Chalk Pit and Hill 70. This, the most serious German movement in the north, was a model of all that a counter-stroke ought not to be, being no more than an abortive frontal attack against a prepared enemy. According to Sir John French's dispatch, twenty-eight battalions were used in first line, and there were large supports. Twelve battalions advanced at the Chalk Pit, from eight to ten against the French at Loos, and six or eight against the Hohenzollern. Such an attack—made by more than two divisions with full reserves—did not suffer from lack of men, and the preliminary bombardment endured long enough to embarrass our defence. But the bombardment was ill-directed, and the tactics of the stroke were ill-conceived. As the result of the day no ground was won, and from eight to nine thousand of the enemy were left dead on the field.

On the 13th the British themselves attacked. Their object was to ease the position at the Hohenzollern, where their line was commanded by the German trenches and redoubts to the north. The morning broke in a Scots mist and driving rain, but before midday, when the bombardment began, it had cleared to a bright autumn day. The area selected was from the Hohenzollern to a point 600 yards south-west of Hulluch—roughly, the area which the 9th, 7th, and 1st Divisions had operated in on 25th September. At one o'clock a gas attack was launched from their front trenches, and at 2 p.m. the infantry crossed the parapets. On the right we captured 1,000 yards of trenches south-west of Hulluch, but the artillery fire, exactly ranged, forbade us to remain in them. Farther north we took and held the section of German trenches south-west of Cité St. Elie, in the angle between the Vermelles–Hulluch and the Hulluch–La Bassée roads, carried the south-western edge of the famous Quarries, and won a trench on their north-western face. But the heaviest contest was on the left, where the 46th (North Midland) Division of Territorials was engaged at the Hohenzollern, and showed themselves not less resolute in attack than the Londoners at Loos a fortnight earlier. At the moment we held only the western and southern rims of the Redoubt. The communication trenches, Big Willie and Little Willie, were in German hands, and the whole of Fosse 8, the houses behind it, and the Fosse trench, running east of the Redoubt, were one nest of machine guns. The first rush gave us the main trench of the Hohenzollern. But swift progress was impossible under the machine-gun fire, and the attack resolved itself into a struggle of bombing parties. The fight, which lasted for three days, till the 2nd Guards Brigade relieved the North Midland men, resulted in the gain of the main trench of the Redoubt and no more. The artillery preparation had been insufficient to make progress possible across that sinister ground.

On the afternoon of the 19th there was another sporadic German effort in the Loos area, when an attack was made against the front from the Quarries to Hulluch. It was of the usual type—first a bombardment, then an infantry advance across open ground, which was stopped dead by our machine-gun and rifle fire. It was followed by a number of bombing attacks against the Hohenzollern, which had a better chance, since the enemy held the maze of communication trenches east of the main trench of the Redoubt. These too, failed, and the Germans suffered considerable losses without the gain of a single position. But in Champagne on that day a counter-stroke was attempted better judged than the futile efforts in the north. The French advance in September had on the west a German salient between Auberive and Rheims. If this salient could be advanced, then the Rheims–Châlons railway might be cut, and the French forces forced back behind the river Vesle and the Vesle Canal. Such a success would be followed by a combined attack on Rheims, which would then be in danger of envelopment. Observers in Britain throughout the campaign were inclined to forget the strategic significance of Rheims, that great junction of road, railway, and water communications. It was not less important than Verdun. Had Germany in these months been able to adopt a serious offensive in the West, it is likely that Rheims would have been the point chosen at which to break the French line. As it was, that area offered the best chance for a counter-attack which might nullify all the gains to the eastward. On the night of the 18th the Germans began a great bombardment upon the six miles of the French front which lay roughly along the road from La Pompelle, one of the Rheims forts, to the village of Prosnes. For three hours high explosives rained on the French front lines, while a curtain of asphyxiating shells was dropped behind them. Early on the 19th the " preparation " was renewed, and a wave of gas was loosed. Just after dawn the German infantry attacked in four successive lines with an interval of some 300 yards between them. The first two lines were blotted out before they reached the French trenches. The third gained a momentary footing, but was driven out by bombs. The fourth succeeded better, and managed to effect a lodging in some parts of the advanced trenches. In the afternoon, however, the French reinforcements pushed through the curtain of fire, counter-attacked, and drove back the assailants with enormous losses. Next day another effort was made farther to the west, around the village of Prunay, seven miles south-east of Rheims. The front was much the same, a little over five miles. After a long bombardment and a gas attack the infantry three times tried to rush the French lines, and three times were driven back. No man got farther than the wire entanglements in front of the trenches.

On Sunday, 24th October, it was the turn of the French. After the capture of Tahure the German salient north of Le Mesnil, including the Butte of Mesnil, remained unconquered, though the French had bitten into its sides. In the south-west part of this salient, which was a redoubt in advance of the German final position, lay a work called La Courtine. It was a typical German fortress, 1,200 yards long, 250 yards deep, and embracing three or four lines of trenches connected by subterranean tunnels—another such redoubt as the Hohenzollern in the north. On Sunday, after desperate fighting, the French carried La Courtine, and found it choked with German dead. On Monday they had to face a counter-attack, which failed. On the Tuesday night there was another German attack, which was also beaten off, and the action left the French with their front in this section appreciably straightened, and a dangerous redoubt on their flank obliterated.

The last incident of the month, the last counter-stroke of the autumn battles, came on Saturday, the 30th. The Germans, strongly reinforced, attacked all along the Tahure section on a front of four miles, but especially at La Courtine and at the Butte of Tahure. The La Courtine effort, four times repeated, failed; but at the Butte their artillery preparation drove the French from the crest, and the Germans retook the summit. This forced the French back to the southern side of the hill just below the crest, where they had the advantage of the kind of position which the German reserve lines had enjoyed in the September battles. The German movement was a resolute attempt to break the French line at Tahure by a frontal advance, combined with a flanking attack from the Mesnil salient. It failed in its main purpose, but by driving the French from the top of the Butte it gave a further lease of life to the Bazancourt–Grand Pré railway, and eased the German position in the coming winter stagnation.

The great action which began on 25th September had wholly ceased by the beginning of November. Both sides had settled down to the modern equivalent for winter quarters—trench warfare unrelieved by any concerted attack on a large scale. There was some fighting at Hartmannsweilerkopf in the Vosges towards the end of December. On the 19th of the month, after a heavy bombardment, the enemy released gas on the north-east side of the Ypres salient, but our counter-bombardment pinned the attacking infantry to their trenches, and the affair became a fiasco. For the rest, the tale of the second winter in the West is one of minor local attacks and counter-attacks, and an incessant struggle with nature. The weather was open and wet. There was a week of frost and a little snow in November, and in the Vosges there were frequent snowfalls, but generally the days were mild and damp. The Allies had learned much from the previous winter. Their trenches were better drained and better placed; the men were furnished with rubber boots; and there was less of the long, heart-breaking spells in one section of the line which had been inevitable the year before owing to shortage of men. But no ingenuity in alignment, no pumping, no flooring or revetments could make the trenches in most parts other than desperately wet and comfortless. In the loose chalk of the Artois, where the ground dried rapidly, rain made the parapets crumble, and the battalions had to be continuously at work repairing them. In water-logged regions like the Ypres salient and the Festubert and Givenchy areas there was nothing for it but endless pumping. The solid earth dissolved after a few hours' rain, and the deeper the trenches were made the deeper the water in their bottoms. The Germans on large parts of the front still held the higher and more easily drained positions. When our line was on a slope, a drain could be made by cutting a tunnel through the parapet or parados; but when we were on the flats the men were wet from the moment they entered the place till they returned to billets. The last two months of 1915 were wonderfully mild for the time of year, and the sun shone more often than in the gloomy preceding winter; but the damp remained, and damp is a greater enemy to armies than the most hyperborean cold.

It was the business of the Allies to keep the German strength stretched taut, and few days were without their incidents. Upon the Belgian coast the British monitors punctually shelled the German flank, and from Nieuport to Belfort there were daily artillery bombardments. The men in the trenches were not idle, for, apart from local offensives, they had the heavy task of keeping their section in good order. Everything depended upon the battalion commander. When he was energetic and business-like, the trenches were reasonably safe and comfortable; when he was inert they often became mere ruinous ditches. To keep even a peaceful bit of line in good condition needed constant care. In some cases, where much-depleted battalions held a line properly allotted to a battalion at full strength, there were simply not enough men for the work, and the relieving troops fell heir to a dilapidated dwelling-place.* When it is remembered that, in addition to this artisan's

---

* Some of the Territorial battalions, which, owing to the system of second-line units, had great difficulties in getting their drafts, were now reduced to a third and even a quarter of their original strength, but were still treated as complete battalions. The same thing happened in the American Civil War, when the North, instead of recruiting for the seasoned battalions, allowed the formation of new regiments. Only Wisconsin created no new units, but kept her original regiments up to full strength, so that, as Sherman said, a Wisconsin regiment was equal to an ordinary brigade.

labour, the men were required to keep up various forms of aggression, and to repel the enemy's efforts in the same direction, it will be seen that the winter trench life was no sinecure.

The British army had immensely improved its fighting machinery since the preceding winter. Our trench mortars were no longer improvised affairs like mediæval cannon, as dangerous to the users as to the enemy, We had standardized and perfected our system of bombs. Our artillery was far more numerous and better supplied. We had so many men engaged on expert duties that distracted battalion commanders complained that the ordinary infantryman was becoming rare. Two special activities deserve a word. In some parts of the front, notably in that held by the British Third Army, our sniping had been brought to high perfection with the assistance of various officers who were experienced big-game hunters. In each battalion several men were taught how to locate the enemy sniper, and how to use stalking-glasses and telescopic sights. The result was that we began to have a body of sharpshooters equal to the forest rangers of South Germany. Again, our work in mining and counter-mining had reached the level of a science. We had recruited a special detachment from expert mining and tunnelling engineers—men from all the great mining areas of the world—and with their help we blew up mines at Ypres and Givenchy, and turned the centre of the Hohenzollern Redoubt into one vast crater. The enemy retaliated in kind, but less successfully. An interesting feature of the winter warfare, as showing the spirit of the offensive in our troops, was the new fashion of raids on the enemy's trenches. The Canadian Corps seem to have begun it. A small detachment selected a piece of line where the barbed wire entanglements could be most easily cut. Under cover of darkness they raced across the intervening ground, took a section of the German front lines with bombs and the bayonet, and held it till the Germans began to push in from both ends. Then they retired, usually taking with them some prisoners. These affairs were represented in the German reports as serious British offensives which broke down before the strength of the defence. On the contrary, they were isolated exploits of battalions intended to annoy the enemy and keep him in a state of suspense, an object which they completely achieved. The raiding parties were always small, and they stayed in the enemy's lines no longer time than permitted of a safe return. Their adroit management was proved by their inconsiderable losses.

During these months wholesale changes had been made in the

British dispositions. New divisions were arriving from home, and three new corps were formed, destined to compose the Fourth Army. One corps went east to Salonika, and all the old corps were altered in their constituents. There were many promotions of brigadiers, who had won their spurs in the field, to divisional commands. The cavalry brigades were broken up temporarily into dismounted battalions, who took their places with the infantry in the trenches. The most notable change was the disappearance of the Indian Corps, both the Meerut and Lahore Divisions departing for the East, taking with them their white regular battalions. No more were the French roads filled with the turbans of the Sikhs and the cowboy hats of the Gurkhas, and the French fields with their bivouac fires and the babel of strange tongues. The country folk, to whom the Indians were figures of sheer romance, watched with a certain sadness the going of their Eastern allies. The great experiment had succeeded. In many hard-fought battles of the campaign—at Givenchy and Neuve Chapelle in the last months of 1914, at Neuve Chapelle again in March 1915, at Fromelles in May, and in the holding battles of September—the Indian soldiers had shown surpassing loyalty and courage. They had faced the brunt of the white man's war, and endured the miseries of the northern winter, and had at all times and under all terrors been true to their salt. They were to win yet higher renown in climes more akin to their own, by the marshes of the Tigris and on the sands of Syria.

If a soldier who had fought in the trenches during the winters of 1914 and 1915 had been asked as to the chief difference between the two years, he would probably have pointed to the better supply of guns and shells. We have seen that the Christmas attack at Ypres was checked by our artillery alone. No longer were the guns limited to an inconsiderable number of rounds a day. From hour to hour the men in the trenches were cheered by that most welcome of sounds, the busy talk of the great ordnance behind the front. We had not yet reached the ideal in munitions that we were striving for, but we were immeasurably better off than we had been in the summer, and our supplies were daily increasing. In a speech in the House of Commons on 20th December Mr. Lloyd George gave an account of his stewardship. He recalled the black days of the previous May, when we turned out each day 2,500 high explosive and 13,000 shrapnel shells, as compared with the German 250,000, mostly high explosive. He dealt in detail with the different types of arms—heavy guns, field guns, machine guns, small arms, trench mortars. On the whole his report was cheering. But he repudiated with passion the suggestion that we were overdoing production—that we could possibly overdo production. "The most fatuous way of economizing is to produce an inadequate supply. A good margin is a sensible insurance. Less than enough is a foolish piece of extravagance. It is not merely that. What you spare in money you spill in blood." And he concluded with an earnest appeal to employers and workmen to make certain that over the portals of their workshops they should not have to inscribe "Too late."

A sense of the gravity of the situation, but not less a recognition of its good hope, were the notes of that speech, and they were also the notes of the British temper. The nation had by now realized the meaning of a world war. The British losses up to January 9, 1916, were 549,467, of whom 128,138 were dead. It was a scale of casualties far beyond anything in our history. Again, even the most thoughtless were becoming aware of the economic strain which must be met. At the outset many had deluded themselves with the hopes of a short war, since it was generally believed that the stress of combat under modern conditions was too great to be long endured by mortal men. All the wars of the nineteenth century had been brief. The Austro-Prussian War of 1866 had lasted only six weeks, the Franco-Prussian War of 1870 six months, the recent Balkan wars only a few weeks, so far as the actual struggle went. Even the Crimean War had endured for little more than a year, the Russo-Turkish War of 1877 and the Russo-Japanese War of 1904 for less than eighteen months. But now we were approaching the eighteenth month of a war which in intensity of sacrifice had had no equal, and, though the goal was nearer, it was not yet in sight. None of the easy protracted campaigns of Britain in the past, from the Hundred Years' War to the South African War, afforded any parallel. But there was one nineteenth-century struggle which was felt to give some kind of precedent—the desperate four years of the American Civil War. In that war as in this there could be no indecisive peace. The North had to win a complete victory or lose everything. In that war the greater potential strength in men and wealth was with the North, as it was now with the Allies. The problem of the North, as it was the problem of the Allies, was how to use that strength—how to mobilize and train its man-power, to blockade and weaken its enemy, and finally to force his line and defeat him in a field battle. The North, like the Allies, had fumbled at the beginning. It had to learn its lesson, and the learning was costly. But when it had truly mobilized its strength, and used it with undivided purpose to crush the main enemy forces, the North had won a decisive victory. That was a precedent both to cheer and to solemnize. It demanded the concentration of every atom of our natural assets, but it promised for such effort and sacrifice a full reward.

On the 15th of December it was announced that Sir John French had been transferred to the command of the forces at home, and that Sir Douglas Haig had been appointed as his successor. Haig stood in the very first rank of British soldiers. He had played a chief part in the most hotly contested battles of the campaign —at First Ypres, at Neuve Chapelle, at Festubert, at Loos. Chary of speech, bold in design, resolute in execution, he had raised the First Army under his command to a foremost place among the British forces. He had the confidence of his men, and had earned the admiration of all who worked with him, for he was at once a scientific soldier after the most modern plan, and a true leader. Among his many merits not the least was that he had been a brilliant staff officer, and had a proper understanding of the functions of a staff. He was a young man, too, as modern generals went—only fifty-five; the youngest, except Gouraud, of all the great Army chiefs in the West. He was succeeded in the command of the First Army by Sir Charles Monro, who returned from the Mediterranean Expeditionary Force, and who in turn was succeeded by Sir Archibald Murray, who had acted for three months as Chief of Staff at home and had done something to reconstitute the necessary General Staff in London. It was now possible for Kitchener to bring back Sir William Robertson from France, and make him Chief of the Imperial General Staff in Whitehall. This last appointment was in many ways the most important made since the beginning of the war. It affirmed a vital principle of military organization which for more than a year had been neglected, and if the mere revival of the post was of the first importance, not less so was the choice of the man to fill it. A learned and capable soldier, and an administrator of the first rank, Sir William Robertson had wrought marvels as Quartermaster-General in the early months of the Western campaign. As Chief of Staff to Sir John French he had done good service, but his new task called for exceptional powers of character and mind, since he became the supreme military adviser to the Cabinet on the conduct of the war. He was no military pedant, and might be trusted to take a broad view of what constituted armed strength;

but he was also a professional soldier, and would not suffer vital military necessities to be forgotten in the complexities of civil politics. The nation breathed more freely when it learned of his appointment, for it realized that the Government had now that expert guidance without which the national effort must be dissipated and weakened.

On the 18th of December Sir John French issued a farewell address to his troops. Such leave-takings are not easy, and in the Field-Marshal's words there was a note of honest emotion and affection. He was a British soldier of the elder school, and he had that power of making his personality known throughout his command which is of inestimable value to a general, and which was not possessed by his far abler successor. He had also in a high degree the quality which the British soldier knows and honours as "stout-heartedness," and in dark days his vigorous optimism did much to nerve and stiffen his armies. He received a viscounty, and took his title from Ypres, before which he had fought his greatest battle—a fitting choice, for his name will always be linked with that most miraculous achievement in the history of British campaigning. But if he was a gallant leader and a devoted public servant, it had nevertheless long been clear that he was not the man to carry his country to victory. His optimism was too often unthinking, the fruit of a buoyant temperament rather than of a penetrating mind. After the blunders of Loos no government could have retained him in supreme command. He had not the vigour of intellect and the elevation of character for the task of moulding the new levies of Britain into great armies, of solving the infinite problems of the new form of war, of adjusting the military difficulties of an alliance and the political intricacies of a strife of peoples in which the army was but a part of the national weapon. For such a duty there was needed a more exact and scientific judgment, a more flexible and resourceful mind, a grim patience and an unshakable serenity of soul, and that quality of statesmanship which only a few soldiers have possessed, and these the greatest.

CHAPTER XLV.

THE POLITICAL SITUATION IN FRANCE AND BRITAIN.
October 1, 1915–January 26, 1916.

Popular Anxiety—The New Ministry in France—Criticism of the French Staff—The Situation in Britain—The Censorship—Edith Cavell—The New General Staff—British Finance—The Recruiting Problem—The Derby Report—The Military Service Bill—Parallel with American Civil War.

THE beginning of October saw a recrudescence in France and Britain of that uneasiness with the conduct of the war which had been noticeable in May. The purport of recent events was writ too large for the most casual to miss. The situation in the Near East was ugly, and the Allied Governments seemed to speak with an uncertain voice. The first exhilaration after the September advance in the West had been succeeded by a doleful reaction, in which the results gained were unduly depreciated. Germany seized the occasion to revive the peace talk of early September, and this put the finishing touch to French impatience. October saw the formation of a new Ministry, which M Delcassé's resignation on the 13th had made inevitable. Reasons of health, combined with disagreement with his colleagues on their Balkan policy, forced from office the man who of all living French statesmen had rendered the most conspicuous service to his country. M. Delcassé had never been strong, and he was one who habitually worked at high pressure, and drew most of the activities of his department into his own hand. He combined a bold imagination with great tenacity of purpose, and, like Joffre, his fellow-Southerner, he was a man of few words. Along with King Edward VII. and Lord Lansdowne, he had been the architect of the Anglo-French *entente*, and for a decade he had been the man in all France most feared by Berlin. In the war he saw the justification of his policy, and since its start he had laboured without rest. He had played a main part in the negotiations which preceded Italy's entrance into the contest, and had been the architect of those conventions by which all the Allies bound themselves to entertain no proposals for a separate peace. Ten years before, in June 1905, he had been driven from office, and the event had been regarded as a portent in every capital in Europe. His last resignation could have no such effects, for the centre of gravity had moved away from Chambers and Chancelleries. But it had one instantaneous result. The Ministry must be reconstructed. The National Cabinet formed during the German sweep on Paris had been a coalition of parties, and had aimed at representing all the groups rather than at being a mobilization of the best available talent. Administratively it had done well, though M. Millerand's handling of the War Office had been the object of much criticism from the Army Committee of the Chamber, but it was weak in deliberative talent. In Britain Ministers seemed to be embedded in office, and wholesale changes were looked upon by those who professed to be versed in political affairs as a disaster too grave to be envisaged. In France Ministries dissolved with ease if for any reason they found themselves out of tune with the nation. The superior elasticity of the group system as it obtained in France came as a painful surprise to those who had extolled the merits of the British party arrangement. The truth was that in France the people's eyes were not on the Chamber, and a change of Ministry produced only a slight impression. It was the same in Britain; but our statesmen—less wise than the French—were unwilling to admit the unpalatable fact. They continued to believe that the continuance of each in office was indispensable to the country.

A new French Ministry was formed, with M. Briand as Premier. It represented an effort to secure the highest administrative efficiency combined with the advisory value of the men most experienced in public life. It was, therefore, a blend of experts and elder statesmen. M. Briand was one of the most interesting figures in French politics. Though only fifty-four, he had changed violently many times in his career. He had been a revolutionary, and he had crushed the great railway strike of 1910. He had been a bitter anti-clerical, and he had been also the peacemaker between Church and State. But his very adaptability inspired confidence in a crisis. He was a " swallower of formulas," with an eye for facts rather than a memory for dogmas, and the situation needed a man who could bring to the instant need of things an alert and unshackled mind. He had also, from his Breton birth, the Celtic fire which made him, like Mr. Lloyd George, an inspiring and magnetic leader in war. He took the portfolio of Foreign Affairs, with the assistance of M. Jules Cambon, formerly French Ambassador at Berlin, and the diplomatist who above all others had emerged with distinction from the stormy negotiations preceding the war. General Galliéni succeeded Millerand at the War Office, and Admiral Lacaze went to the Ministry of Marine. Some of the representatives of extreme groups who had been included in the former Cabinet retained their positions; M. Painlevé, the President of the Army Committee of the Chamber, and famous as a mathematician, had a seat, as had M. Albert Thomas, who had done valuable work in the Munition Department. But apart from the experts like M. Jules Cambon, General Galliéni, and Admiral Lacaze, the most remarkable feature of the new Ministry was its strength in that deliberative talent which comes from ripe experience. There were no fewer than eight men who had already held the office of Premier—M. Briand himself, M. Viviani, and M. Doumergue among the younger men, and among the elder M. Combes, M. Ribot, M. Méline, M. Léon Bourgeois, and M. de Freycinet. It was a Ministry which not only represented every phase of opinion, like its predecessor, but contained the highest practical talent which the nation could show. France, turning her eyes for one moment from the enemy lines, approved the change.

As the winter proceeded, much criticism began to be heard of the General Staff, both in the Chamber and among the people. The formalism and arrogance of a certain type of staff officer irritated the officers of the new levies, drawn as they were from every class and profession of civil life. Men began to ask themselves whether the General Staff had shown much prescience in the first weeks of war; whether, with the exception of the Marne, there had been any great intelligence in the leadership. The reputation of Joffre himself was not left unassailed; the very qualities which made him a tower of strength in the early months seemed to be a weakness now that the military problem had become endlessly ramified. His notion of the "*guerre d'usure*" seemed to many a confession of stupidity, his optimisim had begun to pall, and the pirouettings about the Vosges crest, which were the chief incidents of the winter months, first amused and then exasperated. The see-saw fortunes of Hartmannsweilerkopf—"*vieil Armand*"—came to be a bitter jest. Moreover, there was much grumbling among the troops because of scanty leave, bad transport arrangements, and the fact that the rural manhood had been drawn upon for the army beyond all reasonable proportion, since the industrials were wanted for munition-making, and, said the countrymen, had greater power with the politicians. In December Joffre was given command over all the French armies in every theatre of war, and Castelnau was taken from his group command and made Chief of the General Staff. This latter was a popular appointment, but it led to friction at Headquarters, and the year closed with a feeling of a general lack of confidence in the High Command abroad in the nation. There was need of some conspicuous operation, either in attack or defence, to pull the people together; and such an operation the new year was to provide.

The situation in Britain was much the same. Our losses, as announced up to 9th October, were close on half a million, or five times the strength of our original Expeditionary Force. On the Western front they amounted to 365,000, of whom 67,000 were dead. Thirteen months of incessant fighting had shown a glorious record for our men, but could the same thing be said of our leaders? All our actions had been, like Albuera and Inkerman, soldiers' battles; people were beginning to suggest that Vittoria and Salamanca were better examples to follow, and that a generals' battle would be a welcome change. For the first time criticism of our leadership in the field began to be heard in responsible mouths, while the Government in general suffered considerable discredit for the calamitous results of their Balkan policy. A whipping-boy was discovered in the censorship. Upon the censorship we visited for a little the irritation and doubt which had been engendered in the popular mind by the obvious difficulties into which we had blundered. That institution from the beginning had had few friends, and it had not been conducted with much consistency or reason. It had sanctioned the publication of news which seriously hampered our diplomacy, such as the offer of Cyprus to Greece, or exasperated our Allies, like the South Wales strike; while it repressed for weeks all information about the exploits of our battalions—information necessary both to encourage recruiting at home and to give our troops in the field the confidence that their work was not neglected. This secrecy was not the work of the much-criticized Press Bureau, which acted mainly as a post office, but of the military authorities themselves, who were inclined to forget what was needed by a country whose armies were still volunteers. Ministers, too, showed a disposition to shelter themselves behind the censorship, and claim immunity from criticism.

The speeches of Lord Curzon, Lord Lansdowne, and Lord Buckmaster in a debate in the House of Lords a month later seemed to demand for the actions of the Government a protection from hostile comment which was manifestly inconsistent with our constitutional practice. Britain was not a bureaucracy. Her Ministers were not experts but amateurs, who had won their positions as exponents of popular opinion, and held them on the condition that the people could scrutinize their work, and, if necessary, ask for their dismissal. Such a system was meaningless unless popular opinion had a chance of making itself felt. Stupid attacks upon Ministers were to be deprecated, but even stupid attacks were better than compulsory silence. Our political system gave us no guarantee for administrative capacity in our Ministers. They might possess it, but if so, it was by accident; they had reached their position by being good politicians, by their skill in dealing with words and formulas and not with facts. It was the nation's business in a life-and-death struggle to make a zealous search for competence, and for this free criticism was essential. Ministers were responsible *to* the nation, and the nation was responsible *for* Ministers. Failure should be met by dismissal, for the nation was partly to blame. The other way, the old way, when the nation had no responsibility, was to send blundering statesmen to the scaffold. That was the logical culmination of the policy of suppressing criticism and disowning the nation's partnership.

In this atmosphere of unsettlement fell the 110th anniversary of Trafalgar. As in 1805, that day came in the midst of a great war. The name served to recall to men's minds that at other times in her history Britain had been beset with enemies, and had eventually triumphed. On October 21, 1805, Pitt was within three months of his end; Napoleon, after meditating the invasion of England, was turning east to win the greatest of his victories; never had the power by land of our adversaries been stronger, and it had not yet reached its summit. But Trafalgar was the death-blow to the French emperor's hopes of world domination, and though it took years to finish the war, his cause was lost when on that autumn afternoon the shattered navies of France and Spain fled in the teeth of the rising gale. Trafalgar Day was a reminder, too, of what the British fleet had already accomplished. Germany had imitated Napoleon's Berlin and Milan decrees by her barbarous submarine warfare, but she had so far failed, as Napoleon had failed, to relax the economic pressure of Britain. Our mercantile navy was increasing under her threats. To our Fleet alone we owed it that we could wage war at will in any part of the globe, and continue that sea-borne commerce which was the breath of our life. Our sea power could not by itself bring about the victory we needed, but it had compelled Germany to fling her armies madly about Europe in the effort to win a military decision while yet there was time.

But it was the death of one Englishwoman which did more than any other incident of the war—more than the sinking of the *Lusitania* or the tragedy of Belgium—to key the temper of Britain to that point where resolution acquires the impetus of a passion. Miss Edith Cavell, a lady of forty-three, the daughter of a Norfolk clergyman, had been since 1906 the head of a nursing institute in Brussels. When the war broke out she was in England, but she returned at once to Belgium, and transformed her institute into a hospital for wounded soldiers. There she nursed without discrimination British, French, Belgians, and Germans. During her year's work she succeeded, with the help of friends in Brussels, in conveying many of the wounded Allied soldiers into Holland, whence they could return to their armies, and also in assisting the escape of Belgian civilians of military age. Her activities were discovered by the German authorities, and on 5th August she was arrested and lodged in the military prison of St. Gilles. There she was kept in solitary confinement, and no word of her arrest reached her friends till three weeks later. On 26th August Sir Edward Grey asked the American Ambassador in London to request Mr. Brand Whitlock, the American Minister at Brussels, to inquire into the case. Mr. Whitlock took up the matter energetically, and on 31st August addressed an inquiry to Baron von der Lancken, the chief of the political department of the German Military Government in Belgium. He waited ten days without receiving an answer, and then wrote again. On 12th September he was informed that Miss Cavell by her own confession had admitted the offence with which she was charged, that her defence was already in the hands of a Belgian advocate, and that as a matter of principle no interview could be permitted with accused persons. Upon this M. de Leval, the legal adviser to the American Legation, took action. With admirable assiduity he endeavoured to get into touch with Miss Cavell and her so-called advocates, but found endless difficulties put in the way. It was not till 4th October that he was informed that the trial was fixed for the following Thursday, 7th October. On that date—nine weeks after the arrest and without the production to the defence of any documents of the prosecution—the trial of the thirty-five prisoners began. Miss Cavell by frankly admitting the charge had given the prosecution evidence which could not have been otherwise obtained. Under the German Military Code, paragraphs 58, 90, and 160, the offence was treason and punishable by death, and the penalty was applicable to foreigners as well as to German citizens. The court rose next day, and judgment was reserved.

During the week-end M. de Leval tried in vain to find out what was happening. On Monday Mr. Hugh Gibson, the young Secretary of the American Legation, spent the whole day interrogating the German authorities, and as late as 6.20 p.m. he was officially informed that the decision of the court had not been pronounced. At 8 p.m. M. de Leval heard by accident that sentence had been passed at 5 p.m., and that Miss Cavell was to be shot at 2 a.m. on the following morning. The American Legation made a last effort. Two pleas for mercy were drawn up, addressed to Baron von der Lancken and to Baron von Bissing, the German Governor-General. Mr. Whitlock was ill in bed, but he wrote a personal letter to von Bissing, and Mr. Gibson, M. de Leval, and the Spanish Ambassador, the Marquis de Villalobar, called on Baron von der Lancken about 10 p.m. The only power to grant a reprieve belonged to Baron von Bissing, a military pedant of the narrowest type, and the deputation, after an earnest appeal, was dismissed about midnight. That night at ten o'clock a British chaplain was admitted to Miss Cavell's cell. From him we have an account of her last hours. She asked him to tell her friends that she died willingly for her country, without fear or shrinking, and in the true spirit of Christian humility she forgave her enemies. "This I would say, standing as I do in view of God and eternity, I realize that patriotism is not enough. I must have no hatred or bitterness towards any one." At two in the morning she died, her courage and cheerfulness, on the admission of the German chaplain, being unweakened to the end.

Miss Cavell's execution was a judicial murder. It was judicial since, on the letter of the German military law, she was liable to the extreme penalty. But in the case of a woman and a nurse, who had ministered to German sick and wounded, the pedantry which exacted that penalty was an outrage on human decency.* That the German authorities were uneasy about their work was shown by the secrecy upon which they insisted, and which Sir Edward

---

* As was pointed out at the time, a close parallel was to be found in the execution of Dame Alice Lisle by Jeffreys at the Bloody Assize.

Grey in his letter to Mr. Page rightly denounced. There was little comment in the German press, and there was evidence that the incident was by no means applauded by Germany at large. Herr Zimmermann, the German Under-Secretary for Foreign Affairs, could only defend it by a legend of a " world-wide conspiracy," and by the familiar plea of the necessity of " frightfulness " in a crisis " to frighten those who may presume on their sex to take part in enterprises punishable with death." In France and Britain, in Holland and America, the murder woke a profound horror, and revealed as in a flashlight the psychology of that German " culture " which proposed to regenerate the world. Von Bissing and his colleagues stood clear in all their lean and mechanical poverty of soul, cruel by rule, brutal by the text-books, ruthless after a sealed pattern, but yet without the courage of their barbarity, for their policy was furtively pursued and safeguarded with deceit. Against that dark background the spirit of the lonely Englishwoman shone the brighter. We dare not tarnish so noble a deed with facile praise. Her heroism had led captivity captive, and for her death was swallowed up in victory. She was not the least of the sisterhood of great-hearted women who have taught the bravest men a lesson in courage. M. Clemenceau spoke the tribute of the people of France. " The profound truth is that she honoured her country by dying for what is finest in the human soul—that grandeur of which all of us dream but only the rare elect have the chance of attaining. Since the day of Joan of Arc, to whose memory I know that our Allies will one day seek to erect a statue, England has owed us this return. She has nobly given it."

Apart from vague popular uneasiness there were certain urgent problems which weighed upon the public mind, problems which were more difficult for Britain than for her Allies. These problems were the reform of her military machine; her economics and finance; and the policy to be pursued in mobilizing her man-power.

As to the first, it was clear that she lacked a consistent and fully-thought-out strategic policy. She had made adventures without counting the cost; she had drifted into impossible situations, and had suffered Germany to dictate her line of conduct. The words which Demosthenes long ago addressed to his countrymen were singularly applicable at the moment to Britain. " In the business of war and its preparation all is confused, without method or programme. The time to act is lost in preliminaries; the favourable occasions do not wait on our slowness and our timidity. The forces that were judged sufficient reveal themselves insufficient on the day of crisis. . . . These are truths, unfortunately, and without doubt disagreeable to hear. If we were assured that in suppressing all the facts that displease us we should succeed in suppressing them in reality, we would give the people only pleasant news. But if smooth speeches cannot do away with the ugly facts, it would be criminal to delude you by concealment. Learn therefore, that for the war to be well conducted we ought to put ourselves not behind, but at the head of, events. Wisdom lies in directing events, as a general ought to direct his troops, in order to impose his will on them, instead of being reduced to follow the *fait accompli*. Now you, Athenians, who have the greatest resources in cavalry, infantry, revenue, it is not right that you make war against Philip in the way a barbarian boxes. A barbarian, as soon as he is hit, catches hold of the sore place, and if you hit him on the other side, there go his hands. He knows not and wishes not to cover himself in advance, or to foresee the attack. Thus do you. If you learn that Philip is in the Chersonese, you decide on an expedition to that country; if he is at Thermopylæ you race there; if he is elsewhere, no matter where, you follow him there. Here or there, it is he who leads you. You never take an advantageous military initiative. You never foresee anything till you learn that it is either accomplished or about to be accomplished. These tactics have been good enough in other times, but now the crisis has come, and they are no longer tolerable." *

Reasonable men were beginning to look askance at schemes for mere political change, and to direct their attention to some reform of our military machine, especially as concerned its higher control. That, and not a shuffling of Ministers, was the vital need. It had long been evident that the uncertainty in our policy was largely due to the absence of a competent General Staff at home. We had possessed such a Staff in connection with our pre-war army, but the dispatch of the Expeditionary Force had carried it off to the front in the West, and no attempt had been made to replace it. For fourteen months Lord Kitchener had acted as his own General Staff, an arrangement which was the worst conceivable. It was the business of a General Staff to advise the Cabinet on questions of military policy, and to frame strategic plans, and since we were fighting in Europe in alliance with five Powers, the task was highly complex. The whole immense theatre of operations had to be brought under view, and the work of not one British force but half a dozen had to be directed. The absence of a Gen-

* *Philippics*, I., § 36-41.

eral Staff in London meant that the burden of the work fell upon the Secretary of State for War; as the most prominent British soldier, he was the sole military adviser of the British Cabinet; and in addition, he had the tasks of raising and organizing the new armies, and for many months of arranging their munitionment—each more than enough to fill the time of the ablest man. There was the further difficulty that Lord Kitchener's great career had scarcely fitted him for the direction of a European strategy. He had been engaged all his life in laborious undertakings in extra-European fields, and could not be expected to be closely in touch with the most recent developments of military science. The arrangement was one which could only end in failure. The Cabinet were uninformed, and there was no machinery to provide them with that knowledge on which alone a coherent national strategy could be based.

Early in October a beginning was made with the construction of a better machine. The General Staff at Whitehall was reconstituted, with Lieutenant-General Sir Archibald Murray, who had formerly been Sir John French's Chief of Staff in France, at its head. This was the first of a number of changes and experiments, which culminated, as we have seen, in the return of Sir William Robertson to the War Office. In a lengthy speech by the Prime Minister on 2nd November, a new Committee of the Cabinet was announced, which should act as a War Council,* but should communicate its findings before final decision to the Cabinet at large. In the same speech it was made clear that the Dardanelles expedition was not the venture of any one Minister, but a decision of the whole Cabinet. Mr. Churchill, thus exonerated from the wild charges with which for months he had been assailed, took the opportunity soon afterwards of making his own vindication in the House of Commons, and then resigned the sinecure of the Chancellorship of the Duchy of Lancaster, and joined his regiment in France.

In his speech on 2nd November the Prime Minister had referred to the financial position as serious, but as affording no grounds for pessimism. A mere speculation as to the staying powers of the rival belligerents was a barren enterprise, unless the difference between the demands on their endurance was realized. On the general question the Prime Minister was right. " I do not think our position compares unfavourably with that of the Governments

* The Committee was made up of the Prime Minister, Mr Balfour, Mr Lloyd George, Mr. Bonar Law, and Mr. McKenna.

who are opposed to us. The consumption of the German Government and the German nation has been far in excess of what they have been able to produce or import, and their stocks of available commodities are, from all we hear, rapidly diminishing and dwindling. Further, the standard of life of the greater part of the population of Germany has been depressed to a point at which there is little or no margin of reserve. We in these respects apparently and ostensibly stand in a better position." But he was no less right when he went on to insist that if Britain was to sustain the burden there was need of sacrifices and of a universal retrenchment unparalleled in her history. For the German difficulty was one of gradual pinching and embarrassment, but in Britain's problem there were elements which might bring the whole economic machine to a sudden standstill.

Germany, as we have seen, was virtually a complete economic unit, self-sustained and self-sufficing. That is to say, she was only concerned with internal payments, and these, so long as her people believed in the certainty of victory, could be made with ease. She could increase paper currency indefinitely so long as she had printing presses to make the notes. The "goods" were in Germany; she had only to manufacture the "money" to facilitate their transference to the hands of the Government; and while her people trusted to the credit of the state there would be no trouble about the transfer. The wheels of war have never stopped in deference to an economic purism. Britain had this problem also. She had to raise money internally to pay her troops in the field and the sailors on her fleets, and her own producers for that part of the war material which was manufactured at home. But she had to do more. She, like France, was still an open country, with commercial relations throughout the entire globe. She had to import for herself and her Allies large quantities of war stores, and she had also to import great amounts of raw material and food to keep her civilian life going. And for these imports she must make payments which the foreign exporters would accept. She could pay her own subjects with her War Loan stock, but that was her own kind of money, not the kind which was current in foreign countries. The British financial problem was therefore twofold—to raise funds internally for domestic payments, and to provide some means of meeting our liability to foreign exporters.

The first problem was the simpler. In the last resort an indefinite amount could be raised, even if we were compelled to inflate our currency or resort to forced loans. No belligerent Government which retains the confidence of the nation need ever be stopped short by any domestic payments. The aim of Britain was so to manipulate her levies as to produce the minimum of economic dislocation. The cost of the war had steadily risen. In June it was estimated at £2,660,000 a day ; in September it was £3,500,000 ; in November it was £4,000,000 ; and for the year 1916–17 it was calculated at £5,000,000. For the year 1915–16 the Chancellor of the Exchequer put the total British expenditure at close on £1,600,000,000, of which £190,000,000 was allocated to the Navy, £715,000,000 to the Army, and £423,000,000 as loans to our Allies and Colonies.

In earlier chapters we have seen the results of the two loans of November 1914 and July 1915. Borrowing on a still vaster scale was in the near prospect, but when the Chancellor of the Exchequer introduced the second War Budget in the House of Commons on 21st September he did not specify any fresh loans. He confined himself to dealing with the amount to be raised by new taxation— over £300,000,000, leaving nearly £1,300,000,000, to be met by borrowing. The income tax was increased by adding 40 per cent. to the existing rates ; and as this increase was not accompanied by any revision of the complicated system which had grown up during the preceding seventy years, the result was an exceedingly intricate and difficult scale of charges. Generally speaking, the effect was to assess large unearned incomes at about 3s. 6d. in the pound, and earned incomes under £1,500 at a fraction over 2s. 1d. All incomes in excess of £130 were made liable to taxation, and the amount allowed to go free was reduced to £120, though the deduction for each child was increased from £20 to £25. The tax, so far as employees engaged in manual labour were concerned, was to be paid quarterly, and employers were allowed to deduct it from salaries. The super-tax, too, was increased on incomes over £8,000. There were a number of other financial expedients. The customs dues on commodities already taxed were increased, and a new 33⅓ per cent. *ad valorem* duty was imposed on certain foreign articles of luxury, such as motor cars, cinema films, clocks, and musical instruments. The aim of this impost was restrictive as well as revenue-producing, in order to lower our imports from abroad of non-essential commodities. An excess profits tax of 50 per cent. was imposed on all business profits made during the war, excess profits being defined as those in excess of an average of recent years, allowances being made for any extra capital employed. These most substantial imposts, which bore very heavily on the middle and professional classes, were accepted without murmuring, even with alacrity, by the nation. " It has been my duty," said the Chancellor of the Exchequer, "to ask the country to assent to taxes on a gigantic scale. Surely it must have been a subject of congratulation to every member of the House that the country has accepted these burdens with almost unanimous willingness, and it is without precedent in a great war of any country that the nation has come forward and literally asked to be taxed."

Far more complex, and at the same time far more urgent, was the question of how to pay for our foreign imports. In the case of an importing country like Britain there is usually an excess of imports over the value of her exports. This balance was normally liquidated partly by her earnings from freights, partly from her banking commissions, and partly from the interest on foreign securities in British hands. In time of war it was obvious that the first two sources would greatly decline, since so much of her mercantile marine was being used for war purposes, and since the usual financial activity of the London market was restricted. Moreover, by the import of war stores the balance against her was hugely increased. In the case of the United States it was possible to get a calculation approximately exact. For the year ending June 30, 1914, the excess of American exports over British imports was £60,000,000. For the year ending June 30, 1915, it was £131,000,000. If we take the figure of £60,000,000 as the excess which could be met in the normal way of trade, then £71,000,000 had to be met by extraordinary measures—that is, by other means than freight earnings or the interest on British-owned American securities. The result of this abnormal situation, which the Government appeared to be slow in recognizing, was that the American exchange went steadily against Britain. Early in November it was as much as thirty-six cents below the normal. This meant that to settle her debts to America she must pay considerably more than the amount of the debts. One result, partly attributable to this fact, was a great inflation of prices. For the nine months ending September 1915 she imported 17,000,000 cwts. less of grain and flour than for the same period in 1913, but they cost her £20,000,000 more. She imported 2,300,000 cwts. less meat, but at an increased cost of £26,000,000.

To meet this grave situation there were various possible expedients. One was to increase her civil production, and, therefore, her exports, but this war conditions forbade. Another was to reduce her imports of all non-essential commodities, and the thrift campaign in Britain and the import duties of the September Budget were steps to this end. A third was to export capital—gold and foreign securities. A fourth was to induce foreign exporting countries to make her a loan and grant her commercial credits. Both the third and fourth plans were adopted. Some gold was exported, but there were obvious limits to this method. The Government took steps to prepare a register of American securities in British hands, an easy task so far as the chief holders —the banks and insurance companies—were concerned. The amount so held was believed to be between £500,000,000 and £700,000,000. It was proposed that they should be sold to the Government, who would pay for them with War Loan stock and use them to meet our debts in the United States. Meantime, early in September, an Anglo-French Commission arrived in New York to attempt to arrange an American loan. In spite of the furious opposition of the German sympathisers in America, a 5 per cent. loan for £100,000,000 was arranged, a large figure when we remember the aversion of American investors to foreign securities, and the high rate of interest to which they had been accustomed. There seems little doubt that the loan was floated by pro-Ally sentiment rather than by purely business considerations. The proceeds were to be employed exclusively in America for the purpose of steadying the exchange, and at the same time, private commercial credits were arranged in the United States for the same end to the amount of some £30,000,000. These various expedients did not clear the situation, but they eased it, and they pointed a way to a continuous policy on the subject based upon the friendly co-operation of American business men.

Meanwhile a vigorous effort was being made to solve the recruiting problem without adopting legal compulsion. The National Register had been compiled in August, and in September a conference of Trade Union representatives decided to organize throughout the country a special Labour Recruiting Campaign. On 11th October Lord Derby, who had served as Postmaster-General in the last Unionist Ministry, and was the most popular and influential figure in the north of England, was appointed Director of Recruiting, and a vast activity was inaugurated. The campaign was regarded as the final trial of the " voluntary " system. If before a date in the beginning of December sufficient recruits were not forthcoming, the Prime Minister in his speech of 2nd November had foreshadowed—with many qualifications—a conscriptive method as the only alternative. Early in October it was clear that the rate of voluntary recruiting had fallen dangerously low. To keep our existing units at strength, a steady flow of at least 35,000 recruits per week was required, and the actual weekly average was far short of this figure. There were in the country over two million single men of military age unenlisted, and there were great numbers of married men who were willing to join the army, but who not unnaturally objected to taking the step while the unmarried hung back. Lord Derby's appeal was directed to both classes. By enlisting men in groups, which should not come up till called on, the path was made easier for those who had special and terminable difficulties in their way. Once a man enlisted he could appeal to a local tribunal to consider his case, and either exempt him or transfer him to a later group; but he must first enlist. If he liked, he could join a regiment immediately; if he preferred to be relegated to a group, he was attested, and returned to his civilian occupation till he was called up. Groups were to be called up strictly in order, the younger unmarried men before the older, and all the single before the married.

The first limit of enlistment was fixed as 30th November. The work began with great impetus and enthusiasm, and the Trade Union and political leaders flung themselves heartily into it. Enlistment among the married men was especially large; but they wished for some enlightenment as to what would be their status if the scheme failed. If, for example, few single men attested, would the married groups be called up at once? The Prime Minister in the House of Commons on 2nd November attempted to answer this question. " So far as I am concerned," he said, " I should certainly say that the obligation of the married man to enlist ought not to be enforced or binding upon him unless and until—I hope by voluntary effort, and if not, by some other means—the unmarried men are dealt with first." This seemed too much like an expression of personal opinion to be satisfactory, so on 11th November Lord Derby officially announced that he had been authorized by the Prime Minister to say that he had pledged his Government as well as himself. In a further statement, published on 20th November, after a reply by the Prime Minister in Parliament had once more clouded the subject with uncertainty, the matter was put clearly and finally. If the young unmarried men did not come forward voluntarily, then either the married men would be released from their pledge, **or a bill** would be passed compelling the young men to serve.

During the last week of November recruiting activities reached their height. Every effort was made to increase the gross total. Men from "starred" industries enlisted; civil servants were invited to attest; the eyesight test for recruits was postponed till their group should be called up. The date for the conclusion of the canvass was extended to 11th December, and then to 12th December, after which day the group system should cease. The rush to the recruiting offices during the few days before 12th December resembled the stress in the first months of war. All comers were accepted, and since it was found impossible to attest all who applied before midnight on 12th December, the names of those still unattested were taken, and the group system was kept open for them three days longer. The great effort had now been made, and it remained to await its results. The next fortnight was filled with rumours. It was known that the gross attestation had been large, but that owing to the indiscriminating character of the recruiting a great number must be subsequently rejected, and it was also believed that a very substantial proportion of the unmarried had refused to enlist. Speculation was set at rest on January 4, 1916, by the publication of Lord Derby's report.

The grand total of men of military age, excluding those who joined the army between August 15 and October 23, 1915, was 5,011,441. Of these 2,829,263 men had enlisted, attested, or had been rejected. These large figures, however, would require to be cut down, as they included many "starred" men, and nearly a million who had not been medically examined. It was certain that the local tribunals would make further reductions, as many who had attested would be regarded as "indispensable." Further analysis was necessarily speculative. It was estimated that of the 840,000 single men attested, not more than 343,386 would be available; of the 1,344,979 married men, not more than 487,676. This gave a total yield from the canvass of a little over 830,000. Again, according to the Prime Minister's pledge, the men in the married groups could only be called up if no more than a negligible quantity of single men remained unaccounted for. But out of the 2,179,231 single men available, only 1,150,000 were accounted for under the Derby canvass. If from these figures the number of "starred" single men unattested—378,071—was deducted, it left a total of 651,160 unstarred single men who had not come forward. "This," wrote Lord Derby, "is far from being a negligible quantity, and, under the circumstances, I am very distinctly of opinion that in order to redeem the pledge mentioned above it will not be possible to hold married men to their attestation unless and until the services of single men have been obtained by other means, the present system having failed to bring them to the colours." Lord Derby pointed out some of the difficulties under which he had laboured. The enormous list of " reserved " occupations had had a most detrimental effect on recruiting. The previous " starring," too, had led to many obvious abuses. Nevertheless, including those rejected on medical grounds, a total of nearly 3,000,000 men had placed themselves at the disposal of their country. Men had offered themselves from foreign towns wherever there was a British community, and from the remotest parts of the British possessions. " The canvass," Lord Derby concluded, " shows very distinctly that it is not want of courage that is keeping men back, nor is there the slightest sign but that the country as a whole is as determined to support the Prime Minister in his pledge made at the Guildhall on November 9, 1914, as it was when the pledge was made. There is abundant evidence of a determination to see the war through to a successful conclusion."

The publication of the Derby Report cleared the air of rumours, and focussed national opinion. The situation had been simplified. A campaign of voluntary enlistment, conducted with every conceivable device to stimulate enthusiasm and awaken the sense of duty, had yielded less than 900,000 men. Of these more than half would not be available, according to the Prime Minister's pledge, unless steps were taken to compel the enlistment of the large unattested balance of single men. The view of the overwhelming majority of the nation was never for a moment in doubt. The Prime Minister could not be false to an explicit undertaking, given after due consideration and many times repeated. On Wednesday, January 5, 1916, Mr. Asquith introduced the Military Service Bill into Parliament.

So far as opinion went, the case may be briefly summarized. There was no considerable section of the people against the application of legal compulsion, except the official organization of the Labour Party and the Trade Unions. A handful of extreme Radicals, who were very generally repudiated by their constituencies, purported to oppose the measure on principle, and there were a number of small doctrinaire bodies, religious and secular, throughout the land which followed suit. Those who objected to all war and the few who specifically objected to the present war were naturally in opposition. Within the Cabinet itself there were three doubting Ministers. The Chancellor of the Exchequer, Mr.

McKenna, had scruples from the point of view of national finance in withdrawing any further large number of men from productive industry; the President of the Board of Trade, Mr. Runciman, knowing the shortage of skilled labour, feared the effect of wholesale recruiting; the Home Secretary, Sir John Simon, was understood to have a conscientious objection to any departure from voluntaryism, though he had assented to Acts which compelled time-expired marines and soldiers to remain under service. The difficulties of the first two Ministers were very real, and worthy of all respect. A nation in a struggle for life must fight with all its weapons, and for Britain her wealth and industries were not the least part of her armoury. The financial position was anxious, and if our financial strength weakened it would mean as much as the loss of armies to the Allied cause. We were short of labour for munitions and shipbuilding, for war services as well as for civilian life. Clearly a balance must be struck between rival interests, all equally vital to the conduct of the war. On the other hand, it was to be said that the wholesale "starring" and reservation of industries had met a large part of these Ministers' claims, and that, if priority was to be given to any one need, it should be to the demand for fighting men. An army may conquer, even if it be badly supplied and its pay in arrears, but it cannot conquer if it is too small.

The debate on the Military Service Bill was one of the few occasions during the war when the centre of interest was the House of Commons, and the Prime Minister's adroitness and power of conciliation served a true national purpose. The Bill—which was not extended to Ireland—applied to all single men and widowers without children dependent on them between the ages of eighteen and forty-one on August 15, 1915. The Derby groups were revived, and men were given the opportunity of voluntarily joining them. If not, from a day five weeks after the passing of the Bill, unless in the interval they had been exempted, they would be held to have enlisted for the duration of the war. Exemption was granted to ministers of religion of all denominations, to men holding certificates of exemption, to those who had been medically rejected, to those required for indispensable industries and employments, to those who supported relations or dependents, to necessary civil servants, and to "conscientious objectors" to war in any form.

The Cabinet was now unanimous, with the exception of the Home Secretary, who resigned his office and led the meagre opposition against the Bill. His speech did more than that of any of the advocates of the measure to convince the country of its necessity, for the best case which so able a lawyer as Sir John Simon could make out against the policy was weak and captious. The most striking speeches in support of the Bill were made by Mr. Balfour, Mr. Bonar Law, Mr. John Ward, now colonel of the Navvies Battalion, and Brigadier-General Seely, who had returned that day from the front. The first reading was carried by 403 against 105—a majority of 298. The second reading was sanctioned by a majority of 392. On 24th January, the Bill passed the House of Commons, the minority vote being no more than 36.

The attitude of the Labour Party and of organized labour throughout the country deserves a brief notice, for it was one of the most characteristically British performances in the campaign. The three Labour members of the Government, Mr. Arthur Henderson, Mr. Brace, and Mr. G. H. Roberts, were supporters of the Bill. On 6th January, a Congress of Labour delegates met in London to consider the question. The Congress was composed of delegates from three Labour bodies—the Trade Union Congress, the General Federation of Trade Unions, and the Labour Party. It did not represent the bulk of the working-classes, nor did it represent all the unions, which themselves were a minority of wage-earners; but it was a conference of real importance, representing the management side of the various workers' organizations, and therefore the more advanced leaders of working-class thought. The debate showed that the members were not convinced that compulsion was required by military needs and suspected a device of capitalism, and, above all, that they feared that the law might be so worked as to bring pressure to bear on the men in the workshops and to establish industrial slavery. By a majority of a million—according to the curious system of card votes—the delegates instructed the Labour Party in Parliament to oppose the measure. The three Labour members of the Government accordingly placed their resignations in the Prime Minister's hands, not because they objected to the Bill but because they approved of it. On 12th January a conference took place between the Prime Minister and various delegates of Labour, when Mr. Asquith undertook to provide safeguards that the Bill should not have the effect of introducing industrial compulsion. The resignations of the three Ministers were withdrawn pending the annual Conference of the Labour Party, which was due at Bristol on 26th

January. Meantime the South Wales Miners' Federation held a meeting at Cardiff and passed a "down tools" resolution to give effect to their opposition, a move which did not secure the assent of the other mining districts in the country. On 13th January the Miners' Federation of Great Britain met in London, and decided by a majority of over half a million to oppose the Bill. Nottinghamshire, the only district where a plebiscite of the members had been taken, dissented, and Cleveland, North Wales, and South Derbyshire did not vote. The British Labour Congress, in which the miners were represented, met on 26th January, after the passing of the Bill through the House of Commons. By a majority of nearly a million they approved the war. By large majorities they repudiated conscription and disapproved of the Military Service Bill. By a small majority, the miners not voting, they decided not to agitate for repeal when the measure had become law; and by a very large majority they agreed that the three Labour members should retain their posts in the Government.

This curious result, which only the thoughtless would label inconsistency, was a typical product of our national temperament. We were loth to give up cherished dogmas even under the stress of a dire necessity. We were determined to make the omelette, but not less determined to smash no single egg in the process. But we were also a practical people, and the practical argument in the long run prevailed. The Merthyr by-election, where in a constituency formerly represented by an extreme Socialist a wholehearted advocate of compulsion was elected by several thousands, and the plebiscite of the Notts miners showed the true temper of the average citizen. Had a General Election been forced over the Bill, there can be no question but that few, if any, of its opponents would have returned to Parliament. The Labour delegates were honest men in a quandary. They could not easily give up the vague political creed which they had preached for years on every platform. But they were practical men and Englishmen, and they recognized compelling facts. If they could not formally repudiate their dogmas, they could neglect them. That has been the way of Britain for a thousand years. Her theory may be belated, but it is too dear and ancient for sacrilegious hands; in a crisis her practice will be guided by common sense.

The importance of the Derby Scheme did not lie in its numerical results. These were terribly whittled away by the chaotic methods of "starring" men and "reserving" industries. It lay in the fact that, after a fair trial, it had exposed to the nation the inadequacy of any voluntary system to meet our needs, and had brought the country to that great decision by which the whole of its manhood was placed at the disposal of the State. Once the sacrifice had been faced, proper methods of procedure would discover themselves. The effect upon our Allies was immediate and beneficent, and the impression produced on the enemy might be judged from the strenuous efforts of the German press to belittle the event. Britain had at last slipped the foil from her weapon. She had given the most solemn proof that for her there was no turning back.

Opponents of the Military Service Bill cried "Ichabod" because we had departed from a cherished British tradition. "There are some," said Sir John Simon, "who regard the principle of voluntary enlistment as a real heritage of the English people." The view was bad history, for in reality we had returned to the custom of our forefathers. "Commissions of Array" had provided a large part of the armies which the kings of England led to France. King Harry summoned his archers before Agincourt almost on the terms of the Bill.* Cromwell's New Model Army was not a voluntary army; for eight years, from 1643 to 1651, more than half the infantry were pressed men, summoned by the county committees; and it was only when the Army ruled the land that its power and prestige brought forth sufficient voluntary recruits. The principle of compulsion for land service at home was accepted in the Napoleonic wars, and the Navy which fought at Trafalgar was not voluntarily enlisted. The truth was that in recent years Britain had tended to have a short historical memory. The doctrines of the mid-nineteenth century—by no means the most fruitful epoch of our political thought—with their insistence upon an intense individualism in economics and social duty, were accepted as an integral part of the constitution and the national temper. They were in reality abnormal and parvenu growths, the mules of political theory "without pride of ancestry or hope of posterity."

The most interesting parallel to the step now taken by Britain was the course followed by Lincoln in the second year of the American Civil War. At the beginning of the struggle he had about 18,000 regulars, most of them serving on the western frontier, and he had four-fifths of the regular officers. He showed how little

* " Recruit me Lancashire and Cheshire both,
   And Derbyshire hills that are so free,
  But no married man, nor no widow's son,
    For no woman's curse shall go with me."

he appreciated the magnitude of the coming conflict by asking for only 75,000 volunteers, and these to serve for no more than three months. Then came the battle of Bull Run, which opened his eyes. He was empowered by Congress to raise 500,000 volunteers for three years' service, and presently that number was increased to 1,000,000. Recruits came in freely; and, if the small population of the North be remembered, the effort must rank as one of the most remarkable ever made by a system of voluntary enlistment. Lincoln began by asking for 600,000, and he got 700,000. After Fredericksburg he asked for 300,000 men, and he got 430,000. Then he asked for another 300,000, of which each state should provide its quota. But he only got 87,000, a little more than a quarter of his requirements. The South, meanwhile, had for many months adopted conscription. It was now a year and a half since the first battle, and the campaign had entered upon that period of drag which was the time of blackest depression in the North.

Then Lincoln took the great step. Of all parts of the world at the moment the North was that in which the idea of individual liberty was most deeply implanted. It was a land which had always gloried in being unmilitary in contradistinction to the effete monarchies of Europe; the American Constitution had shown the most scrupulous regard for individual rights; the press was unbridled and most powerful; the country, too, was full of philosophic idealists who preferred dogmas to facts and made their voices heard in the papers and on the platform. Moreover, there was a General Election approaching, and, since the war had gone badly, there was a good chance that Lincoln might be defeated if he in any way impaired his popularity. There were not wanting crowds of men—some of them of great ability and prestige—who declared that it was far better to lose the war than to win it by transgressing one article of the current political creed. There were others, Lincoln's friends and advisers, who warned him solemnly that no hint of compulsion would ever be tolerated by free-born Americans, and that if he dared to propose the thing he would have an internal revolution to add to his troubles. Again and again he was told, in language that has a familiar sound, that the true friends of the enemy were the compulsionists. Lincoln was in the fullest sense of the word a democratic statesman, believing that government must be not only for the people but by the people. When he was faced with the necessity of finding some other way of raising men than as volunteers, he was faced with the task of jettisoning—not the principles, for they are hardier things—but all the sentiments and traditions of his political life.

But Lincoln knew that it was the business of a statesman to lead the people, to act, to initiate a policy, and not to wait like a dumb lackey in the antechamber of his masters. He knew that policy should be not an abstract dogma but a working code based upon realities. He knew also that in a crisis it is wisest to grasp the nettle. He saw the magnitude of the crisis, that it was a question of life or death, whatever journalists and demagogues might say. So he took the plunge, and on 3rd March, 1863, a law was passed to raise armies by conscription. He did not hesitate to employ drastic measures against those who encouraged resistance. He met the " thin end of the wedge " argument in words which deserve to be remembered: that " he did not believe that a man could contract so strong a taste for emetics during a temporary illness as to insist upon feeding upon them during the remainder of a healthful life." There were violent mass meetings and much wild talk, and there were riots in New York and elsewhere in which a number of lives were lost; but in a very little time the good sense of the country prevailed. It was one of the two greatest acts of Lincoln's life; the other was when he decided to fight for the integrity of the nation. And like all great acts of courage it had its reward. Four months later Gettysburg was won, Vicksburg surrendered to Grant, and the tide turned. The recruits came in—300,000 in October 1863, nearly 1,300,000 in 1864, and it is an interesting fact that 85 per cent. of these were volunteers; the effect of conscription was to revive voluntary enlistment. The men had been found, the resources of the country had been fully mobilized, and two years after the passing of the Act came that April day when Lee surrendered to Grant at Appomattox.

CHAPTER XLVI.

SOME SIDE-LIGHTS ON THE GERMAN TEMPER.

The Growth of the *Politiques*—German Military Opinion—Views of German Financiers—The Popular Mind—Bethmann-Hollweg.

In an earlier chapter we discussed some of the fundamentals of that German psychology which precipitated the war, and which, so long as it endured, made peace unthinkable save by unconditional surrender. In the present chapter it is proposed to review the temper of Germany after eighteen months of fighting. A protracted struggle is a great dissolvent of dreams. The touchstone of suffering rejects many grandiose theories. The second winter of such a war inevitably compelled reflection and a stock-taking on the part of all the belligerents. The first careless rapture gave place to prudential considerations, and Germany was forced to envisage the future in the light not of what she desired but of what she could compass. There is always a difficulty in assessing the temper of a hostile people, more especially when that people is beleaguered and blockaded. To the student the evidence available was contained in the speeches and messages of German statesmen, the German newspapers and journals, and in the reports of neutral travellers. Through Switzerland, Holland, and Scandinavia there filtered also a good deal of information, in the form of records of private conversations by neutrals with German leaders in politics and finance. But the evidence demanded cautious use, for public opinion in Germany was at the best incoherent and ill-organized. The voice of a disciplined nation is the voice of its masters, till the spell is suddenly broken and a babel of tongues is loosed. Hence in assessing the German temper it was not safe to dogmatize. Tendencies could be fairly recognized, but as yet they were tendencies only and not proven facts.

There had always been a good deal of peace talk. Proposals for a settlement were suggested to neutral Powers, especially

America, but they were in the nature of " feelers" rather than considered terms. The Allies had made no secret of their irreducible minimum. Germany was clearly unable to do this, and she contented herself with stating her maximum, to see how the world received it. The first suggestion of terms was merely preposterous, and was probably intended for domestic effect rather than to create an impression of reasonableness abroad. But by the middle of the winter of 1915, when overtures for a separate peace had been rejected by Russia, and when the temper of France showed clearly enough what her answer was likely to be, it became the fashion among German journalists who had access to the neutral press to lay the blame for the continuance of the war solely on Britain Germany was represented as a magnanimous conqueror who was willing to use her victories with moderation. She asked only for security for her legitimate national developments, and Britain, in her insensate commercial jealousy, would hear of no terms except her ruin. The doctrine of the " Hymn of Hate " was repeated in more decorous language. There was " one foe and one alone—England." In Austria, on the other hand, there was a tendency to a different view. In more than one inspired article it was urged that the world was large enough to allow both Britain and Germany room for commercial expansion, and that the time was ripe for an understanding. But such articles also laid it down as a condition precedent that Germany, as the victor, must be given substantial compensation for her sacrifices. This probably represented the broadest stratum of opinion in the Central Empires. " We have won, but circumstances forbid us to reap the just fruits of our victory. Let our success be acknowledged, and we will accept a very modest reward, for if the war goes on much longer the whole of Europe will be ruined." It was futile to discuss these *ballons d'essai*, for there was no clear or consistent national will behind them. The German mind was in confusion. The great initial plan, elaborated with such care and precision, had failed. Germany had not yet adjusted her point of view to the changed conditions, and she hesitated between the old bluster and a rather clumsy diplomacy. The problem had so many sides that it is worth while to examine it in more detail.

The military question, on which all others depended, was not discussed with any great freedom. The German censorship forbade it. The experts wrote from a brief, and there was none of that informed and candid criticism of operations which was found in France, and, to a small extent, in Britain. But it was possible to detect a change in the strategic reviews which appeared from time to time in the German press. In the first place, they began to reveal some perplexity of mind. So long as the great initial plan was feasible, so long even as Falkenhayn's revised version promised success, they spoke with one undivided voice. But early in the winter they showed a certain wavering. Bernhardi, for example, was a distinguished soldier who wrote with real authority on military subjects. But he was allowed to contribute to the American press articles which were sheer foolishness. He prophesied wildly from day to day, and all his prophecies failed. Now, Bernhardi did not write nonsense without a cause, and his journalistic vagaries suggested a certain confusion in the minds of those behind him.

In the second place, the old contempt for their opponents had gone. It had been succeeded by a genuine respect for Britain. It was very generally recognized that the lines in East and West had become rigid, and, whatever flamboyant writers might say to the contrary, that the German adventures in the Near East, though they might annoy the Allies, could not gain victory. The meaning of sea-power was tardily recognized. The war had reached a stalemate, and was rapidly becoming a trial of economic endurance. An ambitious offensive on the part of Germany would not better matters. The Imperial Chancellor, in an interview given about Christmas time to an American journalist, quoted a " high military authority " to this effect :—

" Germany could take Paris. It would only be a question of how many men we were willing to sacrifice. But that would not bring England to terms, and therefore would not end the war. We could take Petrograd. But suppose we drove the Tsar out of his capital —England would not care. We could drive the Italian army into the sea—it would make no difference to England. The more territory we occupy the thinner our front and the greater difficulty in supplying it. Going ahead on such lines would help England more than us."

These were candid words, very different from the official talk of a year before. It would appear that the High Command had come to the conclusion that no further offensives on the grand scale could profitably be taken. Endurance was the *mot d'ordre*, and they believed that they could endure. They were wholly convinced that no Allied attack could pierce the iron walls on East and West. So, at any rate, they said, and they had some reason for the belief in the events of the past autumn. How much the capacity for endurance of army and people filled the thoughts of the generals was shown by an interesting letter from Hindenburg to the Imperial

Chancellor, which was published in a Berlin paper.* The Field Marshal appealed to the statesman to do something to ameliorate the life of the lower and lower-middle classes, from whom his soldiers were chiefly drawn. Complaints of their sufferings, he said, came in every letter, and this weakened the spirit of his men. They could not fight with a free mind if they believed that their kinsfolk were in want.

Throughout the German military comments on the situation there ran a curious note of exasperation. By all the text-books their enemies should long ere now have acknowledged defeat. Germany was entrenched on the soil of France and Russia; she had occupied all Belgium and Poland and Serbia; the Allies had failed to break her front in the main theatres, and they had met with costly checks in Gallipoli and Mesopotamia. The Germans had always regarded war as an enlarged form of *Kriegspiel*. Had this been a war game played at some Staff college, Germany would have scored most of the points, and would long ago have been adjudged victor. Her perverse foes did not recognize when they were soundly beaten. Following upon this exasperation, there could be detected a dawning sense that the great German offensive had shot its bolt. She still claimed the initiative, but it was a barren initiative. More successes would get her no nearer victory, though she believed that in the field the Allies were equally debarred from the hope of winning a decision. Her General Staff would appear to have come very near to recognizing that military effort had done its most, and that the future lay in the economic sphere. The Army chiefs were being converted to Tirpitz's creed. It was Britain's command of the sea which barred the way to Germany's hegemony by land. But for that fatal Navy an early decision would have been won. It was that Navy, too, which threatened Germany's economic endurance. The "freedom of the seas" in Germany's sense of the phrase must be the first of Germany's winnings, even if to gain it she had to sacrifice for a little some of her cherished territorial dreams. She could not hope to dictate to the world on land if Britain ruled the water.

The economic situation was not less hard to assess than the military, both as regards the actual facts and the way in which the German people viewed them. Undoubtedly the land was very short of many necessaries, and had to use unpalatable substitutes. A good meal could be had at a restaurant at a lower price than was possible in the Allied cities, but this was largely due to skilful stage

* *Deutsche Tageszeitung* of January 23, 1916.

management. As a matter of fact, luxuries were more plentiful in Germany than many staples. Stage management extended to all the cities and towns which neutral visitors were likely to frequent, but it stopped short of the country districts. There beyond question there was great discomfort, a discomfort which just stopped short of want. Hindenburg's appeal to the Imperial Chancellor put the matter fairly: " It is one of the results of German economic development that the small business man in particular is compelled, almost without exception, to have recourse to loans. In view of the conditions of payment and of the markets produced by the war, the wife and family have the utmost difficulty in keeping the trade or business of the husband or father going." Further, the shortage or stoppage of some of the most popular foodstuffs was a sore trial to a people who were inelastic in their dietary. The result, when these facts were taken in conjunction with the heavy death lists, was a very deep and widespread depression. This depression was easy to overestimate. It had not reached the point where life becomes intolerable to the ordinary man, and he agitates wildly for change. The discipline and the very real courage of the German nation still postponed that day. Its coming might have been assured had the blockade of the Allies been more strictly drawn. Many foodstuffs still entered the country through neutral channels, and vital necessaries of war such as fats and lubricating oils; for though the results of the blockade had been striking, they fell considerably short of that " strangle-hold " which had been the Allied aim.

Economic distress, however slight, is usually intolerable unless there is hope of a speedy relief. The ordinary man was buoyed up in the last resort by the confidence that victory would come, and with it a feast of fat things. The economist, perturbed by the present, and aware that the dream of a lucrative victory had gone, looked farther into the future. He saw at the best an impoverished country, with an immense debt, shut off from many of the chief markets of the world. For exports America was his main hope, and this explained the activity of German agents in the United States, and the general desire among German statesmen to avoid a breach with Washington. In domestic policy he encouraged his soul with the vision of a Central European Empire exploited and administered by a single industrial policy. In the late summer of 1915 a remarkable book was published at Berlin, under the title of *Mittleleuropa*. Its author, Friedrich Naumann, had been a Radical deputy and a Free Trader, and he sought to build out of the wreckage a new economic state. A period of war, he wrote, is always a period of intellectual receptivity ; and as Bismarck laid the foundation of the German Empire amid the roar of the guns of 1870, so, during the stress of this greater conflict, the seed of a new order might be sown. His plan was to make of the Central Powers—Germany and Austria-Hungary—an economic unit. After the war, he argued, the nations would group themselves into large economic units, and it was the business of Germany to look near home and use the means which lay ready to her hand. The new Mid-Europe would include a tenth of the globe and 200 millions of people, to set against the 95 millions of France, the 107 millions of America, the 170 millions of Russia, and the 425 millions of Britain. His scheme was not a mere customs union, but an industrial unity. Austria was backward and half exploited. Her labour conditions were bad, and the lack of opportunity at home drove great numbers of her people to emigrate. Hungary, the granary of Europe, produced only half the yield per acre of agricultural Prussia. In the difficult period after the war it would be necessary for the Central Powers to pool their resources, and for Austria to submit to organization and exploitation on German lines. He dreamed of a great system of syndicates, which, while meeting the just claims of labour, should, with the help of the state, bring the joint production to a maximum. The war had compelled a wholesale state organization of internal production. Let that system continue after peace, for economic victory was to the biggest economic battalions.

This attractive theory found many supporters. It was blessed by the Austrian Prime Minister and by the German Minister of Finance. But it was looked at askance by Hungary and by many Austrian men of business ; and it was vehemently assailed by the " Overseas " school, of which we may take Reventlow and Ballin as representatives. The latter continued to implore Germany not " to turn her eyes away from the sea," and the former argued with some force that the Central Empire school based their views upon a " freedom of the seas," to be obtained from Britain not by coercion but by agreement. By all means, he said, organize Central Europe as an economic unit ; but before that can be done the British supremacy on the ocean must cease. In this plea he was supported not only by the naval school of Tirpitz, but by the army chiefs, who recognized that the most resounding successes of German arms on land were nullified by the Allied strength at sea.

The views of the great German financiers on the situation were in many ways the most instructive of all. It is certain that a very large share of the original responsibility for war must be laid upon their shoulders. They had welcomed hostilities for two reasons; first, because they believed that the war would be short and glorious, and would lead to a world-wide prestige, and an unprecedented commercial expansion; secondly, because the burden of armaments had begun to press heavily upon German industries, and a successful war would permit of a reduction. When the first dream vanished, the great captains of industry and the financiers, such as Rathenau, Gwinner, and Ballin, had played a large part in that domestic concentration and reorganization with which Germany had replied to the Allied blockade. But as the months passed their hearts grew heavy. They saw Germany creating internal credits which could only be redeemed in the event of a crushing victory. They saw the annual interest due on loans rapidly approaching the point when it would exceed the annual increment of the country. As a complete victory receded, they were compelled to face the grim fact that even a draw would involve something very like bankruptcy. They had gambled high, and had lost; it only remained to secure the little that remained from the colossal *débâcle*. Accordingly, during the early winter months many strange overtures, for which Gwinner was chiefly responsible, emanated from the German circles of high finance. French and British men of business were adjured to interfere while there was yet time. It was pointed out that, whatever the sufferings of Germany if the war were prolonged, the sufferings of the Allies in industry and commerce would be little less. Was Europe, it was asked, to make a gift of her trade to America? Such jeremiads were accompanied by suggestions for peace. The terms proposed varied, but their tone was moderation itself compared with the schemes which had filled neutral journals during the summer and autumn. But two essential conditions were common to all. Germany would pay no indemnity, and she demanded the "freedom of the seas." This latter phrase was hard to interpret; but, as so used, it appeared to mean a revival and extension of the ill-fated Declaration of London, the idea being that Britain must be stopped from using her naval power in time of war so as to interfere, by blockade or otherwise, with the success of land operations. In this respect the views of the financiers coincided with those of the General Staff. How such freedom could be won did not appear. The war had taught Britain lessons which she would not readily recant, and the more sober German opinion could not be blind to this obstacle. Nothing but the destruction of the British Fleet would win the licence which they demanded. Hence it seemed probable that the interest of the German High Command was turning more and more to the sea. Germany had had time since the beginning of the war to build ships of a new pattern. Her scientific ingenuity had provided her with vastly improved weapons. Careful watchers of the omens were inclined to think that the first half of 1916 would see some great naval effort—that campaign at which the Imperial Chancellor had hinted, " which would strike a vital blow at England."

To turn to the question of the temper of the ordinary German citizen was to be faced with a complete lack of real data for judgment. There was no public opinion in Germany, self-conscious and vocal, such as could be found in France and Britain. A rigid censorship had smoothed out the press, and the foreign observer was left to deduce German feeling from the kind of public arguments which were used to placate and strengthen it. The censorship, the roseate reports from Headquarters, the robust optimism of statesmen, prevented the ordinary man from realizing the true situation. He knew that Germany had paid a high price, for he saw the circle of his family and his friends shrinking, and he felt in his daily life the rigour of war, but he could not but believe that the reward was assured. Germany had achieved victory, and only the blind folly of her enemies prevented them from yielding. A little more endurance, a little more effort, and their surrender would be compelled. But there were not wanting voices to declare some dissatisfaction. Germany had overrun Poland, Belgium, and part of France. She had won a long series of great battles, in honour of which the cities had been beflagged and the schools given holiday. She had conquered the road to the East, and brought under her influence the leaders of Islam. The end was near, but why were her enemies so blind to its imminence ? It was generally believed that the Imperial Chancellor's speech of 9th December would bring the Allies crowding upon each other's heels to sue for forgiveness. But the stiff-necked generation had shown no signs of grace. Britain had replied by introducing compulsory service, and what this meant in the way of revolution many Germans could guess. Russia had replied with a new offensive in the Bukovina, and France with an advance in the Vosges. Without doubt God had made these nations mad as a preparation for their complete destruction. But a number of sober-minded people began to lean to the other explanation. Since the Allies did not yield, was it possible that the German successes were not so resounding as their leaders claimed ? The Allies might be mad, but on the other hand they might really be unbroken. In the latter case it was an ill look-out for Germany, for she had staked heavily on the efforts of the past year.

Suspicion of the Government was growing, but as yet it was only in its early stages. It was true that a formidable opposition was appearing among the Social Democrats. That group no longer spoke and voted as a unit. In June manifestoes had appeared, signed by names like Ledebour, Haase, Kautsky, and Bernstein, warning the country that the war on Germany's part was no longer defensive but aggressive; the debate on peace terms in the Reichstag on 9th December showed that the Minority Socialists were intractable, and Scheidemann and the Majority leaders were becoming more and more a docile appendage of the Government. But they had with them the vast bulk of their countrymen. The nation still cherished most of its dreams, and the suppression of news was so drastic that there was small material for wavering. The German people were officially presented with a simple picture, in which all virtue and chivalry were on their own side and all the scowling barbarities on the other. Rumours of atrocities in Belgium or on the high seas either did not reach them, or were so presented as to appear the most reasonable acts of war. If a man of ordinary wholesome instincts was told tales of the torture of German soldiers by Belgian irregulars, of desperate sufferings in prison camps, of the persecution of harmless German civilians, of a long-cherished plot on the part of the Allies to root the German race out of Europe, he would not be greatly concerned by the news of the sinking of Allied liners and the bombardment from the air of Allied cities, the less when he was informed officially that the lost liners were heavily armed and carried munitions of war, and that London and Hull were fortresses like Königsberg and Cuxhaven. He learned with amazement that the Allies had brought charges of inhumanity against his countrymen, and he set them down to the craft of a foe who had been beaten in the field. His papers were filled with the German version of the *Baralong* case; and if he heard at all of the sinkings of the *Ancona* or the *Persia*, he believed those who told him that they were legitimate acts of war.

This complete ignorance may explain the apathy of the German Catholics * towards the sufferings of their co-religionists in France and Belgium. The German clergy played a curious part in the

* The statement applies to the majority. There were honourable exceptions.

war. The Lutheran pastors, grateful for the fervid Protestantism of the Imperial family, delivered weekly homilies in which Old Testament precedents were cited on behalf of a war of extermination. Their furious blasphemies exceeded the wildest efforts of the Ranters or Fifth Monarchy men in our own Civil War. The Catholic hierarchy was obedient to the Government, and, with the anxious neutrality of the Vatican as an example, declined to take action on the appeal of their French and Belgian colleagues. On 28th November the Belgian bishops addressed a letter to the German clergy, which was in the main the work of Cardinal Mercier. It was a request for an inquiry into German atrocities based upon a very strong *prima facie* case. No reply was vouchsafed; indeed no reply was possible. But under normal circumstances charges on which three-fourths of the world were agreed must have produced some justification, or at any rate must have caused some uneasiness even among the docile flock of German Catholicism. But the charges failed of effect, for the German people either did not hear them, or, hearing, were fortified by official assurances in a robust incredulity.

But while the people at large were on the whole united in their belligerent purpose, being still fortified by hope, the leaders, the men who had access to the facts, were drawing rapidly into two distinct groups. We may call the parties thus created the *politiques* and the fanatics. The first claimed the Imperial Chancellor, the Foreign Office, and probably most of the civilian ministers; at times the Emperor; many of the army chiefs, and some of the ablest military and naval critics. They recognized that a war of straightforward conquest was no longer possible. They hoped for a draw, a peace in which the conditions should favour Germany. Accordingly they laboured to prepare the public mind of the world for it, and relinquished most of the inflated superman business which had been rampant among them at the outset. They were no longer contemptuous in speech of their opponents. They became complimentary, as towards brave men fighting under a misconception. They talked much of the purity and reasonableness of Germany's aims, of her desire for an honourable peace, and they endeavoured to curb the ardent spirits who had already begun to divide up hostile territories. Above all, they were assiduous in their efforts to explain away the events which led to war, and to get rid of the most damning counts against German policy. These explanations were only aimed in a small degree at their own people, for Germany had been long ago convinced on the subject.

They were addressed to neutral countries, especially America, and to what German statesmen fondly hoped were wavering and uncertain elements among the population of their enemies.

A striking example was found in the speech which the Imperial Chancellor made in the Reichstag on 19th August. Bethmann-Hollweg had never been among the fire-eaters, and had lost popularity in consequence. In that speech he laboured to fasten the guilt of war on British Ministers, who, he said, had already violated Belgian neutrality by a secret agreement, and had refused Germany's offer of a pacific alliance, preferring an offensive pact with France. He tried to prove that Germany, in the crisis of July 1914, had striven for peace, and had not scorned the proposal for a conference. He talked much of the future of Poland when emancipated from Russian tyranny. He declared that Germany must win the freedom of the seas—" not as England did, to rule over them, but that they should serve equally all peoples." Germany, he said, would be the shield of defence in the future for small nations. And he concluded with a hope that the day would come when the belligerent nations would exact a terrible retribution from the leaders who had so gravely misled them. " We do not hate the peoples who have been driven into war by their Governments. We shall hold on through the war till these peoples demand peace from the really guilty, till the road becomes free for the new liberated Europe —free of French intrigues, Muscovite desire of conquest, and English guardianship."

The interesting point in this utterance was the light it shed on the rôle which Germany now desired to play in the world's eyes. She stood for reason, public honour, international decency, and peace, said the Imperial Chancellor. She had been terribly sinned against ; but, like a good Christian, she would forgive her enemies. He laboured to justify Germany's doings by the old-fashioned canons of right and wrong. He was a *politique*, desirous of preparing the way for an advantageous settlement. That was intelligible enough, but the conclusion was inconsequent. It asked for German supremacy, neither more nor less. She was to be mistress, and other nations were to have the measure of freedom which she chose to give them. In Sir Edward Grey's words : " Germany supreme, Germany alone would be free—free to break international treaties ; free to crush when it pleased her ; free to refuse all mediation ; free to go to war when it suited her ; free, when she did go to war, to break again all rules of civilization and humanity on land and at sea ; and, while she may act thus, all her commerce at sea is to remain as free in time of war as all commerce is in time of peace." The Imperial Chancellor's deduction was a *non sequitur*. It did not follow upon his laborious earlier arguments; nay, it clashed sharply with them. It was the same conclusion as that of the fire-eaters, who were the more logical inasmuch as they would have none of the Chancellor's premises. The cautious *politique* had been infected with the same disease as the fanatics.

Who among the leaders of thought were the fanatics? The chief fount of the virus did not lie in any one political party. It did not lie in the army itself, whose chiefs were professional zealots, and did not greatly concern themselves with grandiose political theories. Nor was it to be found exclusively in the coterie of Tirpitz, for whom Reventlow played in the press the part of dancing dervish. Its true home was in that class which Britain was apt to overlook in the enumeration of her enemies—the high financial and industrial circles, with their obedient satellites, the university professors. In May 1915 six Economic Associations had presented to the Chancellor a petition demanding, among other things, the incorporation with Germany of the whole of Belgium and northern France as far as the Somme, and in the East the annexation of a large part of Poland and the Baltic Provinces. Their modest claim was approved by no less a person than Prince Bülow. The financial magnates who prepared the petition had a reason of policy behind their megalomania. They saw that nothing short of a colossal and undisputed victory would safeguard their supremacy. Unless Germany could pay her war bills with indemnities unimagined before in history, there would be bankruptcy to face—bankruptcy which at the best would mean a decade of lean years. The brightest military glory would not restore their overseas trade or redeem the wastes of paper currency. A generation of hard living and preparation for a further effort, which anything less than absolute victory must involve, had no terrors for the hardier souls of the army or the ancient squirearchy. But it seemed the end of all things to the soft and vain-glorious kings of German trade. They became fanatics, partly from policy, and partly because they had the disease in their blood.

They had strong allies in the academic class. Not all, for there were some professors, such as Delbrück, who sounded a note of warning, and one or two who had the courage to speak unpopular truths. But the majority blew a louder trumpet than the fighting men. In a manifesto* of the "leaders of German thought," prepared in June, 1915, and bearing 13,000 signatories, among them names like Meinecke and Oncken, they demanded, but in a more peremptory tone, the annexations in Europe required by the Economic Associations, and they asked also for Egypt, the Persian Gulf, and various other possessions which would enable them to supplant the world-trade of Britain. They embarked, too, on a new philosophy of history of which a pleasing example was found in a little book published in February by Professor Werner Sombart of Berlin, under the title of *Hucksters and Heroes*.† The author was not a profound thinker or a pleasing writer, but his work was typical of the spirit then dominant in his country, for it is the sciolist who has his ear most ready to catch a hint of popular desires, and his work has always documentary value. Two quotations will make clear his meaning. "Our kingdom"—he speaks for Germany—"is of this world. If we desire to remain a strong state we must conquer. A great victory will make it possible not to trouble any more about those who are around us. When the German stands leaning on his mighty sword, clad in steel from his sole to his head, whatsoever will may down below dance around his feet, and the intellectuals and the learned men of England, France, Russia, and Italy may rail at him and throw mud. But in his lofty repose he will not allow himself to be disturbed." The conception of the chosen people was developed in his peroration: "No. We must purge from our soul the last fragments of the old ideal of a progressive development of humanity. . . . The ideal of humanity can only be understood in its highest sense when it attains its highest and richest development in particular noble nations. These for the time being are the representatives of God's thought on earth. Such were the Jews. Such were the Greeks. And the chosen people of these centuries is the German people. . . . Now we understand why other people pursue us with their hatred. They do not understand us, but they are sensible of our enormous spiritual superiority. So the Jews were hated in antiquity, because they were the representatives of God on earth."

Such was the simple philosophy of history which in varying degrees had captured the larger part of the German intellect. It would be unfair to build an indictment on the rhetoric of a second-rate mind like Sombart, but the same conception appeared in the

* The text of the various documents will be found in J. W. Headlam-Morley's *The Issue* (1917).
† *Händler und Helden.*

speeches and writings of men as eminent as Wilamowitz-Mollendorff.* What was a reasoned theory with the scholar became a sullen dogma with the unlearned. It was the existence of this disease which made no terms of peace as yet conceivable. The Imperial Chancellor, seeing whither his country was tending, might seek to diffuse an atmosphere of reasonableness, and pave the way for a settlement. But madness is a prepotent thing, and the fanatics would continue to call the tune till the day of cataclysm. The spirits which had been summoned from the unclean deeps could not be laid by a few puzzled politicians.

* See his inaugural address as Rector Magnificus of Berlin University.

CHAPTER XLVII.

AMERICA AT THE CROSS-ROADS.

The Purpose of the Allies—American Ideals—Mr Wilson's increasing Difficulties—Mr Elihu Root's Speech—The Problem for America narrowed and clarified.

HAD a man asked for what purpose the Allies were fighting, he could not have been answered with a simple formula. They fought each of them for their own national ends. France sought to remove the particular menace which had for so long disturbed her dreams and forced her to bear the burden of a crushing military establishment, and she stood for those principles of pacific national progress to which, for a century, she had never been more than temporarily unfaithful. Russia asked that her racial future should be respected, and that she should be given the chance of that unaggressive development of her vast territory which was her immediate need. Britain, standing a little outside the European family, sought the safety of her shores and her ideal of a free Empire expressed in those lines of Claudian which have never yet found an adequate translator.* Each power had her domestic interests, which by themselves were sufficient to justify her in the contest.

But over and above these special issues there was one purpose not national or racial, but universal. Germany had exalted Force to the throne of the universe. She admitted no rights of state or individual which could not be maintained with the strong arm.

---

* " Haec est in gremium victos quae sola recepit,
    Humanumque genus communi nomine fovit,
    Matris non dominae ritu : civesque vocavit,
    Quos domuit, nexuque pio longinqua revinxit ;
    Huius pacificis debemus moribus omnes
    Quod veluti patriis regionibus utitur hospes,
    Quod sedem mutare licet, quod cernere Thulen
    Lusus, et horrendos quondam penetrare recessus,
    Quod bibimus passim Rhodanum, potamus Orontem
    Quod cuncti gens una sumus."
                               De Consulatu Stilichonis, III., 150–160.

She sought to restore the rule of tooth and claw and the ethics of the Stone Age. Hitherto there had reigned a code of public conduct—vague and diffuse, perhaps, and with faulty sanctions, but none the less a priceless safeguard of peace. The question was whether this, the laborious handiwork of generations, was to be altogether destroyed. If Germany won, public Right became meaningless. The neutral nations would be faced with a world in which nothing was granted to them, in which they could only keep what they were potent enough to hold. This meant for the smaller states a precarious future, with absorption or extinction on the horizon; and for a Power like America, an immediate arming on a colossal scale, and the entrance into that competition in fleets and battalions which she had hitherto happily avoided. On a broad survey of the situation, neutrality seemed inconceivable. All neutral peoples, great and small, had found their ease and protection under the ægis of public Right. If this were challenged, it seemed not only their duty but their vital interest to side with the constable and bring the wrongdoer to book.

It was not easy for the little European states to act upon this view, for the malefactor was too near their threshold; but it might reasonably have been expected that America, who had no cause to fear immediate violence, would have appreciated the real point in the quarrel. America, however, as we have seen, was from the start seriously handicapped for a true perception of her interests. She was as yet less a people than a collection of peoples. Her national consciousness, so far as sound political thinking was concerned, was weak. The Nation found itself frustrated at every turn by the State; her racial " integration," in spite of the efforts of her reformers, was incomplete; the centrifugal forces, to use the common metaphor, were still stronger than the centripetal; she was less a unified Power than a loose federation. It had been different fifty years before; but the America of 1916 was not the America of 1865. Her enormous increase in population had given her masses of men owing diverse allegiances, and, though she had absorbed them so that they soon approximated to one human type, she had not yet given them a common code of political thought. She was always in danger of becoming what Mr. Roosevelt described as a " mere polyglot boarding-house." Again, her immersion in business and her remoteness from the normal interests of the great Powers, had left her ordinary citizens singularly uninstructed in world-politics. She was insular, so far as these matters were concerned—insular in a way no island Power could afford to be. While she had produced many admirable political thinkers and international jurists, it is fair to say that the majority of her people knew less and cared less about the greater matters of world-policy than many nations far lower in the scale of wealth, intelligence, and civilization.

The main difficulty lay in that keen commercial spirit which she cultivated as her chief glory. She was absorbed by one kind of interest, and had small leisure for others; and, like all peoples and individuals in such a case, she tended to take short views even in her favourite province. If a man is set on money-making and is highly successful, the odds are that he will forget about non-commercial problems, even those which, if neglected, will sooner or later tumble his mercantile edifice about his ears. Before the war American economics were in no very comfortable state. Labour troubles on a grand scale threatened, capitalists were regarded with general suspicion, and many of the most advertised enterprises of capital were on the verge of insolvency. The first months of the campaign looked as if they would intensify these difficulties. Then suddenly the situation changed. The sale of food and war munitions at high prices to the Allies caused an unprecedented wave of prosperity to overflow the land. In 1915 the United States had advanced a long way towards becoming a creditor nation. Her exports for the year were more than a thousand million dollars ahead of the highest previous total, and her credit balances were over three hundred millions sterling. She had imported over a hundred millions sterling of gold, and repurchased about three hundred millions sterling worth of American securities held in foreign countries. There was practically no unemployment, and wages had everywhere advanced. Bankrupt railroads were paying good dividends. Her staple industries, such as the production of iron and steel, had increased by 25 per cent. their former maximum production. She had had bumper crops, sold at extravagant prices. Copper had doubled in value. There was a marked revival in shipbuilding. Even the South, though its cotton crop was five million bales less than that of 1914, disposed of it at a higher price, and its other agricultural products reached a record figure. The war had brought to America an unparalleled chance of gain, and she was busy with both hands taking advantage of it. It was on this that the thoughts of the ordinary citizen were fixed, and not on the war itself. International corporations were formed with large capitals to finance foreign enterprises and develop the future export trade. America seemed to herself to be about to win the whole world, and was inclined to be careless whether or not in the process she lost her soul.

In the autumn of 1915 an incident occurred which revealed an apparently impassable gulf between her way of looking at things and that of Western Europe. On 5th November her Government communicated to London and Paris a Note of protest against the Allied maritime policy, which came as a painful surprise to the British and French peoples. Of all Washington's many Notes it was the narrowest in argument and the most captious in spirit. There was nothing judicial in its tone; it was the kind of brief which a competent lawyer can prepare on either side of any question, without breadth of view or balance, a series of meticulous arguments on details. It laid down as settled law many views which were notoriously in dispute. It ignored the changed circumstances, and argued from the books like an old-fashioned conveyancer. The precedents to which it appealed were enumerated, not weighed. It tried, but failed, to explain away some of the embarrassing judgments of the Supreme Court in the Civil War. It complained that American vessels were detained on suspicion, an obvious right of any belligerent with regard to ships or individuals. In its attempt to make the flag decisive proof of the nationality of a merchant vessel it disregarded the most patent facts of a condition of war. It dwelt incessantly upon the inadequacy of our blockade, though it was clear that the work of British submarines in the Baltic was far more effective than had been the efforts of the Federal Navy off the Confederate coasts. The Note was written in that strain of acid rhetoric occasionally found in legal documents. It was the kind of protest which can be manufactured on any subject by men who refuse to look beyond the formal aspect of a question. It was the claim of a commercial people to be exempt from all consequences of a world war, their "general right," in the words of the Note, "to enjoy their international trade free from unusual and arbitrary limitations"—as if a man during an earthquake should protest that he had leased his house with a covenant that provided for quiet enjoyment. As such, it did violence to the common sense of the American people.

But in its concluding words it offended against more sacred canons than good sense and good taste. America was perfectly entitled to consult only American interests and refrain from an unprofitable quixotry; but those responsible for that policy were not entitled to claim for it a loftier motive. "This task," the Note concluded, " of championing the integrity of neutral rights, which have received the sanction of the civilized world, against the lawless conduct of belligerents arising out of the bitterness of the great conflict which is now wasting the countries of Europe, the United States unhesitatingly assumes, and to the accomplishment of that task it will devote its energies, exercising always that impartiality which from the outbreak of the war it has sought to exercise in its relations with the warring nations." Championing the integrity of neutral rights! The world had seen every principle of international law and decency shattered to pieces among the smoking ruins of Belgium. Then Washington had been silent, as she was justly entitled to be. But so soon as commercial interests were touched came the clarion challenge of the trustee of neutrals, the champion of international law. It was an anomaly which all friends of America viewed with deep regret. They could have wished that the author of the *Biglow Papers* had been alive with his honest scorn to prevent this unseemly rhetoric.

The principles which seemed to govern the attitude of Mr. Wilson have been sketched in an earlier chapter. On his conception of the duty of a President he behaved with complete correctness, and he rightly interpreted the wishes of the vast majority of the American people. It was not an easy path to tread for a man of his antecedents, for it involved the deliberate shutting of the eyes to many matters which in his past life had interested him most deeply. But he moved on the tight-rope of legality with perfect balance. Whatever defects his critics might find in him of sympathy and the larger intelligence, it could not be denied that his conduct was resolute, and, in a sense, courageous.

Facts, however, were destined to make his resolution look like weakness. If a man is determined not to fight, and his enemy knows this, it is unlikely that he will escape without finding himself in strangely undignified positions. Mr. Wilson's mind was essentially of the juridical type. He was admirable in formal argument, and had he been pleading before an international court his case would have been good, and the judges would no doubt have found for him. But he was still unable to envisage that rough-and-tumble world where decisions are won not by words but deeds. He still believed that he could secure victory by making debating points against his adversary. This remoteness from facts was shown in the three disastrous years during which, in Mr. Roosevelt's phrase, he "waged peace" against Mexico. It was most conspicuously shown in the situation created by the sinking of the *Lusitania* and by the later outrages. The President stated his case with dignity and force; he was flouted, and he did nothing. Germany, like a street urchin, regarded her mentor with her finger to her nose. Fair words alternated with foul deeds, and though eventually he won an admission of liability from the German Government on the *Lusitania* point and a promise of compensation, it was the most barren of victories, for the outrages continued. The words of the President's severest critic were not without warrant. The Germans "had learned to believe that, no matter how shocked the American Government might be, its resolution would expend itself in words. They had learned to believe that it was safe to kill Americans—and the world believed with them. Measured and restrained expression, backed to the full by serious purpose, is strong and respected. Extreme and belligerent expression, unsupported by resolution, is weak and without effect. No man should draw a pistol who dares not shoot. The Government that shakes its fist first and its finger afterwards falls into contempt." *

And yet, had he known it, all the cards were in the President's hands. Germany at this stage did not dare to quarrel with America. The American market and American money were her sole economic hopes after the war; the adhesion of America to the Allied cause, even if she did not mobilize one man, would at once have settled those financial difficulties on which Germany counted. America was immune from her attack; she was by no means immune from America's. She counted on the large German population in the United States to decide the perplexed President, and she strove by many deeds of violence to show the offensive power of this German leaven. But the menace had no serious import except for the timid. It was rumoured that a certain German statesman told a distinguished American diplomat: "Remember there are half a million Germans of military age in the United States, and that nearly all have had military training;" and that the Ambassador replied, "I calculate, sir, that we have more than half a million lamp-posts." It was the right answer.

Towards the close of 1915, therefore, a curious situation had arisen. The Note of 5th November had shown a spirit of pettifogging criticism which contrasted strongly with America's inertia in the face of notorious German law-breaking, and which encouraged

---

* "*Dogberry.* This is your charge :—you shall comprehend all vagrom men; you are to bid any man stand, in the prince's name.

"*Second Watchman.* How if a' will not stand ?

"*Dogberry* Why, then, take no note of him, but let him go; and presently call the rest of the watch together, and thank God you are rid of a knave."
Much Ado about Nothing, Act III, Sc. 3.

in Berlin the hope that a real quarrel with the Allies might soon arise. On 7th December the President's Message to Congress denounced German intrigues in America, and demanded legislation to deal with them. Following on this, Berlin officially repudiated the campaign of outrage on American soil, though the publication of Captain von Papen's papers, which implicated Count Bernstorff beyond possibility of doubt, gave the lie to this disclaimer. Presently Mr. Wilson set out on a speech-making tour in the Middle West. With the violence of an academic mind defrauded of its dreams, and with the enthusiasm of a convert, he preached a policy of military and naval preparedness which exceeded even Mr. Roosevelt's demands. The sensitive barometer of his mind was beginning to register a slight change in the weather of American popular opinion. But in his speeches he made it very clear that he was exasperated with both sides in the world-war, and this Germany took for a hopeful omen. She made haste to proffer a settlement of the *Lusitania* business, and then promptly put forward a new and exorbitant claim. Mr. Lansing, in an unofficial memorandum to the Allies, had expressed the opinion that merchantmen should not be armed. Presuming on this, on February 10, 1916, the German Government handed to the Ambassadors of the neutral Powers at Berlin a memorandum concerning the treatment of armed merchant vessels, and two days later it was presented by Count Bernstorff to Mr. Lansing, along with his *Lusitania* proposals. Germany announced that from 1st March she would treat all armed merchantmen as belligerent vessels, and attack them at sight wherever they might be encountered, and she warned neutrals that they would journey in them at their peril.

The claim was, of course, preposterous. It was preposterous in fact, since, if a submarine was not obliged to summon and search a vessel, it could not tell whether or not she carried guns. The proposal involved a campaign of complete licence, and the sinking of an unarmed ship would be attributed, as before, to the mistake of the submarine commander. It was no less preposterous in law. The right of a merchantman to carry arms for defence had been for three centuries a canon of maritime practice, and had nowhere been so clearly stated as in America. It had been authorized by an Act of Congress in 1798. Chief-Justice Marshall in the *Nereide* case had laid it down that the right of a neutral to send goods in a belligerent vessel extended to armed as well as to unarmed ships. "As belligerent merchant vessels," he said, "rarely sail unarmed, the exception, if any existed as to armed vessels, would be greater than the rule." Jefferson had also dealt with the matter. " Though she has arms to defend herself in time of war in the course of her regular commerce, this no more makes her a privateer than a husbandman, following his plough in time of war with a knife or pistol in his pocket, is thereby made a soldier.* . . . Were the merchant vessels coming for our produce forbidden to bear any arms for their defence, every adventurer who had a boat, or money enough to buy one, would make her a privateer; our coast would swarm with them; foreign vessels must cease to come."

Germany had manœuvred Washington into an awkward corner; but Mr. Wilson had the courage to throw over his recent suggestion to the Allies, and reject without equivocation the view of Berlin. He waived aside the *Lusitania* settlement, since it was accompanied by such a rider. On 15th February his Cabinet decided not to admit Germany's claim to torpedo armed merchantmen without warning—a step not taken without many futile mutterings of revolt from a section of the Democratic following. In a letter to Senator Stone he put very clearly the view which had the assent of all the better elements in the nation.

" For my own part I cannot consent to any abridgment of the rights of American citizens in any respect. The honour and self-respect of the nation are involved. We covet peace, and shall preserve it at any cost but loss of honour. To forbid our people to exercise their rights for fear we might be called upon to vindicate them would be a deep humiliation indeed. It would be an implicit — all but explicit— acquiescence in the violation of the rights of mankind everywhere, and of whatever nation or allegiance. It would be an abdication of our hitherto proud position as spokesman, even amid the turmoil of war, for law and right. It would make everything this Government has attempted, and everything it has achieved during this terrible struggle of nations, meaningless and futile. It is important to reflect that if in this instance we allowed expediency to take the place of principle, the door would inevitably be opened to still further concessions. Once accept a single abatement of rights, and many other humiliations will certainly follow, and the whole fine fabric of international law might crumble under our hands piece by piece. What we are contending for in this matter is of the very essence of the things that have made of America a sovereign nation. She cannot yield them without conced-

* Germany would have contended that the carrying of arms did make him a soldier. This was also in theory the law of other Continental nations, but they did not press it to the absurdity of a logical conclusion. According to Germany, the non-combatant on land or sea committed a crime if he resisted, or prepared to resist, the armed forces of an enemy state. That is why Count Reventlow denounced the " treachery " of the English civilians who were reported to have fired at a raiding Zeppelin.

ing her own impotency as a nation, and making a virtual surrender of her position among the nations of the world "

It was not, however, in these arguments on detail between the two Governments that the true centre of gravity lay. They were concerned with specific rights, but the question of the basic and primordial right—that of every nation, whether neutral or not, to the maintenance of public Law—had been shelved by the President in the first months of the campaign when he declined to protest against the violation of Belgium. It was inevitable that it should revive as the war progressed, and Germany's intentions became clearer alike in the heat of victory and the chagrin of failure. As we have seen, Germany was beginning to realize that between her and the conquest of the world lay the sea power of the Allies. Her victories by land would avail her little so long as Britain ruled the water. Once again, as of old, that Navy stood between the Superman and his dreams.

The position may be briefly restated. Germany claimed the " freedom of the seas," which on her lips meant that in time of war all traffic should be unimpeded except enemy consignments of munitions and contraband. The land Power should have the free use of its limbs, while the naval Power should be hobbled. With this claim neutrals, on a narrow view of their interests, might be inclined to agree, since the Allied control of the sea did infringe certain of their customary rights. These infringements were set forth precisely in the American Note of November 5, 1915. On the other hand the Allies argued that new conditions must modify accepted practice; that international law, like all human law, must show elasticity and conform to facts. The neutral interests which were infringed were minor matters, the mere trimmings and fringes of the law; but the greatest of all neutral interests, the maintenance of public Right, was the cause for which they were making untold sacrifices. If Germany succeeded, they asked, what would be the freedom of the seas under her control? In time of peace the ocean was free for all honest citizens to go their ways upon. This freedom had been won by the British fleet three hundred years before, and had been maintained by the British fleet ever since. If the Allies failed, there would be an end of such freedom, the German creed being what it was. It was true that Britain claimed supremacy on the water, but this was in no way akin to Germany's desired hegemony on land. A control exercised for the purpose of police is different from a conquest sought for aggrandizement. In the present stage of international relations the sole power capable of bringing a wrongdoer to task was the British navy. At some future period it might be possible to internationalize this duty, but for the present it must be performed by the only nation which could perform it.

Neutrals were not asked to forgo their interests, but they were asked to remember their greatest interest—the protection of public Right. No neutral was entitled to use its lesser interests or rights to impede a Power which was struggling desperately for the greater interest and the fundamental right. A man, if the house next door has been burgled, does not trip up the constable, even if in the excitement of the pursuit that zealous officer may have trodden on his toes. Mr. Wilson's interpretation of American interests had been too narrow. If Britain went down, America's security and prosperity would inevitably follow, or at the best she would be condemned to a feverish struggle against time to prepare armaments on a scale colossal enough to counter her enemy's. It was the British fleet, and not the Monroe doctrine, that had warned off Germany from South America. It was the British fleet that enabled America to reap where she had not sown, and to gather where she had not strawed. Where lay the true American interest? In tripping up the constable, or in taking an honest share in the policing of the world?

It was clear that during the winter this question was coming home with force to the best American minds. Mr. Wilson had been right in the principles he had laid down, but wrong in their application. It appeared to many that a false course had been taken to gain the ends which he had so eloquently defined. There was a reaction against the narrow nationalism which had hitherto predominated, and a growing sense that the international issue was an integral part of the national interests. Some Americans, such as Dr. Eliot of Harvard and Mr. Roosevelt, had always held this view. A "League of Nations to Enforce Peace" was proposed, with men like ex-President Taft among its supporters; branches were formed in many of the States, and the propaganda was approved by a referendum vote of the United States Chamber of Commerce. The New York Bar Association, an eminently discreet body, resolved that the day for a policy of isolation was past, and criticized the aforesaid League of Nations only because it did not go far enough. Many shared this attitude who had no wish to embark on war. They were of Mr. Roosevelt's opinion that " one outspoken and straightforward declaration by this Government against the dreadful iniquities perpetrated in Belgium, Armenia, and Serbia would have been worth to humanity a thousand times as much as all that the professional pacificists have done in the past fifty years." Others, like the American Rights Committee in New York, desired a definite diplomatic breach with the Teutonic Powers. But all shades of this new thought were agreed that it was unseemly for the United States to assert its commercial interests so as to hamper the full effect of sea power used on behalf of public Right. The tone of the Note of 5th November found few defenders among the more thoughtful classes of the American people.

It was left for Mr. Elihu Root to state this point of view in a speech which was in many ways the most remarkable made in any country since the outbreak of war. Mr. Root was an ex-senator, had been Secretary of State under Mr. Roosevelt, and was by common consent the foremost American lawyer of the day. The speech, delivered on 15th February to the Republican Convention in New York City, was to a small extent concerned with party politics; but its significance lay in the fact that for the first time a man of great eminence stated sanely and broadly the true interests of neutrals. He put into eloquent words what had been the national ideal alike of Washington and Jefferson, of Lee and Lincoln.

"The American democracy stands for something more than beef and cotton and grain and manufactures; it stands for something that cannot be measured by rates of exchange, and does not rise or fall with the balance of trade. The American people achieved liberty and schooled themselves to the service of justice before they acquired wealth, and they value their country's liberty and justice above all their pride of possessions. Beneath their comfortable optimism and apparent indifference they have a conception of their great republic as brave and strong and noble to hand down to their children the blessings of freedom and just and equal laws.

"They have embodied their principles of government in fixed rules of right conduct which they jealously preserve, and, with the instinct of individual freedom, they stand for a government of laws and not of men. They deem that the moral laws which formulate the duties of men towards each other are binding upon nations equally with individuals. Informed by their own experience, confirmed by their observation of international life, they have come to see that the independence of nations, the liberty of their peoples, justice and humanity, cannot be maintained upon the complaisance, the good nature, the kindly feeling of the strong toward the weak; that real independence, real liberty, cannot rest upon sufferance; that peace and liberty can be preserved only by the authority and observance of rules of national conduct founded upon the principles of justice and humanity; only by the establishment of Law among nations, responsive to the enlightened public opinion of mankind."

That Law had been shivered on the fields of Belgium. The case was not *sub judice*; Germany had admitted, defended, gloried in her wrong-doing. And that Law was America's own law just as much as any domestic statute.

"We had bound ourselves by it; we had regulated our conduct by it, and we were entitled to have other nations observe it. That law was the protection of our peace and security. It was our safeguard against the necessity of maintaining great armaments and wasting our substance in continual readiness for war. Our interest in having it maintained as the law of nations was a substantial, valuable, permanent interest, just as real as your interest and mine in having maintained and enforced the laws against assault and robbery and arson which protect our personal safety and property."

In another speech at Washington Mr. Root elaborated his argument. "Up to this time breaches of international law have been treated as we treat wrongs under civil procedure—as if they concerned nobody except the particular nation upon which the injury was inflicted and the nation inflicting it. There has been no general recognition of the right of other nations to object. . . . There must be a change of theory. And violations of the law of such a character as to threaten the peace and order of the community of nations must be treated by analogy to criminal law. They must be deemed to be a violation of the right of every civilized nation to have the law maintained."

America did not seek to interfere in the quarrels of Europe. She had a right and a duty to be neutral as to the differences between Germany and Britain; but neutrality was impossible where her own law was outraged. Then she was entitled to be heard, and she was bound to speak. "With the right to speak," said Mr. Root, "came responsibility, and with responsibility came duty —duty of government toward all the peaceful men and women in America not to acquiesce in the destruction of the law which protected them; for if the world assents to this great and signal violation, then the law of nations no longer exists, and we have no protection save in subserviency or force." America was once again at the cross-roads. She and her President had taken the wrong turning, but she was retracing her steps. She was again faced with a decision of incalculable significance for the world and for herself.

CHAPTER XLVIII.

THE POSITION AT SEA.

January 24, 1915–February 29, 1916.

Tirpitz's Plan—The Allied and German Losses at Sea—The German Submarine Campaign—The *Baralong* Incident—The British Blockade—German Commerce Raiders—The Work of the British Fleet.

THE Battle of the Dogger Bank was fought on January 24, 1915. Had any one on that day prophesied that a year would elapse without another naval action he would have found few anywhere to accept his forecast, and none in the British navy. Our sailors looked confidently for many German raids, which should culminate in the appearance of the High Sea Fleet. But the year was one of watching and waiting. Battleships were, indeed, employed in the luckless Gallipoli venture, and suffered many losses; but that was not the engagement of ships with ships, but of ships against forts and land entrenchments. Our armed auxiliaries scoured the seas and controlled neutral traffic; our mine-sweepers were busy at their thankless task from the Pentland Firth to the Channel, from the Shetlands to the Scillies; our gunboats and patrol boats hunted submarines in many waters, from the North Sea to the Dardanelles; our cruiser squadrons kept tireless watch, sweeping the sea by night and day; but our battle-cruisers and capital ships still waited for the chance that did not come. We were paying the penalty of the success we had won in the first six months of war. The enemy was driven to fight with small arms, and not with his great guns, and the warfare he chose was waged in secret and in the dark. We were condemned to the offensive-defensive, as troops who have carried a vital position are compelled to consolidate their ground and thrust back the counter-attack. Hence for that year the history of the war at sea was a history of losses. We were repelling the enemy's assault, and for the most part waging war in our own country rather than carrying it into his.

The German submarine campaign was not ill-conceived. It failed, but it was not futile. As planned by the Great General Staff, it showed a shrewd perception of the economic vulnerability of Britain. In the long run, they argued, it was only the merchant shipping of the world, whether owned by Allies or neutrals, which could checkmate Germany's scheme of conquest. It alone could enable her enemies to perfect their equipment, and create a fighting machine equal to her own. Germany had lost her mercantile marine, but then it was less vital to her purpose. If the Allied shipping could be seriously crippled, there might arise this quandary: either Britain must curtail her military operations, which demanded many ships, or she would find her revenues shrinking seriously from lack of trade, and her population gravely distressed from shortage of food and the vast increase of prices. The Allies were using some 3,000 merchant vessels for the purposes of war; and if Germany could make heavy inroads on the remainder she might effect a true naval success without the sacrifice of one battleship.

In framing this policy she counted upon two possibilities, which failed. She was using as weapons the mine and the submarine, to which there had up to date been no effective antidote devised. She hoped, therefore, to create a panic among Allied seamen, so that merchantmen would limit their activities at the mere threat of danger. She believed, too, that the British Admiralty would be slow to discover any means of defence and reprisal. In both forecasts she was wrong. There was no panic, and our Navy speedily organized a counter-campaign. But the merit of her scheme was that when the thoughts of the Allies dwelt chiefly on armies and navies, she foresaw the economic necessities at the back of armed strength, and struck at them. If she did not succeed, she certainly incommoded her foes. Up to the end of 1915, largely owing to her submarine campaign, nearly 1,000 Allied and neutral ships had been put out of use, and these losses could not be replaced with any readiness. It was different in the Napoleonic wars, when every little English port had its local shipbuilder; but in these days of iron and steel vessels of large tonnage there was none of this decentralized construction, and we could not easily make good the decline in our carrying capacity. The consequence was that freights rose very high. If we compare 1914 and 1915, we find the freights of Burmese rice increased from 21s. to 150s. per ton; Calcutta jute from 18s. to 152s.; Argentine wheat from 18s. to 150s. Even deducting the excess profits tax, the net profits of the shipping industry increased by

543 per cent. One calculation, covering the first nineteen months of war, put the increased cost to the nation at £400,000,000.

Nor was Germany's offensive confined to blows at civilian trade. By means of mine-laying on a large scale she hoped slowly to reduce the strength of our Fleet, with no corresponding loss to her own. Moreover, her submarines took an active part in the only naval campaign after January 1915—that in the Eastern Mediterranean, where their achievements furnished a brilliant page in the still scanty chronicles of submarine war. The Eastern Mediterranean was no doubt an ideal ground for such operations, for our task of supplying and reinforcing by sea a large army provided endless easy targets. But the journey thither, and the provision of bases in out-of-the-way islands and odd corners of the African coast were enterprises which did credit to the new service. It was hastily assumed by many that the narrow entrance to the Mediterranean would enable us to detect and check the approach of submarines. But the nine miles of the Strait of Gibraltar are nearly a thousand feet deep, and its strong currents made netting impossible.

The main naval preoccupation of the Allies in 1915 was therefore the perfecting of means of defence against mine and submarine, and the endeavour to make the enemy's attack as little costly as possible to themselves, and as difficult and burdensome as possible to him. The record of the year was one of losses on both sides— losses the majority of which fell on the Allies. But, taking into account the nature of Germany's plan and the end which she had set herself, it may fairly be said that the balance of success was not with the attack.

In an earlier chapter we have seen our battleship disasters in the Dardanelles, where France lost the *Bouvet*, and Britain the *Irresistible*, the *Queen*, the *Goliath*, the *Triumph*, and the *Majestic*. The year passed without any further wastage of capital ships, but on January 9, 1916, the pre-Dreadnought battleship, *King Edward VII.*, struck a mine in the North Sea and sank, happily without loss of life. The list was heavier in armoured cruisers. The *Argyll*, a ship of an old class, with a speed of 22 knots, and four 7.5-inch guns, stranded on the Scottish coast on October 28, 1915. On 30th December the *Natal*, one of the best gunnery ships in the Navy, was mysteriously blown up in harbour, and lost out of her ship's company over 300 officers and men. On February 11, 1916, the light cruiser *Arethusa*, which had played a great part in the Battle of the Bight of Heligoland as the parent ship of the destroyer flotillas, and had been in action during the Cuxhaven raid and the battle of January 24, 1915, struck a mine off the East Coast, and was lost. She was the first oil-driven cruiser in the Fleet, and bore one of the most historic names in our naval history. France lost a cruiser, the *Léon Gambetta*, in the Ionian Sea in April 1915; and in February 1916 a very old cruiser, the *Amiral Charner*, was torpedoed off the Syrian coast. The losses among destroyers were few, since their speed made them comparatively safe from submarines. The *Maori* was mined off the Belgian coast, the *Lynx* in the North Sea, and the *Louis* stranded in the Eastern Mediterranean. Of submarines we could trace the loss of eight—four in the Dardanelles or Sea of Marmora, two in the North Sea, one in the Baltic, and one in January 1916, wrecked on the Dutch coast. The French lost the *Saphir*, *Joule*, *Mariette*, and *Turquoise* in the Dardanelles, and the *Fresnel* and the *Curie* in the Adriatic.

The largest roll was that of armed merchantmen and fleet auxiliaries, whose size and constant keeping of the sea made them specially vulnerable to mine and submarine. In January 1915 the *Viknor* sank off the coast of Ireland. In February it was followed by the *Clan Macnaughton*, and in March by the *Bayano*. In May the *Princess Irene* was blown up at Sheerness; in August the *Ramsey* was sunk by gun-fire in the North Sea; in September the *India* was torpedoed in the North Sea. In October the *Hythe*, a mine-sweeper, was sunk in collision at the Dardanelles, and next month the *Tara*, an armed boarding steamer, was torpedoed. On February 10, 1916, four mine-sweepers near the Dogger Bank were attacked by German destroyers, and one of them, the *Arabis*, was sunk—an episode which was represented in the German press as a victory over enemy cruisers. The French during the year lost the *Casa Blanca* and the *Indien* in the Ægean. Transports, too, made an easy mark. In September 1915 the *Royal Edward* was torpedoed in the Ægean Sea, with the loss of over a thousand men, mostly drafts for the 29th Division at Gallipoli. In the same month, and in the same waters, the *Ramazan* was sunk by gun-fire, and three hundred perished. In October the *Marquette*, carrying Indian troops, was torpedoed, with the loss of a hundred lives; and in November the *Mercian*, carrying yeomanry, was shelled for several hours by a submarine, but was able to escape with over a hundred killed and injured. In November France lost the transport *Calvados* off Algeria, and early in 1916 *La Provence* was sunk in the Mediterranean, as she was carrying troops to Salonika. To this list may be added the British hospital ship

Anglia, which on 17th November struck a mine in the Channel, and sank with considerable loss of life.

The losses among merchant shipping need not be detailed. Up to October 31, 1915, from the outbreak of war, 264 British merchant ships, aggregating half a million tons, and 158 fishing vessels had been destroyed by enemy action. From the ordinary accidents of the sea we had lost during the same period 167 steamships, 229 sailing ships, and 144 fishing vessels. The most conspicuous losses were the *Lusitania* on 7th May, the *Armenian* on 28th June, the *Iberian* on 30th July, the *Arabic* on 19th August, the *Hesperian* on 4th September, the Italian liner *Ancona* on 8th November, the French liner *Ville de Ciotat* on 24th December, and the *Persia* on 30th December. Two Japanese vessels were also sunk in the Eastern Mediterranean, with the result that Japan sent warships to those waters. The sinking of the *Ancona* was attended with peculiar brutality. She was bound from Naples to New York, carrying Greek and Italian emigrants with their families. While passing to the south of Sardinia a submarine appeared and began to shell her; even after she had stopped the shelling continued. A panic was the result; many were killed on the decks by shrapnel; women and children flung themselves pell-mell into the boats, and while there were subjected to the fire of the submarine. Finally a torpedo was discharged, and the ship sank. Over two hundred persons perished in this outrage. The submarine flew the Austrian flag, and the Government of Vienna acknowledged it as their own; but there is good reason to believe that it was in reality a German boat, and that the Austrian flag was used to avoid further complications with America, and to prevent a declaration of war by Italy on Germany. The tale was one of the most horrid in the campaign, and no explanations could relieve its barbarism. Insult was added to injury by an extraordinary request made by Vienna on 7th December that special preparations should be made to protect from submarine risks certain Austro-Hungarian subjects being conveyed from India by the British steamer *Golconda*, on the ground that the majority of them were "better-class people." The request gave the world an insight into the perverted mind of the Teutonic Powers. Sir Edward Grey replied with vigour and point :—

"I am at a loss to know why 'better-class' people should be thought more entitled to protection from submarine attack than any other non-combatants. But however that may be, the only danger of the character indicated which threatens any of the passengers in the *Golconda* is one for which the Austro-Hungarian and the German Governments are alone responsible. It is they, and they only, who have instituted and carry on a novel and inhuman form of warfare, which disregards all the hitherto accepted principles of international law and necessarily endangers the lives of non-combatants. By asking for special precautions to protect one of their own subjects on board a British merchant vessel, the Austro-Hungarian Government recognizes what are the inevitable consequences of its submarine policy, and admits that the outrages, by which the *Lusitania*, the *Persia*, and numbers of other ships have been sunk without warning, were not the result of the casual brutalities of the officers of enemy submarines, but part of the settled and premeditated policy of the Governments whom they serve."

The German losses were naturally smaller ; for, except in the Baltic, the German warships did not keep the seas, and there was no German commerce left to destroy. One battleship—the *Pommern*—a vessel ten years old, with a displacement of about 13,000 tons, four 11-inch guns, and fourteen 6.7-inch guns, was torpedoed in the Baltic by Commander Max Horton on 2nd July ; more than one transport in the same waters fell to British and Russian submarines ; and in the battle of the Gulf of Riga on 20th August Germany suffered substantial losses in destroyers and cruisers. A tribute should be paid to the efficiency at this period of the Russian Baltic Fleet, and to its skilful handling by Admiral Kanin. It held the Eastern Baltic against German warships, and operated repeatedly with success as a flank guard of the Russian armies. The new spirit introduced by Admiral Essen—whose death was one of the greatest losses suffered by the Allies during the campaign—showed itself in a defiance of weather conditions which might have deterred the boldest sailors, in a complete intimacy with difficult waters, and in a readiness at all times to take the big hazard. With the assistance of British submarines, under commanders like Max Horton and Noel Laurence, Russia throughout the year dominated the Eastern Baltic. In cruisers and battle-cruisers Germany had already lost heavily—the *Scharnhorst, Gneisenau, Yorck, Magdeburg, Köln, Mainz, Hela, Nürnberg, Leipzig, Ariadne, Emden, Karlsruhe.* In the early months of 1915 the list was increased by the *Blücher, Dresden,* and *Königsberg*. In October the *Prinz Adalbert,* in November the *Undine,* and in December the *Bremen* were sunk in the Baltic. At least nine destroyers and seven torpedo boats were lost during 1915. In the class of armed merchantmen and auxiliaries, the *Macedonia* was captured in March at Las Palmas, and the *Kronprinz Wilhelm* and the *Prinz Eitel Friedrich* were interned in an American port. The mine-layer *Albatross* went ashore at Gothland in July, and in August the *Meteor* was blown up in the North Sea. Against Turkey the Allied offensive was conspicuously successful. If the guns of the Dardanelles forts and the German submarines took heavy toll of our large vessels, our submarines in the Straits and in the Marmora played havoc with Turkish shipping. Down to October in those waters we had sunk two battleships, five gunboats, one torpedo boat, and 197 supply ships.

Of the campaign against the enemy submarines few details were published at the time, and no list of achievements—a policy based upon a sound appreciation of the enemy temperament. A sinister silence, without a word of news, was more trying to the nerves of the German under-sea service than any advertisement of success. *Omne ignotum pro magnifico.* Famous submarine commanders went out and never returned. No man setting forth from the Elbe bases knew what he had to face, for some device which meant certain death might be waiting for him in the British coastal waters. A few of our methods of defence were known to the world. The new type of monitors—vast, torpedo-proof rafts carrying 14-inch guns—were able to operate in shallow seas with almost complete immunity from the under-water menace. Elaborate nets were constructed in the main sea-passages, in which more than one submarine was fatally entangled. But of our direct offensive few details were made known. Sometimes an airplane was the weapon; the new " Q " boats—tramps with a concealed armament for the decoy of unwary submarines—had their first success in July 1915; by hundreds of patrol boats, manned largely by fishermen, the submarine was tracked and followed as the old whalers pursued the ringer. Science was called to our aid, and by means of improved microphones we became adepts at detecting the presence of the enemy under water. The doings of these patrols and their quarries make up a record of perhaps the strangest romances of peril and courage in all human history; but here we can only set down the general result. In spite of many losses our commerce had not been seriously crippled; there was no hint of panic among our sea-going folk; and we had organized a counter-campaign which had left Germany aghast. It was not so much that we had depleted her submarine fleet, for her new constructions filled the gaps, but that we had put an end to many of the best and most unreplaceable of her submarine commanders, and diffused over the whole business of attack that atmosphere of terror and uncertainty which should, on Germany's calculation, have been the lot of the defence. The German navy, which had looked for immediate success, was driven to counsel patience with a wry mouth. " Only a child," wrote Captain Persius in the *Berliner Tageblatt*, " would accuse the British of being bad seamen. They know how to defend themselves, and have devised every kind of protection. It becomes more and more difficult for U boats to get near enough to hostile ships to launch a torpedo. An almost miraculous skill is required to avoid all snares, escape from destroyers, and yet make a successful attack."

The consequence was that the German Government was in two minds about the whole business. In September 1915 there was a change in the post of Chief of the Naval Staff, and Bachmann was succeeded by von Holtzendorff, who was no friend of Tirpitz. The difficulties with America depressed the politicians, and the Imperial Chancellor was not in sympathy with the naval and military view of under-sea warfare. In January 1916 Holtzendorff pressed for a revival of the extreme rigour of the campaign, " unhampered by restrictions of a non-military nature," and promised that within six months Britain would be forced to sue for peace. In that month Pohl retired from the command of the High Sea Fleet, and died a few weeks later ; and his successor, von Scheer, the ablest of German sailors, pressed for a clearing up of the submarine position. But in spite of the support of Falkenhayn the opposition of Bethmann-Hollweg proved too strong ; unrestricted submarine warfare was not officially sanctioned. In March—to anticipate—Tirpitz ceased to be Naval Secretary of State, and when, in that month, the French passenger steamer *Sussex*, carrying American citizens, was torpedoed without warning, the German Government formally apologized to Mr. Wilson and undertook that it should not happen again. But the German military and naval chiefs were unconvinced, and only bided their time.

One incident in the submarine campaign deserves special notice, because of its use by Germany to found a charge of barbarism against British seamen. The facts in the *Baralong* case were these. Early in the afternoon of August 19, 1915, the steamer *Nicosian*, with a cargo of army mules, was approaching the Irish coast some sixty miles from Queenstown. There she fell in with the German U boat 27, which a few hours before had sunk the *Arabic*. A torpedo was fired, which struck the *Nicosian*, but without sinking her, upon which the submarine began to shell. Thereupon the captain and crew put off in a boat ; but the American cattlemen who had come over in charge of the mules, having no experience of the ways of submarines, remained on board. The captain of the U boat, desiring to economize his torpedoes, sent a boarding-party to finish off the *Nicosian* with bombs. At that moment the *Baralong* arrived on the scene. She had been got up as a tramp, and was probably destined by the U boat as its next victim; but as she approached she stripped off her disguise, and revealed herself as an armed auxiliary, with the men waiting at their guns She opened musketry fire on the submarine, and then split her in two with shots from her port and stern guns. Upon this the German captain and the rest of the crew put off in a boat to the *Nicosian*, intending, no doubt, to surrender there. The *Baralong's* captain, not knowing their purpose, fired upon them and several were killed. Meantime strange things were happening on the *Nicosian*. The American cattlemen, whose temper had not been improved by the shelling, observed that the boarding-party in the first boat were carrying bombs. They allowed the German seamen to come on deck, and then rushed on them and battered in their heads with furnace bars. Presently in the second boat came the captain and the rest of the crew. They, too, were hunted up and down the ship and disposed of. When a British officer arrived from the *Baralong* he found no Germans left. The *Nicosian's* captain and crew rejoined her, and the vessel proceeded to Avonmouth.

The German Government presently produced a sworn statement by several cattlemen and by the second officer of the *Nicosian*, who had been dismissed, alleging that the men of the *Baralong* murdered the crew of the submarine as they were struggling in the water. It was a fantastic perversion of the facts, and one signatory had not even been at sea when the events of which he claimed to be an eye-witness occurred. Germany demanded the trial of the crew of the *Baralong* for murder; Sir Edward Grey answered that he was very willing that the matter should be investigated by a tribunal composed of American naval officers, provided that Germany agreed to allow the investigation by the same court of the circumstances connected with the sinking of the *Arabic*, the attack on the stranded submarine E13 in Danish waters, and the firing on the crew of the steamer *Ruel* after they had taken to the boats. Germany replied that the three last affairs were not *in pari materia* with the first; and announced that, since Britain refused to make amends for the *Baralong* outrage, " the German Government feels itself compelled to take into its own hands the punishment of this unexpiated crime, and to adopt retaliatory measures." What these could be it was difficult to guess, for a man cannot proceed to stronger measures when he has consistently practised the last extremes of outrage.

The blockade of Germany maintained by British warships was one of our chief weapons in the campaign. We have seen the difficulties which it raised with America on points of law ; towards the end of 1915 it was no less criticized by the British people on the point of fact. Critics urged that it was ineffective. Figures were quoted showing the enormously increased imports of the neutral countries adjoining Germany, principally in the way of foodstuffs. Our ring-fence was condemned as a farce, and the Foreign Office—which was not unnaturally suspected, as the sole begetter of the unfortunate Declaration of London—was enjoined to hand over the blockade to the sailors, who meant business. When these recommendations were examined they were found to fall under two heads. The first was the proposal to regularize our proceedings according to international law, and thereby placate the legally-minded America. It was urged that there was nothing to prevent a large extension of our list of absolute and conditional contraband, since we had thrown over the Declaration of London. Further, we might now declare a legal blockade. Even if it had been impossible before—which was not admitted by those who saw in the Baltic a " closed sea " on a parallel with the American Great Lakes—the success of our submarines in these waters had enabled us now to make it effective. Ever since the summer there had been a real blockade of the German Baltic ports. We had wrecked there both the commerce and the troop transport of the enemy—it was difficult to find German or Swedish underwriters to undertake the risk. German ships had for the most part to keep within territorial waters, and this greatly increased the slowness and the risks of their voyages. The Danish press—which might be taken as an independent witness—had no doubt about the effectiveness in point of fact of the British Baltic blockade.

But a formal blockade would have given us no powers which we had not already arrogated, and the proclamation, while it might have satisfied a few American jurists, would have made the situation still more delicate with regard to European neutrals. More important was the second ground of criticism—that by way of adjacent neutrals a large amount of vital imports was still filtering through to Germany. It was possible for the Government to show that the figures of the critics were exaggerated ; but the fact remained that Germany was making desperate attempts to get sea-borne food and raw materials for the purposes of war, and that our activities, while they had diminished this influx, had by no means put an end to it. It was easier to prove the unpleasant fact than to suggest a policy to prevent it. Talk about handing over the whole business to the Navy had little meaning, for before the Navy could act it must be given directions, and these directions were exactly what it was so hard to arrive at. What seemed to be in the minds of the critics was the action of Britain in the Napoleonic wars, when she stopped all commerce to the continent of Europe. But at that time the whole of Europe was openly or implicitly hostile, and unless we now wished to bring in all neutrals against us, this heroic remedy could scarcely be adopted. With Sweden, in particular, our relations were highly delicate; and Russia had no desire to see Sweden enter the field against the Allies, and appear with an army in Finland on her right rear. In his speech in the House of Commons on January 26, 1916, Sir Edward Grey put the point clearly :—

"If you establish lines of blockade, you must do it consistently with the rights of neutrals. You cannot establish these lines of blockade and say that no ships will go through them at all, or you will stop all traffic of any kind to the neutral ports inside. You would stop all traffic to Christiania, Stockholm, Rotterdam, Copenhagen—all traffic whatever. Well, of course, that is not consistent with the rights of neutrals. You cannot shut off all supplies to neutral countries. You must not try to make the grass grow in the streets of neutral ports. You must let through these lines vessels *bona fide* destined for the neutral ports, with *bona fide* cargoes. Nor can you put every cargo in your Prize Courts and say it has not to go to a neutral port until the Prize Court has examined it. The congestion in this country would be such that you could not deal with it if you did that, and you have no right to say that the British Prize Court is the neck of the bottle through which all trade has to pass. If we had gone, or attempted to go, as far as that, I think the war possibly might be over by now; but it would have been over because the whole world would have risen against us, and we, and our Allies too, would have collapsed under the general resentment of the whole world."

It remained, then, to discriminate between neutral imports intended for neutral use and those which might be passed on to the enemy. Such discrimination was obviously a task of immense intricacy, and involved the certainty of many mistakes. The principle of "rationing" a neutral was accepted, but the method had many grave drawbacks. If the imports prior to the war were taken as the basis, then this involved not only imports required for home consumption, but those re-exported to Germany to meet the balance of trade. It permitted, for example, the German acquisition of foodstuffs, and so was in defiance of the preamble of the Order in Council of March 11, 1915, which announced that " His Majesty had decided to adopt further measures to prevent commodities of any kind from reaching or leaving Germany." If the basis were the home consumption of a particular article, then the following situation might occur. The limit from the point of view of our blockade might be reached early in any year, through a number of ships arriving in neutral ports carrying that article, part of which was secretly destined for Germany. Cargoes arriving later, honestly destined for neutral consumption, we should be compelled to turn back or confiscate. To meet these difficulties, central distributing agencies were arranged in the neutral states which had the control of all consignments. They were responsible to us for the behaviour of their own merchants, and they formed authoritative bodies with which we could negotiate, and arrange from week to week the details of lawful commerce. It was by no means a perfect scheme; but in the circumstances, when we could only seek a balance of difficulties, it was probably the best possible. In the words of Lord Robert Cecil, who in February 1916 entered the Cabinet as Minister of Blockade, we could stop up the holes in the dam as they appeared; but it was inevitable that a good deal of water should run through while the repairs were being made.

The criticism of our blockade policy was soon extended to other naval matters. On one point it was amply justified. The merchant shipping question had been allowed to drift, so that freights had risen to a crazy height, and shipowners made altogether excessive profits. It was urged that shipping companies should be made " controlled establishments," so that the whole of their surplus earnings might be taken for the nation; but this plan, while it might have augmented our revenue, would not have met the real difficulty. It would have been well if the shipping trade had been taken over by the Government, who would have paid it a fixed rate of interest on its capital and drawn up a reasonable schedule of freights. Neutral freights had naturally followed the British lead, and risen to the same extravagant height, and it was idle to hope to lower them by any of the devices proposed—such as, for example, making their coaling facilities in the ports of the Empire depend upon their adherence to a tariff—unless our British scale was lowered and systematized. The reason why some such step was not taken seems to have been the departmentalism which is rampant in any time of stress. Every great question is interdepartmental, and no one can be settled speedily or wisely unless there is a strong central authority to colligate and harmonize the claims of the departments. Finally, in the early days of March, the critics fastened upon naval policy itself — not, indeed, the work of the Fleets and the fighting Admirals, but the alleged supineness of the Board of Admiralty in new construction. Mr. Churchill returned from his battalion in the trenches to make a speech full of dark innuendoes, concluding with a demand for the reinstatement of Lord Fisher at Whitehall. He had a slender parliamentary and journalistic following, but those who most admired his courage and mental alertness could not but regard the performance as ill advised.

In the first months of 1916 speculation was rife, both among sailors and civilians, as to German naval plans. It was known that Germany had been busy at new construction, but it was not clear what form it would take. There were rumours of capital ships armed with 17-inch guns, of new mammoth submarines capable of voyaging a thousand miles from their bases without seeking supplies, and so beaked and armoured that they could sheer through any nets. It was believed that Germany contemplated in the near future an attack by sea and air as a complement to some great offensive by land. The most reasonable forecast seemed to be that she would lay a minefield from some point on the British coast eastwards, and under its cover attempt a raid or a bombardment of our south-eastern shores. If our battleships and battle-cruisers hastened to cut off the raiders, they would be entangled in the minefield and lose heavily. In this way she might hope to reduce our capital ships and prepare for future operations by her High Sea Fleet on more equal terms.

Colour was given to some such forecast by the very remarkable German mine-laying activity at the end of 1915 and during the first months of 1916. A new type of U boat had been specially devised for the laying of mines under water. It carried the mines in a special air-tight chamber which could be shut off from the hull of the submarine, and opened from above to the sea. As the mines descended they were automatically released from their sinker, which went to the bottom and acted as anchor. The mines, being lighter than water, floated at the end of the connecting chain, which kept them at the requisite distance below the surface.

A minefield laid in this way was impossible to trace, except by its consequences, and it necessitated sweeping operations on a far greater scale than hitherto. Hence there tended to be a shortage of smaller auxiliaries, mine-sweepers and the like, attached to the Grand Fleet. The campaign in the Eastern Mediterranean, where our lines of communication lay on the sea, required a very large number of small vessels, and the dearth of skilled labour at home made it difficult to construct new ones in the time. Germany had correctly appreciated the situation, and laid her plans accordingly.

A second evidence of German naval activity was the dispatch of commerce-raiders from her North Sea ports. In December 1915 a vessel of some 4,500 tons, which had been launched as a fruit-ship and christened the *Ponga*, but had been transformed into an auxiliary cruiser carrying 6-inch guns, slipped out of Kiel harbour. She was rebaptized the *Moewe*, after a gunboat sunk at Dar-es-Salaam. Her commander was Count von und zu Dohna-Schlodien, who had been the navigating officer on the battleship *Posen*. Disguised with false sides to look like a tramp, and flying the Swedish flag, she slipped through our watching cruisers in the fog, and, fetching a wide circuit round the north of Scotland, arrived in the Atlantic. There she began a remarkable predatory career. She took the *Corbridge* off Cape Finisterre on January 11, 1916, and presently added the *Author, Trader, Ariadne, Dromonby, Farringford,* and *Clan Mactavish*. The last vessel, which carried a 3-inch gun, put up a gallant fight, and lost eleven men killed. On 15th January the *Appam*, a vessel of nearly 8,000 tons, with the Governor of Sierra Leone on board, was taken in the seas off Madeira. Count Dohna, who behaved with humanity, put the crews and passengers of his different captures into the *Appam*, and sent her off under Lieutenant Berg to Norfolk, Virginia, where she duly arrived on 1st February, and raised a new legal conundrum for the American Government. Meantime the *Moewe* proceeded on her course, haunting the junction of the South American and West Indian trade routes, and added to her bag the *Westburn, Horace, Flamenco, Edinburgh,* and *Saxon Prince*, as well as the French *Maroni* and the Belgian *Luxembourg*. She sent the crews of these vessels in the *Westburn* to Santa Cruz, in Teneriffe, and after landing them blew the ship up. The *Moewe*, having done enough *pour chauffer la gloire*, turned towards home by the same route as she had come, and safely arrived at Kiel on 4th March Her commander deserved all credit for a bold and skilful performance. He had captured fifteen vessels, and cost Britain at least £2,000,000. He brought home with him four British officers, twenty-nine marines and sailors, 166 men from the different crews, and some £50,000 in gold bars. He had proved that the right kind of disguise might give a ship the invisibility of the submarine, and his countrymen were entitled to acclaim his achievement.

Encouraged by his success, and before he had returned, Germany sent out another raider. This was the *Greif*, a big armed merchantman, carrying 7-inch and 4-inch guns, and fitted with torpedo tubes. Disguised as a tramp, and with the Norwegian colours painted on her sides, she made her way through the North Sea, and was steering a course for the Atlantic between the Shetlands and the Faroes, when, on the forenoon of 29th February, she was sighted by the *Alcantara*, a Royal Mail ship of over 15,000 tons, now used as an auxiliary cruiser. The *Alcantara* overhauled her, inquired her name and destination, and lowered a boat. Suddenly the false bulwarks were dropped, and the stranger opened fire at a range of about 1,000 yards. She discharged a torpedo, but without success; and then one of her shells wrecked the *Alcantara*'s steering gear, and a second torpedo found its mark. Meanwhile another British auxiliary, the *Andes*, appeared, and by her gun-fire put the *Greif* out of action. The destroyer *Comus* also joined in from long range, and made accurate shooting. The enemy, now blazing from stem to stern, presently blew up, probably when the fire reached her cargo of mines. From the sinking *Alcantara* the two cruisers rescued all but five officers and twenty-nine men, and picked up five of the *Greif's* officers and 115 of her crew.

The work of our Fleet was so quiet and so little advertised that the ordinary Briton dwelling in the southern towns felt more remote from it than from the Flanders trenches. Only on the seaboard, especially in the north and east, was there evidence for the eye of an intricate and ceaseless activity. As our Army had grown so had our Navy. Men of every class and occupation— yacht owners, fishermen, leisured people with a turn for the sea— had been drawn into the net, and the Royal Navy now included as motley a collection of volunteers in its auxiliary branches as could be found in the ranks of the new battalions. How arduous and anxious was the work only those employed in it could tell. That it was carried on in all weathers and under all discouragements with no surcease of keenness, was a tribute not only to our national character, but to the masterful traditions of the great Service.

Any army, compelled to twenty months of comparative inaction and an unsleeping defensive, would have gone to pieces. But any army was a ragged and amateur business as compared with the British fleet. The ordeal was sustained partly because a ship's life in war is not so different from a ship's life in peace, partly because of the tradition of discipline and wise ceremonial, and partly because of the expertness of the profession. A modern sailor has duties so intricate and technical that they provide his mind with constant occupation. Even in peace neither body nor brain can afford to rust.

The sea has formed the English character, and the essential England is to be found in those who follow it. They have not altered since the days of the Channel skippers who taught Drake his trade, and the adventurers who first drank bilge and ate penguins in far-away oceans. Our seamen have been unmoved by the political storms which raged on land. They have been neither Puritans nor Cavaliers, Whigs nor Tories, but plain Englishmen who were concerned with greater things. From blue water they have learned mercifulness and a certain spacious tolerance for what does not affect their craft, but they have also learned in the grimmest of schools precision and resolution. The sea endures no makeshifts. If a thing is not exactly right it will be vastly wrong. Discipline, courage to the point of madness, contempt for all that is pretentious and insincere, are the teaching of the ocean and the elements, and they have been the qualities in all ages of the British sailor. On the Navy, " under the good Providence of God," it is written in the Articles of War, hang the peace and prosperity of our islands and our Empire. But in this struggle there were still greater issues, for on the British navy especially depended whether law or rapine was henceforth to rule the world. To one who visited the Grand Fleet there came a sense of pride which was more than the traditional devotion of Englishmen to the senior service and the remembrance of a famous past. The great battleships far up in the northern waters, wreathed in mists and beaten upon by snowstorms, the men who for twenty months of nerve-racking strain had kept unimpaired their edge and ardour of mind, were indeed a shining proof of the might and spirit of their land. But in the task before them there was a high duty, which their forefathers, indeed, had shared, but which lay upon them with a more solemn urgency. They were the modern crusaders, the true defenders of the faith, doing battle not only for home and race and fatherland, but for the citadel and sanctities of Christendom.

CHAPTER XLIX.

THE WAR IN THE ÆGEAN AND IN AFRICA.
October 1915–May 1916.

Stalemate at Salonika—Bulgaria's Temper—The Position in Constantinople—The Defences of Egypt—The Defeat of the Senussi—The Conquest of the Cameroons—Germany's Principles of Colonization.

I.

DURING the first months of 1916 the stalemate at Salonika continued. Rumours of impending Bulgarian and German attacks were, indeed, assiduously circulated; but there was small substance behind them. They were not even successful as bluff, for no bluff was needed. Whether the enemy attacked or not, it was imperative that the Salonika occupation once begun should be continued. It was impossible to allow the hesitating neutrality of Greece to be subjected to the pressure of the immediate proximity of the enemy without any Allied force to act as a buffer. It was necessary for political reasons to have a *pied à terre* for the recovery of Serbia. It was especially necessary, in view of the unplumbed chances of the future, to keep the road open for a flank attack on Bulgaria in case the progress of Russia, or the accession of Rumania to the Allies, or the exhaustion of the Turk, should put King Ferdinand in peril. The landing at Salonika in October 1915 was not a step which could be easily retraced, for politics and strategy were inextricably commingled in its purpose.

On purely military grounds stagnation was predetermined. When Sarrail had once completed his lines and blown up the Demir Hissar bridge, he offered an awkward object for attack. The transport problem would be difficult. The Salonika–Monastir railway had no extension to the north, and so could not be used for bringing heavy guns and shells from the Danube. The main railway to Nish had been comprehensively wrecked by the French in its southern section, and the Demir Kapu tunnel especially would take long to repair. The only immediate route by rail was the line from Constantinople and Dedeagatch through Demir Hissar, which was also for the time out of working order. Assuming that these various ways were mended and ready for use, the main Allied position itself was a hard nut to crack. Its eastern half was very strong, and rested in the sea. In the western section only two parts were possible—the twenty odd miles from Lake Langaza to the Vardar, and the eighteen miles of the Vardar valley; and even there the inducements were small. The Allied entrenchments lay for the most part on northward facing slopes, heavily wired in front, and with seven miles before them of swampy plain over which the invaders must move. It would have been for the attack a second Suvla or Achi Baba. Finally, if the assault had been successful, and Sarrail had been driven to embark, what advantage would have been won? Some power of coercing Greece, no doubt; but, to set against that, a position which must be held under the perpetual menace of naval attack. Nor were the Allies better circumstanced for taking the offensive. There were three possible directions for an advance. One was on the left, against Monastir. There the country was open and easy as far as Verria, which was distant from Monastir only some sixty miles as the crow flies. But the advance must move along the winding valley which the railway followed; the hills as far as Vodena would have to be captured and held; and beyond that a series of narrow defiles must be traversed. Any such movement would be in danger of encountering entrenched positions of the Gallipoli type. A second route lay in the centre towards Uskub; but this meant the Vardar valley, a continuous defile for nearly a hundred miles. An advance on the right offered better hopes, and there the enemy seems to have apprehended danger. But it involved ascending the Struma valley, in which there was no railway, and which led through narrow passes between the spurs of Rhodope and the Serbian hills. Moreover, before an advance could begin, the Vardar valley and the routes from Monastir must be blocked, and the country about Lake Doiran must be reoccupied. Such a movement would be costly, laborious, and highly precarious, and no sane commander would have undertaken it unless the general diplomatic and military situation in the Near East had worn a more hopeful complexion than it did in the first months of 1916.

The long spell of inaction at Salonika was employed by the Allies in perfecting their position till the area of defence was nearly impregnable against the enemy forces then arrayed before it. These were now almost wholly Bulgarian, for Germany's commitments in the West had drawn away most of the divisions with which Mackensen had fought the autumn campaign. German submarines began to show some activity in the Greek territorial waters of the Salonika Gulf ; so, in order to make his own communications secure, General Sarrail, on the morning of January 28, 1916, occupied the Greek fortress of Kara Bunar, on the east side of the gulf, about fifteen miles from the city. There was little change for months in the constituents of the Allied army. On 9th May Major-General G. F. Milne succeeded Sir Bryan Mahon as the commander of the British forces. Meantime the remnants of the Serbian army were being refitted and made ready for the field. The capture of Durazzo by the Austrians on February 27, 1916, made it necessary to find some base for refitment inaccessible to the enemy. Accordingly, French and Italian troops landed at Corfu, and the use of the island as a Serbian rest camp began. Then might have been seen the cheering spectacle of the blue caps of the French Chasseurs Alpins amid the rococo splendour of the Achilleion, that classical villa which the German Emperor had used as a summer retreat. Some 100,000 Serbian soldiers were assembled at Corfu, and a considerable part of these were during the early days of May transferred to Salonika. The situation alarmed the Bulgarian High Command, who feared an Allied offensive ; so on 26th May Bulgarian forces advanced on to Greek soil north of Seres and Drama, and occupied Fort Rupel and one or two other works which commanded the line on which they anticipated the Allies might move. The Greek Government acquiesced, on the ground that the tolerance which they had already shown to the one belligerent must be extended to the other. Sarrail's position, uneasy at the best, seemed in danger of being seriously compromised by the behaviour of King Constantine's Government. Every obstacle was placed in the way of the movement of the re-armed Serbian troops through Greek territory, and from Thessaly the assembly of men and munitions was reported, which might have a sinister purpose. It was certain that before long the Allies must take drastic action at Athens.

It was also becoming clear that relations between Bulgaria and her German allies were incompletely harmonious. The peasants who made up the Bulgarian armies had been promised a short and easy campaign; they had, on the contrary, suffered heavy losses, and had been under arms for more than half a year. Germany was exploiting their land and exporting foodstuffs; their farms were going to ruin, they themselves were badly provisioned, and they detested the overbearing manners of their German colleagues. Among the educated classes there was much irritation at the Prussianizing of the capital, and the intrusion of a horde of Germans into the Government service. Finally, few Bulgarians were perfectly happy in a campaign which arrayed them in opposition to the armies of Russia. On the other hand, Bulgaria had already won much of her desires. She had Uskub and Monastir, and all that part of Macedonia which she had claimed. The only further bribe which Germany could offer her was access to the Ægean at Kavala, and such a prospect had not the same influence on the popular mind as the traditional cry of an unredeemed Macedonia. In these circumstances it was natural that the thoughts of many among the Allies should turn to the possibility of attaching Bulgaria to their own cause. It was argued with some truth that the talk about "Bulgarian treachery" had been overdone. Apart from the personal misconduct of the egregious Ferdinand and some of his Ministers, there was no reason to label the ordinary Bulgarian with the name of traitor. He had never professed any love for Serbia; he considered that his country had been shamelessly treated in the Balkan wars; he was bitter against his neighbours and those Allied Powers who had befriended them; he fought for what he considered his bare rights, and he accepted any alliance which would assist him to get them. It was argued, further, that the business of the Allies was to beat Germany, and not to punish the moral delinquencies of this or that statelet. A friendly Bulgaria would block the Teutonic route to the East, and put Turkey in the gravest peril. It would at once release for more fruitful service the quarter of a million troops now stagnant at Salonika, and turn the tables on Germany in the East.

Such a view was not without justification; but the difficulties before its realization were insuperable. The Allies were committed to a doctrine of nationality, and that was in theory the policy also of each Balkan state. But it had never been so in practice. Turkey and Austria between them had displaced and dislocated the Balkan races. Each little state was oppressed, and was herself an oppressor. Serbia at the outbreak of war saw people of her own blood in Bosnia, Dalmatia, and elsewhere under an alien rule; but she herself governed large tracts inhabited by Albanian and

Bulgarian races. It was the same with Greece and the same with Rumania. The Balkan trouble could only be settled by a complete new delimitation of territory on racial grounds, and for this a clean slate and a free hand were needed; and when the day for it came it was very certain that those who had clamoured for it most loudly would raise the gravest obstacles. "Territory according to nationality" was very well as a cry; but no nation was willing to give up land which she had won by arms or by diplomacy, or surrender economic ambitions which had nothing to do with race. The Allies could only placate Bulgaria at the expense of Serbia and Greece. Serbia could not be compensated as she desired until a complete Allied victory was won, and any attempt to use her territory to bargain with at a moment when, largely through the fault of the Allies, she was beggared, would have seemed to the world a monstrous dereliction of principle and honour. Further, any bargaining which would outbid Germany at Sofia would be a flat contradiction of those principles for which the Allies were professedly fighting. Germany offered Bulgaria Nish and part of Old Serbia, and during the winter in these districts the familiar practice of Bulgarization had begun in the schools and the local administration. In that area the population was wholly Serbian. She offered Kavala, where the people were Greek and Turkish, and part of Thrace, where the people were Turkish and Greek. There was no real common ground for dealing between the Allies, with their avowed principles, and King Ferdinand, who had no principles and wanted material gains. Proposals which might have succeeded a year before were simply irrelevant under the changed conditions. Most important of all, the Allies were committed to two aims, both of which were utterly repugnant to Sofia. The first was a greater Serbia; the second was the establishment of Russia on the Bosphorus. So far the Teutonic League could offer Bulgaria not only a bigger territorial bribe, but a scheme of world policy, not indeed without its dangers, but to the Bulgarian mind a thousandfold less repulsive than the professed objects of the Allies.

II.

Constantinople during the first months of 1916 was in a state of misery and confusion which had not been equalled in the memory of its citizens. At first the evacuation of Gallipoli by the Allies raised its spirits; but soon came the fall of Erzerum, which the Government could not conceal, and presently the losses of Mush and Bitlis, and the menace to Trebizond. Starvation laid its hand on the poorer classes. No supplies could reach the city from Bulgaria, and but little from Constanza, since the Russian fleet in the Black Sea barred the Rumanian voyage to all craft but the smallest schooners and feluccas. Germany, never loved by the older Turks or the masses of the people, became highly unpopular, and all German troops were removed from the city. There remained numerous German officers and officials, and several thousand German workmen in the munition factories; but to march German soldiers through the streets of Stamboul might have provoked a revolution. The ordinary Mussulman was concerned for the fate of his religion and his country, and he saw both in the hands of arrogant and sacrilegious infidels. Nor was the Young Turk better regarded. The cooler heads of the Committee, like Djavid, remained quiet, watching the tide of affairs; but Enver and Talaat swaggered in the limelight, and only the most vigilant espionage and the most arbitrary police methods saved them from death. Prince Yussuf-ed-din, the heir to the throne and no friend of the Committee, was murdered in February by Enver's order, according to the old fashion of Yildiz, and this barbarous act roused bitter popular hatred and widespread popular fear. Enver's dominance was based wholly on blood and terror, and had the bullet of some fortunate assassin found his brain, it is probable that the whole edifice he had built would have crumbled in a day, and the Osmanli shaken themselves loose from their unwelcome fetters. To add to the farce, he and Talaat quarrelled violently. Enver, who, to do him justice, was brave and vigorous, departed to Syria to deal with an Arab rising, and his rival had a brief period of absolute power. The situation was scarcely comfortable for the German masters, who found themselves labouring to introduce the most modern Prussian methods into a land which seemed to model itself on some swashbuckling Italian city of the Middle Ages.

The situation in Egypt, since a British Protectorate had been proclaimed and Sultan Hussein placed on the throne of the deposed Khedive, had been one of internal tranquillity. Great masses of British troops had been under training, a Turkish force had reached the banks of the Suez Canal, and later the place had been the base for the Gallipoli operations; but these military doings had small effect on the serenity of the land. Nationalism, in the old sense, was quiescent. Its leaders were either in detention camps or in exile, and the attempts on the life of the Sultan and one of his Ministers were the only flickering of what Germany had hoped would be a consuming fire. The secret of this tranquillity was not to be sought only in the firm hand of the British Military Governor, but in the very real economic prosperity of the country. Egypt was in the rare position of being untouched, so far as her pockets were concerned, by the world-war. The presence of great armies brought money into the country, and provided an inexhaustible market for local produce. Her crops were good; even her cotton crop, which at one moment gave cause for disquiet, belied her fears. The peasant farmer of the Nile valley might owe a shadowy allegiance to the Khalif, but he was first and foremost a man who had to get his living. Lord Cromer had long before discovered that the centre of gravity was economic, and that political stability would be assured if among the labouring masses there was a modest security and comfort.

By the end of the year 1915 the German threats of invasion were very generally discounted. Had Turkey been in earnest preparations for the great assault should have been begun in early December. But in spite of rumours of pipe lines and light railways being built westward from Beersheba, it was clear that no serious effort was being made to prepare the ramshackle Syrian railways for the transport of a great army. The invasion could only succeed if it were conducted on a large scale with elaborate preliminaries, and these neither Djemal at Damascus nor Enver at Constantinople had seriously envisaged. Part of the Syrian army had gone to reinforce Bagdad; part, it was clear, might soon be called for in Transcaucasia. But it behoved the Allies to be ready for all emergencies. Their position in the Eastern Mediterranean was roughly that of an army holding interior lines, and, with the command of the sea, their communications were simple. They needed a training ground for their reserves, and a starting point from which to reinforce their various adjacent battle-grounds. Accordingly, the defence of the Nile valley was combined with the provision of a base for all the other activities in the Near East.

The only cloud which immediately threatened—and it was a very small one—came from the west. The western frontier of Egypt, seven hundred miles long, adjoined the Italian possessions in Tripoli, and Italy was an ally. But the writ of Italy ran feebly in the interior. After the Tripoli war the Italian suzerainty, formally acknowledged in the Treaty of Lausanne, was not made effective beyond the coast-line. Turkish regulars and Turkish guns remained behind to help the Arab and Berber tribes to resist the alien rule. When Italy declared war on Austria the Italian force of occupation fell back to the coast, and the inland tribesmen were left to their own devices. Stirred up by German and Turkish agents, these tribesmen prepared for action. They hoped to gather to their standard the Bedouins of the Libyan plateau, and to win the support of the great Senussi brotherhood. The Senussi formed one of those strange religious fraternities common in North Africa. Their founder had been a firm friend of Britain, and had resisted all overtures from the Mahdi. He had preached a spiritual doctrine which Islam for the most part regarded as heterodox, and his followers were outside the main currents of the Moslem world. In especial they were untainted with Pan-Islamism, and had held themselves aloof from politics. Their headquarters were the oases of the North Libyan desert, and they had no fault to find with British rule in Egypt. Their Grand Sheikh, Sidi Ahmed, had given assurance of friendliness to the Anglo-Egyptian authorities, and his official representatives lived on the Nile banks in cordial relations with the Government. But the overtures of Nuri, a half-brother of Enver, and Gaafer, a Germanized Turk, proved too much for the loosely organized tribesmen of the Senussi, and ultimately for the Grand Senussi himself. It was only at the north end that the Tripoli frontier had to be guarded. South lay the endless impassable wastes of the Libyan desert. But along the coast lay the Libyan plateau, with many little oases linked up by caravan tracks. The Khedival highway ran to Sollum on the border, and when, in the autumn of 1915, trouble threatened, the frontier posts at Sollum and Sidi Barrani were drawn in to Mersa Matruh, which, with a railway only eighty miles distant, and the sea at its door, was well equipped as a base to defend the marches.

The first hostilities began on 13th December, when 1,200 Arabs were driven back with heavy losses. Towards the end of the month a force of 5,000 under Gaafer gathered on the outskirts of Matruh, and on Christmas Day the hastily collected British Western Frontier Force, under General Wallace, went out against this, the first invasion of Egypt from the west since the Fatimites in the tenth century. The enemy was located in a donga some eight miles from Matruh, and was completely routed with a loss of over 500 killed and prisoners. He appeared again early in January 1916, and on the 23rd General Wallace, now reinforced by part of the South African Infantry Brigade, fell upon him some twenty miles west of Matruh and scattered him with heavy losses. But the British column was not yet sufficiently mobile to follow up its successes, and the Senussi remained a cloud on the western horizon.

Meantime the large assembly of troops in Egypt had been increased by a division from Cape Helles. The command, divided between the General Commanding the Mediterranean Expeditionary Force, the General Commanding in Egypt, and the General Commanding the Levant base, reached a pitch of subtle differentiation which it required the soul of a mediæval schoolman to understand. Early in March Sir John Maxwell returned to England, and Sir Archibald Murray, of the Mediterranean Expeditionary Force, was left in undivided charge. By that time the troops had begun to move—one division going to Mesopotamia, and the original Anzac Corps and some of the old 8th Corps to the Western front. There still remained a large force, part of which was in process of training, and during the first months of the year there was a certain activity on the eastern and western borders.

The first task was to finish with the Senussi. Major-General W. E. Peyton, who had commanded the 2nd Mounted Division at Suvla, succeeded General Wallace in command of the Western Frontier Force. On 26th February General Lukin's South African Brigade, supported by mounted troops, defeated the enemy at Agagia, near Barrani, fifty miles east of the border, and captured Gaafer and his staff. On 16th March Peyton occupied Sollum, the Egyptian port on the frontier, which had been evacuated three months before. Sollum lies on the flat shore of a bay, and behind it the escarpment of the Libyan plateau rises steeply to a height of 700 feet. Lukin took the escarpment from behind, by way of the Halfaia Pass, and as soon as the plateau was won the town was ours. Meantime a detachment of the Duke of Westminster's armoured cars performed brilliant service in hampering the enemy's retreat. Airplane reconnaissance on the morning of the 14th showed that the enemy headquarters at Bir Warr, six miles west of Sollum, were empty, and making a detour of thirty miles, the cars started in pursuit. They headed off the fleeing convoy in the south, and, after a fight which stretched for seven miles, collected over fifty dead, some forty prisoners, and all the enemy guns. With the capture of Sollum and the clearing of the frontier the Senussi campaign virtually ended. It had been a brilliant little affair, carried out, too, in trying weather, hailstorms and great cold being diversified with long spells of scorching heat Water there was little of, and most of the supply had to be brought by sea from Alexandria to Matruh, and sent forward by camel train to the front. There was no food in the country, for the usual barley crops had not been raised, and the steps of the British columns were clogged with famishing Arab families. After our humane fashion, we beat the enemy and fed his belongings.

The scene now changed to the eastern frontier of Egypt, where, in the Sinai desert, Turkish forces from the Beersheba base continued their spasmodic operations. As we have seen, there were three main routes across the desert to the canal—the coast route by El Arish to Kantara, the central route from El Audja to Ismailia, and the southern route from Akaba to Suez. British detachments had been pushed east as far as the oasis of Katia, on the northern route, about thirty miles from the canal, and on 13th April an Australian column raided Jifjaffa—on the central route, some sixty miles from the canal—and broke up an enemy detachment which was boring there for water. On Easter Sunday, 23rd April, we were less fortunate. Early in the morning a heavy mist cloaked the desert, and under its cover the Turks effected a surprise attack on Katia village. The place was held by detachments of Yeomanry, and the superior numbers of the enemy, which included a battalion composed of Austrians and Germans, compelled them to fall back, fighting a rearguard action. Reinforcements arrived, and the advance was checked, but not before we had lost heavily in dead and prisoners. Presently the enemy withdrew, having himself suffered many casualties, and our aircraft successfully bombed his retreat. On the same day a bold attack was made much farther west at the post of Dueidar, only fifteen miles from the canal. The place was held by one company of the Royal Scots Fusiliers; the odds were at first about six to one; but the gallant few held their ground till they were reinforced by two other companies of the regiment. The Turks were beaten off with a loss of seventy dead and thirty prisoners, and a squadron of the Australian Light Horse harassed their retirement. During April and May the Turkish posts in the Sinai desert were repeatedly assailed by our aircraft, and buildings, water and petrol tanks, and boring plant destroyed. Meantime preparations were being made to carry the war beyond the desert, by the construction of a railway and a pipe line, for Kitchener had long been convinced that the true defence of Egypt was not on the Canal but on the Palestine border. The first steps were taken in the long advance which was to bring us to Jerusalem, Damascus, and Aleppo.

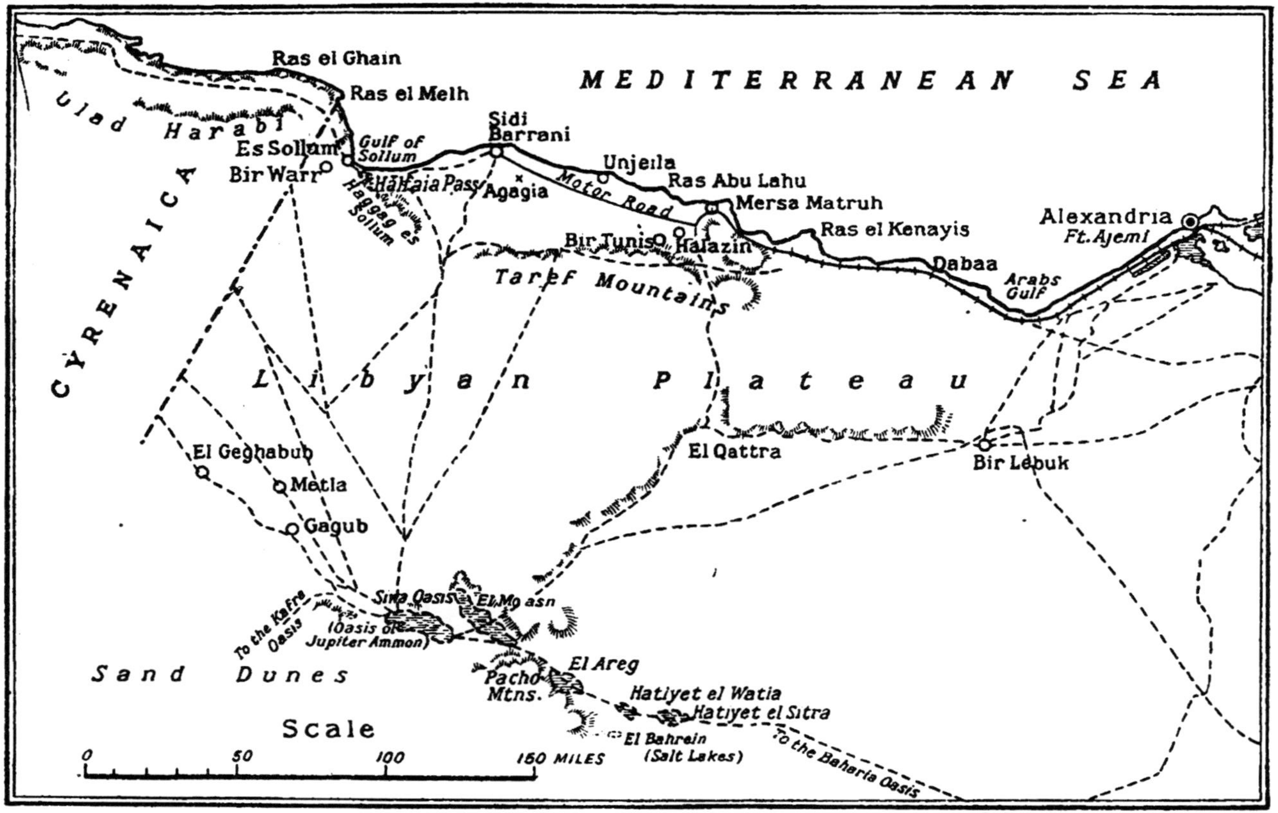

THE MAPPA CO., LTD., LONDON

THE WESTERN FRONTIER OF EGYPT

Meantime in the southern part of the Libyan desert British columns prevented any massing of disaffected tribesmen. Darfur, the most westerly of the Sudan protected states, whose capital, El Fasher, is some five hundred miles south-west of Khartum, had since the beginning of the year given ground for anxiety. Its Sultan, Ali Dinar, had grown truculent, and early in February took to raiding on the Kordofan frontier. Accordingly, the Sirdar of the Egyptian army, Sir Reginald Wingate, concentrated in March a force at El Nahad on that border. The force was conveyed by the Sudan railway to El Obeid, and marched to its concentration point. At the end of March it moved forward to Om Shanga, on the caravan route to El Fasher, where an advanced base was formed. In Sudanese warfare any considerable advance has to be made by successive stages, each point occupied forming a depot where supplies are collected for the next onward move. Early in May the oasis of Abiad, about half-way between Om Shanga and El Fasher, was occupied, and from this point on 15th May a mixed force of all arms marched on El Fasher. On the 22nd the Sultan, with a force of 2,600 riflemen, was utterly defeated at the village of Beringia, twelve miles north of the capital, and an area of 150,000 square miles was regained for the Sudan. El Fasher was occupied, large quantities of military stores were captured, the inhabitants were speedily and peacefully disarmed, and Ali Dinar, with a small following, fled westwards to seek sanctuary among the Fur tribesmen of the Jebel Marra hills. A satisfactory feature of the operations was that this campaign in a difficult desert country was carried to a successful conclusion entirely by the soldiers of the Egyptian army under their British leaders, without the support of any white troops.

III.

We left the Cameroons campaign at the end of June 1915, when the French in the south had captured Lome, the Franco-British column in the north had taken Garua and Ngaundere, and the main force, moving up the midland railway, had reached Eseka and a position short of Wum Biagas, while the whole northern railway was in our hands. The Allied force had now grown to about 9,700, consisting of British, French, Belgian, and Indian native troops, trained and led by white officers and non-commissioned officers. The German strength was at the outset 3,000, including some 250 white officers, and though it was well munitioned, especially in the way of machine guns, the disparity of numbers suggested a short and simple campaign. But the Germans had potent allies in the country and the weather. A territory half as large again as the German Empire in Europe had to be methodically "driven" so that no enemy resistance should anywhere remain, for it was impossible to bring matters to a decision by any one battle. It was a region created by nature for the defence. Food was abundant; there were few roads; the lines of communication for the attack stretched out alarmingly, and every fresh mile lessened their safety. Practically all supplies had to be transported by native carriers, whose loads were from 50 pounds to 60 pounds per man, and to defend the routes blockhouses had to be established every twenty miles whose garrisons greatly depleted the strength of the advancing columns. The country everywhere was difficult to move in, and well fitted for surprise attacks by the defence. In the coastal area there were dense dripping forests choked with undergrowth, and seamed with broad and deep rivers. In the interior the savannahs were covered with elephant grass, sometimes twenty feet high, and broken up by rocky heights whose boulder-strewn slopes were natural entrenchments and redoubts. The climate, too, especially in the coast districts and in the south, was hostile to rapid movement by white men. Tropical diseases, such as malaria, blackwater fever, and dysentery, waited to take toll of the overfatigued and the underfed.

Nevertheless the Cameroons expedition was well within the experience of both France and Britain. It was the kind of campaign with which any Power with a long colonial record was familiar. The problems involved—leadership of native levies, improvisation under difficulties, swift marches through awkward country, the complex tropical transport—were those which Britain especially had faced for two hundred years. In the European theatre we were met by something new in our history, new indeed in the whole history of war.

> "Far other is this battle in the west
> Whereto we move, than when we strove in youth
> And brake the petty kings."

But in the Cameroons we could apply a knowledge which our Allies had learned in Algiers and Tonkin, and we had acquired in a score of campaigns from Burma to Ashanti.

The Allied forces were under the command of Major-General

THE CAMEROONS CAMPAIGN.

Sir Charles Dobell, whose plan was a converging movement upon the German seat of government, which should in its progress sweep up the outlying centres of resistance. It was the same plan which had already been crowned with victory in German South-West Africa. The difficulties were indeed many. The enormous area and the lack of most modern forms of communication made accurate timing almost impossible, and left the details of each section of the fighting largely to the subordinate commanders. After the occupation of Duala on September 27, 1914, the seat of the German Government was transferred to Yaunde, a station on the edge of the interior plateau, south of the Sanaga valley, and about 120 miles from the coast. Yaunde was obviously the proper object for the converging movement, and in March 1915 Dobell arranged with General Aymerich, the officer commanding the French southern columns, for a general advance upon this point. The intricacies of the country held up the attack, and towards the end of June it became necessary to withdraw Colonel Mayer's French force, which had advanced to Eseka and beyond Wum Biagas, to the line of the Kele River. After this came the inevitable lull caused by the rainy season. At the end of August a conference took place at Duala between the Governor-General of French Equatoria, Dobell, and Aymerich, in which a plan for future operations was arrived at.

The different forces and their position at the moment may be briefly summarized. The main army under Dobell was composed of two columns—the British, under Colonel Gorges, on the Sanaga River; and the French, under Colonel Mayer, farther south, on the Kele River. This represented the main thrust at Yaunde, and at the time was within fifty miles of the town. On the northern railway a British force under Lieutenant-Colonel Cotton was at Bare, and a detachment under Major Crookenden was at Ossidinghe, twenty miles from the Nigerian border. Farther north, Brigadier-General Cunliffe's force, which included a French column under Lieutenant-Colonel Brisset, that had marched from Lake Chad, was on the line Ngaundere–Kontcha–Gashaka, on the high ground above the upper streams of the Sanaga. The country in its rear was not wholly cleared, for a strong body of the enemy was holding out in the mountain of Mora, at the northern extremity of the Mandara range. In the south two main forces, under the direction of General Aymerich, had marched up the northern affluents of the Congo. On the east what the French called the Column of the Lobaye, under Lieutenant-Colonel Morisson, had moved west and north-west, taking Bania and Gaza; and another farther west, the Column of the Sangha, under Lieutenant-Colonel Hutin, had gone due north, taking Nola and Lome. The two forces had now joined hands, and were holding Dume and Bertua, about 130 miles east of Yaunde. Finally, a detachment under Lieutenant-Colonel le Meillour was marching up the east side of the Spanish *enclave* of Rio Muni, to cross the Campo River and attack Ebolowa, which lay about sixty miles south by west of Yaunde. The German stronghold was therefore in the position of being ringed round on all sides. The enemy force nearest to its gates was Dobell's main army; the farthest off was Cunliffe's northern columns towards Ngaundere.

The real operations could not commence till early in October, but in the meantime Cunliffe took advantage of the better weather in the north of the colony to make an attempt to reduce the mountain Mora, and so release the investing force for operations farther south. Mora, as he described it, " has a base perimeter of about thirty miles; it rises precipitously to a height of 1,700 feet, and its sides, which are so steep as to be accessible only in a few places to men using both hands and feet, are covered with huge boulders, affording excellent cover to the defenders." He arrived four miles from the fort on 23rd August, and resolved to make the attack from Onatchke, a hill to the north, the summit of which was nearly level with Mora and separated from it by a deep valley 600 yards wide. From Onatchke three separate attacks were launched. In the third a part of the 1st Nigerian Regiment reached the summit but were stopped by a redoubt, which they attempted with the bayonet, but failed to carry. They remained in the position without food or water for forty-eight hours, till they were withdrawn. Cunliffe decided that to take Mora he needed more artillery and more time, and as he was due to co-operate in the main advance he was compelled to relinquish the attempt for the present, and leave troops behind to invest it.

The main movement against Yaunde began on the 9th of October, when the Nigeria and Gold Coast troops of Colonel Gorges's column captured Wum Biagas. Meanwhile Colonel Mayer, advancing from the Kele River, occupied Sende on 25th October, and reached Eseka five days later. There was a short lull, which was occupied in improving the routes. The bush track from Edea to Wum Biagas was converted into a good motor road, and railway communications with Eseka were all but completed. Where the country did not permit of motor or rail traffic, a force of 7,000 carriers was employed. The next advance was on a wide front, Colonel Gorges aiming at the point Dschang Mangas, and Colonel Mayer at the road which connected Yaunde with the coast village of Kribi. The forest part of the advance was hotly contested; but by the beginning of the third week of December Gorges had reached open country, and on the 17th Dschang Mangas was taken. Mayer had an ordeal no less severe; but after five days' fighting he took Mangeles on 21st December. Meanwhile the British column had pushed on, finding the resistance of the enemy everywhere slackening, and on the first day of 1916 it entered Yaunde.

In the north there had been some spirited campaigning. Cunliffe directed Colonel Brisset's French column to move on Tibati, Lieutenant-Colonel Webb-Bowen's column on Galim, and Major Crookenden's force from Ossidinghe on Bamenda. Meanwhile Lieutenant-Colonel Cotton moved from Bare against Dchang. Cunliffe's main body advanced from Kontcha against the mountain Banyo, which was one of the strongest German positions in the colony. On 22nd October Crookenden reached Bamenda, and on 6th November Cotton took Dchang. The two forces then moved on Fumban, which they took on 2nd December with the assistance of a detachment of Cunliffe's troops. Cunliffe himself had been engaged in the reduction of Banyo mountain, a stronghold of the type of Mora, and succeeded at daybreak on the 6th of November, after an action which, in the words of his report, "may be justly described as one of the most arduous ever fought by African troops."

During the action at Banyo the two columns of Colonel Brisset and Colonel Webb-Bowen had entered Tibati. Cunliffe's forces were now converging on the Sanaga River by way of Yoko, which was entered by Brisset on 1st December. On January 4, 1916, the crossing of the Sanaga was achieved at the Nachtigal Rapids, a point only forty miles north of Yaunde, and connection was established with General Aymerich on the east. Brisset and Webb-Bowen entered the German capital immediately after Aymerich, and only a few days after the place had fallen to Gorges. Such precision in concentration would have been admirable in any campaign; it was especially admirable in one involving such vast distances and precarious communications. "It is, I think, a remarkable feat," wrote Dobell in his dispatch, "that troops that had fought and marched for a period of seventeen months should have converged on their objective within a few days of one another."

The rest was merely a matter of sweeping up. The bulk of the German troops not already prisoners fled south-westward towards Spanish territory. Ebolowa was occupied on 19th January, and Colonel Morisson with a strong French force chased the remnants over the Campo River inside the borders of Spanish Guinea. Among the fugitives was the German Governor, Ebermaier, and the German Commander-in-Chief, Zimmermann. There only remained the mountain Mora in the far north, where the garrison still held out. Generous terms were offered—officers to be allowed to retain their swords, native ranks to be released and given free passage to their homes, all Europeans to go to England as prisoners of war—and on 18th February Captain von Raben, the commandant, surrendered. There were now no Germans left in the Cameroons, and the conquest of the country was completed.

Had the Cameroons campaign been the only hostilities in which Britain at the time was engaged, its happy issue would have been a cause of pride to the whole Empire, and would have brought high honour to the men who contrived it. It was economical, well-conceived, and admirably executed. Few tropical wars have involved more intricate problems of transport or more toilsome marches. Take the case of Cunliffe's northern force. When it entered Yaunde in January it had marched and fought continuously over 600 miles since the 18th of September, and its line of communication with the base at Ibi was 400 miles long. The campaign revealed the fine fighting qualities of the West African native troops, both French and British, and Dobell paid tribute to the bravery and unshaken cheerfulness of the Senegalese, and the Nigerians of the West African Frontier force, to whom " no day appears to be too long, no task too difficult." Cunliffe's testimony is worth quoting : " The Nigerian Regiment is composed of men of many different tribes ; their characteristics, traditions, and even their language differ as widely as does the food to which they are accustomed. They have been called upon to take part in a great struggle, the rights and wrongs of which they can scarcely have been expected dimly to perceive. They have been through the, to them, extremely novel experience of facing an enemy armed with modern weapons and led by highly-trained officers. Their rations have been scanty, their barefoot marches long and trying, and their fighting at times extremely arduous, yet they have not been found wanting either in discipline, devotion to their officers, or personal courage." In the case of

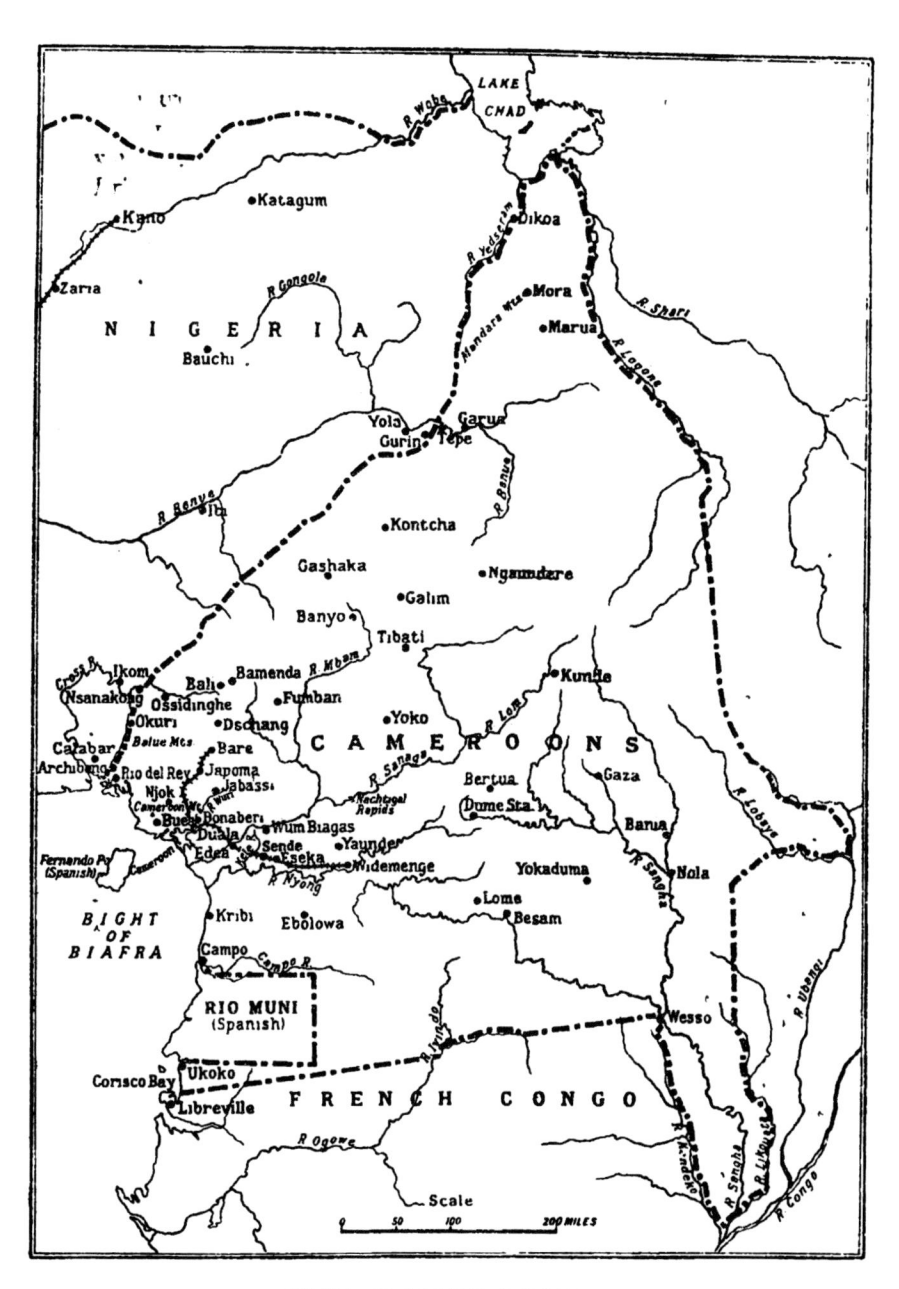

THE CAMEROONS.

such troops everything depended upon the leading. They were like great schoolboys, and, if properly handled, would go anywhere and do anything. The campaign proved that France and Britain had not lost the art of providing the type of regimental officer who by tact and courage can win and retain the affection of savage tribesmen.

The German garrison of the Cameroons—as was clear from captured documents—had confidently believed that they could hold out till the end of the European struggle. Their hopes were disappointed. Germany's grandiose African enterprises had by the middle of February 1916 been reduced to the single colony of East Africa, where General Smuts's columns were already pressing in upon the interior railways. If such far-away happenings seemed trivial compared to the desperate contest on the main battle-ground, the conquest of the German colonies had none the less a vital bearing upon the policy of the war. In striking at German Africa the Allies were not attacking irrelevant and half-forgotten dependencies, but an integral part of the German scheme of world-empire.

In an earlier chapter we have seen why Germany first came to Africa, and how she won her footing. German colonization was a reasoned policy, not the haphazard work of individuals which gradually grows into a national purpose; and, like all reasoned policies, in its first stages it marched fast. She had a clear aim—to provide producing grounds for raw material, military outposts, and observation stations. Such an aim, be it said, was not colonization, which is more than a chain of plantations, and much more than a string of garrisons. Colonization involves *settlement*—the adoption by emigrants of the new land as their home, the administration of that new land with a view to its own interest, and not with regard merely to the ambitions of the parent country. Mere exploitation is not colonization, as the Dutch and the Portuguese found. The inhabitants must get their roots down, must acquire a local patriotism as well as a patriotism of origin. The duty to the land itself must be recognized, and not less the duty to the older masters who continue to live side by side with the new. A true colony is a slow business, an organic growth rather than a mechanical construction, and true colonies the German possessions had never been, for the heart of the matter was neglected. Further, the German colonies, being what they were, were a constant menace to their neighbours. If one man is digging trenches to drain his farm, and another digs to make the foundations of a fort, there is nothing in common between the two, and no possibility of harmonious neighbourship. The German colonies were part of the Pan-Germanist propaganda, like the Bagdad railway or the fortress of Tsing-tau. They represented one side of the plan of expansion, as the control of Mesopotamia represented the other. There was this difference between the two sides, that while the extension south-eastward of the Central European Powers might be possible by military strength only, the maintenance of armed colonies demanded a navy. Again and again the enthusiasts of the German Navy League used the colonial argument to support their pleas; Germany in her striving after *Weltmacht* must have her oversea garrisons, and an omnipotent navy was needed as a link between them. Given that navy, their strategic value would have been great. German East Africa was on the southern flank of the road to India, as Mesopotamia was on the northern. With German influence on both sides of the great waterway to the East, the most vital interests of Britain would have been menaced. The *Drang nach Osten* was largely and subtly conceived.

Shortly after the fall of the Cameroons Professor Ernst Haeckel added to the gaiety of nations by discoursing in an American magazine on Germany's future plans. The world had not hitherto associated Haeckel with high politics; but in these bad times all the *gelehrten* were mobilized, and the venerable author of *Welträthsel* with the rest. He explained that Germany needed an empire, not like England from lust of gold, or like France for vainglory, or like Italy from megalomania, or like Russia because of sheer barbarous greed, but because she was overcrowded at home, and wanted an outlet for her surplus population. Africa was to be a substantial part of that empire; the Congo especially, which would come to Germany as a consequence of the espousal of Belgium. The whole of Central Africa from sea to sea would be German, while the Cape would be restored to Holland, and Egypt to the Turks, and perfidious Britain would depart from the continent altogether. The plea for settlement was out of date, for Germany in recent years had shown no desire for settlers, and the tide of her emigration had long ago ebbed. Haeckel's dream could only come true if the Allies were beaten to the ground. The doom of the German colonies was sounded with the first gun that spoke on the Belgian border. Their continuance was forbidden by every consideration of strategy and common sense, by the Allies' knowledge of what Germany aimed at, of the purpose which she had destined her colonies to serve. She had never shown the true colonizing spirit. As there is an honourable camaraderie among pioneers in wild countries, so there is a certain freemasonry among those Powers which have experimented in colonization. Their object is to make a garden of the desert, to create a new land which, while owing allegiance to the motherland, shall yet be free to follow its own natural development, and shall be administered for its own advantage. If a tropical country, it owes duties to the soil and the former inhabitants; if a white man's land, it seeks settlement and the advent of a new nation. But a colony which is used as an armed post and a point of vantage in some great strategical game is outside this comity. It is eternally a spy, an alien, a potential disturber of the peace. During its life it will be regarded with just suspicion, and its end will be unlamented.

CHAPTER L.

THE RUSSIAN FRONT IN THE SPRING OF 1916.
January 11–April 18.

The Battles of Lake Narotch—Yudenitch takes Erzerum—Capture of Trebizond.

IVANOV's Christmas attack on Czernovitz—which, though it failed in its immediate purpose, to some extent dislocated Germany's Balkan plans—was followed by three months of normal trench fighting. It was generally believed that the spring would see a great effort by Hindenburg to take Dvinsk and Riga. There were two weeks in April when the western entrance to the Gulf of Riga was free from ice, while the northern inlet was still barred to Russia; and it was anticipated that during that time, when the Russian navy could not protect the Russian flank, an attack would be made to force the coast road. But a spring offensive in that region laboured under special difficulties, owing to the melting of the snow and the brimming marshes and rivers, and there were other observers who believed that Hindenburg, if he struck at all, would choose an area due east of Vilna, where the many lakes were divided by high and dry ridges. The allocation of German troops seemed to support the latter view. In the north Hindenburg commanded all the forces from the sea to the river Pripet; almost the whole of his command was German, and the line was strongest in the centre. Russki's health had led to his resignation of the Army of the North to Plehve, who in turn was replaced in February by Kuropatkin, whose administrative talents and assiduous care for his troops made him a good commander in what was pre-eminently a stage of reorganization and adjustment. A great offensive was in train for the early summer, and Russian Headquarters had chosen the Dvinsk salient as its area.

In the Russian northern and southern groups there was little special activity to record during the late winter and the early spring. Every week there were raids and counter-raids, and efforts on both sides to seize knuckles of firm ground and so improve their positions. In the northern sector, between Riga and Dvinsk, on 22nd March, the Russians carried a portion of the German front, taking a village and a wood east of Augustinhof. In the southern sector there was some desperate fighting round the bridgehead of Usciezko, which Tcherbachev had approached on the first day of January, but had failed to take. The place was a natural stronghold, situated on high ground between the Dniester and a tributary. The precipitous slopes, clothed with undergrowth, had been converted into a maze of trenches and galleries, and had been surrounded with immense wire entanglements. During February the Russians laid siege to this fortress, which from its position dominated a large part of their front. On 20th March there was a heavy action, in which the Austrians were driven across the river, and the bridgehead of Usciezko passed definitely into Russian hands.

The main battle of these months was fought by Evert's right, in the neighbourhood of Lake Narotch, against Hindenburg's right centre, the X. Army of Eichhorn. Evert's command consisted of the First, Second, Tenth, Fourth, and Third Armies; and of these the Second, under General Smirnov, extended from halfway between Vidzy and Postavy, past Smorgon, to a point a little south of the river Vilia. It was the largest of all the Russian armies, numbering no less than eleven corps. We are concerned now with the left wing, between Lakes Narotch and Vishnevsky, which was made up of three corps in line, under the charge of General Baluyev. The Russian offensive, which began on 18th March, inaugurated a series of battles which lasted till the middle of April. They were undertaken with one purpose, and one purpose only—to meet the request of the Western Allies for a diversion in the East, since at Verdun the storm had at last burst upon France. The pass between Lakes Narotch and Vishnevsky was the direct road to Vilna and Kovno. Hindenburg could not risk a breach of his front at a point of such strategic importance, and to parry a blow there he must summon all his strength.

The German front in the East, as we have seen, was not the continuous line of fortifications which was found on the West. In places it was only a trench deep, and in some of the marshy regions there were no trenches at all, the ground being held by patrols from both sides, which were constantly engaged in small duels. But in the vital parts there were fortifications on the Western scale, and this was the case in the corridor between Lakes Narotch and Vishnevsky. The chief feature of the place was a big bog about half-way between the lakes, which in March was wholly impassable except by the rare causeways. North of it stretched a line of low sandy slopes to the edge of Lake Narotch, with, behind them to the west, further pockets of bog. The German first line lay along and behind the crown of the slopes, well placed so as to provide enfilading fire against any attack, and protected by five or six lines of wire entanglements. Three hundred yards behind lay their second line, curving back in the north to rest on a small marsh. Between that marsh and the lake was a dry strip, containing a farm and a church tower with a German machine gun on the top. General Baluyev's plan was to attack with his 5th Corps on the right against the main position on the slopes. A division of his 35th Corps was directed to advance in the centre immediately to the north of the Great Marsh, while on the south of the marsh the two divisions of his 36th Corps were to move up a grassy slope similar to the terrain of the 5th Corps. A very considerable concentration of field and heavy guns was provided before the action, with a fair supply of shells, though there was some lack of high explosives for the heavy guns. Before the first attack on 18th March there was a two days' artillery preparation, to which the Germans made little reply. The supply of ammunition for the field guns was calculated for ten days, and each separate attack was preceded by a bombardment of from twelve to forty hours' duration.

In all, eight attacks were made—on 18th March, on the nights of the 21st, 22nd, 25th, 27th, and 31st, on 7th April, and on 14th April. The ground was chiefly won at night, and the last two daylight attacks accomplished little. By 15th April the 5th Corps had carried the first and second German lines opposite, and the low hills behind them which the enemy had used as an observation post—a distance of over a mile. The enemy resisted chiefly with machine guns, of which he had eight per battalion, as against the Russian two. The 35th Corps in the centre had a more difficult task. It carried the German first line, but found the wire intact before the second, and, in spite of splendid courage, was unable to break through. One regiment of the corps swore to carry the position before it; it failed, but when another regiment succeeded later it found four hundred dead of the first still in the German wire. In all, the 35th Corps advanced about half a mile. South of the Great Marsh the 36th Corps was held fast. It carried part of the German first line, but could not hold it, and at the close of the action it had won nothing but a wooded cemetery on the first slope, which it held as an outpost.

So far the attack had been moderately successful, mainly because there had been sufficient artillery preparation to enable the superb Russian infantry to get to grips with the enemy. Evert had performed the task set him, and had occupied Hindenburg's full attention during the critical April weeks. It had been a costly exploit, for he had lost not less than twelve thousand men; but the troops were in good spirits. They had seen their guns dominate those of the enemy, and this was so novel an experience that their hopes ran high. The depleted divisions were filled up from the depots, and, if the wastage of guns and ammunition could be made good, the position was secure. But, unfortunately, ground won by artillery was destined to be lost by its absence. The Russian Staff regarded the operations as concluded, and resolved to move the reserves of guns elsewhere. The total supply was still quite inadequate for the whole front, and the fashion was followed of concentrating in turn at different points. Accordingly the whole of the heavy artillery reserve was removed with the exception of two batteries, and these were left with a scanty supply of shells. Moreover, the airplanes used for "spotting" were packed for removal, and the captive balloons were taken down. The Germans soon perceived what had happened from their air reconnaissance. All the 26th of April they were bringing their guns and ammunition stores forward, and on the 27th they set to work to find the ranges of the Russian front and reserve trenches and their scanty field batteries. That front on the 27th was held by the two divisions of the 36th Corps south of the Great Marsh. Across the marsh ran a line of outposts, partly from the 36th Corps and partly from the 5th Corps; from the marsh to Lake Narotch lay the 5th Corps. The 3rd Siberian Corps was in reserve to the 36th Corps, and the 35th Corps to the 5th Corps. The storm fell entirely on the line of the 5th Corps. At 4.45 on the morning of 28th April 120 heavy guns opened against it, principally on its left flank. Thence the bombardment spread along the whole front, chiefly high explosives; and since there could be no Russian reply, both field and heavy guns were pushed up close to the front line. Before 11 a.m. all telephone communication was cut between the eight battalions of the four regiments in line and their reserves. The half-dried marshes which patched the front did not allow of proper entrenching; often the only defences were parapets of sandbags, and there were no protected approaches from the rear. Long before noon all the breastworks had been obliterated, and the enemy had his field guns firing at close range in his own first line.

About 11 a.m. the German infantry began to advance in skirmishing order. The breach of the Russian left centre opened an alley-way into the Russian position, and the five German divisions of attack poured through. Practically unopposed, they advanced for a mile and a half, passing their old first-line trenches which the Russians had won a month before, and pushing on beyond the slopes where had lain the original Russian line. At this point the two reserve regiments of the 5th Corps came into action. Marching north, they struck at the flank of the German frontal advance. It was now about three o'clock in the afternoon, and the Germans had covered between two and a half and three miles of ground, during which their artillery fire had been suspended. At the sight of the Russian reserves the German infantry retired and left the battle to their guns. The reserves drove back the enemy as far as his original front-line trenches—at least a third of the ground he had occupied; but as they came under the fire of the heavy batteries they were compelled themselves to retreat, leaving to the Germans most of the ground already advanced over. As the night fell the battle died away. In twelve hours all the results of the Russian advance in March and April had been lost, and something more. The casualties in the Russian regiments in line were severe—from two-thirds to three-quarters in each, with three-quarters of the officers.

The Lake Narotch battle was a mere episode in its strategical aspect—a gallant effort at a diversion which failed, for only one division had been drawn in from the enemy's reserve—but it was one of the most instructive actions in the campaign. It revealed in the sharpest relief the old lesson that before superior fighting quality can have its effect the way must be prepared by an adequate fire. The original Russian artillery concentration was small, judged by Western standards; but even an approach to equality in heavy guns was sufficient for the Russian infantry. To withdraw the batteries was an invitation to the enemy to advance to an easy conquest. What he gained he gained wholly by his guns; and it was the first action on the Eastern front where he used his guns on the plan now adopted in the West. Regiments which were half composed of young recruits needed especially the protection of artillery; yet for six hours the Russians withstood a devastating fire, to which they could make no reply, and only fell back when they were outflanked and reduced to a handful. It was a clear proof of Russian *moral*, and of the inexorable need for an adequate artillery machine.

The spring months saw Russian activity in another area, and this activity was also in the nature of a diversion to assist the Western Allies. Ever since, in the previous autumn, the Grand Duke Nicholas had become Governor-General of the Caucasus he had prepared for an offensive westward into Anatolia. The evacuation of Gallipoli had released a large Turkish army; Britain was in difficulties on the Tigris, and it was known that Germany was planning with the Porte an advance on Egypt; the Salonika position was at its best stagnation, and at its worst a peril. If he could threaten Turkey at a vital point he would relieve Britain's anxieties, and might even win from another direction the prize for which the Dardanelles campaign had been vainly fought—a clear road to Constantinople.

The traveller who would visit Erzerum has a choice of three more or less arduous ways. He may embark on a Black Sea coaster and follow the northern shore of Anatolia, where the great plateau breaks down in forested steeps with scarcely a creek or bay to vary the line, till he reaches the ancient walls of Trebizond, the city to which Xenophon's Ten Thousand struggled through the Armenian hills. Thence a good metalled road runs inland to Erzerum, crossing three passes, one of them 8,000 feet in height. The distance from port to fortress is 200 miles, and a week of fine weather is needed for the journey. Or he may travel a thousand miles by the Bagdad line to Ras-el-Ain, in the Euphrates valley, whence he has 250 miles of hill roads through the Armenian Taurus to cover before he reaches the city. Or he may go by railway to Angora, two days' journey from the Bosphorus. After that he will move eastwards by road through the great wheat-lands of Anatolia, where dwells the flower of the Turkish peasantry and the main strength of the Sultan's armies, past the rich city of Sivas, till the Euphrates valley is reached at Erzhingian, and the real highlands begin. Erzerum lies well among the mountains, a true frontier fortress, guarding the road from Russia to the fruitful vales of the ancient Lycus and Halys, the kernel of Asiatic Turkey.

The place stands on a pocket of flat ground, 6,000 feet above the sea. South and north and north-east rise lofty mountains, through which the roads to Mush and Trebizond make their way over high and difficult passes. South-west is the vale of the western Euphrates; east are ranges of hills forming the watershed between the Euphrates and the Araxes. The city, therefore, lies in a much-encumbered trough which provides an avenue from western Anatolia to Transcaucasia. Before the war it was reckoned the strongest fortress in the Turkish dominions. It had a circle of inner works forming a continuous rampart around the city; and to the east, commanding the roads to Olti, Kars, and Mush, a number of forts lined the horseshoe of hill which formed the watershed. Before the war these defences had been allowed to decline in strength. The old inner rampart was wholly out of date, and the outer forts were for the most part too near the town; they dated back, many of them, to the last war with Russia, when Erzerum was invested, and for some time held as a hostage by the armies of the Tsar. In the early winter of 1914 an attempt was made to set the place in order. A German, Posseld Pasha, was now governor; but he left the old redoubts alone, and after the new fashion organized an outer ring of defence on the eastern horseshoe of hills. It was claimed by the Turks that in the Erzerum *enceinte* there were no less than 1,030 pieces of artillery, including 460 heavy guns from Krupp, and about 200 field and mountain guns.

The strength of Erzerum against an army from the east lay in the horseshoe of hill defending it called Deve Boyun, the "neck of the camel." Its weakness lay in the fact that it was a fort pushed into the borderland beyond the area of good communications, so that it could not speedily be munitioned or reinforced from the base. The nearest available railhead was Angora, 440 miles distant as the crow flies. The way from Angora to Sivas traversed 200 miles of hilly country; thence a rough road 230 miles long ran to Erzhingian, and from Erzhingian a good road covered the seventy-five miles to Erzerum. Assuming that convoys covered on an average twenty miles a day, then two days by rail and twenty-five by road lay between the fortress and the Bosphorus; so that, allowing for inevitable delays, we may take thirty days as the minimum time for supplies to travel from that base. The ordinary line of supply was from Trebizond; and there were other roads from Black Sea ports such as Samsun, which fed the main route from Angora. These lines, however, were out of use, for the simple reason that Turkey had lost to Russia the command of that part of the Black Sea. Up to the end of February the Russian light cruisers and torpedo craft had sunk about 4,000

Turkish schooners and feluccas, many of them new vessels. In one cruise of three days, about the middle of January, more than two hundred ships were destroyed. The effect of these naval operations was to cut off all the Turkish supplies by sea, and reduce the communications of Erzerum to the long and difficult land route, which in midwinter was apt to be deep in snow. The Russian army was in a more favourable position. The line from Tiflis to Sarikamish gave them a railhead only eighty miles from the Turkish fortress. Up to the arrival of the Grand Duke Nicholas as Viceroy, the Army of the Caucasus had been about 100,000 strong; but before the end of the year it received two corps from the bases in South Russia as reinforcements. Its commander was General Nicholas Yudenitch, a man of fifty-three, who had been Chief of Staff to Woronzov-Dashkov, and had been mainly responsible for the victories of Sarikamish and Ardahan.

The Turkish forces on the Erzerum front at the beginning of January did not exceed 150,000 men. They had been increased in the autumn on the news of the coming of the Grand Duke Nicholas; but since then three divisions had been dispatched to Mesopotamia. The III. Army, under Kiamil, had the line from the Black Sea to south of Erzerum; while five divisions and a quantity of mounted irregulars covered Bitlis and Mush and the country round Lake Van, where they had the assistance of Kurdish tribesmen. On the left wing of the Erzerum front, holding the mountain passes around Lake Tortum and the defiles of the Olti Chai, lay the 11th Corps. In the centre, defending the upper Araxes valley and the direct route from Sarikamish, were the 9th Corps and part of the 10th; and on the right flank, covering the road from Hassan Kaleh to Mush and Lake Van, was the remainder of the 10th Corps. The German, Posseld, was no longer commandant of Erzerum, his place being filled by the former Turkish commander, Ahmed Fevzi.

In the beginning of January Kiamil had no suspicion of the impending attack. The Grand Duke had kept his counsel well, and the Russian command of the Black Sea enabled him to bring his reinforcements to the Caucasus without advertisement to the enemy. All winter an offensive had been maturing, and the date originally fixed had been the early spring; but in the beginning of January an event happened which compelled him to expedite his plans. On 9th January the last Allied troops left the Gallipoli peninsula, and thereby released at least five Turkish corps for service elsewhere. Some were destined for the Caucasus front, but it would be six weeks at the earliest before they could reach it. The Grand Duke resolved to strike while reinforcements were still impossible, and to fight a winter campaign, as Woronzov-Dashkov had done the January before. It was a bold decision, for winter in the Armenian Taurus is a season of desperate rigour. The normal temperature is 25 degrees, and it sinks often to as much as 40 degrees, below zero. The roads are choked with snow, and the mountain tracks, which are often the only choice, are swept by blizzards and avalanches. Ridges must be crossed more than 10,000 feet high, and the easiest passes are only two or three thousand feet lower. In that country the people still hibernate in pits in the earth, as they did in the days of Xenophon's Ten Thousand. A winter attack would have the merit of surprise, but it ran the risk of being broken by the sheer inclemency of nature.

Yudenitch advanced, as he was bound to do, on a broad front, for he had to guard against a flanking counter-offensive. Fully seventy miles separated the extreme horns of his army. His plan was a converging attack upon Erzerum by three columns. The right column moved from Olti—where, early in January, a Turkish assault had been repulsed—along the narrow glen of the Olti Chai to turn the flank of the Turkish 11th Corps; the central column was directed along the Kars–Erzerum road, towards Hassan Kaleh; while the left column was entrusted with the advance from Alashkert into the valley of the Sharian River to turn the Turkish right, and cut off the Lake Van troops from the main Erzerum defence. The plan in its essence was that of Enver in January 1915, an advance by widely separated forces utilizing the mountain passes and directed towards a concentration on the skirts of the fortress itself.

The movement began on 11th January. The first duty before Yudenitch was to clear his flanks. His right wing, taking the enemy by surprise, thrust him back upon Lake Tortum. Then, creeping over the passes, it so encircled the Turkish left that it was compelled, in order to avoid envelopment, to fall back towards Erzerum by the upper glens of the western Euphrates. The Russian left column followed a similar strategy. By 13th January it had cleared the upper valley of the Sharian, and waited on the advance of the centre, while farther south Russian detachments were pushing the outlying Turkish divisions west of Lake Van. Meantime the main movement, that of the centre, was progressing well. On 16th January it had reached

Kuprikeui, a village which commanded the bridge over the Araxes. Here for two days there was a stubborn battle. The Turks held the houses and the bridgehead with machine guns, and for a little the advance was checked. But on the evening of the 18th, in a heavy snowstorm, a Russian battalion forced the bridge, and in the early darkness the village was taken, and the three Turkish divisions defending it driven in rout along the Erzerum road.

This battle was the crisis of the advance, and Erzerum was lost in the fight for the Araxes crossing. Yudenitch was now only thirty-three miles from the fortress, and his southern column, penetrating wild mountain ranges by crazy paths, had driven in the wedge he designed, and was rolling back the Turkish right towards Mush. The northern column had forced one division clear away from Erzerum, north of the Dumli Dagh, and had compelled the remainder of the 11th Corps to a precipitate retreat, with the loss of several thousand prisoners. On the 19th Yudenitch was at Hassan Kaleh, where a spur of hill separates the upper and middle sections of the upper Araxes valley. It was believed that this strong position would be held in force; but the Turks had been too badly broken at Kuprikeui, and they fought only a slight rearguard action. Next day the retreat had gone westwards behind the horseshoe of the Deve Boyun, and the Russians were at the gates of Erzerum—that ridge which in the last Russo-Turkish War, after the fall of Kars, had been held for months by Mukhtar Pasha.

Up to 26th January, when the final stage of the attack began, the Russian success had been swift and complete. The whole Turkish front had been driven in for fifty miles, and large quantities of supplies and guns, and at least 4,000 prisoners, had been taken. Two Turkish divisions in the south and one in the north had been isolated from the main army, and the rest had been shepherded into the basin of Erzerum. The speed of the Russian advance, especially in the centre, had left many Turkish detachments cut off on ridges and in mountain glens, who had no alternative but to make their way to the coast or Kurdistan, or to surrender. It was Yudenitch's aim to move so swiftly that the enemy should not have time to rally or to improvise new defensive positions. Meantime, in the Black Sea, the Russian fleet was methodically sweeping up the Turkish transports. On the day of the victory at Kuprikeui it destroyed, in the neighbourhood of Trebizond, 163 sailing ships, 73 of which were laden with provisions. On 22nd January 40 more vessels shared the same fate. On the first news of the

Russian advance, 50,000 troops from the Gallipoli army had left Constantinople for Angora ; but it would be more than a month before they could reach the threatened city.

The case of Erzerum was now hopeless. It was short of stores, and the 100,000 men who had won its shelter could not long maintain it against a victorious enemy converging from north, east, and south. The Turkish army was seriously demoralized. The Cossack cavalry, pressing the pursuit, passed on the road hundreds of broken men, huddled together and sleeping in the snow. Parties sent out to collect prisoners found many frozen to death where they lay. Arms and equipment had been flung aside by the fugitives. It was a motley and disheartened force that gathered behind the shelter of the Deve Boyun for a final stand. Rumour ran in the West that Erzerum had been invested, but such a feat was impossible. The numbers of the Russians and the topography of the place alike forbade it. It was Yudenitch's intention to carry the outer defences by assault, for once they crumbled, the city lay open.

From the 26th of January to the 12th of February there was a pause in the main operations. The Russians had to bring up their heavy guns and ammunition, and organize the supply line for their front, and this work, performed over snow-covered mountain roads, could not be completed in a day. Meantime a steady bombardment of the Deve Boyun ridge by field guns and the smaller howitzers prevented the enemy from improving the defence. On the 10th of February the right column, under Prjevalsky, pouring down the valley of the western Euphrates through deep snow and some 50 degrees of frost, arrived at the fort of Kara Gubek, which was the extreme north-east point of the Erzerum defence. The fort stood on a rib between two bold peaks which the Germans had not fortified, since they believed them to be inaccessible for artillery. But a Siberian division managed to work round the left rear of the place, and get their heavy guns in position on the flanking peaks. On the 12th Kara Gubek fell ; and next day, with a heavy bombardment, Fort Tafta was carried, after its magazine had been exploded by a Russian shell.

The fall of Tafta gave Yudenitch access to the rear of the main defences on Deve Boyun. During the next two days the central column pressed hard along the Kars road, and one after another of the forts on the ridge yielded. Meantime the southern column was forcing its way through the passes of the Palantuken range along the roads from Mush and Lake Van. On the evening of the 15th the position was virtually carried, and nothing was left to Erzerum but its old ramparts and neglected inner redoubts. There could be only one course for the defence—to retreat with the best speed possible. The German Headquarters Staff were the first to leave, and presently the bulk of the garrison was streaming north and west and south along the roads to Trebizond and Erzhingian and Diarbekr. On the morning of Wednesday, the 16th, at eight o'clock, the last works were evacuated, and before midday the Cossacks of the central column rode into the city, where they were joined by the southern and northern columns. Erzerum had fallen.

The affair was one of the most skilfully managed episodes in the war. Yudenitch had adopted a plan which demanded careful timing, under conditions where it was almost impossible to work to a time-table. By his three separate operations on different lines, he laid himself open to dangerous counter-attacks on one or other of the six flanks he offered to the enemy. It was a scheme, too, which made immense demands on the resolution of his men. To drag 8-inch guns over rocky saddles clogged with snowdrifts, as Prjevalsky did before Kara Gubek, was a feat which must rank high among the achievements of mountain warfare, and in the whole campaign was only paralleled by some of the operations on the Italian front. Splendid, too, was the drive of the centre which won the bridge at Kuprikeui; and scarcely less memorable were the doings of the southern column, which moved with amazing speed in a wild tangle of pathless hills. The possession of Erzerum was not in itself of the first importance. Russia had pushed her way to the gates of Anatolia; but she had not yet entered them, for Erzerum, as we have seen, was a border fortress situated well in advance of the rich lands it was designed to guard. Not till Erzhingian was passed, and the plain of Sivas was reached, would a blow be struck at the true heart of Asiatic Turkey. Again, in any such advance the flanks must be pushed forward; Trebizond must be taken, and the Russian left must hold the Armenian Taurus and the roads from the south. Yudenitch was not yet clear of the mountains, and he had many difficult miles before his bold strategy could reap its legitimate fruits. What he had achieved was a crushing blow at the Turkish field forces. He had gravely depleted them, and so lessened their power of mischief elsewhere. But he had still to face the divisions released from Gallipoli, and his next steps must be slow and deliberate.

His problem was far from simple. His forces were not large,

and the main line of the Turkish retreat—down the Kara Su or western Euphrates towards Erzhingian — was through difficult mountain country, with positions everywhere capable of a stout defence. He was compelled to advance on a broad front, and while his centre moved west from Erzerum it was essential that his left wing should advance from Mush and Bitlis towards Diarbekr, while his right wing should sweep the country between Erzerum and the Black Sea. He was aware that Enver would strain every nerve to redeem the Turkish defeat. He knew that troops were being hurried eastwards as fast as the wretched communications would allow, while rumour had it that the Aleppo corps was coming north, and that divisions were being sent from Mesopotamia. It would be a week or two before the first Turkish reinforcements could arrive, and the winter weather put a brake upon his own and the enemy's speed. He therefore devoted himself to perfecting his communications, and to disposing his forces in such a way that they would hold all the routes by which an outflanking movement might be possible. His left wing moved slowly on Diarbekr. His left centre advanced down the western Euphrates. His right centre followed the high road from Erzerum to Trebizond, towards the town of Baiburt. A small connecting column took the hill road between Erzerum and the port of Rizeh, and occupied the town of Ispir, in the glen of the upper Chorok. His right wing was directed against Trebizond.

Trebizond was the most famous of the cities of northern Anatolia. Originally a Greek colony from Sinope, it was the last stage in the march of Xenophon's Ten Thousand. When Julius Cæsar conquered the King of Pontus he made it a Roman colony. From its harbour Arrian started on his famous voyage, and on Arrian's advice Hadrian raised it to a great city. Throughout the Middle Ages it was the trade centre through which the merchandise of Persia, India, and China flowed to the markets of Europe. After the coming of the Turks it remained a forlorn remnant of the Eastern Empire till eight years after the fall of Constantinople, when the last emperor submitted to Mohammed the Conqueror. The importance of the place to Russia did not lie in its usefulness to the enemy. Since she had won the control of the Black Sea, Trebizond had been of little value to the Turks as a base for sea-borne supplies. But it would be of immense value to any Russian advance, not only as the best harbour on that coast, but as the focus from which ran all the chief roads in that part of Asia Minor. Its capture would give to the right flank a much-needed security, and would

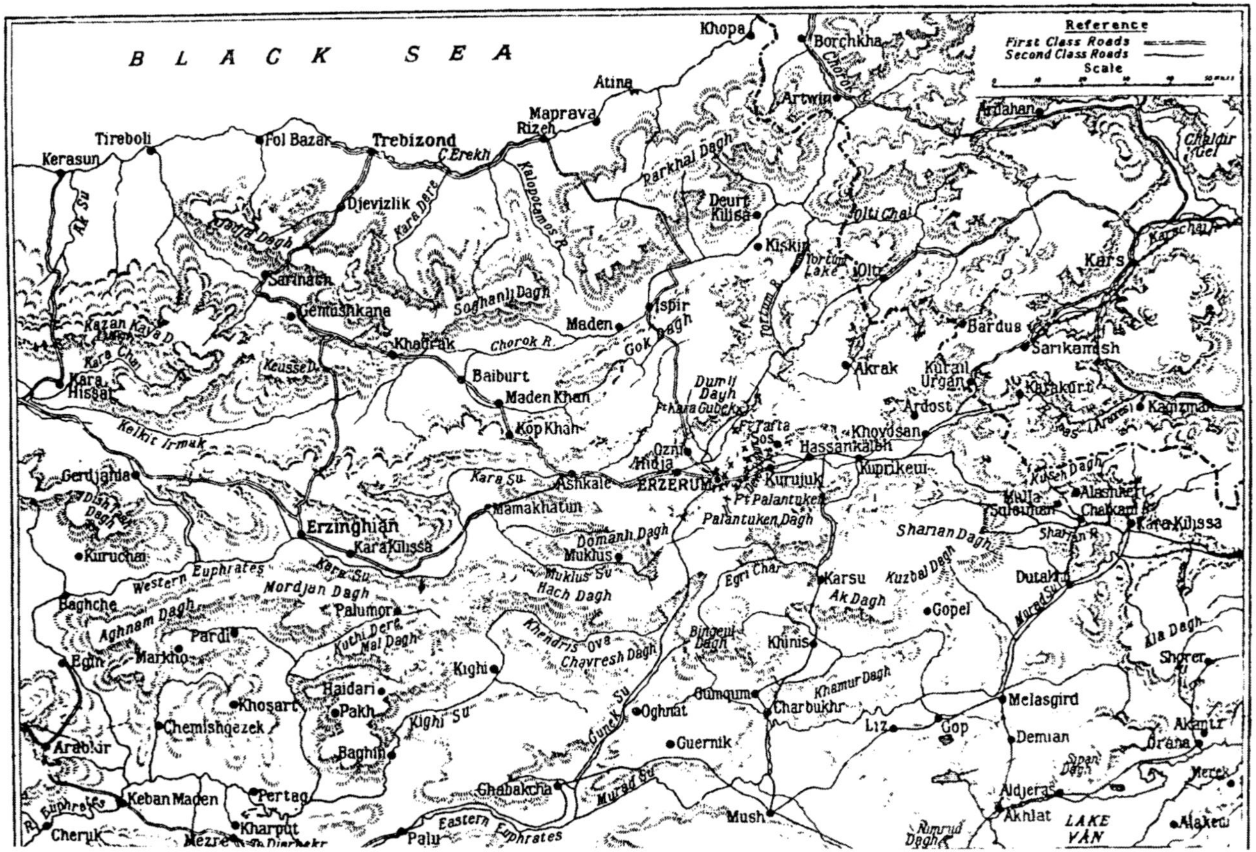
Reference
First Class Roads
Second Class Roads
Scale
BLACK SEA
Khopa
Borchkha
Chorok
Artwin
Ardahan
Atina
Maprava
Rizeh
Tireboli
Fol Bazar
Trebizond
C. Erekli
Kerasun
Ak Su
Djevizlik
Kara Dere
Kalopotamos R.
Parkhal Dagh
Deurt Kilisa
Kiskim
Tortum Lake
Olti
Olti Chai
Kars
Kars Chai
Chaldir Gel
Sarinach
Gemushkana
Soghanli Dagh
Ispir
Maden
Gok Dagh
Bardus
Sarikamish
Kazan Kaya D.
Kara Chai
Kara Hissar
Keussed
Khadrak
Chorok R.
Baiburt
Maden Khan
Kop Khan
Akrak
Kurail Urgan
Karakurt
Ardost
Kaghisman
Khoyosan
Hassankaleh
Kelkit Irmak
Gerdjanda
Dumli Dagh
Ft. Tafta
Sos
Ozni
Ilidja
ERZERUM
Kurujuk
Kuprikeui
Kuseh Dagh
Alashkert
Kara Su
Ashkale
Mamakhatun
Pt. Palantuken
Palantuken Dagh
Mulla Suleiman
Chalkani R.
Kara Kilissa
Dish Tash Dagh
Erzinghian
Kara Kilissa
Kuruchai
Domanli Dagh
Muklus
Muklus Su
Sharian Dagh
Sharian R.
Western Euphrates
Kara Su
Mordjan Dagh
Hach Dagh
Egri Char
Karsu
Kuzbal Dagh
Dutakh
Baghche
Aghnam Dagh
Palumor
Ak Dagh
Gopel
Murad Su
Ala Dagh
Pardi
Kuthi Dere
Mal Dagh
Khendris Ova
Chavresh Dagh
Bingeul Dagh
Khinis
Shorer
Egin
Markho
Kighi
Khamur Dagh
Melasgird
Haidari
Khosart
Pakh
Kighi Su
Gumgum
Charbukhr
Oghnat
Liz
Gop
Demian
Akantr
Chemishgezek
Guernik
Orana
Arabkir
Baghin
Gunek Su
Sipan Dagh
Merek
Keban Maden
Pertag
Ghabakcha
Murad Su
Mush
Aldjeras
Euphrates
Kharput
Eastern Euphrates
Akhlat
LAKE VAN
Alakeu
Cheruk
Mezre
Palu
Rumrud Dagh

afford a new base, thereby shortening the line of communications, and relieving Batum and the Kars railway of the heavy strain which they had hitherto borne. Yudenitch's strategy was to win Trebizond by an advance on all his front, which would pin the enemy to his positions, while the operative force on his right would attempt to reach its goal by means of the sea-coast. His main forces would, therefore, be ready for the enemy reserves when they should arrive, and would distract any part of them from going to the relief of the corps which held Trebizond. In a sense, therefore, the Trebizond campaign was an isolated operation. Almost up to the date of its fall Yudenitch was engaged with the new Turkish divisions on the roads to Erzhingian and Baiburt and Diarbekr. It was the day after Enver's main counter-offensive had decisively failed that the Russians entered the ancient city.

A portion of the attacking force reached the coast by the road from Erzerum to Rizeh, and a certain part from Batum; but in winter these hill roads were so perilous that the larger portion of the army of assault had to be brought by sea. On 4th March, under cover of the fire of warships, Russian troops were landed on the shore at Atina, sixty miles east of Trebizond. They met with little resistance, and next evening had occupied Mapavra, nine miles along the coast to the south-west. On the 8th the enemy was thrown back behind the river Kalopotamos, thirty-five miles from Trebizond. Then came a pause, and in twenty days, owing to the difficulty of the shore road, only five miles were covered. On 6th April the Russians reached the main line of the Trebizond defence, the stream called the Kara Dere, which, issuing from a gorge among precipitous hills, flows through some ten miles of flatter country and enters the sea in a marsh just east of Cape Erekli. The Turks were easily driven from the right bank; but on the left shore, on a ridge 2,000 feet high, they had prepared a strong position which could not be turned by any flank attack to north or south. The frontal assault on the Kara Dere position lasted for nine days. On 15th April the crest was carried, and the enemy fled in precipitate retreat towards the city. Several little streams crossed the intervening ground, and just east of Trebizond was a highish ridge; but the defence was in no condition to tarry. Next day the Russians were only twelve miles from the walls, and on the morning of 18th April, after a further landing had been made west of the city, Trebizond was in their hands. The garrison—what was left of 50,000 men—fled southwards in the direction of Baiburt.

The Trebizond operation was well conceived, and carried out with the same precision as had marked the advance on Erzerum. The steady pressure of Yudenitch's central army virtually isolated the city, and the assaulting force, assisted from the sea, could pursue its course without fear of surprise or sudden enemy reinforcement. The capture of Trebizond gave Russia a flanking point in that front—Trebizond-Erzhingian-Diarbekr—which she must win before she could carry the campaign into the true Turkish stronghold. Till that line was attained she was fighting in the chaos of highland which was, so to speak, the wire entanglement of the main position. Once it was reached the second stage would begin, and she would be striking at the granary of Turkey, the great Anatolian plain, whose loss, more even than that of Constantinople, would mean the downfall of the Osmanli.

The difficulty of transport, which made most campaigns in Turkey self-contained operations, prevented Yudenitch's success from having any immediate effect upon the situation elsewhere in the Near and the Middle East. It failed, in especial, to draw off the enemy from the beleaguered village on the Tigris where now for nineteen weeks a slender British force, broken with sickness and short of every supply, was waiting patiently for the succour that did not come.

CHAPTER LI.

THE FALL OF KUT.

December 3, 1915–April 29, 1916.

The Siege of Kut—The Relieving Force—The Battle of 6th and 7th January—The Battles of 13th and 21st January—The Attempt of 7th to 8th March—The Attempt of 5th April—The Last Efforts—Fall of Kut—The Responsibility of the Government of India.

WE left Townshend on December 3, 1915, when he had found sanctuary in Kut for the remnants of the Bagdad Expedition, with the enemy closing in around him. He had approximately 10,000 men, having lost 4,567 in the Ctesiphon fighting and the subsequent retirement. He had provisions for at least two months, and received assurances from Nixon that within that time he would be relieved. It might have been possible to continue the retreat, but he was rightly averse to a step which would undo the whole results of the Mesopotamian campaign, and his superiors confirmed his decision. From the start he was handicapped, since for political reasons it was considered undesirable to expel the Arab inhabitants and leave them to the tender mercies of the Turks; and these inhabitants numbered 6,000 non-combatants.

The town of Kut lay inside a loop of the Tigris, where the river, some eighty yards wide, runs roughly due east. The loop is shaped like a Moorish arch, and the opening is to the northward. At its widest it is a mile across, and its length is a little under four miles. The houses were mostly in the loop, but across the river stood a liquorice factory with a few hovels round it. From the south-west corner runs the Shatt-el-Hai, the watercourse which, as we have seen, connects the Tigris with the Euphrates at Nasiriyeh. This gave the squalid little town its importance, for connecting with it a caravan route ran north across the Pusht-i-Kuh hills to the Persian border. Its normal population, mostly Arab, was under

4,000, and its narrow, dusty streets and houses with the plaster peeling from the walls made up as dreary a scene as could be found in a habitable land. All around it stretched the flat, sun-baked wastes, broken only by an occasional cluster of palms and a clump or two of prickly bush. In the rains the cracked soil became a sea of mire, with the turbid red flow of the Tigris rolling through it like the freshet of a strong river in a tidal estuary.

By 5th December the siege had begun in earnest. Four Turkish divisions lay around the town, the chief strength being on the north and south-west. On the 7th the enemy summoned the garrison to surrender, and on Townshend's refusal opened a heavy bombardment. Some of the few river craft remaining were set on fire, and we were compelled to give up the bridge to the east of the town, which was destroyed, and to draw in our outposts at that point. The bombardment was heaviest on the 10th and 11th, when the Turkish infantry also attacked; but no result was obtained. We had a few hundred casualties, mainly incurred in our sorties, and Townshend estimated the Turkish losses at not less than 1,000. After that there came a lull. But on the 23rd a new enemy division arrived from Gallipoli, and the Turks made a furious attempt to carry the place by assault. All the morning of the 24th the enemy's fire was concentrated on the northern defences, and in the evening the new division attacked at the north-eastern corner. During the night the enemy pierced the position, but was ejected and fell back to trenches 500 yards in rear of his former first line, with casualties estimated at 700. On the 29th the liquorice factory on the south bank was bombarded, but no infantry attack followed. It was the last of the enemy's attempts to blast his way into the British position. Thenceforth his plan was blockade.

Meantime the relieving force far down the river was beginning to move. Its task was far more complex than would appear from a mere glance at the geographical distances. Compared with the Tigris, the Nile, for all its cataracts, was a respectable river. Interminable windings, endless shifting shoals, and in normal times a depth too shallow for any but the lightest craft, made the problem of water transport almost insoluble. To add to this, the rains were erratic, and when they came the river became a raging flood and the adjacent desert a lagoon. All along the banks, separated by any distance from a hundred yards to several miles, lay wide stretches of marsh, connected by channels with the river. In wet weather, therefore, the whole riverine district was more water-logged than the Yser flats in midwinter. When the snow melted in the Armenian hills the Tigris was well above the level of the surrounding country, and the ill-kept *bunds*, or dykes, were insufficient to restrain it from spreading in lakes over great areas. The consequence was that transport became an incalculable thing, which, whatever the arrangements at the base, must repeatedly break down in an advance. The only real solution was to follow Kitchener's example in the Sudan and build a railway at some distance from the flood region, since the river was wholly untrustworthy. Such a course—far cheaper in the end—was not followed, because the magnitude of the enterprise and the strength of the enemy were from the first gravely underrated. It was an instructive lesson in the folly of conducting a campaign with the left hand.

The difficulties did not end with the transport. There were the trying extremes of the climate to be reckoned with, the treachery of the Arab tribes, and the considerable preponderance in numbers of the Turkish army. Above all, the dead flatness of the land made attack extraordinarily difficult against an enemy who thoroughly understood the art of entrenching. There was no natural cover for the assailant—no villages, hedges, or banks, nothing but a monotonous level of clay or mud. The innumerable marshes gave the Turks excellent flanking defences, and consequently, by constructing comparatively short trenches between the swamps and the river, they could block any advance. The alternative—to fetch a wide circuit through the drier land away from the stream—was impossible, because we had only the Tigris to rely upon for our transport. From start to finish we were compelled to depend upon a precarious and inadequate system of communication.

The Turkish commander drew his lines with the skill of a master. Having completely invested Kut, he set himself to bar the road to any relief. His first line of defence was at Sheikh Saad—about twenty-five miles due east of Kut, but much farther by the river. There he had a position on both sides of the stream; and on his left, since he had no natural obstacle to rest his flank on, he had a line entrenched at right angles to his front, very much as he had done at Ctesiphon. Five miles above Sheikh Saad he had an intermediate line on the left bank along a watercourse called the Wadi, at a place called Orah, where the Tigris makes a sharp bend to the south-east. Above Orah the great Suwaicha marsh flanked the left bank of the river at a distance of a mile or two. Here there was a series of immensely strong positions, all of the same general character, astride the river, and resting on swamps on both wings. From east to west there were the Umm-el-Hanna position, the Falahiyeh position, the very formidable lines at Sanna-i-yat, and last of all, only seven miles from Kut, the Es Sinn position, the strongest of all, which had its right flank drawn back almost at right angles from the Dujailah Redoubt to the Shatt-el-Hai. These defences were not wholly complete at the time when the advance of the relieving force began, but long ere one position could be carried the alternatives in the rear had been prepared.

Sir John Nixon, the commander-in-chief, was compelled by ill-health to resign his post in December, and his place was taken by Lieutenant-General Sir Percy Lake, the Chief of the Indian Staff. At the moment, apart from Townshend's troops, there was nothing available but the remnants of Gorringe's 12th (Indian) Division. A new force, called the Tigris Corps, was constituted under Sir Fenton Aylmer, V.C., the Indian Adjutant-General. It was reinforced by the Lahore Division from the Western front, a considerable part of the Meerut Division, the Indian troops relieved from Gallipoli, and some English Territorial battalions which had been brought from India. The corps was very imperfectly organized and its staff was still in embryo, but, since Townshend's need was urgent, Aylmer considered it his duty to start at once. The transport was still in the same condition as six months before, and what had then been inadequate had now to do duty for a force three times the magnitude of the old The result was that 12,000 of the reinforcements which reached Basra never left the base.

The van, under Major-General Younghusband, moved out from Ali Gharbi on 4th January, and located the enemy at Sheikh Saad, holding him to his trenches on both sides of the river. On the 6th Major-General Kemball's column came in touch on the right bank. The weather was still dry, but the flat, mud-coloured ground, the haze, and the frequent mirages made reconnaissance a difficult task. Kemball entrenched himself over against the enemy lines, and next day advanced to the attack. An infantry brigade got round the enemy's right flank, and accounted for a whole battalion. That day, the 7th, Aylmer's main force came into action on the left bank, and there for two days we fought a costly action. Outflanking was impossible owing to the position of the Turkish left, though our artillery checked an attempt by Turkish cavalry to turn the British right, and the battle was a stubborn infantry frontal attack against a steady and well-directed Turkish fire. On 9th January the enemy, fearing lest our success on the right bank might turn his flank, fell back upon the intermediate position at Orah, where he had the protection of the Wadi watercourse descending from the Pusht-i-Kuh hills.

The rains had now begun. The Tigris rose four feet, and a hurricane blew which made navigation a precarious venture. In biting winds and seas of mud the British troops followed up the enemy to the Wadi watercourse. After a long night march on the 12th, Aylmer attacked on the 13th both in front and flank, having concentrated all his force on the northern bank, while monitors from the river bombarded the enemy's right. The position was carried next day, and the enemy retired. Already the casualties of the relieving force were nearly 6,000. The weather now made reconnaissance hopeless, and any further movement must be very slow. The Turks had only fallen back a mile or two to the Umm-el-Hanna lines, which, as we have seen, were the outermost of the strong positions between the Suwaicha marsh and the river. On 21st January Aylmer attacked them, but failed to carry the ground, and was compelled to entrench himself 1,300 yards from the enemy. Next day there was an armistice for the burial of the dead, and thereafter for more than a month complete stagnation. The general commanding had realized that his force was not sufficient for the task he had set himself, and was waiting on reinforcements. The India Office, by a curious misreading of a telegram, announced that Aylmer was attacking Es Sinn, only seven miles from Kut, when he was only attacking Umm-el-Hanna, twenty-three miles distant, with sixteen miles of fortified ground through which he must force his way before he could join hands with Townshend.

The month of February was one of inaction for Aylmer's army. Early in the month the rains ceased, a cold drying wind blew from the desert, and there was frost at night. It was the right weather to advance, but he did not consider that he had the wherewithal to do it. The control of the expedition had now passed from the Government of India to the Imperial General Staff at home, but the change of direction could not make itself felt for some months. There was some skirmishing with Arab tribes round Nasiriyeh, and on the 23rd of the month Aylmer pushed out a column on the right bank of the river to El Aruk, which enabled him to enfilade the Turkish position at Umm-el-Hanna. Once again inaction reigned.

till on the evening of 7th March he embarked on the boldest venture of his campaign.

This was no less than to turn the main Turkish position at Es Sinn by striking straight across the desert, avoiding the river and the riverine swamps, against its right flank at the Dujailah Redoubt. It was a perfectly sound strategical plan, but it had to face heavy odds. One difficulty was the night march across the desert to effect a surprise. Wolseley, before Tel-el-Kebir, had to move only 13,000 British regulars 3½ miles across easy ground in 3½ hours; Aylmer had to move 20,000 heterogeneous troops from 12 to 16 miles in less than 9 hours. Another lay in the fact that there was no water except in the river, and unless we routed the enemy speedily and completely we should be hard put to it to support our advanced columns. Our only chance lay in an immediate success.

The place of assembly on the evening of 7th March was at the spot known as the Pools of Siloam, on the right bank of the river. The force advanced in three columns over a flat, featureless desert, between the two great belts of swamp, in a direction a point south of west. The night was black as pitch, and guiding was difficult, for no one had been over the ground before. " The silence was so profound that one heard nothing save the howl of a jackal, the cry of flighting geese, and the ungreased wheel of an ammunition limber, or the click of a picketing peg against a stirrup. . . . Sometimes one felt one was moving in a circle. One could swear to lights on the horizon, gesticulating figures on a bank."* That night move was well carried out on the whole, though Kemball's column on the left, which had farthest to go, was 2½ hours behind time. Before the first light came we had reached the Dujailah depression, and saw the fires of the Turkish camp. To the west, eight miles away, our men saw also a sight which they were not destined to see again—the flash of Townshend's guns at Kut. The strategy deserved to succeed, but it failed. We were just too late in starting the attack, and the Turk had his defence ready. Repeatedly during the day we flung ourselves on his breastworks, causing him many casualties, and losing heavily ourselves. But we could not continue the assault on these terms, for we were far from water and supplies; so Aylmer was obliged to fall back to his old position east of Umm-el-Hanna. The beleaguered garrison in Kut had heard with joy the sound of our guns, and waited eagerly to see the familiar khaki on the flats east of the Shatt-el-

* Mr Edmund Candler.

Hai. But the guns died down, and the rescuers did not come. Once more they were shut off from sight or sound of their kin.

Another month of inaction followed. Aylmer was superseded in the command by Gorringe, a soldier with a long record of good service, who had led the expedition to Nasiriyeh in the previous summer. He had now with him the 13th Division, which, it will be remembered, had done gloriously at Gallipoli in the assault on Chunuk Bair in the preceding August. It was decided to deliver a frontal attack upon the Umm-el-Hanna lines, and to this division the task was entrusted. Meantime we had been hard at work underground. Since there was no cover to screen an advance, it was necessary to push our firing-line close to the enemy's, and no less than sixteen miles of sap-work had been completed, which brought us within 100 yards of the Turkish front. The attack was delivered early on the morning of 5th April. At 5 a.m. the 13th Division, under the command of Sir Stanley Maude, rushed from the sap-heads, and in one hour had carried the first three lines of the Umm-el-Hanna position. By 7 a.m. they were through the fourth and fifth lines. It was a clear day, and our airplanes warned us that the Falahiyeh lines 6,000 yards farther west, and the Sanna-i-yat line, the same distance beyond them, were being strongly reinforced. The ground in front of us was very open, so Gorringe deferred the next step till the evening. At 8 p.m. the second advance was made, and the Falahiyeh position fell. It was by far the most successful day in the chronicle of the relief expedition, and the fighting quality which stormed those labyrinths of trenches nine feet deep can scarcely be overpraised. Meanwhile, on the right bank of the river the British left—the Lahore Division under General Keary, which had to its credit a long year of struggle on the Flanders front—had captured all the positions on the enemy's right opposite Falahiyeh. In the afternoon the Turks counter-attacked resolutely, for the loss was vital to them ; but we beat them off, and consolidated the ground won.

Before us now there lay only the lines of Sanna-i-yat and Es Sinn, and it seemed reasonable to hope that the tactics which had carried the first two positions would carry the third and the fourth. For a moment there was hope of Townshend's relief. But once again Nature allied herself with the enemy. The snow was melting in the Armenian hills, and the great flood season of April and May was beginning. The Tigris rose at a bound and spread itself over the landscape. The Suwaicha marsh became a deep lake which ran into our trenches. and the bottle-neck between the river and the swamp was narrowed to a causeway. The Turks suffered as well as ourselves from this invasion of the floods, but the handicap was far greater for the attack than for the defence. Our men camped in mud-holes, and advanced often waist-deep in water. Hailstorms, thunderstorms, and waterspouts added to the misery, and for days we had to bethink ourselves of avoiding drowning instead of forcing back the enemy.

In a blink of fine weather on the 9th Gorringe attacked the main Sanna-i-yat position on the left bank, but failed to make progress. On the afternoon of the 12th he brought the 13th Division to the right bank, and sent it into action across the flooded belt, more than half a mile wide, between the Tigris and the Umm-el-Brahm marsh. The attack did not break through, but it forced the enemy's right wing back a distance varying from one and a half to three miles. We continued to struggle on the south side of the river, and on 17th April, at seven o'clock in the morning, we carried the strong position of Beit Eissa, a fort which was within four miles of Es Sinn, and slightly in rear of the Sanna-i-yat lines on the left bank. That same night the Turks launched on us one of the greatest of their counter-attacks. After a heavy bombardment large masses of troops brought from Es Sinn attacked at Beit Eissa between 7 p m. and 4.30 the next morning, but failed to shake us. In this action the Turkish losses were 400 prisoners, and it was estimated that 3,000 died. German officers led the attack, and some of them were among the slain. One whole Turkish division was in action, and portions of two others—in all some 10,000 men.

There remained the north bank, where was the main Sanna-i-yat line. On 22nd April we attacked and carried the first and second trenches, but Turkish reinforcements drove us out of them. The space between the river and the swamp was so narrow that only one brigade could move in line, and there was no possibility of outflanking. Gorringe had made a gallant effort, but the weather and the countryside had defeated him. He had lost 33 per cent. of his army, and all hope of relief was gone.

The garrison of Kut, it should be remembered, had fought a most arduous campaign during the preceding summer, and they had just finished the march to Ctesiphon, the battle, and the feverish retreat. Already for weeks they had been living on poor rations and enduring the extremest fatigue of which the human body is capable. All December they had been bombarded, and had repulsed repeated attacks. There were many wounded and much sickness. But the spirit of the little force never flagged,

and they set themselves to make the best of the wretched Arab town and their intolerable conditions. On the ground by the liquorice factory they played a kind of cricket and hockey, as long as their strength permitted them, and they tried to supplement their stores by fishing in the river. The gentle art of Izaak Walton was never pursued under stranger circumstances.

From the first day of 1916 onward Townshend's main task was to fight famine. The enemy shelled the place nearly every night with heavy guns, and there were destructive bombing raids by Turkish airplanes; but starvation was the grimmest foe. At first there was plenty of horse meat. On 24th January a large store of grain was discovered; but it could not be ground till millstones were dropped by our aircraft. Townshend, whose high spirits and inexhaustible vitality made him an ideal commander of a beleaguered fortress, set about planting vegetable seeds to provide some relief from the scurvy that was threatening. On 5th February each British soldier was receiving a twelve-ounce loaf of mixed barley and atta, a few dates and groceries, and one pound of horse meat; and each Indian a pound of flour and a small allowance of turmeric, chillies, and ginger. By this time the place had run out of rice and sugar, and there was only milk for ten days in the hospital. In the first week of March the flour ration was reduced; and after Aylmer's failure at Dujailah there was a further reduction all round. On 8th April the mill had to stop working for want of fuel, and hunger began in earnest. After 20th April many of the Arabs, with starvation in front of them, tried to escape down the river by swimming. There had all along been a desperate scarcity of tobacco, though cigarettes used to be dropped by airplanes, and towards the end men were smoking as substitutes lime leaves, ginger, and baked tea-dregs. Even in January English tobacco was selling at eight shillings an ounce. Soon all the horses and mules had gone. One of the last to be slaughtered was an Indian mule which had been in three frontier campaigns, and which the butcher had twice refused to kill.

On 14th February the King had sent a message of thanks and encouragement to Townshend, who had replied cheerfully by wireless. The garrison, almost to the end, believed that they would be relieved. The floods did not affect them greatly, for Kut stands on slightly higher ground than the rest of the plain; they were even an advantage, since they compelled the Turks to withdraw their lines a considerable distance. But about the middle of April, when all the troops were weak with famine, even the stoutest heart had to recognize that the limits of endurance had been reached. The last effort of Gorringe was to try to break the blockade with a river steamer, the *Julnar*, on 24th April. It was a hopeless task, since the boat had to run the gauntlet of the enemy guns on a winding river against a strong flood, and she went ashore four miles east of the town.

The end came on 29th April. At 11.40 a.m. Townshend sent out a wireless message: " Have destroyed my guns, and most of my munitions are being destroyed ; an officer has gone to Khalil, who is at Madug, to say we are ready to surrender. I must have some food here, and cannot hold on any more. Khalil has been told to-day, and a deputation of officers has gone on a launch to bring food from *Julnar*, ship sent night April 24th to carry supplies to garrison Kut." A little later he wired : " Have hoisted the white flag over Kut fort and town, and the guards will be taken over by a Turkish regiment, which is approaching. I shall shortly destroy wireless. The troops go at 2 p.m. to camp near Shumvass." It was a very weary and broken force which laid down their arms : the remnant of the historic 6th (Indian) Division, which had begun with a year of unbroken conquests. Before surrender the troops occupying the first lines had been too weak to march back with their kits, having held their position for a fortnight. In all, the garrison at the date of Kut's fall consisted of 2,070 British troops of all ranks, and some 6,000 Indians.

The Turks behaved at first with apparent chivalry. Khalil, their commander, treated Townshend with extreme respect, in view of his gallant resistance. The sick and wounded were sent downstream to Gorringe, and food and tobacco were at once distributed. Townshend and his staff were taken to Constantinople, and the rest to internment in Anatolian camps. The decency shown at the surrender was soon forgotten, and the rank and file and the junior officers were condemned to unparalleled sufferings and barbarities. Of the British prisoners more than one-half perished ; of the Indian at least a third.*

Kut had resisted for 147 days—a fine record when we consider the condition of Townshend's force at the beginning of the siege. It shared with Przemysl the distinction of being the only place in the war which was taken by blockade ; but, unlike Przemysl, its surrender brought no stigma to the garrison. They resisted to the utmost limits of human endurance, and officers and men shared the same hardships. Its fall was a misfortune, but not a disaster.

* See *Report on Treatment of British Prisoners of War in Turkey*, Cd. 9208.

RESPONSIBILITY OF INDIAN GOVERNMENT.

The temporary loss of 8,000 troops was not a crushing blow to an armed force which now numbered millions Moreover, the campaign in Mesopotamia, unfortunate as was its immediate issue for Britain, had achieved a real strategic purpose, even in its melancholy later stages. But for the reinforcements sent by the Turks to the Tigris, and their preoccupation with the capture of Kut, it is probable that the Russians in the Caucasus would not have moved so swiftly, and that Erzerum and Trebizond would not have fallen. It should be said, in common justice to the relieving force, that it showed singular gallantry and devotion. All that man could do it did to cut its way through to Townshend. The fault lay in the earlier decision which had created a problem that could not be solved in the scanty time permitted.

But as the news filtered through from Mesopotamia, it became clear to the ordinary man that a mistake in strategy had not been the sole blunder. The transport service from the first had been utterly inadequate; and though the campaign in Mesopotamia had begun as early as November 1914, the conditions of that appalling country had never been seriously faced. Until February 1916 no special hospital boat had been provided to take down the wounded from the fighting line, though admirably equipped hospital ships ran between Basra and Bombay. In the same way there was no proper transport from the field to the river. Badly wounded men had to endure agonies in springless carts. There was also a shortage of coolie labour, and far too little attention to sanitation. The British soldier, white or coloured, is an uncomplaining being; he was desperately uncomfortable, but he could joke about it; but even from his lips a cry was wrung. " If you put 500 badly wounded," wrote one officer, " on a paddle steamer in pouring rain, all lying on the hard deck with an awning which does not keep out the rain; give them one doctor, no attendants, no food, scanty blankets, no sanitary arrangements; leave them there for twelve hours or more, then send them on a twelve hours' journey or more—it must be trying, to say the least of it. But this is a true picture, and people should know of it." It would be hard from the whole war—on the British side, at any rate—to parallel the misery of the severely wounded, lying packed together for hours in pools of water on decks sodden with dirt and animal refuse. The story was the same in every detail of the service. Everywhere there had been lack of foresight, a narrow preoccupation with India's supposed domestic requirements, a genius for confusion, and as a consequence, unimaginable suffering for the men. The evidence published by the Mesopotamia Commission is one of the grimmest and least creditable chapters in British imperial history. The main responsibility, as we have seen, for the initial strategic mistake lay with the British Government; but for the graver faults which condemned thousands of human beings to avoidable torture, we must look to the Government of India. The immediate blame must rest with the Indian Medical and Transport services, but the whole Indian administration, from Lord Hardinge downward, was implicated in the tragic blunder.

The news of the fall of Kut, the capture of Erzerum and Trebizond, the conquest of the Cameroons, and the engagements on the Egyptian frontier, fell in Europe on ears which since the third week of February had been dulled to all other sounds but the noise of battle on the Meuse. It is time to turn to the fight at Verdun, where Germany made the third of her great bids for victory in the West.

CHAPTER LII.

THE BATTLE OF VERDUN: FIRST STAGE.
February 21–April 10, 1916.

The Reasons for Falkenhayn's Plan—Nature of Verdun Area—The French Position—The Attack of 21st February—The Crisis at Douaumont—Pétain's Scheme of Defence—The German Attack west of the Meuse—The Struggle for Vaux—The Flank Attack at Avocourt—The Position on 10th April—Pétain—The Achievement of the French Soldier.

I.

IN January 1916 the Allies seemed in a favourable position for the campaign of the new year. They had considerably increased their strength in men and material. France had trained her 1916 and 1917 classes, but had not yet used them at the front; Britain had by the Derby scheme and the Military Service Act provided, along with troops in home camps, a potential force nearly twice the size of that which she had in the field; Italy had large numbers at her depots, and had not yet called up the greater part of her possible reserves; Russia was only waiting for small-arms to bring forward reinforcements as great as her field army, and her recruiting ground was still enormous. In Britain the manufacture of munitions, as we have seen, was very different from the lean days a year before; and in France, where trade union restrictions were wholly set aside, the daily output exceeded even her past records. Great offensives had accordingly been planned for 1916 both in East and West: by Russia in the Dvinsk salient, and by France and Britain on both sides of the river Somme.

Faced with such a prospect it was impossible for the Teutonic League to sit still. Germany, in the weeks before Christmas 1915, had to face a problem scarcely less difficult than that which had confronted her after her initial failure at the Marne. She had made an immense effort during the winter to provide stocks of munitions. The poor type of German shell which was noticed on our front about this time was a bad omen; the same thing had happened in the preceding year before Mackensen's supreme effort on the Donajetz. She had to consider her people, now growing impatient of victories which brought no decision and the hope of peace deferred. She had the prestige of her dynasty to think of, and the whole military and bureaucratic system built round it. She had in her mind two wavering neutrals, who must be constantly presented with new proofs of her might. Above all, she was faced with her dwindling man power, and an economic stress which could not be indefinitely endured. It was becoming clear that the first great movement of 1916 must be undertaken on her initiative. She was confronted by two alternatives. She might stand as before on the defensive in the West, and look to the East for a decision; or she might attack in the West, and then turn in triumph to take order with Russia.

At Christmas Falkenhayn had presented to the Emperor a memorandum in which he enumerated cogently and lucidly the factors in the case. No immediate danger was to be looked for from Russia or Italy, and both might be expected to grow weaker, if left alone, from internal maladies. The worst peril was Britain; but German armies could not reach her shores, and the only true weapon against her was the submarine. An attack on her Flanders front would, even if successful, bring no real decision, and the early spring was an ill time for Flemish campaigning. But if Britain was the most deadly foe, France was the one nearest exhaustion, and the French army was Britain's chief weapon. It might be possible to strike at France in a part so vital that she would bleed to death, and so "England's best sword would be knocked from her hand." A break through in the ordinary sense was not contemplated. He sought to inflict on France the utmost injury with the least expense to Germany, and for this a section at once acutely sensitive and highly embarrassing for the defence was required. Germany must be free to accelerate or draw out her offensive, to intensify it or break it off from time to time as suited her purpose. Two such areas suggested themselves—Belfort and Verdun, and the argument leaned towards the latter.

Even if the major purpose failed, one certain result could be looked for. The German armies would take a famous city. Verdun was more noted than Ypres or Arras; it was still intact, and these were shells; it was called a fortress, a title no longer given to Rheims; it had been desperately battled for already, so that its conquest would give the greater glory; it was less than eight miles from the German lines; it was in the area of the Imperial Crown Prince's command, so that its fall would raise the waning prestige of the dynasty. It would be possible to present to the German people and to the neutral nations the glorious news that the most famous fortress of eastern France, the key of the eastern gate, had fallen to the valour of German arms.

This was mainly a political consideration, for the taking of Verdun could not be rated as a military success of the first order. But there was another reason, which of the three was the most important, because, unlike the first, it dealt not with the possible but the probable, and, unlike the second, it was based on purely military considerations. A strong offensive in the West might induce the Allies to make a premature counter-attack. Germany feared lest, as soon as Russia was ready, France, Britain, Russia, and Italy should make a concerted offensive, exactly timed, so that the old device of rushing reinforcements across Europe would be forbidden her. To prevent this, she must take her enemies one at a time. If Verdun were threatened, the Allies would be induced to throw in their main reserves to defend it, to expend a large part of their stores of shells, and to make an advance elsewhere on the Western front to ease the pressure. The great offensive of 1916 would then go off at half-cock, and would have the support of neither Italy nor Russia. Germany counted on this result, counted on it securely, as was proved by her dispositions. During the battle which we are about to consider she had some ninety divisions lying quiescent at other parts of the front, and there was no subsidiary movement to aid the great stroke at Verdun. That was not the German theory of war, it was in flat defiance of the teaching of Clausewitz and Moltke, and it was at variance with her previous practice in the campaign. There could be only one explanation. The ninety divisions were destined to meet and take heavy toll of the expected Allied counter-attack.

The first step was a gigantic concentration of artillery, brought from the interior factories and the Eastern front, and consisting mainly of the more mobile howitzers—between six and twelve inches—though a certain number of the large siege pieces were also present. Some of the best corps in the West, such as the 3rd of Brandenburg, were taken out of the line and rested, to prepare them for the great effort. The Crown Prince was holding his section at Christmas with two corps. During January he received the equivalent of three new corps, including one of Mackensen's divisions from Serbia. By the middle of February at least thirteen new divisions had appeared mysteriously in the West, and seemed to be located in and around the Champagne, Argonne, and Lorraine fronts. It was an extravagant concentration on a section which did not exceed twenty miles. The Crown Prince was in immediate command, and he had as his adviser the old Marshal von Haeseler, at one time the tutor—and the trenchant critic—of the Emperor in military affairs. Strantz's detachment in the Woëvre, Falkenhausen's Lorraine contingent, and Gaede's group in Alsace were attached to him. The major strategy was Falkenhayn's, and it was based upon two principles. The first was that no first-class artillery effort had yet been made against the Western entrenchments, and that, with an adequate concentration, the guns might be used to win the battle. The great movement was divided into stages. Each stage should be conquered by the artillery, and then occupied by the infantry with —it was hoped—insignificant losses. Again, for each infantry advance against a new position fresh troops were to be used—an endless wheel of reserves, so that every stage should have the support of an unexhausted human impetus. There was to be no vain hurling of men against unbroken positions. The infantry should only advance to occupy the ground conquered by the guns.

As a preliminary the enemy must be puzzled and distracted, so from the first week of January the Allied front was " felt " in all its length from Nieuport to the Alps. In an ordinary campaign each of these attempts would have been reckoned a substantial battle, but now they ranked as no more than episodes, and must be briefly chronicled. The French line was attacked in Champagne at the Butte de Tahure, at Massiges, near Navarin Farm, and east of the Tahure–Somme–Py road. There were attempts to cross the Yser in the neighbourhood of Steenstraate and Het Sas, and heavy fighting near the Hohenzollern and Hulluch, and on the Vimy heights. South of the Somme, between Frise and Dompierre, there were violent bombardments and a considerable German success. There was an attack on the Aisne front north of Soissons, some fighting in the St. Dié district, and activity in upper Alsace. The Allied High Command was uncertain how to regard these adventures, whether as feints or as an honest " feeling " of their front to find a weak point. It was noticeable that all the places attacked were salients which might form a reasonably good starting-point for an enemy offensive. As it turned out, these diversions were not " feelers " but feints, for the terrain of the main attack had long been decided upon. Under their cover Germany continued to accumulate troops and *matériel* in the Verdun hinterland.

It was vital for the enemy to prevent aerial scouting over his lines. In January the Fokker appeared—a German copy of the French Morane machine—which, from its high speed and quickness in rising, made an admirable weapon of defence. It scored many successes against British and French airmen, and it was observed that the German machines had become bolder, and were frequently inside our front. As before the Allied attack of September 1915, attempts were made to bomb from the air the line of communications and all nodal points of transport. The fact that these energies seemed to be concentrated on the district between Châlons and Verdun was sufficient in itself to give a clue to the German plans. Zeppelins were also busy in that sector, and on 21st February, the first day of the battle, one of them was destroyed by an anti-aircraft gun near Revigny, on the Vitry–Bar-le-Duc railway. An incendiary shell kindled a fire in the stern of the airship; this was extinguished, and she slewed round, when a second shell raked her from stern to bow. In a moment the great machine was a crooked wisp of flame, and there fell to the ground a tangle of *débris* and some charred human remains.

The French Headquarters Staff were not unaware of what was impending, but there was some division in their councils. General Herr, who commanded the fortified region of Verdun, had done his best, and had prepared three defence lines and in some sections a fourth, but he had not the men to hold them. Colonel Driant, who commanded a Chasseur battalion and sat in the Chamber as deputy for Nancy, protested that the place was in peril, and in December Galliéni asked Joffre for a reassurance and received a sharp answer. But in January the Commander-in-Chief sent Castelnau down to report, and from 1st February the defence work was accelerated, and two Territorial divisions added as reinforcements. The equivalent of four corps was assembled in the rear, plans were made for supplying a force of a quarter of a million men on the right bank of the Meuse should the necessity arise, and, since railway communication would at once be cut by an attack, the great road from Bar-le-Duc was prepared as a main artery of transport. The lure of Verdun was sufficiently obvious, and every day brought news of training camps, rehearsals, and the arrival of new units behind the enemy front, while deserters, awed by the impending carnage, crept over the French lines with tales of unexampled preparation. But the French Staff was not clear on the matter; its Intelligence section differed from its Operations section, which thought Champagne and Artois as likely areas of attack; and General Herr was left with no more than nine infantry divisions and six regiments of heavy artillery to hold both banks of the Meuse. French Headquarters had decided that the attack on Verdun might be only a feint to prepare for a blow elsewhere, and that it was necessary, above all things, to keep their reserves mobile. Besides, the concentration of which they had evidence might be used equally for an assault in eastern Champagne, in the Argonne, and north of Nancy. In the third week of February all along the Allied front there was a restless anticipation. A blow was imminent, its general character could be diagnosed, but its exact incidence was still unproved.

Verdun since the days of the Romans had been a famous city. A prince-bishop had his seat there in the Middle Ages, when the place was under the German Empire. The Constable de Montmorency in the time of Henry II. conquered it for France, and under Louis XIV. Vauban fortified it with his system of bastions, revelines, and ditches. In 1792 it surrendered readily to the Duke of Brunswick, and was consequently the indirect cause of the September massacres in Paris. But in the war of 1870 it made a stout resistance. Waldersbach in vain tried to batter his way in; but the place held out for ten weeks, and fell only when the investment was complete and supplies failed. After the loss of Alsace-Lorraine it became, along with Belfort, Toul, and Epinal, one of the eastern bulwarks of France, and was a vital point in the defensive plans of Seré de Rivières. In 1875 the entrenched camp of Verdun formed the left wing of the fortifications of the Heights of the Meuse. It barred the crossing of that river on the main line of advance from Metz to the passes of the Argonne and the upper Marne valley. It was the meeting-place of the great road from Paris eastwards, and the highway which followed the Meuse. It was the junction of five railway lines It was only a day's march from the German frontier and the fortress of Metz.

Verdun, therefore, was naturally made the strongest of the four entrenched camps. It was fortified with an inner line of redoubts—Belleville, St. Michel, Belrupt, La Chaume, and de Regret. Beyond this an outer line of forts and batteries was pushed out in a circuit of some thirty miles. These were, on the east, Chatillon, Manezel, Moulainville, Eix, Mardi Gras, Laufée, Vaux, and Hardaumont, with Tavannes in their rear guarding the Metz–Verdun railway; on the north, Douaumont, Thiaumont, Belle-Épine, Marre, Bourrus, and Bruyères; on the south, Rozellier, St Symphorien, and Haudainville; on the west, Germonville, Bois de Sartelles, Bois du Chapitre, Landrecourt, and Dugny, with Choisel, Chana, and Sartelles in support. In all there were thirty-six redoubts of various sizes, and at its greatest the diameter of the camp was nine miles. It was the last word in the old science of fortification, and it had not been neglected like Lille and Rheims and Laon. Before the war all the forts had been brought up to date: concrete and steel had replaced the former masonry and earthworks, and heavy guns after Brialmont's fashion had been mounted in sinking turrets. The first month of the campaign, which saw the famous "*dégringolade de forteresses*," put Verdun in dire jeopardy. Hastily it was attempted to construct entrenchments far in advance of the forts, and the work had scarcely begun when the Imperial Crown Prince was at its gates. The city was held by Sarrail with his field army, and was all but invested when the German failure at the Marne compelled the general retreat of the invader. During the battle of the Aisne the Crown Prince attacked from Montfaucon, and held the Argonne as far south as the Vienne–Varennes road. Strantz won a bridgehead at St. Mihiel, but failed to link himself up with the Crown Prince's left. After that there was for long no serious attempt on Verdun. In the spring of 1915 the French won Les Eparges, which gave them an advanced position in the Woevre, but they could not cut off the St. Mihiel salient. The Crown Prince hammered for sixteen months in the Argonne, striving for his old objective—an advance sufficiently far south to join hands with Strantz at St. Mihiel. But in spite of some small successes, the German front at Verdun remained a horse-shoe and not a ring.

The city lay on both sides of the river in a pocket of plain. West and north on the left bank rose at some distance low hills, of which the nearest and most conspicuous was the ridge of Charny, bearing the outer works of de Rivières' system. On the right bank the Heights of the Meuse rose steeply from the stream to some five hundred feet above the water-level of the valley. These heights from west to east were five to six miles broad, and broke sharply down to the clayey flats of the Woevre. They were not a range of hills but a plateau, showing in places a gentle rise to inconsiderable crests. The summit was largely cultivated, and diversified with great woods of beech, oak, and chestnut. The ravines which descended to the Meuse and the Woevre were deeply cut and filled with scrub. Little villages and farms were scattered over it, and several roads followed the natural hollows of the tableland. One, which was conspicuous in the coming battle, ran from Vacherauville, on the Meuse, by Beaumont, to Ville and Chaumont in the Woëvre; another followed the crest of the heights from Bras by Louvemont to Herbebois and Ornes. The Metz railway tunnelled the range to Eix; a little line crossed by the gorge of Vaux, and skirted the east side of the hills to Damvillers and the vale of the Loison; the main line to Sedan and the north followed the western side of the Meuse trench. The inner circle of forts kept the first crest of the rise; the outer circle was farther over on the tableland, corresponding to what was its line of greatest elevation.

A man standing in February on the summit of the Côte de Froide-Terre saw to the north a rolling level almost flat to the eye, and broken up here and there with the grey-brown of winter woods. Behind him Verdun, with its old citadel and walls, smoked far down in the hollow. West and north-west lay the river valley, with low ridges running to the dark hump of the Argonne. East the blue plain of the Woëvre, blurred with forests, and showing the glint of meres and streams, ran into the haze which was Germany. Such a spectator would not have seen the French lines. On 20th February they lay nine miles north of the city, and eight miles to the east, right out in the Woëvre flats. They represented the limits of success won by Sarrail's far-flung defensive. From just south of Boureuilles, on the east side of the Argonne, the first position curved north-eastwards in a broad salient. It held Forges and the glen which fell to the Meuse, but not the Wood of Forges on the north side. Crossing the Meuse, it ran just south of Consenvoye, covered Brabant and Haumont and the Wood of Caures, skirted the north side of the Wood of Ville, and passed along the eastern heights to Herbebois and Ornes. It then struck out into the Woëvre, covered Fromezey, came within a mile of Etain, followed the Orne valley, fell back to cover Fresnes, and then by the ridge of Les Eparges regained the highlands, across which it bent to the river at St. Mihiel. The second position was defined by the points Samogneux, Hill 344, Mormont Farm, Beaumont village, the Woods of Fosses, La Chaume and Les Caurières, Bézonvaux and Dieppe. The third position was roughly the outer line of de Rivières' forts—Bras village, Douaumont, Hardaumont, Vaux, Laufée, and the village of Eix. Between the second and the third position intermediate lines had been prepared on the Côte de Talou, commanding the angle of the Meuse, on the Côte du

Poivre, and on the southern slopes between Louvemont and Douaumont, around the farm of Haudromont.

It was a strong position, and in the early winter of 1914 Sarrail had laboured to make it impregnable. A network of wire had been stretched at all points of danger, gun positions were carefully chosen and cunningly concealed, sheltered roads were constructed, the old forts were dismantled and their guns used to arm the outer lines. A fort was now no more than a few yards of ground in a defensive position; the true fortification was the labyrinth of trenches. But no forethought could altogether get rid of the difficulties of the position. It was a pronounced salient, and therefore was at once a threat to the German front and a temptation to their attack. The Germans, holding the Wood of Forges on the west and the two humps called the Twins of Ornes on the east, had good flanking observation posts and a shelter for dangerous gun positions Moreover, it was a bridgehead. Verdun was, like Ypres, the neck of a bottle. All supplies and reinforcements for the lines on the heights must cross the bridges of Verdun and go through its gates. Again, the railway communications of Verdun might be menaced. The main Meuse valley line was cut at St. Mihiel, the Paris line by St. Menehould was exposed to the enemy's long-range guns, and there remained only the little branch line from Bar-le-Duc. It was, indeed, a position which invited a grand attack, since the French would be caught in a wedge of upland, with at their back a bombarded city and shattered railways, and a river swollen to a width of a thousand yards by the winter rains.

A desultory bombardment began on Wednesday, 16th February. It was nothing unusual, but it was noticed that the German guns were busy on a long front—from Montfaucon on their right to Fromezey on their left, a curving front of some twenty-one miles. Verdun, too, was bombarded by heavy pieces, and the Governor of the city cleared it of its last civilian inhabitants. The French guns replied, trying to search out the enemy's batteries, which seemed to be massed in the Wood of Forges, the big Wood of Consenvoye, and in the Forest of Spincourt in the Woëvre. French airmen reported that in the little Wood of Gremilly, north of the Twins of Ornes, the batteries were massed as close as apples in a basket. The omens portended some mighty effort, but as yet there had been none of that dense " preparation " which had preceded the Allied attacks. The French waited for that, as a sure and final proof that Verdun was the enemy's objective.

It came at a quarter past seven on the morning of Monday, the

21st. For twelve and a half hours guns of every calibre poured 100,000 shells per hour on a front of six miles. History had never seen so furious a fire. It blotted out the French first lines, it shattered the communication trenches, it tore the woods into splinters, and altered the very shape of the hills. At a quarter to five in the evening the German infantry moved forward to what they had been told would be an easy and uncostly triumph. They looked to be in Verdun in four days.

II.

The vale of the Meuse is a nursery of winter fogs. From the Woëvre clay and the deep trench of the river they rise to cloak every fold of the intervening plateau. On this February day the air was thick and damp, and a raw wind blew from the east. The short season of premature springtide, which the early weeks of the month saw, had given place to the cold brume of November. It was perfect weather for the German attack. Their guns, massed far behind in the open wheel to wheel, were firing by the map, and had the exact range of the French line. The French guns could not find them to speak back, for the limit of visibility was low. We are to picture a sudden overwhelming blast of fire, precisely directed and fed from accumulations delivered by no less than fourteen new strategic lines, suddenly unloosed upon a front prepared for no more than the average field bombardment. Its success must be immediate and overwhelming. The French first line disappeared, and the German infantry, when at dusk they advanced, promenaded into possession.

A front on which there has been much fighting bears a strange appearance on the map. It is curiously distorted, and its shape represents not the decision of the High Command, but the accidents of battalion successes and failures. The Brabant–Herbebois front was cut up into angles and loops, salients and re-entrants, as had been the Champagne front before the September battle. Behind the fire trenches 100 yards off were the support trenches, which had a more regular outline. Behind them again, and still part of the first position, was a third line, which was intended to be the true reserve line in case of an attack. The wise French habit had always been to hold their firing trenches and first support lines lightly, to fall back from them under a bombardment, and let the enemy occupy them, and then to deal with him faithfully by means of the 75's and an infantry counter-attack from the reserve position. Under the blast of that terrible Monday the thin screen of Territorials, Chasseurs, and Colonials from the 51st and 72nd Divisions who held the front fell back, not without loss, to the reserve lines. But now appeared the consequences of neglect. These lines were poor, they gave bad cover for assembling troops, and the ways up to and out of them were ill devised. Moreover, in this kind of battle the immediate odds were with the assault. It had the range determined; its guns were concealed; it was moving against a fixed object from a fixed base. The success of the first movement was assured. The German artillery was brilliantly handled; by the testimony of the French gunners, its work had not been surpassed in the campaign. The barrage of fire held off for the moment any aid from the French rear. The German infantry, when the guns lengthened range, advanced in scouting parties to reconnoitre the effects of the bombardment. Then came a screen of bomb-throwers and pioneers to prepare the new position, and then the troops to occupy it. It all went by clockwork in the first stage. The firing trenches and most of the first support lines were carried in the centre, in the Wood of Haumont, and the Wood of Caures. The flanks of the French centre, Brabant and Herbebois, were still intact, and since the old line had been a blunt salient, the immediate effect of the German onslaught was only to straighten it. The order was for the troops in front to resist till the last moment, while preparations were made for falling back to new ground, for by now the weight of the enemy's effort was correctly understood.

Before dawn next day, Tuesday, the 22nd, a fresh bombardment began. On the left, in the woods around Brabant, there was an attack with liquid fire, and on all the front there was a torrent of shrapnel, high explosives, and lachrymatory shells. Once again the wings held, though the north-east corner of the Herbebois position fell into German hands. The French counter-attacked in the Wood of Haumont, but without avail, and the day resolved itself into a desperate struggle for the southern halves of the Haumont and Caures Woods on both sides of the Vacherauville-Longuyon road. Every point in rear of the French was drenched in shells, and the hamlet of Haumont was soon destroyed. Nevertheless its defenders clung on amid the debris, and it was not till six o'clock in the evening that the first Germans fought their way into its ruins. Farther east, in the Wood of Caures, wave after wave of the enemy's infantry was slowly pressing the defence southwards towards the shallow depression where lay Beaumont village. Here Colonel Driant's Chasseurs made their final stand. The order for retreat had been given from headquarters, and the commander insisted on being the last to go. In the darkness he fell, with many of his famous battalion around him. He was such a deputy as might have been looked for from that city which for so long spoke with the enemies of France in the gates.

That night a further retreat was resolved upon, and this time it must be on a greater scale. We must regard the French centre at this period as pivoting on Ornes. There the hills fell steeply to the plain, and the maze of gullies around the glen of the Orne stream provided shelter from the German guns in the Forest of Spincourt. With this as its eastern pivot, the line had slowly bent south, keeping also a fixed point in the west at Brabant. But now the loss of Haumont had made Brabant a perilous salient, and during the darkness of that night of the 22nd it was evacuated. When morning came the French had fallen back to an almost straight front, running from Samogneux on the Meuse, and cutting the Longuyon road just north of Beaumont village. Thence it bent a little north, taking in part of the coppice of Wavrilles and the south end of Herbebois. Roughly the position covered two broad lumps of plateau, separated by the valley at Beaumont, up which ran the Longuyon road, and defended at the extremities by the steepness of the ground. It was a stage in the retirement of which the preparation had been begun on the first day of the attack, but it was only a stage, and no continuing city. The French aim was with each phase of the German assault to fall back a little, but to take heavy toll in each phase; then, when their final position had been reached, to stand at all costs, after the edge had been taken off the enemy's ardour.

Wednesday, the 23rd, saw an intense bombardment of the new lines, but necessarily without the deadly precision of the first day. At Samogneux a counter-attack was tried, but the artillery fire broke it up. All the positions in the front suffered, especially the farm of Anglemont, and on the right, from 6 a.m. onward, there was fierce fighting around Wavrilles and Herbebois. In these hours the French were to all intents fighting in the open—"*la guerre en rase campagne.*" Their guns served them wonderfully in breaking the advance of the enemy's infantry; but masses poured on where masses fell, and by the evening, while the wings held fast, all the centre was in a state of flux. The Germans were close upon Beaumont village, and on the northern skirts of Fosses and

La Chaume. As the darkness closed in the French line was Samogneux–Hill 344–Beaumont–Ornes, and it was a very bad line. Meantime the posts far out in the Woèvre were being menaced by an increased artillery bombardment. That night must see a drastic retirement if the defence was not to crumble prematurely.

Accordingly it was decided that the pivot of Ornes must be relinquished. During the darkness Samogneux was evacuated, save for a small rearguard. The line in the Woevre was drawn in close to the skirts of the hills, an average of four miles. The flanking points of the centre were now the village of Champneuville, in the crook of the Meuse, and a ravine in the Wood of Caurières north-west of Bézonvaux. On the morning of Thursday, the 24th, all the Longuyon road around Beaumont was the theatre of desperate fighting. The French counter-attacked towards Wavrilles; but in the afternoon the enemy had penetrated to the east of the Fosses Wood, and Beaumont was isolated. By that evening the Fosses and La Chaume Woods were gone; Ornes was given up, and its garrison managed to reach Bézonvaux; and on the west, after heavy losses, the Germans carried the crest of Hill 344, between Samogneux and Louvemont. More deadly still, the enemy's centre just at the darkening attacked between Louvemont and the point marked 347 on the Vacherauville–Ornes road. This was getting very near the final French position, and that position the French had not yet occupied.

That night of Thursday, the 24th, represents one of the great efforts of the first stage of the battle. The same troops, which had been in action without a rest for four days against five times their strength in men and ten times their strength in guns, made a supreme rally, which permitted the High Command to carry out successfully the culminating stage of the retreat. Positions had been prepared upon the Côte de Talou and the Côte du Poivre. The first, situated within the bend of the river, was of small use to either side. It was destined to become no-man's-land, being swept at will by the opposing guns. Champneuville was given up, and only a small detachment left on the Hill of Talou. The new position ran from the Meuse at Vacherauville along the Côte du Poivre, just south of the village of Louvemont and the farm of Les Chambrettes, and then south by the woods of La Vauche and Hardaumont to the edge of the hills at the gorge of Vaux. It represented roughly the highest ground on the plateau. It represented also the last French defensive position covering Verdun. Not, indeed, all of it, for the ground held on the morning of Friday, the 25th, was for the most part a little in advance of the actual keys. These were the Côte du Poivre and the Douaumont plateau. If from direct or flank attack either should be lost the defences of Verdun must crumble.

Early on Friday morning the snow began—a heavy, dead fall, with little wind, but accompanied by a grinding frost. With the first light the German batteries opened, and on all parts of the front the assault started. The French were in a slightly better case, for this was a prepared position skilfully chosen, and they had more cover from the incessant shell-fire. Moreover, they had their strength increased by two divisions, the first arrivals from the reserve. It was now the fifth day of the battle, and the Germans were behind their time-table. According to schedule they should that day have been in Verdun. They knew as well as the French that this was the last position, and they flung themselves on it with the certainty of speedy conquest. Always fresh troops moved forward for every effort; the French were still, for the most part, the same remnant that had taken the first shock—a remnant now most pitifully reduced. For another twenty-four hours they must hold the fort.

The area of the great central attack was now limited to a space of some four and a half miles—from the Côte du Poivre to the spur of Hardaumont, above the gorge of Vaux. For a clear understanding of the battle it is necessary to grasp the details of this strip of plateau. On the west the slopes of Poivre were steep above the river. In the hollow between it and Talou ran the road from Vacherauville to Beaumont, while another track climbed from the Meuse and followed the crest to Louvemont. South another road ran from Bras to Louvemont, and sent off a branch to Douaumont and Bézonvaux. Poivre was itself a spur of the big Louvemont plateau, and due east of it, across a slight dip, was another spur, on which stood Haudromont Farm. East, again, was the long stretch of what we may call the subordinate plateau of Douaumont. To the north-east it sent out spurs, separated by deep ravines, to the glen of Bézonvaux. These spurs were muffled in trees, and the most westerly was called the Wood of La Vauche, and the most easterly the Wood of Hardaumont. Just south of the plateau was the gorge of Vaux, through which ran the Verdun–Damvillers line. The whole plateau was as fantastic as a jigsaw puzzle, but Douaumont itself was a clear feature. The village of one street lay at the cross-roads—a little place which held in peace some three hundred inhabitants. About six hundred yards south-east of it was the Fort of Douaumont, one of de Rivières' main positions, but dismantled these five months. Two hundred and fifty yards east, again, stood a redoubt, which was a position in the French field line. Douaumont had a good field of fire to north and northeast, where the ground sloped gently to the edge of the tableland. It was nearly six hundred feet above the level of the Meuse, the highest point in all the neighbourhood, and from it the eye had an unimpeded view of the towers of Verdun, less than five miles distant.

The German attack on that Friday was directed against the two ends of the position—Poivre and Douaumont. The French withdrew their last men from Talou, and held their lines a little on the south side of the Poivre crest The big retreat of the night before meant that the enemy had to bring his guns forward and get new ranges, and consequently his bombardment took some time to reach its height. The attack on Poivre was doomed to failure. The ground on west and south-west was too steep, and, moreover, it was commanded by the French artillery on the Charny ridge across the river. The advance from the north across the west end of the Louvemont plateau was broken up time and again by the French gunners. Nevertheless the attempt was made all through that snowy Friday, with the result that Louvemont village was occupied about 3 p.m.; but its violence was less than the simultaneous assault on Douaumont in the east. There the enemy pushed along the ridge between the woods of Fosses and Caurières, up the woods on the spur of La Vauche, and up the tributary gullies from Bézonvaux glen.

The attack reached a pitch of unprecedented violence, since it was the culmination of the German effort, the last blow before which the fortress must crumble. The order had been issued that at all costs Douaumont must be taken, since Douaumont was the key of Verdun. The Emperor with his staff was somewhere on the Twins of Ornes, watching through his glasses the scarp of the plateau where the German shells were bursting. Victory was taken for granted; it was already bruited in Berlin, and the capital only waited the word of confirmation to fly its flags and make holiday. The infantry poured up the wooded spur of La Vauche and the side ravines, using the cover of the splintered trees, won the edge of the plateau, and then struggled to advance across the deadly glacis, 300 yards broad, to the French position on the crest. Again and yet again the French guns caught them in the open and stopped them. But there could be no going back under the

Emperor's eye. It was noted that the first ranks seemed to be dazed and insensitive, moving forward, singing, with glassy eyes, as if under the influence of the drug which the Old Man of the Mountain gave to the Assassins—mere cannon-fodder, to screen the picked troops behind them. Wave after wave rolled on, broke, and ebbed, and then one mightier than the rest covered the glacis and reached the French trenches. Two companies of the 24th Regiment of Brandenburg penetrated without opposition to the old fort, and captured the garrison of sixty or seventy, who mistook them for their own men. To the west the French still held the village, and to the east the redoubt, but at the fort itself the Brandenburgers had broken their position. The achievement, gallant as it was, had no military value, but it was enough for the watching Emperor. The tidings were flashed to Berlin, and promptly came the proud announcement that Douaumont, the key of the last defence line of Verdun, was in German hands.*

About seven that morning Castelnau had arrived. He saw Langle, the group commander, and he decided that the right bank of the Meuse should be held, that Pétain should be put in charge of the section, and that the Second Army, now being built up from reserves in the back area, should be moved to Verdun. That day Pétain met Joffre at Chantilly, who gave him his orders, ending cheerfully as usual with "Eh bien! mon ami, maintenant vous êtes tranquille." Next day, the 26th, he reached Verdun by motor car, a general in advance of his army. He did not arrive an hour too soon. In four days four miles of ground had been lost, and with them gun positions which made the task of the defence almost impossible. He had to reorganize communications which were already terribly threatened, and reconstruct and perfect entrenchments which had been neglected. He had to bring up supports over difficult ground to meet the greater man-power of the enemy, and to organize the French artillery to counteract the hammer-blows of the colossal German concentration of guns. All this he had to do against a stronger enemy who believed that victory was already won. In the night it had been bitter frost, and the wounded left out were corpses in the morning. Looking from the parapets in the faint light, both sides saw dark figures apparently crawling in the white no-man's-land between the lines.

* The story is brilliantly told by C. von Brandis, one of the company commanders, in his *Die Sturmer von Douaumont*, 1919. He and his men were left for four weeks in the fort without light, and when they emerged their faces were like corpses.

Marshal Henri-Philippe Pétain

At first they suspected a night attack, but soon they saw it was an army of the dead.

With the morning came a change, and on the Douaumont plateau was launched the first counter-attack. The famous 20th Corps of Nancy—the men who, with Castelnau, had held the Grand Couronné at the crisis of the Marne battle—swept from behind the crest and checked the invaders. The two divisions, under General Balfourier, pushed the Brandenburgers to the rim of the plateau, all except the handful who held out in the ruins of the fort.

Balfourier's action represented the end of the first and most critical phase of the great fight. The French had been assailed on an awkward and somewhat neglected position, and their High Command was not prepared for the contingency. Accordingly the two weak divisions had to fall back yard by yard, exacting a heavy price for all they gave. The German aim was by one torrential assault to sweep the defence off the heights before it could be reorganized and supplemented. Had the French yielded, as they might well have done, to that terrific momentum, Verdun would have fallen in less than the four days of the German schedule. But they retired only at the last extremity, and compelled the enemy to split his endeavour into small stages, each of which required a fresh infantry attack and a new artillery preparation. After the first day the chances of the offence grew less certain. The German guns were now firing from positions where they had not registered; the unequalled French gunners could reply, and the momentum did not gain but declined. Henceforth the battle was to be fought by the French with fresh troops and an ampler munitionment, and under the eye of a brilliant and tireless general. But let all honour be paid to that forlorn hope which took the first shock of the onslaught and held the gap long enough to check the tide.

III.

On the afternoon of Saturday, 26th February, the German assault had failed on the two wings at the Côte du Poivre and at Douaumont. The great advance which began on the Monday before was stayed, but as yet the enemy did not know it. All he perceived was a check to the movement on his flanks, and he attempted to counterbalance this with a blow by his centre, where the farm of Haudromont marked the westernmost spur of the subsidiary Douaumont plateau. At the same time with his left he attacked the most easterly spur, where the Wood of Hardaumont looked over the Woëvre. The tactics were not unlike those of Wagram, if we take the central attack as corresponding to Macdonald's advance with the 5th Corps on Süssenbraun, and the attack on the spur of Hardaumont as paralleled by Davoust's assault on Markgrafneusiedl. The struggle raged far into the night, but everywhere the French lines held. Meantime, on the extreme French right, the drawing in of the Woëvre posts was successfully completed

That night the snow fell heavily, and all Sunday, the 27th, and Monday, the 28th, the combat continued. On the west the attack on the Poivre ridge came to a standstill, largely because of the French guns on the left bank of the Meuse, which dominated every movement on the western slopes. The French held the south side of the ridge and the Germans the end towards Louvemont, but neither side could advance, since the German guns around Beaumont and the French guns on the Charny height between them compelled a stalemate. The isolated hill of Talou had long been untenable by either side. A violent artillery attack was made on the Douaumont position, and the two divisions of the Brandenburg corps attacked successively, but without avail. An attack on the Wood of Hardaumont likewise failed, and the battle lines lengthened southwards, where the German left strove to turn the French right in the Woëvre. On the Sunday the enemy, advancing along the Metz railway, came in contact with the French holding the station of Eix, about a mile and a half from the village of that name. South of the station is a hillock marked on the map 255 metres, about seventy feet above the level of the plain. The French held this height against all attacks during the Sunday and Monday. On the latter day the Germans pushed against the village of Manheulles, six miles south of Eix, where the road from Metz joined that which followed the skirts of the hills, and against Fresnes, a mile to the south-east. About half Manheulles village fell into their hands, but with this success they had to content themselves. Their aim was clear. If they could advance on to the heights by way of the Fresnes–Verdun road they would have won a position in rear of the main defence.

Now at the close of February fell one of those lulls which are a notable feature of modern battles. The German assault on the Verdun salient had followed a different method from their many salient battles on the Eastern front. There they had endeavoured to strike in from the flanks and cut at the roots; at Verdun they drove straight on the apex, as they had done during the early stages of the First Battle of Ypres. The reason is not far to seek. The Verdun salient was shallow, no more than a bulge in the front, and it provided no tempting re-entrant angles, save at St. Mihiel, where the precariousness of the German communications made a great forward movement difficult. But it made up for this disadvantage by being split in two by a broad and swollen river. All that part on the eastern bank of the Meuse formed, so to speak, a salient within a salient. If the French could be driven back in confusion there would be a desperate muddle on the few roads and a desperate congestion at the neck of the bottle, the bridges of Verdun. It therefore seemed wise to them to hammer in this segment by frontal attacks as being the shorter and simpler road to their goal—the possession of Verdun and the cutting off of large numbers of French troops and guns. That frontal attack all but succeeded. But by the end of February it had clearly failed, so far as any hope of instant success went. The carefully planned stages of the battle had somehow miscarried. They had been too slow to have the proper cumulative effect. Between each the French had rallied, and each new step had to be taken against a prepared and wholly undemoralized opponent. Why, with their weight of men and guns, and in view of the slender numbers of the defence, the Germans did not succeed better is something of a mystery. Partly it may have been that in that winter weather and difficult upland country there was undue delay in the succession of the stages, in moving forward artillery, in bringing up shell supplies, and in refitting troops. Partly it may have been, as the French maintained, that the infantry attacks, in spite of their complete disregard of human life, were not delivered with the fire and resolution which bears down all opposition. The German troops had been told that the guns would do the work for them; but when the guns stopped short of destroying a position they were puzzled and dispirited. They died heroically, but they did not exact the full price of their sacrifice. Again, it is clear that the untouched French gun positions on the left bank of the river unduly narrowed the German front in attack, and prevented the wings from giving the proper support to the centre. A frontal attack is well enough, but it must have its flanks safe.

Accordingly, at the end of February, the German High Command revised its plan. Slowness to revise had never been a fault of

German strategy, even when it meant an arduous readjustment of details. The heavy howitzers had been fixed in their emplacements in the Woods of Spincourt and Hingry, and could scarcely be moved, but many mobile batteries were taken across the river to the woods of Septsarges, just east of Montfaucon. The main German route of supply for the whole front was the railway from Metz to Conflans and Spincourt, whence a new line had been constructed westwards to Dun in the Meuse valley, on the Verdun-Sedan line. A branch had been recently made from Dun to Montfaucon. So far as communications went—and without them the great guns could not be munitioned—the Germans were well equipped for fighting on both banks of the river. The new plan, which Ludendorff had always advocated, was to strike at the French positions on the west side of the salient, drive them in, and menace Verdun from the north-west. Such a stroke would get rid of the handicap to the central advance from the French artillery on the left bank of the Meuse, and would, moreover, if pushed even a short mile, threaten the main rail and road communication of Verdun itself. At the same time, as the battle developed, the right side of the salient at Vaux should be attacked. The German plan was now a return to a favourite battle-order of Napoleon's—blows on each flank, followed at the proper moment by a thrust at the centre. For it is clear that, as the consequence of this flanking operation, the German Staff still looked to a victory on the Poivre–Douaumont front, in the unlikely case of the French troops on the heights not having voluntarily retired as the clouds darkened.

It may be asked why the Germans did not contemplate a turning movement from the Woëvre against the French right. As we have seen, they attacked at various points on the edge of the heights; but from a casual survey of the map it might appear that a movement, say along the Verdun–Fresnes road, would have given them better and speedier results than an advance up the western bank of the Meuse. The latter would drive in a wedge on Verdun's flank, but the former would take the whole position in rear. The reason must be found in the configuration of the Woëvre itself. It has a stiff clay soil, which in an open winter makes it a mass of swamps and brimming ponds, so that, as in Poland, the only routes for heavy transport were the causewayed roads and railways. Besides the Damvillers and Metz railways, there were from Vaux southwards to Fresnes four roads which ran up to the edge of the hills—the Vaux–Dieppe road, the main Verdun–Longuyon highway through Etain, a little road from Chatillon to Moranville, and the great Paris–Metz road which passed through Manheulles. Along each of these highways the Germans attacked with their columns, but the soft soil on both sides did not permit of easy deployment. Worse still, the whole plain was under observation from the heights, and all the roads and cross-roads were commanded at long range by the south-eastern forts of the Verdun *enceinte*. Hence the German attack, being delivered in winter conditions, was perforce confined to the northern, north-western, and north-eastern sections, where their communications were ample and well-screened, and they had underfoot the dry soil of the hills.

The new plan involved an adjustment of the command. The Imperial Crown Prince remained in charge of the operations, but the attacking force was divided into two groups, that on the right bank of the Meuse being under Mudra, and that on the left under Gallwitz, who had been summoned from the XI. Army in Macedonia.* Meantime Pétain had not been idle. His Second Army had been taken out of Langle's group, and was under the direct control of Joffre, who came frequently to Verdun and gave minute personal attention to every detail. The robust cheerfulness of the Commander-in-Chief was an admirable complement to the meticulous industry and resourcefulness of the army commander. Pétain divided the area into sections, and his forces into groups; he perfected the arrangements for motor transport; he quadrupled the field guns and doubled the heavy pieces; he constructed four successive positions of defence: above all, he diffused throughout the army a spirit of reasoned confidence and sober resolution.

On Thursday, 2nd March, it was noted by the French command that the German guns had become active against their front between the Argonne and the Meuse at Forges. The French lines there, unchanged for many months, ran from the river up the narrow marshy valley of the Forges brook, covering Forges village. The Germans had the Wood of Forges just north of the debouchment of the stream; but farther west the French had the ridge on the north bank, covered Bethincourt, and turned north-westwards in a salient to within two miles of Montfaucon, the isolated hill which had once been the Crown Prince's headquarters. They covered Malancourt and Haucourt, turned south through the Wood of Malancourt, passed between the Wood of Cheppy and the Forest of Hesse, covering Avocourt, and then by way of Vauquois reached the Aire at Boureuilles, and joined the Argonne front toward the

* In April Mudra was succeeded by Lochow, and in July, when the Battle of the Somme began, von François took the place of Gallwitz.

Fille Morte and Haute Chevauchée. It is important to note the configuration of the ground just inside the French lines. The brook of Forges splits at Bethincourt into two branches, one coming from Malancourt in the west, and the other running due north in a well-marked valley from the village of Esnes and the Wood of Bourrus. This latter branch needs some attention. On its right bank, between it and the Meuse, is a long ridge of hills which is known as the Goose's Crest. At its western end this ridge has various summits, of which the chief one is Mort Homme, 295 metres high, and to the north, just above Bethincourt, the lesser height marked 265. From these points the ridge runs eastwards, with a mass of woodland, the Wood of Cumières—called in its northern part the Crows' Wood—clothing its southern flank, and just peeping over the crest. It sinks steeply to the Meuse at Regnéville, opposite Samogneux, and on the south of it, at the bend of the river, lies the considerable village of Cumières. On the other side of the southern branch of the Forges brook is a slightly higher ridge, rising at one part to 304 metres, separating it from the woods between Avocourt and Malancourt.

In any attack upon the French position west of the Meuse this ridge, called the Goose's Crest, must play a deciding part. If it fell, then there could be no halting for the French short of the ridge of Charny, nearly four miles distant, on which the outer line of de Rivières' forts protected Verdun. Such a retreat would not necessarily lead to the fall of the city—for that the Charny height must be forced—but it would have one immediately beneficial result for the German attack. It would strip from the west bank of the river all those artillery defences which had prevented any outflanking of the centre by way of the Côte du Poivre. It would then be possible to swing south from the Louvemont plateau and take the Douaumont position on its left flank. But to obtain this result it was necessary to carry the Goose's Crest in its entirety; and especially the hill of Mort Homme, which was its highest point. For this operation there were only two possible ways, since the flank above the Meuse was too steep for any large movement of troops and guns. There might be a frontal attack from the line of the Forges brook, between Forges and Malancourt; or there might be a flanking movement on the west from the Avocourt Woods against the summit 304, which, as we have seen, confronted the Mort Homme across the southern branch of the Forges stream. Either, if pushed to a finish, would give the Germans Mort Homme, and without Mort Homme no success could be final. It was the key of the western bank, as the Douaumont crest was the key of the eastern heights.

The bombardment which began on 2nd March from the batteries in the woods of Forges and Septsarges was directed at the French firing trenches along the Forges glen, at Forges itself, at Malancourt, at the reserve lines on the Goose's Crest and Mort Homme, and especially at the Crows' Wood and the Wood of Cumières, which concealed the French guns. Moreover, all the hinterland was "watered," and the Clermont–Verdun railway, for long in danger, became impracticable. The French transport was now almost wholly by road and motor, and an endless chain of convoys passed and repassed between Verdun and the railhead by that "Sacred Way," which became the most famous of the roads of the campaign. It was a task which involved a terrific strain for the men. "Each outing," wrote a French transport driver, "represents for us from fifteen to twenty-five hours at the wheel—when it is not thirty—and for our lorries 150 to 200 kilometres. This night and day. On arriving here, we did the journey twice almost without stopping—that is to say, forty-eight hours without sleep, and almost without food. It was so hard that it was decided that there should be only one chauffeur per lorry, and that we should take it in turns. Can you imagine what it means to drive one of these lorries, weighing five tons, and carrying an equal weight of shells, either during a descent of 12 or 14 in the 100, and with a lorry just in front and one just behind, or driving during a frosty night, or without lights for short intervals when nearing the front ? Can you see the driver alone on his lorry, whose eyes are shutting when a shock wakes him up suddenly, who is obliged to sing, to sit very upright, to swear at himself, so as not to sleep, or throw his lorry into a ravine, or get it stuck in the mud, or knock the one in front to pieces ? And then the hundreds and hundreds of cars coming in the contrary direction, whose lights blind him!"

For four days the bombardment continued. It was a clue to the enemy's purpose ; but in order to prevent the reinforcement by the French of the Malancourt–Forges line, a vigorous attack was made on the Douaumont position. The main advance was against the village itself, and from the Wood of Hardaumont towards the hamlet of Vaux. The Germans got into Douaumont village, now only a heap of ruins ; but the French held the higher slopes to the south, for the village was well short of the crest of the plateau. During the remainder of the week there was a series of small actions between Haudromont and Hardaumont. These were, from the German point of view, containing battles, while the main stroke was preparing elsewhere. The bombardment was now general on the whole front, from Fresnes to the Argonne. German aircraft attempted to bomb the villages west of Verdun, where the French reserves were accumulating, and the city itself was heavily attacked by the long-range howitzers and naval guns. Pétain had correctly divined the enemy's plan, and had made all preparations to meet the threat on the west bank. At dawn on Monday, 6th March, the guns fell silent, and two German divisions descended upon the Forges glen.

The French first position was clearly untenable in an attack. Its right flank was in the air, for across the Meuse from Forges the Germans held all the bank for three miles up to the debatable land of the Côte de Talou, and so could assail the French wing with converging fire. Accordingly the French fell back, fighting obstinately, to their prepared position behind the Goose's Crest. Forges fell by midday, and the Germans, pushing along the railway, took Regnéville by the evening, and had advanced some way up the slopes of the ridge. Before the darkness had quite fallen they had won the eastern crest, and had penetrated the Crows' Wood, all that portion of it which overflows on the north side of the ridge. On Tuesday morning the French still held Bethincourt, but had been forced back from the Forges glen across the Goose's Crest at the Crows' Wood, and held the southern slopes of that ridge through the Wood of Cumières to a point on the Meuse between Cumières and Regnéville. It was a repetition of what had happened on 21st February between Brabant and Herbebois. The covering troops were withdrawn with little loss from the first lines to the position where they proposed to make their stand.

Next day, Tuesday, the 7th, came the first attack against the new French line. It was supported by two subsidiary movements on the east—an attack on Fresnes, which took the place and several hundred prisoners, and a successful assault on the redoubt in Hardaumont Wood, which gave the enemy a position against Vaux. But the main fighting was at the Goose's Crest. There the French counter-attacked, and won back most of the Crows' Wood, but had to face a fierce German pressure east and west of Bethincourt. Next day, the 8th, the struggle for the Crows' Wood continued, and the French recovered all of it except the eastern end, while they continued to hold their ground at Bethincourt. That night the German effort swung to the other flank, according to their fashion, and centred on Vaux.

Looking up from the Woëvre flats, the traveller could note a small glen, like one of the folds in our own South Downs, with steep sides crowned with clumps of wood. A railway and road ran up the hollow, and half-way there was a straggling village of one street with a church at the eastern end. To the north rose the Wood of Hardaumont, and peeping over its summit a little to the left he caught a glimpse of the round top of the Douaumont fort. On the south side the height was capped with the old fort of Vaux, around which stretched the Chenois Wood. On that Wednesday night the Germans held the Hardaumont crest, and so could safeguard any advance up the glen from flanking fire. Just after midnight, when the moon had set, the 3rd Brandenburg Corps, now replenished from the depots, and an infantry brigade from Posen, attacked up the ravine, and for a moment carried the ruins of Vaux village. The French counter-attacked, and promptly drove them out with the bayonet. When daylight came the Germans returned to the charge, advancing not only against the village, but to the south up the steep slopes of the Chenois Wood against the old fort on the escarpment. The attack was delivered with great resolution, but by the evening it was checked, and no ground was gained. That day saw the end of the Brandenburgers as a unit so far as this battle was concerned. They were withdrawn from the line in a state of utter disintegration. On Friday, the 10th, the enemy, now largely reinforced, came on again, but was caught by the French guns before he could get to close quarters. Saturday, the 11th, saw the final effort. In the early morning the Germans swept up the ravine and took the eastern end of the village and the ruins of the church. On their left they pressed up the hill, losing heavily on the slopes, but their impetus slackened before they reached the crest, and they were stayed at the wire entanglements round the fort. Next day there was no infantry fighting, but only an intermittent bombardment.

The attack on Vaux, had it succeeded, would have turned the Douaumont position as successfully as if the Côte du Poivre had been carried. Simultaneously all along the Woëvre side there were attempts to advance, notably in the woods south-east of Damloup, at Eix, and at Manheulles. All were unsuccessful, and like clockwork the effort see-sawed to the other wing. The German strategy was that of a woodcutter who strikes first on one side of the trunk and then on the other. But the method is useless unless each stroke of the axe cuts out a substantial wedge, and this the German blows had failed to achieve. It was as if a forester, after cutting off the loose bark, had come to an inner core so hard that it turned the edge of his tool.

From Thursday, the 9th, to Tuesday, the 14th, the struggle went on between Bethincourt and the Goose's Crest. On the 10th a fresh division was launched against the Crows' Wood, and the Germans advanced their front to the edge of the Wood of Cumières. Next day the French first line, running from Bethincourt southeast up the slope of the ridge on the Cumières road, was carried, but the French regained part of it by the evening. On Sunday, the 12th, there was a great bombardment of all the ground from Bethincourt to the river, especially the French lines in the Wood of Cumières below the Goose's Crest. Next day it was discovered that the bombardment was extended at long range to the Charny ridge and the Wood of Bourrus, as if to cut off French reinforcements preparatory to a general attack. That night the artillery never ceased, and on the morning of Tuesday, the 14th, came the expected thrust for the Mort Homme.

The French line at that moment formed a salient, of which Bethincourt was the apex. From Bethincourt it ran in front of the country road leading over the shoulder of the Goose's Crest to Cumières. This road, a mile and a quarter south-east of Bethincourt, crossed the spur of the Mort Homme marked 265 metres. The French lay on the northern slopes of this, and then bent back over the Goose's Crest, behind the Crows' Wood, and so to the Meuse. The Germans based their attack on the Crows' Wood, which they now held, and directed it south-west towards the point 265 behind the French trenches. A Silesian division advanced in the centre, while a brigade moved on the right up the slopes of 265 from the Forges brook, and another brigade on the left advanced directly against Hill 295, the highest point of the Mort Homme *massif*. The striking force was scarcely less than 25,000 men. The centre, coming on in five successive waves, pushed back the French behind the Bethincourt-Cumières road. Its flank was caught by the French guns and checked, but the Silesians managed before nightfall to win two positions just under the crest of Hill 265, which made that hillock no longer tenable. The mile of ground between it and the Crows' Wood was now in their hands. Berlin announced the capture of the Mort Homme, but the news was false. The French still held the key position, and all that had been lost was an outlying spur. There was a lull on Wednesday, the 15th; but that night a new artillery preparation began, and at three o'clock in the afternoon of Thursday, the 16th, a second attack was made on the same method as the first. It was caught by field and machine guns in flank, and completely broken up. A counter-attack by the French right drove part of it in disorder with heavy losses back to the shelter of the Crows' Wood.

That same night there was a new assault on Vaux. Twice the ruins of the village were attacked, but the enemy was held back just west of the church. Three other attacks, based on the cemetery, attempted to scale the slopes to the fort. They were caught by the French searchlights from the heights, and broken up by the French guns. The woodman's strokes on both sides of the trunk had struck an adamantine core.

So closed the second phase of the battle, on the twenty-second day since the guns had opened between Brabant and Herbebois. The result of the blow on the west bank of the Meuse had been to win a triangle, less than a mile deep, between the brook of Forges and the Bethincourt–Cumières road. It had sharpened the Bethincourt salient, but it had not yet secured the key-point of the Mort Homme. On the east bank most of the Wood of Hardaumont had gone, and the Germans were up to Vaux village, but they were no nearer carrying the Douaumont plateau. Till now the attack had suffered in scarcely less proportion than the defence, but the Germans could not cut their losses and break off a barren struggle. They had claimed victory too brazenly, and must go on for very shame's sake till they won some apparent decision. They were faced with a new syllogism: Verdun depended on Douaumont and Charny; these in turn depended upon the Mort Homme; the Mort Homme refused to yield to a frontal attack, therefore an effort must be made to take it in flank.

Only one flank was possible. Accordingly, on Friday, the 17th, the German guns opened in a fresh bombardment between Avocourt and Bethincourt. The new assault on the key-point was coming from the west.

IV.

With the opening of the new phase the great struggle changed its character. The original plan had gone to pieces. The Battle of Verdun, as conceived by Falkenhayn before 21st February, was lost by the end of the first week. The swift surprise which would have given the Germans the city—and thereby a resounding advertisement for German arms—and which in certain circumstances might have broken the French front, had died away into a war of trenches. Verdun might still be won, but its winning would have less military meaning. It was not a key-point but merely an insignificant heap of ruins, since the French front was held not by fortresses but by entrenched field armies. Its capture would be a certain gain, but only if the price exacted were reasonable. Had the Crown Prince entered it on 26th February he would have paid much for his victory, but it might reasonably have been considered to be worth the cost. By the middle of March it was very clear that Verdun, even if it fell next day, would have been bought too high. The essence of war is to win something from the enemy at a fair price. In every battle both sides have losses; if the loss to one side, whether in position or in men, is proportionately greater than the loss to the other, then the latter has won. If a man at a sale bids fifty pounds for a picture and secures it, he may have a bargain; if he pays a hundred pounds it may still be worth while; but if the price is run up to a thousand, and he persists, he may have blundered into folly. The analogy is not exact, for a buyer at an auction is not compelled to pay unless he gets the coveted object, whereas in the case of Verdun the enemy paid cash down at every bid, and had no security of any gain.

The Allied counter-attack, for which the rest of the German front was waiting, did not come. The great armies of the north and centre remained fast in their trenches, and save for an inconsiderable attack at the Navarin Farm in Champagne, there was no auxiliary movement during these days to divert Allied reserves or confuse the Allied strategy. It is clear that on this point the calculations of the German High Command were completely upset.[*] What they had counted on did not come to pass, and they sat still in the expectation of it, while with every hour their chances of victory declined.

The struggle on the Meuse Heights could only have been justified at this stage if the attack were taking toll of the defence out of all proportion to its own losses. But though the French casualties were the higher, the disproportion was not enough. The pick of the German regiments were flung desperately forward, hideously mauled, their gaping ranks replenished from local reserves, and sent in again. In some cases as much as 60 per cent. of the effectives perished.[†] That was inevitable from the nature of the fighting.

---

[*] See Falkenhayn's comments, *General Headquarters*, Eng. trans., pp. 239–40.
[†] The 3rd (Brandenburg) Corps is a case in point. It started on 21st February with over 20,000 bayonets. By 28th February it had lost two-thirds of its officers

Verdun on the Meuse, before Bombardment
From a painting by A. Renaud

What was more important, the original tactical plan was relinquished. The artillery bombardment, which should have made the infantry advance easy, grew less complete as the days passed. There was less precision in registering, greater delay in bringing up supplies of heavy shell, and the halts between each stage enabled the defence to prepare for the next blow. The fresh troops used for the attack became patently inferior in quality, since the best had been used up with tragic speed, and there was not now the promise of swift victory to give heart to the assault. Again, the general advance on a broad front, which had been the second stage as originally planned, was growing impossible. Armies tire like individuals, and a great sweep, once it has been checked, cannot be easily repeated. Accordingly we find a series of local attacks at widely separated sections, which could not correctly be said to have any cumulative effect. Had the salient been narrow the blows at its neck might have been formidable, but the Verdun position was not properly a salient at all. The base was too broad for the cutting-off tactics which had served Germany well in the Eastern campaign. The battle was now to all intents a frontal attack upon the French lines. It had resolved itself on the German side into an effort to create little salients, and then push them in. If we return to the simile of the woodcutter, we may say that the attempt to cut great wedges on each side of the tree had failed, and had been replaced by a number of small and casual gashes. Such a method may serve to bring down a sapling, but in this case the trunk was broad and hard, and its roots deep.

Strategically the French held the command. In Joffre's Order of the Day to the Verdun defenders, issued during the first weeks of March, the situation was accurately described: "For three weeks you have been undergoing the most formidable assaults which the enemy has yet attempted against us. Germany counted on the success of this effort, which she believed to be irresistible, and to which she devoted her best troops and much powerful artillery. She hoped that the capture of Verdun would revive the courage of her allies, and convince neutral states of German superiority. She had reckoned without you. Night and day, in spite of a bombardment without precedent, you have resisted all

and non-commissioned officers, and more than half its effectives. Between 29th February and 8th March it was taken out for rest and refitment. On the latter day it went again into action, still—in spite of drafts—some 40 per cent. below strength; and two days later was withdrawn from the battle a mere shadow of its former self. It had lost in ten days' fighting 22,000 men, or rather more than its total original strength.

attacks and maintained our positions. The struggle is not yet at an end, for the Germans need a victory. You will succeed in wresting it from them." *The Germans needed a victory.* This was the only explanation of a strategy which refused to count its losses, and persisted in a game which under no conceivable circumstances could now be worth the candle. Such needs, in essence not military but political, are in war the fruitful parents of disaster. Tactically, too, Pétain was master of the situation. He followed the traditional French practice of holding his first line lightly, of surrendering it under attack, and of winning it back, if necessary, with the counter-stroke. When a desperate push was made he was prepared to fall back a little, provided he could take sufficient toll of the enemy. In certain cases, such as the Douaumont crest or the Mort Homme, where the position was vital for his plan, he was prepared to push the counter-attack with resolution, and lose men on a heavy scale. But his general purpose was to incur no needless losses, and to make the enemy pay soundly for every yard of ground surrendered. His attitude was that of the trader who has wares to sell to any one who will give his figure. He regarded no village or crest, not even Verdun itself, as immune from this grim bargaining. The Germans may have any ground they want—so ran his argument—provided they pay a high enough price. It was the destruction of the enemy's forces, not the sacrosanctity of a strip of land, which would gain for France the victory.

The new bombardment on the west bank of the Meuse, which began on 17th March, reached its height by midday of the 20th. That afternoon the first infantry attack was made on the Avocourt–Malancourt line. The Mort Homme, as we have seen, was the key of the left bank; its one accessible flank was the western, and of that the key was Hill 304. That hill, again, could only be approached from the west and north-west, where it sent down long gentle slopes to the upper feeders of the Forges brook. On the west the Wood of Avocourt covered the slopes of an underfeature which ran up to Hill 304. To the north, in the hollow, lay the conjoined hamlets of Malancourt and Haucourt, at the foot of another easy spur. If the Germans could take the Wood of Avocourt, they would have won a position well up the slopes of 304, and would have excellent cover for the final rush for the summit. If at the same time they could press beyond Malancourt and Haucourt, and win the northern slopes, the hill, which was the key of Mort Homme, must presently be in their hands.

On that Monday afternoon, the 20th of March, a Bavarian

division, supported by a discharge of liquid fire, fought its way into the eastern part of the Avocourt Wood. By night fresh troops were brought up, and towards evening, in spite of the brilliant work of the French batteries at Esnes, the German line was pushed to the edge of the trees where the hill pastures began. All Tuesday the Germans were busy putting a barrage behind Hill 304, and hammering at the point of the Malancourt salient. On Wednesday they built a redoubt in the captured Avocourt Wood as a base for the next advance on the hill, and their infantry attacked on a line between the corner of the wood and Malancourt village. They gained a footing on the little hill south-west of Haucourt, but failed to win the French redoubt there. On Thursday and Friday the bombardment continued, and a few more trenches were won at Haucourt. The Malancourt salient was now being pinched very thin, and the vital point—the west slope of 304—was gravely threatened by the enemy.

Then came a short lull. From Saturday, the 25th, to Monday, the 27th, there was nothing but intermittent artillery fire, which by the Monday evening had grown to that intensity which heralds a fresh attack. On Tuesday that attack came at Malancourt, where battalion after battalion was hurled on the weak French troops in the village. In this fight the French heavy guns played a great part, and the waves of the assault, descending the slopes to the Forges glen, were terribly shattered by their fire. The real danger-point was not there but at the Avocourt Wood, and on the Wednesday afternoon Pétain resolved on one of those rare counter-strokes which he used only to win back some vital position. It was completely successful. The Germans were driven in for more than 300 yards, and the redoubt they had made fell into French hands. Counter-attacks followed, but they failed to retrieve the loss. Meanwhile at Malancourt the Germans managed to fight their way into the north-west corner of the village. Next day there was a pause, broken only by futile counter-attacks from the Avocourt Wood. But during the night, having brought up reinforcements, the Germans again flung themselves on Malancourt. The French garrison repelled the first attack at 9 p.m. with heavy loss to the enemy, and again at 11; but about 1 a.m. in the morning of Friday, the last day of March, the invaders won the south-west corner of the hamlet.

The loss of Malancourt was now only a matter of hours. The strength of a full division had been used against its kilometre of front, and the price had been paid which the French required.

Fighting desperately among the ruins, the garrison fell back to Haucourt, and the capture of Malancourt was announced in Berlin. Pétain went farther. On that Friday night he quietly drew his troops at Haucourt across the little stream to a strong position on the lower slopes of Hill 304. The Germans were ignorant of this move, and for several days continued to bombard empty trenches. The salient had been blunted, the French lines adjusted, and the enemy could make nothing of his gains. He could not debouch from his new position because of the French command of Hill 304 and Mort Homme. In that bare little glen there was no friendly Crows' Wood to give him cover.

On the night that the French were filing silently across the Forges stream a new attack was launched on Vaux. There had been two abortive assaults on the Thursday night, and from midday on Friday a heavy bombardment had been loosed along the front from Poivre to Hardaumont. Late on Friday night the enemy returned to the charge, and the second of two attacks gave him the western houses of Vaux village, up to the point where the roads forked around a little pond. The one on the right climbed steeply between the Hardaumont and Caillette Woods, and reached the plateau near the old fort of Douaumont. On the morning of Saturday, 1st April, the enemy struggled to advance up this road, which was carried in a shallow ravine among the trees, but the French guns from the south held him. Next day, Sunday, on that narrow front of little over a mile, he launched the equivalent of a division in four columns. He penetrated most of the Caillette Wood, pressing up the ravine, and also from the Wood of Hardaumont. This was a substantial success, for he had made of the French lines behind Douaumont village a difficult salient, and he had also made a salient of the old Vaux Fort and the bluff it stood on.

As at Avocourt the French counter-attacked with purpose, for the ground must be won back to safeguard this position. General Nivelle had arrived with the 3rd Corps, in which General Mangin commanded the 5th Division. That night their guns were active, and at dawn on Monday, the 3rd, Mangin pressed the invader out of the Caillette Wood—all except the slender horn of it close to the Douaumont redoubt—recovered the ravine and the ground round Vaux Pond, and with a last fine effort won back the western skirts of the village. That day's fight was one of the severest struggles in the whole battle. The narrow glen of Vaux, up which the German columns moved, was soon a charnel-house, choked with the dead and dying. Through these human barriers the German heavy guns blasted a road for the reinforcements that came on time and again to breast the hill. In the advance which gave them the Caillette Wood and—for a moment—the rim of the plateau, the Germans lost desperately; but in the subsequent counter-attack the French, after their fashion, spent their strength freely to redeem a real tactical loss. On the balance the enemy had paid the heavier price, and he had no gain to counterbalance it.

Meanwhile the battle had been resumed on the western flanks. On Monday, the 3rd, an attack on the line Haucourt–Bethincourt took the Germans into the trenches north of the Forges brook, which the French had evacuated on the last night of March. For the next two days there was a lull; but on Thursday, 6th April, in the afternoon, the Germans finally entered Haucourt village, and attacked Bethincourt, which was now the apex of a perilous salient. That night part of the French first-line trenches were carried between Bethincourt and Hill 265 along the Cumières road, and all the next day was filled with a new and intense bombardment. Under its cover during the night the enemy flung his horns south and east of Haucourt, and gained a footing in two small woods situated between the village and the spur of Hill 304. That day there was also fighting at Bethincourt, which, it was very clear, must soon be relinquished. When darkness fell the garrison was withdrawn, and on Saturday morning the enemy was in possession. The French front now ran from the redoubt in Avocourt Wood, along the slopes of Hill 304, to the Forges stream north-east of Haucourt, and thence to a point a little south of the Bethincourt–Esnes and Bethincourt–Cumières cross-roads. It continued just south of Hill 265, and behind the Goose's Crest to the Meuse, north of Cumières. Since 17th March, when the flanking attack on Mort Homme began, on the average less than one mile of ground had been relinquished on a front of six.

The adjustment of the French lines was completed just in time, for on Sunday, the 9th, an attack was delivered on the Mort Homme position, which, except for that February Friday at Douaumont, was perhaps the fiercest engagement so far witnessed in the battle. On the Friday Pétain had been aware of a great concentration behind the heights which run from Forges to Malancourt. It was not less than five divisions strong, and two of these divisions had not yet appeared in action. Hitherto the Germans had attacked Mort Homme first from the north and east, and then by way of Hill 304 from the west. But now they aimed at a general assault on the whole front west of the river, the first of the kind since the main effort for Douaumont failed on 26th February. Two divisions were to push through the Avocourt and Malancourt Woods against Hill 304, and they were to be followed by two divisions moving from the Crows' Wood directly on the Mort Homme. These two main assaults were to be supported by efforts on the extreme flanks, against Cumières on the east, and Avocourt on the west. At the same time, across the river there was to be an attack on the Côte du Poivre, and a constant bombardment of the east bank was designed to mislead the French as to the true point of danger.

At eight o'clock on the Sunday morning the attack from the Wood of Avocourt began, an attack in dense formation after the familiar German pattern. It never got out of the trees, it never even reached the French trenches. It was driven back by the French field guns and the big pieces around Esnes. But it was well covered, and its retirement was free from serious losses. At 10 a.m. came the attack from the Crows' Wood, the old theatre of the first bid for Mort Homme. This effort failed disastrously, and the troops were mown down in swathes. Presently came the first flank assault, along the flat riverside meadows between Regnéville and Cumières, between the Goose's Crest and the Meuse. It penetrated into the ruins of Cumières, but was broken up and destroyed before it found a lodgment. All the afternoon these attacks were repeated, and at one point on a front of about 400 yards the first French trenches were carried at the Mort Homme. There the contest was fierce till the darkness, and great glory was won by the 151st Regiment of the line, by the 16th Battalion of Chasseurs, and by the 8th, that famous battalion which on September 22, 1843, had held Sidi-Brahim as the Spartans held Thermopylæ. Late in the evening, while the world was lit by a fantastic sunset, came the assault on the extreme western flank at Avocourt by a Bavarian brigade. This had some of the elements of a surprise, but the ground it won was regained by a counter-stroke before the darkness fell.

Next day the battle still raged all along the front, and at the Côte du Poivre the Germans won a ravine on the south-eastern edge. But by Tuesday, the 11th, it was clear that they had failed. They had used some nine divisions; indeed, they had used them up. At every point the great assault was held and checked, and the constant supplies of new troops only added to the carnage. The general assault was no more fortunate than the local assaults,

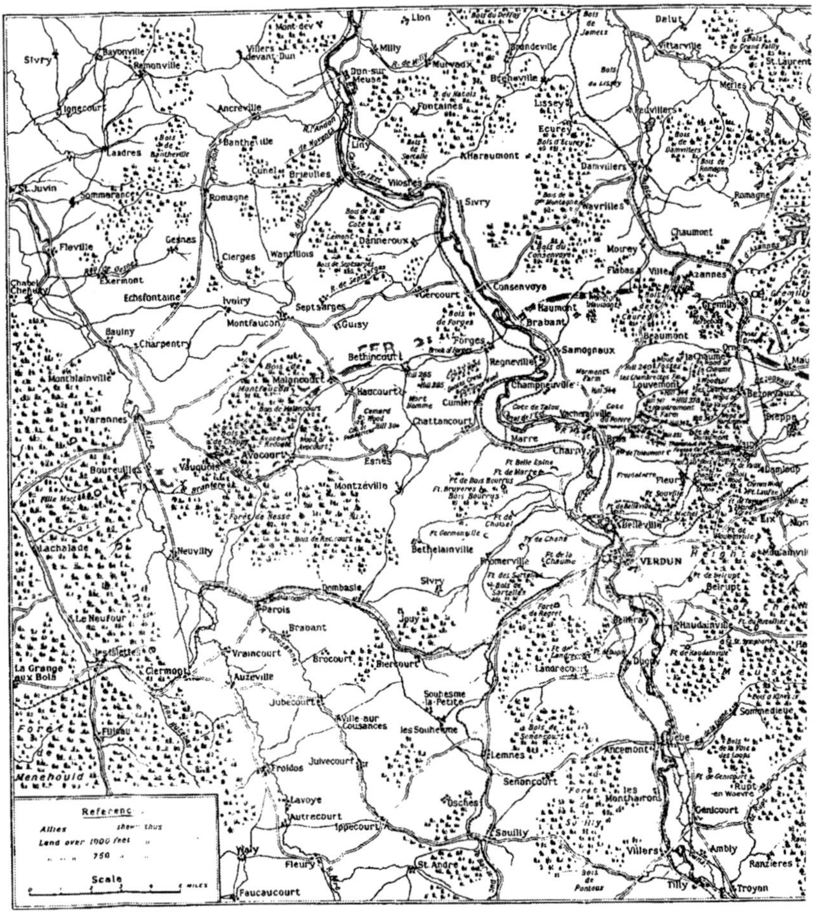

Reference
Allies shown thus
Land over 1000 feet
750
Scale
Sivry
Bayonville
Remonville
Landres
St. Juvin
Sommerance
Fleville
Exermont
Echsfontaine
Ivoiry
Montfaucon
Septsarges
Cierges
Romagne
Cunel
Brieulles
Bantheville
Ancreville
Dun-sur-Meuse
Milly
Murvaux
Fontaines
Liny
Vilosnes
Haraumont
Sivry
Lion
Brandeville
Bréheville
Lissey
Ecurey
Damvillers
Wavrilles
Moirey
Flabas
Ville
Azannes
Chaumont
Romagne
Merles
Peuvillers
Vittarville
Dalut
St. Laurent
Danneroux
Gercourt
Consenvoye
Haumont
Brabant
Samogneux
Beaumont
Regnéville
Champneuville
Forges
Bethincourt
Malancourt
Haucourt
Cumières
Chattancourt
Avocourt
Esnes
Montzéville
Vauquois
Varennes
Boureuilles
Montblainville
Charpentry
Baulny
Lachalade
Le Neufour
Les Islettes
Clermont
Neuvilly
La Grange aux Bois
Futeau
Forêt
Menehould
Parois
Brabant
Vraincourt
Auzéville
Brocourt
Jubécourt
Dombasle
Jouy
Sivry
Bethelainville
Marre
Charny
Vacherauville
Louvemont
Bezonvaux
Fleury
Douaumont
Belleville
VERDUN
Belrupt
Haudainville
Dugny
Landrecourt
Ancemont
Senoncourt
Lemmes
Souilly
Villers
Tilly
Ambly
Génicourt
Rupt en Woevre
Sommedieue
Troyon
Ranzières
Osches
St. André
Ippécourt
Fleury
Autrecourt
Lavoye
Froidos
Julvécourt
Waly
Faucaucourt
Souhesme la Petite
les Souhesme
Ville aur Cousances
Eix
Hill 304
Mort Homme
Forêt de Hesse

flank attack had failed like frontal attack, and no one of the key-points of Verdun was in the enemy's power.

The 9th of April marked the end of the third phase—the lateral movement on Mort Homme. The repulse by Pétain of the combined effort from Avocourt to Poivre marked the end also of the main German plan. Each item of that proud enterprise had crumbled. The scheme which was to give Verdun into their hands in four days had failed to give it in forty-eight. Henceforth system went out of the German tactics. Wild rushes were diversified by spells of inert weariness, and in both action and inaction they were bleeding to death.

V.

Few battles nowadays have a clean and satisfactory close. Some never end, or end only with the campaign. Fighting did not cease at Ypres and Loos, Champagne and Arras. But there comes a moment when the chances of the attacker's main purpose have gone, when the initiative in any real sense has departed from him, and when he is compelled to look for some means of breaking off the engagement without a naked confession of failure, or of continuing it on different lines. The advent of such a moment may be guessed from various signs: the lack of a serious strategical purpose in attack—fighting, so to speak, only to pass the time; the supersession of generals; lengthy official explanations that the purpose of the movement is something quite different from what was stated at the start; a claim of victory with bogus figures added in proof; the sudden resumption of activity elsewhere.

If we look for these signs we shall find some of them apparent about the middle of April. The attack of April 9-10 was not the end of the battle, but it was the culmination of the German effort. "The Germans will without doubt attack again," said Pétain in his Order of the Day. They did attack during the following weeks—at the Caillette Wood near Douaumont, at the ravine between Poivre and Haudromont, at Mort Homme, at Hill 304—violent attacks sometimes mustering a strength of two divisions. The tide of battle rolled as far south as Les Eparges, where, on 19th April, three fruitless efforts were made to pierce the French position. But these assaults were no more than a local offensive; they were not colligated and directed by any conceivable strategical plan. The battle for Verdun had gone against them. Presently came other proofs. Marshal von Haeseler, the Crown Prince's mentor, returned to Berlin a discredited man, and more than one corps commander followed. The German Press was filled with long *exposés* of the true objects of the Verdun struggle, which, it was claimed, had succeeded. Sour grapes were cried : Verdun itself was of no importance, and whether or not the city fell was immaterial to the High Command ; what they had done was to weaken the French field armies and use up their reserves. Following on this, totals of unwounded prisoners were published, and the German Staff gave rein to their fancy. Figures were given for certain days and areas in which the number of French prisoners claimed greatly exceeded the total French casualties, and fell little short of the troops actually engaged. Finally, by the middle of April the French themselves began to take the offensive—at Vaux, at Haucourt, at the Mort Homme. It was no general counter-attack—that was not the French strategy— but only the winning of a position here and a position there to ease the front. A wrestler, when his opponent's fierce effort has begun to slacken, will shift his grip a little to lighten the strain and get a better stand.

So ebbed the first stage of the Battle of Verdun, so far the longest continuous battle in history. It had stretched from the snows of February into the spring sunlight of April. When the first shots were fired the copses of the Meuse Heights were brown and leafless, but by its close young green was breaking in waves over the scarred soil, the almond trees were blossoming, and the waterside meadows were gay with marigolds. No less spectacular battle was ever fought. On that arc of thirty miles the better part of a million men stood to arms, but to the observer from any point— from the ridge of Charny, or the southern forts, or the shattered Verdun streets—they seemed to have been swallowed up in the earth. Only the dull unceasing rattle of the guns, the fleecy puffs of shrapnel on the ridges, and at times mushrooms of dark smoke told of the struggle. These, and the endless stream of transport choking every road, where the might of France moved up to the lines of her defence.

The result had been a signal French victory. If Verdun represented a less critical moment than the Marne, it was a far more deadly struggle, and it bit deeper into the enemy's strength. Of all that she had set out to win Germany had gained nothing. She had not broken the French front ; she had not set foot in Verdun city, and thereby won the right to proclaim the fall of a famous fortress to expectant citizens and dubious neutrals ; she had not lured the Allies into a premature offensive ; she had not even taken undue toll of the French ranks. She had hoped to deliver such a blow as would shake the nerve of France and compel a separate peace. But the spirit of France never burned brighter and stronger than when her armies lay on those shattered heights, weary but unconquered Germany had compelled the expenditure of large stores of shell, and thereby delayed the Allied offensive, and she had won a few square miles of barren highlands. It was the sum of her achievement. As against it, she had proclaimed certain victory on the housetops, and suffered the discredit of those who anticipate successes and fail. And she had lost troops that she could not replace Many a famous corps left Verdun a shadow which could never again in the campaign regain its old substance.

If we ask the secret of Germany's failure we shall find it largely in the neglect of that military doctrine which enjoins the economy of force. Her tactical plan was sound, but the soundest plan may miscarry, and when the immediate success was denied her, she continued to spend herself for a victory which was every day of diminishing value. Verdun to her was worth a price, but it was not worth any price ; and it was beyond doubt not worth the price she offered after 26th February. Her political commitments prevented her from cutting her losses and following the true principles of war. She was wrong in her premise, for even if she had succeeded in her aim she would not have dealt a fatal blow to the armies of France ; but she would have won a solid and marketable success. Failing that success, she could not go back to where she began ; the absence of victory meant for her a grave and indubitable defeat. Tactically it may be said that she overrated the power of artillery in action. Her successes in the East against an ill-equipped foe had distorted her vision. She inclined to regard her infantry as if it were a mere escort for the guns. But it is infantry which wins the decision ; its *rôle* is the principal one ; it is still the " queen of battles." An artillery " preparation " can never be more than the means to the occupation by the infantry of the enemy's trenches. It is clear that time and again her men had not the stamina or the *élan* to complete the work which the guns had begun. Small blame to the German infantryman. He was tried too high ; his nerve was weakened by impossible demands ; his units, through their misuse and grave depletion, lost all corporate vigour. Germany treated her human material as if it were a lifeless mechanism, and outraged human nature reacted and foiled her plan.

The achievement of France was brilliant to a superlative degree whether we regard her generalship or the fighting quality of her men. The first of the great French soldiers, Foch, had emerged into the clear light of fame at the Marne; Verdun brought into prominence a second. Henri Philippe Pétain had begun the war as a colonel of infantry, had won his spurs in the Artois fighting in the summer of 1915, and had commanded with great distinction an army in the Champagne battles of September. His mind was firm, elastic, crystal clear, infinitely resourceful; his brain was masterful in detail, without ever losing its grasp of principle and a broad perspective; his knowledge of human nature was profound, and few soldiers have been greater adepts at the training of raw troops and the reorganization of dispirited units. He had a character of singular elevation and strength—simple, modest, patient, gentle, and brave. His devoutness—as deep as that of Foch and Castelnau—had in it something of the rigour of northern France, something of the iron fatalism of his great compatriot, Calvin. He had nothing of Joffre's fatherly benignity and gargantuan cheerfulness, or Foch's southern vivacity and sudden lightning-flashes of imagination, but in a crisis his grave, wise face was to every one who saw it a refuge and an inspiration. No threat could weaken his nerve, and no fog of war cloud the calm lucidity of his mind. For dealing with a certain kind of crisis he had no equal. With perfect clearness he grasped the situation on that hectic 26th of February, and with perfect coolness he made his schemes to meet it. He declined to be hurried into irrelevant counter-strokes, even when a tempting chance offered; he refused to be misled by the enemy's feints; calmly he made his plan, and resolutely he abode by it. His aim was to hold Verdun at the minimum cost, and to spend men only when he could make the enemy spend in a fantastic ratio. But for all this generous parsimony he never let a strategic position slip from his grasp; he would give up an irrelevant mile, but strike hard to win back an essential yard. During the battle he drew on many divisions from a wide section of front, but he wasted none of them. When one had done its part it withdrew, and fresh troops took its place. He was equally adroit in his handling of artillery. The 75's far forward in the line of battle again and again broke up the enemy's advance, and the heavy guns, cunningly placed among the folds of the hills, and served by excellent observation posts, defended from afar the key positions.

What shall be said of the soldiers themselves, who for these two months rolled back the invader? Not the Ypres salient or the nightmare Labyrinth was more dreadful than those shattered Meuse uplands, churned into grey mud by the punctual shells, till they seemed like some lunar desert where life was forbidden. It was a struggle on the defensive, a contest of stark endurance waged with the knowledge that ground must some time be ceded, but with the resolve that the cession should be dearly bought. Such a task puts the sternest strain on human nature. It requires not the exhilaration of hot blood and high spirits, but cold patience and disciplined sacrifice. The glib commentators who before the war praised French *élan* and denied French fortitude were utterly put to shame. It was the fortitude and the stoicism of the French that were their most shining endowments. They showed it under Castelnau at Nancy and under Maud'huy at Arras; but Verdun was the apotheosis of the quality. "*Passeront-pas*" sang the soldiers, and held the gate, a living wall stronger than concrete or steel. Through days of giddiness and torture, when the solid earth seemed crumbling beneath them, they maintained their ground. Advanced posts, as at Malancourt and Haucourt, drew on the enemy and stood at bay, with odds of one to six, till the precise moment arrived for which retreat was designed. Nor did the long doggedness of defence impair the spirit of the offensive; when a counter-attack was needed it came as if from fresh troops who had never in their lives done anything but move forward.

Conspicuous among the merits of the French infantry were the discipline and initiative of the smallest units, even of individuals. Men had constantly to act without orders, at any rate in the first days of the battle, and they showed that austere conscience as to what was personally required of them which belongs to an army which is no mechanism but a living weapon. Left to himself to decide, the soldier in nine cases out of ten chose the more arduous duty. In some words to his chasseurs before his death at the Wood of Caures Colonel Driant spoke of the task which was before each man. " In a struggle like that which awaits us, far-stretched and parcelled out, no one can entrench himself behind the absence of orders and remain inert. Often there will be occasions when fractions of units will be left to their own devices. To stand fast, to stay the enemy by every means, must be each man's dominant thought." Again, this active intelligence and sense of responsibility were maintained, not for hours or days, but for weeks and months. This was the immense achievement of the

French. They did not weary in well-doing. They could preserve on the defensive that fine tenacity of spirit which wears down the enemy as the harder metal wears down the softer. The phrase of the poet on the eve of his death on the battlefield, "On n'a jamais fini de faire son devoir," was the keynote of the whole struggle. Soberly and methodically the French faced a sacrifice to which there could be no limits, a duty which knew no ending.* They did this cheerfully and without complaint, because their minds were utterly made up. There was no alternative but victory. The race was ready to perish on the battlefield sooner than accept a German domination. There was something so matter-of-fact in this resolution, which appeared in every word and deed of the nation, that the casual observer forgot how great it was. Its completeness gave them peace and confidence. The renunciation was so absolute, the offering so unreserved, that no one doubted of the issue. Many would die, but of a surety France, in whose eternity they were but a moment, would survive. Such faith seemed to be less a human thing than some slow and secret process of nature which, like spring or morning, insensibly renews the world.

* These words were found scribbled on the wooden casing of a bomb-proof shelter in the French firing-line:—

"Mon corps à la terre,
Mon âme à Dieu,
Mon cœur à la France."

They are almost translated by Sir Walter Scott's lines:—

"The body to its place,
The soul to Heaven's grace,
And the rest in God's own time!"

END OF VOLUME II.

BIBLIOLIFE

Old Books Deserve a New Life
www.bibliolife.com

Did you know that you can get most of our titles in our trademark **EasyScript**™ print format? **EasyScript**™ provides readers with a larger than average typeface, for a reading experience that's easier on the eyes.

Did you know that we have an ever-growing collection of books in many languages?

Order online:
www.bibliolife.com/store

Or to exclusively browse our **EasyScript**™ collection:
www.bibliogrande.com

At BiblioLife, we aim to make knowledge more accessible by making thousands of titles available to you – quickly and affordably.

Contact us:
BiblioLife
PO Box 21206
Charleston, SC 29413